ASP DEVELOPER'S GUIDE

ASP
Developer's
Guide

Greg Buczek

McGraw-Hill
New York   San Francisco   Washington, D.C.   Auckland
Bogotá   Caracas   Lisbon   London   Madrid   Mexico City
Milan   Montreal   New Delhi   San Juan   Singapore
Sydney   Tokyo   Toronto

Library of Congress Cataloging-in-Publication Data

Buczek, Greg.
    ASP developer's guide / Greg Buczek.
       p.   cm.
    Includes index.
    ISBN 0-07-212294-3
    I. Title.
    QA76.625.B82   1999
    005.2'76—dc21   99-057026
                                            CIP

McGraw-Hill

A Division of The McGraw·Hill Companies

P/N 0-07-212292-7   PART OF ISBN 0-07-212294-3

The sponsoring editor for this book was Michael Sprague, the editing supervisor was Curt Berkowitz, and the production supervisor was Claire Stanley. It was set in Century Schoolbook by Priscilla Beer of McGraw-Hill's desktop composition unit in cooperation with Spring Point Publishing Services.

Printed and bound by Quebecor/Martinsburg.

Throughout this book, trademarked names are used. Rather than put a trademark symbol after every occurrence of a trademarked name, we used the names in an editorial fashion only, and to the benefit of the trademark owner, with no intention of infringement of the trademark. Where such designations appear in this book, they have been printed with initial caps.

This book is printed on recycled, acid-free paper containing a minimum of 50% recycled, de-inked fiber.

This book is dedicated to every precious moment we have in this life.

CONTENTS AT A GLANCE

CONTENTS

Contents

PREFACE

Active Server Pages, or ASP, provide a means for Web developers to activate their Web sites with dynamic live database-driven content. The code that produces this rich content is all *server side*, which means that it runs on the server. The benefit of server-side scripting is that the end result is raw HTML. So you don't have to worry if the visitor to your site is compatible with the language or tools you are using. Another benefit of server-side scripting is that you can utilize components on your server without requiring the visitor to install any particular program.

This book shows you in great detail all the components involved in working with Active Server Pages. First, you will learn about the ASP object model. Then we will look at numerous components involved in working with Active Server Page applications. After that, we will review working with a database and creating components. Finally, in the last three chapters will use all these tools to create an e-commerce site.

Who Should Read This Book

The book is designed to meet the needs of those new and already familiar with ASP, as well as Visual Basic developers.

For those who are familiar with ASP, this book provides a good overview of all the components involved that you can use as a reference and makes sure you have covered all the bases.

For those who are Web developers, this book can be the tool to help you understand how to activate your site. You will get a strong overall understanding of how to add dynamic content to your site.

Visual Basic developers who are looking to expand their horizons will not be disappointed with ASP. Your Visual Basic skills will bring you up to speed in no time.

Final Note

The best way that you can learn a new technology or bring your skills to a higher level is to get your hands dirty. Remember that every minute you spend messing around with ASP is another minute in your experience. So find a project to work on, and work and work at it. In time it will all become clear.

Acknowledgments

I wish to acknowledge Joyce Buczek. I greatly appreciate all the help you have given me on this book. I also appreciate your putting up with me on those long, demanding days and nights.

—GREG BUCZEK

1

Developing Dynamic Internet Applications

Where the Web Has Been

Over the past years the Internet has impacted so much of our lives. The World Wide Web is now a huge conglomeration of information. Now when we want to find the address or even a map to a business we can look for it on the Web. You want to know what is playing at your local theaters? You can look for it on the Web. Need to check on your stock prices? You can do that on the Web. Searching for a job in Des Moines? You can do that on the Web.

But the Web hasn't always been that informative.

The Internet has its roots in the sharing of information among researchers. The creation of the *HyperText Markup Language*, or HTML, was a common way of presenting information on diverse platforms and operating systems. The computers that were viewing the HTML pages had

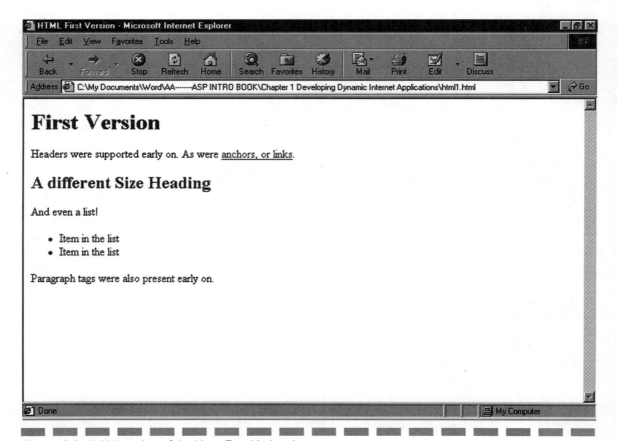

Figure 1-1   Initial version of the HyperText Markup Language.

client programs and browsers, which read and interpreted the HTML code and presented this interpretation to the person viewing the page.

That basic reason has remained the impetus and force behind the Internet, but the way the information is presented has changed drastically.

An early Web page may have looked like the one in Figure 1-1.

Notice that this first version of HTML contained the basics for presenting information as well as the ability to navigate to other documents. This early version also supported the notion that tags that were not understood were ignored. This is still an important part of HTML and is used by developers all the time. But in this 1992 version, there was no way of presenting graphical information such as pictures, tables, or objects. Note also that there was no way of retrieving information from the person viewing the Web page.

HTML 2 Specification

The next version of HTML included tremendous enhancements. Figure 1-2 shows some of the things a page could include in version 2 of the HTML specification.

Probably the most important new features in version 2 of the HTML specification were the table, image, and form tags. The *table tag*, for the first time, allowed information to be displayed in a tabular format. But that was just its initial, intended use. Quickly it became the dream come true for those Web developers who wanted better placement of elements on a page. Developers now use the table tags extensively to precisely place items on a Web page.

The *image tag* allowed developers to decorate their page. Now they could include company logos, employee pictures, and event pictures. Graphics were also used to decorate the layout of the page. Additionally, small invisible images were used to aid in the placement of other elements on a Web page. For example, some developers would place a blank image of a certain size to provide for an indent.

The HTML 2 specification also included the addition of *forms*. Prior to forms, interaction with visitors to the page was very limited. With forms and the standard form elements, we could now gather rich information about visitors, and that information could be used to supply them with an appropriate page, gather personal information, add them to a mailing list, or numerous other applications.

The contents of the forms were submitted to *Common Gateway Interface* (CGI) programs as a byte stream for processing. The CGI pro-

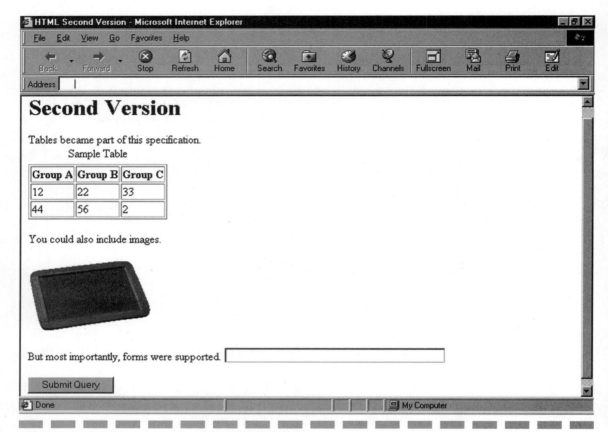

Figure 1-2 *Sample page using the HTML 2 specifications.*

gram, often written in PERL or C, would parse out the data in the stream. The data would then be processed and the CGI program would return result information back to the browser.

HTML 3.2 Specification

The next major version of the HTML specification released by the W3C Consortium was version 3.2. This more recent version brought us close to where the specification is today. It added numerous parameters and enhancements to existing tags as well as a slew of new tags, the most important of which was the applet tag.

The *applet tag* allowed developers to insert JAVA applications right into their Web pages. These JAVA applets could be full applications that performed a tremendous variety of tasks. You could create a slide show of images with a JAVA applet that sent visitors to a different location whenever they clicked on a specific image. You could have a JAVA applet present updated information on the prices of stock quotes. You could use a JAVA applet to present the current weather conditions. You could write a JAVA applet that was a children's paint program. The use and applications were numerous, and the tag ripped the Web wide open.

HTML 4 Specification

HTML 4 is the current HTML specification released by the W3C Consortium. Major additions to this specification are the Object, Script, and Style Sheet tags.

The *Style Sheet* tags allow developers to create common styles for elements on a Web page. Once a style is defined, it can be referenced from another page. For example, this allows developers to define once the color, size, and font of a header element. Then that style can be referenced from numerous pages. If it is deemed necessary to change that header style, the change needs to occur only in a single location, the definition of the element, for that change to be propagated to all the pages that use that tag.

The *Script tag* allowed for the inclusion of what is referred to as *client-side scripts*. This means that embedded within the HTML is code that is run by the browser on the client's machine. We look at client-side scripts later in this chapter as we discuss the benefits and pitfalls of this type of scripting.

The other major enhancement made with this specification was the inclusion of the *Object tag*, which provided the mechanism for multimedia and other objects to be placed within the confines of a Web page. For example, an Object tag might be used when you visit a news site to bring up a streaming audio/video plug-in you have on your computer when you want to view some news clip; or, an Object tag might be used to bring up a 3D-world viewer that is another add-in installed on your computer.

Dynamic vs. Static Content

Again, early on, the majority of the content on the Internet was *static*, which means that every time you view a Web page you see exactly the same page. All the text is the same, all the graphics are the same, the formatting, everything. For the content of the page to change, the developer must manually modify the text of the page and place it back on the Internet.

This technique provides for a stale Web site. You may get visitors to come once or twice, but if your pages do not change visitors will likely not feel compelled to return to your Web site.

In recent years, Web developers have realized that static content is not enough. So more and more companies started posting dynamic Web content for at least part of their Web site. Today, it is pretty uncommon to find a major Web site that does not supply some kind of dynamic content.

Dynamic Web content refers to Web pages that have content that changes over time. For example, the page shown in Figure 1-3 displays one set of content if the current day of the week is the weekend; and if

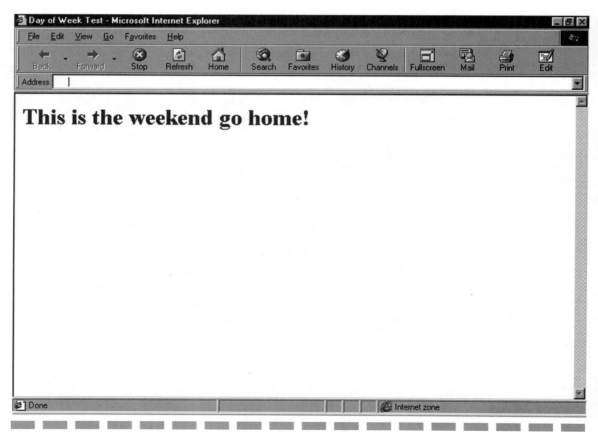

Figure 1-3 Sample page displaying content for a weekend day.

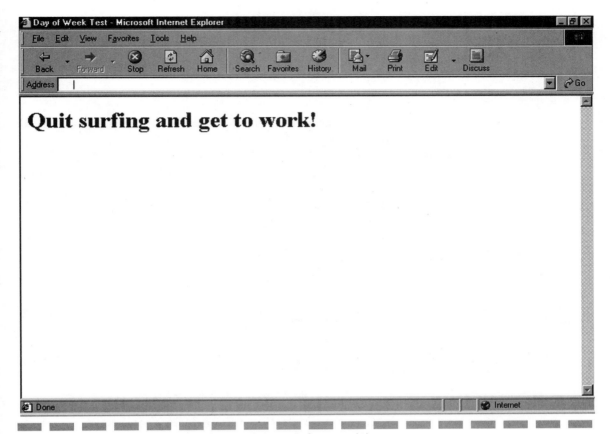

Figure 1-4   *Same sample page now showing content for a weekday.*

the current day of the week is Monday, Tuesday, Wednesday, Thursday, or Friday, then the page will display the content shown in Figure 1-4.

As you can see, the page in Figure 1-4 contains dynamic content. The content of the page can change over time. It can change with each viewing or at random or regular intervals. The important point is that it does change. Developing these dynamic Internet applications is the focus of this book.

The code involved in creating dynamic content can be implemented in a variety of mechanisms. The code in the previous example was created through VBScript on an Active Server Page as shown below.

```
<%
if weekday(Date) = 7 or weekday(Date) = 1 then
%>
<H1>This is the weekend go home!</H1>
```

```
<%
else
%>
<H1>Quit surfing and get to work!</H1>
<%
end if
%>
```

Don't worry if you can't read this code now; we go into it in great detail throughout the chapters of this book.

But the preceding code didn't have to be written as an Active Server Page with VBScript. It could have been implemented through a component written in C++. It could have been implemented though a filtering library that looks for pages with certain extensions and processes these pages accordingly. It could have been written in JavaScript.

In the next section, you will see that the code could have been written on either the client side or the server side.

Client-Side and Server-Side Scripting

Client-Side Scripting

Scripting in this context refers to the location where the code is processed. In this case, *client-side* scripting means that the code runs on the client's machine. When a visitor requests a page to view, the HTML and any code within the HTML page are downloaded to the visitor's browser. The browser then parses the HTML and runs any recognizable code on the page. The result of that parsing and the running of that code are displayed in the browser to the visitor. For example, notice in Figure 1-5 the graphic at the bottom of the window that says "Welcome to NetStats2000—NetStats Live."

Now look at the same page when the mouse hovers over the graphic as shown in Figure 1-6. Notice now that the graphic says "Click here to contact us." This is done with client-side code. The visitor to the page requests the page and processes any code on the page. In this example, the code is written in JavaScript and appears like this to the browser:

```
<SCRIPT LANG="Javascript"><!—
browserName = navigator.appName;
browserVer = parseInt(navigator.appVersion);
```

Figure 1-5
Client-side sample
graphic.

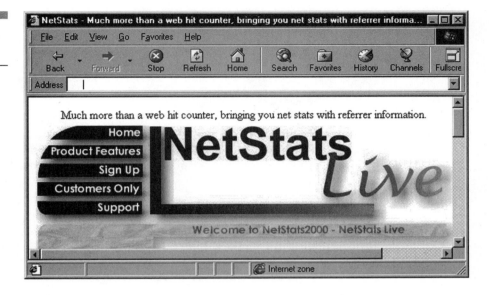

```
if (((navigator.appName == "Netscape") &&
    (parseInt(navigator.appVersion) >= 3 )) ||
    ((navigator.appName == "Microsoft Internet Explorer") &&
    (parseInt(navigator.appVersion) >= 4 ))) version = "ok";
else version = "x";
if (version == "ok")
{
    img6off = new Image();
```

Figure 1-6
Same page with
mouse hovering over
image.

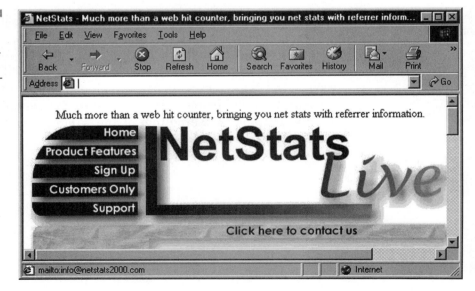

```
    img6off.src = "./assets/images/baroff.jpg";
    img6on = new Image();
    img6on.src = "./assets/images/baron.jpg";
}
function imgover(imgName)
{   if (version == "ok")
    { document[imgName].src = eval(imgName + "on.src"); } }
function imgoff(imgName)
{ if (version == "ok")
    { document[imgName].src = eval(imgName + "off.src"); } }
// -></SCRIPT>
```

And then within the image element we have the following code that uses the preceding functions and variables:

```
<A HREF="mailto:info@netstats2000.com"
onmouseover="imgover('img6')" onmouseout="imgoff('img6')">
<IMG HEIGHT=33 WIDTH=569 SRC="./assets/images/baroff.jpg"
BORDER=0 ALT="Click here to contact us" name=img6></A>
```

Notice that the code is surrounded in *Script tags*, which tell the browser that what follows is going to be code. But a very important consideration is that not all browsers support code. So what happens if a browser that doesn't support the Script tag tries to parse this page? The entire block is ignored because tags that are not recognized are skipped.

In this example we don't mind. If visitors do not see our *rollovers*—the graphic that appears when they hover their mouse over the image—no real functionality is lost.

But let's take a look at another example where this omission might not be so trivial (Figure 1-7).

In this sample client-side script, we are relying on the code to validate user entry before visitors can submit a request. If visitors leave the field blank, they see the message that is displayed in Figure 1-8.

If the visitor enters a value in the field, the form is validated and the visitor is sent to the responding page. The code that performs the validation is:

```
<SCRIPT language="JavaScript">
<!--
function IsPresent(PassedValue)
{
    var ReturnTest = 0;
    var LocalPassedValue = PassedValue;
    if (LocalPassedValue)
    {
    for (var i=0; i<LocalPassedValue.length; i++)
        {
        if (LocalPassedValue.charAt(i) != " ")
```

Figure 1-7
Sample client-side
script using field
validation.

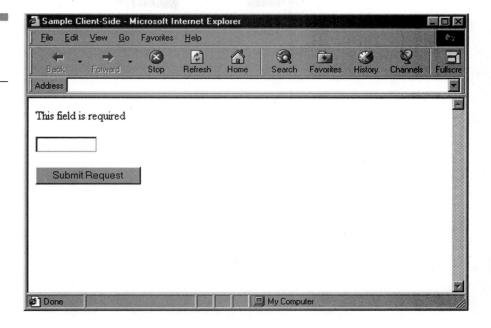

```
                    {
                    ReturnTest = 1;
                    }
                }
            }
        if (!ReturnTest)
            {
            return 0;
            }
            return 1;
            }
    function CheckForm()
    {
        var TheMessage = "";
        if (!(IsPresent(document.sampleform.reqField.value)))
            {
```

Figure 1-8
Message displayed
to visitors if they
leave the field blank
when the form is
submitted.

```
        TheMessage += "Please enter a value.\n";
        }
    if (TheMessage != "")
        {
        alert(TheMessage);
        }
    else
        {
        document.location.href = "result.htm";
        }
}
// ->
</SCRIPT>
```

The code for the SUBMIT button looks like this:

```
<INPUT TYPE="button" NAME="submitButton" VALUE="Submit Request"
onClick="CheckForm();">
```

Remember what happens when the browser doesn't support the Script tag, or for that matter the language used in the script? All the code between the Script tags is ignored, so this page becomes useless for browsers that don't support Script. Visitors would see the page, but when they pressed the SUBMIT button, nothing would happen.

This is a risk you have to weigh. Clearly, client-side scripting has its benefits. You reduce the work of your server since the processing is done on the client-side; you reduce your network traffic since fewer calls are made; and the visitor doesn't have to wait for additional calls to your browser.

There is also an added danger. All of your code is exposed to visitors, so if your visitors choose to see the source of the page through a menu option on their browser, they will see every line of your code.

Server-Side Scripting

The focus of this book is on server-side scripting. Again, what we are talking about in this topic is the location where the code is run. In client-side scripting the code is run on the visitor's browser. With *server-side scripting*, the code is processed on the server before it is sent to the visitor's browser.

Visitors request a Web page by typing the name of that page in their browser window or by clicking on a link. The Internet Server then receives that request and retrieves the page. Any server-side code is then processed. The page can then be returned as pure HTML. The browser then parses the basic HTML and displays it to the visitors. Thus server-side scripting does not require any special functionality from the browser. The browser does not know how to read any kind of script, since it is processed on the server side and just basic HTML is returned.

Also your code is protected. Frequently, you don't want the rest of the world to be able to see your source code. The code may be proprietary to your company or it could contain hidden system information that should not be viewable by an anonymous user. Server-side scripting addresses this problem by returning only the result of the code, not the code itself. So if a visitor requests to see a page that contains some code to log into a database, you don't want the visitor to be able to see how your queries are run, the field names, the validation technique, and so forth. With server-side, the visitor sees only the result of that code.

Let's take a look at a few examples of using server-side script. The page displayed in Figure 1-9 shows a standard Log In form. This page validates a user's entrance into a fictitious Web site. The page allows visitors to enter their user name and password. If they enter an invalid password, they see the page displayed in Figure 1-10.

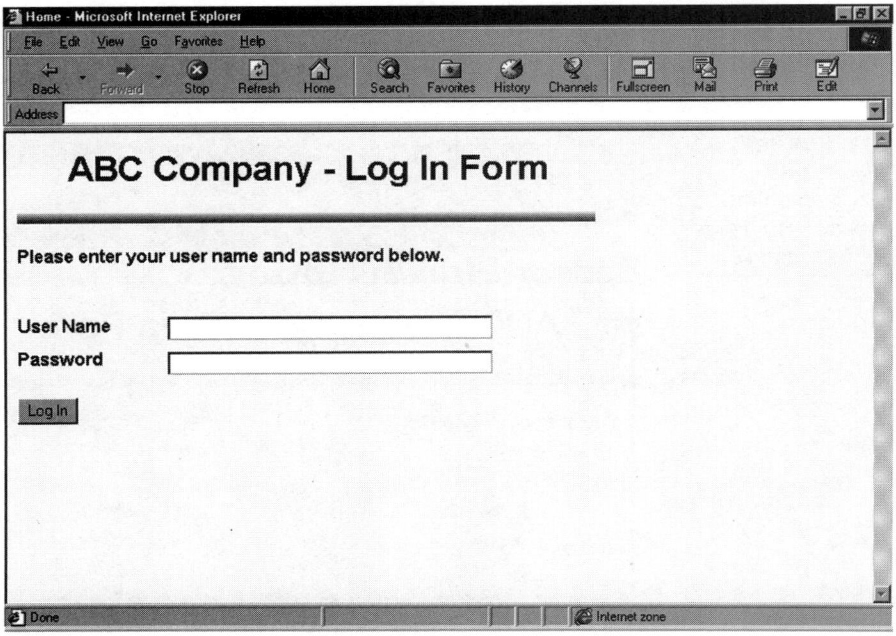

Figure 1-9
Log In page showing initial view.

Figure 1-10
Sample Log In site
displaying error mes-
sage when an invalid
entry is attempted.

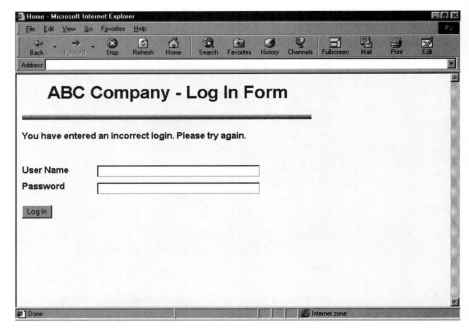

Figure 1-10
Sample Log In site
displaying error mes-
sage when an invalid
entry is attempted.

Visitors receive a message informing them that the information they entered was not found. If they enter a correct log in, they see the page shown in Figure 1-11.

The Log In page is implemented as a single Active Server Page. The code for the page follows. Again, don't worry if you don't understand the

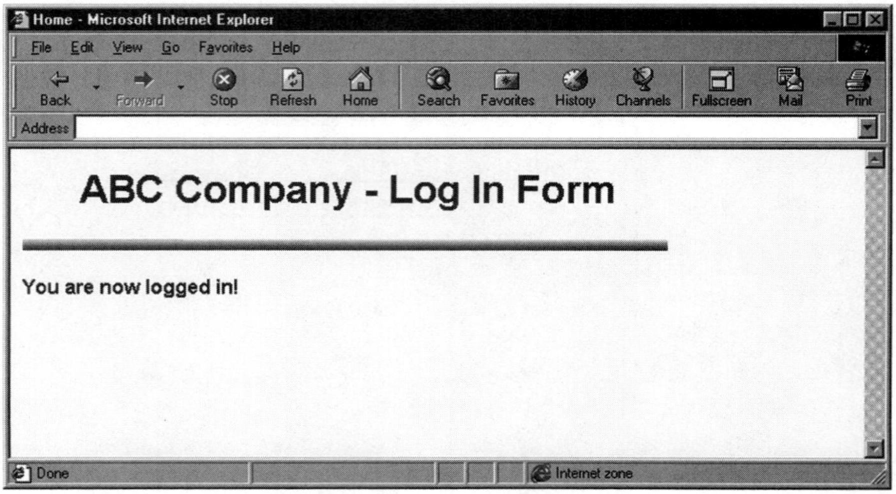

Figure 1-11
Text seen on the Log
In page with a suc-
cessful entrance.

details at this point—just try to read through it. Later in the book we discuss code like this at great length.

```
<%@ Language=VBScript %>
<%
if not isempty(Request.Form("LogIn")) then
   set conn = server.createobject ("adodb.connection")
   conn.open "ASPBook", "sa", "yourpassword"
   set RSUser = conn.Execute("select UserName from C1Login " _
      & "where UserName = '" & Request.Form("UserName") _
      & "' and Password = '" & Request.Form("Password") _
      & "'")
   if RSUser.EOF then
      TheMessage = "You have entered an incorrect login. " _
         & "Please try again."
   else
      TheMessage = "You are now logged in!"
   end if
else
   TheMessage = "Please enter your user name and password below."
end if
%>
```

Briefly, the code is first checking to see if the LOGIN button was pressed. If it was, the code queries the database to see if the user name and password exist in a single record. If a record does exist, then the user has entered a valid record and an appropriate message will be displayed. If a record is not found, the visitor has entered an invalid entry and a different message is prepared. The last message supplies the content for the initial view of the page.

Think about what would happen if we tried to implement this as client-side script. One thing would be that it would run on only recent versions of Internet Explorer, since the code is written in VBScript. Another problem is that we would be exposing the database password within the source that would be sent out to the browser.

With server-side script we don't have these concerns. The code will be processed on the server and none of the preceding code block will be visible to the visitor; plus, we don't have to concern ourselves with the type of browser that our visitor is using since the browser receives only HTML as the result of this page.

Another major advantage of server-side scripting is that the server can use components to process the page that may not be available on the client's machine. For example, let's say that I wanted to create a loan calculator on my Web site. It would be implemented like the page shown in Figure 1-12.

Visitors would enter the data needed to complete the calculation. When they press the CALCULATE button, they would have code that

Figure 1-12
Loan calculator
sample page.

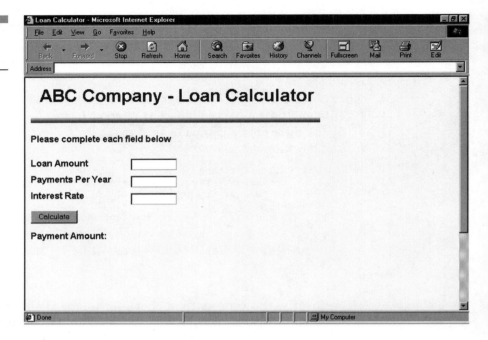

would compute the payment amount based on their specifications. As we have seen, you have a few options for where this code is located and how it is implemented.

You already know that the code is better protected from being pirated by another developer if you use server-side scripting. You also know that you won't have to worry about the browser being able to interpret the code that you have written with server-side scripting. But now you have a third advantage.

If you have ever tried to write loan calculations from scratch, you know this is error-prone, tedious work. Why not take advantage of components on your server that can do the calculations for you? For example, Microsoft Excel contains a rich set of financial calculations. You can harness that component's power within your server-side script and remove the need to rewrite code that you already have. So with server-side scripting you can use the power of any creatable components on your server to assist you with your application's needs without worrying whether visitors have the component on their machine.

Components of Dynamic Internet Solutions

So far we have looked at what makes a Web page dynamic or static. We have looked at different ways to make your pages dynamic and the benefits and pitfalls of the different methodologies. In this section, we look at the different components that make up a dynamic Internet solution and how they interact.

A dynamic Internet solution can contain a variety of components. First, it contains the HTML. Usually even for the most dynamic page there is some raw static HTML that binds together the dynamic elements. Frequently a dynamic page or site contains a database, where the dynamic content is often derived. More advanced solutions will contain server components. These components often contain business rules and act as an intermediary between the database and the dynamic portions of the Web page. The page will also contain some kind of code that inserts the dynamic content onto the page, like ASP code. And a dynamic solution usually will utilize some type of Web server like Internet Information Server that, in receiving the request from the browser, processes any code on the page and returns the result.

Quiz Page Walk-Through

To demonstrate each of the components involved in a dynamic solution, a sample Quiz is presented in the next few pages. The Quiz uses HTML for static elements of the page. It uses a database to store the questions and answers. A Visual Basic component provides calls to the database for retrieving the questions and answers and for checking the answers. The Quiz page is implemented as an Active Server Page and contains code to dynamically display the Quiz based on the current question; and the Quiz is implemented on an Internet Information Server that processes the code and returns the results to the browser.

The Quiz is implemented as a single Web page. When visitors first enter the page they see what is shown in Figure 1-13. When visitors first enter the Quiz they see the first question. They select what they think is the correct answer first and then press the CHECK ANSWER button. When that button is pressed they see the page shown in Figure 1-14. This

Figure 1-13
First page from the
Quiz.

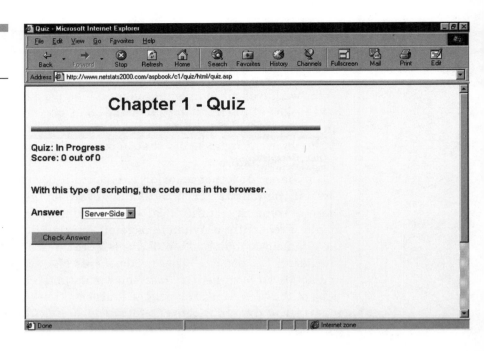

Figure 1-14
Second question
from the Quiz page.

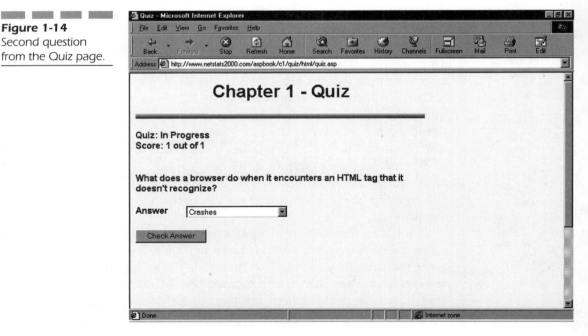

Figure 1-15
Final page for the Quiz.

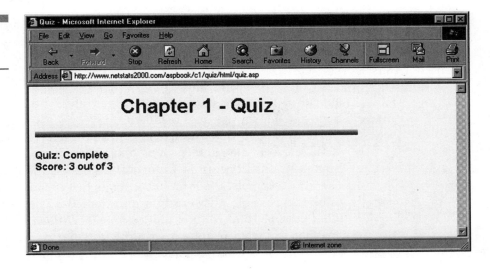

process continues until those taking the Quiz answer the last question and they see the page shown in Figure 1-15.

Notice that at the end of the Quiz, visitors do not see any additional questions nor is the ANSWER QUESTION button present. As you will see further in this discussion, the ASP code controls this output on to the page.

HTML

Within this dynamic Internet environment, the HTML is the combination of any static HTML in the originally requested page and the output of the code run by the server. So when visitors request to see the first question of the Quiz, they receive and see only HTML. For example, even though the Quiz question is dynamic, based on the current question requested, the HTML outputted for the question is this:

```
<P><B><FONT FACE="Arial,Helvetica">
With this type of scripting, the code runs in the browser.
</B></FONT>
```

And the Select control, the drop-down box on the form that contains the possible answers to the question, contains different values for each question but appears like the example below if the visitor selects to see the source for the page:

```
<SELECT NAME="Answer" >
   <OPTION VALUE="Server-Side">Server-Side</OPTION>
   <OPTION VALUE="Client-Side">Client-Side</OPTION>
</SELECT>
```

In fact, from the visitor's point of view, this single page site would appear as if it were four separate pages: one for each of the three questions and one for the final results page.

The HTML in this example also includes a *form*, which is a grouping of HTML form elements such as text boxes, free-form text boxes (called TEXTAREA), Select controls, radio buttons, and checkboxes to name a few.

In this example, the form has a single Select control element that contains the possible answers to a question. But the form also has a few other controls that contain hidden values. *Hidden elements* contain values that you want to submit with the form but you don't want visitors to see. In the next example page, three hidden elements are used.

```
<INPUT TYPE=HIDDEN NAME="CurrentQuestion" VALUE = "1">
<INPUT TYPE=HIDDEN NAME="QuestionsTaken" VALUE = "0">
<INPUT TYPE=HIDDEN NAME="NumberCorrect" VALUE = "0">
```

The first hidden element contains the number for the current question. We need this value so we can check to see if the visitor has selected the correct answer for this question. The QuestionsTaken hidden element stores the number of questions that the visitor has responded to. The NumberCorrect value contains the number of questions that the visitor entered correctly.

These three hidden values and the one Select control value that contains the answer that they selected for this question are submitted with this form when visitors press the button labeled CHECK ANSWER. What this means is that the browser sends these fields as a stream of bytes to the address specified in the Form tag:

```
<FORM ACTION="./quiz.asp" METHOD=POST>
```

So these values are sent back to the same page that created this page—this is how we get the multiple pages out of the single Web page. Each time visitors answer a question, that question number, along with their answer and the other two values, is sent back to this same page for processing.

One more item is passed with the page when it is submitted. The name of the button pressed is also passed:

```
<INPUT TYPE="submit" NAME="Calculate" VALUE="Check Answer" >
```

You will see this code used frequently in this book and in your own code. The presence of this button or the presence of whichever button is pressed is used to determine what action to take.

When the page is processed, raw HTML exists side by side with the code on the page. For example, on the unprocessed page the Select control described earlier looks like this:

```
<SELECT NAME="Answer" ><% response.write AnswerText %></SELECT>
```

And the HTML with the code in the unprocessed page for the hidden elements appears like this:

```
<INPUT TYPE=HIDDEN NAME="CurrentQuestion" VALUE = "
    <% Response.Write CurrentQuestion %>">
<INPUT TYPE=HIDDEN NAME="QuestionsTaken" VALUE = "
    <% Response.Write QuestionsTaken %>">
<INPUT TYPE=HIDDEN NAME="NumberCorrect" VALUE = "
    <% Response.Write NumberCorrect %>">
```

Further on in this section, we look at how the Active Server Page code works with the HTML to provide for the dynamic content displayed to visitors.

Database Component

Many of the Internet/intranet solutions that you create will have some kind of a database component to them. If you are logging users into your site, you will need a table of users to validate their entry into your site. If you have your company's catalog online, you will probably have a series of tables relating to the products that deal with names, descriptions, inventory, prices, specials, and so forth. If your site contains the current weather conditions where you are located, you probably store that data for retrieval in a database.

So the *database component* of a dynamic Internet application often contains the source for the dynamic content. In our sample Quiz project, the requests for the database come from the Active Server Page. The request passes through our *server component* that queries the database. The database returns the request to the server component, which then passes the data back to our Active Server Page.

As you will see in greater detail in Chapter 13, the code requesting

Figure 1-16
ODBC Data Source
Administrator.

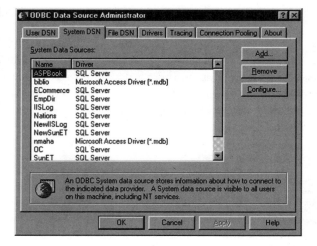

the data from the database, whether in the Active Server Page or in the server component, must have a way of locating that database. This can be achieved through the *Open Database Connectivity* (ODBC). With ODBC we create a Data Source Name (DSN) through the ODBC Data Source Administrator as shown in Figure 1-16. By clicking on the ADD button we can set up a connection with any reachable database for which we have an ODBC driver.

In this sample site we are connecting to an SQL Server 6.5 database called *ASPBook*. The DSN is created to allow communication between SQL Server and the Active Server Page. When this connection was initially created, the database type, the IP Address of the server, and the name of the database were supplied. Some of this you can see in Figure 1-17.

Figure 1-17
ODBC DSN
Configuration.

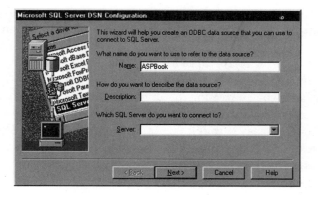

TABLE 1-1

C1Questions Fields

Field Name	Field Type	Notes
QuestionID	int	Primary Key
Question	varchar	Text of the question
Answer	varchar	Text of the correct answer

The data in the database for our Quiz sample contain the text of the question, the correct answer for the question, and all possible answers to be listed in the Select control on the Web page. Two tables are used to satisfy the data needs. One table is called *C1Questions*; this table contains the data for the question itself. The names of the fields, type, and use are displayed in Table 1-1.

The *QuestionID* is the primary key for the table. That means it contains a value that is unique for this field. So if one record has a QuestionID of 45, no other record can have that same value. This uniqueness provides the mechanism for us to retrieve the proper question in code. The data type is *int*, meaning that the value for this field is a whole number.

The Question field contains the text of the question itself. This is the data you see on the Web page when a question is displayed. The data type listed here is *varchar*, which means that this field will hold letters and/or numbers. The length of the field can vary from 0 to 255 characters.

The Answer field contains the correct answer for the question. This text field is used to check visitors' answers with the correct answer to determine if they answered the question correctly. The field can contain 0 to 100 characters.

The second table used in this sample Quiz page contains all the possible answers to the Questions. The table is called *C1Answers* and the fields for that table are displayed in Table 1-2.

TABLE 1-2

C1Answers Fields

Field Name	Field Type	Notes
AnswerID	int	Primary Key and Identity Column
QuestionID	int	Foreign Key
Answer	varchar	Text of the correct answer

The data in Table 1-2 are used to populate the Select control on the Web page. Each question has one or more answers that appear in this table. In code, we query this table looking for all the answers that go with our current question and then display those choices in the Select control.

The *AnswerID* is the primary key for the table. As mentioned earlier, a *primary key* uniquely identifies a record across a table. The field is also an Identity Column. This means that when a new record is added to this table, you can leave this field blank and SQL Server will automatically populate it with a Unique value. As you will see in Chapter 13, when you create a field like this in SQL Server, you can specify a number to start with and how much to increment the number from record to record.

The QuestionID is used as a *foreign key* in this table, which means that it is used to connect this table with the C1Questions table. When we populate the Select control with possible answers, we don't want to see all the possible answers across all the questions. We want to see just the answers that go with the current question. This field provides that filtering. When an Answer is entered in to this table, a value for the QuestionID must also be supplied. This QuestionID refers to the question that goes with this answer.

The last field in this table is the Answer field, which contains the text of the Answer itself. These data end up in the Select control.

One of the records in the C1Questions table is displayed in Table 1-3.

TABLE 1-3

C1Questions Sample Record

Field Name	Value
QuestionID	1
Question	With this type of scripting the code runs in the browser
Answer	Client-Side

TABLE 1-4

C1Answers Sample Record

Field Name	Value
AnswerID	1
QuestionID	1
Answer	Server-Side

A sample record from the C1Answers table is shown in Table 1-4.

Server Components

Not all of your Internet/intranet solutions need server components. In fact, at first you may not use them at all. But there will come a time when you find that you cannot achieve the solution at hand with just ASP; or, maybe you will find that your ASP is getting overly complicated and needs to be segregated into objects; or, you may need to split the complexity of the task between entry-level programmers and more advanced programmers.

Using or creating a server component will often satisfy these requirements. *Server components* are code modules that you access through your ASP, or from within other programming environments, to accomplish some programming task.

Some server components are built into your system. For example, IIS comes with the Collaborative Data Objects that make it simple for you to send email through your code, as you will see in Chapter 9. Another component that comes with IIS is the *Browser Capabilities* component, which provides methods for determining the browser and other information about the visitor as you will read in Chapter 10.

Other components are available for purchase or may be downloaded from vendors. These are usually more specific in their task. For example, if you find that you need to create a graphic in code that is made up of a pie chart, you can find a component to take care of that need. So, frequently you can save yourself time and money by purchasing a component to assist in your programming needs.

Your other option is to create your own component. Creating your own component can satisfy a variety of needs, one of which is performance. If you create a component, it is implemented as compiled code, which differs from Active Server Page code, which is script that must be recompiled with each use.

Another very important reason to create components is to split off your business rules from the interface of your application. For example, say that you need to create a site that adds new employees to your employee database. You may have a variety of ways to accomplish this. You may have an Access application that your Human Resources people use to enter the employee into the database. You may also have your ASP application that is used to enter an employee into the database.

The database is probably set up in such a way that certain fields are required and some fields need to be a certain type and within a specific range. These rules, business rules, are much more easily modified and quality-controlled if they are in a single location. A server component is often implemented in such a way.

An additional reason to create server components is to remove the complexity of certain code blocks out of the hands of more junior programmers. You may, for instance, have a procedure that calculates some predicted future value of stock based on a set of parameters and calculations. This code could be placed into all the locations that need it. But a programmer who is not familiar with the code may not implement correctly. If you create a server component you can provide your programmers with just a single call to achieve the same task.

In Chapter 10 we discuss in great detail the creation of server components. So for this discussion we will just introduce the use of server components.

For the Quiz page, a server component was created by compiling an ActiveX DLL created in Visual Basic. The component provides the database interface between our front-end code, the ASP, and the database itself. The component was created by selecting an ActiveX DLL project from within Visual Basic, as shown in Figure 1-18.

When we select an ActiveX DLL as the project, we are setting up the template for creating a DLL server component. Within the project the

Figure 1-18
Creating an ActiveX
DLL from Visual
Basic.

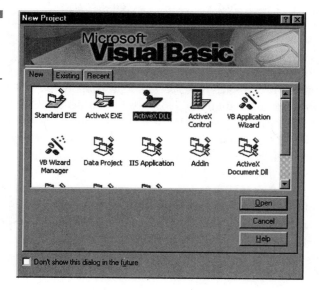

Figure 1-19
Naming the server
component.

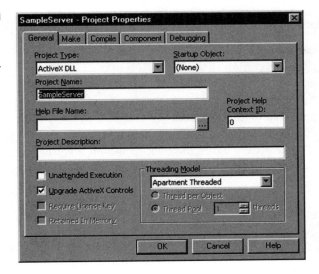

name of the project takes on special meaning because that name will be used below in our ASP code to call the procedures in this server component. You do this by selecting the Project Properties menu item from the Project menu. The resulting dialog box is shown in Figure 1-19, from which you set the name of the project in the PROJECT NAME text box.

Within an ActiveX DLL server you have *classes*, where the procedures actually go. A server can have one or more classes. Classes are usually implemented by putting together the procedures that are common. For example, the server component used in this example contains a single class. The class contains the procedures that retrieve the question, answer, and check an answer. But if we expanded this application we may add pages that allowed users to add questions to the test. The procedures that took those actions would probably be in a separate class. Or maybe you would add another class that allowed users to log in to your Quiz application so they could keep track of their progress. You would probably implement the procedures for that functionality in another class.

As with the project, the class has a name. The name of the class is important—like the *project* name—because it will be used in our ASP code to call the procedures that we have in this server. Within Visual Basic you do this by viewing the properties for a class as shown in Figure 1-20.

Now that we have our server defined and the class defined within that server we are ready to create procedures or methods within the

Figure 1-20
Naming the class.

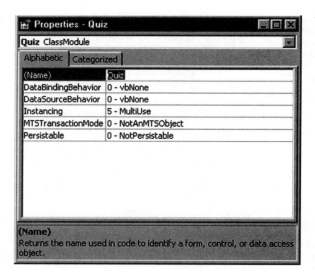

class. The *methods* are code blocks that we write to achieve some programming task. These methods will be called from the Active Server Page code that we discuss later.

This Quiz class that we created previously has three methods. The first method retrieves the text of the question based on the QuestionID passed into the procedure. The code for this procedure is:

```
Public Function GetQuestion(QuestionID)
Dim RSQuestion As ADODB.Recordset
Set RSQuestion = Conn.Execute("select Question from C1Questions " _
    & "where QuestionID = " & QuestionID)
If RSQuestion.EOF Then
    GetQuestion = "NA"
Else
    GetQuestion = RSQuestion("Question")
End If
End Function
```

Note that the method is called *GetQuestion*. In the ASP Code, this is the name we use to call this procedure. The code in this procedure connects to the database and retrieves the text of the question based on the QuestionID. If the QuestionID is not valid, then the text NA is returned; otherwise, the text of the question is returned.

The next procedure returns the text needed to populate the Select control on the HTML form with the possible answers for a question. The code for that procedure is:

```
Public Function GetAnswer(QuestionID)
Dim RSAnswers As ADODB.Recordset
Dim TempList As String
Set RSAnswers = Conn.Execute("select Answer from ClAnswers " _
    & "where QuestionID = " & QuestionID)
Do Until RSAnswers.EOF
    TempList = TempList & "<OPTION VALUE=""" _
        & RSAnswers("answer") & """>" _
        & RSAnswers("Answer") & "</OPTION>"
    RSAnswers.MoveNext
Loop
GetAnswer = TempList
End Function
```

This method is called *GetAnswer*. When this method is called it is passed a QuestionID. All possible answers for that question are retrieved from the database. The code then iterates or loops through each of the answers, building the necessary HTML text for a Select control with each answer being an Option in the Select control. That raw HTML is then returned from this method.

The final method, or procedure, in the Quiz Class of the SampleServer server is called *CheckAnswer*. This procedure checks to see if the answer supplied is the correct answer for a question. The code is:

```
Public Function CheckAnswer(QuestionID, AnswerText)
Dim RSAnswer As ADODB.Recordset
Set RSAnswer = Conn.Execute("select Answer from ClQuestions " _
    & "where QuestionID = " & QuestionID)
    If RSAnswer("Answer") = AnswerText Then
        CheckAnswer = 1
    Else
        CheckAnswer = 0
    End If
End Function
```

The CheckAnswer procedure requires two values passed into it, the QuestionID of the question to be checked and the Answer to test for correctness. The code connects to the database retrieving the correct answer for the desired question. That answer is then compared to the one passed into this procedure. If the two match, then the answer being checked is correct and the procedure returns a 1. If the answer was not correct, the procedure returns a 0. These values and the return values from the other procedures will be used within the ASP code discussed later.

The class that we create within Visual Basic has a place for us to put what we want to run when the class is first called, or *instantiated*. This location is called the *Initialize event* and contains this code:

```
Private Sub Class_Initialize()
    Conn.Open "ASPBook", "sa", "yourpassword"
End Sub
```

This code supplies our connection with the database. Remember in our discussion on the database portion of the Quiz that we needed to set up a Data Source Name or DSN. The preceding line of code uses that DSN to connect to the database. Then the other procedures within this class use that connection to retrieve the data.

Active Server Page

So far we have looked at the raw HTML that is sent to the browser as well as its static use within our dynamic page. We have looked at the database that contains the Quiz questions and answers, and we have looked at the component created in Visual Basic that connects to the database. Now we will look at the Active Server Page code.

The *ASP Code* is what is read and processed by IIS when our visitor requests the page. This code completes the necessary calls to produce the desired output to the browser. In our Quiz sample the code must retrieve the questions and answers. It must also keep track of the current question, the number of correct answers, and the questions answered. The code must also format the page so the Answers field and the button do not appear if the visitor is done with the Quiz. We go into great detail in Chapter 4 about the specific layout of this code, so for now just try to read through it.

At the top of the Active Server Page we have the following code:

```
<%@ Language=VBScript %>
<%
set objQuiz = server.CreateObject("SampleServer.Quiz")
if isempty(Request.Form("Calculate")) then
  CurrentQuestion = 1
  QuestionsTaken = 0
  NumberCorrect = 0
else
  if objQuiz.CheckAnswer(Request.Form("CurrentQuestion"), _
    Request.Form("Answer")) = 1 then
    NumberCorrect = Request.Form("NumberCorrect") + 1
  else
    NumberCorrect = Request.Form("NumberCorrect")
  end if
  QuestionsTaken = Request.Form("QuestionsTaken") + 1
  CurrentQuestion = Request.Form("CurrentQuestion") + 1
end if
QuestionText = objQuiz.GetQuestion(CurrentQuestion)
```

```
if QuestionText = "NA" then
  TheMessage = "Quiz: Complete"
else
  TheMessage = "Quiz: In Progress"
  AnswerText = objQuiz.GetAnswer(CurrentQuestion)
end if
%>
```

The first line of code simply tells the compiler the scripting language we are using, VBScript.

Next we create an instance of the class within the server that we discussed in the last section. In other words, we are connecting to the server component because we want to use the procedures it contains:

```
set objQuiz = server.CreateObject("SampleServer.Quiz")
```

Notice when we created the procedure that we used the Project name and the class name, SampleServer.Quiz.

Remember in our discussion on the HTML that we discussed looking for the SUBMIT button to determine what action to take. That is what we are doing here:

```
if isempty(Request.Form("Calculate")) then
```

We are saying that if visitors haven't pressed the CALCULATE button, then they must have just entered the page. If that is the case, then we need to set the page up for the first question:

```
CurrentQuestion = 1
QuestionsTaken = 0
NumberCorrect = 0
```

If the CALCULATE button is present, then visitors must be submitting questions that need to be scored:

```
Else
```

The code then calls our component to see if visitors entered the correct answer. If they did, then we need to give them credit for a correct answer:

```
if objQuiz.CheckAnswer(Request.Form("CurrentQuestion"), _
Request.Form("Answer")) = 1 then
NumberCorrect = Request.Form("NumberCorrect") + 1
```

Otherwise, the current number correct is just how many they have correct so far:

```
else
  NumberCorrect = Request.Form("NumberCorrect")
```

Now we need to retrieve the text for the next question by calling the GetQuestion procedure of our server component:

```
QuestionText = objQuiz.GetQuestion(CurrentQuestion)
```

If an additional question was not found, the procedure returns an NA as we defined in the previous section.

```
if QuestionText = "NA" then
```

That means we should prepare a message to visitors that tells them that the quiz is complete:

```
TheMessage = "Quiz: Complete"
```

Otherwise we have retrieved a valid question and the answers to the question need to be retrieved through the GetAnswer procedure:

```
else
  TheMessage = "Quiz: In Progress"
  AnswerText = objQuiz.GetAnswer(CurrentQuestion)

end if
```

Scattered throughout the HTML are additional lines of script that insert the variables created earlier. For example, the text of the question is written within the HMTL like this:

```
<P><B><FONT FACE="Arial,Helvetica">
<% response.write QuestionText %></B></FONT>
```

The answers for the Select control are written with this line of code:

```
<SELECT NAME="Answer" ><% response.write AnswerText %></SELECT>
```

And the running tally of the visitor's Quiz score is written within the HMTL in this form:

```
<P><B><FONT FACE="Arial,Helvetica">
<% Response.Write TheMessage %><BR>Score:
<% Response.Write NumberCorrect %> out of
<% Response.Write QuestionsTaken %></B></FONT>
```

So the ASP performs a very important task!

Making It All Work with an Internet Server

All the preceding code does not do a thing without an Internet Server to pull everything together. The Internet Server waits for requests from browsers. The Internet Server retrieves the requested page. Depending on the type of page, it will check it for ASP code. If the code is present, the Internet Server will process the code and any will connect to any server components requested by the ASP code. Once the processing is complete, the Internet Server sends the HTML out to the requesting browser.

In our example we are using Microsoft's Internet Information Server on a Windows NT operating system. When someone on the Internet or on our intranet requests the `quiz.asp` file, IIS retrieves that page. IIS notes that the page ends in the extension `.asp`. This tells IIS that this is an ASP page and it needs to have its code processed. IIS runs the code on our Quiz page. It creates an instance of our Quiz class from the SampleServer server. The resulting HTML is then sent by IIS back to the browser that requested the page.

In the next chapter, we look more deeply at IIS. We will see how to configure and use IIS from a developer's perspective.

Not Just for NT IIS Anymore

The focus of this book is on using Active Server Pages on a Windows NT server running the Internet Information Server. But the popularity of ASP is quickly going beyond this framework. Numerous companies are creating tools and add-ins for other Internet servers and operating systems that allow ASP developers to use their skills outside the Microsoft model.

In the coming years expect ASP to continue to grow as it provides a vital role in connecting the client and the server.

2

IIS: A Developer's Perspective

What Is IIS?

Microsoft's *Internet Information Server* (IIS) is the connection between the client and the server in an Internet/intranet browser-based development solution. In this type of solution, the *client* is the browser like Internet Explorer, Netscape Navigator, or any other browser. The *server* is the combination of tools and applications that we use on our Web site to produce the content. On some pages, the role of IIS will be just to send out some static HTML; on other pages, IIS has a much greater role and will facilitate in the connection of a multitude of resources on your server.

Figure 2-1 shows the steps involved in a request made in this client/server environment. We discuss this process in more detail in Chapter 4, but for now note the involvement of IIS. Visitors type a request in to their browser for a page on your server. The request is routed through the Internet to your server, which then routes the request to IIS. IIS retrieves the page requested and, based on the name of the file requested, it decides what to do with the page. If the file has an .asp extension or the file is some other type associated with some kind of processing on your machine, IIS processes the code on that page.

That processing can involve other components as well. If the code needs to connect to SQL Server to retrieve some data, then the necessary components are instantiated. If the code requires some graph drawing program to render a graph, then that component is started. Or, if the code calls one of your own components, it will also be instantiated.

The result of the code and all the components loaded for this page is sent back to the requesting browser. The browser then parses what is sent and displays the page to the visitor. If the page does not contain an

Figure 2-1
Steps involved in a request made by the browser.

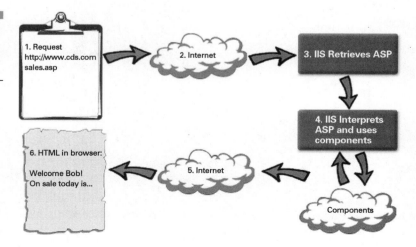

extension or name that IIS notes needs to be processed, it is just sent to the browser without any components being instantiated or any processing done.

Getting a Copy of IIS

Microsoft's Internet Information Server 4.0 for Windows NT 4.0 comes with the Windows NT 4.0 Option Pack. You can download the Option Pack for free from Microsoft's Web site. New copies of the NT 4.0 CD come with IIS 4.0, so you may already have IIS running on your server—you will need to have at least version 4.0 of IIS on your server. Previous versions will not allow you to take advantage of all the tools and techniques presented in this book. You can determine if you have the Windows NT 4.0 Option Pack installed by looking for the Option Pack folder as shown in Figure 2-2.

Comprehensive installation instructions for IIS can also be found at Microsoft's Web site. The remainder of this chapter deals with configuring IIS from a developer's perspective. You will learn how to work with the Microsoft Management Console, configure the WWW service, add new

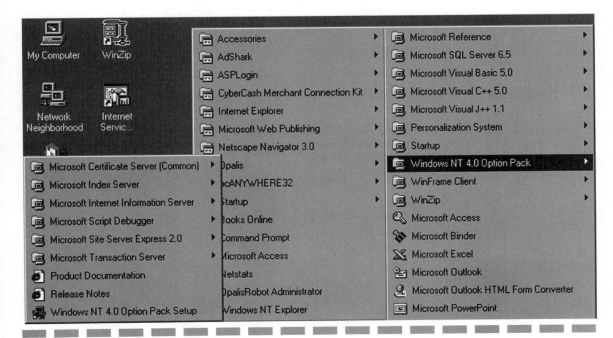

Figure 2-2   Windows NT 4.0 Option Pack folder.

sites, configure sites, work with ASP applications, use and configure the FTP service, and monitor your Internet Information Server's performance.

Microsoft Management Console

The *Microsoft Management Console*, or MMC, is the tool that you use to configure IIS. MMC is new to Windows NT and is also used to configure numerous other administrative tasks in the NT environment. The tool works by using Snap-Ins for each application that needs to take advantage of MMC.

MMC is a framework for configuring services. A product that requires its administrators to use MMC for configurations provides a Snap-In for MMC. The *Snap-In* provides a hierarchical view of the objects within the utility and the actions that can be taken on each object.

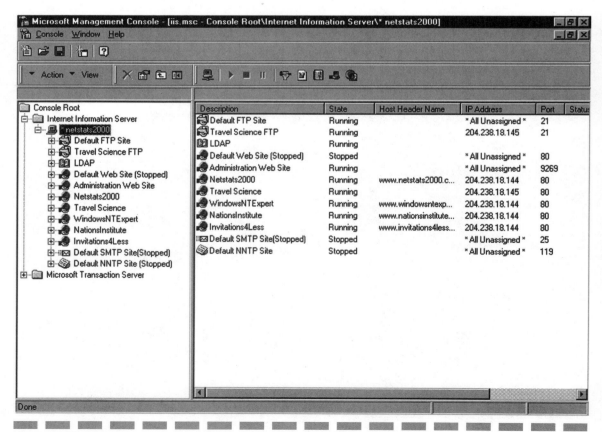

Figure 2-3   Microsoft Management Console with the IIS Snap-In in use.

To launch the MMC for the Internet Information Server, select Internet Service Manager from the Microsoft Internet Information Server shown in Figure 2-2 and you should see the management console similar to the one in Figure 2-3.

On the left is the hierarchical list of objects within the IIS Snap-In. You expand and contract the list just as you would with the Windows Explorer by clicking on the plus sign to expand and on the minus sign to contract. When you click on one of the objects on the left side you see a list of all the items within that object on the right side of the window.

Each *object* can have *actions*, which are things you do with or to an object. You can view the list of actions for an object by right-clicking on the object or by first selecting it and then clicking on the ACTION button in the toolbar as shown in Figure 2-4.

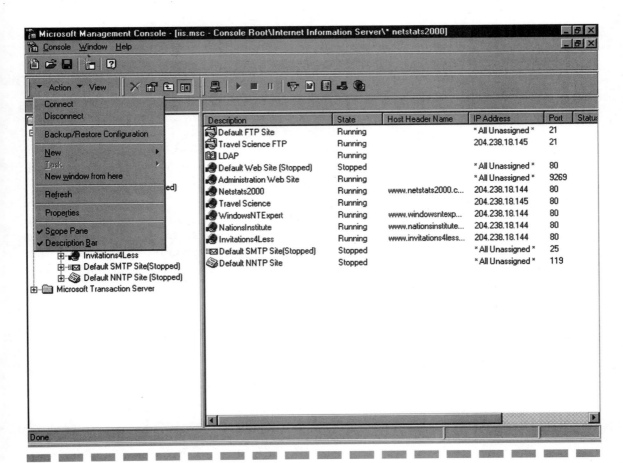

Figure 2-4   Action menu in the MMC.

Each object can also have *properties*, which are attributes of an object. To view the properties of an object, right-click on the object and select Properties. You can also view the properties of an object by clicking on the Action menu and selecting Properties or by pressing the PROPERTIES icon on the toolbar.

A Snap-In can also provide additional functionality through the toolbars that aren't related to a specific object. For example, you can view the Performance Monitor or the Event Viewer by selecting the related icon from the toolbar.

WWW Service Properties

The Internet Information Server includes the WWW Service as one of its services. This service has its own properties that you can modify to affect the way WWW Service is configured. The WWW Service contains many properties that are also properties of an individual Web site. When you create a new Web site, the properties it uses are inherited by the properties of the WWW Service, so setting the service up properly from the beginning will save you time down the road when you have numerous Web sites on your server.

To open the properties for the WWW Service within MMC, right-click on the name of the computer that contains the WWW Service you wish to configure and select Properties. See the dialog shown in Figure 2-5.

Note the ENABLE BANDWIDTH THROTTLING check box. If you check this, the text box beneath it becomes enabled. You can then specify how much of your network bandwidth you would like to use for this service. This value is a maximum value, not a reserved amount of bandwidth—what it means is that no matter how much bandwidth is available you may use no more than the value listed here.

Web Site Properties

Under the MASTER PROPERTIES box, select WWW Service and click on EDIT. You should now see the main properties dialog for the WWW Service as shown in Figure 2-6.

Make sure that you are on the tab called WEB SITE. The first thing you can enter is a description for this service. This has no effect on the service and is just for your own identification. In the middle of this prop-

Figure 2-5
Master Properties
selection dialog.

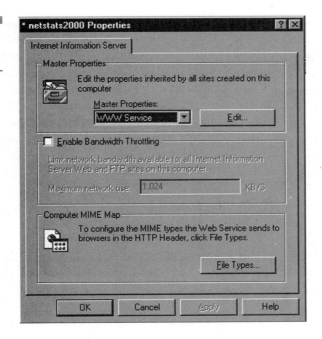

Figure 2-6
WWW Service
Properties.

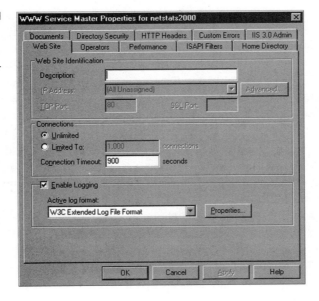

erty sheet you can configure connections. Here you can allow for an unlimited number of simultaneous visitors connected to your IIS WWW Server or you can limit that. You can also provide a *Connection Timeout* value, which represents the number of seconds a user can remain inactive without being disconnected from your WWW Service.

At the bottom of the property sheet, select whether you want logging and if so what type of logging you want. *Logging* in the WWW Service refers to the tracking you want to do on visitors to your site. If logging in is enabled, every item requested from the Web server is entered as a record in a database or a text file. Fields that are entered can include the date and time of the request, the IP address of the requestor, the file being requested, and much more. You have four choices for the log format: Microsoft IIS Log File Format, NCSA Common Log File Format, W3C Extended Log Format, and ODBC Logging.

The *Microsoft IIS Log File Format* is a specific file format used just by IIS. The log produced is an ASCII text file. When you click on the properties for this type, you can select where the log will be located and how often a new log is generated.

The *NCSA Common Log File Format* is more of a standard log format that is found on Internet Servers outside the Microsoft world. You may need to use this type of format if you are using a third-party Log Analysis tool.

The *W3C Extended Log Format* is similar to the NCSA Common Log File Format, but provides additional fields that you can track. You can also select which fields you do and don't want to collect. If you press the PROPERTIES button for this logging type, you will see the Extended Logging Properties as shown in Figure 2-7.

If you click on the EXTENDED PROPERTIES tab you will see the different fields that you can track. The User Name field works only if the person is actually logged on to your server. If the page that the person was visiting at your site was http://www.somewhere.com/search.asp?query=VB, then the URL Stem would be the www.somewhere.com/search.asp part and the query=VB the URI Query field. The User Agent field contains information about the browser that made the request. The Referrer field contains the name of the page that the visitor was at prior to this page if the visitor clicked on a link to get to this page and if the browser supports the Referrer field. If the requested item is a graphic on a page, then the Referrer field contains the name of the page that the graphic is on.

The fourth type of logging is *ODBC Logging*, which is the most resource-heavy but provides you with the greatest possible analysis

Figure 2-7
Extended Logging
Properties dialog box.

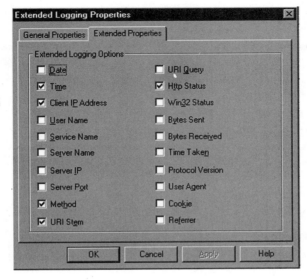

capabilities. With ODBC logging each request made to your server is logged as a record into a database. You use the properties for this type to specify the Data Source Name (DSN) of the database that you wish to use. When you use this type you must first create a table to store the request records in. This table has to be of a specific format as described for SQL Server in Table 2-1.

After you create the table, you will need to create a DSN through the ODBC Administrator that you will then reference from the properties dialog box for the ODBC Logging. See Chapter 13 for additional information on creating a DSN.

NOTE: *Since logging requires that the request be written to a file or database, it uses resources. When you are not using logging you may want to disable it.*

Performance Properties

Select the PERFORMANCE tab from the WWW Service Properties and you should see a property sheet like the one in Figure 2-8.

The Performance Tuning property should be set to the number of connections that you estimate you get per day. You don't want to set this to

TABLE 2-1

ODBC Logging
Table Definitions

Field Name	Value
ClientHost	varchar(255)
Username	varchar(255)
LogTime	datetime
Service	varchar(255)
Machine	varchar(255)
ServerIP	varchar(50)
ProcessingTime	int
BytesRecvd	int
BytesSent	int
ServerStatus	int
Win32Status	int
Operation	varchar(255)
Target	varchar(255)
Parameters	varchar(255)

Figure 2-8
WWW Service
Performance
Properties.

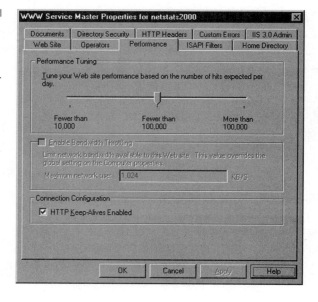

the top level unless you really get that many connections, since resources would be wasted.

Notice that the Enable Bandwidth Throttling is disabled. This property can be set only for an individual Web site. We discuss this property later in this chapter in the "Web Site Properties" section.

When checked, the HTTP Keep-Alives Enabled allows a browser to maintain a connection across page requests instead of requiring the browser to reconnect with each request. This field is enabled by default.

ISAPI Filters Property

One of the more advanced functions with IIS is to create an *ISAPI filter*, which allows you to take your own custom action when some event occurs within IIS. Instead of IIS processing the event in its own usual way, it allows your program to process the event. These programs are frequently written in Visual C++ and also frequently involve a customization of logging. So if you don't like the formats available for logging that we discussed in an earlier section of this chapter, you could write your own.

To do this, you add an ISAPI filter through the ISAPI Filters property as shown in Figure 2-9. You can add an ISAPI filter by clicking on the

Figure 2-9
ISAPI filters dialog.

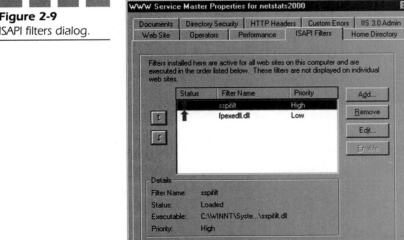

ADD button and browsing to the library file. The order that these filters appear in is important, because the first filter found to handle an event runs before other filters do. When these files are loaded they remain in memory, so take care not to overuse them.

Home Directory Properties

Next let's examine the properties of the Home Directory property sheet, as shown in Figure 2-10.

Note that some of the items on this page are disabled because they don't apply to the WWW Service scope and are discussed later in this chapter when we review the properties for Web sites and ASP applications.

As you set the properties in the WWW Service, remember that, when you create a new Web site on IIS, it will inherit the properties that you supply here—so be careful.

The ACCESS PERMISSIONS refer to what the anonymous visitor can do with files. If READ is selected, the visitor can view files. If WRITE is selected, then the visitor can upload files to the server.

You can check the LOG ACCESS check box to include the files in a site or directory within the log file. If DIRECTORY BROWSING is checked, visitors can see the contents of the directory if there is no default page in the directory they are in. You usually don't want this on, because you

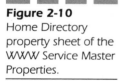

Figure 2-10
Home Directory property sheet of the WWW Service Master Properties.

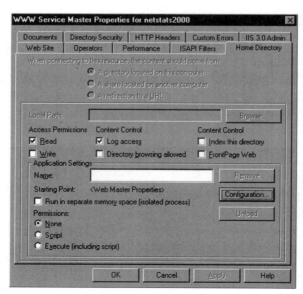

want visitors to navigate to pages at your site through links instead of just seeing a list of pages at your site.

If INDEX THIS DIRECTORY is checked, the pages within the site or directory will be included in automated indexing, which creates a database that you can use to allow visitors to search the content of your site.

The rest of the properties on this tab are discussed later in this chapter.

Documents

The Documents property sheet from the WWW Service Properties dialog is displayed in Figure 2-11.

When you type in a Web address like http://www.something.com, you are really going to a page at that site, like http://www.something.com/index.html or http://www.something.com/default.asp. This is referred to as the *default page*. If you don't specify a page to go to, the server assumes you want the default page for that site or directory; on many servers that is a fixed name like index.html.

Within IIS, not only can you specify the name of the default page, but you can also specify more than one. You do this by pressing the ADD button on the DOCUMENTS tab. Once specified, you can then set the order in which IIS should look for a default page. For example, using the pages

Figure 2-11
Documents property
sheet.

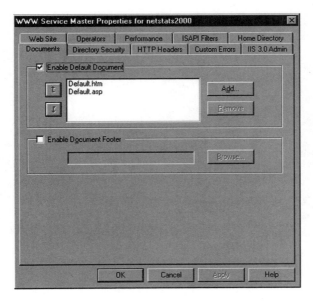

listed in Figure 2-11, IIS will first look for a page named default.htm. If it doesn't find one, it will then look for a page named default.asp.

If you check ENABLE DOCUMENT FOOTER and specify a page name, IIS will insert that page at the bottom of every page requested. You could use this feature to automatically add copyright information to every page on your site without having to modify any page just by specifying the name of a page that contained the copyright information in the Document Footer field.

Customer Errors

The Customer Errors properties page is displayed in Figure 2-12.

When you try to go to a Web page that doesn't exist, you get an error message that says the page doesn't exist. Most Web sites just show this error message in a raw format that shows the error number and the description of the error. But other sites provide you with a more rich error message that doesn't leave you feeling like you are stuck with no further options. IIS gives you the capability of returning whatever customized page you want when an error occurs.

For example, instead of showing visitors a stale message that the page wasn't found, maybe you want to give them the capability of searching for a page within your site, or maybe you want to give them

Figure 2-12
Customer Errors
property sheet.

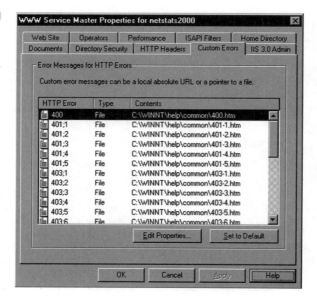

contact information so they can supply you with the name of the dead link.

You supply the name of the page you want displayed by clicking on EDIT PROPERTIES when the error number you want to work with is highlighted. You can then supply the name of the page to be displayed.

Web Sites Within IIS

As you can see from Figure 2-13, you can have numerous Web sites within IIS. The Web sites within IIS are noted with an icon that has a hand holding the earth. In the preceding example, there are seven Web sites installed; Default Web Site, Administration Web Site,

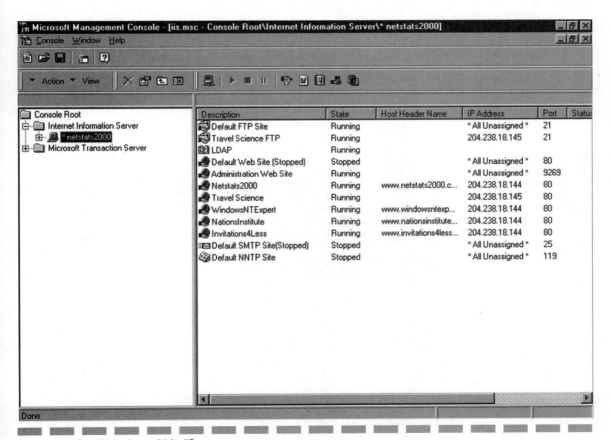

Figure 2-13   Web sites within IIS.

NetStats2000, Travel Science, WindowsNTExpert, NationsInstitute, and Invitations4Less.

Notice the second column after the name of the site is called *state*. This column tells you whether the site is currently running, paused, or stopped. A *running* Web site is up and reachable by current and new connections; a *paused* Web site can be reached only by those already connected; a *stopped* Web site is shut down and cannot be reached by any connection.

To start, stop, or pause a Web site, right-click on the site in the right half of the MMC and select START, STOP, or PAUSE, as shown in Figure 2-14. You can also start, stop, or pause a Web site by clicking on the Action menu item or by clicking on the START, STOP, and PAUSE icons from the toolbar.

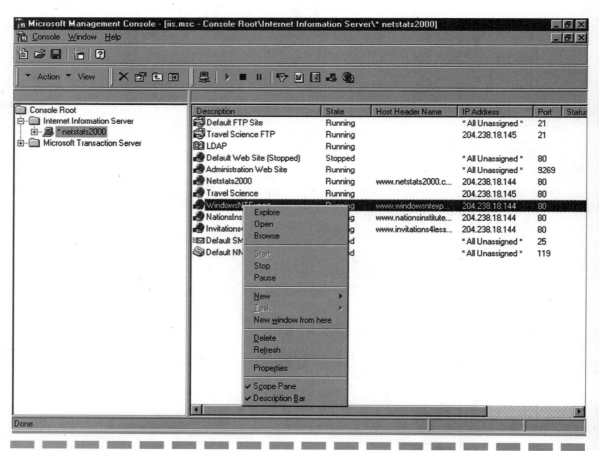

Figure 2-14 Starting, stopping, and pausing a Web site.

Adding a Web Site

You can add a Web site to IIS by using the New Web Site Wizard. You access the wizard by right-clicking on the computer that you want to host the Web site on and selecting NEW followed by WEB SITE as shown in Figure 2-15.

The wizard takes you through the steps of adding a new Web site to IIS. The first step is to supply a common name for the Web site, as shown in Figure 2-16. This name is for your own identification purposes. In the second step you configure the IP Address and Port Number for this Web site, as shown in Figure 2-17.

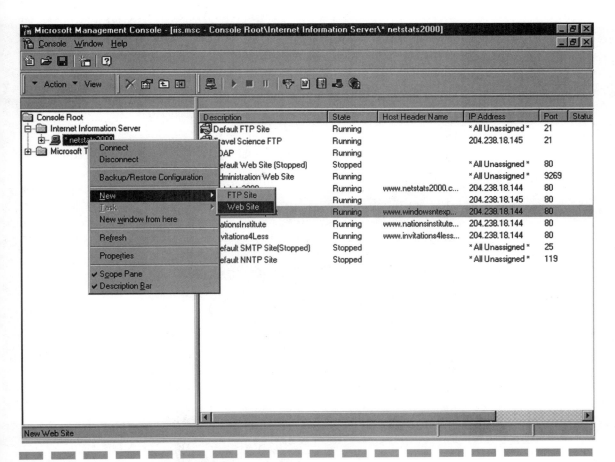

Figure 2-15   Selecting the New Web Site Wizard.

Figure 2-16
New Web Site
Wizard Step 1.

The first step is to select the IP address for your server. If your server has a single IP Address, you can select that value from the list. If your server has multiple IP Addresses, you will need to know which IP Address your domain name is registered to. If you do not know this, contact your ISP or network administrator and they should be able to tell you.

As you will see later in this chapter, one of the greatest changes made to version 4 of IIS is that you can host multiple Web sites on a single IP Address—so you really need only a single IP Address.

The port numbers should be left alone. These are the default values that a browser sends out. If you enter a different value, visitors to your site will have to know that port number to access the pages to your site. For example, if you left the value alone for the TCP port, visitors would access your site like this: http://www.somewhere.com. If you changed the port number to 9269, then visitors would have to make that port num-

Figure 2-17
New Web Site
Wizard Step 2.

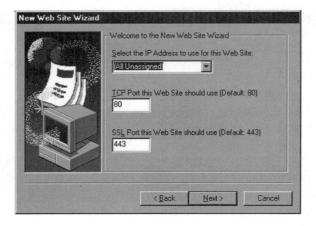

Figure 2-18
New Web Site
Wizard Step 3.

ber part of the address they went to: http://www.somewhere.com:9269.

Usually you wouldn't want to do this because this would be confusing to your visitors since they rarely would enter a port number. But this is a technique for allowing a different entry into a Web server without having an additional domain name. For example, another way to administer IIS is through the Web. You do this by going to your usual domain name but supplying a port number after the name.

In the third step of the wizard, you supply the physical location of the Web site files on your server, which is shown in Figure 2-18.

Press the BROWSE button to select the directory that contains the top-level of the Web site. All the files for the Web site need to be contained within this directory and its subdirectories, unless you create a virtual directory, discussed later in this chapter. The top-level directory can be any directory on your server. If you check the ALLOW ANONYMOUS ACCESS box, any visitor can access the files in this Web site; otherwise, the visitor must have the necessary permissions to access this directory.

NOTE: *You can also change the values you are setting for this site by viewing the properties for the site once it is created.*

In the final step of the wizard you select the access permissions for the Web site (Figure 2-19). If ALLOW READ ACCESS is checked, visitors can view the content of the site. If ALLOW SCRIPT ACCESS is checked, then scripts like ASP scripts can be run on this site. Note though that you may want to place your scripts in a single folder and then allow scripts to be run only in that folder instead of the whole site.

ALLOW EXECUTE ACCESS means that executable program files can be

Figure 2-19
New Web Site
Wizard Step 4.

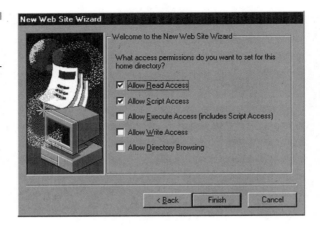

activated and run through this Web site. This is not normally checked because you don't want your visitors launching applications on your server through the Internet.

If ALLOW WRITE ACCESS is checked, visitors can upload files to this site. If ALLOW DIRECTORY BROWSING is checked, visitors can see the names of all the files listed in each of the directories of the Web site.

When you click the FINISH button, the site you just created is added to IIS and should be seen in the MMC. But note that when the site is first created it is stopped. You will need to start the site by right-clicking on it and selecting START. With that complete, your site should now be accessible.

Web Site Properties

Many of the Web site properties are inherited by the properties you set up in the WWW Service earlier in this chapter. If you modify them at the Web-site level, then the Web site's properties overwrite the inherited ones.

In this section we review some of the properties for a Web site, but read the preceding section for further information on the properties that are not covered here.

Multiple Sites on the Same IP Address

A new feature to IIS version 4.0 is the ability to map more than one site to the same IP Address. To do this, you need to follow the steps outlined

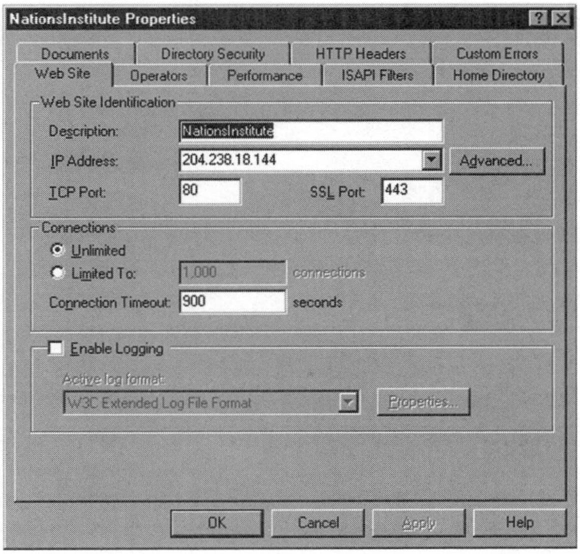

Figure 2-20
Web Site properties.

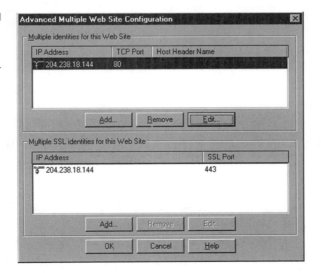

below for each of the sites that are on the same IP Address. Right-click on the Web site from within the MMC and select properties. Select the WEB SITE tab to see the property sheet displayed in Figure 2-20.

Now press the ADVANCED button to see the dialog box shown in Figure 2-21. Notice the entry at the top of this dialog under MULTIPLE

Figure 2-21
Advanced Web Site
properties.

Figure 2-22
Advanced Web Site
Identification dialog
box.

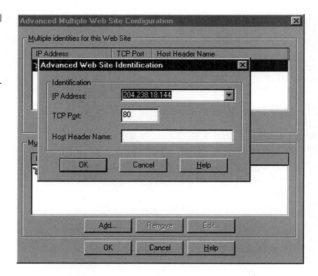

IDENTITIES FOR THIS WEB SITE lists an IP Address and a port number but no *Host Header Name*, which is the domain name for this site and we need to supply a value for this field. Press the EDIT button to edit this entry and now you should see the dialog shown in Figure 2-22.

Enter the domain name for this Web site in the HOST HEADER NAME text box and press OK. Now when IIS receives a request for this domain name, even though it is listed under the same IP Address as other Web sites on this server, it routes the request to the proper Web site.

Web Site Property Sheet Properties

Notice the other properties of the Web Site property sheet shown in Figure 2-20. You can modify the name of the Web site that is used for your own identification through here.

You can also specify the maximum number of connections allowed to this Web site. This is useful in a multiple domain scenario, where you may charge a hosting fee to the Web sites that you host based on the maximum number of connections allowed.

You can also decide how you want the logging of requests made to this

Figure 2-23
Home Directory
properties.

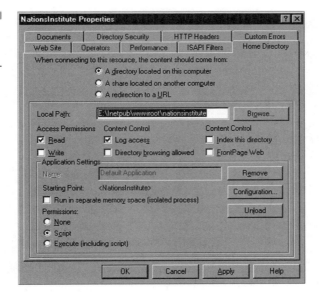

site. Remember that, by default, the property is set to the value you entered under the WWW Service properties.

Home Directory Properties

Now select the HOME DIRECTORY tab as shown in Figure 2-23. The first thing you can set on this property sheet is where the files for this Web site are located. Depending on what you choose here, the bottom portion of the form changes.

If you select a directory on this computer, you then can select the local path and any of the bottom properties. If you select a shared directory, you are then asked to supply the name of the server and the shared folder in the form of \\[server]\[share].

You can also select a *redirection*, which means that when visitors attempt to reach this Web site they are sent to a different Web site somewhere else on the Internet. When you select this option, you are prompted for the URL of the redirection and cannot supply any of the other properties on this page.

The Application Settings properties are discussed in the "Application Properties" section later in this chapter.

Exploring a Site

Now that you have added and configured the Web site, you can browse the contents of the site, as you do with the Windows Explorer. You can expand directories as shown in Figure 2-24.

Virtual Directories

You can view the contents of any folder within your Web site. These files and folders correspond to the logical files and folders that are within the root directory structure for this site. But you can also create virtual directories.

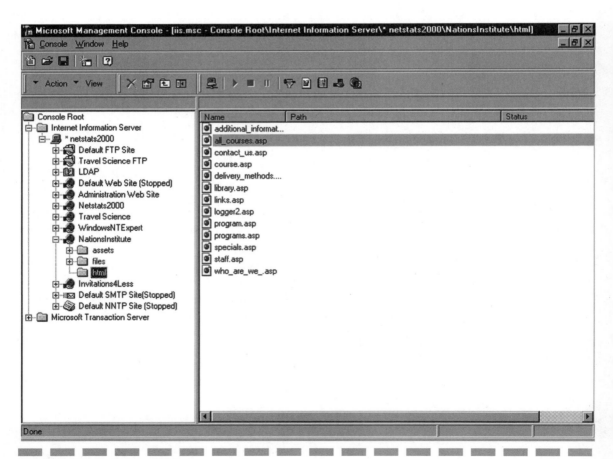

Figure 2-24 Exploring a Web site.

Virtual directories are folders that are outside of the physical directory structure of the Web site but you want to include them within the
Web site. For example, say you have a Web site that contains the subdirectories `html` and `scripts`. You address those directories by specifying
the domain name followed by the name of the subdirectory:
http://www.somewhere.com/html/welcome.html. But let's say that you
have another directory on your server that contains some video files that
you want accessible through your Web site in a directory called `avi`. In
the current configuration, the files are not accessible by your site since
they are outside your site's physical directory structure. But we can create a virtual directory that points to the `avi` directory so it can be
included within the logical structure of our Web site.

To create a virtual directory, right-click on the Web site or folder
where the virtual directory needs to be added and select NEW followed
by VIRTUAL DIRECTORY, as shown in Figure 2-25. Selecting this item

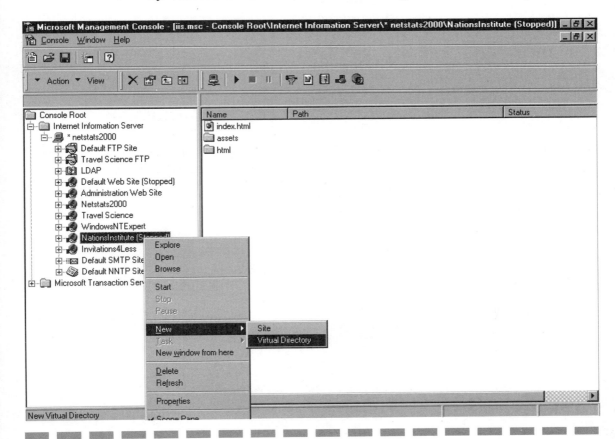

Figure 2-25 Adding a Virtual Directory.

Figure 2-26
New Virtual Wizard
Step 1.

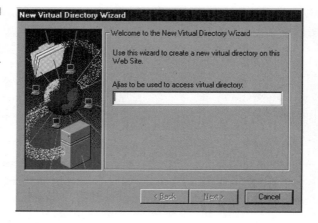

launches the New Virtual Directory Wizard. The first step is shown in Figure 2-26.

The first thing you enter into the wizard is the name that this virtual directory should go by when it is accessed through your Web site. In other words, if the physical directory was called PublicVideos but you wanted it called Videos when accessed from the Web, you would supply the name Videos here for the alias.

In step 2 of the wizard you supply the physical location of the virtual directory as shown in Figure 2-27. Press the BROWSE button and browse to the location of the physical directory.

In step 3, shown in Figure 2-28, you can set the access properties to this virtual directory. Then press the FINISH button and you now have a virtual directory that is physically located outside your Web site but is accessible through your Web site.

Figure 2-27
New Virtual Directory
Wizard Step 2.

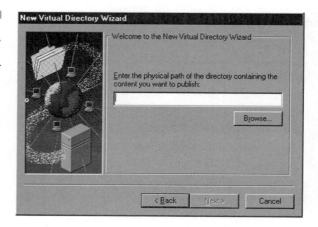

Figure 2-28
New Virtual Directory
Wizard Step 3.

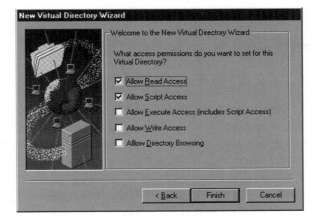

Folder and File Properties

You've seen that you can set properties for the WWW Service itself. You've also seen that you can set properties for individual Web sites that are inherited from the WWW Service. You can also set properties for the folders and files within a Web site. The properties for folders are accessed by right-clicking on a folder and selecting PROPERTIES. You should then see the dialog shown in Figure 2-29.

The folder properties are inherited by the Web site properties so you usually do not need to set them. But this gives you the ability to fine-

Figure 2-29
Folder properties.

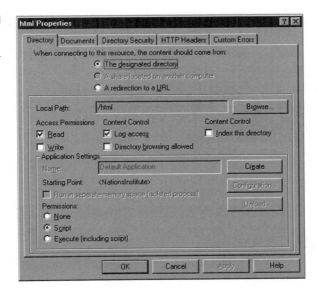

Figure 2-30
File properties.

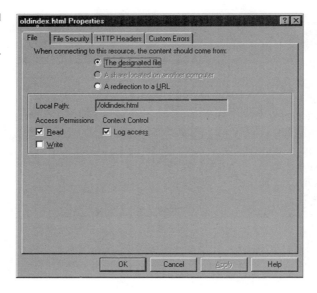

tune the configuration of your Web site. For example, you may want to configure a single folder to hold your scripts. Then you would set the Script permission for this folder; or if you want to log access to only a single folder, you can do that through the Folder Properties.

Each of the files within each folder also has properties. The properties for files are shown in Figure 2-30. The properties for a file are inherited from the folder properties, so the hierarchy of inheritance goes from the WWW Service to the Web site to a folder down to a file.

ASP Applications

Scope and Life

An *ASP application* is a fancy name for a group of Active Server Pages that are located in the same directory structure that you wish to conceptually work with as an application.

An Active Server Page by itself is an island and does not share information stored in variables with other Active Server Pages. An Active Server Page that is part of an ASP application can share and keep the life of variables beyond the single page and store variables that are in a scope outside itself. *Life* of a variable means that a variable stays around after a page ends. *Scope* means that a variable can be visible outside the current page. So with an ASP application you can create variables that stay around after a visitor leaves a page and the variables are visible by other pages in the ASP application.

For example, let's say that you have a secure site and you want visitors to log in to your site before viewing any other pages. You want them to log in to a single page and be able to know somehow from the other pages that the visitor has logged in. You can do that with an ASP application because you could create a variable called UserID that stored the ID of a user. If this variable had a number in it, you would know that the visitor had logged in to the site.

In Chapter 1 we looked at a Quiz page. The page allowed visitors to answer question after question and we maintained their score. This was done on a single page. If we were to expand this tool, we may need additional pages to allow for an alternatively formatted question. Or maybe we would want a page that allowed visitors to review their choices. We would need a way to pass information between the pages regarding the test visitors took, their score, and so on. We need an ASP application to achieve this.

Or maybe you want to build a utility that allowed you to track visitors as they went from page to page across your site. You would need a way to identify the specific visitor so you could make the appropriate entry into some usage table. You would want to store something like a ConnectionID in a variable that was available between pages. You could do this with an ASP application.

Events

Events are code that you write in response to some action that happens. For example, in Visual Basic when users click on a button they fire the Click event; or when users leave a text box they fire the Lost Focus event. The action they are taking makes an event occur.

You can write code that runs when an event is called. When visitors click on a button maybe you close a form, or when they leave a text box maybe you have code that validates their entry.

As you will discover more deeply in Chapter 8 when we discuss the global.asa file, when you have an ASP application you have four events that you can write code to run when the event occurs.

You can write code for the Application_OnStart event. The code in this procedure would run whenever your ASP application starts. An ASP application starts when the first ASP page is accessed by any visitor.

You can write code for the Session_OnStart event. This event fires when a visitor views the first ASP page of your application. This is different from the Application_OnStart in that it fires for each visitor instead of just once.

Another event that you can code for is the Session_OnEnd event. This event fires when the visitor is no longer connected to your site. Specifically this happens when the visitors' session times out or when you programmatically end their session.

The final event that you can program for within an ASP application is the Application_OnEnd event. The code in this procedure fires when the Web site that the ASP application is part of is stopped.

Creating an ASP Application

Now that you know why you would create an ASP application, let's take a look at how you perform this task within IIS. As mentioned before, an ASP application consists of a directory and all of its subdirectories. A directory is part of only one ASP application, so if the main directory was part of another ASP application and then you create it as a new ASP application, it is just part of the new ASP application.

Within the MMC, right-click on the directory that contains the files you want to turn into an ASP application and select PROPERTIES. Make sure you are on the DIRECTORY tab and you should see the property sheet like the one in Figure 2-31.

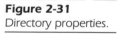

Figure 2-31
Directory properties.

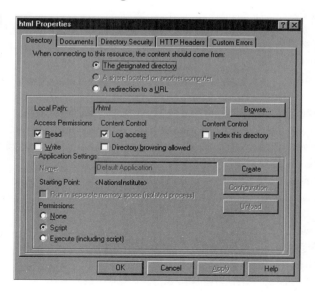

Figure 2-32
Directory properties
with the application
name enabled.

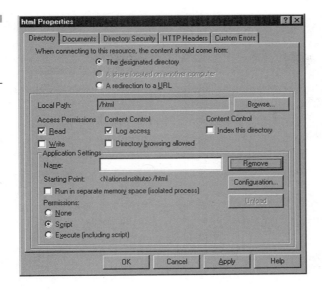

The area that we will be working with is the part at the bottom of the property sheet called *Application Settings*. Click on the CREATE button. When you do, the name for the application becomes enabled like the one shown in Figure 2-32.

Type in the name of your ASP Application in the NAME text box. The name you give it is for your own identification. Press OK and you have created an ASP application. Notice that the icon for the directory has changed from a folder to a box with a small green X in it.

To remove an ASP application, just return to the directories properties and press the REMOVE button.

Configuring an ASP Application

Notice the check box in Figure 2-32 that says "Run in separate memory space (isolated process)". If this item is checked, your ASP application will run outside of IIS. So if your application causes some severe error and needs to be closed it will not bring down other applications or IIS itself. The negative side of taking this action is that it requires additional resources.

To view the other configuration options for your application, click on the CONFIGURATION button from the Directory Properties and you should see a dialog like the one in Figure 2-33.

Figure 2-33
Application
Mappings.

The first tab contains the APPLICATION MAPPINGS. These mappings tell IIS what support program to run when a page that has an extension listed here is requested. For example, click on the .asp extension in the preceding list and select EDIT. You should see the settings shown in Figure 2-34.

The first box contains the name of the program that will process the page. The second box contains the name of the extension that the page must have for it to be processed by the executable. In the third box you can include any HTTP methods that you do not want run with this executable. For ASP you would want to indicate that it is a script engine. The CHECK THAT FILE EXISTS check box is not needed for ASP.

Figure 2-34
Application Extension
Mapping.

NOTE: *If you ever find yourself in a situation where you are trying to view an ASP page and all that you see is the raw ASP code, you are probably missing the entry in Figure 2-34. Just add the entry back to your Application Mappings.*

Now go to the second tab on the ASP APPLICATION properties, the APP OPTIONS tab as shown in Figure 2-35.

The first thing you can do on this property sheet is to enable session state. As mentioned in a previous section, state refers to the ability to store variables that are visible to all the pages outside of a page in an application. To allow for this you need to enable session state. Then you can set the Session timeout property. This value represents the number of minutes that are allowed between page views before the visitor's session is considered over. So if property is set to 20 min, the visitor must go to another page before 20 min or all the session information is lost.

If ENABLE BUFFERING is checked, then the ASP Page must complete all processing before any of the resulting HTML is sent to the browser. The ENABLE PARENT PATHS checkbox allows for the relative addressing of the parent directory if it is checked. The Default ASP Language refers to the script used by default on your ASP Pages. The ASP Script timeout prop-

Figure 2-35
Application Option
properties.

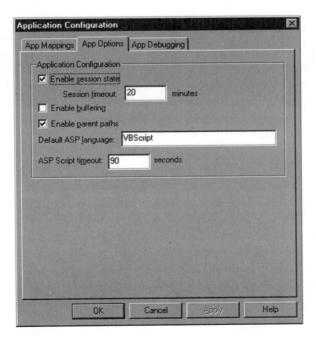

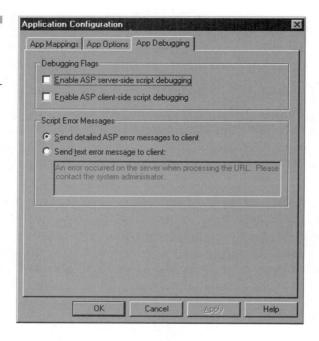

erty stores the number of seconds a page can take to complete its code before it should timeout. This can happen because of a variety of reasons, such as the server is too busy, the amount of data being returned is too large, or the code is in an endless loop.

The third tab contains debugging options and is displayed in Figure 2-36.

If you check the Server-Side Script Debugging option you can set break points for your code to stop while running and a debugger will come up for you to analyze your code. Debugging is discussed further in Chapter 12. The Enable Client-Side Debugging option currently has no significance. Later versions of IIS may use this value.

When an error occurs within your code, the browser is sent a message. You can have the message be a detailed one with the error number, description, and the line of code on which the error occurred. To use this feature, select DETAILED ERROR MESSAGES. Your other option is to display a generic text message.

FTP Sites

In addition to hosting Web sites, the Internet Information Server can also host an *FTP site*, which gives you the capability to easily upload and download files from your server. A default FTP site is installed with IIS. To install a new FTP site you can run the wizard by right-clicking on the computer where you want to add the FTP site then select NEW followed by FTP SITE.

You can configure your FTP site by right-clicking on it and selecting PROPERTIES. You should then see the properties page like the one in Figure 2-37.

Note that, like the Web Service properties, the FTP Service also has properties that you can set and are inherited by the FTP sites. From this first property sheet, you can set the identification for this site. You can also set the maximum number of connections as well as a connection timeout. The *timeout* represents the number of seconds of inactivity that can pass before visitors are disconnected.

Like the Web sites, you can log activity to the FTP site. If you click on the CURRENT SESSIONS button you see a list of all the current visitors to the FTP site. From the SECURITY tab, shown in Figure 2-38, you select who can access your FTP site.

Figure 2-37
FTP Site properties.

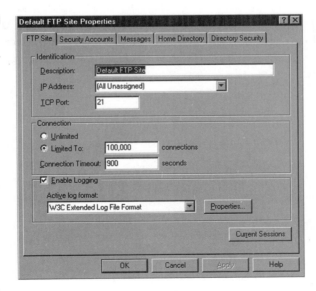

Figure 2-38
FTP Security
Accounts.

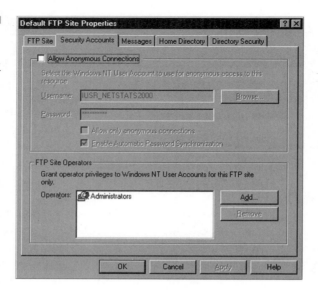

If you select ANONYMOUS ACCESS, anyone can enter your FTP site. You probably want to allow only certain visitors to your FTP site since it allows a powerful amount of modification. You can do this through the bottom part of this property sheet.

Some of the other properties of the FTP site allow you to specify welcome and exit messages that the visitor sees when using the FTP site. You can also specify the name of the physical directory that acts as the entry point for the FTP site. You can also reject certain IP Addresses or allow only certain IP Addresses.

Tools of the Trade

Development Applications Review

In this chapter we look at tools that you can use to develop Web sites, HTML, forms, and especially Active Server Pages. Our discussion begins with a look at the most basic development tool that you should already have, Notepad. You will see that even with just Notepad you can create your own Active Server Pages.

We then look at a couple of tools that you can use to develop Web pages. These tools, FrontPage 2000 and NetObjects Fusion, provide you with a quick and intuitive interface for building sites and pages. We also look at adding elements to pages with these tools and we look at creating forms.

We then turn our attention to tools used to create the code in Active Server Pages, first with a look at NetObjects ScriptBuilder 3.0. This development tool includes a wonderful interface that makes building and creating code blocks a snap. We also look at Microsoft's Visual InterDev. If you are familiar with any of the products in the Visual Studio series, you will enjoy the similar layout and functionality.

Notepad

If you have a computer with some version of Windows on it, you already have a tool for creating and working with Active Server Pages—the tool is *Notepad*.

A Web page and Active Server Pages are just raw text pages, so all you need to create one or work with one is a text editor. Notepad would work, or really any text editor would do fine, for creating or editing an HTML page or an Active Server Page.

Sometimes this is all you really need. I personally have a variety of tools for developing Web pages, sites, and Active Server Pages but I still use Notepad from time to time. The simplicity of loading a text editor versus a huge development suite is one reason. Another reason to consider a text editor is when you are away from your main development machine. You should always be able to find a text editor, and if you can connect to your Internet server, you can still make modifications.

Moreover, it is important with straight HTML to periodically review your raw code. You will find that many tools used to create Web pages or Web sites add numerous lines of table layout code that can simply be deleted, making your page much smaller in size and much more rapidly downloaded.

For example, take a look at the following HTML that was generated with a Web site development tool called *NetObjects Fusion* that we discuss later in this chapter.

```
<TABLE BORDER=0 CELLSPACING=0 CELLPADDING=0 WIDTH=570>
 <TR VALIGN="top" ALIGN="left">
<TD WIDTH=68 HEIGHT =7><IMG SRC="./assets/images/dot_clear.gif"
  WIDTH =68 HEIGHT =1 BORDER=0></TD>
<TD WIDTH=27><IMG SRC="./assets/images/dot_clear.gif" WIDTH =27
  HEIGHT =1 BORDER=0></TD>
<TD WIDTH=95><IMG SRC="./assets/images/dot_clear.gif" WIDTH =95
  HEIGHT =1 BORDER=0></TD>
<TD WIDTH=95><IMG SRC="./assets/images/dot_clear.gif" WIDTH =95
  HEIGHT =1 BORDER=0></TD>
<TD WIDTH=95><IMG SRC="./assets/images/dot_clear.gif" WIDTH =95
  HEIGHT =1 BORDER=0></TD>
<TD WIDTH=95><IMG SRC="./assets/images/dot_clear.gif" WIDTH =95
  HEIGHT =1 BORDER=0></TD>
<TD WIDTH=61><IMG SRC="./assets/images/dot_clear.gif" WIDTH =61
  HEIGHT =1 BORDER=0></TD>
<TD WIDTH=34><IMG SRC="./assets/images/dot_clear.gif" WIDTH =34
  HEIGHT =1 BORDER=0></TD>
</TR>
<TR VALIGN="top" ALIGN="left">
<TD></TD>
<TD WIDTH=468 COLSPAN=6><P ALIGN="center"><B>
  <FONT COLOR="#800000" SIZE="+2" FACE="Arial,Helvetica">
  All invitations and accessories priced at a 25% discount!</B>
  </FONT></P></TD>
<TD></TD>
</TR>
  <TR VALIGN="top" ALIGN="left">
  <TD COLSPAN=8 HEIGHT =39></TD>
  </TR>
</TABLE>
```

An almost identical output could be produced with this HTML:

```
<p ALIGN="center"><b><font SIZE="+2" FACE="Arial,Helvetica">
All invitations and accessories priced at a 25% discount!
</b></font></p>
```

The code is a fraction of the size, so the page would be displayed much more rapidly.

One thing to remember when you use Notepad as your Active Server Page editor is to make sure that you give the file the correct extension. By default, Notepad assigns the extension .txt. So when you save a file using Notepad, make sure to include the proper extension as shown in Figure 3-1.

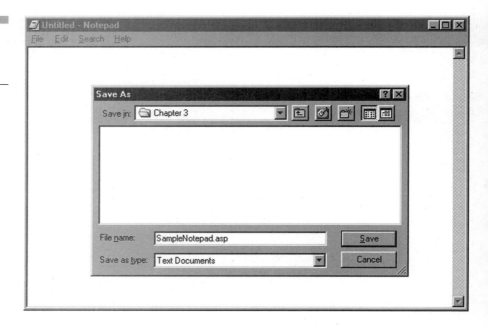

Figure 3-1
Using the proper
extension within
Notepad.

FrontPage 2000

FrontPage 2000 is a Microsoft tool that you can use to develop individual Web pages or Web sites. Since FrontPage is a Microsoft product, it is designed to work well with the Internet Information Server, making changes to your Web site more immediate; with other tools you generally have to upload your pages to the server.

Development Environment

Figure 3-2 shows the development environment with a Web page currently being viewed. The view shown in this figure is the Page view, which is viewed by pressing the PAGE button on the left toolbar. When this button is pressed, a middle pane in the Window displays the contents of the current folder. In this case, the root of a FrontPage Web is called *fpsample*.

In the right pane of the FrontPage, *Page* view is the contents of the currently selected Web page. By clicking on a Web page in the middle

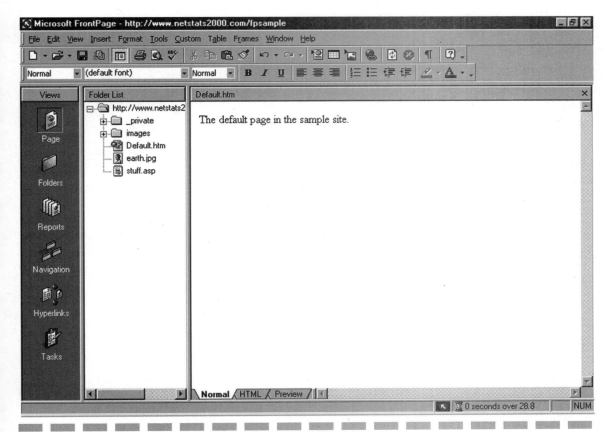

Figure 3-2 FrontPage development environment with a Web page being viewed.

page, it becomes the active page in the right pane. Within this right pane, you have three views for the page. The first view, which is shown in Figure 3-2, is the *Normal* view, where you can graphically add elements and edit elements on the page. If you change the view to *HTML*, you will see the raw HTML as shown in Figure 3-3. From the Normal view you can edit the raw HTML to add script or ASP. You can also use it as a learning tool to see what happens when you add different elements.

The third view for the Page is the *Preview* view. With this view, as shown in Figure 3-4, you can see what the page will look like in a browser. This simple option allows you to quickly see what the output of your page will look like.

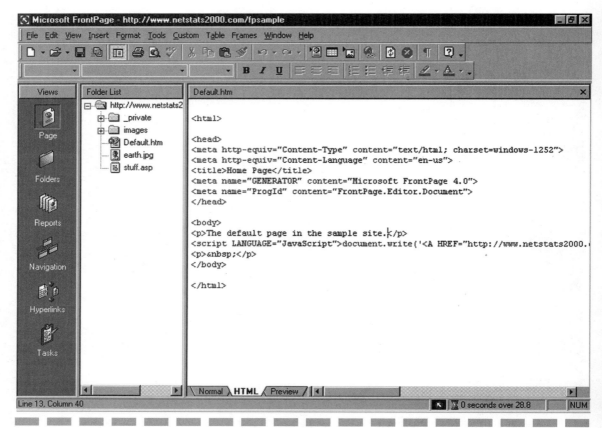

Figure 3-3 HTML view of a Web page within FrontPage.

NOTE: *The Preview view runs on the client-side. That means that any client-side code will also be previewed but none of your Active Server Page will be processed.*

The next main view is the Folder view, which is shown in Figure 3-5. The *Folder* view is where you manage the files and folders within your Web site. You use the middle pane to navigate to the different directories within your site. The right pane then shows the contents of the current folder. Extended information about each of the items—such as the name, title, date modified, and comments—is displayed in the right pane. So with this view you can easily locate files, add tasks to them, note their structure, and sort them by any of the fields.

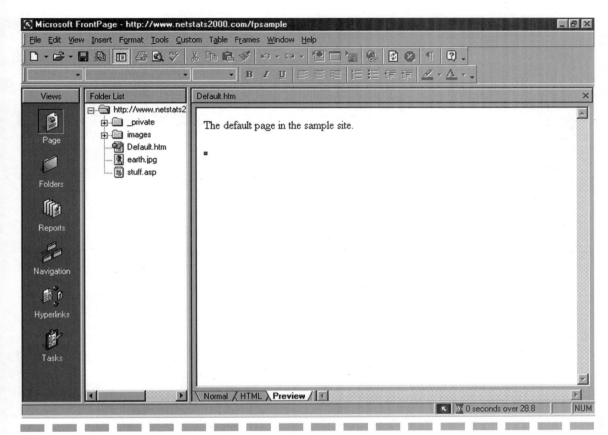

Figure 3-4 Preview view.

To add a comment to a file, just right-click on it and select PROPERTIES. Then click on the SUMMARY tab and enter your comment as shown in Figure 3-6. You can add a comment to any file within your Web.

The next view is the *Report* view, which allows you to see a variety of reports about your Web. The default summary report is displayed in Figure 3-7.

Additional reports can be viewed by selecting Reports from the View menu item. With these reports, you can generate a list of slow pages, old files, recently added files, a broken links report, and many more. Some of the reports are even configurable. You can configure the reports by selecting Tools—Options from the menu and then viewing the REPORTS

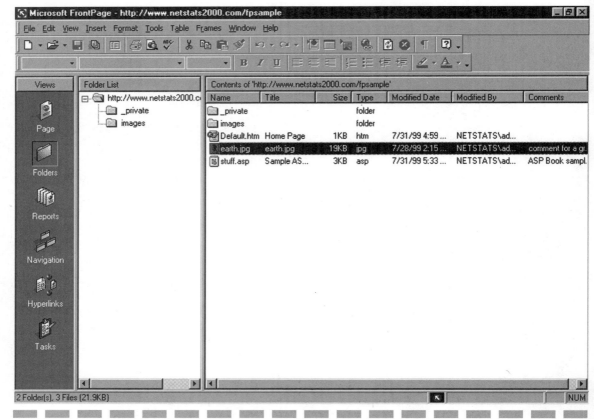

Figure 3-5 Folder view within FrontPage.

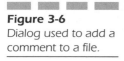

Figure 3-6
Dialog used to add a
comment to a file.

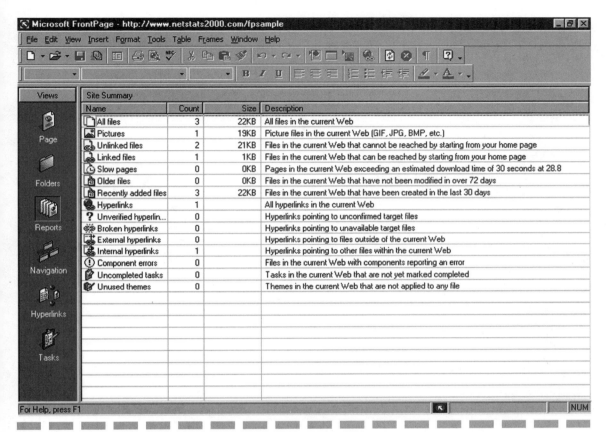

Figure 3-7 Reports view.

VIEW tab. From there you define how many days old a file must be less than to qualify as a new file. You can set the number of days a file reported as old must be. You can also set the number of seconds a page must take to download to qualify as a slow page.

The next view is the Navigation view, shown in Figure 3-8. The *Navigation* view allows you to design the logical layout of your Web site. Here you can add pages to the diagram by dragging them from the folder list to the right pane. Once in the right pane, the pages can be connected in their logical layout. You can remove a page from the Navigation view by deleting it without removing the file from the Web itself.

The *Hyperlinks* view provides you with another graphical view of your Web site. With this view you select a page from the folder list. The right pane then displays all the links related to this page.

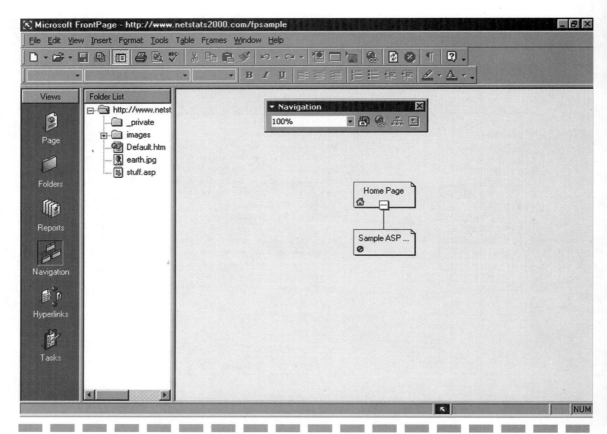

Figure 3-8   Navigation view within FrontPage 2000.

One final view is the *Tasks* view, which is shown in Figure 3-9. *Tasks* are action items needed to be taken by someone involved in the development of the Web site. A task is assigned to an individual—it has a priority, status, date, and description.

You can have a general task that is not related to any particular item. For example, you may assign the task of registering the site on a search engine; or, maybe you could have as a task the completion of the site diagram. To add a general task, first make sure you are on the Tasks view. Then from the menu select Edit—Tasks—Add Task. You should then see a screen like the one shown in Figure 3-10.

From the New Task dialog, you assign the task to a specific person. You can also set the priority of the task and supply a description for it. Once you press the OK button you should see your task added to the Task view.

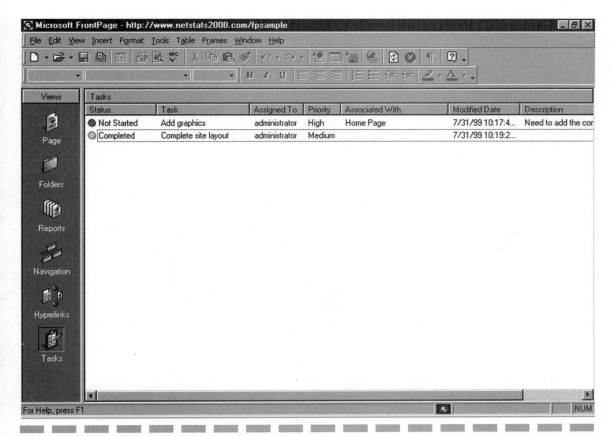

Figure 3-9 Tasks view within FrontPage 2000.

Figure 3-10
Adding a task
through the New
Task dialog.

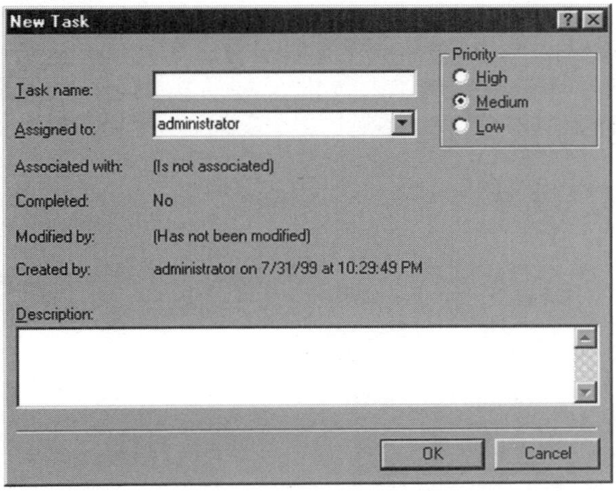

You can also assign a task to a page or file within the Web site. You do that by selecting the page from the folder list. Then right-click on the page and choose ADD TASK. You then add the task in the same way as a general task.

The Tasks view is used to manage a task. By right-clicking on a task, you can select *Start Task*, which then takes you to the file that is associated with the task. You can also mark a task as completed by right-clicking on it. A completed task has a different icon, making it easily distinguished from those tasks not completed.

Creating a Web

In FrontPage, the term *Web* refers to a domain name or subdirectory where you will place a Web site. FrontPage comes with a wizard that you can use to create a new Web. To use the wizard, select New followed by Web from the File menu. You should then see the Web Site selection dialog displayed in Figure 3-11.

Regardless of the type of Web you choose to create, you need to supply

Figure 3-11
Web Site selection dialog.

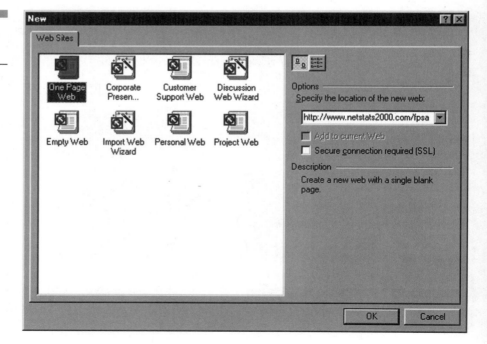

a location for the Web site. If the server is on a remote computer, you may be asked to supply a user name and password for the NT machine that IIS is installed on. This location is where your site will be created. As you work on the site and save your changes, those changes are immediately placed on the server.

Note that there are a variety of choices for your Web. If you choose a single-page Web, then this is the only step of the wizard. A page is created and the necessary files are placed on the server. Other wizards, however, are more complex. For example, take the Corporate Presence Wizard. With this wizard you first select the pages that you want included in your Web site like the ones shown in Figure 3-12.

With each page you select the items that you want to appear on the page. Once the wizard generates that page, it takes your input to create a template that has places for you to place additional content.

The wizard also asks you to select a *theme*, which is a look and feel for your Web site—it is a combination of banners, background, font style, and other elements. FrontPage comes with numerous themes. You can also select a theme or change the theme for your site by selecting Format—Theme from the menu. When you do, you will see the dialog displayed in Figure 3-13.

You can apply a theme to some or all of the pages at your site. You can also modify the look of a theme. Be careful about using these prebuilt themes for your Web site, however. Remember that FrontPage is very popular and every developer who uses FrontPage has these same themes. So a visitor to your site who has been to other sites generated with FrontPage will think that your site does not have a unique design.

Figure 3-12
Corporate Presence
page selection.

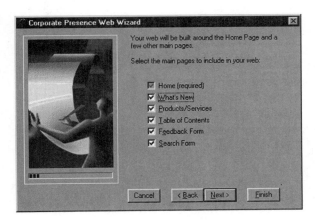

Figure 3-13
Selecting a theme for
your site.

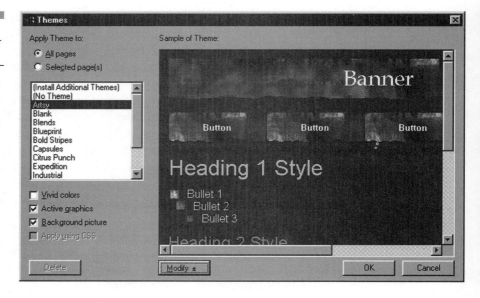

Viewing a Page

As we saw earlier in this chapter, the simplest and quickest way to view
a page that you are working with is to select the Preview view while in
Page mode—but this is just for a quick view. You will want to see how
your page looks within the confines of a standalone browser. You can do
that within FrontPage by selecting Preview in Browser from the File
menu. The resulting dialog is shown in Figure 3-14.

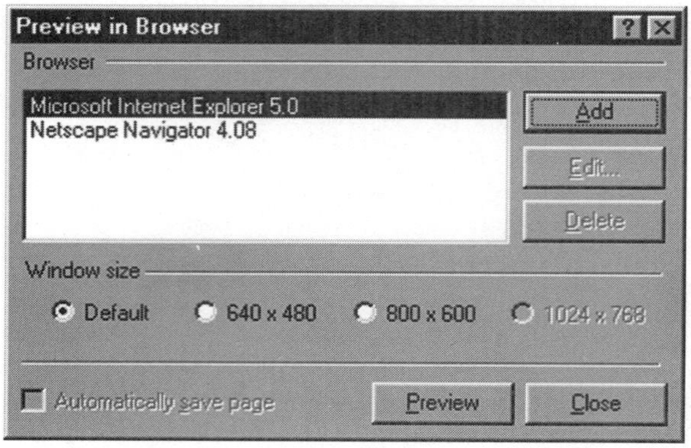

Figure 3-14
Preview in Browser
dialog.

This powerful preview tool allows you to select the browser you want to view the Web page with. It is very important to view your Web site in the different browsers you suspect your audience will use because the page can sometimes behave differently based on the browser being used.

You can also add additional browsers with which you want to view the page by clicking the ADD button. You then supply a name for the browser that will appear in this list and the executable for that browser.

Also note the window size selection. Remember that your visitors may not have the same size monitor you have. So you will want to view your Web site in the different screen sizes that your visitors may be using. You may then want to adjust the look of the site based on that review.

FrontPage has another tool that can help you work with the differences of the different browsers. While in the Normal Page view, select Tools followed by Page Options. Then select the COMPATIBILITY tab. You should see the dialog displayed in Figure 3-15. From this dialog you select the target browser for this page, the version of the target browser, and the server where the page will be posted. Based on those selections, the different checkboxes in the bottom of the page will become *enabled* or *disabled*. Also, menu items within FrontPage will become enabled and disabled based on your selection.

Figure 3-15
Page compatibility.

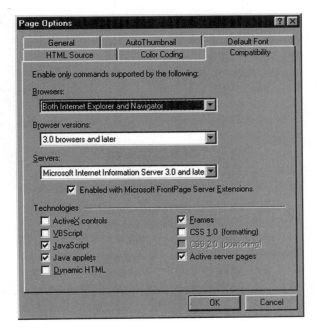

You can also choose Custom for the browser type, browser version, and/or server type. When you do this, you can manually set the specific technologies that you wish the page to support by checking and unchecking the options at the bottom of the page.

Adding a Page

You can add a new Web page or an Active Server Page to your Web within FrontPage by selecting New—Page from the File menu. When you do, you should see a new page selection screen as shown in Figure 3-16. From this dialog you can select from numerous template pages. The template pages take you through a wizard, as when you create a new Web and you supply the information about the page that is married with the template to create a near completed page. You can also select a Normal Page, which is just a blank page. The FRAMES PAGES tab contains more templates, but these templates are built using frames.

Once you make your way through the wizard, your new page will be displayed for you. The next time you save it, you are prompted for the title of the page and the file name for the page. This is where you set

Figure 3-16
New Web page selection dialog.

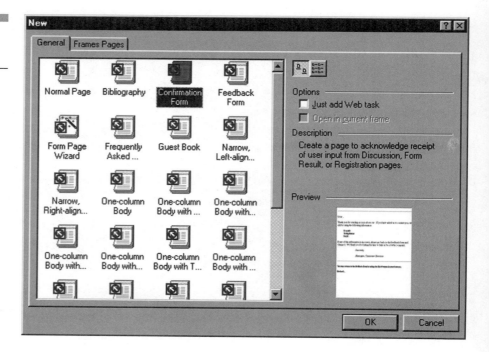

whether the page is an Active Server Page or some other type of page. Just supply the appropriate extension to the file name.

Remember, though, even if you name the file with an .asp extension the server-side code will not work unless the page is being viewed through the server. Once you create the page as an Active Server Page, you can go to the HTML view and manually add your code to the page.

Working with a Page

From the Normal Page view you can just start typing to begin adding text content to your page. You can also format the text as you do with any other Microsoft Office program by using the Formatting toolbar, shown in Figure 3-17.

The first pull-down list in the toolbar allows you to select the type of HTML element to use for this text, such as H1 or OL. You can then apply font, font size, and other font and paragraph attributes. If you then look at the HTML page view you will see that your changes are turned into the necessary HTML tags.

As shown in Figure 3-18, you add other HTML elements to your Web page from the Insert menu.

Most of the items that you add to your page from this list contain a short wizard or dialog that retrieves from you the information needed to complete the element. For example, if you select HyperLink, you are prompted for the location of the file to link to, or you can select a page within the current Web.

You add Form elements to your page in the same way, through the Insert menu and then a sub-item from the Form option. You can add forms in two ways. You can add a form with a single element by inserting that element. For example, if you wanted a form with a single text box, you would select the text-box item from the Form menu and FrontPage would add the element within its own Form tag to your Web page and produce the view shown in Figure 3-19.

You could then supply the action to be taken and other form properties by right-clicking anywhere on the form and selecting Form

Figure 3-17   Formatting toolbar.

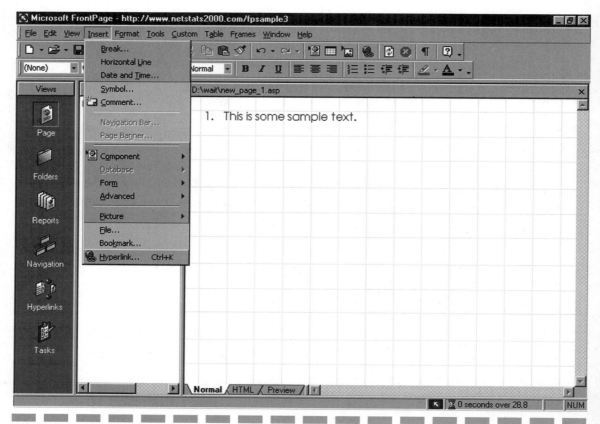

Figure 3-18 Insert menu for a Web page.

Properties. You can then add additional forms to your page in the same way.

If you have a more complex form, you can also select the Form item in the submenu. When you take that action, a form with SUBMIT and RESET buttons is created. You then add elements to that form by selecting them from the submenu while the form has the focus.

If you right-click on any of the Form elements, you can view the properties of the element by selecting Form Field Properties. The Form Field Properties dialog is shown in Figure 3-20.

The different types of form elements have dialog that corresponds to their types. The VALIDATE button allows you to create a client-side restraint on the type and value that the visitor can enter into the field.

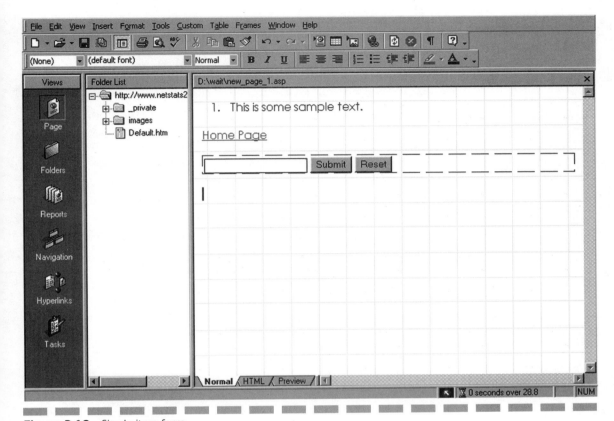

Figure 3-19 Single item form.

Figure 3-20
Form field properties.

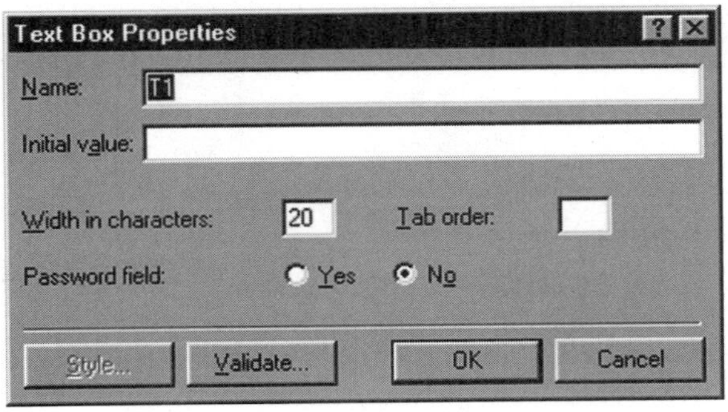

NetObjects Fusion

Another great Web site development tool is *NetObjects Fusion*, http://www.netobjects.com. NetObjects has a variety of tools to assist in Web development. Later in this chapter, we look at another one of their tools called *ScriptBuilder*, which provides an excellent interface for working with code in your Active Server Pages. You can download a fully functional 30-day trial version of their tool from their Web site.

As you will see later in this chapter, the greatest benefit of working with NetObjects Fusion is the control you have over the layout of the elements on the page. The tool allows you to draw elements anywhere on the page, as if you were designing a form within Visual Basic or Access. NetObjects relies on invisible tables and graphics generated in the HTML to provide you with complete freedom over the layout of elements on a page.

Development Environment

Fusion has five main views: Site, Page, Style, Assets, and Publish. You change views by clicking on the toolbar just below the menu that has the view names listed.

The view displayed when Site is chosen is shown in Figure 3-21. The *Site* view is probably the place where you would start the development process for it is here that you can view, add, and remove pages from your Web site. The pages are presented in a logical hierarchical format. This is a logical view, not a physical view, so you are not prevented from linking to pages outside the hierarchy. The view is used by the developer to think through the logic of the site and to plan out the structure.

You add a page to the site by pressing the INSERT key on your keyboard. The page will be added as a child page to whatever page has the focus at that time. In Figure 3-21, Home has the focus, so pressing the INSERT key would add a child page to Home. You remove a page by clicking on it and pressing the DELETE key.

Each page has properties that are displayed in the small Properties dialog on the PAGE tab. That dialog is shown in the bottom right corner of Figure 3-21.

From the Properties dialog you can change the name of the current page by entering it into the NAME text box. If you press the CUSTOM NAMES button you should see a screen like the one in Figure 3-22.

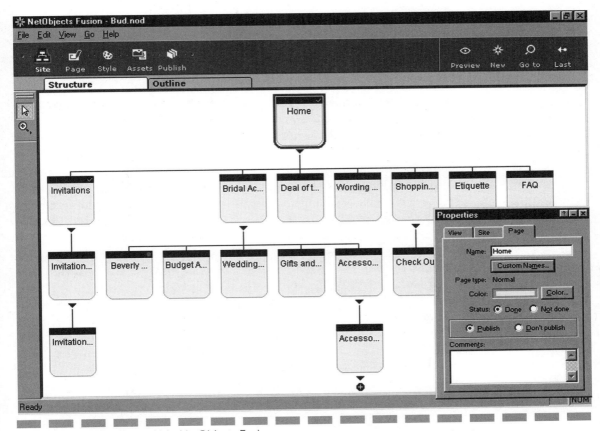

Figure 3-21   Site view within NetObjects Fusion.

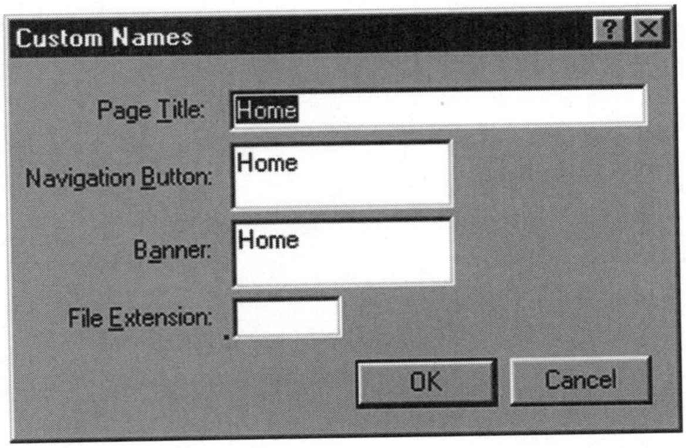

Figure 3-22
Customer Names
dialog.

When you are on a page in NetObjects, you can add a BANNER and NAVIGATION button to a page. In the Custom Names dialog you specify the text that should appear for this page when those elements are added. You can also supply the file extension for the page here.

From the Page Properties dialog you can also supply information for your own site management purposes. You can select a background color for the page that is used just for the background within the hierarchy view. You can also set whether the page is completed and whether it should be published. An additional text box allows you to supply comments for the page.

An additional view within the Site view is the *Outline* view, which shows the pages in an outline format such as Windows Explorer. On the left is the list of pages in their respective places within the site hierarchy and on the right are all the child pages of the current page.

The *Page* view is where you work on a page. To get to Page view, double-click on whatever page you want to work on from the Site view. See Figure 3-23.

Once in the Page view, you can get to other pages in a variety of ways. You can use the arrows in the lower-left corner of the page to move in the hierarchy up a level, down a level, to the page to the left, or to the page to the right. The page you go to when you press the arrows uses the logic of the Site Hierarchy.

You can also press the FOUR-ARROW button next to the single errors. When that button is pressed, a small window lists all the pages in the site in their hierarchical format.

You can also search for a page in your site by pressing the Go To button in the upper-right corner of the screen. When that button is pressed, you are then asked to supply part of the name of the page you wish to go to. If you press the last button, located in the upper-right corner, you are taken to the last page or view that you had open.

Along the left side of the Window are some of the numerous elements and components that you can add to your page. More are available by selecting View—Toolbars from the menu and then selecting the toolbars that are not currently displayed. We look more deeply at a few of these elements later in this section.

The Page itself has a variety of properties you can set. You can view those properties by right-clicking on the page and selecting Layout Properties. From the GENERAL tab, you can use this dialog to set the size of the page and how the layout of the page is accomplished.

The second tab in the Layout properties is the BACKGROUND tab. Here you can set the background color of the page, the background picture, and any background sound desired.

Figure 3-23 Page view within Fusion.

The next main view within Fusion is the *Style* view, which refers to the default fonts, colors, buttons, and graphics of the site, the default look and feel. The Style view is displayed in Figure 3-24. On the left is a long list of styles. On the right is a preview of the style that has been selected. You can preview any of the styles by clicking on them. Once you have selected a style for your site, just click on the SET STYLE button.

You can also edit any of the elements from the existing styles. For example, say you liked the Urban Legend style but you wanted to use a different background for your site. You can modify the background used for this style by selecting Style—Edit Element—Background. You would then be presented with a dialog like the one in Figure 3-25. You can similarly edit the other elements of a style.

Figure 3-24 Style view within Fusion.

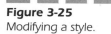

Figure 3-25
Modifying a style.

If you don't like the built-in styles you can create your own. Just select Style—New Style from the menu. You are then asked to supply a name for your style and then you can begin building the different elements of your style.

The next main view within Fusion is the *Assets* view, which lists all the Files, Links Data Objects, and Variables that have ever been associated with your site. This view is displayed in Figure 3-26.

NetObjects Fusion keeps track of all the files and links that have ever been associated with your site. So when you then choose to add a link or picture to your site you can choose from a list of files and links that are already part of your site.

You can also use this view to remove unwanted elements from your site. Just select the element that is no longer desired and click the DELETE key.

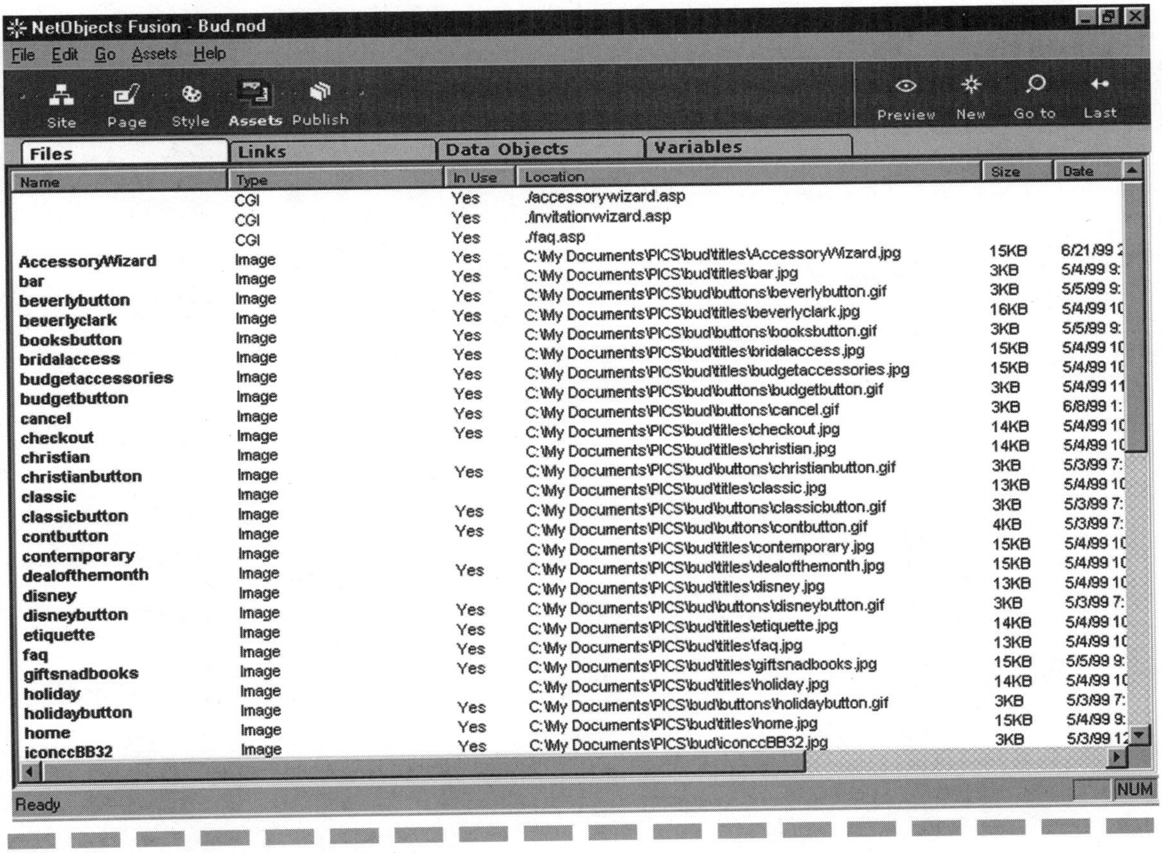

Figure 3-26 Assets view within Fusion.

You can also use the Assets screen to globally replace an Asset. For example, say that you have a link to a site outside of your own that you link to from numerous locations within your site. If you want to change that link to some new link and have the change be global through your site you can by finding the link in the Links list. Then just double-click on the link and supply the new URL for the link.

The last main program view is the *Publish* view, from which you work with how and where your site is to be published. The view is displayed in Figure 3-27, and shows you how your pages will be physically stored when the site is published. In Figure 3-27, the files are shown as they would be placed if the files were published by their type. You can also choose to have the files published all within the same directory or in their logical hierarchical positions. To change how the files are published and other properties of this feature, press the SETUP button. You should see the dialog shown in Figure 3-28.

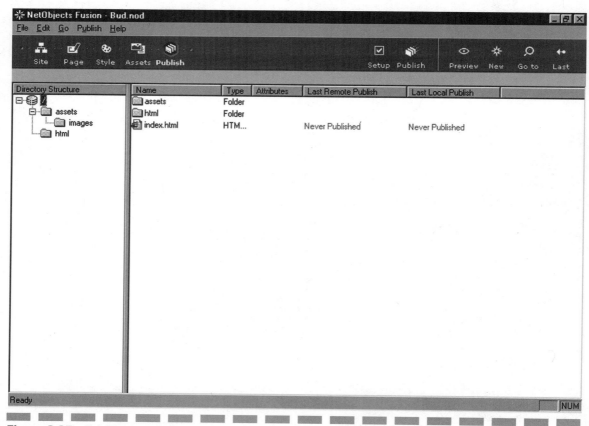

Figure 3-27   Publish view within Fusion.

Figure 3-28
Publish Setup dialog.

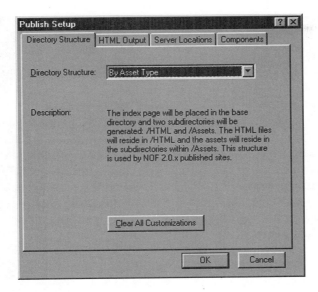

Figure 3-28
Publish Setup dialog.

From this first tab, the DIRECTORY STRUCTURE tab, you select how you want the physical location of the files to be placed. The second tab, HTML OUTPUT, provides you with the ability to change how the site layout is generated and the character set to use. In the third tab, SERVER LOCATIONS, you create the location(s) that you want to publish your site to. This tab is shown in Figure 3-29.

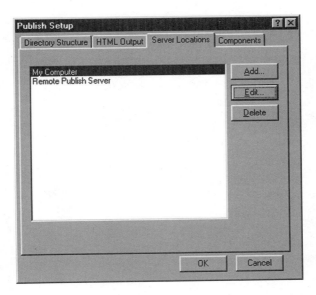

Figure 3-29
Server Locations tab of the Publish Setup dialog.

There are two types of publications you can do: Local and Remote. You can add either of these publications by clicking on the ADD button. If you select LOCAL, then you simply supply the directory where you want the site to be published on your machine or on your Network. If you select REMOTE, then you must supply the location of the remote host, your user name for the host, and your password.

The fourth tab of the setup dialog lists the components, if any, that will be published with the site.

Once you have completed the setup portion of the Publish task you are now ready to publish your site. You do this by clicking on the PUBLISH button. When you do, you are presented with a list of publish locations that you have set up in the SERVER LOCATIONS tab. Then just press OK and your site is generated.

Creating a Web Site Using Fusion

To create a new site within Fusion just select File—New Site. You are then presented with three options, as shown in Figure 3-30. If you select *Blank Site*, a single page Web site is created; if you select *From Template*, you are presented with a bunch of prebuilt sites that you can use as the starting point for your site; if you choose *From Existing Web Site*, then Fusion imports an entire Web site into a new Fusion site.

Figure 3-30
Creating a New Site.

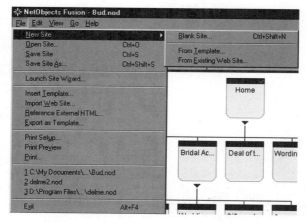

Working with a Page

If you've ever worked with Visual Basic or designed forms within Microsoft Access, you will be relatively comfortable working with pages within Fusion. All elements are drawn on a page. Once the element is on the page, you set its various properties to achieve the desired effect. For example, if you wanted to add text to a page you would select the TEXT icon from the left toolbar in the Page view. Then you would draw the element on your page, making it the desired size. Figure 3-31 shows a page with a text element just drawn.

Now that the element has been drawn on the page you can set its properties. First, you can type the text that you want to appear in the

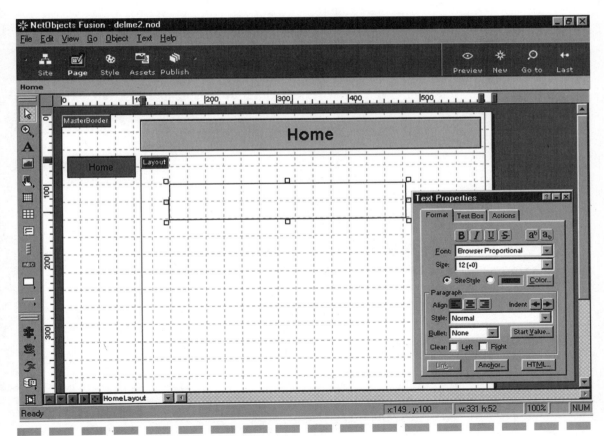

Figure 3-31 Page after text box was added.

element. Then you can set the style for the text, its background, and numerous other properties using the properties dialog box. You use this same procedure to add other elements to your pages.

NetObjects ScriptBuilder

Another great tool from NetObjects is their ScriptBuilder tool. Not only is it a great tool for developing Active Server Pages, but it also can be used for developing client-side scripts as well as working with raw HTML. In this section of the chapter you will see how you can use NetObjects ScriptBuilder to develop your Active Server Pages. You will also see how you can use features of the tool to make adding frequently used script easy and how you can validate your script.

Program Environment

The main window within ScriptBuilder consists of a left pane and a right pane. The *left pane* usually contains a list of actions or options based on the selected tab. The *right pane* contains the Active Server or HTML page or pages that you are working with.

To open a page into the right pane select File—Open. The resulting dialog allows you to browse to the file you wish to open. When you want to create a new file to work with, select File—New. You are then presented with the dialog shown in Figure 3-32.

Figure 3-32
New file dialog from ScriptBuilder.

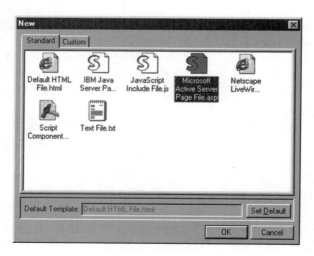

You can then select from one of the templates presented that represents the type of page you wish to create. The template then generates the basic tags for the type of page you selected. For example, if you selected that you wanted to create an Active Server Page, the template would produce a page that contained the basic language, HTML, head, title, and body tags.

But you can also modify these templates, so each time you create a new template they contain the code you always want with that type of file. For example, let's say you have library files that you always include in your Active Server Pages. To do this you always need to add Include lines for those files. You could modify the Active Server Page template so that it would include that code. To modify a template, edit the files located in the `Templates\Standard` folder off of the main `ScriptBuilder` folder.

You can also create your own custom templates. Maybe you frequently need an Active Server Page that has code that connects to a certain database, or maybe you frequently have a page that has code that draws a graph based on data in a recordset—you can create your own templates that include this common code. To create a template, just create the page like any other Active Server or HTML Page and place it in the `Templates\Custom` folder. Those files are then available when you select File—New and view the CUSTOM tab.

In the left pane you select the tab that corresponds with the options or actions you need to work with. If you select the REFERENCE tab you should see something like the picture shown in Figure 3-33. What is displayed in the left pane when you select the REFERENCE tab is a generous library for the different languages and technologies that you can use within ScriptBuilder.

NOTE: *If you don't see the drop-down list where you can type in a search term, click the small arrow in the top right corner of the right pane.*

Most of the reference material comes from online resources, which has positive and negative value. You must be connected to see the reference and some of the reference items point to pages that no longer exist. But the plus is that the content stays up to date since it comes from major online reference areas like Microsoft and Netscape.

You can also use the reference to insert tags and code right into your page. For example, say that you wanted to insert an HTML numbered list. You would drill down to the tag in the HTML reference. Then if you

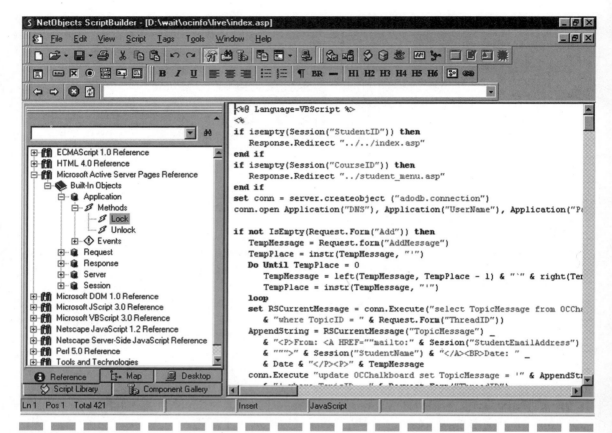

Figure 3-33 Reference view in left window pane.

right-click on the entry and select Insert, the tags for a numbered list would be inserted into the page in the right pane where your insertion point is located.

You can also add additional references to the library. If you right-click anywhere in the REFERENCE tab you should see an item called Settings. Click on that and you will be presented with all the books available in the library. You can set other options for the REFERENCE by selecting Options from the Tools menu.

When you select the Map tag you should see something like what is displayed in Figure 3-34. The map referred to here represents the document you are working with in the right-pane. What is mapped are the tags and components within that document, so you can use the lists in the REFERENCE pane to quickly navigate to the place in your code where

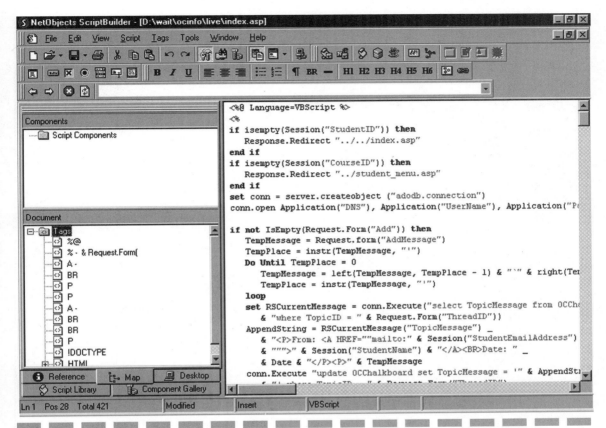

Figure 3-34 Map view within ScriptBuilder.

some tag is. Say you want to locate where you placed a <BR> tag. Just double-click on it and the line that contains a <BR> tag will be high-lighted within your document.

The *Desktop* view, shown in Figure 3-35, allows you to navigate through your system to work with files within a Web site or to locate files that you want to work with. If you double-click on a file it is opened into the right-pane. If you right-click in the Desktop area you can create a folder and view file properties.

One of the most powerful features of ScriptBuilder is the Script Library. Select the SCRIPT LIBRARY tab and you should see the screen shown in Figure 3-36. The Script Library allows you to easily insert pre-built code blocks into your Web page. ScriptBuilder comes with numer-

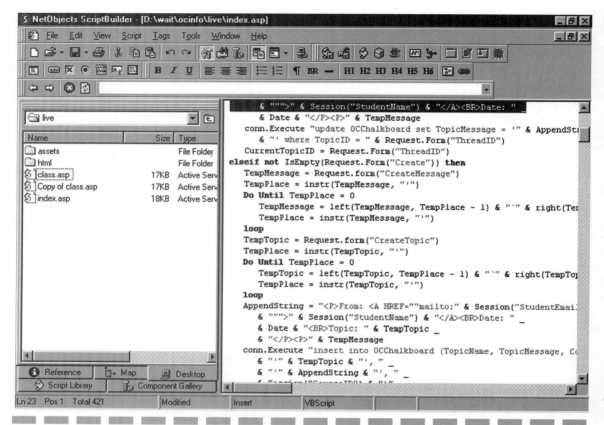

Figure 3-35 Desktop view within ScriptBuilder.

ous server-side and client-side scripts that you can insert into your Active Server Page or your HTML page.

The list in the Script Library can be sorted by any column by clicking on the column head. The columns display the name of the script, the language or technology the script is used for, a description of the script, and the version of Navigator and Explorer that support the script.

To insert a script on to your page just place the insertion point where you want the code to go and then double-click on the script that you want to insert from the Script Library. For example, if you needed a procedure that read a cookie from the visitor's machine you would place your cursor at the point in your Active Server Page where you wanted the procedure to appear. Then you would locate the ReadCookie procedure from the Script Library and double-click on it. The procedure is now part of your code.

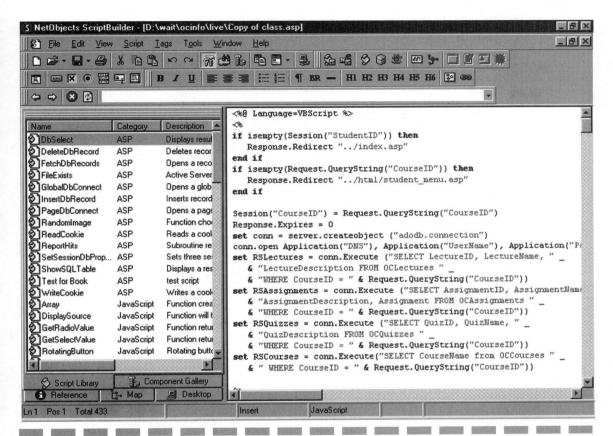

Figure 3-36 Script Library view from within ScriptBuilder.

The built-in scripts are entirely configurable and rewriteable. To change the properties for a script, right-click on it and select Properties. You should see the dialog shown in Figure 3-37. From this dialog you can change the name and description for the script. You should also choose an appropriate language or technology that the script is used for. You can also set what versions of Navigator and Explorer support this script.

You can modify the code for the script by selecting the CODE tab. The window expands to show you the code in a window like the one shown in Figure 3-38. From the code window you can modify the script of any of the prebuilt scripts. For example, I prefer that the ASP procedures (like the one in Figure 3-38) have the ASP code block tags <% and %> already part of the code block. So I can add that in by modifying the script. When you close the code window you are prompted to save or discard your changes.

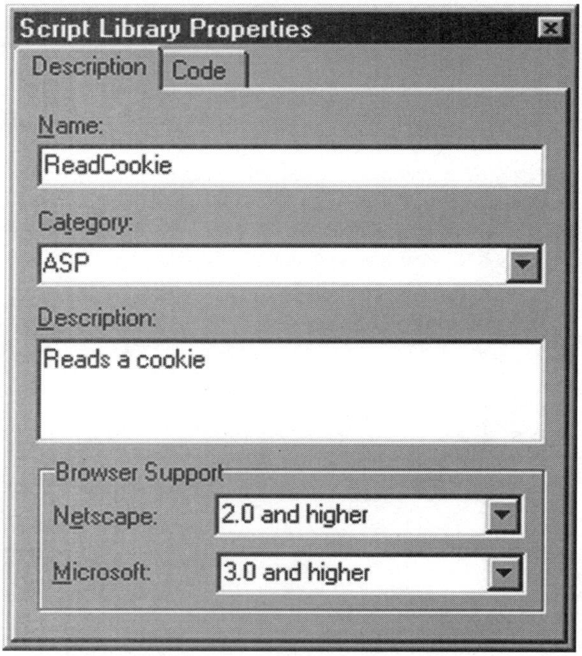

Figure 3-37
Script Library
Properties dialog.

A personal favorite of mine is the ability to add your own scripts to the Script Library. I find that there are so many short blocks of code that are not appropriate for a procedure that I write over and over again. A great way to handle this is to place the script in the Script Library and it is just a double-click away when you are ready for it.

You can add your script to the library in one of two ways. You can right-

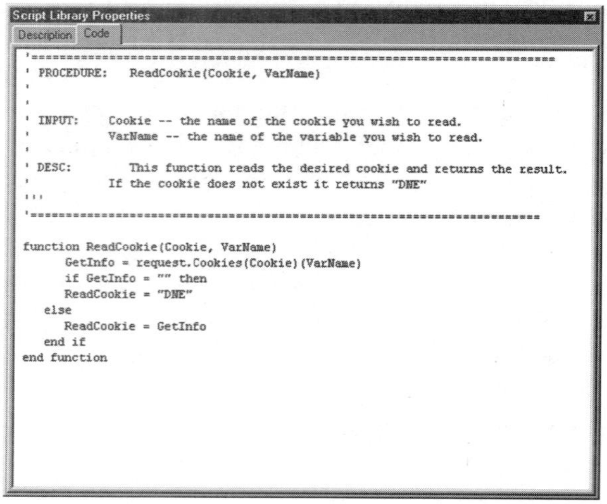

Figure 3-38
Code window for
script editing.

```
'=====================================================================
' PROCEDURE:   ReadCookie(Cookie, VarName)
'
'
' INPUT:    Cookie -- the name of the cookie you wish to read.
'           VarName -- the name of the variable you wish to read.
'
' DESC:       This function reads the desired cookie and returns the result.
'             If the cookie does not exist it returns "DNE"
' ''
'=====================================================================

function ReadCookie(Cookie, VarName)
     GetInfo = request.Cookies(Cookie)(VarName)
     if GetInfo = "" then
       ReadCookie = "DNE"
   else
       ReadCookie = GetInfo
   end if
end function
```

click anywhere in the Script Library and select ADD. You are then presented with a blank code window. This is the same code window you see when you are editing an existing script. You then enter your code for the script. Once completed, you can switch to the DESCRIPTION tab. Here you will see a dialog where you supply the name of the script and a brief description. You also supply the technology or language that uses the code as well as the version support for the script within Navigator and Explorer.

The other way you can add a procedure to the Script Library is to grab it from an existing page. You do this by highlighting text within a document and then right-clicking on the text and selecting Add to Script Library.

For example, say that you connect to a database on many Active Server Pages in the same way and you want the connection code to be part of the Script Library. Highlight the code with your mouse and then right-click on it as shown in Figure 3-39.

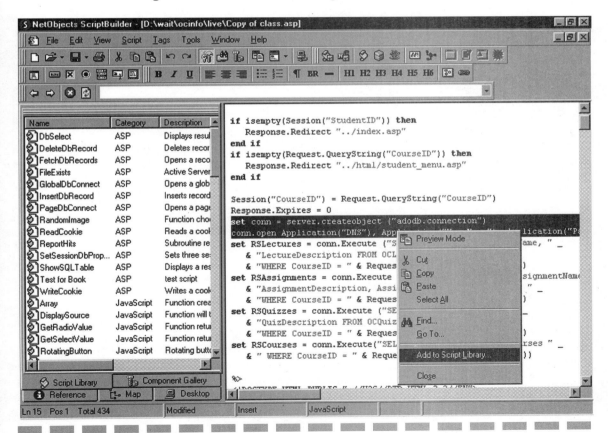

Figure 3-39 Adding code to the Script Library.

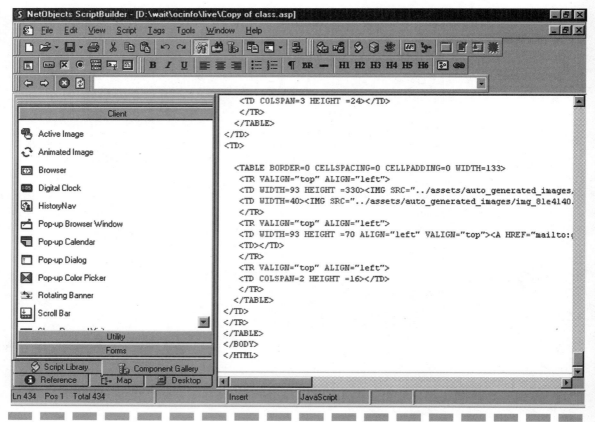

Figure 3-40 *Component Gallery within ScriptBuilder.*

If you then select the Add to Script Library option the code is added to a new library entry. You then supply the name, description, language/technology, and compatibility information for the script. Once completed, the code is part of the Script Library and can be inserted into other pages.

The final tab available in the left pane of ScriptBuilder's main Window is the COMPONENT GALLERY tab. The contents of the tab are displayed in Figure 3-40. The Component Gallery makes working with insertable, programmable components easy. You can include one of the provided components by dragging the component to the place in your Active Serve or HTML Page where you want the component initialized.

You can then use the properties, methods, or events of the component by right-clicking on it and selecting the appropriate action. The template for the property, method, or event is then added to your page. You can also insert your own component into the environment by right-clicking anywhere in the Component Gallery and selecting Add to Gallery.

Working with Code in ScriptBuilder

ScriptBuilder has numerous tools that assist you in writing and working with your code. ScriptBuilder provides color coding for your code lines to make them more readable and distinguishable from HTML. To do this, however, it needs to know what language you are working with. So one of the first things you will want to do is set the default language that it uses for highlighting; to do this select View—Highlighted Language—VBScript from the menu as shown in Figure 3-41.

Once the default language is set, the code is then properly color-coded so that it is easier to read. Also, now that ScriptBuilder knows what language you are using, it can automatically assist you with completing your code blocks. For example, when you type this code with a space:

```
If
```

it then completes the block for you:

```
If expression Then

End If
```

Figure 3-41
Setting the default Highlighted Language.

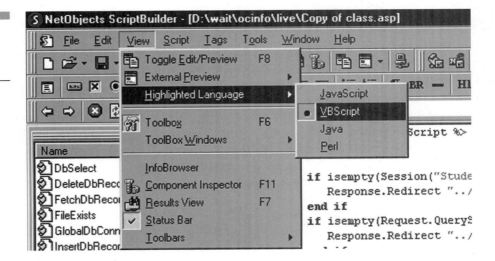

It even highlights the phrase `expression` for you so you can immediately type in your own expression. If you were to type in this code followed by a space:

```
Select
```

ScriptBuilder would build this code block for you with the word `Expression` highlighted:

```
Select Case expression
       Case value

       Case Else

End Select
```

You can even modify this autoscripting feature so that different code appears with each of these statements. For example, say that you want your `If` block to always have an `Else` with it. You could do this by selecting Tools—AutoScripting from the menu. When you do this you will see the complete list of autoscripting options available like those shown in Figure 3-42.

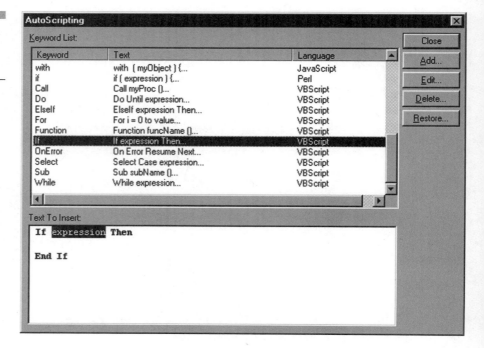

Figure 3-43
Editing code in the
AutoScripting feature.

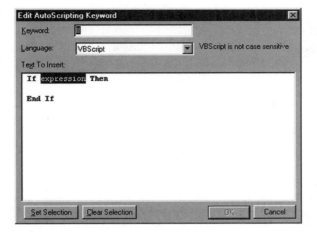

Figure 3-43
Editing code in the
AutoScripting feature.

Note that the list contains statements for VBScript and other languages. In the list you scroll to the If statement under VBScript. Then click EDIT. You are presented with a screen like the one shown in Figure 3-43. From here you could modify the If statement to add the Else statement or any other modification you want. Notice that the word expression is highlighted. When you typed in If on the code page, the word expression was highlighted.

You can also add your own code blocks through the AutoScripting feature by pressing the NEW button in the AutoScripting dialog. When you do this, you are presented with the Add AutoScripting Keyword, which is the same dialog as the one you use to edit a keyword. You just need to supply the keyword, the name you want to type in for the code to appear. You also provide the programming language used in the code and, of course, the code itself.

You can also use this feature to provide yourself with a shorthand code method. For example, as you will learn in the next chapter, you frequently want to include the line Option Explicit in your code to make debugging easier. You could provide yourself a shortcut for typing this line by creating a new AutoScripting entry. First, you provide for the keyword the phrase:

```
ooo
```

Then for the Text to Insert field you would enter:

```
Option Explicit
```

followed by a new line. Now all you need to do is enter ooo on any of your pages and Option Explicit followed by a new line will appear.

Under the Script—Menu is an option called *Server Block*, which produces the following code:

```
<%

%>
```

So it creates a server block for you. If you go to the Tools—Options menu item and change to the CODE tab you should see the screen shown in Figure 3-44. From this tab, you can change the syntax of the code block that is used by setting the Tag Type field.

On that same dialog, note the Function Blocks section. Here you provide the fields that you want to appear automatically in a comment block when you insert a procedure. If you want your name to appear, type it in the Username field. You can then check that you want the user name and current date included in a function comment header.

This information is used when you select Script—Function Block from the menu. When you do, you are presented with the dialog shown in Figure 3-45.

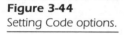

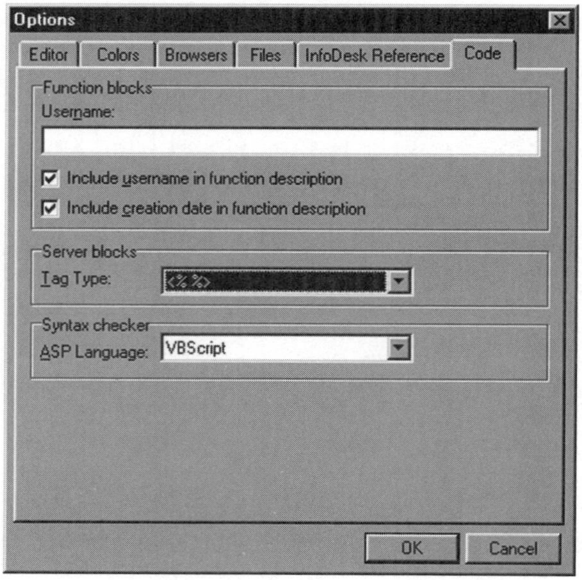

Figure 3-44
Setting Code options.

Figure 3-45
Inserting a Function
Block.

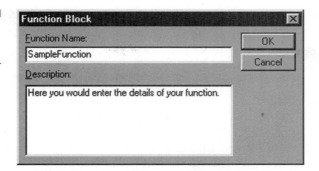

You then enter the name of your function followed by a description of what the function does. When you press OK, the data you entered here is combined with your selections on the Options dialog to produce this code block:

```
'*******************************************************************
'     SampleFunction()
'
'          Here you would enter the details of your function.
'
'     Author: Greg Buczek
'     Date Created: 8/4/99
'*******************************************************************
*/
Function SampleFunction()
End Function
```

As you have seen thus far, ScriptBuilder is not a tool for visually designing pages. You can easily preview pages, but you don't drag and drop visual elements onto a page. In ScriptBuilder you are working with the raw HTML and code.

But the HTML Tags toolbar at least helps you with inserting the tags. The toolbar is shown in Figure 3-46. When these buttons are pressed, an appropriate tag is inserted into your document at the insertion point, so if you press the B button, the <B> and </B> tags are inserted into your document. If you first highlight some text that you want bold, the tags will be placed around that text.

Figure 3-46
HTML Tags toolbar.

Pressing any of the alignment buttons would produce the appropriate paragraph tags to create the desired alignment. For example, pressing the left-alignment button produces this HTML:

```
<P ALIGN=LEFT></P>
```

The alignment icons are followed by the list, numbered list, paragraph, line break, and horizontal line buttons that produce the respective tags when pressed.

The H1 though H6 buttons produce the corresponding heading tags, so pressing the H1 button produces this HTML:

```
<H1></H1>
```

The insertion point is moved between the tags so you can start entering the text for this tag.

The last two buttons on the toolbar produce image and link tags, respectively. Each of the buttons brings up a dialog for you to supply the necessary information. When you press the IMAGE icon, you see the dialog shown in Figure 3-47.

You supply the HTML path to the image, the text you want to appear with or instead of the image, the alignment, border size, image size, and spacing. Based on your entry, an image tag is inserted into your document.

When you press the LINK button you see the dialog shown in Figure 3-48. In this dialog, you supply the location to go to when the link is clicked on, the text to display for the link on the page, optionally a name

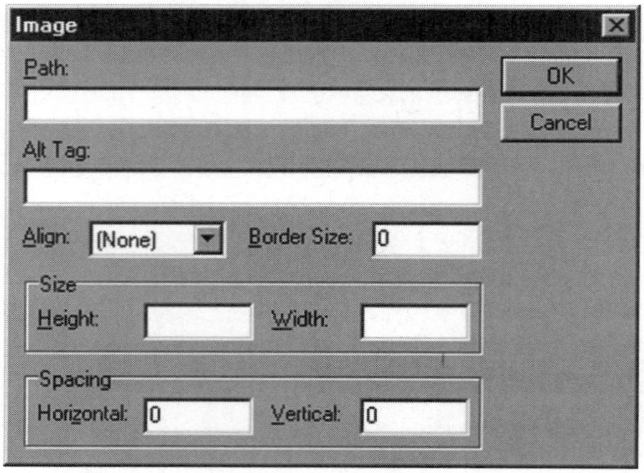

Figure 3-47
Inserting an HTML image tag.

Figure 3-48
Inserting an HTML
link tag.

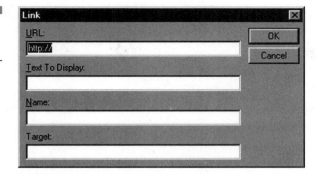

for the link, and the target for the link. The *Target* refers to what
browser or frame to output the resulting page to. Once you enter in the
information and press OK the appropriate tag is produced.

ScriptBuilder also has a toolbar that has buttons for form elements.
This toolbar is shown in Figure 3-49. Each of the buttons displays a different dialog that retrieves the necessary parameters from you to create
the desired tag. The first button creates the form tag itself. When you
press this button, you see a dialog that asks you for the name of the
form, what frame or browser window you want to output the results of
the form output to, the encoding type, and the location of the page to go
to when the form is submitted for processing. You also supply the
method used for submitting the form, Get or Post. The difference
between these methods is discussed in Chapter 5.

The result of filling in the fields for the Forms dialog produces a form
tag at the insertion point like this one:

```
<FORM NAME="MoreInfoForm" TARGET="New"


  ACTION="http://www.whatever.com/page.asp" METHOD="post"
  ENCODE="application/x-www-form-urlencoded">

</FORM>
```

The buttons for the form elements prompt you for slightly different
information based on the type of form element that was selected. For

Figure 3-49
Form Elements
toolbar.

example, the Text field asks you for the name of the field, the value, the length, and whether it is a Password field. It produces a tag like this:

```
<INPUT TYPE="text" SIZE=20 MAXLENGTH=50 NAME="FirstName">
```

But when you press the button for a text area form element, you are asked to supply the name of the field, default text, the size of the field, and how wrapping will work.

Verifying Code in ScriptBuilder

ScriptBuilder also has a couple of tools that assist you greatly in checking your code: the *Syntax Checker* and the *Script Inspector*.

One of the things that frequently occurs when I write Active Server Pages is that I will forget a parenthesis in a line of code like this:

```
If isempty(Request.Form(" OK") then
```

I upload the page to the server thinking that the page is fine and when I run the page I get an error on the preceding line of code. I know the problem but have to edit the page and upload it back to the server.

The Syntax Checker helps with this problem. It won't find errors like the wrong method or property used with an object and it certainly won't find logic errors but it will find syntax errors like the previous one.

Let's say that you have a code block on a page like this:

```
<%
if isempty(Session("StudentID")) then
  Response.Redirect "../index.asp"
end if
if isempty(Request.QueryString("CourseID") then
  Response.Redirect "../html/student_menu.asp"
end if
%>
```

You are now ready to post your page to the server but want to check it for syntax errors. From the Tools menu select Syntax Checker. When you do, the results pane will be added to ScriptBuilder window as shown in Figure 3-50.

Notice the RESULTS pane in the bottom of the window. It lists an error on the page at line 6. The Results will show you a list of all the syntax errors found on the page. If you double-click on the error message it will take you to the line of code that produced the error.

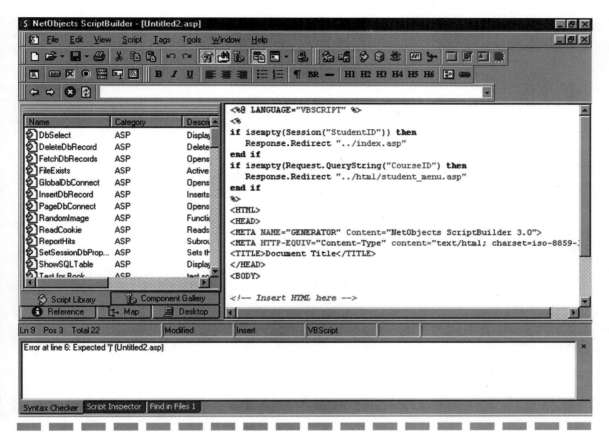

Figure 3-50   Result of using the Syntax Checker.

The Syntax Checker will find a variety of errors like this one. It will tell you if you have an `If` statement without an `End  If` or a `For` without a `Next`. But I've also seen it think there was a syntax error when there wasn't one. Take this line of code which appears as a single line of an Active Server Page:

```
<A HREF="../html/lecturerouter.asp?LectureID=
<% Response.write RSLectures("LectureID") %>">
<IMG HEIGHT=28 WIDTH=35 SRC="<% Response.Write iconpath %>"
BORDER=0 ></A>
```

The line produces an error even though there is no error. What throws off the ScriptBuilder is when you have ASP code like this in line with the HTML.

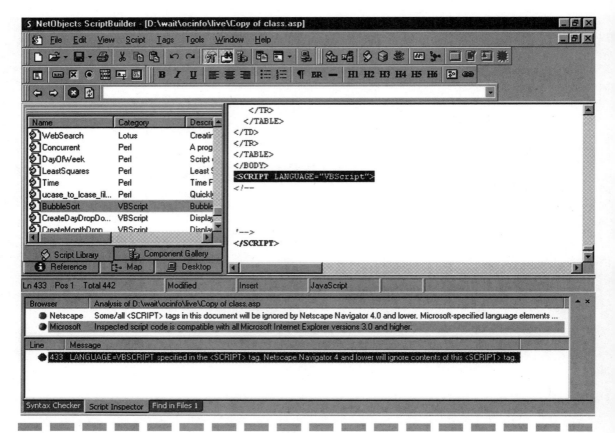

Figure 3-51   Result of running the Script Inspector.

The other verification tool is the Script Inspector. The Script Inspector will look at your HTML, server-side code, and client-side code and will report to you the versions of Navigator and Explorer that are needed to run your code.

To use the tool, open the page you want to test and select Tools—Script Inspector from the menu. The RESULTS pane then appears at the bottom of the program window like the screen shown in Figure 3-51. If you don't see the two result panes at the bottom like the one shown, you need to right-click in the RESULTS pane and select Show Details.

Note that the Script Inspector found a client-side VBScript tag that is not supported by the most recent version of Navigator. When you double-click on the error line in the far bottom pane you are taken to the line that produced the problem.

Microsoft Visual InterDev 6.0

Another helpful tool you can use to develop your Active Server Pages is Microsoft Visual InterDev 6.0. Since it is produced by Microsoft, Visual InterDev has a close connection with the Internet Information Server and NT. From a developer's perspective, its most powerful features are the visual highlighting it provides and the autocompletion of code.

Figure 3-52 displays an Active Server Page open within Visual InterDev. Visual InterDev, through the use of font color, background color, and bold text, makes the page very readable. It is very easy to see where a code block starts and ends; and within the code blocks, statements are bold.

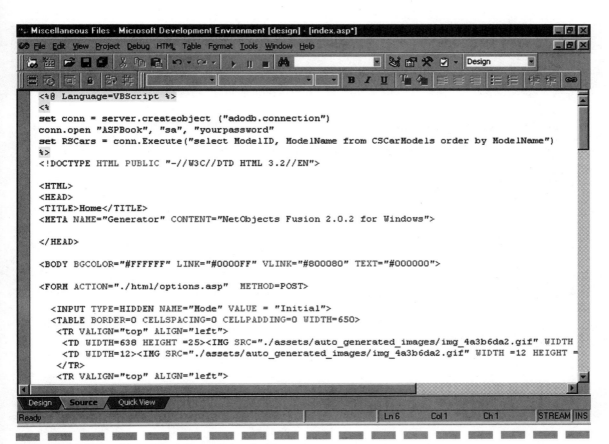

Figure 3-52 Visual InterDev 6.0 program window.

Notice the three VIEW tabs for the page: DESIGN, SOURCE, and QUICK VIEW. Unfortunately once you start including ASP code within HTML— which is almost all of your pages—the DESIGN tab does not work; and the QUICK VIEW tab doesn't work since it cannot process the server-side code. So the only view that you can use all the time is the SOURCE view.

The other super helpful feature of Visual InterDev is the code completion lists, generated when you use the dot syntax for one of the built-in ASP objects. For example, one of the main ASP objects is the Response object. This object is used to communicate back to the browser that called your Active Server Page. The object has numerous properties and methods that allow you to take action. Within Visual InterDev if you type in this code:

```
Response.
```

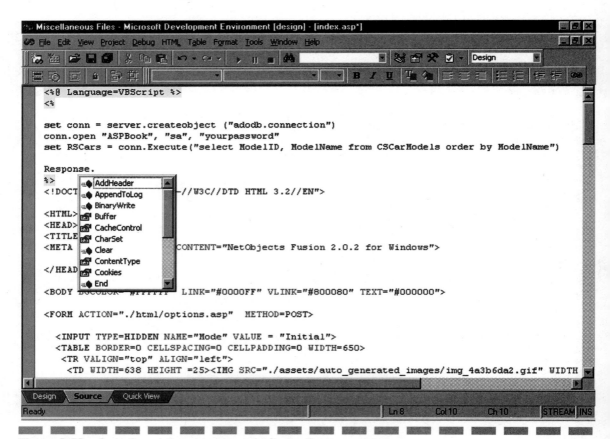

Figure 3-53 Code Completion drop down list for the Response object.

you will see the list shown in Figure 3-53. The list contains all the methods and properties for the Response object. You can then start typing the method you want to use or you can scroll down in the list and select the item you want.

Final Thought on Tools

Regardless of the tools you use, remember that they are tools—the right tools for the job make the work much easier. You should explore their full potential because most have wonderful features that are frequently buried in the menu. Try to avoid being complacent with the same product. Numerous new products and utilities enter the market all the time and can frequently save you enough time to make them quickly worthwhile.

ASP Basics

ASP Code Construction

Active Server Pages are made up of *static HTML* and *dynamic ASP code*. The two can be combined in a variety of ways as this section discusses: HTML can be within code, code can be within HTML, and server-side scripting can be within client-side scripting.

<% = X %> Tag

To differentiate where the code starts and where it ends you need some sort of tag. The simplest tag is as follows:

```
<% = X %>
```

This tells the compiler to print out the result of the expression X. For example, if you wanted to create a Web page that displayed the current date and time you could code it like this:

```
<HTML>
<HEAD>
<TITLE>Simple Tag Page</TITLE>
</HEAD>
<BODY>
<H1>Welcome to the clock page</H1>
<P>It is now: <% = Now() %><P>
</BODY>
</HTML>
```

The page is made up of standard HTML until you get to this line:

```
<P>It is now: <% = Now() %><P>
```

The first part of the line is standard HTML but then the basic ASP tag appears. This tells the compiler that what follows between the <% and the %> is ASP code. Since the opening <% is followed by an equal sign, this further tells the compiler that what follows should be evaluated and the result should be sent as HTML.

In this case, what is being output is the result of the function Now(). As you will learn later in this chapter, Now() returns the current system date and time. So the preceding line returns this to the browser:

```
<P>It is now: 7/21/99 12:10:14 PM<P>
```

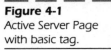
Figure 4-1
Active Server Page
with basic tag.

The result of this Active Server Page is shown in Figure 4-1.

<% Single Line of Code %>

Another way to place your code within an Active Server Page is to place a single line of code between the <% tag and the %> tag. For example, the page uses this syntax to display the number of days until Christmas:

```
<HTML>
<HEAD>
<TITLE>Days Until Christmas</TITLE>
</HEAD>
<BODY>
<H1>How much time is left?</H1>
<P>Days until Christmas: <% Response.Write
DateDiff("d",Date,"12/25/" & Year(Date)) %>
<P>
</BODY>
</HTML>
```

The page is made up of standard HTML until we get to this line:

```
<P>Days until Christmas: <% Response.Write
DateDiff("d",Date,"12/25/" & Year(Date)) %>
```

Figure 4-2
Active Server Page
with single line of
ASP code.

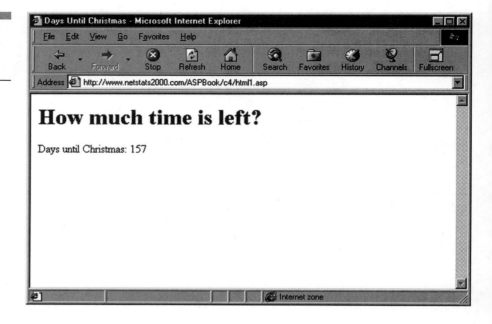

The ASP compiler sees the <% tag and knows that everything between that point and the %> tag is code that needs to be processed. In this case we are using a method called Write of an object called Response to send output to the browser. (This object is discussed in great detail in Chapter 6.) Specifically what is written to the browser is the number of days until Christmas as derived by subtracting the number of days between the current date and Christmas of the current year.

The line of code evaluates to this:

```
<P>Days until Christmas: 157<P>
```

The result of the page is shown in Figure 4-2.

<% Code Block %>

You can also use the <% tag and the %> tag to create a block of code, which is a series of lines that achieve some task. For example, let's say you need to create a Web page that sends, or redirects, visitors to a certain page based on the day of the week. This code block would accomplish that task:

```
<%
If WeekDay(Date) = 1 then
   Response.Redirect "Sunday.html"
ElseIf WeekDay(Date) = 2 then
   Response.Redirect "Monday.html"
ElseIf WeekDay(Date) = 3 then
   Response.Redirect "Tuesday.html"
ElseIf WeekDay(Date) = 4 then
   Response.Redirect "Wednesday.html"
ElseIf WeekDay(Date) = 5 then
   Response.Redirect "Thursday.html"
ElseIf WeekDay(Date) = 6 then
   Response.Redirect "Friday.html"
Else
   Response.Redirect "Saturday.html"
End If
%>
```

This would be the entire content of the page. The page has no output and is made up of just ASP code. The code checks for the numeric day of the week based on the current date and then routes visitors to the correct page based on that number.

<Script> Code </Script>

If you already work with client-side script, you are probably familiar with the <Script> tag. As an alternative to the tags presented thus far, you can also use this tag with Active Server Pages. But you must use the RunAt parameter and set it to server or your ASP code will be passed on to the browser for processing. Below is the code for a Web page that uses the <Script> tag.

```
<HTML>
<HEAD>
<TITLE>Session Object</TITLE>
</HEAD>
<BODY>
<H1>Timeout Property</H1>
<P>The session is set to timeout in (minutes):
<SCRIPT LANGUAGE=VBScript RUNAT=Server >
   Response.Write Session.Timeout
</SCRIPT>
</BODY>
</HTML>
```

The page looks like normal HTML until you get to the <Script> tag:

```
<SCRIPT LANGUAGE=VBScript RUNAT=Server >
```

Figure 4-3
Active Server Page
using the <Script>
tag.

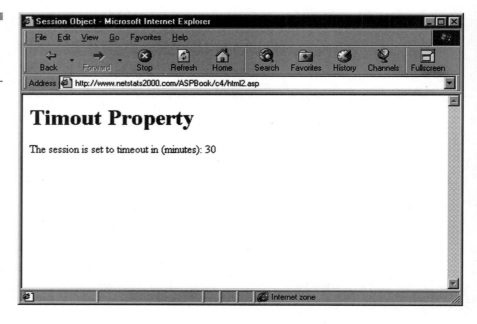

Notice that the language being used is specified and that the code is set to run on the server-side. Next we have the one line of code that writes the number of minutes the session TimeOut property is set to:

```
Response.Write Session.Timeout
```

The code ends with the </Script> tag. When viewed in the browser the code evaluates to this:

```
30
```

The output of the page is shown in Figure 4-3.

HTML in Code

So far we have looked at code within HTML, but we can also do just the opposite. We can put HTML in the code. For example, we could write code that displays one background color if it is during the day and a different background color if it is the night, as shown in the following code:

```
<HTML>
<HEAD>
<TITLE>Change the Light</TITLE>
</HEAD>
<%
  if hour(Time) > 6 and Hour(Time) < 19 then
    Response.Write "<BODY BGCOLOR=""#FFFFD7"">"
  else
    Response.Write "<BODY BGCOLOR=""#808080"">"
  end if
%>
<H1>We turn down the light at night.</H1>
</BODY>
</HTML>
```

Notice what the block of code is doing. It is writing one body tag if the time of day is between 7:00 AM and 6:00 PM and a different body tag during the other hours of the day. So during the evening, the code block produces this HTML:

```
<BODY BGCOLOR="#808080">
```

Figure 4-4 shows what the page looks like in the evening.

Figure 4-4
Change the Light page during the evening hours.

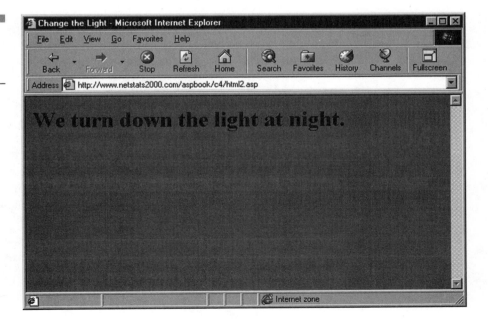

Figure 4-5
Change the Light
page during the day
hours.

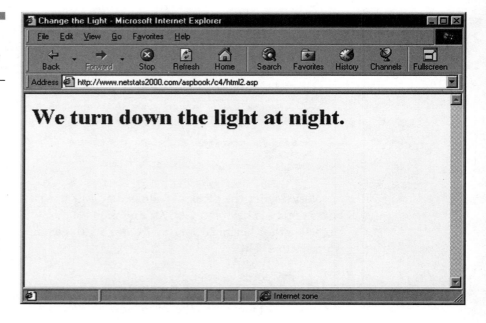

During the day the code outputs this body tag:

```
<BODY BGCOLOR="#FFFFD7">
```

That tag produces the page shown in Figure 4-5.

Script Within Script

You can also include the results of your server-side script within client-side script, so that you can have your server-side code run and place text or code within your client-side code that will run on the browser.

To demonstrate this use, let's say that we have a price calculator that customers can use to determine how much a certain quantity of a product will cost. If the customer is a preferred customer we want to charge one price, otherwise we have a different price. We want to have the price calculated on the client-side to reduce the number of connections and the speed so our customers can easily play with prices. But we need the client-script to charge the price based on the type of customer, which is stored in a server-side variable. The following code combines server-side and client-side script to accomplish this task:

```
<HTML>
<HEAD><TITLE>Client and Server</TITLE>
<%
If Session("CustomerType") = "Preferred" then
  TheRate = 25
else
  TheRate = 50
end if
%>
<SCRIPT language="JavaScript">
<!--
function CheckPrice()
{
  var TheMessage = 0;
  TheMessage = <% response.write TheRate %> * document.sampleform.
    Quantity.value
  alert("Your price is $" + TheMessage);
}
// -->
</SCRIPT>
<BODY>
<FORM NAME="sampleform">
Enter Quantity to determine price
<p>
<INPUT TYPE="text" NAME="Quantity" SIZE=10>
<p>
<INPUT TYPE="button" NAME="submitButton" VALUE="Get Price"
  onClick="CheckPrice();">
</FORM>
</BODY>
</HTML>
```

The first code block is VBScript server-side ASP code. We know that
from the tags used:

```
<%
If Session("CustomerType") = "Preferred" then
  TheRate = 25
else
  TheRate = 50
end if
%>
```

The code checks the value of a session variable, which is discussed more
in Chapter 8. The code sets a variable called TheRate to a value based
on the CustomerType.

The next code block inserts the result of server-side code within a
client-side code block.

```
<SCRIPT language="JavaScript">
<!--
function CheckPrice()
{
  var TheMessage = 0;
```

```
    TheMessage = <% response.write TheRate %> *
document.sampleform.Quantity.value
    alert("Your price is $" + TheMessage);
}
// -->
</SCRIPT>
```

The Script tag without an indication that it is to run on the server is our indication that this is client-side code. Notice that within the middle of this code block we have server-side ASP code:

```
<% response.write TheRate %>
```

The server-side code runs before the code block is sent to the browser. So if the visitor is not a preferred customer the browser receives this HTML:

```
<HTML>
<HEAD><TITLE> Client and Server</TITLE>
<SCRIPT language="JavaScript">
<!--
function CheckPrice()
{
  var TheMessage = 0;
  TheMessage = 50 * document.sampleform.Quantity.value
  alert("Your price is $" + TheMessage);
}
// -->
</SCRIPT>
<BODY>
<FORM NAME="sampleform">
Enter Quantity to determine price
<p>
<INPUT TYPE="text" NAME="Quantity" SIZE=10>
<p>
<INPUT TYPE="button" NAME="submitButton" VALUE="Get Price"
  onClick="CheckPrice();">
</FORM>
</BODY>
</HTML>
```

The first thing you should notice is the absence of the first code block. That code block is gone since it was server-side code and we are now looking at what is sent to the client. Also notice, within the script tags, the variable TheRate has been replaced with the value 50, so all the server-side code is gone and the browser now has a customized version of the CheckPrice procedure that is based on the type of customer.

Figure 4-6 shows the resulting Web page and Figure 4-7 shows the message box that is displayed when the price is calculated.

If the visitor was a preferred customer the price the visitor would see

Figure 4-6
Server and client
code page.

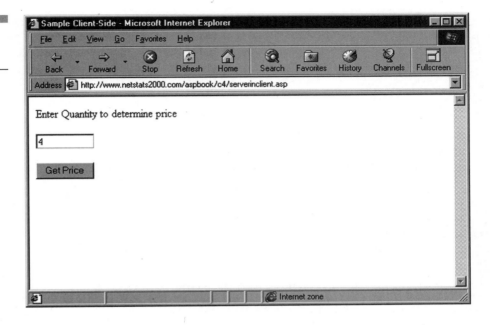

Figure 4-7
Result of the visitor
pressing the GET PRICE
button.

would be based on $25 per unit. The client-side script would have this
line instead of the previous one:

```
TheMessage = 25 * document.sampleform.Quantity.value
```

Processing Directive

By default, IIS expects your ASP code to be VBScript. You can explicitly
state that you will be using VBScript as your code by putting this
Processing Directive at the top of your page:

```
<%@ LANGUAGE=VBSCRIPT %>
```

Note that this line must be the first one on the page. This line tells the compiler that the programming language used on this page is VBScript. If you wish to use JScript then the directive should look like this:

```
<%@ LANGUAGE=JSCRIPT %>
```

Include Files

Why Use Them

As your Active Server Pages grow you will note that your code grows into very large code blocks and you will find that you are rewriting the same procedure over and over again. Include files can help you with this problem, as they are a way for you to put your code in one file and then call that code from an Active Server Page.

For example, let's say that you have standard procedures for validating the data that the visitor enters on a form on a page. You may check Date fields in a certain way, have fields that are required, check for numbers, and check for ranges in numbers. This kind of code would probably be included in many of your pages. If you then needed to modify how one of the procedures worked, you would need to modify the code in each of the pages that used the procedure. Instead, you could put your validation code in a single separate text file and then just link your pages that need the code to that file.

Include files help to clean up overly crowded pages, making them easier to debug. They help because the code is centrally located, which makes modification easier. Another reason to place your code in an Include file is to protect programmers from the complexity of the code.

You may have one programmer at your company that is an expert with the Collaborative Data Objects (CDO). CDO is used to send out email through your Active Server Pages and to interact with Microsoft Exchange. This programmer might have some complicated procedures that manage Exchange calendars. If this programmer was to hand over his or her code to other programmers to place on their Active Server Pages, there is a risk that the code may not be used correctly due to the other programmers' not understanding the code. If the CDO programmer placed his or her code in an Include file, the other programmers would not need to know the intricacies of the underlying code. They would just include the CDO file and call its procedures.

Including a File

To include a file within an Active Server Page you just use an `Include` tag:

```
<SCRIPT LANGUAGE="vbscript" RUNAT="server">
  <!-- #include file="FieldValidation.inc" -->
</SCRIPT>
```

The `Include` line is surrounded by script tags. Note that this `Include` file is called `FieldValidation.inc` and must be located in the same directory as the Active Server Page that calls it. But you can also use a relative path to indicate the location of the `Include` file:

```
<SCRIPT LANGUAGE="vbscript" RUNAT="server">
  <!-- #include virtual="../lib/FieldValidation.inc" -->
</SCRIPT>
```

In this example, the `Include` file needs to be located in a directory called `Lib` that is one directory level up from the current directory.

Including a file has the effect of placing all the code in that file in the exact location where the `Include` line is placed. Every line of code that is in the `Include` file is not part of the Active Server Page that has included it.

The Include File—Structure and Example

The `Include` file is simply a text file that contains your code. Like any other ASP the code has the following structure:

```
<%
'code block goes here
%>
```

The code starts with the `<%` tag and ends with the `%>` tag.

For example, this `Include` file, saved as `FieldValidation.inc`, contains a procedure that tests to see if the data supplied is a date and falls within a specified range. It also contains procedures that check to see if some field is a number and that number falls in a specific range, verify that a numeric value is a valid birthdate and that a zip code value is valid.

```
<%
Function DateRange(DateToTest, StartDate, EndDate)
  if not isdate(DateToTest) then
    DateRange = 0
  elseif cdate(DateToTest) < cdate(StartDate) or _
```

```
        cdate(DateToTest) > cdate(EndDate) then
        DateRange = 0
    else
        DateRange = -1
    end if
End Function

Function NumberRange(FieldToTest, MinNumber, MaxNumber)
    If Not IsNumeric(FieldToTest) Then
        NumberRange = 0
    ElseIf CSng(FieldToTest) < MinNumber Or _
        CSng(FieldToTest) > MaxNumber Then
        NumberRange = 0
    Else
        NumberRange = -1
    End If
End Function

Function Birthdate(FieldToTest)
    If Not IsDate(FieldToTest) Then
        Birthdate = 0
    ElseIf CDate(FieldToTest) > Date Then
        Birthdate = 0
    Else
        Birthdate = -1
    End If
End Function

Function ZipCode(FieldToTest)
    If Len(FieldToTest) = 5 Then
        If IsNumeric(FieldToTest) Then
            ZipCode = -1
        Else
            ZipCode = 0
        End If
    ElseIf Len(FieldToTest) = 10 Then
        If IsNumeric(Left(FieldToTest, 5)) And _
            IsNumeric(Right(FieldToTest, 4)) Then
            ZipCode = -1
        Else
            ZipCode = 0
        End If
    Else
        ZipCode = 0
    End If
End Function
%>
```

Pulling It Together

You could use the Include file mentioned in the last section by using
this syntax in your Active Server Page:

```
<SCRIPT LANGUAGE="vbscript" RUNAT="server">
  <!— #include file="FieldValidation.inc" —>
</SCRIPT>
```

A file named FieldValidation.inc must be in the same directory as the Active Server Page that is calling it. The code of the entire Include file would then be placed by the compiler in the location where the tag appears. Now, from within the code of the Active Server Page, the procedures in the Include file can be called:

```
Response1 = DateRange(Request.Form("Test1"), _
  "12/1/99", "12/15/99")
Response1 = NumberRange(Request.Form("Test1"), _
7, 10)
Response1 = Birthdate(Request.Form("Test1"))
Response1 = ZipCode(Request.Form("Test1"))
```

Later in this chapter we discuss procedures, so don't be concerned if the structure of the Include file doesn't make sense. Also note the use of the Request object in the preceding calls. That object will be discussed at length in Chapter 6. What's important here is to understand that you can take your code out of an Active Server Page and place it in an Include file.

ASP Code in Use

In this section we dive into VBScript, the language most often used with Active Server Pages. You will learn how to use the Data Types, Operators, Statements, and Functions built into VBScript to create Active Server Page code blocks and procedures.

Comments, Case, and White Space

In VBScript, as well as Visual Basic and Visual Basic for Applications, comments are denoted with the *tick* or *single-quote*. You can place a comment at the end of a line of code:

```
If Year(Request.Form("StartDate")) = Year(Date) then 'this is a
  comment on a single line of code
```

You can also use the tick to indicate that the whole line is a comment:

```
If Year(Request.Form("StartDate")) = Year(Date) then
 'the code will enter this point only if the supplied date is
   within the current year
```

You can also create a *comment block*, which is frequently found at the top of a procedure or Active Server Page. It might name either the author, date created, name of the procedure, what it does, the parameters, or return values, or it might describe all of these items.

```
'''''''''''''''''''''''''''''''''''''''''''''''''''''''''''''''''''''''''''''''
'
'   Programmer: Greg Buczek
'   Date Created: 2/1/2000
'   Procedure Name: DateRange
'   Procedure Description: This procedure is used to determine if
        the value
'   passed in is a date. If it is, it is also checked to see if it
        is in a
'   range.
'   Parameters: 3 parameters are passed in, the data to be tested,
        the low
'   value for the data and the high value.
'   Return Value: The procedure returns -1 if the value is a date
        and within
'   the range. It returns a 0 if not.
'''''''''''''''''''''''''''''''''''''''''''''''''''''''''''''''''''''''''''''''
```

Once you start a line as a comment, the whole line must be a comment. For example:

```
'Some comment ' x = 5
```

The code x = 5 will not be executed because it is part of a comment line.

Comments are skipped by the compiler so you should use them liberally. Remember that the programmer after you may not be able to read through your code without good explanation, or you may not be able to remember why it was that you did something a certain way years from now. Comments also help you think through what it is you need to do. They can be used to help you outline for yourself how the code must flow and what situations you need to program for.

Another way to make your code easier to read by yourself or some other programmer is by making good use of *white space*, which refers to the tabs, extra lines, and spaces that you surround your code with.

For example, look at the readability of this code block:

```
if isempty(Session("StudentID")) then
Response.Redirect "../index.asp"
end if
if isempty(Request.Form("QuizID")) then
Response.Redirect "../index.asp"
end if
```

```
set conn=server.createobject("adodb.connection")
conn.open "ASPBook","sa","yourpassword"
set RSQuiz=conn.execute("SELECT CourseID, QuizName, " _
& "CorrectToPass FROM " _
& "OCQuizzes where QuizID = " & Request.Form("QuizID"))
NumberCorrect=0
for each Question in Request.Form
if Question<>"TestIt" then
set RSQuestion=conn.Execute("select QuizAnswer from " _
& "OCQuizQuestions where QuizQuestionID = " _
& Question)
if Request.Form(Question)=RSQuestion("QuizAnswer") then
NumberCorrect=NumberCorrect + 1
end if
end if
next
```

The code block has had all the extra white space removed. It is very difficult to read. As your eyes scan down the page you are not sure what code goes in what loop and where a full line of code starts and stops. Now look at the same code block with its white space:

```
if isempty(Session("StudentID")) then
  Response.Redirect "../index.asp"
end if
if isempty(Request.Form("QuizID")) then
  Response.Redirect "../index.asp"
end if

set conn = server.createobject ("adodb.connection")
conn.open "ASPBook", "sa", "yourpassword"
set RSQuiz = conn.execute ("SELECT CourseID, QuizName,
CorrectToPass " _
  & "From OCQuizzes where QuizID = " & Request.Form("QuizID"))
NumberCorrect = 0
for each Question in Request.Form
  if Question <> "TestIt" then
    set RSQuestion = conn.Execute("select QuizAnswer from " _
      & "OCQuizQuestions where QuizQuestionID = " _
      & Question)
    if Request.Form(Question) = RSQuestion("QuizAnswer") then
      NumberCorrect = NumberCorrect + 1
    end if
  end if
next
```

With the white space in place the code is much more readable. We can tell where an If statement begins and ends. Where we have an If statement within another If statement, we know which code would run in any condition.

The addition of white space does not affect the execution of our code. A lot of white space would make an Active Server Page a little bigger but that is a small price to pay to make the code more readable.

VBScript as well as Visual Basic and Visual Basic for Applications is case insensitive. This means that this variable:

```
NumCorrect
```

is the same as this variable:

```
numcorrect
```

as is this:

```
nUMcORRECT
```

If you have programmed in a language that is case sensitive like C++, you will have to be very careful with the names of your variables and procedures.

The built-in ASP object model and the functions and constructs within VBScript are also case insensitive. So you can refer to the write method like this:

```
Response.Write
```

Or you can refer to it like this:

```
response.write
```

To make your code more readable, you should try to be consistent. If you create a variable as shown here:

```
Dim OrderTotal
```

then you should always write it that way in your code.

Variables

Variables are items you create to store information in your code. In VBScript, variables must start with a letter and cannot be longer than 255 characters. They can contain letters and numbers but cannot contain periods and other special characters. The following are valid variable names:

```
Dim x
```

```
Dim ABC
Dim A241
Dim AveryLongVariableNameThisIsLegal
```

These declarations are not legal:

```
Dim 2C
Dim ABC+
Dim AB.3
```

In VBScript you are not required to first declare your variables—you can just use a variable. For example, the first line of your code could be this:

```
X = 3
```

Although you don't have to declare your variables, you may find it much easier to debug your code if you do it in combination with the `Option Explicit` statement. If you put this line of code at the top of your page:

```
Option Explicit
```

you are telling the compiler that you will declare all your variables. If the compiler finds a variable that was not declared then it will generate an error.

Consider this code block:

```
MyVariable = 2
MyVariable = MyVariable * 3
MyVariable = MyVaraible + 1
Response.Write MyVariable
```

What number is written to the browser? The answer is 1. Notice on the third line the variable is spelled wrong. Since you don't have `Option Explicit` on the compiler, it thinks you are creating a new variable with that name. A new variable would have a zero value; so zero plus one is one.

This is one of the most difficult errors to deal with since the code ran without an error; only the result was in error. If, instead, the code block was written like this:

```
Option Explicit
Dim MyVariable
MyVariable = 2
MyVariable = MyVariable * 3
```

```
MyVariable = MyVaraible + 1
Response.Write MyVariable
```

the compiler would throw an error pointing at line three. We would know we had a problem and it would be pretty simple to find. With four lines of code this is not as big a deal. But when you have a procedure that is a few hundred lines long this can be a big help.

Data Types

In most languages you have a variety of data types to choose from when you create your variables. For example, in Visual Basic you could create variables of these types:

```
Dim X as Long
Dim Y as Currency
Cim Z as String
```

In C++ you can create variables of specific types like this:

```
int TheNumber;
char TheName[100];
float TheFloat;
```

In VBScript, however, you have just one data type that is implied when you say:

```
Dim X
```

The type is called *variant*. This special data type can act like any type that you can create in Visual Basic as well as an object data type. When you place a value in a variant data type it decides for you how the value should be stored. So in this code:

```
Dim X
X = 5
```

the data type of the variant is a type of number, probably a byte. If you then assign a value to the same variable like this:

```
X = "Hello"
```

the variable is now a string type. The same would be true if you assigned it a date or any other type. So over the life of a variant data type, it can change types. The variant data type can also be an object:

```
Dim X
Set X = Server.CreatePbject("adodb.connection")
```

Notice that when we use a variant to store an object the Set statement is used. This is discussed later on in this chapter.

Scope and Life

With regard to a variable, *scope* refers to where the variable is accessible. For example, if a variable is accessible throughout an application, it has Public or Global scope.

Life refers to the period of time during which a variable is accessible. For example, the life of a variable declared within a procedure begins when the procedure begins and ends when the procedure ends.

When you declare a variable within an Active Server Page that is outside a procedure it has *page scope*, which means that the variable is available to any line of code on that page or within any procedure. For example, given the following code:

```
<%
Option Explicit
Dim MyString
MyString = "Hello"
Procedure1
Response.Write MyString
%>
HTML goes here
<%
Sub Procedure1
   MyString = "GoodBye"
End Sub
%>
```

in the second line of code the variable MyString is declared. Since it is declared within the main block of code, not a procedure, it has page-wide scope. The next line of code sets the variable to the string "Hello". The code then calls a procedure called Procedure1, which is at the bottom of the page. The procedure sets the same variable to the value "Goodbye". The procedure ends and the variable MyString is written to the browser. Goodbye appears in the browser.

Now take a look at this code block.

```
<%
Option Explicit
MyString = "Hello"
Procedure1
Response.Write MyString
%>
HTML goes here
<%
Sub Procedure1
  Dim MyString
  MyString = "GoodBye"
End Sub
%>
```

Here the variable `MyString` is declared within the procedure `Procedure1`. The variable is available only in this procedure. So the compiler generates an error on line 3 when we try to set `MyString` to `"Hello"`. The error occurs because the variable has not been declared for the page code.

Now look at this code block and see if you can decide what, if anything, would be sent to the browser.

```
<%
Option Explicit
Dim MyString
MyString = "Hello"
Procedure1
Response.Write MyString
%>
HTML goes here
<%
Sub Procedure1
  Dim MyString
  MyString = "GoodBye"
End Sub
%>
```

This time we have two variables called `MyString`; one that is in the general code and the other that is in `Procedure1`. In the `Procedure1` block, when we set the variable `MyString` to `"Goodbye"` we are setting the one that is declared within that code block. So the `"Hello"` one does not get changed and `"Hello"` is sent out to the browser. (In Chapter 8 we look at variables you can create that are viewable across many pages.)

The life of a variable also depends upon where it is declared. Variables declared in the page code last until the page is finished processing—they start with the page and end with the page.

Variables declared within a procedure begin and end their life with the procedure. Each time the procedure is called, the variable is redefined. So if you call a procedure and a variable declared in that procedure gets assigned a value at the end of that procedure, the value is wiped out.

Operators

Within Active Server Pages using VBScript you can perform a variety of mathematical operations. You can perform the standard basic operations of addition, subtraction, multiplication, and division using the +, -, *, and / operators.

You can also perform *integer division*, which returns the whole number portion of division, no decimal or remainder. Integer division is performed with the \ operator. So if you perform integer division like this:

```
X = 3 \ 2
```

you would be assigning 1 to X.

You also have a function called the `Modulus Operator` that will assign to you the value of the remainder from a division. For example, if you coded this:

```
X = 5 MOD 3
```

X would be assigned to 2 because 2 is the remainder from the division.

This kind of operation is very helpful when you want to perform a task on only certain intervals within a loop. Let's say you were displaying rows of information by iterating through all the records in a table, and to make the lines of information more readable, every 10 records you were going to reprint the header information. Here's how you could code for that:

```
<%
'this line loops us through each record in the table
Do until RS.EOF
  'this line writes the record
  Response.Write RS("TheData")
  'increment the position counter
  RecordsPrinted = RecordsPrinted + 1
  'check to see if ten records have been printed
  if RecordsPrinted MOD 10 = 0 then
      Response.Write "Header Stuff"
  End if
  'move to the next record
  RS.MoveNext
Loop
%>
```

The header information will be printed out only every ten records since `RecordsPrinted MOD 10` will only result in zero if the number is divisible by zero.

Combining strings together into a single string is referred to as *concatenation*, which you perform with the & symbol. Given the following code:

```
<%
Dim OneString
Dim TwoString
OneString = "Hello"
TwoString = OneString & " World!"
Response.Write TwoString
%>
```

the text `"Hello World!"` would be sent to the browser. You can also perform concatenation to pass more than one string as a single parameter:

```
<%
Dim OneString
Dim TwoString
OneString = "Hello"
TwoString = " World!"
Response.Write OneString & TwoString
%>
```

You can round numbers in your code to a whole number in a couple of different mechanisms. You can use the `Int` function to simply chop off the whole number:

```
<%
Dim X
Dim Y
X = 3.14
Y = int(x)
Response.Write Y
%>
```

The preceding code would result in the number 3 being written to the browser. You can also round numbers using the `Round` function. You pass to the function the number to round and the number of decimal places to round to. If you leave off the number of decimal places the number is rounded to a whole number.

```
<%
Dim X
'rounds to 3
X = Round(3.199)
'rounds to 3.2
```

```
X = Round(3.199, 1)
'also rounds to 3.2
X = Round(3.199, 2)
%>
```

Conditions

Frequently in code you need to check some value and perform a task based on a value and a different task based on another value. When coding your Active Server Pages with VBScript you can do that with an If statement or a Select Case statement.

An If statement allows you to check for a condition. If the condition evaluates to True, then the code within the If statement executes. If the condition does not evaluate to True, either no code is run or code within an Else portion of an If statement executes.

The compiler interprets any nonzero evaluation as True; and only zero evaluates to False. So when we could code:

```
If 5 then
```

that would always evaluate to True because the number 5 is a nonzero number. You will frequently see syntax similar to that where no comparison is made, just a simple evaluation. For example, if we needed a procedure that checked for a character within a string and, if found, it would replace the first occurrence of the character with another character we would code like this:

```
<%
Function ConvertIt(StringToConvert, ReplaceChar, ConversionChar)
  If Instr(StringToCOnvert, ReplaceChar) then
    'code to convert string goes here
  end if
End Function
%>
```

Notice the If statement. Nothing is being directly compared; we are evaluating an expression. The function we are using in our evaluation is Instr, which tests for the presence of a string within a string. If the test string is found, it returns the position of the first occurrence. A call like this:

```
Instr("Hello", "l")
```

would return the number 3 because that is the position of the first occurrence of the search character. If we were searching for the letter "z" in the preceding expression, a 0 would return since the search string was not found. So what the preceding If statement is saying is that if the search character is found anywhere the Instr function will return a nonzero value and the If statement evaluates to True. If the search string is not found, the expression evaluates to False since 0 is returned by the Instr function.

So the important thing to remember is that you can use a simple comparison in an If statement but you can also just use the evaluation of an expression to determine the behavior of an If statement.

You can use the If statement in a few different ways. First you can use the If statement on a single line:

```
<%
If Request.QueryString("TheNumber") = 5 then _
   Response.Write "You are correct!<BR>"
Response.Write "That's it"
%>
```

First notice the "_" character on the first line. You will see this used throughout the book. This is called the *continuation character* and is used to place a single line of code across more than one line of text, to make the code more readable.

The If statement in the previous example is a single-line If statement. It evaluates the expression, and if visitors entered the number 5, the expression would evaluate to True and they would see the text You are correct! in the browser window as shown in Figure 4-8.

Notice that visitors also see the text from the next line of code That's it. If visitors entered a number other than 5 they would not see the You are Correct! text but would see the That's it text because that line is outside the If statement.

You can also include an Else statement within the single line If statement. The code in that line would run only if the expression evaluated to False. The code below shows how that would be done.

```
<%
If Request.QueryString("TheNumber") = 5 then _
   Response.Write "You are correct!<BR>" else _
   Response.Write "Wrong!<BR>"
Response.Write "That's it"
%>
```

The same text will be sent to the browser if visitors enter the correct answer, but if they enter an incorrect answer they will now see the additional text Wrong! as shown in Figure 4-9.

Figure 4-8
Result of entering the correct number.

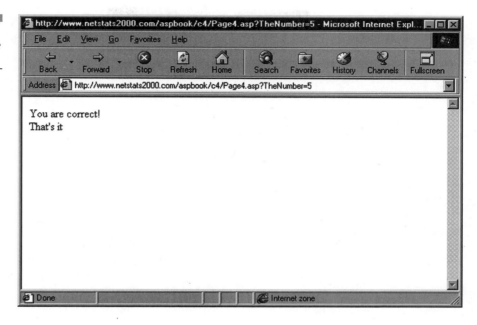

Figure 4-8
Result of entering the correct number.

Figure 4-9
Result of entering an incorrect answer.

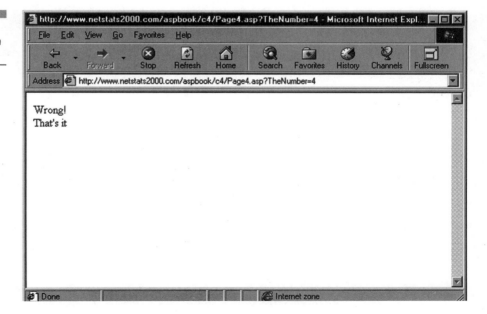

Figure 4-9
Result of entering an incorrect answer.

You are not limited to having just a single line of code running within an `If` statement. You can create code blocks for both the `If` portion and the `Else` portion.

```
<%
If Request.QueryString("TheNumber") = 5 then
  Response.Write "<FONT SIZE=""+2"">"
  Response.Write "You are correct!<BR>"
  Response.Write "</FONT>"
else
  Response.Write "<FONT SIZE=""-2"">"
  Response.Write "Wrong!<BR>"
  Response.Write "</FONT>"
end if
Response.Write "That's it"
%>
```

First, notice that the continuation character is gone. Each of these lines is a line of code. Also notice the double-quotes before and after the +2. This is how you embed a quote character within a string.

Now with the code blocks, an evaluation of True for the expression in the `If` statement executes all the lines of code above the `Else` statement. An evaluation of False allows the execution of the three lines of code underneath the `Else` statement. Then regardless of the condition, the last line of code would execute. The result of an incorrect response is shown in Figure 4-10.

Figure 4-10
Result of an incorrect answer with the code block sample.

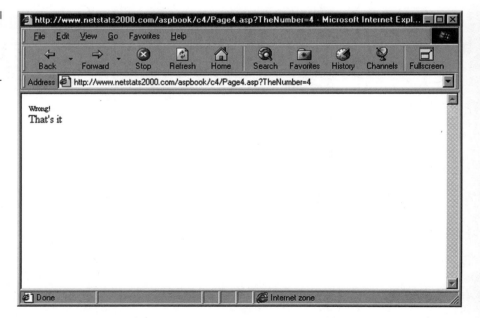

Within an `If` statement you can also include an `ElseIf` statement, which checks an additional condition if the original `If` condition is not True. Take a look at this code block:

```
<%
If Request.QueryString("TheAge") < 13 then
  Response.Write "You are a youngster"
ElseIf Request.QueryString("TheAge") < 20 then
  Response.Write "You are a teenager"
ElseIf Request.QueryString("TheAge") < 40 then
  Response.Write "You are a young adult"
ElseIf Request.QueryString("TheAge") < 60 then
  Response.Write "You have the experience"
Else
  Response.Write "You are having fun"
End If
%>
```

This code block will display a message based on the person's age. The code first evaluates the initial `If` statement. If `TheAge` is less than 13 they will see the first message and the code then flows down to the `End If` statement, and no other conditions are checked.

If the first `If` statement does not evaluate to True then `TheAge` must be at least 13. So in the second evaluation:

```
ElseIf Request.QueryString("TheAge") < 20 then
```

The question is not just less than 20 but the person must already be greater than 12. If not, the code would have entered the first block and then it would have flowed down to the `End If` statement. If `TheAge` is less than 20, then the code enters this block before heading down to the `End If` statement.

The code continues this way through all the `ElseIf` statements. If none of the `If` or `ElseIf` statements evaluate to True then the code flows in to the `Else` block. Note that you are not required to have an `Else` statement. If one is not present and none of the conditions was met, the code flows out of the `If` statement.

You can also nest `If` statements, which means you have an `If` statement inside an `If` statement:

```
<%
If Request.QueryString("TheAge") < 13 then
  Response.Write "You are a young "
  If Request.QueryString("Sex") = "Female" then
    Response.Write "girl"
  else
    Response.Write "boy"
  end if
```

```
      Response.Write "."
ElseIf Request.QueryString("TheAge") < 20 then
      Response.Write "You are a teenager"
ElseIf Request.QueryString("TheAge") < 40 then
      Response.Write "You are a young adult"
ElseIf Request.QueryString("TheAge") < 60 then
      Response.Write "You have the experience"
Else
      Response.Write "You are having fun"
end if
%>
```

This code is similar to the last example except for the addition of the embedded If statement. Now if the first code block evaluates to True, the text You are a young is written to the browser. Next another condition is met. Based on whether the person is a male or female, different text is written. Then regardless of that question, a period is written to the browser. So with embedded If statements you have the ability to have code run at the beginning of the block then break apart based on a condition and then have more code execute after the embedded If statement. If statements can be embedded very deep, so many options are possible.

You can also use Ands and Ors in your If statement. If an And is used, both conditions must be met. For example:

```
If Request.QueryString("TheAge") < 13 and _
Request.QueryString("Sex") = "Female" then
```

Both of the conditions must be met to enter this If statement. The age must be less than 13 and the user must be a female. That code differs from this line:

```
If Request.QueryString("TheAge") < 13 or _
 Request.QueryString("Sex") = "Female" then
```

This If statement would include all females. It would also include everyone less than 13 years old. Either condition must evaluate to True.

You can combine Ands and Ors to create complex conditions, but you will want to use parentheses to indicate the order of precedence for the evaluation. For example:

```
If (LastName = "Flintstone" and FirstName = "Fred") _
 Or FirstName = "Wilma" then
```

Notice where the parentheses are, this expression would evaluate to

True if the person's name was Fred Flintstone. The expression would also evaluate to True for anybody with the first name Wilma. That is very different from this:

```
If LastName = "Flintstone" and (FirstName = "Fred" _
 Or FirstName = "Wilma") then
```

Notice the only difference in this example compared to the last is the placement of the parentheses. This one evaluates to True for a person with the name Fred Flintstone or a person with the name Wilma Flintstone.

Another option you have with conditional statements is a Select...Case statement, which behaves very similarly to an If statement with ElseIfs. Take a look at this example:

```
<%
Select Case Request.QueryString("Quantity")
  Case 1
    Response.Write "$50"
  Case 2
    Response.Write "$90"
  Case 3
    Response.Write "$130"
  Case 4
    Response.Write "$150"
  Case Else
    Response.Write "$" & Request.QueryString("Quantity") * 40
End Select
%>
```

The first line of a Select...Case statement is the item being tested:

```
Select Case Request.QueryString("Quantity")
```

That is followed with a series of match lists. The first case matches against the number 1:

```
Case 1
 Response.Write "$50"
```

If the text variable is equal to 1, or any other item in the list, then the code enters this block. As with an If statement, once a block is entered no other blocks will be entered, so the code would flow down to the End Select statement.

If the first condition is not met, the code flows and tests each condition until one is met. If no conditions are met, the code flows to the Case Else, which is like the Else portion of an If statement.

Looping

In code, *looping* refers to performing the same block of code zero or more times. In this section, we look at three mechanisms for looping: Do, For...Next, and For...Each.

With a Do loop a task is performed until an expression evaluates to True. For example:

```
X = 4
Do Until X = 5
  Response.Write X
  X = X + 1
Loop
```

This code would iterate through the loop one time. When the code entered the loop, X would be compared to 5. Since at first entrance it is 4, the expression would evaluate to False. When an expression evaluates to False, the code in the loop executes. Within the code block we add 1 to X so it now is set to 5. When the code loops back to the Do Until line, it again checks to see if X is equal to 5. It now is, so the code exits out of the loop.

In this example, the code in the loop never runs:

```
X = 5
Do Until X = 5
  Response.Write X
  X = X + 1
Loop
```

Since X is set to 5 from the start when the Do expression is evaluated it is found to be True and the code flows past the Loop statement.

In this example, the code flows through the loop three times:

```
X = 4
Do Until X > 5
  Response.Write X
  X = X + 1
Loop
```

The first time through the loop X is set to 4, then the second time, 5. Since 5 is not greater than 5, the code enters the loop again and X is set to 6. The code then exits the loop.

Frequently you will use the Do Until statement to iterate through a set of records in a database. Often you will grab some records from a database and will manipulate them or you will present them to the user.

Look at this code block that displays all the items a visitor has in a shopping cart.

```
<%
set conn = server.createobject ("adodb.connection")
conn.open "Ecommerce", "sa", "yourpassword"
set RSOrderItems = conn.Execute("select ItemID, " _
  & "ItemName, ItemType, Quantity, TotalPrice, " _
  & "DetailText from WIOrderItems where " _
  & SessionID = " & Session("SessionID"))
do until RSOrderItems.EOF
  %>
  <P>Item Name: <% Response.Write RSOrderItems("ItemType") %>
  <% Response.Write RSOrderItems("ItemName") %>
  <BR>Quantity: <% Response.Write RSOrderItems("Quantity") %>
  <BR>Price: <% Response.Write RSOrderItems("TotalPrice") %>
<%
  RSOrderItems.MoveNext
Loop
%>
```

We will talk about connecting to and working with databases at great length in Chapter 14, so don't worry about that code if it is unfamiliar to you.

First, notice that the code is made up of three blocks: the *first block*, code only, contains initialization information; the *second block* contains HTML with code embedded in it; the *third block* contains the code that loops us back to the first block.

The loop starts with this line:

```
do until RSOrderItems.EOF
```

We will loop through the code until we are out of records to process. If there are no records in the first place, then the code in the loop will not be processed at all. So the code in the loop will be executed zero or more times.

Within the loop, each item in the shopping cart is written to the browser. For example, this line writes the quantity:

```
<BR>Quantity: <% Response.Write RSOrderItems("Quantity") %>
```

At the bottom of the loop the code moves to the next record so that it can be processed:

```
RSOrderItems.MoveNext
```

Then the loop keyword indicates that the code should flow back to the

`Do` portion and evaluate the expression. If there were four records to print then the code would loop four times. If there were zero records the code would loop zero times.

Another way that you can iterate through code is with a `For Next` loop. Code in a `For Next` loop have a more specific number of times that they run. Instead of checking an expression like the `Do` loop, the `For` loop starts at one number and ends with another number. For example:

```
<%
Option Explicit
Dim I
For I = 1 to 3
  Response.Write I & "<BR>"
Next
%>
```

In the preceding example, the code will enter the `For` block three times. When the code starts I is set to 1. Since 1 is in the range of 1 to 3, the code enters the `For` code block. Next time up, 1 is added to I. Now it is set to 2, which is still in the range of 1 to 3. The code loops through again and I is set to 3. Again looping I is set to 4, which is outside the range 1 to 3, so the code progresses past the loop.

A loop doesn't have to start with 1 though. Take a look at this code sample:

```
<%
Option Explicit
Dim I
For I = -3 to 6
  Response.Write "<FONT SIZE=""" & I & """>Hello</FONT><BR>"
Next
%>
```

This loop starts at -3 and loops until I is past 6. The result of this page is shown in Figure 4-11.

Another tool you can use for looping through a block of code is the `For Each` statement, which is similar to the `For Next` statement, except it iterates through a collection of items. This code block iterates through a collection called `ServerVariables`:

```
<%
Option Explicit
Dim TheVariable
For Each TheVariable in Request.ServerVariables
  Response.Write TheVariable & " - " _
    & Request.ServerVariables(TheVariable) _
```

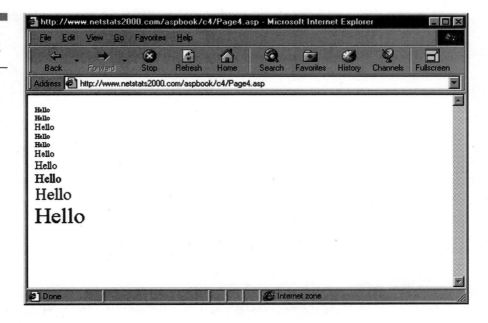

Figure 4-11
Result of the For
Next code sample.

```
      & "<BR>"
Next
%>
```

As discussed in Chapter 7, the ServerVariables collection contains information about visitors and their browser. The code is iterating through each item in the collection. Every loop through the For Each statement is working with a different server variable. The code loops until there are no more server variables to display. The output of the code is shown in Figure 4-12.

Converting Variables

Try to read through this code:

```
<%
If "12/1/1999" > "9/1/1966" then
  Response.Write "It worked"
else
  Response.Write "This shouldn't be seen"
end if
%>
```

Figure 4-12
ServerVariables
output.

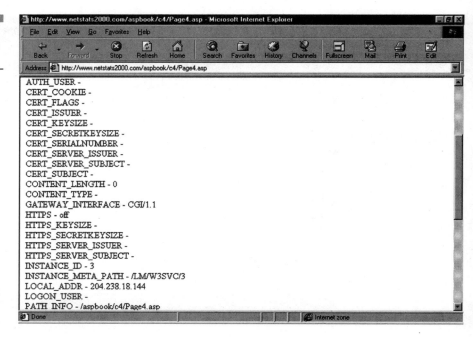

The date December 1, 1999, is greater than the date September 1, 1966. So you would expect that displayed in the browser would be the text It worked. But look at the result of the page shown in Figure 4-13. The text printed was not what was expected. The problem is that the compiler performed a text comparison instead of a date comparison. In a *text comparison*, characters are looked at one at a time until one is determined to be greater. So the first two digits were compared: the 1 and the 9. The 9 was found to be greater than 1, so the expression evaluated to False and we entered the Else portion of the If statement.

Because of this kind of unexpected error, you will occasionally need to convert your data. Within Active Server Pages you can use a variety of conversion functions. If we changed the preceding code to this:

```
<%
If CDate("12/1/1999") > CDate("9/1/1966") then
  Response.Write "It worked"
else
  Response.Write "This shouldn't be seen"
end if
%>
```

we would now see the correct result, which is displayed in Figure 4-14.

Figure 4-13
Result of the date comparison.

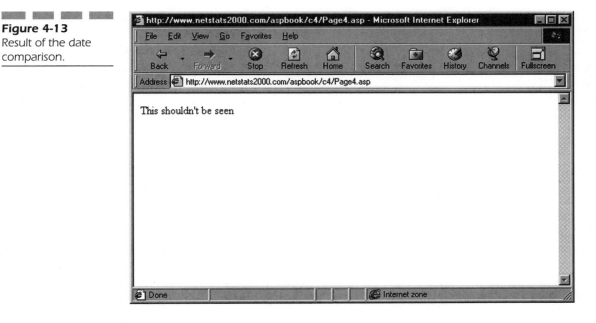

Figure 4-14
Result of converted dates page.

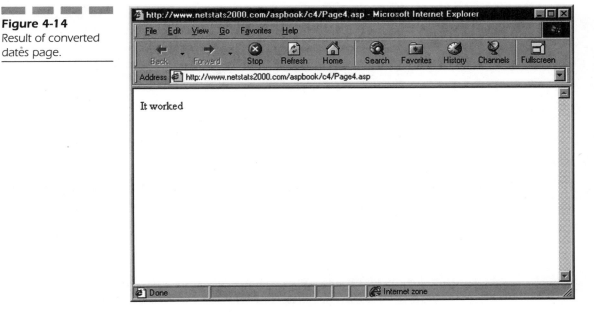

The difference between the two code blocks is the use of the `CDate` function, which converts a variable to a date. If the variable is not a date then the function returns an error. VBScript provides several functions like the `Cdate`. They all start with the letter `C`, which stands for *conversion* and then they contain the name of the type the function will convert to. For example, `CInt` converts to an integer and `CBool` converts to a Boolean.

Date and Time Functions

As you have already seen in a few of the code samples, you will frequently need to manipulate dates. Within VBScript you have a variety of functions from which to choose.

Sometimes you will find that you need to display or use the current date and/or time. You may need to create a query that grabs records from today or you may want to place a time stamp on a record in a database; or, maybe you want to display the current data and time to visitors on a Web page.

Three functions can help you with that: `Date`, `Time`, and `Now`. `Date` returns the current system date, `Time` returns the current system time, and `Now` returns the current system date and time. Note that *current system* means the date and time that the server says it is. The syntax for the functions is below:

```
<%
Response.Write Date & "<BR>"
Response.Write Time & "<BR>"
Response.Write Now
%>
```

Note that the Response.Write method (which is discussed in Chapter 6) writes text to the browser.

The functions take no parameters and produce the output shown in Figure 4-15.

You frequently need to parse out parts of a date. For example, you may want to grab just the month from a date to build an employee birthday list for the current month:

```
If Month(RS("BirthDate")) = Month(Date) then
```

This code would accomplish that. The `Month` function extracts just the numeric month from a date. After the equal sign the `Date` function,

Figure 4-15
Result of the Date,
Time, and Now
functions.

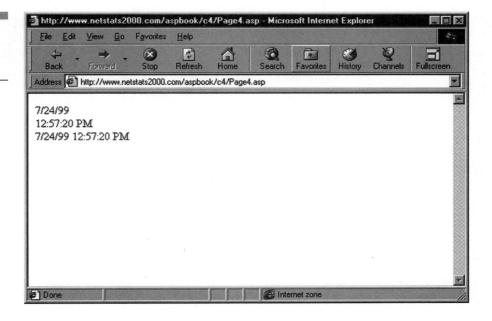

which as you learned earlier returns the system date, and the Month function parses out the current month from that.

A variety of functions are available to parse out a piece of a date or time. The following code reviews the different functions:

```
<%
Response.Write "Year: " & Year(Date) & "<BR>"
Response.Write "Month Number: " & Month(Date) & "<BR>"
Response.Write "Day of Month: " & Day(Date) & "<BR>"
Response.Write "Weekday Number: " & WeekDay(Date) & "<BR>"
Response.Write "Hour: " & Hour(Time) & "<BR>"
Response.Write "Minute: " & Minute(Time) & "<BR>"
Response.Write "Second: " & Second(Time) & "<BR>"
%>
```

The result of this page is shown in Figure 4-16.

Frequently you need to know the difference between two dates. You may need to know how late a customer is on paying a bill. You may need to calculate how long an employee has been with your company; or, you may need to calculate someone's age. The DateDiff function can help you with such a task.

The DateDiff function subtracts the amount of time between two dates and returns the results to you in the unit you desire. By unit, you

Figure 4-16
Result of the Date
and Time parsing
functions.

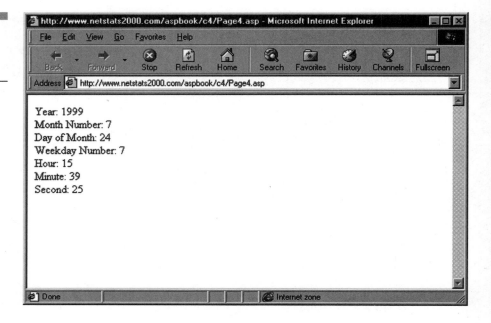

```
http://www.netstats2000.com/aspbook/c4/Page4.asp - Microsoft Internet Explorer
File   Edit   View   Go   Favorites   Help

Back   Forward   Stop   Refresh   Home   Search   Favorites   History   Channels   Fullscreen

Address  http://www.netstats2000.com/aspbook/c4/Page4.asp

Year: 1999
Month Number: 7
Day of Month: 24
Weekday Number: 7
Hour: 15
Minute: 39
Second: 25

Done                                                        Internet zone
```

can get the result in hours, for example, or years. The format of the function is below:

```
DateDiff(UnitForResult, DateSubtracting, DateSubtractedFrom)
```

The options for the first parameter are listed in Table 4-1.

TABLE 4-1

Options for Units in
DateDiff
Function

Unit	Meaning
yyyy	Year
q	Quarter
m	Month
d	Day
h	Hour
n	Minute
s	Second

So, if you wanted to know how many months it has been since the beginning of the twentieth century you would code this:

```
<%
Response.Write DateDiff("m", "1/1/1901", Date)
%>
```

If you wanted to know how many days a customer was past due on payment you would have something like this:

```
<%
Response.Write DateDiff("d", RS("DueDate"), Date)
%>
```

Or if you needed to calculate the age of an employee:

```
<%
Response.Write DateDiff("yyyy", RS("EmpAge"), Date)
%>
```

Sometimes, however, you need to calculate what date it will be based on another date. You may need to calculate what the date will be tomorrow to indicate when a product will be shipped; you may need to calculate a due date based on payment due 30 days after being billed; or, maybe you need to schedule a task based on a request.

All the items require that you add or subtract values from dates. The DateAdd function can perform this task. The DateAdd function contains the following format:

```
DateAdd(Unit, Amount, DateToChange)
```

The first parameter, Unit, represents what you want to add or subtract. You could add years, months, and so on, as indicated in Table 4-1. The second parameter, Amount, represents how many of that unit you wish to add or subtract. The third parameter, DateToChange, is the date that you wish to add or subtract. The function returns the date based on the modification.

If you wanted to calculate tomorrow's date you could do this:

```
<%
Response.Write DateAdd("d", 1, Date)
%>
```

If you need to calculate what the date was one month ago you would use "m" for the Unit and -1 for the Amount:

```
<%
Response.Write DateAdd("m", -1, Date)
%>
```

To calculate the time 3 hours from now you would code like this:

```
<%
Response.Write DateAdd("h", 3, Time)
%>
```

Sometimes you will need to combine more than one function discussed in this section to retrieve the result you need. Say you need to write to the browser the Year to Date, you could do this:

```
<%
Response.Write "1/1/" & Year(Date) & " to " & Date
%>
```

If you needed to calculate the last day of the current month, you could do this:

```
<%
Response.Write DateAdd("d", -1, Month(DateAdd("m",1,Date)) _
  & "/1/" & Year(DateAdd("m",1,Date)))
%>
```

The best way to read code like that is from the inside out, which is also a very good way to think through the logic of creating code like this. At the deepest level is the Date function, which returns the current date. The first occurrence of the Date function is used by the DateAdd function to determine the date a month from now.

From that value the month is parsed. That month is concatenated with "/1/". So now we have a month and day. We now concatenate to that the Year it will be 1 month from now. At this point, this whole string

```
Month(DateAdd("m",1,Date)) & "/1/" & Year(DateAdd("m",1,Date))
```

evaluates to the first day of the next month. That value is then used as the third parameter of the DateAdd function where we subtract one day from that date to get the end of the current month.

Validating Data Types and Existence

When you are getting input from visitors to your site, you sometimes need to validate the data they enter. You may need to know that the data is a date, or that it is a number. You may need to test to see if a field was submitted. You may also need to check and see if data are within a valid range. In this section, we look at functions that help you achieve these tasks.

One of the functions you will see used frequently is the `IsEmpty` function, which checks for the presence of an item. This is often used to check if a field on an HTML form was submitted. Using such a text mechanism helps you determine whether a form has been submitted.

Often you will want to encapsulate all the functionality of a form within a single Active Server Page. The page in one state would display the form with the fields the visitor needs to supply. In the other state, the visitor has submitted the form by pressing a SUBMIT button or a graphic you have set up. When the form is submitted, your code on the Active Server Page would need to take some action to process the data. The way that you could determine the state is by checking for the presence of the SUBMIT button using the `IsEmpty` function.

Take this simple form shown in Figure 4-17.

When visitors first go to this page they should see the form. Then when they press the LOG IN button, they should a different page like the one shown in Figure 4-18.

Figure 4-17
Sample form that determines state using the `IsEmpty` function.

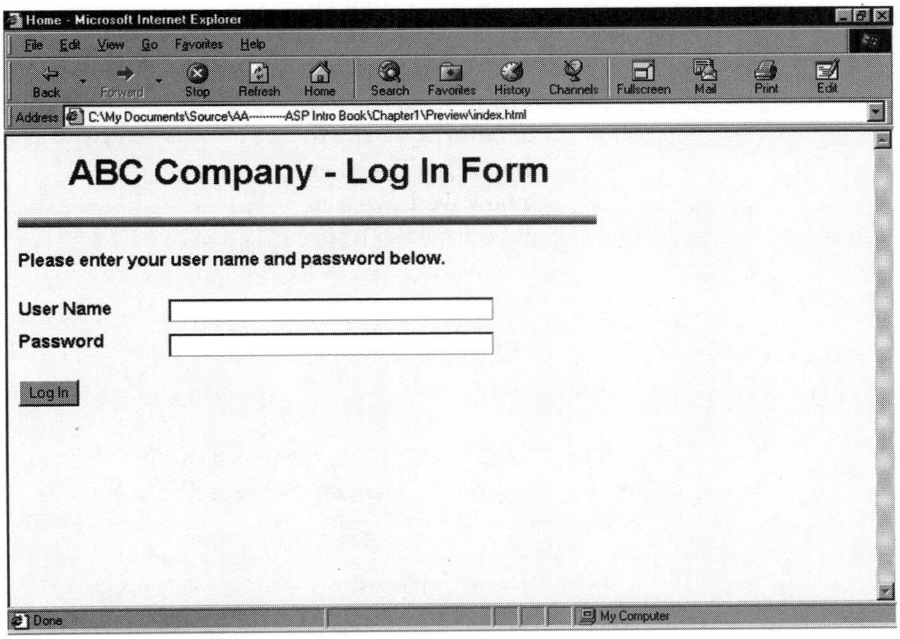

Figure 4-18
Page view after the
form was submitted.

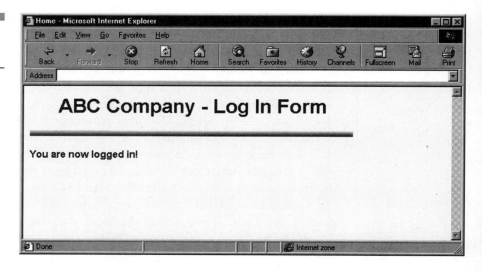

If both pages are to be produced from the same Active Server Page,
you need to use the `IsEmpty` function to determine if the LOG IN button
is present and take the appropriate action based on that knowledge:

```
<%
if not isempty(Request.Form("LogIn")) then
  set conn = server.createobject ("adodb.connection")
  conn.open "ASPBook", "sa", "yourpassword"
  set RSUser = conn.Execute("select UserName from ClLogin " _
    & "where UserName = '" & Request.Form("UserName") _
    & "' and Password = '" & Request.Form("Password") _
    & "'")
  if RSUser.EOF then
    TheMessage = "You have entered an incorrect login. " _
      & "Please try again."
  else
    TheMessage = "You are now logged in!"
  end if
else
  TheMessage = "Please enter your user name and password below."
end if
%>
```

The `IsEmpty` function returns True if the item being tested is empty,
or not present. It returns False if the item has a value. So in the `If`
statement:

```
if not isempty(Request.Form("LogIn")) then
```

with the use of the Not operator, we are saying if the LOG IN button is not empty, if it is present, then enter this code block to process the fields on the form.

When you are adding data to a database, or when you need to do a calculation on some data, both of which would be from user input, you need to identify that the value entered is of the type requested. You need to know that a date is a date and a number is a number. To test some piece of data to see if it is a date, you can use the IsDate function, which returns True if the value passed to it is a date and False if it is not. If you had an HTML form, you could use the IsDate function to test what the visitor has entered into a form field:

```
<%
Option Explicit
Dim TheMessage
If IsDate(Request.Form("BirthDate")) then
  TheMessage = "You entered a date!"
Else
  TheMessage = "You entered an invalid value in the birth date
    field!"
End If
%>
```

Here the IsDate function is testing a field from an HTML form BirthDate. The code then creates a message string that will be displayed to the visitor later in the HTML based on the visitor's input.

To test and see if a variable, property, or database field is a number, you can use the IsNumeric function. Like the IsDate function, the IsNumeric function returns True or False. It returns True if the value passed to it is a number and False if it is not. If you wanted to use the function to test a visitor's input on an HTML form field, you could code something like this:

```
<%
Option Explicit
Dim TheMessage
If IsNumeric(Request.Form("Quantity")) then
  TheMessage = "You entered a valid quantity!"
Else
  TheMessage = "You entered an invalid value in the quantity
    field!"
End If
%>
```

The code would display a message based on the value entered by the visitor.

Data Validation Techniques

You will often also need to validate the range of a number or date. For example, a Birth Date field does need to be a date, but it also should not be in the future; or, a quantity for a product should not be negative or beyond some upper limit. In this section, we look at the code needed to solve such validation concerns.

If you did need to validate that a birth date was not in the future you would code something like this:

```
<%
Option Explicit
Dim TheMessage
If IsDate(Request.Form("BirthDate")) then
  If Cdate(Request.Form("BirthDate")) <= Date then
    TheMessage = "Value OK"
  Else
    TheMessage = "Birth date can not be in the future!"
  End If
Else
  TheMessage = "The value you entered is not a date"
End If
%>
```

Note the embedded If statement and the readability of the If structures based on indentation. Also note that the Date function is used to compare the date entered with the current system date. As you learned earlier in this chapter, the use of the CDate function is needed so the comparison made in the If statement is a date comparison, not a text comparison.

You may also want to trap for a lower limit on a birth date, say 150 years. The code below adds that check:

```
<%
Option Explicit
Dim TheMessage
If IsDate(Request.Form("BirthDate")) then
  If Cdate(Request.Form("BirthDate")) > Date then
    TheMessage = "Birth date can not be in the future!"
  ElseIf DateDiff("yyyy", Request.Form("BirthDate"), Date) > 150
    TheMessage = "A valid birth date was not entered!"
  Else
    TheMessage = "Value OK"
  End If
Else
  TheMessage = "The value you entered is not a date"
End If
%>
```

Notice the addition of the `ElseIf` statement that uses the `DateDiff` function to determine the amount of time in years between the current date and the birth date entered by the visitor. If the difference was more than 150, an error message is created.

With numbers, you also frequently have upper and lower bounds into which the data must fall. If you had a Quantity field that the visitor to your site entered, you would not want it to be below one and you wouldn't want it to be above some logical upper limit. The code below provides such functionality:

```
<%
Option Explicit
Dim TheMessage
If IsNumeirc(Request.Form("Quantity")) then
  If CInt(Request.Form("Quantity")) < 1 then
    TheMessage = "You must order at least one item!"
  ElseIf CInt(Request.Form("Quantity")) > 250 then
    TheMessage = "Quantity can not be 250 or above!"
  Else
    TheMessage = "Order Added"
  End If
Else
  TheMessage = "Quantity must be a number!"
End If
%>
```

Note the use of the `CInt` function used in the preceding code. It converts the value to an integer, so a numeric comparison is made instead of a text comparison.

Formatting Numbers, Dates, and Money

When you display information to your visitor on an Active Server Page you will want to display numbers, dates, and money with the appropriate punctuation. For example, you want your numbers to have the commas in the right place or a date to have a / between the month, the day, and the year. In this section, we explore functions that assist in these tasks.

The `FormatDateTime` function allows you to format a date or a time or both. The function has this form:

```
FormatDateTime(DateToFormat, HowToFormat)
```

The first parameter is the date/time you wish to format. In the second parameter, you indicate how you want the date/time to be displayed. The following code takes you through the different allowable formats:

```
<%
Response.Write "General Format (Default): "
Response.Write FormatDateTime(Now,0) & "<P>"
Response.Write "Long Date: "
Response.Write FormatDateTime(Now,1) & "<P>"
Response.Write "Short Date: "
Response.Write FormatDateTime(Now,2) & "<P>"
Response.Write "Long Time: "
Response.Write FormatDateTime(Now,3) & "<P>"
Response.Write "Short Time: "
Response.Write FormatDateTime(Now,4)
%>
```

The results of using the different formats for the time are displayed in Figure 4-19.

Note that the General Format is the default, so if you leave off this parameter you get this format. Also note that Now was used with the function calls and, because of the formatting, the date and time were chopped from some of the results.

The FormatCurrency function allows you to format money. Note that it will format the money to whatever is the default currency symbol

Figure 4-19
Output of the FormatDateTime function.

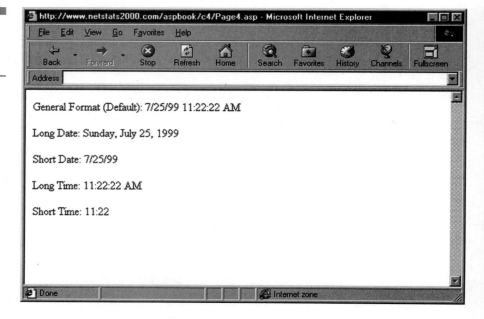

as defined on the visitor's computer. The function has the following form:

```
FormatCurrency(ValueToConvert, NumDecimalPlaces, LeadingZero, _
   NegsInParans, GroupNumbers)
```

The function returns the currency formatted as a string. All the parameters, except the first, are optional. All of the parameters default to whatever is the default on the visitor's system. So you usually call this function without the optional parameters.

The first parameter, `ValueToConvert`, is the value you want to format. The second parameter, `NumDecimal Places`, represents the number of places to the right of the decimal point that you want displayed. The third parameter, `LeadingZero`, allows you to include or exclude a leading zero for numbers that are less than 1. The `NegsInParans` parameter allows you to display a negative number with a negative sign or in parentheses. The last parameter, `GroupNumbers`, indicates whether you want large numbers to be grouped together as the currency type indicates.

A few calls to the function are below:

```
<%
Response.Write FormatCurrency(12345.67) & "<P>"
Response.Write FormatCurrency(-12345.67) & "<P>"
Response.Write FormatCurrency(12345.67,3) & "<P>"
Response.Write FormatCurrency(.67, ,0) & "<P>"
Response.Write FormatCurrency(-12345.67,,,0) & "<P>"
Response.Write FormatCurrency(12345.67,,,,0) & "<P>"
%>
```

Notice in the calls that you can skip some of the optional parameters if you want to include others in the list with just an extra comma. The output of this code is shown in Figure 4-20.

The `FormatNumber` function is very similar to the `FormatCurrency` function, except that it does not have a currency symbol. It has the following format:

```
FormatNumber(ValueToConvert, NumDecimalPlaces, LeadingZero, _
   NegsInParans, GroupNumbers)
```

Like the `FormatCurrency` function, the `FormatNumber` function has parameters for you to specify how many decimal places you want, whether you want a leading zero, whether you want a negative symbol for negative numbers, and whether you want the numbers grouped.

Figure 4-20
Output of
`FormatCurrency`
function.

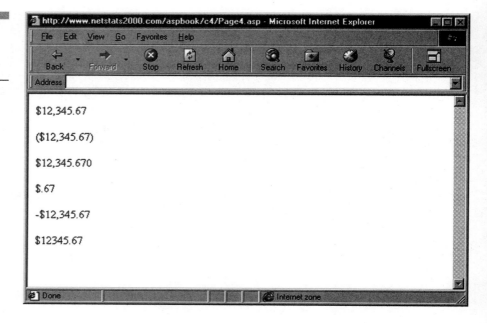

Sample uses of the function are below:

```
<%
Response.Write FormatNumber(.67) & "<P>"
Response.Write FormatNumber(-12345.67) & "<P>"
Response.Write FormatNumber(12345.67123456,5) & "<P>"
Response.Write FormatNumber(.67, ,0) & "<P>"
Response.Write FormatNumber(-12345.67,,,0) & "<P>"
Response.Write FormatNumber(987654321.1234,,,,0) & "<P>"
%>
```

The results of these calls are displayed in Figure 4-21.

One other formatting function to mention in this section is the
`FormatPercent` function. This function is similar to the last two,
except that it takes the number passed, multiplies it by 100, and adds a
trailing percent symbol. It takes the following form:

```
FormatPercent(ValueToConvert, NumDecimalPlaces, LeadingZero, _
    NegsInParans, GroupNumbers)
```

The first parameter is the number to format, and is multiplied by
100. All the other parameters are optional and they default to the system default. Calls to the function look like this:

Figure 4-21
Output of the
`FormatNumber`
function.

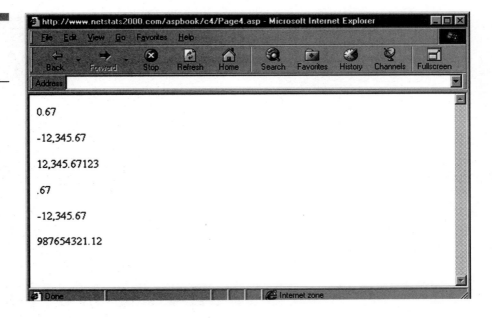

```
http://www.netstats2000.com/aspbook/c4/Page4.asp - Microsoft Internet Explorer
File   Edit   View   Go   Favorites   Help
Back   Forward   Stop   Refresh   Home   Search   Favorites   History   Channels   Fullscreen
Address

0.67

-12,345.67

12,345.67123

.67

-12,345.67

987654321.12

Done                                          Internet zone
```

```
<%
Response.Write FormatPercent(.67) & "<P>"
Response.Write FormatPercent(-.67) & "<P>"
Response.Write FormatPercent(23.67) & "<P>"
Response.Write FormatPercent(23.67, 0) & "<P>"
%>
```

The output of these calls is displayed in Figure 4-22.

Sometimes, though, the calls are not enough. Especially with dates, you will find that you need to go beyond the previous formats to create some specific custom format. Using the date functions discussed earlier in this chapter to parse out the date parts and concatenation you can come up with a solution for your needs.

Manipulating Strings

Whether displaying information to your visitors or retrieving information from them, you will find that you need to manipulate strings. You may need to change case, chop strings, change strings, or find strings. In this section, we look at a variety of functions to help you with these types of tasks.

Figure 4-22
Output of the
FormatPercent
function.

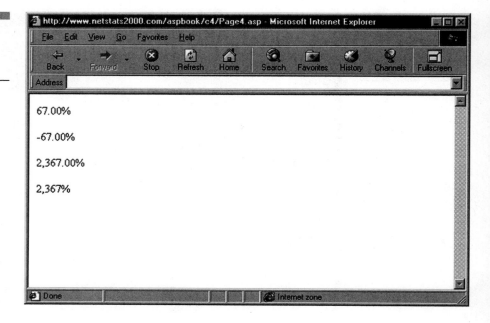

The first two functions we look at are LCase and UCase—both of
them affect the case of a string. LCase converts a string entirely to lowercase and UCase converts a string entirely to uppercase.

A sample use of LCase is below:

```
<%
Option Explicit
Dim StringToConvert
StringToConvert = "HELLO"
Response.Write LCase(StringToConvert")
%>
```

Written to the browser would be the string "hello".

The sample use for UCase is below:

```
<%
Option Explicit
Dim StringToConvert
StringToConvert = "hello"
Response.Write UCase(StringToConvert")
%>
```

This time the string "HELLO" would be written to the browser.

You may find these functions useful when working with older database systems that do not allow lowercase. Another use is when you want to ignore case with database systems that are case-sensitive with text.

The ability to chop apart strings in your Active Server Pages is made simple with the Left, Right, and Mid functions. Chopping apart strings is sometimes necessary when dealing with data passed in to your code as one string but which needs to be displayed as separate fields.

The Left, Mid, and Right functions can help perform those tasks but, as you will see below, you often will need to employ the Instr function and the Len function to figure out where to chop a string.

But first, the Left function chops characters off the left side of a string. The syntax for the function is:

```
Left(StringToChop, NumCharacters)
```

The first parameter is the string that you want to chop from. The second parameter contains the number of characters that you want to chop off. Take this example:

```
<%
Option Explicit
Dim StringToChop
StringToChop = "New Mexico"
Response.Write Left(StringToChop, 3)
%>
```

Written to the browser would be the text "New".

The Right function chops bytes off the end of a string. The syntax for that function is below:

```
Right(StringToChop, NumCharacters)
```

The first parameter is the string that you want to chop bytes from. The second parameter is the number of characters that you want to chop off as shown below:

```
<%
Option Explicit
Dim StringToChop
StringToChop = "New Mexico"
Response.Write Right(StringToChop, 6)
%>
```

This time printed to the browser will be the text "Mexico".

The `Mid` function returns characters from the middle of the string. The syntax of the `Mid` function is a little different from the other two:

```
Mid(StringToChop, StartPosition, NumCharacters)
```

The first parameter is the string you want to parse characters from. The second parameter is the position in which you want the chopping to begin. The third parameter, which is optional, represents the number of characters that you want taken from the middle of the string. If you leave off this parameter, all the characters from the start position to the end of the string are returned.

The following code demonstrates the use of the `Mid` function:

```
<%
Option Explicit
Dim StringToChop
StringToChop = "New Mexico"
Response.Write Mid(StringToChop, 5, 3)
Response.Write Mid(StringToChop, 5)
%>
```

The first text written to the browser would be `"Mex"` since the parameters indicate a start position of 5 retrieving 3 characters. The second line writes the text `"Mexico"` to the browser. The start position is the same but since the third parameter is left off, all the bytes from the start position to the end of the string are written.

As mentioned earlier, to solve the parsing needs that you will have in your code, you will need to use these functions with the `Len` function and the `Instr` function.

The `Len` function returns the length, in characters, of a string. It has the following syntax:

```
Len(StringToMeasure)
```

Passed to the function is the string to you want to know the length of. That length is returned from the function. For example:

```
<%
Option Explicit
Dim StringToMeasure
StringToMeasure = "New Mexico"
Response.Write Len(StringToMeasure)
%>
```

The number 10 is written to the browser.

The `Instr` function looks for a string within a string. If the search string is found, the function returns the character position where that string was found. If the string is not found, the function returns 0. The syntax for the function is below:

```
Instr(StartingPosition, String2Search, SearchString,
   ComparisonType)
```

The middle two parameters are required. The second is the string that you are searching. The third parameter is the string or character that you are searching for. The first parameter, optional, represents the position in which you want the search to begin. If left out, the start position is the beginning of the string.

The comparison type refers to text or binary comparison. Comparison at the binary level means that case is sensitive; so looking for a "B" in "big" would not be found. Text comparison is case-insensitive, so a "B" in "big" would be found. The default is binary comparison; use 0 for binary and 1 for text.

A few examples will help explain the use of this function.

```
<%
Option Explicit
Dim String2Search
Dim SearchString
String2Search = "Mississippi"
SearchString = "s"
Response.Write Instr(String2Search, SearchString)
'3 is written to the browser
Response.Write Instr(3, String2Search, SearchString)
'3 is still written to the browser since 3 is the starting point
Response.Write Instr(5, String2Search, SearchString)
'6 is written to the browser
SearchString = "Z"
Response.Write Instr(String2Search, SearchString)
'since the string is not found 0 is written
SearchString = "P"
Response.Write Instr(String2Search, SearchString)
 '0 again since case is sensitive
Response.Write Instr(1 ,String2Search, SearchString, 1)
'Text comparison so 9 is written to the browser
%>
```

Another function very similar to the `Instr` function is the `InstrRev` function. The difference between the two is that the `InstrRev` function starts its search at the end of the string and works its way to the front. The syntax for the function is below:

```
InstrRev(StartingPosition, String2Search, SearchString,
   ComparisonType)
```

The second parameter is the string that you are searching. The third parameter is the string you are searching for. The other two parameters are optional. The first parameter is the position to start the search. And the last parameter is the type of comparison you want to perform, binary or text.

The code block below demonstrates the use of the function:

```
<%
Option Explicit
Dim String2Search
Dim SearchString
String2Search = "Mississippi"
SearchString = "s"
Response.Write InstrRev(String2Search, SearchString)
%>
```

The number 7, which is the position of the first occurrence of an "s" within Mississippi starting from the end of the string, is written to the browser.

But you really get the power out of these functions by combining them. For example, let's say that you needed a procedure that validated that what the visitor entered was what you would expect from an email address. The code below shows how this could be done:

```
<%
Option Explicit
Dim TheAt
Dim TheDot
Dim FieldToTest
FieldToTest = "bob@somewhere.com"
If Len(FieldToTest) < 6 then
  Response.Write "Email Address Invalid!"
Else
  TheAt = InStr(2, FieldToTest, "@")
  If TheAt = 0 Then
    Response.Write "Email Address Invalid!"
  Else
    TheDot = InStr(cint(TheAt) + 2, FieldToTest, ".")
    If TheDot = 0 Then
      Response.Write "Email Address Invalid!"
    ElseIf cint(TheDot) + 1 > Len(FieldToTest) Then
      Response.Write "Email Address Invalid!"
    Else
      Response.Write "Email Address is valid!"
    End If
  End If
End If
%>
```

First, the `Len` function is used to make sure the email address is at least six characters long:

```
If Len(FieldToTest) < 6 then
```

The email address must contain an "@" symbol. This code checks for that:

```
TheAt = InStr(2, FieldToTest, "@")
If TheAt = 0 Then
```

The `Instr` function is used to search for the presence of the "@" symbol. If it is not present, the function would return a 0. Next, the same check is used for a period in the email address:

```
TheDot = InStr(cint(TheAt) + 2, FieldToTest, ".")
If TheDot = 0 Then
 Response.Write "Eamil Address Invalid!"
```

Note here that the start position for searching for the period is 2 characters beyond the position where the "@" was found. So, not only does the email address need a period, but also its position must be as expected.

The code then checks for characters after the period:

```
ElseIf cint(TheDot) + 1 > Len(FieldToTest) Then
```

This would be the com portion of an email address.

Next, let's take a look at code that would write out just the last name from a field in a database that started a name as a full name.

```
<%
Option Explicit
'Database connection code here
If Instr(RS("FullName"), " ") then
  Response.Write Mid(RS("FullName"), Instr(RS("FullName"), " ") +
1)
Else
  Response.Write RS("FullName")
End If
%>
```

The Full Name field may contain a first name and a last name or just a last name. To account for this, the code first checks to see if there is a space in the full name:

```
If Instr(RS("FullName"), " ") then
```

If there is a space, it is assumed in this code that what follows the space would be the last name, or everything after the first name. The Mid function is then used to return all the characters after the space:

```
Response.Write Mid(RS("FullName"), Instr(RS("FullName"), " ") + 1)
```

Always keep the handful of functions in mind. You will find many of your coding problems will rely on these functions for their solutions.

Sometimes you need to have a string that contains a nonprintable character like a tab or a new line. For example, if you needed to send an email through your code, you would need new line characters to space out the text. You can use the Chr function to perform such a task:

```
TheText = "Hello" & Chr(13) & "World"
```

The variable TheText would now contain a new line character between the two words.

The function Replace allows you to replace one with another string within a target string. The function has the following format:

```
Replace(String2Change, SearchString, ReplaceString, _
StartPosition, NumberOfChanges, ComparisonType)
```

The first parameter is the string that you wish to change. The second parameter is the string, or character within the target string, that you wish to change. The third parameter stores the string or character that you wish to change to. The rest of the parameters are optional. The fourth parameter represents the position in which you want the changes to begin. The next parameter represents the maximum number of changes you want to make. And the last parameter stores whether you want to perform a text, case-insensitive, or binary, case-sensitive search for the string to change.

A few examples of the Replace function are shown below:

```
<%
'normal replace
Response.Write Replace("Mississippi", "s", "x") & "<P>"
'start at position number 5
Response.Write Replace("Mississippi", "s", "x", 5) & "<P>"
'start at position 1 and make to replacements
Response.Write Replace("Mississippi", "s", "x", 1, 2) & "<P>"
'start at position 4 and make two replacements
Response.Write Replace("Mississippi", "s", "x", 4, 2) & "<P>"
```

```
'standard replace but character not found
Response.Write Replace("Mississippi", "S", "x") & "<P>"
'same test but now a text comparison
Response.Write Replace("Mississippi", "S", "x", 1, 4, 1)
%>
```

The results of this code are shown in Figure 4-23.

Random Numbers

If your Active Server Page work takes you into the realm of games or gaming, you will need to work with random numbers. Sometimes random numbers are used for creating identities. Two items are used when working with random numbers: Randomize and Rnd.

Randomize is just a statement and it seeds the random number generator; Rnd generates a random number between 0 and 1, not very helpful. But you use it within a mathematic expression to generate numbers in a specified range. The formula has the following format:

```
Int((Rnd * TopValue) + LowValue)
```

In this expression, LowValue means the lowest number you want and TopValue + LowValue represents the highest number in your range.

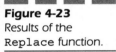

Figure 4-23
Results of the
Replace function.

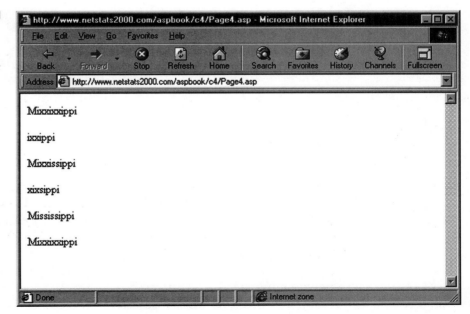

Figure 4-24
Results of the random number page.

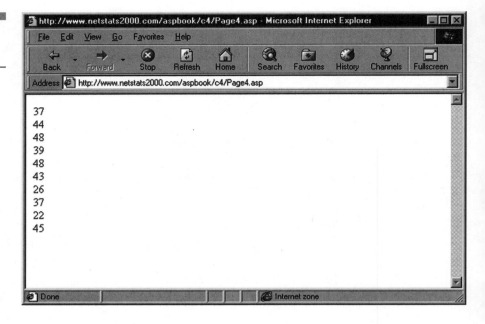

The following code generates 10 numbers in the range of 20 to 50:

```
<%
Option Explicit
Randomize
Dim I
For I = 1 to 10
  Response.Write Int((Rnd * 30) + 20) & "<BR>"
Next
%>
```

The results of the code are shown in Figure 4-24.

Procedures

Now that you know how to create code blocks that can solve a variety of problems, you will want to encapsulate the code blocks into *procedures*, which are a way for you to break out chunks of code that you may use more than once in your Active Server Page and then call that code block from where the functionality is needed.

For example, earlier in this chapter we created a procedure that validated email addresses. We could have placed the code into a procedure and then called that procedure where it was needed.

There are two types of procedures, subs and functions. The main difference between the two is that function returns something when it is called and sub does not. Take this sample code block:

```
<%
WriteMessage
%>
<%
Sub WriteMessage()
  Response.Write "TheStuff"
End Sub
%>
```

The code calls the sub WriteMessage, which then writes a message out to the browser. Nothing is returned by the sub. Notice the structure of the Sub. It starts with the word Sub followed by the name of the sub and then any parameters. The sub ends with the End Sub statement.

A function would be written like this:

```
<%
Response.Write WriteMessage
%>
<%
Function WriteMessage()
  WriteMessage = "TheStuff"
End Function
%>
```

Notice now that the call to WriteMessage expects something back, which is then written to the browser with the Write method of the Response object. The Function has a similar structure to the sub. It starts with the keyword Function followed by the name of the function. Then somewhere in the code block you would set the return value by setting the name of the function equal to something. The function ends with the End Function statement.

Your procedures can also include parameters. Take a look at this code block that changes the email address validation code block to a Function.

```
<%
Option Explicit
Dim LocalTest
LocalTest = "mary@somewhere.com"
Response.Write ValidateEmailAddress(LocalTest)
%>
<%
Function ValidateEmailAddress(FieldToTest)
Dim TheAt
Dim TheDot
```

```
If Len(FieldToTest) < 6 then
  ValidateEmailAddress = "Email Address Invalid!"
Else
  TheAt = InStr(2, FieldToTest, "@")
  If TheAt = 0 Then
    ValidateEmailAddress = "Email Address Invalid!"
  Else
    TheDot = InStr(cint(TheAt) + 2, FieldToTest, ".")
    If TheDot = 0 Then
      ValidateEmailAddress = "Email Address Invalid!"
    ElseIf cint(TheDot) + 1 > Len(FieldToTest) Then
      ValidateEmailAddress = "Email Address Invalid!"
    Else
      ValidateEmailAddress = "Email Address is valid!"
    End If
  End If
End If
End Sub
%>
```

Notice now that the `function` has a parameter passed in to it from the main code block:

```
Response.Write ValidateEmailAddress(LocalTest)
```

Also notice that the `function` returns the message to be printed by setting the function name to the value to be returned.

Request Object

ASP Object Model and Hierarchy

What Are Object Hierarchies?

To provide for a consistent logic in programming under the Windows environment, Microsoft has implemented object hierarchies and others have followed their lead. Object hierarchies make it easy to program other applications' objects from your own code because they follow a consistent and predictable style.

First, what are objects? In the real world, objects are things like a bicycle or a desk or a chair. They are objects; they are things. In computer development, *objects* are things like a spreadsheet or a document or an employee or a shopping cart.

Most of us know what a hierarchy is. We think of company hierarchies that are made up of directors, managers, laborers, and so forth. So *object hierarchies* are a collection of objects that follow some logic. In the computer world, an example of an object hierarchy is the collection of objects in Excel. At the top level we have the Application object, which is Excel itself. Under that we have the Workbook object, and beneath the Workbook object we have the Worksheet object. So again, what we have is a collection of objects organized in a logical manner, or an object hierarchy.

Objects have properties, methods, events, and collections. Properties are *attributes* or ways by which we describe the object. *Methods* are actions we take on an object. *Events* are notifications that we receive that an action has occurred. *Collections* are a group of subobjects.

As mentioned earlier, a bicycle is an object and it has properties, methods, events, and collections. Properties or attributes of a bike are things like its color, the tire size, whether it has thorn-proof tires, and the height of the seat. Methods or actions we take on a bicycle are things like pedaling, steering, or painting. Events are notifications that we receive such as the status of the bike has changed: it is now stopped, it is now moving, and so on. We can then take some action based on that notification. Collections of a bike are things like spokes or brake pads. The items in a collection are objects themselves and also can have properties, methods, events, and collections.

Note that a method can change a property and an event can be fired because a method was invoked or a property changed. If we paint the bike, we would change the color property.

A *worksheet* in Excel is an object and also has properties, methods, events, and collections. A worksheet has a background color, font type, and default width for the columns—these are all properties. *Methods* of a worksheet include copying text onto the clipboard, creating a formula field, or generating a graph from spreadsheet data. *Events* for a worksheet include the notification that it was activated, that the contents have changed, or that the worksheet has been deactivated. A worksheet also has collections like cells, columns, rows, and comments. And since each of those *collections* contains a collection of objects, each of the items in the collection can have properties, methods, events, and collections.

We access a property, a method, or a collection by what is referred to as *dot syntax*. The dot is a period. So if we wanted to refer to the color property of our bicycle we would code:

```
If Bicycle.Color = "Red" then
   Response.Write "You have a red bike."
End if
```

On the second line in the preceding code example we are using the dot syntax to refer to the write method of the response object. The You have a red bike is referred to as a *parameter*, which is information you supply to a method for detail about the action you are taking. Here's another example of a property and a method that we access using dot syntax.

```
Server.ScriptTimeOut = 90
Response.Write Request.Form("NameOfPicture")
Response.BinaryWrite ThePicture
```

First, we are setting the *ScriptTimeOut property* of the Server object, which is how many seconds maximum the script can take to complete before quitting. Next we use the *Form collection*, which is a collection of the fields that were submitted with the page when the request for this page was made. The value for the item NameOfPicture in the Form collection is passed as a parameter to the Write method of the Response object, which returns text back to the visitor's browser.

Then we call the BinaryWrite method of the Response object and pass it a parameter called ThePicture. The *BinaryWrite method* allows us to send nontextual data, such as a picture, to the browser.

So again, objects contain properties, methods, and collections that we call and manipulate using dot syntax.

Events are not referenced directly like the properties, methods, and collections. We write code for events that will run when some event occurs. For example, if we wanted to run code that stored the time that a visitor entered our Web site, we could use the Session_OnStart event. This event is discussed at great length in Chapter 8, but for now just note that every time a visitor enters your site and runs an Active Server Page any code you have in the Session_OnStart event will fire. So to store the time that a visitor entered a site we would code this:

```
Sub Session_OnStart
  Session("StartTime") = Now
End Sub
```

Object hierarchies are the grouping of objects into a logical manner. ASP has a rich collection of objects with numerous properties, methods, collections, and events that we discuss in this chapter and in later chapters.

ASP Object Model

The *ASP Object model* defines five primary objects: the Request object, the Response object, the Application object, the Server object, and the Session object. These objects are discussed below and summarized in Table 5-1.

Through HTML we can send data to the server in the form of Post or Get methods. Retrieving this information is the responsibility of the *Request object*, which supplies us with simple groupings of properties called *collections*, enabling us to retrieve the submitted information. For example, if we have an HTML form on our server with a text field called *Login*, we could retrieve the value of the Login with the following code:

```
Response.Write "Hello and Welcome to: " & Request.Form("Login")
```

TABLE 5-1

ASP Object Model Summary

Object	Purpose
Request object	Supplies you with information from your visitor.
Response object	Methods and properties for building your response to the visitor.
Application object	Deals with properties that govern a grouping of Web pages referred to as an *application*.
Session object	Methods and properties pertaining to a particular visitor.
Server object	Deals with the creation of server components and server settings

With the Request object, we can also retrieve information about the visitor's browser as shown in this code segment:

```
Request.ServerVariables("REMOTE_HOST")
```

This method would return the Internet name or IP address of the visitor's computer. The Request object is discussed in this chapter.

The Response object, as we have already seen, is used to send information back to the visitor's browser. For example, users might be at a form-based page on our site that is a quiz. Users select the answer to the question from a list of possible answers that are in an Option drop-down list. The name of the Option list is "Answer." Once visitors select an answer, they hit the SUBMIT button. This action sends the answer they have selected to our .asp page, which will respond to their choice with this code:

```
If Request.Form("Answer") = "42" then
   Response.Write "You got the correct answer!"
Else
   Response.Write "WRONG! Try again..."
End If
```

So again we are displaying dynamic content to visitors based on their choice. We can also set other browser properties that deal with how to display the response. The Response object is discussed in Chapter 6.

When we group together Active Server Pages that are related to each other into a collection we have an *ASP application*. For example, if we had a set of pages that deal with adding, editing, deleting, and viewing contacts for our company, we can group them together into an ASP application. The *Application object* contains properties at that level. We also have the ability to write code, an event procedure, that runs the first time someone views one of the pages in our application, which would allow us to initialize variables; and we can have code run when our application ends.

Visitors at your site may visit more than one page. They may, for example, browse through your catalog, search for a specific item, view the sales, order a few items, and then check out. The visitor stepping through each of these pages is called a *session*. The *Session object* contains methods and properties to help us keep track of who the visitor is.

Since Active Server Pages stand alone, we need a way to tie them together. We wouldn't want our visitors to have to log in to every page they visited at our site so we could maintain an order—we use the Session object instead. For example, on most of our E-Commerce store pages we will want to make sure that visitors have logged in before they start shopping around. This will allow us to customize the pages they see to match the type of products that they most often are looking for. Therefore, we will want to have this code before any other content appears on our pages.

```
If IsEmpty(Session("UserName") then
  Response.Redirect "http://www.whatever.com/login.asp"
Else
  'show normal page
End If
```

In the first line of code, we check to see if users have logged in. If they haven't, the UserName property of the Session object will contain nothing or be empty. If that is the case, we send them off to the Login page. The Application object and the Session object are covered in Chapter 8.

The main use of the Server object is to allow us to connect to other components that we create or have installed on our system. For example, there is a component that comes with IIS called *Collaborative Data Objects* (CDO). With CDO sending an email from our ASP requires just a few lines of code:

```
Set TheMail = Server.CreateObject("CDONTS.NewMail")
TheMail.Send "gbuczek@somewhere.com", "you@woknows.com","What's
  Up?", "The Text of the message..."
Set TheMail = Nothing
```

Here we use the *CreateObject method* of the Server object to use the CDO component. Then, since CDO obeys the standard object model we discussed, we use dot syntax to call the "Send" method to send the email. Note that we have four parameters in the Send method; a comma separates each parameter. The first parameter is who the message is from, the second parameter is who the message is to, the third parameter is the subject of the message, and the fourth parameter is the body of the message. The Server object is discussed in Chapter 7.

Getting Information from the Visitor

In this section we discuss the Request object. As mentioned in the previous section, the Request object is how you get information from the visitor that is accessing your Active Server Page.

When visitors fill in the fields on a form you created, they usually press a SUBMIT button. Those data are sent to the server and are available to you through the Request object. You can also retrieve the visitor's cookies through the Request object. The Request object can also supply you with header information about the visitor as well as client security certificates.

Request Object Collections

The Request object contains five collections, which are discussed below and summarized in Table 5-2.

Form Collection

Most Web sites contain forms. If you want to add visitors to your mailing list, you have a form for them to supply you with their email address. If you have an e-commerce site, you eventually need a form to get billing and shipping information from visitors; or, you may have a site that polls visitors in current events and the visitors' opinions are retrieved through a form.

Visitors then send or submit the information on the form by clicking on a button, a graphic, or just by pressing ENTER. The data that visitors supplied through the fields on the form are submitted to whatever page you supply in the Form tag. For example:

```
<FORM ACTION="http://www.whatever.com/shoppingcart.asp" METHOD=GET>
```

would send the contents of the form to the shoppingcart.asp page.

When you place a Form tag on your Web page, you provide the

TABLE 5-2

Request Object
Collections

Object	Purpose
Form Collection	Fields submitted from a form through the Post method.
QueryString Collection	Fields submitted from a form through the Get method.
ServerVariables Collection	Header fields available through the visitor's browser when a page is requested.
Cookies Collection	Retrieves cookies from the visitor.
ClientCertificate Collection	Retrieves the client certificate fields from the visitor's browser.

`Action` parameter that indicates how the data should be sent. You can use the Post method as in this example:

```
<FORM ACTION="http://www.whatever.com/shoppingcart.asp"
  METHOD=POST>
```

When you use the Post method, the fields are sent as a binary stream and are not viewed as part of the link to a page. You can also use the Get method:

```
<FORM ACTION="http://www.whatever.com/shoppingcart.asp" METHOD=GET>
```

When the Get method is used, the number of bytes sent is limited and the fields appear as part of the link to the page. For example, take a look at a search engine page like Infoseek. When you enter a keyword for a search, it becomes part of the URL in the results page like the one shown in Figure 5-1.

The search I typed into the search field was Active Server Pages. Notice that that phrase is part of the URL in the ADDRESS box of Internet Explorer. This is because the Get method was used when the form was submitted.

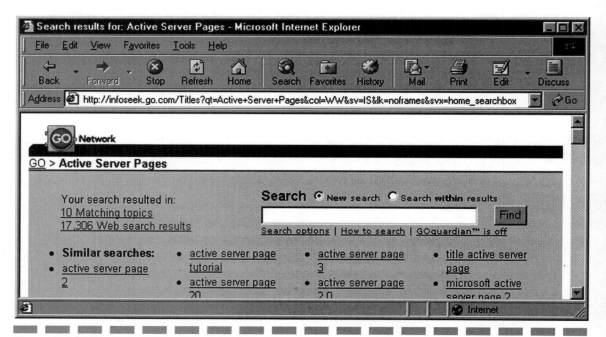

Figure 5-1 URL displays Form fields.

When the form is submitted with the Post method, the fields are available through the Form collection. When they are submitted with the Get method, the QueryString collection contains the submitted data.

When you create a form on a Web page, you include form fields like text, textarea, password, and hidden. When you define these elements on a Web page you give each element a name. For example, if you had a Request For More Information page the form might be defined like this:

```
<FORM ACTION="http://www.somewhere.com/processform.asp"
  METHOD="POST">
Name:<BR>
<INPUT TYPE="text" SIZE=30 MAXLENGTH=50 NAME="Name">
<P>Email Address:<BR>
<INPUT TYPE="text" SIZE=30 MAXLENGTH=50 NAME="EmailAddress">
<P>Interests:<BR>
<SELECT NAME="Interests" SIZE=4 MULTIPLE>
<OPTION VALUE="News">News
<OPTION VALUE="Sports">Sports
<OPTION VALUE="Hiking">Hiking
<OPTION VALUE="Other">Other
</SELECT>
<P><INPUT TYPE="submit" NAME="SubmitButton" VALUE="OK">
</FORM>
```

The form uses the Post method, so the fields will be available through the Form collection. The form is sent to the page processform.asp as specified in the `Action` parameter of the `Form` tag. On the process-form.asp page we can refer to any of the elements that were submitted with the form through the Form collection. So if we wanted to access the Name field we would code this:

```
TheName = Request.Form("Name")
```

The variable `TheName` would contain whatever the visitor entered into that text field, so to reference the field within the Form collection, we specify the name of the field and the value for that field is returned. We could similarly access the field EmailAddress:

```
SendToAddress = Request.Form("EmailAddress")
```

You can use the same procedure to access hidden fields. Even the button that the visitor presses is part of the form and is submitted. So the following:

```
ButtonValue = Request.Form("SubmitButton")
```

would store the value "OK" in the variable `ButtonValue`.

Notice the Select field called *Interests* allows the visitor to select more than one value, since the `Multiple` keyword is in the tag. The values are supplied in a comma-delimited list. So if our processform.asp page contained this code:

```
response.write request.form("Interests")
```

and the visitor selected Sports, then the browser would display:

```
Sports
```

If a visitor selected Sports and News:

```
Sports, News
```

would be displayed in the browser.

When a Form field contains multiple values like this, you can refer to each item individually, so a field that has more than one selection is a *collection of selections*. You can find out the number of selections made by using the *Count property*. This code:

```
response.write request.form("Interests").count
```

would output the number 2 to the browser based on the two earlier selections. We can refer to each element in the array of selections like this:

```
response.write request.form("Interests")(1) & "<P>"
response.write request.form("Interests")(2)
```

Output to the browser this time would be:

```
Sports
News
```

If the visitor made only one selection, the second line of the preceding code would produce an error, so it is best to use the Count property to reference each item in the form element.

We can also reference each item in the collection by using a For Each code block:

```
For Each TheStuff in Request.Form("Interests")
    'insert code that would process each item
    response.write TheStuff & "<BR>"
Next
```

A *For Each code block* iterates through each item in a collection. The variable TheStuff is assigned the value for each element in the Interests collection. So if the visitor selects Sports and News the first time through the code block, TheStuff will be set to Sports and the next time the variable TheStuff will be set to News. After the two iterations, the code block would be out of items in the collection and would not enter the block again.

QueryString Collection

As mentioned before, when a form is submitted, the fields on the form can be submitted using the Get and the Post methods. The previous section looked at the Post method, which uses the Form collection. In this section, we look at the *QueryString collection*, which is populated by the Get method.

You could use the Get method, but on a form you generally use the Post method so you don't have to worry about the length restrictions. Where the QueryString collection is really used is when you need to pass parameters through a link. Say, for example, that you had a page that listed the products you sold. When visitors click on a product, you want them to be able to see the details of the product that they selected. You could have hundreds of pages that displayed each product or you could have a single Active Server Page that could display any product. It would require just a ProductID and would then look up the details of the product in a database. To pass the ProductID on to the page through a link you would be using the QueryString collection.

You would display the product name as a link to the product details page like this:

```
<A
HREF="http://www.somewhere.com/productdetails.asp?ProductID
  =2355">Toothpaste</A>
```

The visitor who clicks on the word Toothpaste is then linked to the productdetails.asp page. The ProductID for the toothpaste, 2355, is sent to that page. Notice the structure of the link. The .asp is followed by a question mark, which indicates that parameters follow. Each parameter is a pairing of the parameter name and value. If more than one parameter is needed, each is separated with an ampersand. So if we had a second parameter for CustomerType, the link would look like this:

```
http://www.somewhere.com/productdetails.asp?ProductID=2355&Customer
  Type=Normal
```

The code on the productdetails.asp page would be responsible for using the ProductID passed into it to determine which product should be displayed. To retrieve the ProductID, the QueryString would be used:

```
TheStuff = Request.QueryString("NameOfField")
```

NameOfField is the field that you want to retrieve the value which would be assigned to the variable `TheStuff`. In the productdetails.asp page the code that used the ProductID would look something like this:

```
<%
Option Explicit
Dim conn
Dim RSProduct
set conn = server.createobject ("adodb.connection")
conn.open "ASPBook", "sa", "yourpassword"
set RSProduct = conn.Execute("select * from Products where " _
   & "ProductID = " & Request.QueryString("ProductID"))
%>
```

The code is using ADO to connect to the database. (We discuss ADO in Chapter 14.) But note that the QueryString is used to retrieve the desired ProductID, which is used in this SQL statement to retrieve, from the database, the product information for the matching record.

If you do submit a form using the Get method, you can use the QueryString collection to retrieve the values for the forms submitted. The same rules apply to this collection as apply to the Form collection. You just use the name of the form field to retrieve the value submitted:

```
TheName = Request.QueryString("Name")
```

If the field has multiple values like those in a Select field, you can reference them by specifying the number of the element you wish to retrieve:

```
response.write request.querystring("Interests")(2)
```

We can also refer to each item in the QueryString collection in a similar fashion. So if we used the Get method for the `Form` tag, the form would be completed as displayed in Figure 5-2.

We could have code on our processform.asp page that iterated through each Form field like this:

```
For Each TheStuff in Request.QueryString
   Response.Write TheStuff & ": " & Request.QueryString(TheStuff) &
"<P>"
Next
```

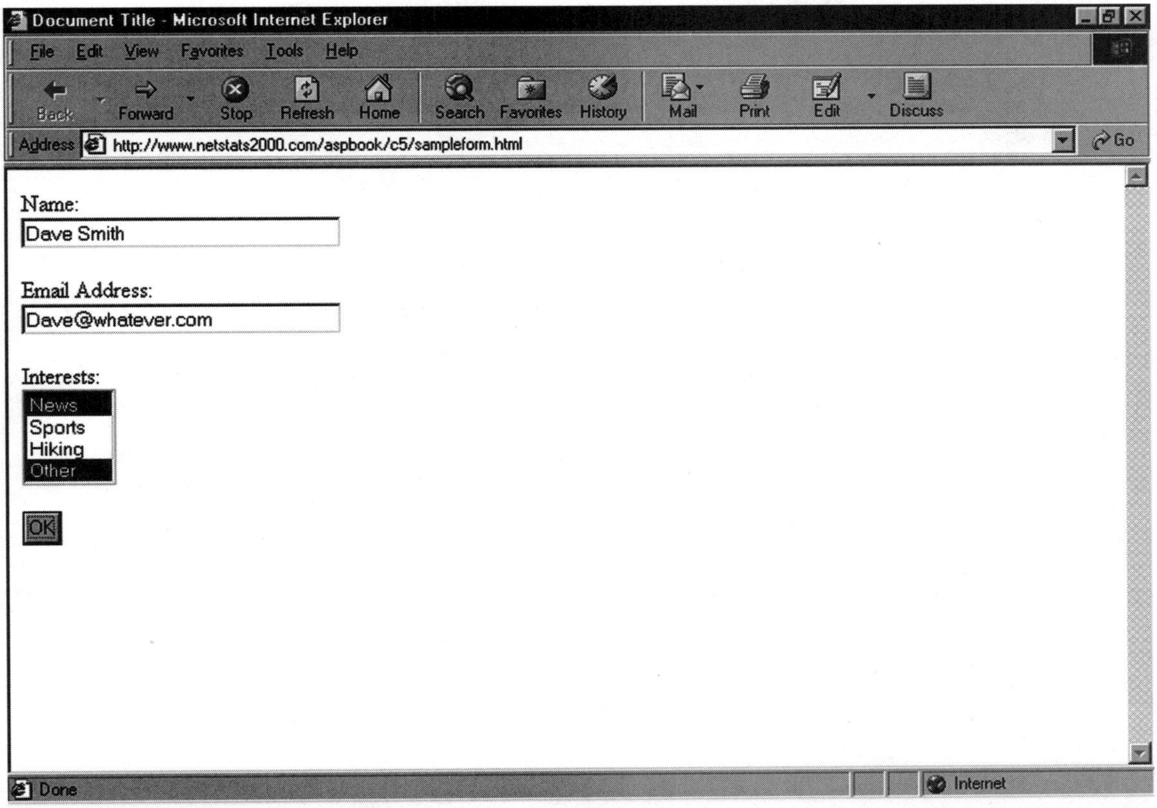

Figure 5-2 Sample form using the Get method.

The code produces the output displayed in Figure 5-3.

Notice a couple of things in the output page. Look at the address for the page. Since the Get method was used, all the Form fields are part of the link. Also notice that the SUBMIT button is listed on the page. That is because it too is part of the HTML form fields. You can use this in your code as a way to provide your visitor with more than one button to choose to take some action. Only the button that is pressed is passed.

In the code block, note that we are using the For Each to iterate through the QueryString collection. The variable TheStuff is set to each of the form elements in turn as the code loops through the For Each structure. The variable TheStuff actually contains the name of the field; that is why it is used to retrieve the correct value for the specific field.

Figure 5-3 Results of processing the page.

ServerVariables Collection

The *ServerVariables collection* retrieves numerous header fields and environmental variables. For example, you can use the ServerVariables collection to retrieve the type of form submission made, the name of the referring page, the path to the current page, the IP Address of the visitor, and the type of Internet Server.

Retrieving one of the items in the ServerVariables collection is simple—just specify the name of the server variable you want to retrieve. For example, if you want to retrieve the path to the current page you would code this:

```
ThePath = Request.ServerVariables("PATH_INFO")
```

If you want to display back to the browser the name of the referring page you could code this:

```
Response.Write Request.ServerVariables("HTTP_REFERER")
```

Some of the header fields and environmental variables should always be available. Those are displayed in Table 5-3. Other server variables that are not always available, but can be very important, are listed in Table 5-4.

TABLE 5-3

Standard Server Variables

Server Variable	Purpose
ALL_HTTP	Contains the entire list of nonstandard headers in the form of HTTP_NAME: value.
ALL_RAW	Similar to the ALL_HTTP except that they appear just as they are received without the HTTP prefix and other formatting.
APPL_MD_PATH	Contains the logical metabase path.
APPL_PHYSICAL_PATH	Contains the physical metabase path.
AUTH_PASSWORD	A password entered if basic authentification is used.
AUTH_TYPE	Type of security authentification that was used.
AUTH_USER	Name of authenticated user.
CERT_COOKIE	String containing a unique identifier for the client certificate.
CERT_FLAGS	First flag is set if a client certificate is present. Second flag is set if the Certificate Authority is a trusted source.
CERT_ISSUER	Client certificate issuer.
CERT_KEYSIZE	Number of bits in the SSL security key.
CERT_SECRETKEYSIZE	Number of bits in the SSL security key for the server.
CERT_SERIALNUMBER	Serial number of the client certificate.
CERT_SERVER_ISSUER	Certificate Authority issuing the server certificate.
CERT_SERVER_SUBJECT	Subject field for the server certificate.
CERT_SUBJECT	Subject field for the client certificate.
CONTENT_LENGTH	Number of bytes reported by the client sent to the server with the request.
CONTENT_TYPE	Type of request made.
GATEWAY_INTERFACE	CGI version in the form of CGI/version number.

TABLE 5-3

Continued

Server Variable	Purpose
HTTPS	Contains the string on if this is a secure request and off if it is not.
HTTPS_KEYSIZE	Number of SSL bits used with the request.
HTTPS_SECRETKEYSIZE	Number of bits used on the server end.
HTTPS_SERVER_ISSUER	Certificate Authority for the server certificate.
HTTPS_SERVER_SUBJECT	Subject field from the server certificate.
INSTANCE_ID	Web server instance identification number.
INSTANCE_META_PATH	Metabase path for this specific instance.
LOCAL_ADDR	IP Address of the server.
LOGON_USER	If the user is logged on to the NT System, this field contains that user's name.
PATH_INFO	Path to the requested page beyond the domain name root.
PATH_TRANSLATED	Physical path of the request.
QUERY_STRING	Any data submitted through the Get method or after a question mark on a link.
REMOTE_ADDR	IP Address of the machine making the request.
REMOTE_HOST	Translated name of the requestor if available. If not, the field contains the IP Address.
REMOTE_USER	Name of the user if sent by the visitor.
REQUEST_METHOD	Request method used, that is, Post, Get.
SCRIPT_NAME	Virtual file location of the script being requested.
SERVER_NAME	Host name of the server.
SERVER_PORT	Port used with the request.
SERVER_PORT_SECURE	If the request is being made through a secure connection, then this field contains the value 1; if not, the field contains the value 0.
SERVER_PROTOCOL	Protocol being used with version number, that is, HTTP/1.1.
SERVER_SOFTWARE	Name and version of the Web server software being run by the server.
URL	Path of requested page.

Server Variable	Purpose
HTTP_CONNECTION	Type of connection between server and client.
HTTP_REFERER	Page that the visitor was at before entering the current page if the progression was made through a link.
HTTP_USER_AGENT	Browser type and version as well as the visitor's operating system.

TABLE 5-4

Non-Standard
Server Variables

To explore the values of all the server variables and the available types you could use the following code within an Active Server Page:

```
For Each TheStuff in Request.ServerVariables
    Response.Write TheStuff & ": " _
       & Request.ServerVariables(TheStuff) & "<P>"
Next
```

This code would produce a list of all the server variables with their values in the form of:

```
Server Variable: Value
```

Cookies Collection

Cookies are a way for you to store nuggets of information on the visitor's computer. You can then use your code to retrieve the values stored on the visitor's machine.

For example, you could store the visitor's user name within a cookie. Then when visitors returned to your site, you would know who they were. With cookies, you could also store visitor preferences, such as their favorite product types or their location.

But since the data are on the visitor's system, you cannot use cookies as your only way to identify visitors. The concern is that visitors could delete the cookie from their machine; or, they may have a cookie-eating program installed that deletes cookies as soon as they are added; or, your visitor may be accessing your Web site from a machine that is different from where the cookie was placed.

You retrieve a cookie through the *Cookies collection*. If you stored a cookie named UserName on the visitor's system, you would retrieve it like this:

```
TheValue = request.cookies("UserName")
```

The variable `TheValue` would contain the value of the cookie UserName. If the UserName cookie did not exist, then `TheValue` would be set to nothing.

Cookies can also be complex. They can contain more than one value within a single cookie. So if you needed to retrieve the visitor's name and favorite product category that were within the same cookie called *Preferences*, you would code this:

```
UserName = Request.Cookies("Preferences")("UserName")
FavCategory = Request.Cookies("Preferences")("FavCategory")
```

You can test to see if a cookie is simple or complex through a property of a cookie called *HasKeys*. If the cookie is complex, it contains more than one value. In this case, the HasKeys property is set to True. If the cookie is a simple cookie, HasKeys is set to False. You reference the property like this:

```
If Request.Cookies("Prefences").HasKeys then
   Response.Write "Complex Cookie"
Else
   Response.Write "Simple Cookie"
End if
```

In the following code, we display the contents of two cookies: one simple and one complex. The HasKeys property is also displayed:

```
response.write "Simple Cookie: " _
   & request.cookies("SampleCookie1") & "<P>"
response.write "Cookie 1 has keys?: " _
   & request.cookies("SampleCookie1").HasKeys & "<P>"
response.write "Complex Cookie All: " _
   & request.cookies("SampleCookie2") & "<P>"
response.write "Cookie 2 has keys?: " _
   & request.cookies("SampleCookie2").HasKeys & "<P>"
response.write "Complex Cookie Part 1: " _
   & request.cookies("SampleCookie2")("Part1") & "<P>"
response.write "Complex Cookie Part 2: " _
   & request.cookies("SampleCookie2")("Part2")
```

The code would produce the output displayed in Figure 5-4.

ClientCertificate Collection

More and more being able to positively identify visitors is necessary, particularly in the area of e-commerce. One of the ways you can do that is through *client certificates*.

Users can purchase a client certificate from an organization referred to as a *Certificate Authority* (CA), which is a company that creates cer-

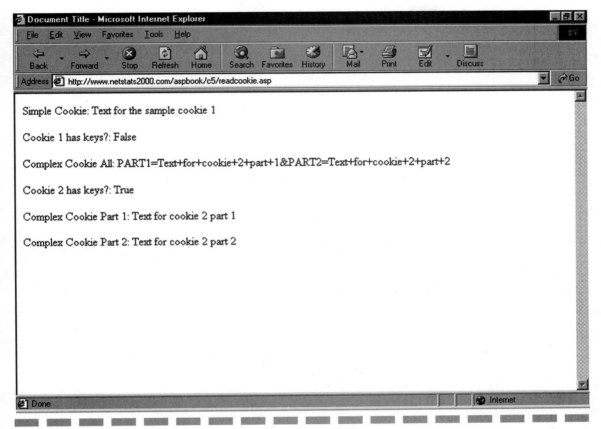

Figure 5-4 Output of cookie sample.

tificates for individuals. The certificate is usually tied to an email address and a password.

Normally, when you work with certificates you decide what Certificate Authorities you trust. To say that you *trust* a Certificate Authority means that you accept certificates issued by their company. Two of the main players in the CA industry are Thawte (http://www.thawte.com) and Verisign (http://www.verisign.com).

You use the *ClientCertificate collection* of the Request object to query the values of the visitor's certificate. Say you wanted to retrieve the date that the certificate expires. You would code this:

```
ExpDate = Request.ClientCertificate("ValidUntil")
```

Some of the objects in the ClientCertificate collection contain subkeys. For example, one of the items in the collection is the issuer of the certificate, the CA. If you wanted to retrieve the specific name of the CA you would code this:

```
CAName = Request.ClientCertificate("IssuerO")
```

The following code iterates through all the values in the ClientCertificate collection:

```
For Each CCValue in Request.ClientCertificate
  Response.Write CCValue & ": " &
Request.ClientCertificate(CCValue) & "<P>"
Next
```

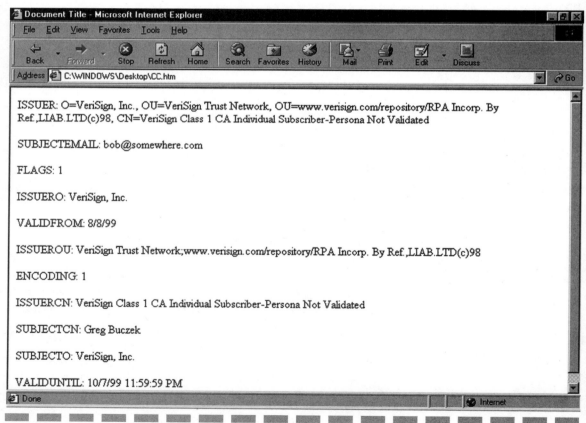

Figure 5-5 Output of ClientCertifcate page.

The more readable output of this code is displayed in Figure 5-5.

Later in this chapter, we look at a practical sample of using the ClientCertificate collection and the steps necessary to retrieve certificates and to require them through IIS.

Request Object Property

The Request object contains only one property, which is discussed below and summarized in Table 5-5.

TotalBytes Property

The *TotalBytes property* contains the number of bytes that are in the parameter portion of an Active Server Page call. If you had a page with the following form:

```
<FORM ACTION="./processform.asp" METHOD="POST">
Name:<BR><INPUT TYPE="text" SIZE=30 MAXLENGTH=50 NAME="Name">
<P>Email Address:<BR><INPUT TYPE="text" SIZE=30 MAXLENGTH=50
  NAME="EmailAddress">
<P>Interests:<BR><SELECT NAME="Interests" SIZE=4 MULTIPLE>
  <OPTION VALUE="News">News
  <OPTION VALUE="Sports">Sports
  <OPTION VALUE="Hiking">Hiking
  <OPTION VALUE="Other">Other
</SELECT>
<P><INPUT TYPE="submit" NAME="SubmitButton" VALUE="OK">
</FORM>
```

and the visitor was to enter the name Dave in the name field, nothing for the email address field, and News for the Interests, the following would display 54:

```
Response.Write Request.TotalBytes
```

TABLE 5-5

Request Object
Property

Object	Purpose
TotalBytes	Number of bytes sent when a page is requested.

The number 54 is the count of bytes or characters in the request if you add the fields submitted with the names of the fields on the form:

```
Field Name: = 4 bytes
Field Name: EmailAddress = 12
Field Name: Interests = 9
Field Name: SubmitButton = 12
Data Entered: Dave = 4
Data Entered: Email (NA) = 0
Data Entered: News = 4
Data Entered: OK (Submit Button) = 2
Ampersands: 3
Equal Signs: 4
Total Bytes: 54
```

If you were to use the Get method with the form submittal, then TotalBytes property would return 0. The property is available only when a form is submitted with the Post method.

Request Object Method

The Request object contains one method, which is discussed below and summarized in Table 5-6.

BinaryRead Method

The *BinaryRead method* returns the data submitted with a form in its low-level raw form. The bytes are returned just as they were submitted instead of through the processed method of using the Form collection.

The method takes the following form:

```
TheStuff = Request.BinaryRead(NumberOfBytesToRetrieve)
```

NumberOfBytesToRetrieve represents the count of the number of bytes you want extracted from the data submitted. TheStuff is set to an array of those bytes. After the call, NumberOfBytesToRetrieve contains

TABLE 5-6

Request Object Method

Object	Purpose
BinaryRead	Returns raw data submitted with a form.

the count of the bytes that were retrieved. To retrieve all the bytes submitted you could code this:

```
TheStuff = Request.BinaryRead(Request.TotalBytes)
```

Almost exclusively, it is much easier to work with the data submitted to a form by using the Form collection. This method of retrieving the data submitted is really suited only for times when you need low-level access to the submission because a binary file accompanied the submission of the form.

Request Object in Action

In this section of the chapter, we look at a variety of sample pages and solutions that utilize the Request object.

First we look at the steps needed to use client certificates. In this sample, you will see how you set up IIS to receive client certificates and how the client gets one. Then we look at a utility that takes the contents of any form and emails it to whoever is indicated by the form. A similar Active Server Page will take the data and save them to a database table. Then we look at a Log In sample. The sample allows visitors to log on to your site. It uses cookies to recognize existing users and allows users to log in if they are new or if their cookie is not present.

Client Certificate Sample

One of the ways that you can identify a user at your site is through *client certificates*, which tell you that persons visiting your site are who they say they are. Users get a certificate from a Certificate Authority. Since anyone can start a Certificate Authority, you decide which ones you will trust. A Certificate Authority then acts as the identifying agent between you and visitors to your site.

To set up a page so that it uses Client Certificates you need to use the Microsoft Management Console for IIS. Browse to the page you wish to secure with Client Certificates and right-click on it; then select Properties. You should see the dialog displayed in Figure 5-6.

Switch to the FILE SECURITY tab and press the EDIT button in the Secure Communications section. You should see the dialog shown in Figure 5-7.

Figure 5-6
File Properties dialog
as displayed within
IIS.

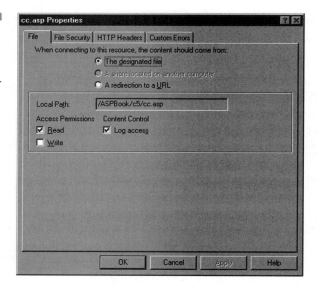

Figure 5-6
File Properties dialog
as displayed within
IIS.

To require a secure channel when the page is accessed you need to check the REQUIRE SECURE CHANNEL WHEN ACCESSING THIS RESOURCE checkbox. Once you do that, you can then select the Require Client Certificates option.

You can also use Client Certificates as a way to map users to specific NT accounts. You do this by checking the ENABLE CLIENT CERTIFICATE MAPPING checkbox and then pressing the EDIT button. When you do that you see the dialog displayed in Figure 5-8.

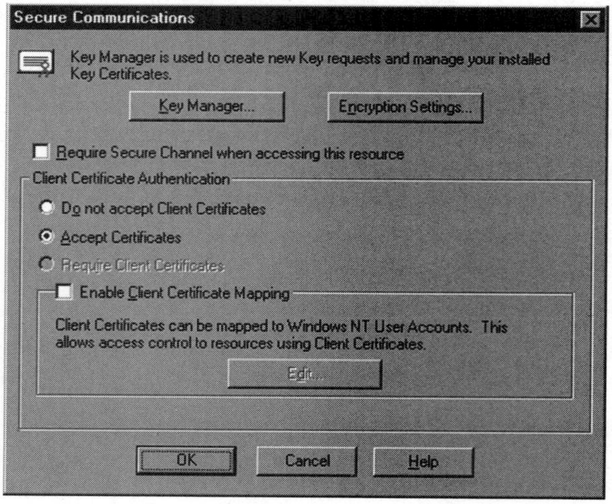

Figure 5-7
Secure
Communications
dialog.

Figure 5-8
Basic Account
Mappings dialog.

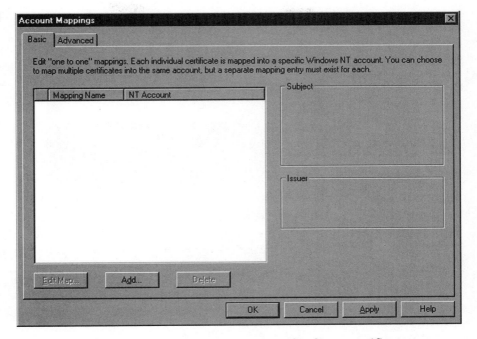

From the BASIC tab you can assign a specific client certificate to a specific account by clicking on the ADD button. More robust are the capabilities under the ADVANCED tab, which allows you to use *Wildcards* to map groups of individuals to specific NT Accounts. You could, for example, map everyone from one Certificate Authority to a specific NT Account; or, you could do the mapping based on the organization connected with the owner of the client certificate.

To add multiple certificates to a single NT Account, click on the ADD button from the ADVANCED tab. You should see the first step of the wizard shown in Figure 5-9.

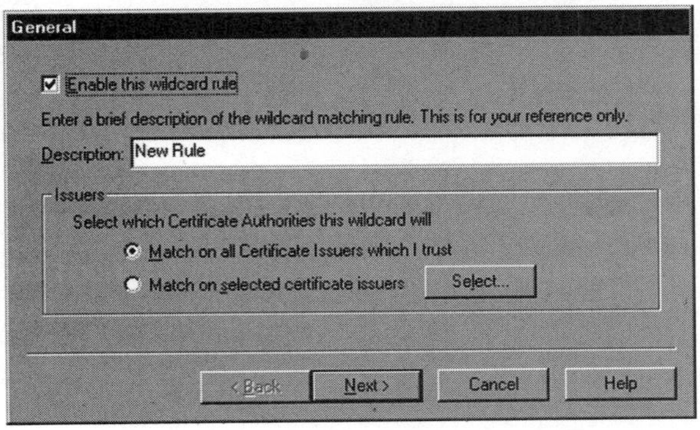

Figure 5-9
Adding an Advanced
Mapping step 1.

Figure 5-10
Rules for the
mapping.

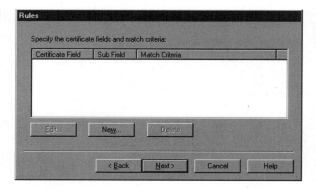

First, you supply some name for your rule, which is purely for your own recognition. The first filtering you supply is whether you want to map to all Certificate Authorities or just selected ones. To limit the Certificate Authorities, press the SELECT button and you will see the list of Authorities.

After selecting the Issuers option press the NEXT button to see the dialog shown in Figure 5-10.

In the Rules portion of the dialog you Add, Edit, and Delete the specific filtering rules for this mapping. Pressing the NEW button displays the dialog in Figure 5-11, where you create a rule based on the field to test and the criteria that that field must match. The rule in Figure 5-11 looks for a company name that starts with ABC within the Organization

Figure 5-11
Sample rule.

Edit Rule Element

Edit the rule element by choosing what major of the certificate is to be matched against. Then choose an appropriate subfield. Finally, enter a matching string. You can use wildcards for the match.

Valid subfields are short strings indicating a sub-value in a certificate field. Example: "O" stands for Organization.

New subfield strings may be defined at a later date. Please refer to current documentation for the latest codes.

☑ Match Capitalization

Certificate Field: Subject

Sub Field: O

Criteria: ABC*

A chart of some of the sub-fields already defined is below.

O   Organization - a company or business
OU Organization Unit - department
CN Common Name - a net address - e.g. "microsoft.com"
C   Country - A short pre-defined code e.g. "US" or "FR"
S   State or Province
L   Locality - city

OK   Cancel   Help

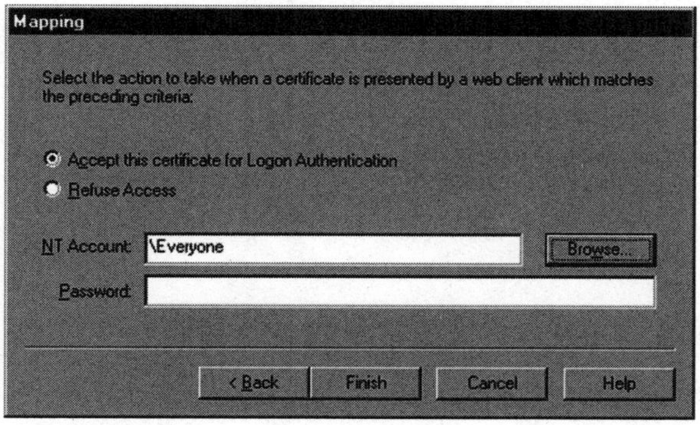

Figure 5-12
Mapping the rule to
a specific account.

subkey of the Subject key. Press OK to accept this rule and then click on the NEXT button. You should see the third step of this wizard as shown in Figure 5-12.

From this third step you select the account to which you want to map this rule, or, you can choose to refuse access to certificates matching this rule. Next press the FINISH button and your Advanced Mapping is complete.

The other end of this secure equation is your visitor getting a Client Certificate. The process to do this involves your visitor going to a Certificate Authority Web site like Verisign or Thawte, where they generally have a wizard for creating Client Certificates that differ from site to site. Most of the major Certificate Authorities do charge for this service.

Once these two pieces are in place, your visitors can enter your secure site and provide trusted information about who they are. The page, now secure, requires that the URL be addressed through https:// instead of http://. If they try to enter the page and they do not have a certificate, they will see a warning like the one shown for Netscape Navigator in Figure 5-13. They then see a message from the browser telling them they need to get a client certificate to view the page.

Visitors that do have a certificate will receive a message from their browser advising them that their client certificate is being requested and asking them to choose one. That dialog is shown in Figure 5-14. They then see the secured page. On the page you can use the Request.ClientCertificate collection to acknowledge the visitor. One code use of the page would be to use the Serial Number field to look up visitors in your database so you know who they are. You could then use data

Figure 5-13
Warning message
displayed in
Netscape Navigator.

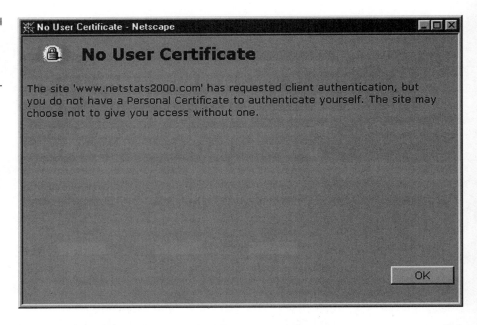

stored there to display your site in the manner that your visitors prefer.
You could code something like this:

```
<%
Option Explicit
Dim conn
Dim RSVisitor
```

Figure 5-14
Message that Client
Certificate is
requested.

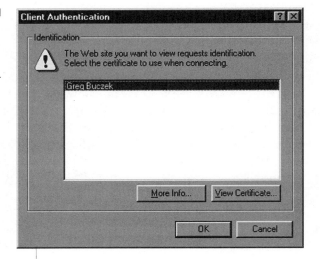

```
set conn = server.createobject ("adodb.connection")
conn.open "DBName", "sa", "yourpassword"
set RSVisitor = conn.Execute("select * from Visitors where
  SerialNumber = " _
  & Request.ClientCertificate("SerialNumber"))
If RSVisitor.EOF Then
  conn.execute "insert into Visitors (SerialNumber) values " _
      & Request.ClientCertificate("SerialNumber")
  Response.Redirect "./config.asp?User=" _
      & Request.ClientCertificate("SerialNumber") & "&Type=New"
Else
  Layout = RSVisitor("Layout")
  FavCat = RSVisitor("FavCat")
End If
%>
```

The database code is discussed more deeply in Chapters 13 and 14. But the code first connects to the database:

```
set conn = server.createobject ("adodb.connection")
conn.open "DBName", "sa", "yourpassword"
```

The code then uses the serial number from the visitors' certificates to look for their record in the database:

```
set RSVisitor = conn.Execute("select * from Visitors where
  SerialNumber = " _
  & Request.ClientCertificate("SerialNumber"))
```

If the visitors are not found, then the following flag will be set:

```
If RSVisitor.EOF Then
```

In that case, they are added to the database:

```
conn.execute "insert into Visitors (SerialNumber) values " _
  & Request.ClientCertificate("SerialNumber")
```

and are sent to a different page to set their preferences:

```
Response.Redirect "./config.asp?User=" _
  & Request.ClientCertificate("SerialNumber") & "&Type=New"
```

otherwise, the data in the database are used to set aspects of the page that they will be shown:

```
Layout = RSVisitor("Layout")
FavCat = RSVisitor("FavCat")
```

Form Email Processor

One of the pages almost all sites have is a *More Information form*. This page usually asks visitors to supply information about themselves and they are given the opportunity to ask a question. The contents of the form are then sent to whomever you indicate. The sample site presents such a page. More important, however, is the code used to process the form. The code presents a way to have any form submitted to it and the contents of that form are then emailed to whomever is indicated in a special field on the form.

The first page of the tool is the *Request for More Information*, which is displayed in Figure 5-15. The form on the page can contain whatever types and quantity of elements that you want, but it includes two special hidden form elements:

```
<INPUT TYPE=HIDDEN NAME="SendTo" VALUE="gbuczek@thuntek.net">
<INPUT TYPE=HIDDEN NAME="CompleteMessage"
VALUE="Thanks for supplying the information requested.">
```

The *SendTo field* stores the email address of the person that the contents of the form should be sent to. The other special field is the

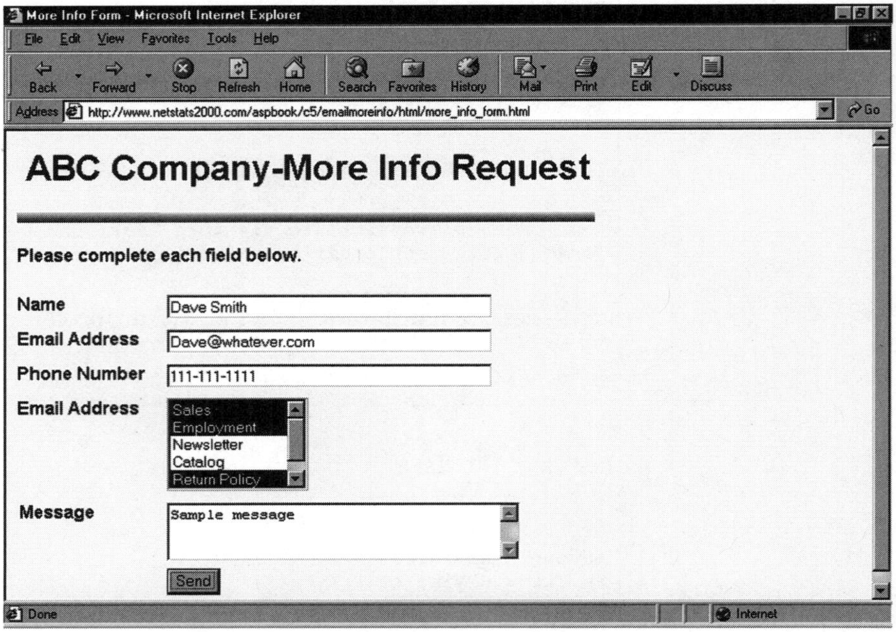

Figure 5-15
More Info Request form.

CompleteMessage field, which contains the text displayed to the visitor after the form is submitted. Another field of interest is the SUBMIT button:

```
<INPUT TYPE=SUBMIT NAME="SubmitButton" VALUE="Send">
```

Remember from our earlier discussion that the SUBMIT button is sent with all the other fields on the form. As you will see when we look at the code, if the SUBMIT button is named SubmitButton, it is not sent with the rest of the fields on the form.

Figure 5-16 shows the page displayed to the visitor after the SUBMIT button is pressed. Notice the message on this page. This is the text that was sent to the form through the CompleteMessage field.

The code then sends an email to the person indicated in the SendTo field. The text of the email message based on the preceding entry would look like this:

```
Name: Dave Smith
EmailAddress: Dave@whatever.com
PhoneNumber: 111-111-1111
Interest(3): Sales, Employment, Return Policy
Message: Sample message
```

Figure 5-16

Page seen after the More Info Request form is submitted.

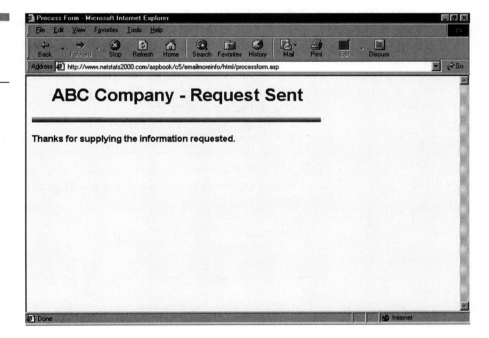

The contents of the form are sent to an Active Server Page that creates the email. The main code block for that page is:

```
<%
Option Explicit
Dim TheMessage
Dim TheFormField
For Each TheFormField in Request.Form
  If TheFormField <> "SendTo" and TheFormField <>
    "CompleteMessage" _
    and TheFormField <> "SubmitButton" Then
    If Request.Form(TheFormField).Count > 1 Then
      TheMessage = TheMessage & TheFormField & "(" _
          & Request.Form(TheFormField).Count & "): " _
          & Request.Form(TheFormField) & chr(13)
    else
      TheMessage = TheMessage & TheFormField & ": " _
          & Request.Form(TheFormField) & chr(13)
    end if
  end if
Next
Dim ObjMail
Set objMail = CreateObject("CDONTS.NewMail")
objMail.Send "na@na.com", cstr(Request.Form("SendTo")), _
  "New More Info Request", cstr(TheMessage)
Set objMail = Nothing
%>
```

NOTE: *The code uses a few objects we haven't yet discussed but which are needed to complete the example.*

The code sets up a loop that will iterate through each field that was submitted. In the loop, the variable TheFormField is set to each of the items in the Form collection:

```
For Each TheFormField in Request.Form
```

The email sent out should not include these special fields that indicate to whom the message is sent, the message displayed to the visitor, and the SUBMIT button:

```
If TheFormField <> "SendTo" and TheFormField <> "CompleteMessage" _
  and TheFormField <> "SubmitButton" Then
```

If the form element is part of a complex field, the number of elements is indicated:

```
If Request.Form(TheFormField).Count > 1 Then
```

```
TheMessage = TheMessage & TheFormField & "(" _
    & Request.Form(TheFormField).Count & "): " _
        & Request.Form(TheFormField) & chr(13)
```

otherwise, just the field name and value are stored in the email message text variable:

```
TheMessage = TheMessage & TheFormField & ": " _
    & Request.Form(TheFormField) & chr(13)
```

The code then loops to the next field:

```
Next
```

The rest of the code uses the Collaborative Data object (discussed in Chapter 9) to send an email to the person indicated in the SendTo field:

```
Dim ObjMail
Set objMail = CreateObject("CDONTS.NewMail")
objMail.Send "na@na.com", cstr(Request.Form("SendTo")), _
    "New More Info Request", cstr(TheMessage)
Set objMail = Nothing
```

Form Database Processor

Another task frequently needed with many forms is the ability to store the data submitted into a database table. The Request object is once again used to pass hidden and visitor-supplied fields to the processing form.

In this sample, we will look at a survey. The visitor comes to our site and completes a survey. The contents of the survey are inserted into a database table, but the code could be used to write any form data to a database. The code uses the Request object to retrieve the field names and values, the table name, and the message to be displayed to the visitor.

The survey page is shown in Figure 5-17. The survey page can contain a variety of Form fields. The name of each of the form elements must be the same as the name of the field within the target table where the record will be added. For example, this Form field:

```
<TEXTAREA WRAP=PHYSICAL NAME="Service" ROWS=3 COLS=61></TEXTAREA>
```

requires that the table has a field named *Service*. The HTML form also contains hidden fields as follows:

Figure 5-17
Survey page.

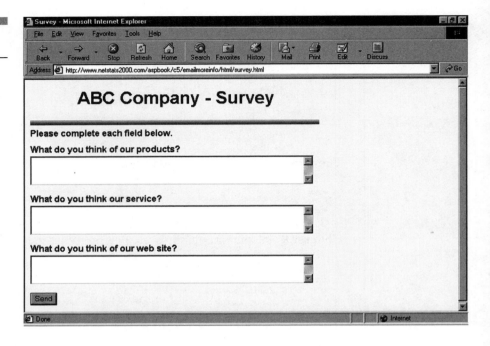

```
<INPUT TYPE=HIDDEN NAME="CompleteMessage"
  VALUE="Thanks for supplying the information requested.">
<INPUT TYPE=HIDDEN NAME="TableName" VALUE="C5Survey">
```

The CompleteMessage hidden field stores the message that will be displayed after the form is submitted. The TableName field stores the name of the table where the data are to be written.

When visitors press the SEND button they see the page shown in Figure 5-18. The code on the process_form.asp page takes the data submitted and adds them to a database. The main code block is:

```
<%
Option Explicit
Dim TheFields
Dim TheValues
Dim TheFormField
Dim TheQuery
For Each TheFormField in Request.Form
  If TheFormField <> "TableName" and TheFormField <>
"CompleteMessage" _
    and TheFormField <> "SubmitButton" Then
      TheFields = TheFields & TheFormField & ", "
      TheValues = TheValues & "'" & Request.Form(TheFormField) &
"', "
  end if
```

Figure 5-18
Page displayed after
visitors submit their
survey.

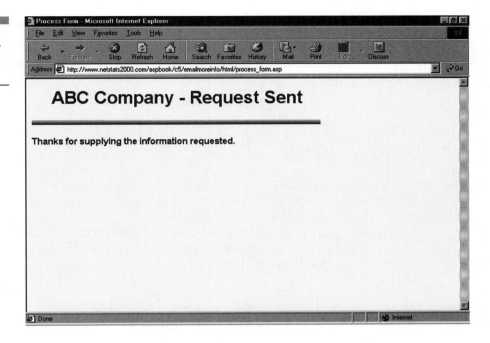

```
Next
TheFields = left(TheFields, Len(TheFields) - 2)
TheValues = left(TheValues, Len(TheValues) - 2)
Dim conn
set conn = server.createobject ("adodb.connection")
conn.open "ASPBook", "sa", "yourpassword"
conn.execute "insert into " & Request.Form("TableName") _
  & " (" & TheFields & ") values (" & TheValues & ")"
%>
```

The code iterates through all the fields that were submitted and are
available through the Form collection:

```
For Each TheFormField in Request.Form
```

The code skips the processing of the following fields, since they are not
meant to be added to the database:

```
If TheFormField <> "TableName" and TheFormField <>
  "CompleteMessage" _
and TheFormField <> "SubmitButton" Then
```

All the other fields and their values are concatenated together, as they
will be needed to create the proper query:

```
TheFields = TheFields & TheFormField & ", "
TheValues = TheValues & "'" & Request.Form(TheFormField) & "', "
```

The code then moves on to the next Form collection item:

```
Next
```

Each of the strings created previously will, at this point, have an extra comma and space at the end. This code removes those unwanted characters:

```
TheFields = left(TheFields, Len(TheFields) - 2)
TheValues = left(TheValues, Len(TheValues) - 2)
```

Finally, database code (which is discussed more thoroughly in Chapters 13 and 14) adds the data submitted to the data passed through the TableName field within the Form collection:

```
Dim conn
set conn = server.createobject ("adodb.connection")
conn.open "ASPBook", "sa", "yourpassword"
conn.execute "insert into " & Request.Form("TableName") _
   & " (" & TheFields & ") values (" & TheValues & ")"
```

Site Log In

Many sites have a private area that visitors must first log in to before they can enter. Sometimes entire sites are of this type. This tool shows you how to create a login page that uses cookies to store the login information about the visitor. The tool also stores visitors' information in a database so they will be allowed entry even if their cookies are not present.

The tool shows you how you can use the Request object to gather information from visitors. The information is gathered through visitors from the Form collection and through their computer from the Cookies collection.

The first time visitors enter the site they see a screen like the one shown in Figure 5-19. Since this is their first visit to the site, they do not have the cookie on their system. The code doesn't know whether these are existing visitors with missing cookies or if these are new visitors. If these are new visitors, they can click on the link and are sent to the New page shown in Figure 5-20.

Here visitors supply us with their name, password, and interest. The

Figure 5-19
Log In form.

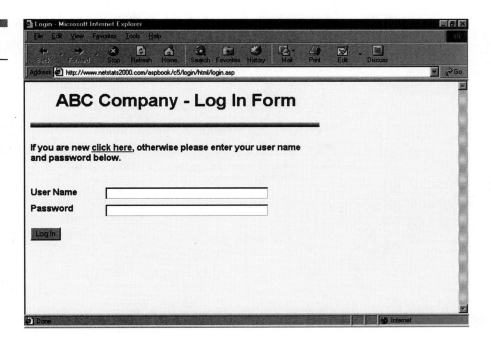

Figure 5-20
New User page.

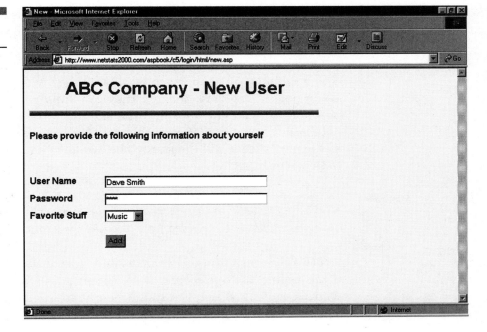

Figure 5-21
Welcome page from
the login site.

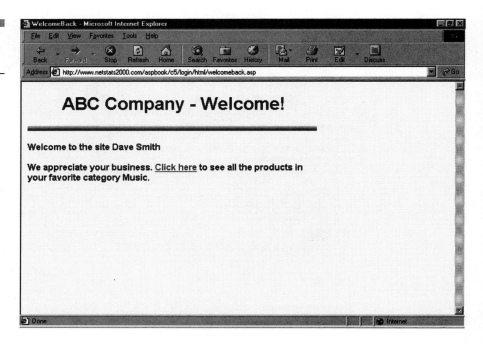

code writes that information to the database and also writes the cookie to visitors' systems for future entries. Once they add themselves, they see a page like the one shown in Figure 5-21.

On subsequent visits they will be taken straight to this page if a cookie is found on their machine; if not, they will be sent back to the Login page. This time, though, they can supply their user name and password to gain entrance into the site since the data are now in the database. Their information is then written to a cookie on their machine so the next time it will (hopefully!) be available and they can go straight to this page.

NOTE: *The code in this sample includes topics that have not yet been discussed. They are included here to make the sample more complete.*

The entry page into this sample site is responsible for checking to see if the visitor has our cookie. If so, the page is displayed with its customized content. If not, the visitor is sent to the Login page. The main code block for this page is:

```
<%
Option Explicit
If not Len(Request.Cookies("Login")("UserName")) > 1 Then
    Response.Redirect "./login.asp"
End If
%>
```

The code uses the Request object to check for the cookie. The cookie is of the complex type since it contains more than one field. The length of the cookie is checked to see if it exists.

```
If not Len(Request.Cookies("Login")("UserName")) > 1 Then
```

If the length of the cookie is not at least one character, it is not present and visitors are sent to the Login page:

```
Response.Redirect "./login.asp"
```

otherwise, the page is displayed with the customization of visitors' name and their favorite category based on the retrieved cookie:

```
Welcome to the site
<% Response. Write Request.Cookies("Login")("UserName") %>
your favorite category
<% Response. Write Request.Cookies("Login")("FavCat") %>.
```

Notice again that this is a complex cookie. The main cookie name is Login and the subkeys are UserName and FavCat.

The Login page allows visitors to log in to the site if they are found in the database. If they are, the cookie is written to their system and they are sent back to the Welcome page.

```
<%
Option Explicit
Dim RSUser
Dim conn
If not isempty(Request.Form("Login")) Then
  set conn = server.createobject ("adodb.connection")
  conn.open "ASPBook", "sa", "yourpassword"
  set RSUser = conn.Execute("select * from C5Login where " _
    & "UserName = '" & Request.Form("UserName") & "' and " _
    & "Password = '" & Request.Form("Password") & "'")
  If not RSUser.EOF Then
    response.cookies("Login")("UserName") = request.form
      ("username")
    response.cookies("Login")("FavCat") = request.form("FavCat")
    response.cookies("Login").Expires = "2/2/2002"
    response.redirect "./welcomeback.asp"
  end if
End If
%>
```

The page has two states. Either visitors have just entered the page and the form needs to be displayed or they have submitted the form and the information needs to be checked against the database. The IsEmpty function is used to check for the presence of the LOGIN button. If it is present, then the form has been submitted:

```
If not isempty(Request.Form("Login")) Then
```

In that case, we will need to look for the visitor in our database:

```
set conn = server.createobject ("adodb.connection")
conn.open "ASPBook", "sa", "yourpassword"
set RSUser = conn.Execute("select * from C5Login where " _
   & "UserName = '" & Request.Form("UserName") & "' and " _
   & "Password = '" & Request.Form("Password") & "'")
```

If a record for the visitor is found, an EOF flag will be set:

```
If not RSUser.EOF Then
```

We then need to write the cookie to the visitors' system and set the expiration date for the cookie:

```
response.cookies("Login")("UserName") = request.form("username")
response.cookies("Login")("FavCat") = request.form("FavCat")
response.cookies("Login").Expires = "2/2/2002"
```

They are then sent to the Welcome page.

```
response.redirect "./welcomeback.asp"
```

The code on the new page adds new visitors to the database, writes their cookie, and sends them to the Welcome page. The code for the page is:

```
<%
Option Explicit
Dim conn
If not isempty(Request.Form("Add")) Then
    set conn = server.createobject ("adodb.connection")
    conn.open "ASPBook", "sa", "yourpassword"
    conn.execute "insert into C5Login (UserName, Password, FavCat) " _
       & "values (" _
       & "'" & Request.Form("UserName") & "', " _
       & "'" & Request.Form("Password") & "', " _
       & "'" & Request.Form("FavCat") & "')"
    response.cookies("Login")("UserName") = request.form("username")
    response.cookies("Login")("FavCat") = request.form("FavCat")
    response.cookies("Login").Expires = "2/2/2002"
```

```
    response.redirect "./welcomeback.asp"
End If
%>
```

Like the Login page, this page has two states. The page either is in Form view or in Process view. The Form view displays just the form so visitors can supply their information. The Process view processes what they entered on the form. The state is determined by looking for the ADD button:

```
If not isempty(Request.Form("Add")) Then
```

If the button is present, we need to add the visitor to the database:

```
set conn = server.createobject ("adodb.connection")
conn.open "ASPBook", "sa", "yourpassword"
conn.execute "insert into C5Login (UserName, Password, FavCat) "
   & "values (" _
   & "'" & Request.Form("UserName") & "', " _
   & "'" & Request.Form("Password") & "', " _
 & "'" & Request.Form("FavCat") & "')"
```

Next, the cookie and expiration date are written to the visitors' system:

```
response.cookies("Login")("UserName") = request.form("username")
response.cookies("Login")("FavCat") = request.form("FavCat")
response.cookies("Login").Expires = "2/2/2002"
```

and visitors are sent to the welcome page.

```
response.redirect "./welcomeback.asp"
```

CHAPTER 6

Response
Object

Sending Information Back to Visitors

In the last chapter, we reviewed the step in the process that allowed visitors to supply us explicitly and implicitly with information about their request and environment. In this chapter, we look at the other side of the process, getting information back to visitors and to their system.

Take a look at Figure 6-1. The circled section shows you the role of the *Response object*, which allows you to communicate your dynamic Web content back to the browser. You use the information collected by the visitor and other components on your system to prepare text, graphics, and much more that you want sent back to the visitor. This is done through the Response object.

In this chapter we cover the Collection, Properties, and Methods of the Response object. You will learn how to write cookies to the visitor's browser. You will learn how to control when the results of your code are sent to the visitor. You will learn how to write headers to the browser. We also look at sending data other than text, such as graphics, as output to the browser.

At the end of the chapter, we then look at a few practical uses of the Response object.

Figure 6-1
Response object's role in the ASP process.

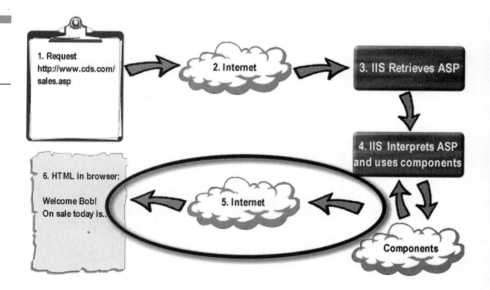

Response Object Collection

The Response object includes just a single collection, which is discussed below and summarized in Table 6-1.

Cookies Collection

As mentioned in the last chapter, cookies are a way for you to store nuggets of information on the visitor's computer. You can then use your code to retrieve the values stored on the visitor's system at a later time.

For example, you could store the most recent searches a visitor has made on your Web site in a cookie. Then, when visitors search again, you could present them with their last five search criteria; or, you could store visitors' location in a cookie and when they return to your site, you could display local information for your visitors.

But since the data are on the visitor's system, you cannot use cookies as your only way to identify visitors or in situations where the cookie must be present. You should always try to provide an alternative to cookies. Remember that visitors could delete the code at any time, they could have a program on their machine that blocks cookies, or they may be visiting your site from a different system.

You place cookies on the visitor's machine by using the Cookies collection of the Response object. To write a single simple cookie to the visitor's system you would code this:

```
Response.Cookies("NameOfCookies") = "Value"
```

The *NameOfCookie* is the name you want to store the cookie as on the visitor's system. The value represents the text to store in the cookie. So if you coded this:

```
Response.Cookies("SearchCriteria1") = "ASP"
```

TABLE 6-1

Response Object
Collections

Object	Purpose
Cookies	Allows you to write cookies to the visitor's browser.

this would add the cookie with the name SearchCriteria1 to the visitor's system. The cookie would contain the value ASP. If the cookie already exists, the old value will be overwritten.

The preceding creates a simple cookie that contains a single value. But cookies can also be complex and contain subkeys. You refer to subkeys by specifying the name of the cookie with the name of the subkey in this form:

```
Response.Cookies("NameOfCookie")("NameOfKey") = "Value"
```

In this example, NameOfCookie is the name of the main cookie and NameOfKey represents the name of the subkey being referred to. Value would be what you want to set the cookie to.

In our search criteria example, we could store the five most recent searches in a complex cookie. Take a look at Figure 6-2. This is what our search page, in simplified form, would look like the first time the visitor came to the search page. The Recent Searches field is blank. But after the visitor has made a few searches, the select element would be populated with those searches as shown in Figure 6-3.

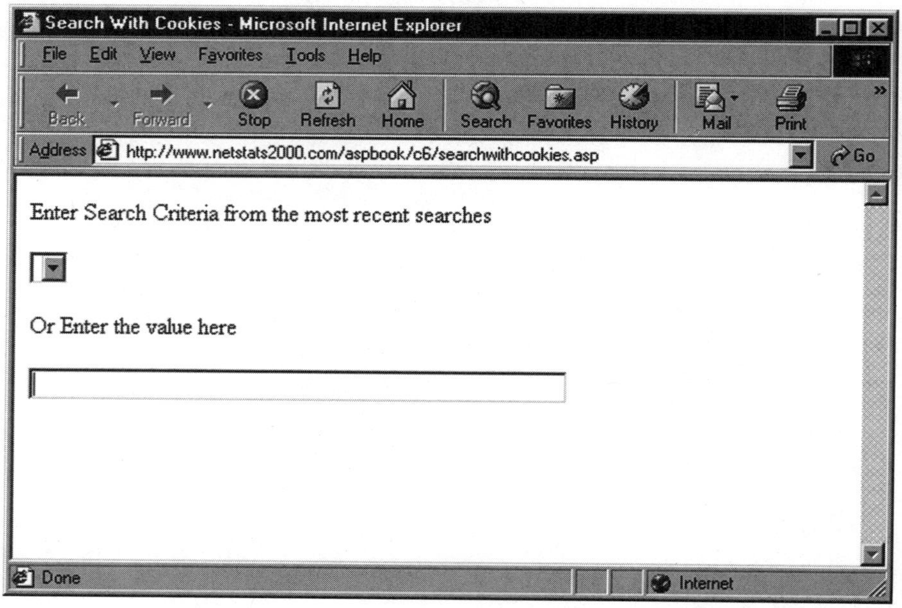

Figure 6-2
Search page without recent searches.

Figure 6-3
Search page after
search is complete.

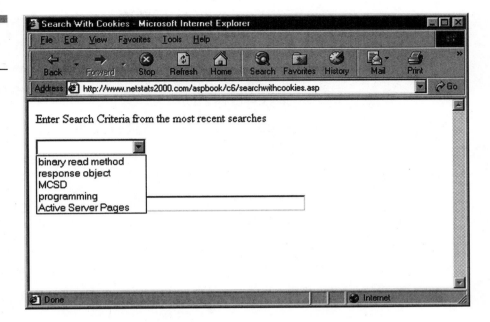

The code that accomplished this task uses cookies. A code block at the top of the page writes the cookies:

```
<%
If Len(Request.Form("Search")) > 0 Then
  Response.Cookies("SearchCriteria")("5") = Request.Cookies
    ("SearchCriteria")("4")
  Response.Cookies("SearchCriteria")("4") = Request.Cookies
    ("SearchCriteria")("3")
  Response.Cookies("SearchCriteria")("3") = Request.Cookies
    ("SearchCriteria")("2")
  Response.Cookies("SearchCriteria")("2") = Request.Cookies
    ("SearchCriteria")("1")
  Response.Cookies("SearchCriteria")("1") = Request.Form("Search")
End If
%>
```

First, the code makes sure that visitors entered a new search:

```
If Len(Request.Form("Search")) > 0 Then
```

If they have, each of the cookies is bounced up one level. The fourth most-recent search becomes the fifth, the third becomes the fourth, and so on:

```
Response.Cookies("SearchCriteria")("5") = Request.Cookies
  ("SearchCriteria")("4")
Response.Cookies("SearchCriteria")("4") = Request.Cookies
  ("SearchCriteria")("3")
Response.Cookies("SearchCriteria")("3") = Request.Cookies
  ("SearchCriteria")("2")
Response.Cookies("SearchCriteria")("2") = Request.Cookies
  ("SearchCriteria")("1")
```

Then the criterion they just entered is used to populate the most recent search criterion:

```
Response.Cookies("SearchCriteria")("1") = Request.Form("Search")
```

On the HTML form the Select control is populated with these cookies each time the page is loaded:

```
<SELECT NAME="OldSearch" SIZE=1>
  <OPTION VALUE="<% Response.Write
    Request.Cookies("SearchCriteria")("1") %>"><% Response.Write
      Request.Cookies("SearchCriteria")("1") %>
  <OPTION VALUE="<% Response.Write
    Request.Cookies("SearchCriteria")("2") %>"><% Response.Write
      Request.Cookies("SearchCriteria")("2") %>
  <OPTION VALUE="<% Response.Write
    Request.Cookies("SearchCriteria")("3") %>"><% Response.Write
      Request.Cookies("SearchCriteria")("3") %>
  <OPTION VALUE="<% Response.Write
    Request.Cookies("SearchCriteria")("4") %>"><% Response.Write
      Request.Cookies("SearchCriteria")("4") %>
  <OPTION VALUE="<% Response.Write
    Request.Cookies("SearchCriteria")("5") %>"><% Response.Write
      Request.Cookies("SearchCriteria")("5") %>
</SELECT>
```

But this cookie would persist only while the visitor was connected to your site. You need to set the *Expires property* of the cookie to some date and/or time that it should remain on the visitor's system. The syntax for the Expires property is as follows:

```
Response.Cookies("NameOfCookie").Expires = Date
```

Date is the date and/or time that the cookie will expire. *NameOfCookie* is the name of the cookie for which you want to set the expiration date. In our search criteria example, we would code like this:

```
Response.Cookies("SearchCriteria").Expires = "5/1/2005"
```

There are three other properties of a cookie that you can set: Domain, Path, and Secure. You can limit the cookie to a single domain name with the Domain property. So if we coded this:

```
Response.Cookies("SearchCriteria").Domain = "whatever.com"
```

the cookie would be limited to the domain name `whatever.com`. We can go deeper and limit the cookie to just a particular path directory within our domain with the Path property. If we wanted to limit the search criteria cookie to a directory called `Docs` we would code this:

```
Response.Cookies("SearchCriteria").Path = "/docs/"
```

The last property to discuss for the Cookies collection is the *Secure property*. This Boolean property stores whether the cookie is securely transmitted when it is sent or retrieved. You code the property like this:

```
Response.Cookies("SearchCriteria").Secure = FALSE
```

Response Object Properties

Properties of the Response object allow you to control how data are sent to the visitor's browser. The properties are discussed below and summarized in Table 6-2.

TABLE 6-2

Response Object Properties

Object	Purpose
Buffer	Boolean property that determines whether the ASP output is sent as it occurs or as a block.
CacheControl	Used to indicate caching instructions to proxies.
Charset	Used to set the character type which is appended to the content type header.
ContentType	Specifies the content type header which states the type of data returned, that is, HTML, image.
Expires	Number of minutes before a cached page expires.
ExpiresAbsolute	The specific date and/or time that a cached page expires.
IsClientConnected	Boolean property that returns whether the client is still connected to the site.
PICS	Appends pic-label fields to the returned headers.
Status	Status line header returned to the browser.

Buffer Property

The *Buffer property* is a Boolean property that determines whether the output of your ASP is sent as it runs or it is stored until all the code is complete or the Flush method is called. When you use the Buffer property, it must be used before any information is written to the browser.

As stated previously, it is a *Boolean property*, which means that it is set to True or False. Let's take a look at how a couple of code blocks would differ based on the setting of the Buffer property. The first code block is buffered.

```
<%
Option Explicit
Response.Buffer = True
Response.Write "Running query..."
Dim conn
Dim RSTotalSales
set conn = server.createobject ("adodb.connection")
conn.open "Sales", "sa", "YourPassword"
set RSTotalSales = conn.Execute("select Sum(TotalAmount) as
 TotalSales " _
  & "from Sales")
Response.Write RSTotalSales("TotalAmount")
%>
```

The scenario of this code block is that we are presenting a page that shows the total amount of sales for all records in a database table. We will estimate that the query will take 20 s to run. The buffer is on. So when the code gets to this line:

```
Response.Write "Running query..."
```

the text is placed in the buffer and is not sent to the browser. The code continues and 20 s later the code completes. The text `Running query...` as well as the result of the query are now sent to the browser.

Now think about the flow of this code block:

```
<%
Option Explicit
Response.Buffer = False
Response.Write "Running query..."
Dim conn
Dim RSTotalSales
set conn = server.createobject ("adodb.connection")
conn.open "Sales", "sa", "YourPassword"
set RSTotalSales = conn.Execute("select Sum(TotalAmount) as
 TotalSales " _
  & "from Sales")
Response.Write RSTotalSales("TotalAmount")
%>
```

This time when the code gets here:

```
Response.Write "Running query..."
```

the text is immediately sent to the browser. So now visitors receive the feedback that something is happening while they are waiting for the query to run. This technique of giving the visitor gradual feedback is very important for procedures that take more than a few seconds to complete. Without the feedback, especially on the Internet, visitors may assume something is wrong and leave your site.

CacheControl Property

Many visitors access the Internet through a Proxy. The visitors submit their request through their browser and the request is then sent to a *Proxy*, which serves as a funnel for many computers making requests to the Internet. One of the things the Proxy does is store a cache of pages requested by all the users of the Proxy. So instead of retrieving the same page many times from the Internet, the Proxy merely returns the cached page to the person making the request.

With static HTML pages this usually works OK, although with dynamic Active Server Pages you frequently don't want your pages cached. The *CacheControl property* is your way of instructing the Proxy to cache or not to cache. The code must precede any HTML and takes the following form:

```
Response.CacheControl = "Public"
```

or

```
Response.CacheControl = "Private"
```

By default, the property is set to *Private*, which indicates that the content should not be buffered. If you do want the text of your Active Server Page buffered, simply set the property to Private.

Charset Property

The *Charset property* allows you to modify the Charset parameter of the content-type header. The code has the following syntax:

```
Response.Charset = "CharSetValue"
```

The Charset value represents the name of the character set you wish to use. If you include more than one line of code that modifies the Charset property, only the last value is used. Since the line of code modifies a header, it must precede any HTML outputted to the browser.

ContentType Property

When you send content back to the browser, regardless of whether it is through HTML or your code, you indicate the *content type*, which tells the browser what type of data is being returned. Are you returning HTML, a picture, video, audio, and so forth? This is what you tell the browser through content type.

You can set this value in code using the *ContentType property*. For example, if you wanted to indicate that you were returning HTML, you would code this:

```
Response.ContentType = "text/HTML"
```

If you wanted to indicate that you were returning a GIF image you would code this:

```
Response.ContentType = "image/GIF"
```

The default value for this property is text/HTML. The first part of the value indicates the type, which is followed by the subtype. Table 6-3 summarizes the main top-level types.

TABLE 6-3

Content-type Summary

Type	Definition
Application	Unspecified binary information.
Audio	Indicates that the data being transmitted comprise an audio format.
Image	A graphic is being transmitted, typically gif or jpeg.
Message	The body of a message.
Multipart	The data being transmitted is of multiple data types.
Text	Just text is being sent, like plain or HTML.
Video	The data being sent are of video format, like avi or mpeg.

Expires Property

The visitor's browser contains a *cache*, which is a storage area on the visitor's system where previously viewed pages are stored. This allows visitors to view a Web page without having to download it again if it hasn't changed.

With HTML pages this usually works just fine—the page is in the buffer until it is noted as updated and then the page is downloaded again. But with Active Server Pages you may need to have more control over how long a page stays in the visitor's cache without explicitly updating with your server. One of the ways you can do that is with the *Expires property*, which sets the number of minutes that an Active Server Page is available in the visitor's cache.

The property has the following syntax:

```
Response.Expires = NumMinutes
```

where *NumMinutes* represents the number of minutes for which the page is cacheable.

Take this simple code sample:

```
<%
Response.Expires = 2
Response.write Now
%>
```

It produces the output shown in Figure 6-4.

The code writes the current system date and time, based on the server, to the browser. But note the Expires property that is set to 2. If visitors close their browser and return to this page within 2 min, they will see the exact date and time displayed. If at the time they return it has been more than 2 min, the page will be updated.

So the property sets the amount of time that must go by before the page is updated, unless visitors use the REFRESH button in their browser. This type of code is helpful in situations where you might have a page that is getting hits much more frequently than it is changing. You could have the page cached for the number of minutes for which it would be valid.

ExpiresAbsolute Property

Another way that you can define how long your page is cached for is with the *ExpiresAbsolute property*, which allows you to set a point in

Figure 6-4

Output of code using the Expires property.

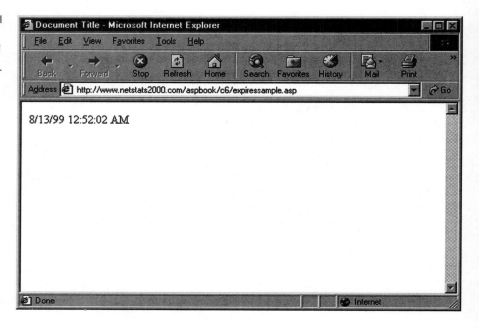

time until which the page is valid. The property can be set to a date and/or a time and has the following form:

```
Response.ExpiresAbsolte = "5/14/2004 14:13"
```

A good use of this property is to save your server the bandwidth and processing needed to send out a page with a visit even if it changes only once in a while. For example, your site may have a weather forecast page. That page may change only once a day. If visitors return to the page in less time than that, you wouldn't want to have to send them a new page. It could just be cached.

Or, say you have a Job Listings page, which you update every Friday. If someone viewed the page on Monday, you would not want the server to continue to dish out the page to visitors if they return on a daily basis until Friday. To solve this problem you could provide code like this:

```
<%
Option Explicit
Dim TheExpireDate
If WeekDay(Date) = 1 then
  TheExpireDate = DateAdd("d", 5, Date)
ElseIf WeekDay(Date) = 2 then
  TheExpireDate = DateAdd("d", 4, Date)
ElseIf WeekDay(Date) = 3 then
  TheExpireDate = DateAdd("d", 3, Date)
```

```
ElseIf WeekDay(Date) = 4 then
   TheExpireDate = DateAdd("d", 2, Date)
ElseIf WeekDay(Date) = 5 then
   TheExpireDate = DateAdd("d", 1, Date)
ElseIf WeekDay(Date) = 6 then
   TheExpireDate = DateAdd("d", 7, Date)
Else
   TheExpireDate = DateAdd("d", 6, Date)
End If
Response.ExpiresAbsolute = TheExpireDate
%>
```

First, we use the `Option Explicit` directive, which tells the compiler that we intend to declare all our variables:

```
Option Explicit
```

Then we declare the variable `TheExpireDate`, which stores the date on which the page will expire:

```
Dim TheExpireDate
```

Remember that the Job Listing page is updated every Friday, so if today's date is a Sunday, the page should expire in 5 days:

```
If WeekDay(Date) = 1 then
   TheExpireDate = DateAdd("d", 5, Date)
```

If today is a Monday, the page should expire in 4 days:

```
ElseIf WeekDay(Date) = 2 then
   TheExpireDate = DateAdd("d", 4, Date)
```

If the current date is a Tuesday, then we need to add 3 days to get to Friday:

```
ElseIf WeekDay(Date) = 3 then
   TheExpireDate = DateAdd("d", 3, Date)
```

Four would be a Wednesday, so 2 days is added to the current date:

```
ElseIf WeekDay(Date) = 4 then
   TheExpireDate = DateAdd("d", 2, Date)
```

We add 1 day to the current date if the current system date is a Thursday:

```
ElseIf WeekDay(Date) = 5 then
   TheExpireDate = DateAdd("d", 1, Date)
```

If today is a Friday, the page is good for a whole week:

```
ElseIf WeekDay(Date) = 6 then
  TheExpireDate = DateAdd("d", 7, Date)
```

For the `Else` condition to evaluate, the day of the week must be Saturday. So 6 days are added:

```
Else
  TheExpireDate = DateAdd("d", 6, Date)
```

The code then uses the `TheExpireDate` variable to set the ExpiresAbsolute property:

```
Response.ExpiresAbsolute = TheExpireDate
```

IsClientConnected Property

The *IsClientConnected property* tells you whether the visitor is still connected to your site. This read-only Boolean property returns a True or False value. If the property returns True, the visitor is still connected. If the property returns False, the visitor has left your page.

The property is usually used in an `If` statement like this:

```
If Response.IsClientConnected = True then
```

But remember that an `If` statement evaluates the expression, so all you need to code is this:

```
If Response.IsClientConnected then
```

You will want to use this property on pages that have code that may take more than a few seconds to run. If the visitor leaves while the code is running, then the code should stop so you can save your system resources. Take a look at this code block:

```
<%
Option Explicit
Dim conn
Dim RSTotals
Response.Buffer = False
set conn = server.createobject ("adodb.connection")
conn.open "Sales", "sa", "yourpassword"
set RSTotals = conn.Execute("select Sum(Sales) as TotalSales from
  Sales99")
response.write RSTotals("TotalSales") & "<P>"
```

```
     If Response.IsClientConnected Then
       set RSTotals = conn.Execute("select Sum(Sales) as TotalSales from
         Sales98")
     response.write RSTotals("TotalSales") & "<P>"
     If Response.IsClientConnected Then
       set RSTotals = conn.Execute("select Sum(Sales) as TotalSales
         from Sales97")
       response.write RSTotals("TotalSales") & "<P>"
     End If
   End If
   %>
```

First, the `Option Explicit` declarative is set and a couple of variables declared:

```
Option Explicit
Dim conn
Dim RSTotals
```

The scenario in this page is that we have a few queries to run and each will take a while to run, so we don't want the page buffered. We want visitors to see the results of each query as they come in, so buffering is turned off:

```
Response.Buffer = False
```

Next, we connect to a database and run a query:

```
set conn = server.createobject ("adodb.connection")
conn.open "Sales", "sa", "yourpassword"
set RSTotals = conn.Execute("select Sum(Sales) as TotalSales from
  Sales99")
```

The code then sends the result of the query to the browser:

```
response.write RSTotals("TotalSales") & "<P>"
```

Next, we should make sure that visitors are still connected because we don't want to run another query if they have left the page:

```
If Response.IsClientConnected Then
```

If they are still connected, the next query runs and writes its result to the browser:

```
set RSTotals = conn.Execute("select Sum(Sales) as TotalSales from
  Sales98")
response.write RSTotals("TotalSales") & "<P>"
```

Then the code checks to see if visitors are still connected before running the final query:

```
If Response.IsClientConnected Then
  set RSTotals = conn.Execute("select Sum(Sales) as TotalSales from
    Sales97")
  response.write RSTotals("TotalSales") & "<P>"
```

PICS Property

The *PICS property* allows you to add a PICS-LABEL to the response header. The property has the following syntax:

```
Response.PICS = Value
```

where the variable `Value` represents the text of the PICS label that you wish to add.

Generally, PICS labels are used to indicate the rating, in terms of its contents. Some browsers and third-party add-on tools look for this tag to determine whether to display a page based on the filtering of the visitor, such as parental content control.

You would use this tag on an Active Server Page that had content that could vary, based on your code. To learn more about rating systems, you may want to visit the Recreational Software Advisory Council at http://www.rsac.org.

Status Property

The last property to look at for the Response object is the *Status property*, which allows you to set the returned status header. For example, you could use this code to fool the browser into thinking the page was not found:

```
Response.Status = 404
```

This code would produce the output shown in Figure 6-5. This can be useful in circumstances where you need to dynamically create a condition that is not really true. Setting the status can also be helpful for debugging purposes to see what will happen when a specific status occurs.

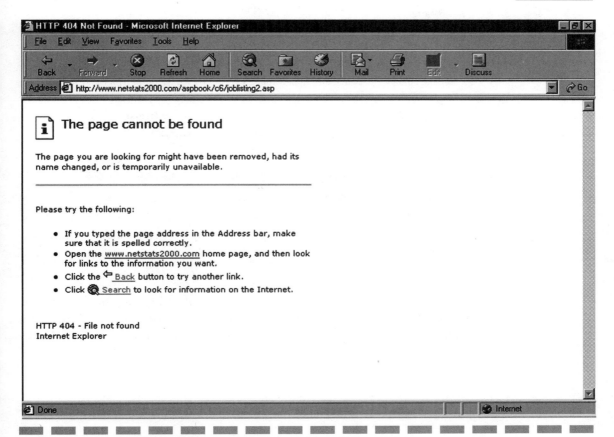

Figure 6-5 Result of setting the status to 404 as viewed from IE 5.

Response Object Methods

The methods of the Response object are discussed below and summarized in Table 6-4.

AddHeader Method

You can use the *AddHeader* to add your own custom header to the output of an HTML page. The method takes the following form:

```
Response.AddHeader NameOfHeader, ValueOfHeader
```

TABLE 6-4

Response Object
Methods

Type	Definition
AddHeader	Allows you to add your own custom header to the response.
AppendToLog	This method provides a way for you to write information to the NT log.
BinaryWrite	This method is used to send nontextual information to the browser.
Clear	Removes any output that has been buffered.
End	Explicitly stops any processing of the code on an Active Server Page.
Flush	Sends the contents of the buffer to the browser.
Redirect	Sends the browser to a different page for the response.
Write	Sends text to the browser.

NameOfHeader is the name that you want to use for the header and *ValueOfHeader* is the value you want sent for the header. Since this method writes to the HTTP header, it must be called prior to any HTML output. For example:

```
Response.AddHeader "StorageValue", "Red63"
```

would create a header entry called StorageValue with the value Red63.

AppendToLog Method

The very handy *AppendToLog method* allows you to add text to the Web Server Log for a specific request. The text can be up to 80 characters and cannot contain commas. The method takes the following form:

```
Response.AddToLog Text2Add
```

`Text2Add` is a variable that contains the text you wish to add to the log. To use this feature, you must have logging turned on for the site in which the page is located. You can do this through the Microsoft Management Console by selecting the WEB SITE and then right-clicking on it and selecting Properties. Select the WEB SITE tab and you should see the dialog displayed in Figure 6-6. Make sure that you have the ENABLE LOGGING checkbox checked.

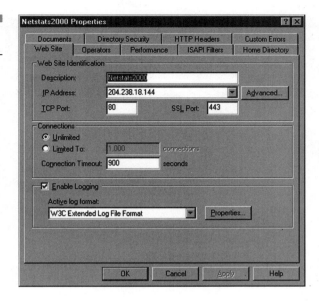

Figure 6-6
Web Site Properties.

If you were to code this:

```
Response.AppendToLog "mymessage"
```

in a W3C formatted log, the entry would be this:

```
1999-08-14 16:27:40 207.66.52.164 - W3SVC3 NETSTATS2000
204.238.18.144 GET
/aspbook/c6/logtry.asp mymessage 200 0 429 382 47088 80 HTTP/1.1
Mozilla/4.0+(compatible;+MSIE+5.0;+Windows+98;+DigExt)
Login=FAVCAT=Music&USERNAME=Dave+Smith;
+NSCookie=207%2E66%2E52%2E130%3A8%2F14%2F99+9%3A45%3A50+AM;
+ASPSESSIONIDQGQQQQPF=GACBAFHAFIIOKEDDDBPAMJHJ -
```

Note that the text we added to the log entry is in the middle of this entry and is in bold. Note also that the text will appear only for a log entry to this specific page.

BinaryWrite Method

The *BinaryWrite method* allows you to send nontextual, raw binary information to the browser. The method takes the following form:

```
Response.BinaryWrite DateToWrite
```

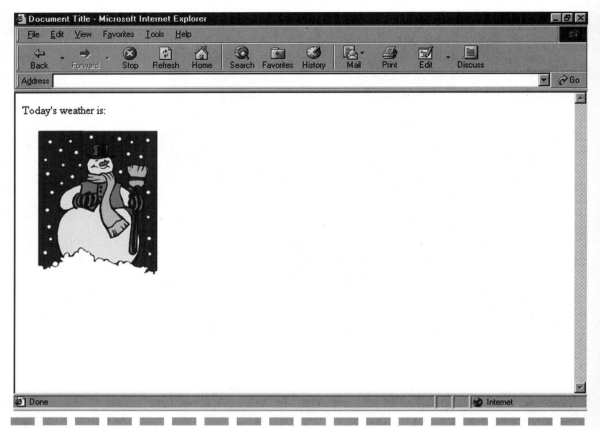

Figure 6-7 Weather page.

The `DataToWrite` variable contains the binary information that you want to send to the browser. Typically, this is used to send data—such as sound or images to a browser—instead of text.

A very nice use of this feature is to use it so you can place an `Active Server Page` tag as the source of an image within a standard HTML page.

For example, say that on your Web site you have a weather page like the one displayed in Figure 6-7. This simple page is produced by the following HTML:

```
<HTML>
<HEAD>
<TITLE>Weatehr</TITLE>
</HEAD>
<BODY>
```

```
<P>Today's whether is:<P>
<IMG SRC="./snowy.gif">
</BODY>
</HTML>
```

The image tag pulls up a picture representing the current weather. You could have the image tag be the output of an Active Server Page by changing the source of the image tag to this:

```
<IMG SRC="./weatherpict.asp">
```

Then within the weatherpict.asp page you would use the BinaryWrite method to return the binary information for the picture that you wanted displayed in that spot on the HTML page. The code on that Active Server Page would be something like this:

```
<%
Option Explicit
Dim conn
Dim RSWeather
Dim ThePicture
set conn = server.createobject ("adodb.connection")
conn.open "Weather", "sa", "yourpassword"
set RSWeather = conn.Execute("select PathToCurrentWeather from
 WeatherCond " _
  & "where WeatherDate = '" & Date & "'")
response.contenttype = "image/gif"
set ObjBin = server.createobject("bin.binary")
ThePicture = ObjBin.ReadFile(RSWeather("PathToCurrentWeather"))
response.binarywrite(ThePicture)
set ObjBin = Nothing
%>
```

First, we tell the browser that we plan on declaring all our variables:

```
Option Explicit
```

Then a couple of database variables are declared:

```
Dim conn
Dim RSWeather
```

Next, a variable is declared that will store the binary data of an image:

```
Dim ThePicture
```

Database code then retrieves the picture representing the current weather:

```
set conn = server.createobject ("adodb.connection")
conn.open "Weather", "sa", "yourpassword"
set RSWeather = conn.Execute("select PathToCurrentWeather from
WeatherCond " _
 & "where WeatherDate = '" & Date & "'")
```

The default return of a page is HTML. This page will return a gif representing the current weather conditions, so the content type needs to be set to reflect that return:

```
response.contenttype = "image/gif"
```

Then we use one of the many third-party controls on the market that allow you to open a binary file:

```
set ObjBin = server.createobject("bin.binary")
ThePicture = ObjBin.ReadFile(RSWeather("PathToCurrentWeather"))
```

That binary file is then written to the browser using the BinaryWrite method of the response object:

```
response.binarywrite(ThePicture)
```

Clear Method

The *Clear method* empties the buffer. Since the method works with the buffer, you must have the Buffer set on or an error will occur. The method has the following syntax:

```
Response.Clear
```

Take a look at this code:

```
<%
Response.Buffer = True
Response.Write "Hello"
Response.Write " World!"
%>
```

This code sends "Hello World!" to the browser. This code:

```
<%
Response.Buffer = True
Response.Write "Hello"
Response.Clear
Response.Write " World!"
%>
```

writes just "World!" to the browser. The "Hello" was in the buffer when the buffer was empty.

Note what this code block would do:

```
<%
Response.Write "Hello"
Response.Clear
Response.Write " World!"
%>
```

This code block produces an error because the buffer was not set to be on.

End Method

The *End method* of the Response object tells the compiler to stop processing any remaining code. It takes the following form:

```
Response.End
```

So using the example in the last section, this:

```
<%
Response.Write "Hello"
Response.Write " World!"
%>
```

would write the text "Hello World!" to the browser. But this:

```
<%
Response.Write "Hello"
Response.End
Response.Write " World!"
%>
```

would write just the text "Hello" to the browser.

If you are buffering your output, the contents of the buffer are sent to the browser when the End method is called. This method is typically used in an If statement. You check some condition, and if the condition is met, you end the processing. For example, if you are adding an employee record to a table, you may check that certain fields are present or of a certain type. If they are not, then you create an error message to display to the visitor and you stop processing.

Flush Method

In this chapter, we have looked at a few properties that control when and what data are sent to the browser. We have looked at the Buffer property, which allows you to hold data before being sent to the browser; we looked at the Clear method, which empties the buffer; and we looked at the End method, which stops the processing of any further code.

One more method allows us to control this type of behavior of the output: the *Flush method*, which sends any buffered output and immediately sends it to the browser. Since the method clears the buffer, an error will occur if the Buffer is not on. The method has the following syntax:

```
Response.Flush
```

With the combination of the Buffer property and the Flush method, you have complete control over at what point different results of your code are sent to the browser.

For example, say you had a page that produces a series of reports in the form of HTML tables that are based on the results of queries run against a sales database. Such a page could look something like the page displayed in Figure 6-8. The page takes 30 seconds to load. Each year takes about 15 seconds and each month takes a few seconds. You have decided that you want to show the visitor each year as the year is done being processed as a single unit. You can accomplish this task by setting the Buffer property to True. Then after each year's code was complete, you could call the Flush method to send that data immediately to the browser.

Redirect Method

The *Redirect method* sends the browser to a different page to receive a response. The method takes the following form:

```
Response.Redirect URL
```

In this case, URL is the page to which the browser is sent.

You will find this method very useful for a variety of uses. The generic main use of the method is to process a request in some way and then

Figure 6-8
Sales Report.

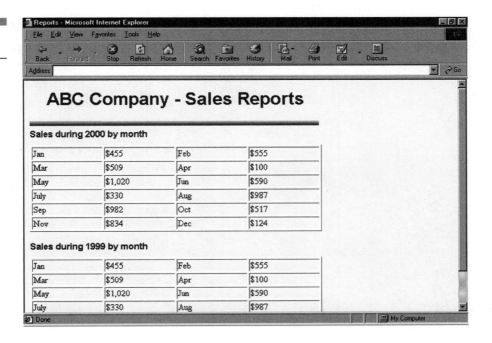

send the person to a different, sometimes non-Active Server Page to view.

For example, you may have a catalog that displays information about your products, such as their price, description, and so forth. You may have a button that the visitor clicks on to place an order that goes to an Active Server Page. The page could also include an icon picture of the product. Such a page is shown in Figure 6-9. When visitors click on the icon of the product, they are shown a larger picture of the product. Typically, this link is just to an image. But for your marketing information you may want to track how many people are requesting to see the larger image of the product. You could do this by linking to an Active Server Page that recorded the request in a database and then redirecting the visitor to the product's large picture.

Another frequent use of the redirect method is with *banner ads*, which are pictures you place on your site that advertise some other site. When visitors click on the banner, they are taken to the advertiser's site. The number of visitors that click on an ad is very important because it is often used in determining how the advertiser is charged.

You would probably want an Active Server Page between the banner ad and the advertiser's site. When the visitor clicks on the banner, the

Figure 6-9
Sample Product
Catalog.

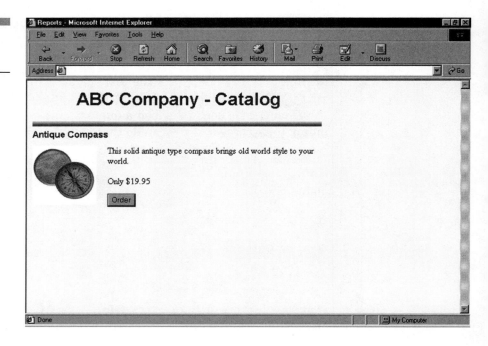

request is sent to an Active Server Page that records the click on the banner ad. The code in the Active Server Page then redirects the visitor to the advertiser's site.

Write Method

The Write Method, which has been used frequently in the last few chapters, is probably the method you will use the most. The *Write method* allows you to return nonbinary data to the browser.

The method takes the following form:

```
Response.Write Text2Write
```

when `Text2Write` is the text you wish to send to the browser. For example, this line of code:

```
Response.Write "Hello World!"
```

would send the text `"Hello World!"` to the browser in the spot where the code was written. You can write text, dates, numbers, and so forth.

You can also embed HTML in the text sent through the Write method:

```
Response.Write "<B>Hello World!</B>"
```

This line of code would write the text `"Hello World!"` to the browser with the HTML tags for bold.

You sometimes need to embed a quote within your string that you are sending to the browser. You can do that by coding like this:

```
Response.Write "Bob said, ""Hello World!"""
```

A double-quote indicates that you want a quote within a quote.

Response Object in Action

In this section, we look at some examples of using the methods, properties, and collection of the Response object to create utilities that you can start using right now. The first sample we look at adds a Select control to a home page that visitors can use to quickly navigate to the most popular page on the site.

We then look at a tool that implements a *Progress Bar*, which is similar to a bar line on a graph but it indicates the amount of progress complete on a task. The tool will utilize buffering to accomplish this task.

After that, we look at a page that allows visitors to store their personal viewing preferences for the site. The Cookies collection is used to store the fonts and colors visitors prefer and the write method is used to customize the look of the page.

NOTE: *This section contains some objects and methods that have not yet been discussed. They are used here to add to the completeness of the demonstration.*

Redirect with a Select

In this sample site, the home page contains standard navigational links to main sections of the Web site. But it also contains a Select control that visitors can use to view the most popular pages on the site. The site utilizes the redirect method to send the visitor to the page in the Select

Figure 6-10
Welcome page using
the select redirect.

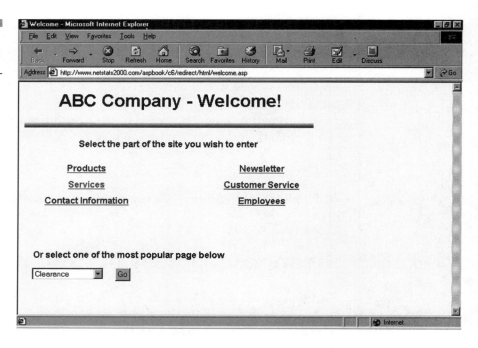

control. It also uses the Write method to populate the Select control. The Home page is shown in Figure 6-10.

The *Select control*, which displays a list of the most popular pages on the Web site, is populated from a list of pages and their locations from a table in the database. Visitors select a page from the list and when they press GO, they are taken to another page of the site. One of the items in the list is the Deal of the Month page. When visitors select it from the list and press the GO button, they are transported to the Deal of the Month page like the one shown in Figure 6-11.

The Select control is populated from a table in an SQL Server database. The table contains the names of the pages that are displayed in the Select control and the URL for the page that is stored as the submitted value for the Select control.

The specifications for the table are displayed in Table 6-5.

The *PageName* field stores the name of the page that is displayed in the Select control to the visitor. The *PageURL* field stores the location of that page.

Code on the Home Page retrieves the data from the C6Redirect table.

```
<%
Option Explicit
```

Figure 6-11

Deal of the Month
page viewed after
clicking on the Select
control.

Figure 6-11
Deal of the Month
page viewed after
clicking on the Select
control.

```
Dim conn
Dim RSMostPopular
set conn = server.createobject ("adodb.connection")
conn.open "ASPBook", "sa", "yourpassword"
set RSMostPopular = conn.Execute("select * from C6Redirect")
%>
```

First, the code tells the compiler that we plan on declaring all our
variables:

```
Option Explicit
```

Then two variables that will be used to connect to the database and to
retrieve the needed data are declared:

```
Dim conn
Dim RSMostPopular
```

TABLE 6-5

C6Redirect Field
Specifications

Field Name	Field Type	Notes
PageName	varchar	Length = 100
PageUrl	varchar	Length = 100

The code then connects to the database and retrieves the data from the most popular pages:

```
set conn = server.createobject ("adodb.connection")
conn.open "ASPBook", "sa", "yourpassword"
set RSMostPopular = conn.Execute("select * from C6Redirect")
```

The data retrieved from the database are used in a second code block that builds the Select control.

```
<SELECT NAME="RedirectTo">
<%
  Do Until RSMostPopular.EOF
%>
  <OPTION VALUE="<% response.write RSMostPopular("PageURL") %>">
    <% response.write RSMostPopular("PageName") %></OPTION>
<%
    RSMostPopular.MoveNext
  Loop
%>
</SELECT>
```

The Select control is called RedirectTo:

```
<SELECT NAME="RedirectTo">
```

Next, the code starts a loop that will take it through all the records in the most popular pages table:

```
<%
  Do Until RSMostPopular.EOF
%>
```

The Write method of the response object is used to add options to the Select control. Notice that the Write method is in line with the HTML. Also notice that there are two writes per record: the *first write* stores the internal value for the option, the page to go to if the visitor selects that page; the *second write* contains the name of the page that is displayed to the visitor:

```
<OPTION VALUE="<% response.write RSMostPopular("PageURL") %>">
  <% response.write RSMostPopular("PageName") %></OPTION>
```

The code then moves on to the next record before looping:

```
<%
    RSMostPopular.MoveNext
  Loop
%>
```

TABLE 6-6

C6Redirect Table
Sample Records

Page	Definition
Clearance	./clearance.asp
Deal of the Month	./deal_of_the_month.html
Phone Numbers	../index.html
Email Us	mailto:jsmith@whatever.com

Table 6-6 shows some sample records that could be entered into the table. The sample records in Table 6-6 would produce the following HTML:

```
<SELECT NAME="RedirectTo">
  <OPTION VALUE="./clearance.asp ">Clearance</OPTION>
  <OPTION VALUE="./deal_of_the_month.html">Deal of the
Month</OPTION>
  <OPTION VALUE="../index.html">Phone Numbers</OPTION>
  <OPTION VALUE="mailto:jsmith@whatever.com">Email Us</OPTION>
</SELECT>
```

Notice the Email Us entry, which will work just like an email link and will open an email on the visitor's system that is addressed to the address in the value field.

When the visitor presses the *Go* button, the form is submitted to the redirectcombo.asp page as specified in the Form tag:

```
<FORM NAME="LAYOUTFORM" ACTION="./redirectcombo.asp" METHOD=POST>
```

The code on that page redirects the visitor as requested:

```
<%
If not isempty(Request.Form("RedirectTo")) Then
  Response.Redirect Request.Form("RedirectTo")
else
  Response.Redirect "../index.html"
End If
%>
```

First, the code makes sure that the form field RedirectTo was submitted with the form:

```
If not isempty(Request.Form("RedirectTo")) Then
```

If it was, visitors are sent to the URL specified in the RedirectTo field:

```
Response.Redirect Request.Form("RedirectTo")
```

otherwise, they have entered this page in a way by which it was not meant to be accessed. So the visitor is sent to the Home Page:

```
Response.Redirect "../index.html"
```

Progress Bar

This sample page shows you how you can create a *Progress Bar* that provides the visitor with the visual cue of how far a task is in the progress of its completion. The tool utilizes the Write method to control the output of the HTML. It also sets buffering on and it uses the Flush method to control exactly when certain output is displayed to the visitor.

When visitors first enter the page, they see a page like the one in Figure 6-12. The page then starts its lengthy process to create the report. The Progress Bar indicates where the process is, as shown in Figure 6-13.

Figure 6-12
Progress Bar in its initial state.

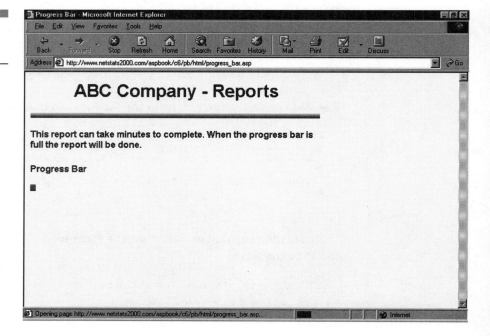

Figure 6-13
Progress Bar with process half complete.

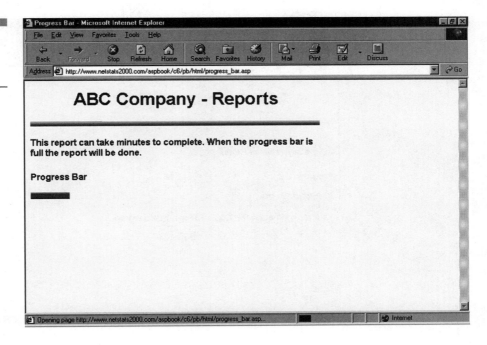

The Progress Bar continues to show the visitor that the page is still working, until the page finally is complete and the visitor sees the results as shown in Figure 6-14.

The code to create the progress bar uses some time delays to simulate the lengthy running of code to create the report. The first code block is:

```
<%
Option Explicit
Response.Buffer = True
Dim DelayTime
%>
```

First, the compiler is told that we will declare our variables:

```
Option Explicit
```

Then we set the Buffer on since we will be using the Flush method:

```
Response.Buffer = True
```

A variable that will hold the delay time is then created to simulate a lengthy process:

```
Dim DelayTime
```

Figure 6-14
The Progress Bar is
now complete.

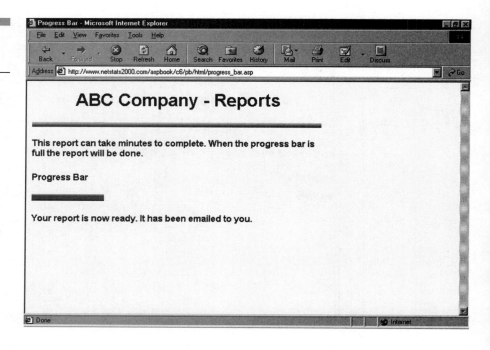

The next code block draws the Progress Bar:

```
<%
Response.Write "<IMG HEIGHT=12 WIDTH=10 SRC=""../assets/images/
  redbar2.gif"" BORDER=0>"
Response.Flush
DelayTime = Second(Time) + 10
If DelayTime > 59 Then
   DelayTime = DelayTime - 60
End If
Do Until Second(Time) = DelayTime
Loop
Response.Write "<IMG HEIGHT=12 WIDTH=10
SRC=""../assets/images/redbar2.gif"" BORDER=0>"
Response.Write "<IMG HEIGHT=12 WIDTH=10
SRC=""../assets/images/redbar2.gif"" BORDER=0>"
Response.Flush
DelayTime = Second(Time) + 5
If DelayTime > 59 Then
   DelayTime = DelayTime - 60
End If
Do Until Second(Time) = DelayTime
Loop
Response.Write "<IMG HEIGHT=12 WIDTH=10
SRC=""../assets/images/redbar2.gif"" BORDER=0>"
Response.Flush
DelayTime = Second(Time) + 16
If DelayTime > 59 Then
   DelayTime = DelayTime - 60
```

```
End If
Do Until Second(Time) = DelayTime
Loop
Response.Write "<IMG HEIGHT=12 WIDTH=10
SRC=""../assets/images/redbar2.gif"" BORDER=0>"
Response.Write "<IMG HEIGHT=12 WIDTH=10
SRC=""../assets/images/redbar2.gif"" BORDER=0>"
Response.Write "<IMG HEIGHT=12 WIDTH=10
SRC=""../assets/images/redbar2.gif"" BORDER=0>"
Response.Flush
DelayTime = Second(Time) + 1
If DelayTime > 59 Then
   DelayTime = DelayTime - 60
End If
Do Until Second(Time) = DelayTime
Loop
Response.Write "<IMG HEIGHT=12 WIDTH=10
SRC=""../assets/images/redbar2.gif"" BORDER=0>"
Response.Flush
DelayTime = Second(Time) + 1
If DelayTime > 59 Then
   DelayTime = DelayTime - 60
End If
Do Until Second(Time) = DelayTime
Loop
Response.Write "<IMG HEIGHT=12 WIDTH=10 RC=""../assets/images/
   redbar2.gif"" BORDER=0>"
Response.Flush
DelayTime = Second(Time) + 1
If DelayTime > 59 Then
   DelayTime = DelayTime - 60
End If
Do Until Second(Time) = DelayTime
Loop
Response.Write "<IMG HEIGHT=12 WIDTH=10
SRC=""../assets/images/redbar2.gif"" BORDER=0>"
Response.Flush
DelayTime = Second(Time) + 1
If DelayTime > 59 Then
   DelayTime = DelayTime - 60
End If
Do Until Second(Time) = DelayTime
Loop
Response.Write "<IMG HEIGHT=12 WIDTH=10
SRC=""../assets/images/redbar2.gif"" BORDER=0>"
Response.Write "<IMG HEIGHT=12 WIDTH=10
SRC=""../assets/images/redbar2.gif"" BORDER=0>"
Response.Write "<IMG HEIGHT=12 WIDTH=10
SRC=""../assets/images/redbar2.gif"" BORDER=0>"
Response.Flush
%>
```

First, the Write method is used to place the first bar of the Progress Bar so the visitor sees some progress from the start.

```
Response.Write "<IMG HEIGHT=12 WIDTH=10 SRC=""../assets/images/
   redbar2.gif"" BORDER=0>"
```

Notice that the Write method is writing an HTML image tag. Also notice the double-quotes, which indicate a quote within a quote.

That HTML tag is then flushed from the Buffer:

```
Response.Flush
```

Next, to simulate a delay, the current seconds of the time is retrieved. Ten is added to that value to simulate a delay of 10 s:

```
DelayTime = Second(Time) + 10
```

Since adding 10 to the current seconds on the time could bring that value above 59, it is checked:

```
If DelayTime > 59 Then
```

If the number is above 59, 60 is subtracted to bring the seconds back in range:

```
DelayTime = DelayTime - 60
```

The code then delays for 10 s to demonstrate the use of the Progress Bar:

```
Do Until Second(Time) = DelayTime
Loop
```

Then progress images are written to the Buffer to indicate the progress made by completing this section of the code:

```
Response.Write "<IMG HEIGHT=12 WIDTH=10
SRC=""../assets/images/redbar2.gif"" BORDER=0>"
Response.Write "<IMG HEIGHT=12 WIDTH=10
SRC=""../assets/images/redbar2.gif"" BORDER=0>"
```

Those lines are then flushed from the buffer and sent to the browser:

```
Response.Flush
```

The process then repeats itself as more progress is made on the overall task. As you look through the code block, notice that different code blocks receive differing amounts of progress images. You should apply this type of weighting to your code blocks. Think about how long a task will take and give it a proportional amount of progress indication compared to the other code blocks within the overall progress.

Preferences Page

The *Preferences page* shows you how you can store the look and feel of your site chosen by visitors, who are allowed to select the fonts and colors of the page. Then when they return to the site, they see the page based on their preferences.

The page uses the Cookies collection to store and retrieve visitors' preferences. The Write method is used to display the contents of the page in the format requested by visitors.

When visitors first view the page, they see default color scheme displayed in Figure 6-15.

Visitors can then select their color and font scheme. When they press the SAVE button, their preferences are saved and they see their chosen view of the page like the one shown in Figure 6-16.

Since the preferences are stored in a cookie, the next time visitors enter the page, they see the page the way in which they have selected the look and feel. If the cookie is gone, or they are on a different system, visitors see the page again with the original color scheme.

The code on the page stores and retrieves the cookie values. The code determines whether the form has been submitted and takes appropriate

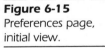

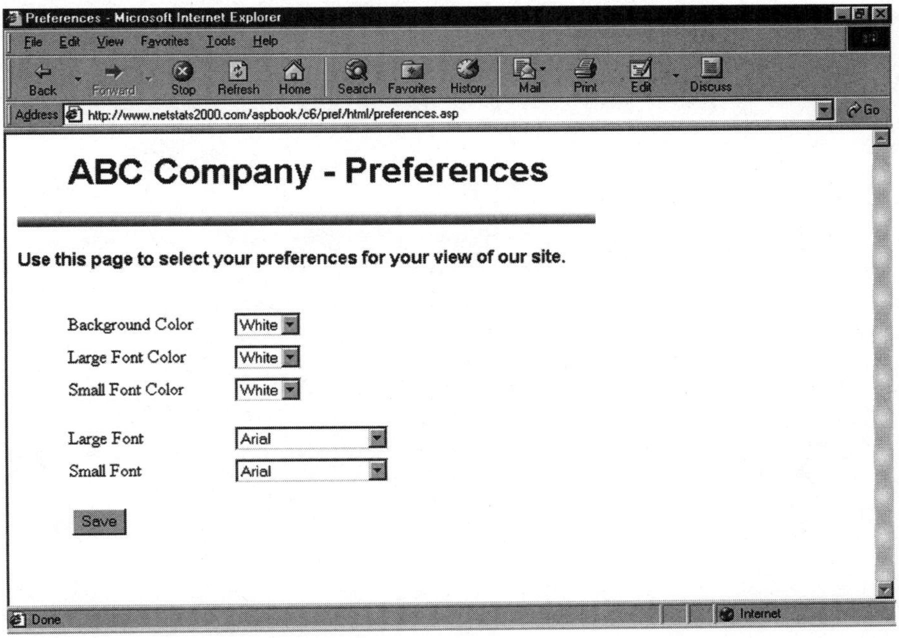

Figure 6-15
Preferences page, initial view.

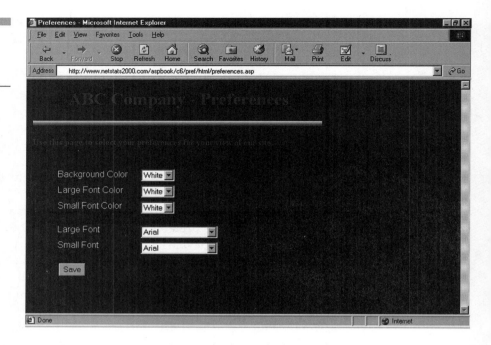

action based on that condition. The code also formats the page itself based on the visitor's selection. The main code block is:

```
<%
Option Explicit
Dim BackgroundColor
Dim LargeFontColor
Dim SmallFontColor
Dim LargeFont
Dim SmallFont
If IsEmpty(Request.Form("Save")) Then
  If not len(Request.Cookies("Prefs")("BackgroundColor")) > 0 Then
     Response.Cookies("Prefs")("BackgroundColor") = "#FFFFFF"
     BackgroundColor = "#FFFFFF"
     Response.Cookies("Prefs")("LargeFontColor") = "#000000"
     LargeFontColor = "#000000"
     Response.Cookies("Prefs")("SmallFontColor") = "#000000"
     SmallFontColor = "#000000"
     Response.Cookies("Prefs")("LargeFont") =
"Arial,Helvetica,Univers,Zurich BT"
     LargeFont = "Arial,Helvetica,Univers,Zurich BT"
     Response.Cookies("Prefs")("SmallFont") = "Times New
Roman,Times,Times NewRoman"
     SmallFont = "Times New Roman,Times,Times NewRoman"
     Response.Cookies("Prefs").Expires = "2/2/2002"
  Else
     BackgroundColor = Request.Cookies("Prefs")("BackgroundColor")
```

```
      LargeFontColor = Request.Cookies("Prefs")("LargeFontColor")
      SmallFontColor = Request.Cookies("Prefs")("SmallFontColor")
      LargeFont = Request.Cookies("Prefs")("LargeFont")
      SmallFont = Request.Cookies("Prefs")("SmallFont")
   End If
else
   Response.Cookies("Prefs")("BackgroundColor") = Request.Form
      ("BackgroundColor")
   BackgroundColor = Request.Form("BackgroundColor")
   Response.Cookies("Prefs")("LargeFontColor") = Request.Form
      ("LargeFontColor")
   LargeFontColor = Request.Form("LargeFontColor")
   Response.Cookies("Prefs")("SmallFontColor") = Request.Form
      ("SmallFontColor")
   SmallFontColor = Request.Form("SmallFontColor")
   Response.Cookies("Prefs")("LargeFont") = Request.Form
      ("LargeFont")
   LargeFont = Request.Form("LargeFont")
   Response.Cookies("Prefs")("SmallFont") = Request.Form
      ("SmallFont")
   SmallFont = Request.Form("SmallFont")
   Response.Cookies("Prefs").Expires = "2/2/2002"
end if
%>
```

The code first lets the compiler know that the variables will be declared:

```
Option Explicit
```

Then the variables that will store the visitor's preferences or the default preferences are declared:

```
Dim BackgroundColor
Dim LargeFontColor
Dim SmallFontColor
Dim LargeFont
Dim SmallFont
```

Next, the state is determined. If the SAVE button is not present, then the form has not been submitted:

```
If IsEmpty(Request.Form("Save")) Then
```

That means this is the first viewing of the page in this session. The code then checks to see if visitors have the Preferences cookie on their machine by using the Len function to test the length of one of the sub-keys of the Preferences cookie:

```
If not len(Request.Cookies("Prefs")("BackgroundColor")) > 0 Then
```

If the cookie is not present, a cookie is created that places the default preferences on the visitor's system:

```
Response.Cookies("Prefs")("BackgroundColor") = "#FFFFFF"
```

Next, a variable that is used to modify the page inline is set to the default preference:

```
BackgroundColor = "#FFFFFF"
```

The same method is used to store the other preferences:

```
Response.Cookies("Prefs")("LargeFontColor") = "#000000"
LargeFontColor = "#000000"
Response.Cookies("Prefs")("SmallFontColor") = "#000000"
SmallFontColor = "#000000"
Response.Cookies("Prefs")("LargeFont") = "Arial,Helvetica,
    Univers,Zurich BT"
LargeFont = "Arial,Helvetica,Univers,Zurich BT"
Response.Cookies("Prefs")("SmallFont") = "Times New Roman,Times,
    Times NewRoman"
SmallFont = "Times New Roman,Times,Times NewRoman"
```

Next, an expiration date is set for the cookie:

```
Response.Cookies("Prefs").Expires = "2/2/2002"
```

The `Else` portion of the second-level `If` statement means that visitors are just entering this page but have been here before. So they have the Preferences cookie and that cookie is used to set the variables that will be used to define the look and feel of this page:

```
BackgroundColor = Request.Cookies("Prefs")("BackgroundColor")
LargeFontColor = Request.Cookies("Prefs")("LargeFontColor")
SmallFontColor = Request.Cookies("Prefs")("SmallFontColor")
LargeFont = Request.Cookies("Prefs")("LargeFont")
SmallFont = Request.Cookies("Prefs")("SmallFont")
```

The `Else` portion of the main `If` statement is for the condition in which the form has been submitted. In that case, the submitted values are used to repopulate the cookie:

```
Response.Cookies("Prefs")("BackgroundColor") = Request.Form
    ("BackgroundColor")
```

It is also used to set the value for the default preferences for the current page:

```
BackgroundColor = Request.Form("BackgroundColor")
```

The same is done for the other preferences:

```
Response.Cookies("Prefs")("LargeFontColor") = Request.Form
  ("LargeFontColor")
LargeFontColor = Request.Form("LargeFontColor")
Response.Cookies("Prefs")("SmallFontColor") = Request.Form
  ("SmallFontColor")
SmallFontColor = Request.Form("SmallFontColor")
Response.Cookies("Prefs")("LargeFont") = Request.Form("LargeFont")
LargeFont = Request.Form("LargeFont")
Response.Cookies("Prefs")("SmallFont") = Request.Form("SmallFont")
SmallFont = Request.Form("SmallFont")
```

And an expiration date is set for the cookie:

```
Response.Cookies("Prefs").Expires = "2/2/2002"
```

In line with the HTML, the page is formatted according to the default preferences or the preferences selected by the visitor. For example, this line of code sets the value for the background color:

```
<BODY BGCOLOR="<% response.Write BackgroundColor %>">
```

And this line of code sets the font and color for one of the lines of text:

```
<FONT FACE="<% response.Write LargeFont %>" Color="
<% response.Write LargeFontColor %>">
```

Server Object

Getting in at the Top

So far we have looked at the Request object that, as you have seen, allows you to get information about the visitor. We have also looked at the Response object, which we used to send information back to the visitor's browser. In this chapter, we look at another object from the Active Server Page object model, the Server object.

The *Server object* provides you with one property and four methods that allow you to communicate and use functionality of the *Internet Information Server* (IIS). You communicate with IIS in the sense that you can change how the server works with a page. The functionality of the Server object allows you to take actions in your script for which the script itself doesn't supply the mechanism.

Figure 7-1 displays the role of the Server object in the Active Server Page processing model. Following the model, visitors type in the page they want to see or they click on a link or part of the page they are on, which is an Active Server Page. The request travels through the Internet to your server. Your server retrieves the requested page and, if it is an Active Server Page, it begins processing. The role of the Server object is, at this point, when the code is being processed. The Server object allows you to bring other components into the processing of the page and allows you to communicate with the server itself. The processed page is then sent to the visitor's browser.

Figure 7-1
Role of the Server object in the Active Server Page object model.

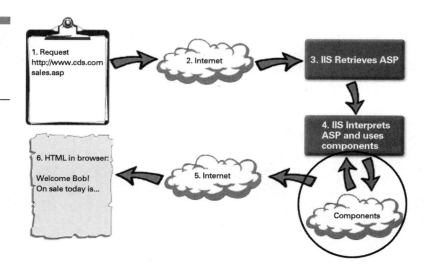

Server Object Property

The Server object contains just one property that allows you to communicate with the Server. That property is discussed below and summarized in Table 7-1.

ScriptTimeout Property

For a variety of reasons, your code can take a long time to process. The server may be very busy, a component may be stuck in a loop, or your own programming logic may have the code repeating endlessly. Mainly for those reasons, you can set the maximum amount of time your script should be allowed to run before it stops and returns an error to the browser making the request.

You can set this maximum run time at the Web-server level by viewing its properties and pressing the CONFIGURATION button on the HOME DIRECTORY tab. You can set this property at the Web-site level in the same way. You can also set the property at the ASP Application level by right-clicking on the application within the Microsoft Management Console view of IIS and selecting Properties. Then if you click on the DIRECTORY tab, followed by the CONFIGURATION button, you should see the dialog shown in Figure 7-2.

On the APP OPTIONS tab of this dialog is the text box labeled ASP SCRIPT TIMEOUT. Here you can set the maximum number of seconds that a script is allowed to run.

From within your code, you can extend the amount of time you allow the script to run by using the *ScriptTimeout property* of the Server object. The property has the following syntax:

```
Sever.ScriptTimeout = NumberOfSeconds
```

The variable `NumberOfSeconds` is the number of seconds the script can run for before it times out.

	Property	Purpose
TABLE 7-1 Server Object Property	ScriptTimeout	Seconds an Active Server Page can run before it times out.

Figure 7-2
Setting the maximum
time an Active Server
Page can run.

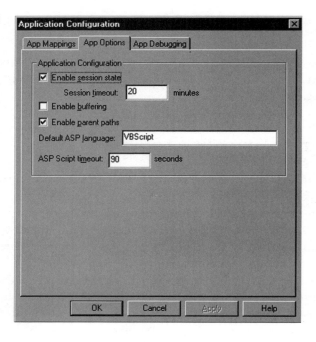

You can view the value of this property in the browser window by writing code like this:

```
<%
Response.Write "<B>This page can run for "
Response.Write Server.ScriptTimeout
Response.Write " seconds before it times out.</B>"
%>
```

The page will print out the default value for the property as shown in Figure 7-3.

You can also set the value of the property in code to give your code a longer period of time to complete its processing. This code set the maximum time allowed to 200 seconds:

```
<%
Server.ScriptTimeout = 200
Response.Write "<B>This page can run for "
Response.Write Server.ScriptTimeout
Response.Write " seconds before it times out.</B>"
%>
```

The output of this code shows you that the value has been changed and is displayed in Figure 7-4. The value you place in the property must be a number and it must be above zero; if it is not, an error will occur.

Figure 7-3
Output of displaying
the ScriptTimeout
property.

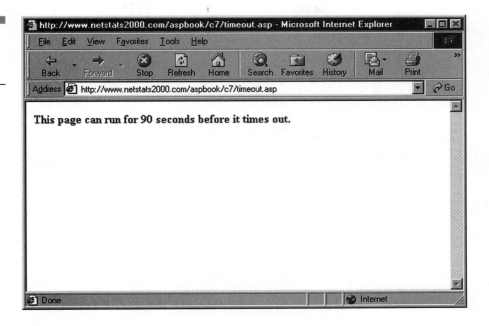

Figure 7-4
Output of program-
matically changed
property value.

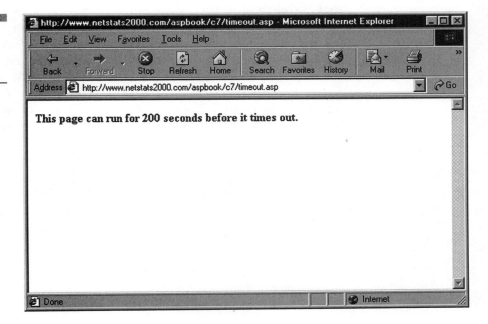

Server Object Method

The Server object has four methods that you can use for a variety of tasks. The methods are discussed below and summarized in Table 7-2.

CreateObject Method

You've already seen this method used frequently in this book. Without it, in fact, Active Server Pages would be so limited in functionality that they would rarely be used.

The CreateObject method allows you to instantiate a *server component*, which refers to an object, usually a DLL, on your server that has its own objects, collections, methods, properties, and/or events. The term *instantiate* means that in your code you can access the server component.

You can think of these server components in three different categories. There are server components that come with the Internet Information Server. These components are specifically provided because they are designed to extend what you can do with Active Server Pages. These components include the *Browser Capabilities component*, which provides you with information about the browser making the request; *Ad Rotator component*, which provides you with an easy way to include and manage banner ads on your site; and the *Page Counter component* that can be used to provide hit information.

The second type of server component you will use are those that are on your server that provide some other additional functionality to your page but are not necessarily designed for Active Server Pages. This type of server component would include *Microsoft Word*, which you could use to format text in the form of a Word document; a *Graph Generator*, which would create a graph image based on your input on the fly that you could include on your Web page; or an advanced mathematical pro-

TABLE 7-2

Server Object
Methods

Object	Purpose
CreateObject	Allows for the creation of a server component.
HTMLEncode	Encodes text into an HTML encoded format.
MapPath	Returns the physical path for a virtual or relative path.
URLEncode	Modifies the text passed so that it is encoded in URL format.

gram whose code you would use to provide some scientific calculation result on your page.

The final type of server component would be the ones you create yourself. At some point, you will need to create a procedure that you can't do from within Active Server Pages and for which you can't find an existing server. On occasion you will create such a component as a workaround for some bug or deficiency within Active Server Pages. Another reason that you may create your own server components is for purposes of *encapsulation*, which means that you want to place code in one place and then use the code in a variety of locations; then, if the code needs to be changed, it needs to be changed in only one location.

The method has the following format:

```
Set MyObject = Server.CreateObject(NameOfAppClass)
```

You must start the declaration with the keyword Set. If you do not (which is easy to forget) you will see an error like the one displayed in Figure 7-5.

The difficult part about dealing with this error is that the error message isn't descriptive. Also, the error doesn't occur at the point where you use the CreateObject statement; it occurs where the object is first used through its methods and properties.

Figure 7-5
CreateObject error.

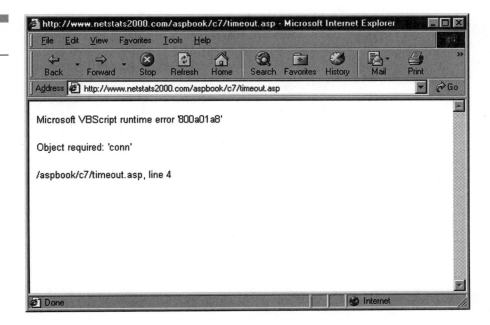

Microsoft VBScript runtime error '800a01a8'

Object required: 'conn'

/aspbook/c7/timeout.asp, line 4

In the preceding syntax of the call, `MyObject` is the variable that will become the instance of the Server object. The single parameter `NameOfAppClass` is passed to the CreateObject method. This parameter is generally a string and contains the name of the server and the class within the server that you wish to create. So the form of the string is referred to as the *App.Class*.

For example, if you wanted to create a connection to a database you could code like this:

```
set Conn = server.createobject ("ADODB.Connection")
```

In this example, the application server's name is ADODB. The class within that server that you wish to create is called *Connection*. The object being created is placed in the variable `Conn`.

Let's take a look at another example:

```
set MyWord = createobject("Word.Application")
```

Here the variable called `MyWord` will be an object provided by the Word server component's class called *Application*.

Once you create your object you can start using the methods, properties, and collections of that object. This example shows how you would do that.

```
<%
Option Explicit
Dim conn
Dim RSEmp
set conn = server.createobject ("adodb.connection")
conn.open "ASPBook", "sa", "yourpassword"
conn.execute "delete from Emps where EmpID = " &
Request.Form("EmpID")
set RSEmp = conn.Execute("select * from Emps where EmpID = " _
  & Request.Form("NewEmpID"))
Response.Write "<P>" & RSEmp("FirstName")
Response.Write "<P>" & RSEmp("LastName")
set conn = Nothing
set RSEmp = Nothing
%>
```

First, the compiler is told that we will be declaring our variables. Remember that this aids greatly in debugging large Active Server Pages:

```
Option Explicit
```

Next, two variables are defined. One will store a connection object to a database:

```
Dim conn
```

The other will hold a recordset of data from a database:

```
Dim RSEmp
```

Here the CreateObject method is used to create an object of the ADODB application of class-type Connection:

```
set conn = server.createobject ("adodb.connection")
```

Now that we have created this connection, we can start using it. Here the Open method of the Connection object is used to connect to a specific Data Source Name:

```
conn.open "ASPBook", "sa", "yourpassword"
```

Next, the Execute method of the Connection object is used to delete a record from the database:

```
conn.execute "delete from Emps where EmpID = " & Request.Form
  ("EmpID")
```

In the next line of code, the Execute method is once again used, but this time it is used to return another object:

```
set RSEmp = conn.Execute("select * from Emps where EmpID = " _
  & Request.Form("NewEmpID"))
```

The variable RSEmp is created not with the CreateObject method but with a method of the Execute method of the connection object. But RSEmp is an object and it is an object of the Recordset type. The type contains a Fields collection that is used to retrieve data from the fields in the database:

```
Response.Write "<P>" & RSEmp("FirstName")
Response.Write "<P>" & RSEmp("LastName")
```

Since these are objects that are more complex than just a standard variable that would store a number or some text, they use more resources. You can release the resources used by an object by setting it to equal nothing, like this:

```
set conn = Nothing
set RSEmp = Nothing
```

In this next code example, an instance of the Collaborative Data object is created. This object is used to send email and to work through code with Microsoft Exchange.

```
<%
Option Explicit
Dim objMail
Set objMail = CreateObject("CDONTS.NewMail")
objMail.Send "susan@whatever.com", "jill@whatever.com", "Hello",
  "How are you?"
Set objMail = Nothing
%>
```

First, we state that we will declare our variables:

```
Option Explicit
```

Then a variable to hold the email object is created:

```
Dim objMail
```

The CreateObject method is used to create an instance of the NewMail class of the CDONTS server:

```
Set objMail = CreateObject("CDONTS.NewMail")
```

The Send method of the NewMail object is used to send an email message. Four parameters are passed into the method:

```
objMail.Send "susan@whatever.com", "jill@whatever.com", _
"Hello", "How are you?"
```

The resources of the object are then released:

```
Set objMail = Nothing
```

HTML Encode Method

Say you have a Web page that displays quiz questions through an Active Server Page that tests the students' understanding of numeric comparison. For example, let's say you want to display a question like that shown in Figure 7-6.

Figure 7-6
Quiz page sample.

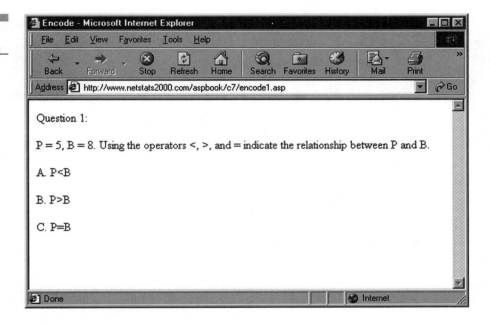

Notice the use of the < and > signs, which of course have special meaning on a Web page. If the Active Server Page contained the following code, you would not get the desired output:

```
<%
Response.Write "Question 1:" & "<P>"
Response.Write "P = 5, B = 8. Using the operators <, >, and =
 indicate " _
  & "the relationship between P and B." & "<P>"
Response.Write "A. P<B" & "<P>"
Response.Write "B. P>B" & "<P>"
Response.Write "C. P=B" & "<P>"
%>
```

Instead you would get the page shown in Figure 7-7. Notice that the answers on the page are not what were desired. That is because some of the text was interpreted by the browser as HTML tags.

You can get around this problem using the HTML encode method of the server object, which has the following syntax:

```
ConvertedText = Server.HTMLEncode(TextToConvert)
```

The `TextToConvert` variable is the text you wish to convert. The `ConvertedText` is the HTML encoded text returned by the method. So if we changed our code in the previous example to this:

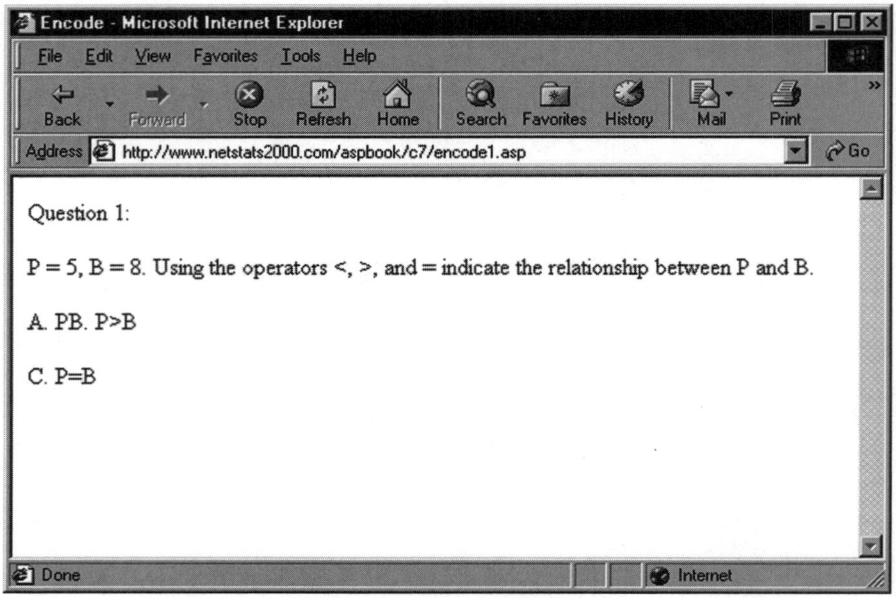

Figure 7-7
Text incorrect on
Quiz page.

```
<%
Response.Write "Question 1:" & "<P>"
Response.Write "P = 5, B = 8. Using the operators <, >, and =
  indicate " _
  & "the relationship between P and B." & "<P>"
Response.Write Server.HTMLEncode("A. P<B") & "<P>"
Response.Write Server.HTMLEncode("B. P>B") & "<P>"
Response.Write Server.HTMLEncode("C. P=B") & "<P>"
%>
```

we would then get the desired output because the text would have the proper HTML encoded escape sequences as shown here:

```
A. P&lt;B<P>B. P&gt;B<P>C. P=B<P>
```

MapPath Method

The *MapPath method* of the Server object converts a virtual or relative path as viewed through the Web server into its real physical path. The method takes the following syntax:

```
ConvertedPath = Server.MapPath(PathToConvert)
```

The `PathToConvert` variable is the path you wish to convert and the `ConvertedPath` variable is the path converted into its physical directory.

For example:

```
<%
Response.Write "Path to parent directory: " & "<BR>"
Response.Write Server.MapPath("../") & "<P>" & "<P>"
Response.Write "Path to current directory: " & "<BR>"
Response.Write Server.MapPath ("./") & "<P>" & "<P>"
Response.Write "Path to file in current directory: " & "<BR>"
Response.Write Server.MapPath ("myfile.txt") & "<P>" & "<P>"
Response.Write "Path to root directory: " & "<BR>"
Response.Write Server.MapPath ("/") & "<P>" & "<P>"
%>
```

First, the path to the current directory is mapped:

```
Response.Write Server.MapPath("../") & "<P>" & "<P>"
```

Next, the path of the current directory is mapped:

```
Response.Write Server.MapPath ("./") & "<P>" & "<P>"
```

Then, a file in the current directory is mapped:

```
Response.Write Server.MapPath ("myfile.txt") & "<P>" & "<P>"
```

Last, the server root is mapped:

```
Response.Write Server.MapPath ("/") & "<P>" & "<P>"
```

The output of the code is shown in Figure 7-8.

URLEncode Method

When you submit a form through the Post method, or you provide a link with a query string, the text in the query string needs to exclude certain characters since the text becomes part of the link.

For example, say that you want to search for the meaning of http:// and you go to a search engine to look it up. When you type in that search and press the SUBMIT button, you will see the results of your search. Part of the link to the search result is your search query. Notice that now your search string of http:// is converted to this:

```
http%3A%2F%2F
```

The character of the colon is converted to something that won't be rejected or confusing to your browser and the server. You can accomplish

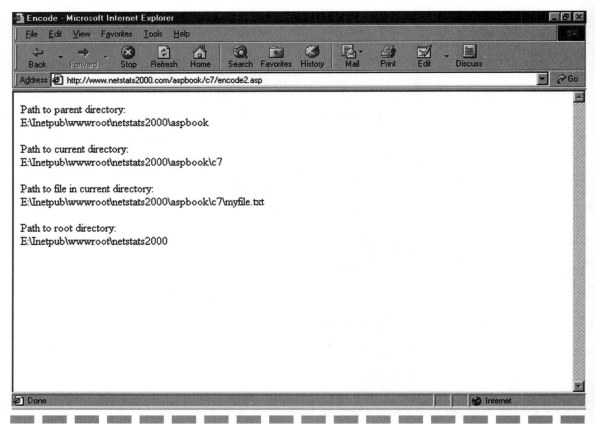

Figure 7-8 Output of the MapPath method.

this task in your code manually using the URLEncode method, which has the following syntax:

```
ConvertedText = Server.URLEncode(Text2Convert)
```

where Text2Convert is the text that you wish to convert and ConvertedText is the result of the method. Take this code example:

```
<%
Response.Write Server.URLEncode("Hello? World!") & "<P>"
Response.Write Server.URLEncode("http://www.whatever.com") & "<P>"
Response.Write Server.URLEncode("Yes, 10% of $20.") & "<P>"
Response.Write Server.URLEncode("`;:[]{}") & "<P>"
%>
```

Figure 7-9
Result of the
URLEncode code.

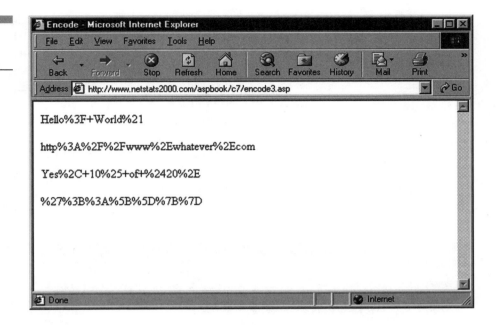

The result of this code is displayed in Figure 7-9.

Server Object in Action

In this section, we look at a solution that uses the Server object and the other objects we discussed thus far. The example looks at using the CreateObject method of the Server object to create an instance of Microsoft Word that we will use to create custom Word documents.

Office Automation

In this sample, we use the Microsoft Word server in code to generate a Word document. The visitor will supply us with specific data for the Word document; that information will be married with a template document. The customized Word document is then displayed to the visitor.

The code utilizes the CreateObject method of the server to instantiate Word. The code also uses the MapPath method of the Server object to indicate the physical location of the template file and the physical location of the resulting Word document. The Request and Response objects are also used to retrieve the visitor's input and to send the visitor to the resulting Word document.

Before we look at the code, take a look at what the code actually does. When visitors first enter the tool, they see a menu like the one displayed in Figure 7-10. You would list on this page all the form letters that were available. If visitors select the Balance Due Form Letter, they will see the form shown in Figure 7-11.

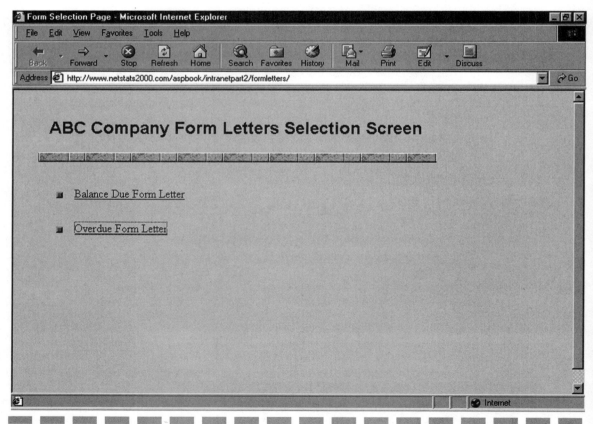

Figure 7-10 Menu for Word Form Letter tool.

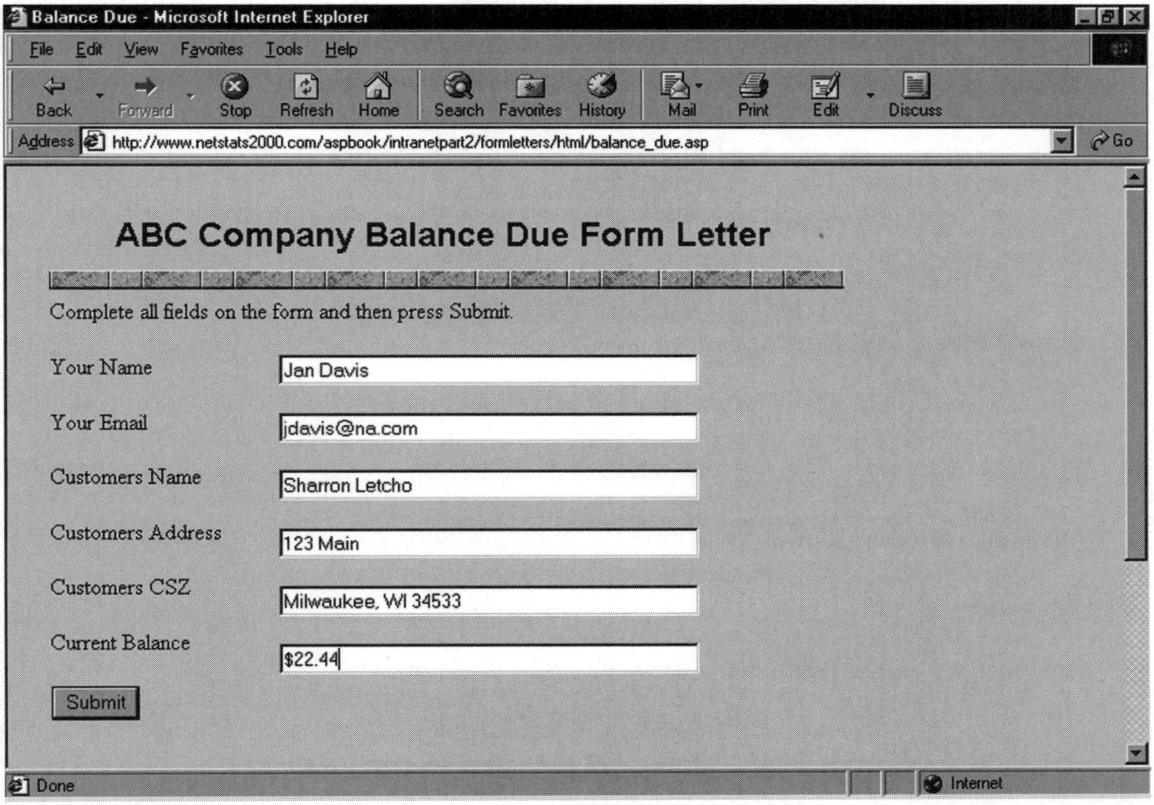

Figure 7-11 Balance Due Form Letter.

Most of the fields on the Balance Due form refer to bookmarks in the Word template where the text of these fields will go. The form submits the data entered back to itself for processing:

```
<FORM ACTION="./balance_due.asp" METHOD=POST>
```

The code determines whether to display the form by checking for the presence of the SUBMIT button. If it is there, then the form must have been submitted.

When the visitor presses the SUBMIT button, the server loads an instance of Word to create the document. The visitor is then redirected to that document once it is complete, as shown in Figure 7-12. Notice the text on this page. It contains the data we entered on the previous

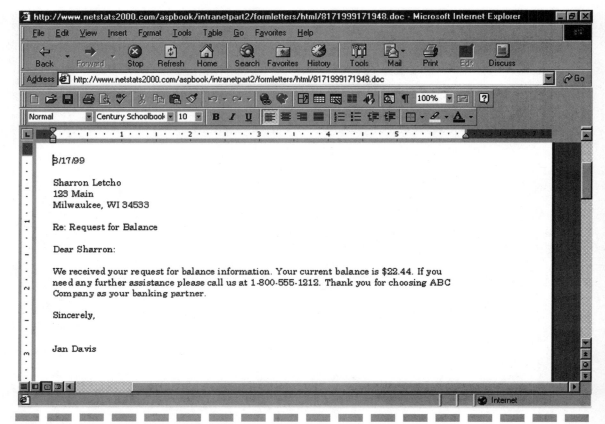

Figure 7-12   Generated Balance Due Form Letter.

form. The code places the data entered into specific areas in the Word document called *bookmarks*. You create the template by using the Insert Bookmark option from the Word menu in the spot where you want one of the form fields.

If visitors click on the Overdue Form Letter from the main menu, they see the form shown in Figure 7-13. The visitor would enter the data requested on this form to generate the Word document displayed in Figure 7-14.

Note that visitors can type whatever they want into the fields on the form. Also note that, since the resulting page is in Word, visitors can print it, save it, and modify it in whatever way they see fit. The code for the Balance Overdue Active Server Page determines the state of the

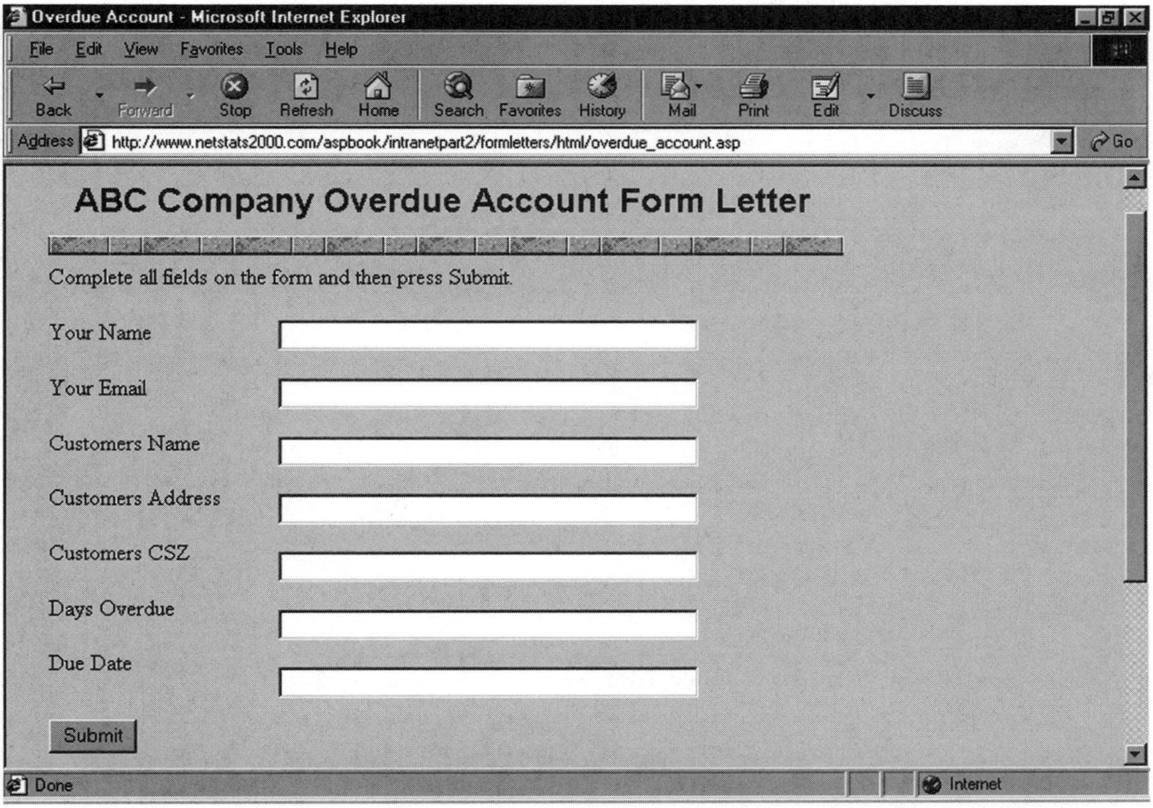

Figure 7-13 Form for gathering the fields needed to complete the Overdue Account Word document.

form. If the form has been submitted, the code creates the Word document and redirects visitors to its location.

The main code block is:

```
<%
Option Explicit
Dim MyWord
Dim Path2File
Dim Path2File1
if not isempty(Request.Form("Submit")) then
  set MyWord = Server.Createobject("Word.Application")
  MyWord.Application.Documents.Open Server.MapPath("../") _
    & "\balancedue.doc"
  MyWord.ActiveWindow.Selection.GoTo -1,,, "CurrentDate"
  MyWord.ActiveWindow.Selection.TypeText cstr(Date)
  MyWord.ActiveWindow.Selection.GoTo -1,,, "CustomersName"
```

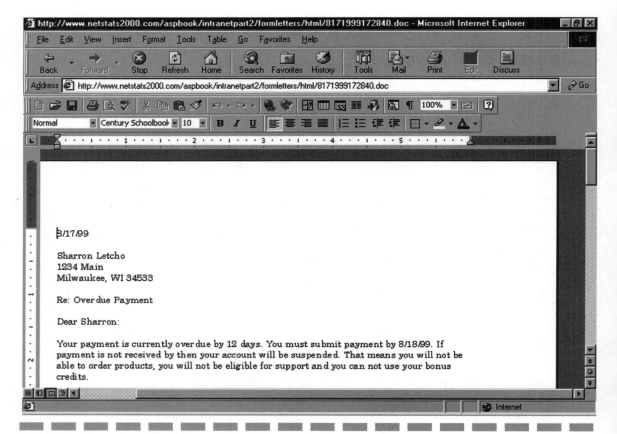

Figure 7-14 Overdue Account Word document.

```
MyWord.ActiveWindow.Selection.TypeText cstr(Request.Form
  ("CustomersName"))
MyWord.ActiveWindow.Selection.GoTo -1,,, "CustomersAddress"
MyWord.ActiveWindow.Selection.TypeText cstr(Request.Form
  ("CustomersAddress"))
MyWord.ActiveWindow.Selection.GoTo -1,,, "CustomersCSZ"
MyWord.ActiveWindow.Selection.TypeText cstr(Request.Form
  ("CustomersCSZ"))
MyWord.ActiveWindow.Selection.GoTo -1,,, "FirstName"
if instr(Request.Form("CustomersName"), " ") > 0 then
  MyWord.ActiveWindow.Selection.TypeText _

cstr(left(Request.Form("CustomersName"),instr(Request.Form
  ("CustomersName"), " ")-1))
else
  MyWord.ActiveWindow.Selection.TypeText cstr(Request.Form
    "CustomersName"))
```

```
  end if
  MyWord.ActiveWindow.Selection.GoTo -1,,, "CurrentBalance"
  MyWord.ActiveWindow.Selection.TypeText
  cstr(Request.Form("CurrentBalance"))
  MyWord.ActiveWindow.Selection.GoTo -1,,, "YourName"
  MyWord.ActiveWindow.Selection.TypeText
  cstr(Request.Form("YourName"))
    Path2File1 = Month(Date) & Day(Date) & Year(Date) _
      & Hour(Time) & Minute(Time) & Second(Time) & ".doc"
    Path2File = Server.MapPath("./") & "\" & Path2File1
    MyWord.ActiveDocument.SaveAs Path2File
    set MyWord = Nothing
    Response.Redirect "./" & Path2File1
  end if
%>
```

First, we tell the compiler that we intend to declare our variables:

```
Option Explicit
```

Then we declare a variable that will store the instance of the Word server:

```
Dim MyWord
```

Two other variables will store path information about the name of the generated file:

```
Dim Path2File
Dim Path2File1
```

Next, we check to see if the form has been submitted. We do this by looking for the SUBMIT button in the Form collection:

```
if not isempty(Request.Form("Submit")) then
```

If it is present, it will not be empty and we need to create the Word document. To do so we will need a connection to the Word server. The CreateObject method of the Server object is used to connect to Word. The variable MyWord will contain our instance of the server:

```
set MyWord = Server.CreateObject("Word.Application")
```

Next, the Open method, a method of the Documents collection, which is a collection of the Application object, which in turn is an object under our MyWord object is used to open the template Word document balancedue.doc. Note that the MapPath method of the Server object is used to locate the physical path of the parent directory:

```
MyWord.Application.Documents.Open Server.MapPath("../") _
& "\balancedue.doc"
```

Next, the Goto method is used to find the bookmark in the Word document we just opened called `CurrentDate`:

```
MyWord.ActiveWindow.Selection.GoTo -1,,, "CurrentDate"
```

The current date, first converted to a string, is placed into that location:

```
MyWord.ActiveWindow.Selection.TypeText cstr(Date)
```

Next, we locate the CustomersName bookmark on our template document:

```
MyWord.ActiveWindow.Selection.GoTo -1,,, "CustomersName"
```

And into that we place the form collection field CustomersName that the visitor submitted with the form:

```
MyWord.ActiveWindow.Selection.TypeText cstr(Request.Form
   ("CustomersName"))
```

The same thing is done for the CustomersAddress and the CustomerCSZ fields:

```
MyWord.ActiveWindow.Selection.GoTo -1,,, "CustomersAddress"
MyWord.ActiveWindow.Selection.TypeText
cstr(Request.Form("CustomersAddress"))
MyWord.ActiveWindow.Selection.GoTo -1,,, "CustomersCSZ"
MyWord.ActiveWindow.Selection.TypeText
cstr(Request.Form("CustomersCSZ"))
```

Next, the code locates the bookmark FirstName:

```
MyWord.ActiveWindow.Selection.GoTo -1,,, "FirstName"
```

Here we will need to place the customer's first name. But all we have is the customer's full name. We assume in our code that if the full name contains a space, then everything to the left of the space is the first name. So first we check to see if there is a space in the full name:

```
if instr(Request.Form("CustomersName"), " ") > 0 then
```

If there is a space, then we place just the text to the left of the space into the bookmark using the TypeText method of the Word object:

```
MyWord.ActiveWindow.Selection.TypeText _
    cstr(left(Request.Form("CustomersName"), _
      instr(Request.Form("CustomersName"), " ")-1))
```

otherwise, we just place the full name in the field:

```
else
  MyWord.ActiveWindow.Selection.TypeText cstr(Request.Form
    ("CustomersName"))
end if
```

Then, the previous code is once again used to write the fields for the CurrentBalance and YourName:

```
MyWord.ActiveWindow.Selection.GoTo -1,,, "CurrentBalance"
MyWord.ActiveWindow.Selection.TypeText cstr(Request.Form
  ("CurrentBalance"))
MyWord.ActiveWindow.Selection.GoTo -1,,, "YourName"
MyWord.ActiveWindow.Selection.TypeText
cstr(Request.Form("YourName"))
```

Now that we have created the Word document, we need to save it in some physical file location. The file will be named based on the current date and time:

```
Path2File1 = Month(Date) & Day(Date) & Year(Date) _
  & Hour(Time) & Minute(Time) & Second(Time) & ".doc"
```

The path to the file will be the same as the Active Server Page we are using. The MapPath method is used to retrieve that location:

```
Path2File = Server.MapPath("./") & "\" & Path2File1
```

Next, the SaveAs method is used to save the file we just created:

```
MyWord.ActiveDocument.SaveAs Path2File
```

Finally, we release the resources used by the document:

```
set MyWord = Nothing
```

The visitor is then redirected to the location where we just saved the file:

```
Response.Redirect "./" & Path2File1
```

Similar code is used on the Overdue Account Active Server Page. The main code block for that page is:

```
<%
Option Explicit
Dim MyWord
Dim Path2File
Dim Path2File1
if not isempty(Request.Form("Submit")) then
  set MyWord = Server.CreateObject("Word.Application")
  MyWord.Application.Documents.Open Server.MapPath("../") _
    & "\overdue.doc"
  MyWord.ActiveWindow.Selection.GoTo -1,,, "CurrentDate"
  MyWord.ActiveWindow.Selection.TypeText cstr(Date)
  MyWord.ActiveWindow.Selection.GoTo -1,,, "CustomersName"
  MyWord.ActiveWindow.Selection.TypeText
cstr(Request.Form("CustomersName"))
  MyWord.ActiveWindow.Selection.GoTo -1,,, "CustomersAddress"
  MyWord.ActiveWindow.Selection.TypeText
cstr(Request.Form("CustomersAddress"))
  MyWord.ActiveWindow.Selection.GoTo -1,,, "CustomersCSZ"
  MyWord.ActiveWindow.Selection.TypeText
cstr(Request.Form("CustomersCSZ"))
  MyWord.ActiveWindow.Selection.GoTo -1,,, "FirstName"
  if instr(Request.Form("CustomersName"), " ") > 0 then
    MyWord.ActiveWindow.Selection.TypeText _
cstr(left(Request.Form("CustomersName"),instr(Request.Form
  ("CustomersName"), " ")-1))
  else
    MyWord.ActiveWindow.Selection.TypeText cstr(Request.Form
      ("CustomersName"))
  end if
  MyWord.ActiveWindow.Selection.GoTo -1,,, "DaysOverDue"
  MyWord.ActiveWindow.Selection.TypeText cstr(Request.Form
    ("DaysOverDue"))
  MyWord.ActiveWindow.Selection.GoTo -1,,, "DueDate"
  MyWord.ActiveWindow.Selection.TypeText cstr(Request.Form
    ("DueDate"))
  MyWord.ActiveWindow.Selection.GoTo -1,,, "YourName"
  MyWord.ActiveWindow.Selection.TypeText cstr(Request.Form
    ("YourName"))
  Path2File1 = Month(Date) & Day(Date) & Year(Date) _
    & Hour(Time) & Minute(Time) & Second(Time) & ".doc"
  Path2File = Server.MapPath("./") & "\" & Path2File1
  MyWord.ActiveDocument.SaveAs Path2File
  set MyWord = Nothing
  Response.Redirect "./" & Path2File1
end if
%>
```

First, we tell the compiler that we will be declaring our variables:

```
Option Explicit
```

Next, we declare the variable that will store the instance of Word:

```
Dim MyWord
```

The variables that will store the file path information are also declared:

```
Dim Path2File
Dim Path2File1
```

Next, we check for the SUBMIT button using the IsEmpty function, which returns True if the form field is not part of the collection. The not reverses that logic so the expression evaluates to True if the field is present:

```
if not isempty(Request.Form("Submit")) then
```

Next, we connect to the Word server using the CreateObject method:

```
set MyWord = Server.CreateObject("Word.Application")
```

Then, the MapPath method of the server object is used to retrieve the physical location of the overdue.doc file based on its being located in the parent directory of this Active Server Page:

```
MyWord.Application.Documents.Open Server.MapPath("../") _
  & "\overdue.doc"
```

The code then uses the Goto method to find the bookmark in our template document called CurrentDate:

```
MyWord.ActiveWindow.Selection.GoTo -1,,, "CurrentDate"
```

Using the TypeText method, we insert the current date into the location of that bookmark:

```
MyWord.ActiveWindow.Selection.TypeText cstr(Date)
```

The same procedure is done for the CustomersName, Customers Address, and CustomersCSZ:

```
MyWord.ActiveWindow.Selection.GoTo -1,,, "CustomersName"
MyWord.ActiveWindow.Selection.TypeText
cstr(Request.Form("CustomersName"))
MyWord.ActiveWindow.Selection.GoTo -1,,, "CustomersAddress"
MyWord.ActiveWindow.Selection.TypeText
```

```
cstr(Request.Form("CustomersAddress"))
MyWord.ActiveWindow.Selection.GoTo -1,,, "CustomersCSZ"
MyWord.ActiveWindow.Selection.TypeText
cstr(Request.Form("CustomersCSZ"))
```

We then locate the bookmark that will be used to place the text for the visitor's first name:

```
MyWord.ActiveWindow.Selection.GoTo -1,,, "FirstName"
```

Since we have only the visitor's full name, the first name will be parsed from that by using all the characters to the left of the first space in the full name:

```
if instr(Request.Form("CustomersName"), " ") > 0 then
  MyWord.ActiveWindow.Selection.TypeText _
cstr(left(Request.Form("CustomersName"),instr(Request.Form
  ("CustomersName"), " ")-1))
  else
  MyWord.ActiveWindow.Selection.TypeText cstr(Request.Form
    ("CustomersName"))
end if
```

Then we go to the other bookmarks and insert their text based on the form collection submitted by the visitor:

```
MyWord.ActiveWindow.Selection.GoTo -1,,, "DaysOverDue"
MyWord.ActiveWindow.Selection.TypeText cstr(Request.Form
  ("DaysOverDue"))
MyWord.ActiveWindow.Selection.GoTo -1,,, "DueDate"
MyWord.ActiveWindow.Selection.TypeText cstr(Request.Form
  ("DueDate"))
MyWord.ActiveWindow.Selection.GoTo -1,,, "YourName"
MyWord.ActiveWindow.Selection.TypeText cstr(Request.Form
  ("YourName"))
```

Now we need to come up with a unique name for the Word document because we do not want to overwrite our template file. The name created here is a number based on the current date and time:

```
Path2File1 = Month(Date) & Day(Date) & Year(Date) _
  & Hour(Time) & Minute(Time) & Second(Time) & ".doc"
```

This file name will be used with the path to the directory where the current Active Server Page is located by using the MapPath method:

```
Path2File = Server.MapPath("./") & "\" & Path2File1
```

The Word document is saved using the SaveAs method. The name of the file that we created earlier is passed to the method:

```
MyWord.ActiveDocument.SaveAs Path2File
```

The Word server is released:

```
set MyWord = Nothing
```

and the visitor is redirected to the Word document we just generated:

```
Response.Redirect "./" & Path2File1
```

The Session Object, the Application Object, and the `global.asa` File

ASP Applications

Thus far in this book, in the code and samples we have looked at we have been able to use the Request object to get data about and from our visitor. We have used the Response object to send data back to the visitor's browser. We have also used the Response object to send information to another page using links or the Redirect method with a query string. We have also looked at communicating with the server. But what we haven't been able to do is to share information across pages for a specific visitor or across pages to all the visitors. This chapter focuses on that issue: the Active Server Page application.

If you are a programmer from another language or have just heard programmers talk, you may be familiar with the word *state*, which refers to the persistence of information across an application. In a stateless application all the data is lost from one procedure to the next. So each call, or in the case of Active Server Pages, each page contains its own set of data. An application that has state is one that maintains information between calls, which can be accessed by one or more procedures within an application or the same procedure more than one time.

If you have ever programmed in Visual Basic, you are probably familiar with Public or Global variables. These variables can be visible to the entire application from the start of the application until the end. In Visual Basic, you declare one like:

```
Public EmpName as String
```

You can set its value from within any procedure:

```
EmpName = "Nancy"
```

When the procedure that sets the value of the variable ends, the variable still contains the text Nancy, so other procedures can refer to it or the same procedure could reference the value that was last set to it. An application like this has state. What we have seen in most of the code examples thus far have not allowed us to do this. We have created variables using the Dim statement within the code of the page:

```
Dim EmpName
```

But as soon as the page is done processing the code, the data in the variable EmpName goes away. No other page can reference the value that one page set if we use variables in this way. We have been creating pages that are stateless.

In this chapter, we look at creating an Active Server Page application that allows us to maintain state. An Active Server Page application provides us with the mechanisms to store information about the state of the application from page to page. This information can be stored at two levels: at the Application level and at the Session level.

The *Application level* refers to all the pages in your Active Server Page application and all the visitors to your application, so you can create a variable in a single location that can be referenced by all the pages in your Active Server Page application and all the visitors to that page. Application information is referenced and created through the Application object.

You can also store state information at the *Session level*, which refers to a single visitor to your site. So state information, in this case, is at a lower level than at the Application level. The information is available for a single visitor across your pages. That means that you can create state information that is only viewable to the code for a single visitor. This state level is coded through the Session object.

As you will discover more deeply in this chapter, the Application and Session objects also have events for which you can provide code when the event occurs, so you can have code that runs when your application starts or have code that runs when a visitor enters your site. These capabilities really provide value to what you can do with your Web sites.

Creating an Active Server Page Application

An *Active Server Page application* is composed of a series of related Active Server Pages and a file called global.asa. All the files in the Active Server Page application must reside in the same root directory structure where the application is defined or in the subdirectories of that root directory.

Take a look at the directory structure displayed in Figure 8-1.

An Active Server Page application is made up of all the files that are in the applications root or any subdirectories unless those subdirectories belong to another Active Server Page application. Using our example, we start at the top level, which isn't defined as an Active Server Page

Figure 8-1
Sample directory
structure.

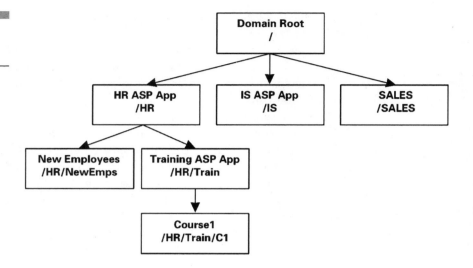

application. We then have a subdirectory called HR that is defined as an
Active Server Page application, so all the Active Server Pages in that
directory are part of the same HR application.

But we also said that the subdirectories are part of the application
unless they are their own Active Server Page application. Under the HR
directory is a directory called NewEmps. This directory is not an Active
Server Page application, so any ASP pages in it belong to the HR application. If the NewEmps directory had any subdirectories, they, too, would
belong to the HR application unless they were defined as their own
Active Server Page application.

The second directory under HR is the Train directory. This directory
is an Active Server Page application itself, so the Active Server Pages in
it do not belong to the HR application. Under the Train directory is a
directory called C1. Since this directory is not an Active Server Page
directory, it belongs to the Train application since that is the next level
up that is an Active Server Page application.

Also off the root is a directory called IS, which is defined as an Active
Server Page application, so the ASP pages in that directory would
belong to IS, not HR or any other Active Server Page application.

The last directory off the root is Sales. This directory is not an Active
Server Page application, so the pages in that directory are stateless.
They do not belong to any Active Server Page application since they are
not in a directory that is a marked as one and no levels above it are
Active Server Page applications.

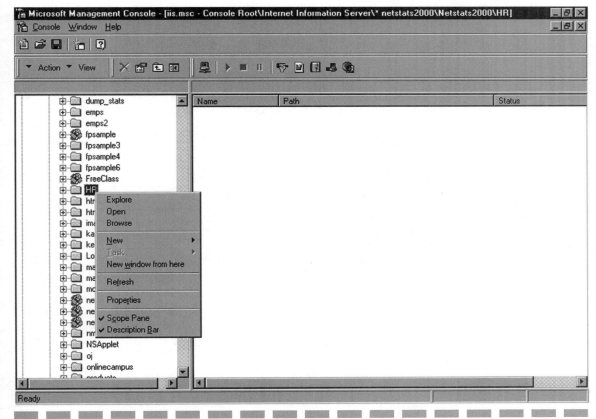

Figure 8-2 Viewing the Properties to create an Active Server Page application.

When you create an Active Server Page application you must be cognizant of where you are placing the ASP in relative position to what pages must be able to share state information. You normally do this by creating a directory somewhere off of the root of your Web site. You then place all the files that are part of that application into that directory.

You are then ready to mark the directory as an Active Server Page application. You do this by right-clicking on the directory within the Microsoft Management Console's view of IIS and selecting Properties, as shown in Figure 8-2.

After selecting Properties you should see the dialog shown in Figure 8-3. Once you are in the Properties for the directory you should be in the DIRECTORY tab; if you are not, change to that tab. Then just press the CREATE button in the Application Settings section of this tab and enter

Figure 8-3
Creating the Active
Server Page
application.

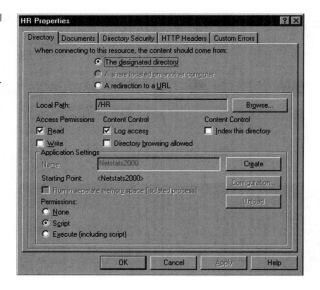

the name that you want to give your application in the NAME text box. Press OK and you now have an Active Server Page application. Now all the Active Server Pages can share information with each through the Session and the Application objects.

Session Object

A *session*, in Active Server Page terms, is a single visitor traversing your Active Server Page application. The session starts when the visitor browses to one of the Active Server Pages in your Active Server Page application or goes to an HTML page that has code that calls one of your Active Server Pages. The session persists until the visitor has left your site.

Visitors to your site can have their session terminated implicitly or explicitly. It ends *implicitly* when they haven't requested one of your pages for a predetermined number of minutes, or the session ends *explicitly* when you call a method that terminates the visitors' session.

While the visitor travels through your site, you can use the Session object to store information about the visitor and to control certain aspects of the visitor's session. The Session object includes collections, properties, and a method that you can code to provide this functionality.

	Collection	Purpose
TABLE 8-1 *Session Object Collections*	Contents Collection	A collection of all the variables that are available at the Session level, excluding any created with the `Object` tag.
	StaticObjects Collection	A collection of all the objects created for the Session level that were created using the `Object` tag in the `global.asa` file.

Session Collections

The Session object contains two collections that you can use to control data that is used in the session-state. The collections are discussed below and summarized in Table 8-1.

Contents Collection

The *Contents collection* is a group of variables that you make available to any of the pages in your Active Server Page application through the Session object. The variables have the Session-level scope, so they are available to any ASP, but the values are not shared by all the visitors. Each visitor would have an individual copy of the variable.

You set the value for an item such as the Contents collection like this:

```
Session.Contents("EmpName") = "Tonya"
```

But since the collection is the default collection you could also write the preceding line of code like this:

```
Session("EmpName") = "Tonya"
```

Either way, the retrieving or setting of an item in the Session Contents collection begins with the Session object and then in parentheses, since this is an item of a collection, you specify the name of the item to which you are referring.

Since the variables are an item of a collection unlike a standard variable, they do not receive the benefit of `Option Explicit`, which makes sense because you might first create the variable on one page and then reference the item on another page. This goes to the real purpose of variables in the Contents collection—they are intended to be retrieved and set from a variety of pages on your Web site.

For example, on one page you could provide code that created a few session variables like this:

```
<%
Session("UserName") = "Bob Tyler"
Session("UserID") = 10
Session("City") = "Portland"
%>
```

Here we are creating three session variables that are now available to any page within our Active Server Page application. First, we create a session variable called UserName and set the value for that variable to the string "Bob Tyler":

```
Session("UserName") = "Bob Tyler"
```

We set this with a string, but the value could have been set by a value in the database or from the user-input through the Form collection of the Request object.

Next, a session variable called UserID that is set to the value 10 is created. Note that we can use session variables for strings, numbers, and also dates:

```
Session("UserID") = 10
```

Finally, we create a third session variable that stores the value "Portland" in the session variable City:

```
Session("City") = "Portland"
```

Now from a second page we can reference or set these session variables or we could create new ones. Take a look at this code:

```
<%
If Session("City") = "Portland" Then
  Session("City") = "Portland, OR"
End If
Response.Write "Hello: " & Session("UserName") & ".<P>"
Response.Write "For your records your account number is: " _
  & Session("UserID") & ".<P>"
Response.Write "How are things in " & Session("City") & "?<P>"
%>
```

First, we retrieve the value of the session variable City within an If statement to see if it is set to the string "Portland":

```
If Session("City") = "Portland" Then
```

If it is, we then set it to a new value:

```
Session("City") = "Portland, OR"
```

Then we use the value of the `UserName` session variable within a Write:

```
Response.Write "Hello: " & Session("UserName") & ".<P>"
```

The values of the `UserID` and the `City` session variables are used for additional output to the browser:

```
Response.Write "For your records your account number is: " _
  & Session("UserID") & ".<P>"
Response.Write "How are things in " & Session("City") & "?<P>"
```

The code would produce the output shown in Figure 8-4.

You can also make objects part of the Contents collection. This is a little dangerous since the resources used by objects can be significantly greater than simple variables, but it allows you to have a Session object

Figure 8-4
Output of code
using the Contents
collection.

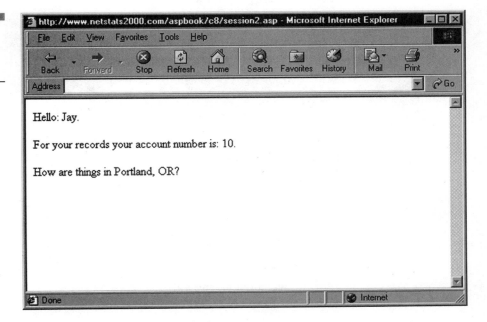

that you create in one place and then use throughout your Active Server Page application.

For example, on one page you could instantiate an object:

```
set Session("Sconn") = Server.CreateObject("adodb.connection")
```

This Session object is now set and using the system resources for this type of object. On another page, or on many pages, you could code using the Session object:

```
Session("Sconn").open "ASPBook", "sa", "yourpassword"
```

Since these fields are all part of a collection we can use the For_Each code block to iterate through each of the session variables and/or objects using code like this:

```
<%
For Each MySession in Session.Contents
  Response.Write "Session Item: " & MySession & "<P>"
Next
%>
```

The output of using this code based on all the session variables we have created thus far is shown in Figure 8-5.

Figure 8-5
Displaying the items in the Session Contents collection.

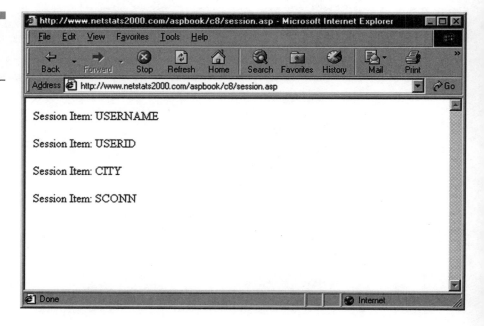

Think about the flow of code in the page where we set the `City` session variable to `"Portland"` and then on another page we modified it to `"Portland, OR"`. If the visitor was to return to the first page, then the session variable would be once again set to `"Portland"`. Many times you will have code that will first create these session variables and give them an initial value. But if they were already created you don't want to change their value. We can use the `IsEmpty` function to determine if the session variable was already created.

So we could modify our code like this:

```
<%
If IsEmpty(Session("City")) Then
    Session("City") = "Portland"
End If
%>
```

Now this code will run only once within the visitor's session. After the session variable is created, the `If` statement will no longer evaluate to True, so the session variable will not be reassigned. Later in this chapter we look at another way to initialize these session variables through the `global.asa` file.

Another use of the session variable is to force visitors to first go to a specific page before entering some other page. Say, for example, that you have quizzes for a class you teach on your Web site. Before visitors take a quiz they need to log in. The problem you are finding is that the students will bookmark the quiz itself and return straight to that page instead of entering the Quiz after they log in.

You could use a session variable to fix this problem. You could have a session variable that contains the `StudentID`, a variable that would be set only from the login page. On the Quiz page itself you would include code like the following that would prevent students from entering the Quiz unless they had first logged in:

```
<%
If IsEmpty(Session("StudentID")) then
    Response.Redirect "./login.asp"
End If
%>
```

Now if students try to go straight to the Quiz page without first logging in, the `StudentID` session variable will be empty and students will be redirected to the Login page.

StaticObjects Collection

Later in this chapter we discuss the `global.asa` file at length. At this point you should be aware that it is part of an Active Server Page application. It provides a way for you to write code that runs when a visitor starts or ends a session. It also provides a way for you to write code that runs when your Active Server Page application starts and stops.

But you can also create Session objects within the `global.asa` file that are then available, like the ones we have discussed thus far, to all the ASP in your Active Server Page application. You create these objects using an `Object` tag and they become available because of the StaticObjects collection.

These Session StaticObjects are declared in the `global.asa` file through an `Object` tag like this:

```
<OBJECT RUNAT=Server SCOPE=Session ID=Sconn PROGID="adodb.
  connection">
</OBJECT>
```

This line of code creates a session-wide object called Sconn that is an ADO connection object. This one:

```
<OBJECT RUNAT=Server SCOPE=Session ID=SobjMail PROGID="CDONTS.
  NewMail">
</OBJECT>
```

creates a Session object called *SobjMail*, which is a Collaborative Data object used to send email.

Once created, you can reference either of these Session objects in the code on any of the ASP that is part of this Active Server Page application like this:

```
<%
Option Explicit
Dim RSUser
Sconn.open "ASPBook", "sa", "yourpassword"
set RSUser = Sconn.Execute("select * from Users")
%>
```

Most important, notice that we reference the StaticObjects collection different from how we referenced the Contents collection. We just specify the name of the collection item without any object before it. In this example, we just use the object name Sconn:

```
Sconn.open "ASPBook", "sa", "yourpassword"
```

Since these are items in a collection we can use a `For...Each` code block to iterate through each of the items in the collection:

```
<%
Option Explicit
Dim MySessionSO
For Each MySessionSO in Session.StaticObjects
  Response.Write "Static Object: " & MySessionSO & "<P>"
Next
%>
```

First, we tell the compiler that we will be declaring our variables:

```
Option Explicit
```

Then we declare a variable that will hold a reference to each of the objects in the StaticObjects collection:

```
Dim MySessionSO
```

A For...Each block is started that will loop through each item in the collection:

```
For Each MySessionSO in Session.StaticObjects
```

The Write method of the Response object is then used to write the name of the StaticObject to the browser before proceeding to the next object in the collection:

```
    Response.Write "Static Object: " & MySessionSO & "<P>"
Next
```

The output of this code, based on the two objects we created, is displayed in Figure 8-6.

Session Object Properties

The properties of the Session object allow you to configure and refer to aspects of the visitor's session. The properties are discussed below and summarized in Table 8-2.

CodePage Property
The *CodePage property* allows you to set the character set that will be used during the session. The character set includes numbers, letters,

Figure 8-6
Output of the
StaticObjects
collection code.

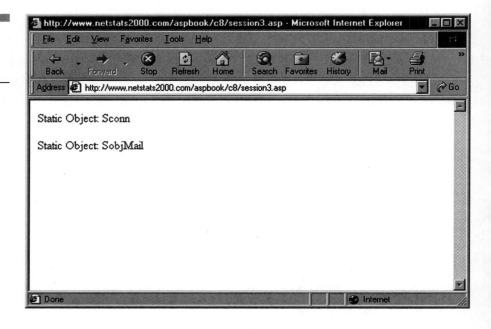

and other characters. Different countries in the world use different character sets, so you can use this property to assist your development if your site provides international content.

The CodePage is a Session property, so what you set it to is what is used by all the pages in your Active Server Page application. The property is read/write and takes the following form:

```
Session.CodePage = CPValue
```

TABLE 8-2

Session Object
Properties

Properties	Purpose
CodePage	Determines the character set used in the session.
LCID	Defines the Locale Identifier for the session.
SessionID	A unique identifier for the visitor's session.
TimeOut	The number of minutes between page views that cannot be exceeded or the visitor's session is assumed to have ended.

where `CPValue` is a number that pertains to the code page that you wish to use. Take a look at this code:

```
<%
Session.CodePage = 1252

Response.Write "CodePage used: " & Session.CodePage & "<P>"
Response.Write "1é æ ç ê ë ì í î ï ð Ê Î Ð" & "<P>"

Session.CodePage = 932
Response.Write "CodePage used: " & Session.CodePage & "<P>"
Response.Write "1é æ ç ê ë ì í î ï ð Ê Î Ð" & "<P>"
%>
```

First, the code page is set to English for the entire session:

```
Session.CodePage = 1252
```

Next, the value of the code page is written to the browser:

```
Response.Write "CodePage used: " & Session.CodePage & "<P>"
```

Then some high number characters are written to the browser:

```
Response.Write "1é æ ç ê ë ì í î ï ð Ê Î Ð" & "<P>"
```

In the next code block the code page is set to Japanese:

```
Session.CodePage = 932
```

The value of the CodePage property is written to the browser:

```
Response.Write "CodePage used: " & Session.CodePage & "<P>"
```

as are some characters beyond the standard characters:

```
Response.Write "1é æ ç ê ë ì í î ï ð Ê Î Ð" & "<P>"
```

LCID Property

The *LCID property* of the Session object allows you to set the locale that the dynamic text should be displayed as. This represents how things like time, numbers, and currency are to be displayed.

Since the property is a Session property, once set, it is for all the pages in your Active Server Page application. The property is read/write and takes the following form:

```
Session.LCID = LocaleID
```

where `LocaleID` represents a number of type long that you wish to set the locale to.

The property provides an additional mechanism for making your site international. You use this property to properly format the dynamic content of your page. For example, take a look at this code block:

```
<%
Session.LCID = 1033 .
Response.Write "US format: " & Now & " " _
   & formatcurrency(1234.56) & "<P>"

Session.LCID = 2057
Response.Write "UK format: " & Now & " " _
   & formatcurrency(1234.56) & "<P>"

Session.LCID = 1049
Response.Write "Russia format: " & Now & " " _
   & formatcurrency(1234.56) & "<P>"

Session.LCID = 1032
Response.Write "Greek format: " & Now & " " _
   & formatcurrency(1234.56) & "<P>"

Session.LCID = 2049
Response.Write "Iraq format: " & Now & " " _
   & formatcurrency(1234.56) & "<P>"

Session.LCID = 3073
Response.Write "Egypt format: " & Now & " " _
   & formatcurrency(1234.56) & "<P>"

Session.LCID = 6154
Response.Write "Panama format: " & Now & " " _
   & formatcurrency(1234.56) & "<P>"
%>
```

First, the code sets the locale to the United States:

```
Session.LCID = 1033
```

Next, the code displays the current date and time as well as currency in the United States format:

```
Response.Write "US format: " & Now & " " _
   & formatcurrency(1234.56) & "<P>"
```

Here the locale is set to the United Kingdom:

```
Session.LCID = 2057
```

and the date/time and money are displayed in United Kingdom format:

```
Response.Write "UK format: " & Now & " " _
   & formatcurrency(1234.56) & "<P>"
```

The same code is used to display the Russia format:

```
Session.LCID = 1049
Response.Write "Russia format: " & Now & " " _
   & formatcurrency(1234.56) & "<P>"
```

Then the Greek format is displayed:

```
Session.LCID = 1032
Response.Write "Greek format: " & Now & " " _
   & formatcurrency(1234.56) & "<P>"
```

Here, the Iraq format is written:

```
Session.LCID = 2049
Response.Write "Iraq format: " & Now & " " _
   & formatcurrency(1234.56) & "<P>"
```

Then the Egypt format for date, time, and money are displayed:

```
Session.LCID = 3073
Response.Write "Egypt format: " & Now & " " _
   & formatcurrency(1234.56) & "<P>"
```

And the same is done for the Panama format:

```
Session.LCID = 6154
Response.Write "Panama format: " & Now & " " _
   & formatcurrency(1234.56) & "<P>"
```

The output of this code is displayed in Figure 8-7.

SessionID

Internally IIS needs a way of tracking visitors as they travel through your site. The way IIS does this is through a *SessionID*. When you are using an Active Server Page application, IIS assigns a random number of type long to all visitors as they enter your site.

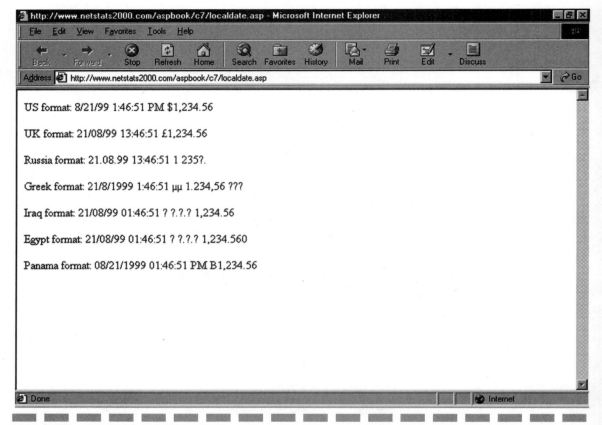

US format: 8/21/99 1:46:51 PM $1,234.56

UK format: 21/08/99 13:46:51 £1,234.56

Russia format: 21.08.99 13:46:51 1 235?.

Greek format: 21/8/1999 1:46:51 μμ 1.234,56 ???

Iraq format: 21/08/99 01:46:51 ? ?.?.? 1,234.56

Egypt format: 21/08/99 01:46:51 ? ?.?.? 1,234.560

Panama format: 08/21/1999 01:46:51 PM B1,234.56

Figure 8-7   Output of the LCID code.

Since the property is used internally by IIS to identify all visitors in their session, it is a read-only property. The property has the following syntax:

```
TheID = Session.SessionID
```

The ID is a variable into which you want to place the ID.

NOTE: *The SessionID is NOT a unique number over time. If you restart your server, the same number can be used again. So do not use this identifier as a primary key in a table.*

TimeOut Property

A session starts when visitors access one of the Active Server Pages in your Active Server Page application or when they access a page that calls code in one of your Active Server Pages. One of the ways a session can end is if visitors do not make a request for one of the pages in your Active Server Page application in a certain number of minutes. That certain number of minutes is set through the *TimeOut property*. The read/write property stores the number of minutes that visitors can take between requests in your Active Server Page application without timing out.

The default for this property is set through the Microsoft Management Console with IIS. Browse to your Active Server Page application and select Properties. Then on the DIRECTORY tab press the CONFIGURATION button. Switch to the APP OPTIONS tab and you should see the dialog displayed in Figure 8-8.

The SESSION TIMEOUT text box contains the default value for the TimeOut property. You can override that value in your code with the

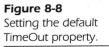

Figure 8-8
Setting the default
TimeOut property.

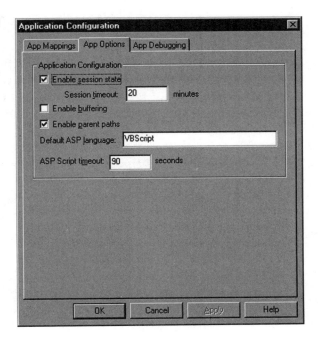

316

Session TimeOut property. The property is read/write and takes the following format:

```
Session.TimeOut = NumMinutes
```

where `NumMinutes` is the number of minutes visitors can go between requests without ending their session.

When the session ends, all the session objects and variables are released and their values are no longer available. If visitors request a page after the timeout has been exceeded, it would be like the request was their first request and a new session would begin.

Session Object Method

The Session object contains a single method you can use to take action on that object. The method is discussed below and summarized in Table 8-3.

Abandon Method

As you saw in the last section, visitors' sessions end if they exceed the number of minutes allowed between requests. The other way the session can be terminated is by calling the Abandon method in code.

The *Abandon method* of the Session object allows you to immediately terminate the visitor's session. This is helpful in situations where visitors take an action that ends some process they have been involved in. For example, if you had an e-commerce site, visitors may traverse through your product catalog and place items in their shopping cart. To manage their state you are using the Session object with a CustomerID, so they are able to add items to their shopping cart and remove items from their shopping cart—and the whole time you maintain their state. At some point they may check out of your online store. When they take that action that means they are done with their shopping cart and you need to process their order. You need to terminate their session. You do that with the Abandon method.

TABLE 8-3

Session Object Method

Method	Purpose
Abandon	Used to explicitly end the visitor's session.

The Abandon method takes the following syntax:

```
Session.Abandon
```

For example, read through this code:

```
<%
Session("UserName") = "Jim Smith"
Response.Write Session("UserName")
Session.Abandon
%>
```

Here a session variable called UserName is created:

```
Session("UserName") = "Jim Smith"
```

The value for that session variable is written to the browser:

```
Response.Write Session("UserName")
```

The session ends:

```
Session.Abandon
```

So once the page is complete, the session variable would no longer be available. When the Abandon method is called, the Session_OnEnd event is fired and all the session variables and objects are released.

Application Object

As you have learned in this chapter, an Active Server Page application is a group of Active Server Pages and the global.asa file in a common directory structure. The *Application object* allows you to programmatically control your application.

With the collections and methods available with this object, you can create variables and objects that are visible throughout your application across all sessions and methods that allow you to control how these variables are changed.

Application Object Collections

The Application object contains two collections that you can use to control variables and objects visible throughout the Active Server Page

Collection	Purpose
Contents Collection	A collection of all the variables that are available at the Application level, excluding any created with the `Object` tag.
StaticObjects Collection	A collection of all the objects created for the Application level that were created using the `Object` tag in the `global.asa` file.

application. The collections are discussed below and summarized in Table 8-4.

Contents Collection

The *Contents collection* is a group of variables that you make available to any of the pages in your Active Server Page application throughout any of the sessions. The variables have the application-level scope so they are available to any ASP and are not shared by all the visitors. The code run for every visitor references the same collection of application variables.

You set the value for an item such as the Contents collection like this:

```
Application.Contents("CurrentDiscount") = .9
```

But since the collection is the default collection of the Application object, you could also write the preceding line of code like this:

```
Application("CurrentDiscount") = .9
```

Either way, the syntax for the retrieving or setting of an item in the Application Contents collection begins with the Application object and then in parentheses, since this is an item of a collection, you specify the name of the item to which you are referring.

Like the Contents collection of the Session object, the Contents collection of the Application object will not trigger an error with `Option Explicit` if the variable has not been referenced before. This makes sense, since the whole point of the Contents collection in either object is to create variables that are available across more than one page.

Application variables provide a mechanism for you to create and set a variable in a single location and then reference the variable in numerous locations. This makes modifying the code much simpler. Take this example:

```
<%
Application("CurrentDiscount") = .9
Application("MinShipHand") = 12
Application("MinQuantity") = 2
Application("ShipHandPercent") = .07
%>
```

Here we have created four application variables. The values in these variables will be available to all the Active Server Pages in our Active Server Page application across all sessions.

First, an application variable named `CurrentDiscount` is created set to the value .9:

```
Application("CurrentDiscount") = .9
```

Next, a variable called `MinShipHand` is created to store the minimum amount of shipping and handling allowed for an order, in this case, $12:

```
Application("MinShipHand") = 12
```

The third application variable, `MinQuantity`, stores the minimum quantity of an item that must be purchased:

```
Application("MinQuantity") = 2
```

And the fourth application variable, `ShipHandPercent`, stores the shipping and handling percentage we charge:

```
Application("ShipHandPercent") = .07
```

Then from any other page in our Active Server Page application we can reference these variables:

```
<%
Option Explicit
Dim OrderTotal
Dim SandH
Dim TotalDue
OrderTotal = Session("OrderTotal") * Application("CurrentDiscount")
SandH = OrderTotal * Application("ShipHandPercent")
If SandH < Application("MinShipHand") Then
   SandH = Application("MinShipHand")
End If
TotalDue = SandH + OrderTotal
%>
```

The sample code block is a simple example of calculating an order total. Notice that there are no hard-coded numbers in the code. The code relies on application variables to determine the charges.

First though, the compiler is told that we plan on declaring our variables:

```
Option Explicit
```

Next, a variable is created that will store the discounted order total:

```
Dim OrderTotal
```

The next variable will store the shipping and handling amount:

```
Dim SandH
```

and the last variable stores the total amount due:

```
Dim TotalDue
```

The order total is derived using the discount stored in the CurrentDiscount application variable:

```
OrderTotal = Session("OrderTotal") * Application("CurrentDiscount")
```

Next, the amount of shipping and handling is derived as a percentage of the OrderTotal based on the ShipHandPercent application variable:

```
SandH = OrderTotal * Application("ShipHandPercent")
```

But we also have a minimum value that the shipping and handling must be. The If statement compares the shipping and handling to the minimum amount stored in the application variable:

```
If SandH < Application("MinShipHand") Then
```

If the calculated shipping and handling is less than the minimum, it is set to the minimum:

```
    SandH = Application("MinShipHand")
End If
```

Finally, the total amount due is derived from the discounted total and the shipping and handling amount:

```
TotalDue = SandH + OrderTotal
```

You can also make objects part of the Contents collection, but be very careful about doing this. Remember that the application variables and objects endure through the entire life of the Active Server Page application, so whatever resources the object is using will be used during the life of your application, which could be a very long time.

When you create an Application-wide object like this:

```
Set Application("Gconn") = Server.CreateObject("adodb.connection")
```

think about what this line of code would do. Throughout the life of your application, which could be weeks, you would have a constant connection to the database.

Since the Contents collection is a collection, we can iterate through the collection with code like this:

```
<%
Option Explicit
Dim MyApp
For Each MyApp in Application.Contents
  Response.Write "Application Variable Name: " & MyApp _
    & " Value: " & Application(MyApp) & "<P>"
Next
%>
```

First, we state that we will declare our variables:

```
Option Explicit
```

Then we declare a variable that will store a reference to each of the items in the collection as we iterate through the loop:

```
Dim MyApp
```

Next, our `For...Each` code block is set to iterate through each of the items in the Contents collection:

```
For Each MyApp in Application.Contents
```

The name of each of the application variables and its value is written to the browser:

```
Response.Write "Application Variable Name: " & MyApp _
    & " Value: " & Application(MyApp) & "<P>"
```

The code then loops to the next item in the collection.

```
Next
```

The Order Processing example discussed earlier would produce the output displayed in Figure 8-9.

StaticObjects Collection

Like the Session object, the Application object has a *StaticObjects collection*, which is created through the global.asa file. Remember that the global.asa is part of an Active Server Page application. It provides a way for you to write code that runs when an Active Server Page application starts or ends, and it provides a way for you to write code that runs when a Session starts and stops.

You create these objects using an Object tag and they become available through the StaticObjects collection. These Application StaticObjects are declared in the global.asa file through an Object tag like this:

```
<OBJECT RUNAT=Server SCOPE=Application ID=Gconn PROGID="adodb.
  connection">
</OBJECT>
```

Figure 8-9
Output of Contents collection iteration code.

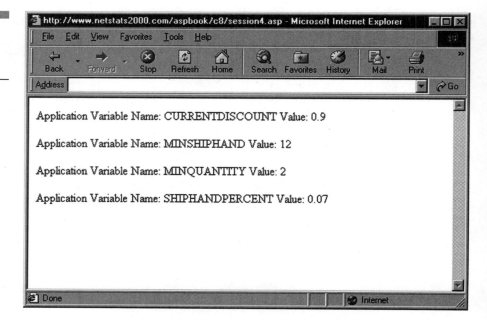

Application Variable Name: CURRENTDISCOUNT Value: 0.9

Application Variable Name: MINSHIPHAND Value: 12

Application Variable Name: MINQUANTITY Value: 2

Application Variable Name: SHIPHANDPERCENT Value: 0.07

This line of code creates an Application-wide object called *Gconn* that is an ADO connection object. Once created, you can reference an item of the StaticObjects collection on any of the pages through any of the sessions of the Active Server Page application:

```
<%
Option Explicit
Dim RSUser
Gconn.open "ASPBook", "sa", "yourpassword"
set RSUser = Sconn.Execute("select * from Users")
%>
```

Notice that references made to the StaticObjects collection are different from how the Contents collection is referenced. The name of the collection item is specified without any object before it. In this example, just the object name Gconn is used:

```
Gconn.open "ASPBook", "sa", "yourpassword"
```

You can also use the For...Each code block to iterate through each of the items in the StaticObjects collection:

```
<%
Option Explicit
Dim MyAppSO
For Each MyAppSO in Application.StaticObjects
  Response.Write "App Object: " & MyAppSO & "<P>"
Next
%>
```

First, Option Explicit is stated, as variable declaration is required:

```
Option Explicit
```

Then a variable is created to store the temporary reference to the collection item:

```
Dim MyAppSO
```

Next, we begin the iteration through the For...Each structure:

```
For Each MyAppSO in Application.StaticObjects
```

The name of the StaticObjects item is written to the browser:

```
    Response.Write "App Object: " & MyAppSO & "<P>"
Next
```

Application Object Methods

The Application object contains two methods that are used to control how the Contents collection items are referenced. The methods are discussed below and summarized in Table 8-5.

Lock Method

One of the problems that can occur with a busy site, or even on occasion with a site that doesn't receive much traffic, is that an application variable may be modified by more than one script at the same time. Remember that an application-level variable is available to all the sessions, so if you have hundreds of simultaneous sessions it becomes likely that more than one session may be trying to change an application variable at the same time.

For example, say you are keeping track of the number of hits to a page by using an application variable. When the application starts you would set the initial value from some field in a database using code similar to this:

```
<%
Option Explicit
Dim conn
Dim RSPageHits
set conn = server.createobject ("adodb.connection")
conn.open "ASPBook", "sa", "yourpassword"
set RSPageHits = conn.Execute("select Hits from RSPageHits")
Application("PageHits") = RSPageHits("Hits")
%>
```

Variable declaration is required:

```
Option Explicit
```

A variable that will store the connection to the database is created:

```
Dim conn
```

TABLE 8-5

Application Object Methods

Method	Purpose
Lock	Locks the application variables so other sessions cannot modify the variable.
Unlock	Releases the lock on the application variables.

Next, a variable is created that will retrieve the hit information from the database:

```
Dim RSPageHits
```

The `Conn` variable is set to be a database Connection object:

```
set conn = server.createobject ("adodb.connection")
```

A connection to the database is established:

```
conn.open "ASPBook", "sa", "yourpassword"
```

A query retrieves the hit data from the database:

```
set RSPageHits = conn.Execute("select Hits from RSPageHits")
```

A `PageHits` application variable is created that will store the number of page hits:

```
Application("PageHits") = RSPageHits("Hits")
```

Then, every time the page is referenced, the `PageHits` application variable is incremented by one:

```
<%
Application("PageHits") = Application("PageHits") + 1
%>
```

So here is the root of the problem. If you have many visitors accessing the same page simultaneously, a possibility exists that more than one session will attempt to change the value of the application variable at the same time. The *Lock method* takes care of this problem by locking the application variables so that only one session can change the value at one time. The method takes the following syntax:

```
Application.Lock
```

We can modify our code therefore to include the Lock method so that only one session will have the ability to change the variable at one time:

```
<%
Application.Lock
Application("PageHits") = Application("PageHits") + 1
%>
```

In this case, all the application variables for this Active Server Page application would be locked until the compiler finished processing all the code on this page. But, as you will see, there is another method to release the lock.

Unlock Method

There are two ways that you can release a lock on the application variables. The first way is as it was earlier, by letting the code run on the page; then when the code finishes, the lock is released. But if the code takes much time to process, you may end up with a bottleneck of other sessions waiting for the application variables to be released. For that reason you should lock your application variables just prior to changing them and then release the lock just after the modification.

You can release the lock in code using the *Unlock method*, which has the following syntax:

```
Application.Unlock
```

So we should modify our page hit example to this properly locked code:

```
<%
Application.Lock
Application("PageHits") = Application("PageHits") + 1
Application.Unlock
%>
```

Just before the modification, the application variables are locked:

```
Application.Lock
```

Then the modification is made to the application variables:

```
Application("PageHits") = Application("PageHits") + 1
```

As soon as the modification is complete the lock is released:

```
Application.Unlock
```

The global.asa File

So far in this chapter we have looked at how you create an Active Server Page application. We have looked at the files that make up and Active Server Page application, the ASP files, and the global.asa file all within the same directory structure. We have looked at the Session and Application objects and how we can create variables and objects that are available across the Active Server Page application.

In this part of the chapter we look at the special file used in Active Server Page applications, the `global.asa` file. First the `global.asa` file is just a text file. You can create one in your favorite text editor or you can use one of the development tools.

The file must be called `global.asa`, and the file must be located in the root directory of the Active Server Page application. The file consists of four events for which you can write procedures and `Object` tags.

The structure of the `global.asa` file is coded as:

```
<OBJECT RUNAT=Server SCOPE=Application ID=Aconn PROGID="adodb.
  connection">
</OBJECT>
<OBJECT RUNAT=Server SCOPE=Session ID=SobjMail PROGID="CDONTS.
  NewMail">
</OBJECT>

<SCRIPT LANGUAGE="VBScript" RUNAT="Server">
Sub Application_OnStart
'code for procedure
End Sub

Sub Session_OnStart
'code for procedure
End Sub

Sub Session_OnEnd
'code for procedure
End Sub

Sub Application_OnEnd
'code for procedure
End Sub
</SCRIPT>
```

At the top of the file are any Application-level objects that are declared with the `Object` tag:

```
<OBJECT RUNAT=Server SCOPE=Application ID=Aconn PROGID="adodb.
  connection">
</OBJECT>
```

That can be followed by any Session-level objects created with the `Object` tag:

```
<OBJECT RUNAT=Server SCOPE=Session ID=SobjMail PROGID="CDONTS.
  NewMail">
</OBJECT>
```

Next, a Script tag indicating the language used and the location to run the code is written:

```
<SCRIPT LANGUAGE="VBScript" RUNAT="Server">
```

Next, you can include code that you want to run when a specific event occurs. You can provide code that runs when the application starts:

```
Sub Application_OnStart
'code for procedure
End Sub
```

You can provide code that runs whenever a session starts:

```
Sub Session_OnStart
'code for procedure
End Sub
```

You can have code that runs when a session ends:

```
Sub Session_OnEnd
'code for procedure
End Sub
```

And you can have code that runs when the application ends:

```
Sub Application_OnEnd
'code for procedure
End Sub
```

The page ends with the end Script tag:

```
</SCRIPT>
```

global.asa Events

Within the global.asa file, you can write code that runs at four different points in the life of your application. The events are discussed below and summarized in Table 8-6.

The structure of the event procedure is as follows:

```
Sub NameOfEvent
   'Event code
End Sub
```

The first line of the procedure starts with the keyword Sub, which is followed with the name of the procedure. On the next line, and the lines

TABLE 8-6

Application and
Session Events

Event	Purpose
Application_OnStart	The event fires when the first page of the application is requested.
Application_OnEnd	Code in this event fires when the IIS shuts down.
Session_OnStart	Fires when the first page of the application is requested for each visitor.
Session_OnEnd	The code in this procedure fires when the session times out or the Abandon method is called.

that follow, is the code that you want to run when the event occurs. The last line of the event procedure contains the keywords End Sub.

Application_OnStart Event

When a visitor requests the first page in your Active Server Page application since the server was started, the Application_OnStart event fires. The event fires before any of the code on the page being requested runs and before the Session_OnStart event fires.

The Application_OnStart event fires only once and will not fire again until the application ends. Your code in this event can access the Application object and the Server object. The Request, Response, and Session objects are not available for you to code.

The event has the following syntax:

```
Sub Application_OnStart
'code for procedure
End Sub
```

This event is typically used for program initialization. This is code that you want to run once at the beginning of your application. This frequently includes creating application variables and objects. The event is also used for notification code.

Previously in this chapter we looked at a page that calculated the total due on an order. The code used application variables declared on an Active Server Page to determine the order total. Those variables should be initialized in the Application_OnStart event:

```
Sub Application_OnStart
  Application("CurrentDiscount") = .9
  Application("MinShipHand") = 12
  Application("MinQuantity") = 2
  Application("ShipHandPercent") = .07
End Sub
```

We don't need to worry about locking the application variables in this event since this event fires and runs before any other code in the Active Server Page application runs.

Another good use for this event is for program customization. Say, for example, that you create an Active Server Page application that is used by many organizations. You want to provide them with a minimal amount of understanding of ASP to use your tool. But the Active Server Page application can be customized from customer to customer and you want them to be able to do that themselves. One way you could accomplish that is by creating a series of configuration variables in the Application_OnStart event. That would give your users a central way of modifying the functionality of the program. Take this example:

```
Sub Application_OnStart
  Application("DNS") = "OC"
  Application("UserName") = "Admin"
  Application("Password") = "yourpassword"
  Application("AllowNew") = "Yes"
  Application("AllowEnroll") = "Yes"
  Application("Path2Logo") = "./images/logo.gif"
  Application("AllowDrop") = "No"
  Application("ChatMode") = "External"
End Sub
```

This code allows users to customize an Online Campus Active Server Page application. First, users can specify the name of the DNS connecting to the Online Campus database:

```
Application("DNS") = "OC"
```

They can also specify the user to log into the database as:

```
Application("UserName") = "Admin"
```

and the password for that user:

```
Application("Password") = "yourpassword"
```

Next, they can control how the program will function. Do they wish to allow new students? If so, code:

```
Application("AllowNew") = "Yes"
```

Do they wish to allow existing students to enroll? If so, code:

```
Application("AllowEnroll") = "Yes"
```

Next, they specify the location of their company's logo:

```
Application("Path2Logo") = "./images/logo.gif"
```

They can specify whether a student can drop themselves from a course:

```
Application("AllowDrop") = "No"
```

And the type of chat program used with the tool:

```
Application("ChatMode") = "External"
```

In your documentation you would provide users with specific instructions on the meaning and values of these application variables. Then in your code you could control the options on a page based on these preferences. For example, here's code from such an Enrollment page:

```
<%
Option Explicit
Dim conn
Dim RSCourses
if Application("AllowEnroll") = "Yes" then
  set conn = server.createobject ("adodb.connection")
  conn.open Application("DNS"), Application("UserName"), _
    Application("Password")
  set RSCourses = conn.execute ("SELECT CourseID, CourseName, " _
    & CourseDescription FROM OCCourses")
%>
  <P ALIGN="CENTER"><B><FONT COLOR="#0000A0" SIZE="+3"
  FACE="Arial,Helvetica">Select a course to enroll</B></FONT>
<%
  do until RSCourses.EOF
%>
  <A HREF="../html/enrolldrop.asp?CourseID=
    <% Response.Write RSCourses("CourseID") %>">
    <IMG HEIGHT=52 WIDTH=56 SRC="../assets/images/p048.gif"
    BORDER=0 ALT="Enroll" ></A>
  <P><B><FONT FACE="Arial,Helvetica">
    <% Response.Write RSCourses("CourseName") %> -
    <% Response.Write RSCourses("CourseDescription") %></B></FONT>
<%
    RSCourses.MoveNext
  loop
end if
%>
```

First, we state that we will declare our variables:

```
Option Explicit
```

Then we create a variable that will be used for the database connection:

```
Dim conn
```

and a variable that will retrieve the course information:

```
Dim RSCourses
```

Here we check the preferences specified in the Application_OnStart event to see whether we should display enrollment information at all:

```
if Application("AllowEnroll") = "Yes" then
```

If the preference is "Yes", then we should. So we create a connection object:

```
set conn = server.createobject ("adodb.connection")
```

Then note that the application variables are used to specify the DNS and the user name and password for connecting to the database:

```
conn.open Application("DNS"), Application("UserName"), _
  Application("Password")
```

Course information is then retrieved from the database:

```
set RSCourses = conn.execute ("SELECT CourseID, CourseName, " _
  & CourseDescription FROM OCCourses")
```

Notice that this HTML is part of our If statement. This will not appear if the AllowEnroll preference is set to anything except "Yes":

```
<P ALIGN="CENTER"><B><FONT COLOR="#0000A0" SIZE="+3"
FACE="Arial,Helvetica">Select a course to enroll</B></FONT>
```

Then we start a loop that will take us through each of the courses in the database:

```
do until RSCourses.EOF
```

Each of the courses is written to the browser as a link that allows the visitor to sign up for a course:

```
<A HREF="../html/enrolldrop.asp?CourseID=
  <% Response.Write RSCourses("CourseID") %>">
```

```
  <IMG HEIGHT=52 WIDTH=56 SRC="../assets/images/p048.gif"
  BORDER=0 ALT="Enroll" ></A>
<P><B><FONT FACE="Arial,Helvetica">
  <% Response.Write RSCourses("CourseName") %> -
<% Response.Write RSCourses("CourseDescription") %></B></FONT>
```

Then we loop back to process the next course:

```
RSCourses.MoveNext
Loop
```

and end the `If` block:

```
end if
```

Application_OnEnd Event

As stated, the application starts when a visitor to your site accesses the first page of your site, just that one time. You provide code for that occurrence through the Application_OnStart event. You can also provide code that runs when the application ends.

The application ends when the server shuts down, so you could provide clean-up or other notification code here. But be very careful about what you include here, since sometimes your application will stop because of an error or a problem on the server. If that happens, your code would never have a chance to run. For that reason, I personally never use this event.

The event has the following syntax:

```
Sub Application_OnEnd
'code for procedure
End Sub
```

You would replace the comment `code for procedure` with whatever code you wanted to run when this event occurred.

Session_OnStart Event

Every time a visitor enters your Active Server Page application, the Session_OnStart event fires and whatever code you place in that event would run. The Session_OnStart event occurs after the Application_OnStart event, if it hasn't yet run, but before any code on the Active Server Page that the visitor is requesting.

When the Session_OnStart event runs, you have all the ASP objects available to code with. The event has the following syntax:

```
Sub Session_OnStart
'code for procedure
End Sub
```

Typically, you place user initialization code here—things like creating a record in a database for the session, starting a shopping cart, setting preferences, and creating session variables and objects are uses of this event.

One of the very helpful things you can do with the Session_OnStart event is to prevent visitors from going to any pages at your site before going to a particular page in your site. For example, you may want to force your visitors to go through your Home Page before going to any other part of your site, or maybe you want them to log in before visiting the rest of the site.

Here is how simple this is to do with the Session_OnStart event:

```
Sub Session_OnStart
  Response.Redirect "./welcome.asp"
End Sub
```

Remember that the Session_OnStart event fires before any code on any of the Active Server Pages in your Active Server Page application fire, so regardless of what ASP the visitor enters in their browser, they are forced to go to the Welcome page.

Take this simple example of using such code. This sample site has two pages, a Welcome page and some other page. When visitors type in the address of the other page in their browser they don't see that page; they see the Welcome page as shown in Figure 8-10. So visitors are not able to go straight to some other page at the site. They must first go to the Welcome page to log in or just to navigate through the site as you wish them to.

If they enter the other page's address in their browser, however, they do see the other page since their session has now begun. See Figure 8-11.

Session_OnEnd Event

The session starts when a visitor accesses the first Active Server Page in your Active Server Page application. The session ends when you call the Abandon method or the visitors' session times out because they didn't make a request in the required number of minutes.

When the session ends, the Session_OnEnd event fires, in which event you can programmatically use the Application, Server, and

Figure 8-10
Figure 8-10
Welcome page to the
sample site.

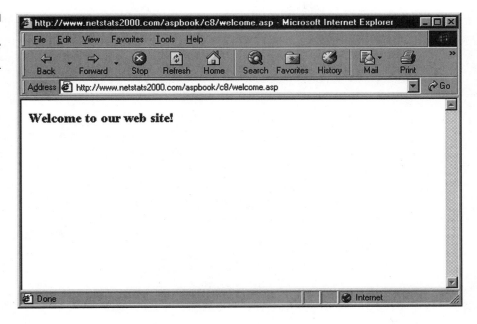

Figure 8-11
Viewing the other
page in the sample
site.

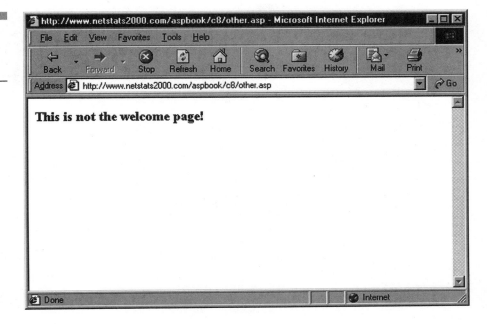

Session objects but the Request and Response objects are no longer available. The event has the following syntax:

```
Sub Session_OnEnd
'code for procedure
End Sub
```

In this event, you would include clean-up code. You may write to the database the date and time that the visitor left a session. You could also use this event to finish processing tasks that still remain opened; or, you could use this event to send out some email notification, if required, using the Collaborative Data objects that are discussed in the next chapter.

Here's a sample of what you might include in the Session_OnEnd event. This procedure places visitors' host name into the database so you can track the identity of the visitors to the site. The value isn't normally available directly through IIS since you usually just get the IP Address of the visitors. The code uses a third-party tool that performs a reverse lookup of the IP Address to determine the Host Name. The problem prior to placing the code in the Session_OnEnd event was that the code was taking too long to process and it was holding up the completion of the visitors' page request in the browser. But now that it is in the Session_OnEnd event, visitors can move on without having to wait for this code to process:

```
Sub Session_OnEnd
  Dim objDNS
  Dim conn
  Dim hostname
  Dim GMT
  set objDNS = server.createobject("INet.DNS.1")
  objDNS.ip = request.servervariables("remote_addr")
  If objDNS.Host <> "" Then
    hostname = objDNS.Host
  Else
    hostname = request.servervariables("remote_addr")
  End If
  GMT = Cstr (dateadd("h", 6, now()))
  set conn = server.createobject ("adodb.connection")
  conn.open "IISLog", "sa", "yourpassword"
  SQL = "update iislog..sessions set session_end = '" & GMT _
    & "', hostname = '" & hostname & "'"
  SQL = SQL & " where Session_id = " & cstr(Session("session_id"))
  conn.Execute SQL
End Sub
```

First, some variables that will be used in this event are declared. One will store an instance of the DNS reverse lookup tool:

```
Dim objDNS
```

Next, a variable is created that will store the connection to the database:

```
Dim conn
```

A variable that will store the visitor's host name is created:

```
Dim hostname
```

and a variable that will store the GMT time is created:

```
Dim GMT
```

The Server object is used to create an instance of the reverse lookup tool:

```
set objDNS = server.createobject("INet.DNS.1")
```

The IP property of that object is set to the IP Address of the visitor's system:

```
objDNS.ip = request.servervariables("remote_addr")
```

The host property of the DNS object is now set to the host name of the visitor's system. But if it is an unknown name, the value will be set to an empty string:

```
If objDNS.Host <> "" Then
```

If it is not, then the host name was found:

```
hostname = objDNS.Host
```

otherwise, the host name was not found and just the IP Address will be used:

```
Else
  hostname = request.servervariables("remote_addr")
End If
```

We also wish to store in the database the date and time that the visitor's session ended. The time is stored in GMT format, which is calculated here as being 6 hours later than the local time zone of the server:

```
GMT = Cstr (dateadd("h", 6, now()))
```

Next, a connection to the database is established:

```
set conn = server.createobject ("adodb.connection")
conn.open "IISLog", "sa", "yourpassword"
```

(Note that the Connection object will be discussed at length in Chapter 14.)

An SQL statement is built using the host name and the time that the session ended. These values will be entered into the record in the database that corresponds with the Session_ID of the visitor:

```
SQL = "update iislog..sessions set session_end = '" & GMT _
    & "', hostname = '" & hostname & "'"
SQL = SQL & " where Session_id = " & cstr(Session("session_id"))
```

That SQL statement is then run to modify the database:

```
conn.Execute SQL
```

Object Declarations in the global.asa

As we saw in the previous sections on the Application object and the Session object, we can create objects at these levels through Object tags in the global.asa. These objects are made available in code through the StaticObjects collections of both the Session and Application objects.

These tags are placed outside the Script tags in the global.asa and have the following format:

```
<OBJECT RUNAT=Server SCOPE=TheScope ID=Name PROGID="App.Class">
</OBJECT>
```

The text TheScope would be replaced with the word Session if you wanted the object created at the Session level or Application if you were creating an Application-level object. Name would be replaced with whatever name you want to give to this object that you will use in your code to refer to this object. An App.Class would be replaced with the name of the server and the class within the server that you wanted to create.

For example, here an Application-level object named Aconn that will be an ADO database connection is created:

```
<OBJECT RUNAT=Server SCOPE=Application ID=Aconn PROGID="adodb.
   connection">
</OBJECT>
```

and here a Session-level object name SobjMail is created that is of the NewMail class of the Collaborative Data objects is created:

```
<OBJECT RUNAT=Server SCOPE=Session ID=SobjMail
PROGID="CDONTS.NewMail">
</OBJECT>
```

Active Server Page Applications in Use

The material covered in this chapter really opens up ASP into what it needs to be so you can create entire solutions in your company's Internet or intranet. Without the Application and Session objects your site would be nothing more than just a series of pages that happened to link to each other. But with these objects you can create robust real-world applications.

Take e-commerce as a case study. Figure 8-12 shows a real-world site that I manage. The page shown in this figure is part of an ordering wizard. The page prompts visitors for the details regarding the specific item that they are ordering. The page relies heavily on the Session object to keep track of visitors so they have the correct items in their shopping cart as shown in this code from that page:

```
if isempty(Session("SessionID")) then
  CurrentDateTime = Now
  conn.Execute "insert into WICustomers (SessionDateTime) values ('" _
    & CurrentDateTime & "')"
  set RSSession = conn.Execute("select SessionID from WICustomers " _
    & "where SessionDateTime = '" & CurrentDateTime & "'")
  Session("SessionID") = RSSession("SessionID")
end if
'''''''''''''
set RSTotal = conn.Execute("select Sum(TotalPrice) as TheTotal from
WIOrderItems " _
  & "where SessionID = " & Session("SessionID"))
if RSTotal("TheTotal") * Application("ShipPercent") > Application
("MinShip") then
  TopShipping = RSTotal("TheTotal") * Application("ShipPercent")
else
  TopShipping = Application("MinShip")
end if
'''''''''''''
Response.Redirect "https://www.netstats2000.com/bud/html/" _
  & shopping_cart.asp?SessionID=" & Session("SessionID")
```

In the first chunk of code, the session variable called `SessionID` is checked to see if it is empty:

```
if isempty(Session("SessionID")) then
```

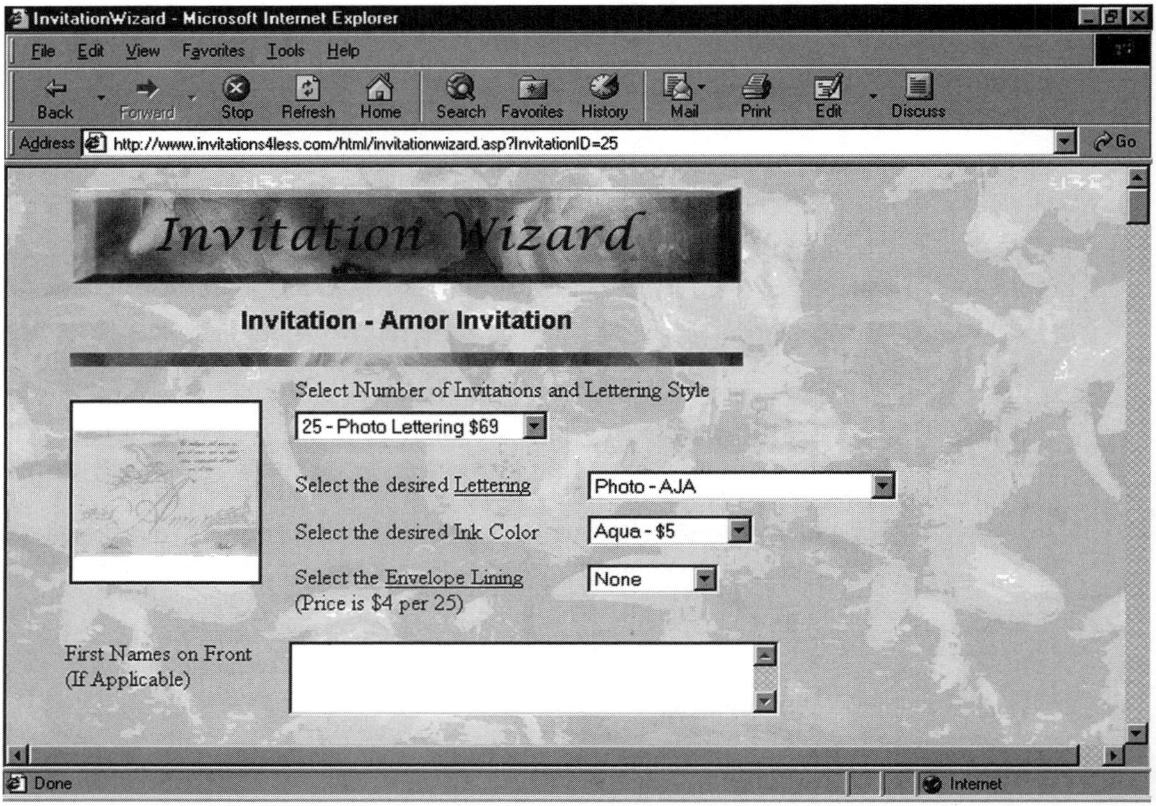

Figure 8-12 Ordering wizard.

If the session variable is empty, that means that visitors have just placed their first item in the shopping cart and a shopping cart record for visitors needs to be created. The current system date and time will be part of the shopping cart record:

```
CurrentDateTime = Now
```

A record is then added to the database:

```
conn.Execute "insert into WICustomers (SessionDateTime) values ('" _
  & CurrentDateTime & "')"
```

The ID for that newly created shopping cart record is retrieved from the database:

```
set RSSession = conn.Execute("select SessionID from WICustomers " _
   & "where SessionDateTime = '" & CurrentDateTime & "'")
```

The `SessionID` session variable is then set to the value from the shopping cart record:

```
Session("SessionID") = RSSession("SessionID")
```

The next chunk of code calculates the shipping for the order. First the order total is derived by retrieving the total for each item in the visitor's shopping cart based on the `SessionID`:

```
set RSTotal = conn.Execute("select Sum(TotalPrice) as TheTotal from
   WIOrderItems " _
   & "where SessionID = " & Session("SessionID"))
```

Then application variables are used to compare the shipping, based on the percent paid for shipping with the minimum amount of shipping due:

```
if RSTotal("TheTotal") * Application("ShipPercent") > Application
   ("MinShip") then
```

If the shipping based on percentage is the greater of the two, it is used:

```
TopShipping = RSTotal("TheTotal") * Application("ShipPercent")
```

otherwise, the minimum amount of shipping would be used:

```
TopShipping = Application("MinShip")
```

So you can see that a well-planned complex Active Server Page application would make full use of the features of the Application object and the Session object.

Collaborative Data Objects for Windows NT Server

Adding Email Messaging Capabilities to Your ASP

The Collaborative Data Objects for Windows NT Server (CDONTS, or CDO for NTS) provide objects that you can instantiate from your Active Server Pages that allow you to send email from your Active Server Pages and your Active Server Page Applications. The CDONTS library exposes a top-level class that we can create, the *NewMail class*, which provides an easy-to-use set of methods and properties that allow you to send email from your Active Server Pages. This chapter focuses on this object.

CDONTS is designed to run on Windows NT Server running IIS 4.0 or later. The library does not require Exchange Server to run. If you do have Exchange Server on your system, it needs to be installed after IIS

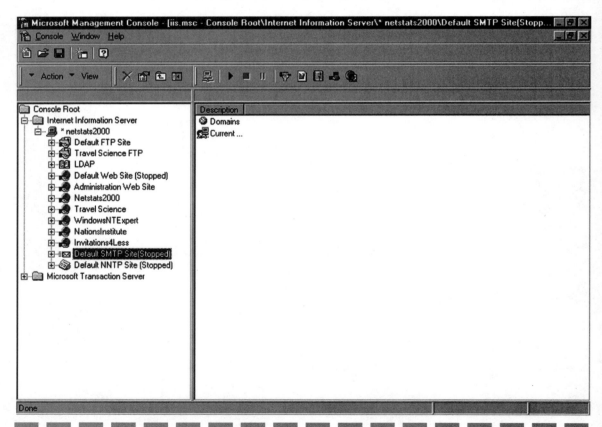

Figure 9-1   *SMTP Site within IIS.*

for the CDONTS library to be properly installed. If you don't have Exchange Server, you will need to be running the SMTP server that comes with IIS for the CDONTS library to function properly. You should see the SMTP Site in IIS as shown in Figure 9-1.

If you don't have Microsoft Exchange, you can configure the SMTP Site from here by viewing its properties. If you don't see the SMTP Site in IIS, then you probably didn't install that component when you installed IIS. Rerun setup and add this component.

NewMail Object

In a few of the examples in this book you have already seen the NewMail object in action. Using the NewMail object, you can send a basic email from your ASP code in just three simple lines:

```
Set objMail = Server.CreateObject("CDONTS.NewMail")
objMail.Send "bob@na.com", "julie@na.com", "Welcome!", _
    "Welcome to the company Julie. We are glad you are here! -- Bob"
Set objMail = Nothing
```

That's all it takes, just those three lines. First, you create a NewMail object from the CDONTS library:

```
Set objMail = Server.CreateObject("CDONTS.NewMail")
```

Then you use the Send method to actually send out the email. The first parameter in the Send method is who the message is from; the second parameter is who the message is to; the third parameter is the subject of the email message; and the last parameter is the text of the message itself:

```
objMail.Send "bob@na.com", "julie@na.com", "Welcome!", _
    "Welcome to the company Julie. We are glad you are here! -- Bob"
```

You then release the resources of the NewMail object by setting it to nothing:

```
Set objMail = Nothing
```

An email is then sent to the recipient. The preceding code would produce an email like the one shown in Figure 9-2. But you can do much

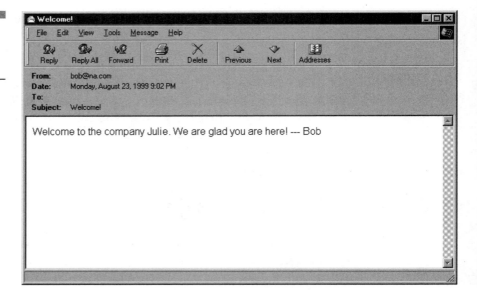

more with the NewMail object than just what is shown in this simple example. In the next part of the chapter, we explore the properties and methods of the NewMail object.

NewMail Object Properties

The properties of the NewMail object allow you to customize how the email message is sent. Table 9-1 summarizes these properties, which are discussed below.

To Property

The *To property* allows you to specify the email address of the recipient. The property has the following form:

```
ObjMail.To = ListofRecipients
```

ObjMail in this code must be an object of the NewMail class of the CDONTS library. The variable `ListofRecipients` is the email address of the person or people to whom you want to send a message. You can address the email to a single person like this:

```
ObjMail.To = "harris@na.com"
```

TABLE 9-1

NewMail Object
Properties

Property	Purpose
To	Email address of the recipient
From	Email address of the sender
Subject	The subject of the message
Body	The text of the email message
CC	Carbon Copy recipients
BCC	Blind Carbon Copy recipients
Importance	Sets the level of importance of the message
BodyFormat	Sets the format of the text of the message, plain text or HTML
MailFormat	Sets the encoding for the message, text or MIME
ContentBase	URL base for all links in the message
ContentLocation	Sets the path for all URL links in the body of the message
Value	User to add additional headers to the message
Version	Returns the version of the CDONTS library

You can also address the email to a list of people by separating each of the recipient's email addresses with a semicolon like the line of code shown here:

```
ObjMail.To = "harris@na.com;julie@na.com;ruth@na.com"
```

Now the email would be sent out to three addresses. Note that you can use the To property to specify the recipients of the message or you can use the parameter of the Send method, so the line preceding would be equivalent to this:

```
objMail.Send "bob@na.com", " harris@na.com;julie@na.com;ruth@na.
  com ", _
"Welcome!", "Welcome to the company Everybody. We are glad you are
here! -- Bob"
```

If you want to use the To property, just leave the second parameter of the Send method blank:

```
ObjMail.To = "harris@na.com;julie@na.com;ruth@na.com"
objMail.Send "bob@na.com", , "Welcome!", _
  "Welcome to the company Everybody. We are glad you are here! --
Bob"
```

If you use both the To property and the Send method parameter, then everyone on both lists will receive an email. So this code:

```
ObjMail.To = "harris@na.com;julie@na.com;ruth@na.com"
objMail.Send "bob@na.com", "nancy@na.com", "Welcome!", _
  "Welcome to the company Everybody. We are glad you are here! --
    Bob"
```

would send an email to four recipients. The email would be sent to the three addresses listed in the To property and the one listed in the second parameter of the Send method.

From Property

The *From property* stores the email address of the sender. The property has the following form:

```
ObjMail.From = EmailAddressofSender
```

Here the ObjMail must be a valid NewMail object of the CDONTS library. The variable `EmailAddressofSender` must be a complete email address like this:

```
ObjMail.From = "marg@na.com"
```

You can include a single sender in this property only. In other words, you can't include a semicolon to indicate multiple senders; if you do, you will get an error in the browser like the one shown in Figure 9-3.

You can use the From property to indicate the sender or you can use the same parameter as the Send method. So this:

```
objMail.To = "julie@na.com;jill@na.com"
objMail.From = "bob@na.com"
objMail.Send , , "Test Mail", _
  "This email was sent to a list of people."
```

is functionally equivalent to this:

```
objMail.To = "julie@na.com;jill@na.com"
objMail.Send "bob@na.com", , "Test Mail", _
  "This email was sent to a list of people."
```

If you specify both, then the sender in the Send method is the one that appears to the recipient of the email message.

Figure 9-3
Error message when
multiple senders are
specified.

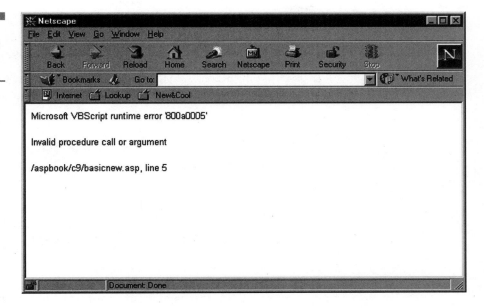

Subject Property

You can use the *Subject property* to specify the subject of the message.
The property has the following format:

```
ObjMail.Subject = TheSubject
```

Here, ObjMail must be a valid NewMail object of the CDONTS server.
TheSubject is a string representing the subject of the message. If you
coded this:

```
ObjMail.Subject = "Welcome!"
```

then the subject of the message would be set to the text "Welcome!"
You can include the subject using the Subject property or by using the
third parameter of the Send method. So this:

```
objMail.To = " julie@na.com;jill@na.com "
objMail.From = "bob@na.com"
objMail.Subject = "Welcome!"
objMail.Send , , , _
  "This email was sent to a list of people."
```

is functionally equivalent to this:

```
objMail.To = " julie@na.com;jill@na.com "
objMail.From = "bob@na.com"
objMail.Send , , "Welcome!", _
 "This email was sent to a list of people."
```

If you include both the Subject property and the third parameter of the Send method, the subject entered in the Send method will be used.

Body Property

The *Body property* sets the text of the message, or HTML, as you will see in a later section. The property has the following form:

```
ObjMail.Body = BodyText
```

ObjMail must be a valid NewMail object of the CDONTS library. BodyText is the text of the message. So if you coded this:

```
objMail.Body = "This email was sent to a list of people."
```

then the text of the message would contain the preceding text. You can use the Body property or the fourth parameter of the Send method to include the body of the email message, so this:

```
objMail.To = " julie@na.com;jill@na.com "
objMail.From = "bob@na.com"
objMail.Subject = "Welcome!"
objMail.Body = "Thanks for stopping by our web site!"
objMail.Send
```

is functionally the same as this:

```
objMail.To = " julie@na.com;jill@na.com "
objMail.From = "bob@na.com"
objMail.Subject = "Welcome!"
objMail.Send , , , "Thanks for stopping by our Web Site!"
```

When you are creating email messages in your code, you will find the need to format them with new line characters to indicate breaks in the text. You can do this with the Chr function that takes a number as a parameter and returns the character for that number. So if you want a new line, you could code this:

```
Chr(13)
```

If you want a tab, you could code this:

```
Chr(9)
```

Another character that you may need to embed within the text of your message is a quote. You can include a quote by inserting two quotes within a quoted string.

Take this code block that includes quotes and new line characters within the body of an email:

```
<%
Option Explicit
Dim objMail
Dim TheMessage
Set objMail = Server.CreateObject("CDONTS.NewMail")
objMail.To = "julie@na.com;jill@na.com"
objMail.From = "bob@na.com"
objMail.Subject = "Welcome!"
TheMessage = "Hello:" & chr(13) & chr(13) _
   & "Thanks for coming to our site!" & chr(13) & chr(13) _
   & """We appreciate your business!"""
objMail.Body = TheMessage
objMail.Send
response.write "done"
Set objMail = Nothing
%>
```

First, we indicate that the variables will be declared:

```
Option Explicit
```

Next, a variable that will hold our NewMail object is created:

```
Dim objMail
```

Another variable that will hold the text of the message is created:

```
Dim TheMessage
```

We then use the CreateObject method of the Server object to instantiate the NewMail object:

```
Set objMail = Server.CreateObject("CDONTS.NewMail")
```

We then specify whom the message is to:

```
objMail.To = "julie@na.com;jill@na.com"
```

whom the message is from:

```
objMail.From = "bob@na.com"
```

then the subject for the message:

```
objMail.Subject = "Welcome!"
```

Here the text of the message is stored in the variable `TheMessage`. Note the use of the `Chr` function to create new lines. Also note the use of the double quotes to indicate a quote within a quote:

```
TheMessage = "Hello:" & chr(13) & chr(13) _
    & "Thanks for coming to our site!" & chr(13) & chr(13) _
    & """We appreciate your business!"""
```

The Body property is set to the `TheMessage` variable:

```
objMail.Body = TheMessage
```

The message is then sent:

```
objMail.Send
```

and the object is released from memory:

```
Set objMail = Nothing
```

The email produced from this code is displayed in Figure 9-4. Notice the location of the quotes and new lines.

Figure 9-4
Email that includes special characters.

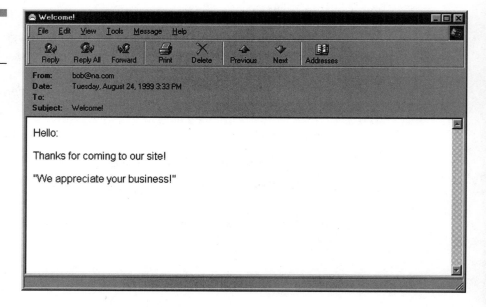

CC Property

The *CC property* allows you to specify recipients of the message that are not part of the main recipients. The CC recipients see the same message but are noted as CC recipients instead of To recipients in the header of the email message.

The property takes the following form:

```
ObjMail.CC = CCList
```

ObjMail must be a valid instance of the NewMail class of the CDONTS library. `CCList` is a string containing the list of email addresses. You can specify a single email address as a CC recipient:

```
ObjMail.CC = "joe@na.com"
```

or, you can include multiple CC email addresses by separating each one with a semicolon:

```
ObjMail.CC = "joe@na.com;kate@na.com"
```

BCC Property

With the *BCC property* you can include blind carbon copy recipients. A BCC addressee receives the same message as those specified in the To and the CC properties but the To and CC recipients are unaware of the BCC email addresses. With this property you can include individuals privately.

The property takes the following form:

```
ObjMail.BCC = BCCList
```

ObjMail must be a valid instance of the NewMail class of the CDONTS library. `BCCList` is a string containing the list of email addresses that are to be blind carbon copy recipients. You can specify a single email address as a BCC recipient:

```
ObjMail.BCC = "joe@na.com"
```

or, you can include multiple BCC email addresses by separating each one with a semicolon:

```
ObjMail.BCC = "joe@na.com;kate@na.com"
```

Importance Property

Different email applications allow you to send an importance level with your email messages. How this importance flag is displayed varies on the system. With the *Importance property*, you can also specify the importance of an email message in your code.

The syntax for this property is:

```
ObjMail.Importance = Value
```

ObjMail must be a valid instance of the NewClass object. The possible values for Value are displayed in Table 9-2.

So we can now add the Importance property to our code block:

```
<%
Option Explicit
Dim objMail
Dim TheMessage
Set objMail = Server.CreateObject("CDONTS.NewMail")
objMail.To = "julie@na.com "
objMail.From = "bob@na.com"
objMail.Subject = "Welcome!"
TheMessage = "Hello:" & chr(13) & chr(13) _
    & "Thanks for coming to our site!" & chr(13) & chr(13) _
    & """We appreciate your business!"""
objMail.Body = TheMessage
objMail.Importance = 2
objMail.Send
Set objMail = Nothing
response.write "done"
%>
```

With Importance set to high, the recipient's email program usually makes the message more visible. Note in Outlook Express the change to the message because of the importance as shown in Figure 9-5.

BodyFormat and MailFormat Properties

So far, all the email we have sent has been in text format. But we can also send our email as an HTML, using the BodyFormat and MailFormat properties.

TABLE 9-2

Importance Property Values

Value	Meaning
0	Low Importance
1	Normal Importance (default)
2	High Importance

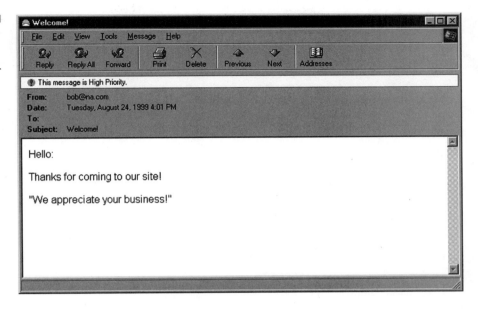

Figure 9-5
Message using the
Importance property.

The *BodyFormat property* has the following syntax:

```
ObjMail.BodyFormat = Value
```

ObjMail is a NewMail object of the CDONTS server. Value can be set to 1, the default that means that the body of the email is text. The other value for the property is 0, which refers to the body containing HTML.

To send an HTML email, you must also use the *MailFormat property*, which sets the encoding type used for the message. The syntax for the property is as follows:

```
ObjMail.MailFormat = Value
```

ObjMail must be a NewMail object. Value can be set to 1 or 0. The default value is 1, which means that the encoding used is text. For HTML email you need to use the value 1, which means that MIME encoding should be used.

This code sample sends an HTML email of high priority.

```
<%
Option Explicit
```

```
Dim objMail
Dim TheMessage
Set objMail = Server.CreateObject("CDONTS.NewMail")
objMail.To = "tim@na.com"
objMail.From = "bob@na.com"
objMail.Subject = "We've gone crazy!"
TheMessage = "<HTML>" _
  & "<HEAD>" _
  & "<TITLE>We've Got A Sale</TITLE>" _
  & "</HEAD>" _
  & "<BODY>" _
  & "<H1><CENTER>Everything is <STRIKE>30%</STRIKE> 50%
    off!</CENTER></H1>" _
  & "<HR>" _
  & "<P>So stop by now! <A HREF=""http://www.na.com"">Click
    here!</A></P>" _
  & "</BODY>" _
  & "</HTML>"
objMail.Body = TheMessage
objMail.Importance = 2
objMail.BodyFormat = 0
objMail.MailFormat = 0
objMail.Send
Set objMail = Nothing
%>
```

First, we specify that we will declare our variables:

```
Option Explicit
```

We then declare the NewMail object variable:

```
Dim objMail
```

and a variable that will hold the HTML email body:

```
Dim TheMessage
```

The objMail variable is instantiated:

```
Set objMail = Server.CreateObject("CDONTS.NewMail")
```

and the recipient of the message is specified:

```
objMail.To = "tim@na.com"
```

Next, the sender is noted through the From property:

```
objMail.From = "bob@na.com"
```

The email is given a subject:

```
objMail.Subject = "We've gone crazy!"
```

Then we build the body of our message as raw HTML. Included are a variety of HTML tags. Notice the embedded quotes within the text:

```
TheMessage = "<HTML>" _
    & "<HEAD>" _
    & "<TITLE>We've Got A Sale</TITLE>" _
    & "</HEAD>" _
    & "<BODY>" _
    & "<H1><CENTER>Everything is <STRIKE>30%</STRIKE> 50%
      off!</CENTER></H1>" _
    & "<HR>" _
    & "<P>So stop by now! <A HREF=""http://www.na.com"">Click
      here!</A></P>" _
    & "</BODY>" _
& "</HTML>"
```

We then set the value of the body to the HTML:

```
objMail.Body = TheMessage
```

The importance of the message is then set:

```
objMail.Importance = 2
```

We indicate that the body is HTML:

```
objMail.BodyFormat = 0
```

The encoding format used should be MIME:

```
objMail.MailFormat = 0
```

and the Send method is used to send the email:

```
objMail.Send
```

The resources of the message are then released:

```
Set objMail = Nothing
```

The recipient of the email message would see the message displayed in Figure 9-6.

Figure 9-6
HTML email message.

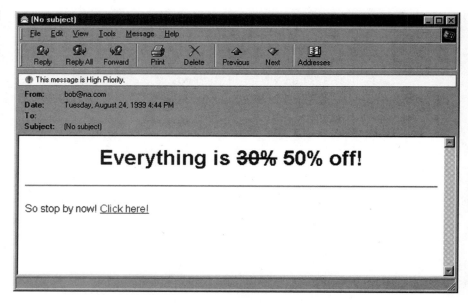

Remember, though, not all email clients can view HTML. Some programs may display just the text of the email message like that shown in Figure 9-7. The program does attempt to show the text in the email, but note how the meaning has changed. In the HTML document, the 30% was crossed out in favor of the 50%. Here we see both of the percentages.

ContentBase and ContentLocation Properties

The ContentBase and ContentLocation properties allow you to specify the location of relative references within your HTML. The *ContentBase property* normally stores the high-level location for the URLs and the *ContentLocation property* normally stores the directory path from the ContentLocation.

The ContentBase property has the following syntax:

```
ObjMail.ContentBase = Path
```

ObjMail must be a valid instance of the NewMail class. The path is usually a domain path. So you may include something like this:

```
ObjMail.ContentBase = "http://www.whatever.com/"
```

If that was all that you included, then the paths on your HTML email would use this as their relative reference in locating images and links.

Figure 9-7
HTML email viewed
by a client that does
not support HTML.

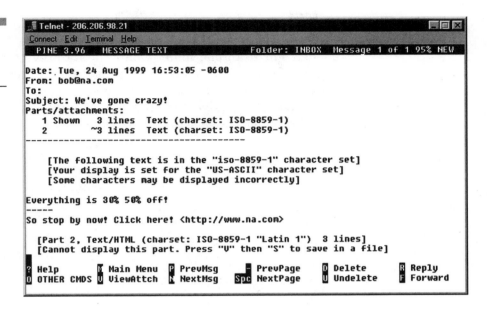

You can also use the ContentLocation property to specify the directory beneath the domain name where the links and files are located. The syntax for the ContentLocation property is as follows:

```
ObjMail.ContentLocation = Path
```

ObjMail is an instance of the NewMail class. The Path would be the location for the files and links. For example, if you coded this:

```
ObjMail.ContentLocation = "emailreports/december/"
```

an image tag in the body of the HTML email would use the ContentBase together with the ContentLocation to determine the physical location of the image.

Value Property

Depending on the email client that the recipient of an email has, there are a variety of other settings that an email message can have. You can add these additional settings through the Value property.

The *Value property* adds an additional Header to the email message and has the following format:

```
ObjMail.Value(HeaderName) = HeaderValue
```

ObjMail must be a valid NewMail object. HeaderName is an instance of the header you wish to add, and HeaderValue is the value for that header. For example, many email clients provide for a From email address as well as a Reply-To email address. If recipients click on the REPLY button in their email client application, it will use the Reply-To email address instead of the From email address.

For example, take a look at this code:

```
<%
Option Explicit
Dim objMail
Set objMail = Server.CreateObject("CDONTS.NewMail")
objMail.To = "kate@na.com"
objMail.From = "bob@na.com"
objMail.Subject = "We've gone crazy!"
objMail.Body = "Send me an email for details!"
objMail.Importance = 2
objMail.Value("Reply-To") = "sales Staff<sales@na.com>"
objMail.Send
Set objMail = Nothing
%>
```

First, we tell the compiler that we will declare our variables:

```
Option Explicit
```

Then we declare the NewMail variable:

```
Dim objMail
```

Then we instantiate the NewMail object:

```
Set objMail = Server.CreateObject("CDONTS.NewMail")
```

The To property is set:

```
objMail.To = "kate@na.com"
```

as is the From property:

```
objMail.From = "bob@na.com"
```

Next, the subject and body of the message are set:

```
objMail.Subject = "We've gone crazy!"
objMail.Body = "Send me an email for details!"
```

Figure 9-8
Message that used
the Reply-To header.

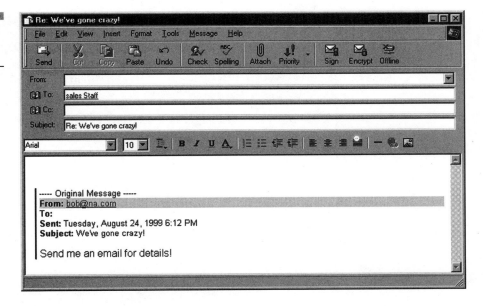

We indicate that the message has high importance:

```
objMail.Importance = 2
```

Then we add the Reply-To header:

```
objMail.Value("Reply-To") = "sales Staff<sales@na.com>"
```

before sending the message and releasing its resources:

```
objMail.Send
Set objMail = Nothing
```

When visitors click the REPLY button from their email client, the message is addressed to the Reply-To address instead of the From address, as shown in Figure 9-8.

Version Property

One final property of the NewMail object to talk about is the *Version property*, which returns the version of the CDONTS library. This read-only property takes the following form:

```
ObjMail.Version
```

Figure 9-9
Version property
displayed.

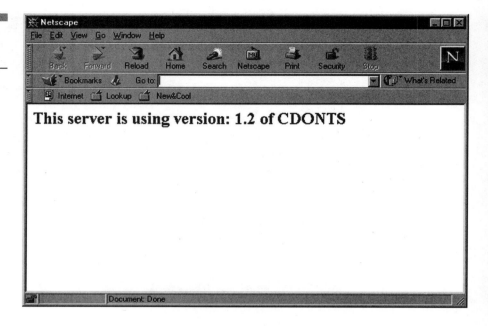

ObjMail has to be a valid NewMail object. Returned from the function is the version of the library, so the following code:

```
<%
Option Explicit
Dim objMail
Set objMail = Server.CreateObject("CDONTS.NewMail")
Response.Write "<H2>This server is using version: " _
  & objMail.Version & " of CDONTS</H2>"
%>
```

would display the version of CDONTS being used as shown in Figure 9-9.

NewMail Object Methods

The methods of the NewMail object allow you to take actions with your NewMail object. The methods are discussed below and summarized in Table 9-3.

Send Method
As you have seen throughout this chapter, the *Send method* is used to send out the email message. The Send method has the following syntax:

```
ObjMail.Send From, To, Subject, Body, Importance
```

TABLE 9-3

NewMail Object
Methods

Method	Meaning
Send	Sends the email message
AttachFile	Allows you to attach a file to an email message
AttachURL	Attach files that are part of an HTML email
SetLocaleIDs	Set Locale information

ObjMail must be a NewMail object. All the parameters of the method are optional. As you have seen, each of the parameters also has a property that you can use to supply the value.

So this code:

```
<%
Option Explicit
Dim objMail
Set objMail = Server.CreateObject("CDONTS.NewMail")
objMail.Send "bob@na.com", "tom@na.com", "Test Message", _
  "Text of the message!", 2
Set objMail = Nothing
%>
```

is functionally equivalent to this code:

```
<%
Option Explicit
Dim objMail
Set objMail = Server.CreateObject("CDONTS.NewMail")
objMail.To = "bob@na.com"
objMail.From = "tom@na.com"
objMail.Subject = "Test Message"
objMail.Body = "Text of the message!"
objMail.Importance = 2
objMail.Send
Set objMail = Nothing
%>
```

You can include any or all of the parameters in the method or in the parameters. If you want to include the Importance property in the method but want to specify the rest of the parameters as properties instead, just use commas as place holders, like this:

```
<%
Option Explicit
Dim objMail
Set objMail = Server.CreateObject("CDONTS.NewMail")
objMail.To = "bob@na.com"
objMail.From = "tom@na.com"
```

```
objMail.Subject = "Test Message"
objMail.Body = "Text of the message!"
objMail.Send , , , , 2
Set objMail = Nothing
%>
```

With the exception of the To parameter, the parameters in this method will override the values of the properties. If both the To property and parameter are used, then all email addresses in both lists will receive an email message.

AttachFile Method

The *AttachFile method* provides a mechanism for you to attach files to the email message. The AttachFile method has the following syntax:

```
ObjMail.AttachFile FileLocation, FileName, EncodingType
```

ObjMail must be a valid NewMail object of the CDONTS library. The `FileLocation` parameter is required and contains the physical location, whereas the `FileName` parameter is optional. If included, that is the name that is displayed as the attachment when in the client email program. If you leave off this parameter, then the name of the file will be displayed here. The `EncodingType` parameter is also optional and is used to indicate the encoding used. By default, the value 0 indicates UUEncode. If you specify a 1 here, then base 64 encoding is used.

The sample code below attaches a file called `Company Log` to the email message.

```
<%
Option Explicit
Dim objMail
Set objMail = Server.CreateObject("CDONTS.NewMail")
objMail.To = "sue@na.com"
objMail.From = "bob@na.com"
objMail.Subject = "Your file"
objMail.Body = "Attached is the file you requested."
objMail.AttachFile "e:\inetpub\logo.gif", "Company Logo"
objMail.Send
Set objMail = Nothing
%>
```

First, `Option Explicit` is used to require variable declaration:

```
Option Explicit
```

Then the NewMail object is declared and instantiated:

```
Dim objMail
Set objMail = Server.CreateObject("CDONTS.NewMail")
```

The To and From properties are set:

```
objMail.To = "sue@na.com"
objMail.From = "bob@na.com"
```

Then the Subject and Body properties are set:

```
objMail.Subject = "Your file"
objMail.Body = "Attached is the file you requested."
```

The AttachFile method is used to attach a file to the message. The first parameter is the physical path to the file that is being attached. The second parameter is the name that we want to use for the file:

```
objMail.AttachFile "e:\inetpub\logo.gif", "Company Logo"
```

The message is sent and the resources used by the object are released:

```
objMail.Send
Set objMail = Nothing
```

The email message received is displayed in Figure 9-10. Notice the name of the file attached.

AttachURL Method

If you are sending an HTML email, you may have graphics or other files that you want included. One way you can do that is by specifying the path to the file through the Internet in the tag for the item, like the `Image` tag. The other way you can include the file is right with the email message itself. You do that with the *AttachURL method*, which allows you to include a file with the email message that is part of the HTML email body. The method has the following syntax:

```
ObjMail.AttachURL PathToFile, FileName, ContentBase, EncodingType
```

ObjMail must be a valid CDONTS NewMail object. The `PathToFile` parameter is required and is the physical location of the file. The `FileName` parameter is the name of the file as used in the HTML and is also required. `ContentBase` is optional and is the URL base for the attachment. The `EncodingType` parameter is also optional. By

Figure 9-10
Email message with attachment.

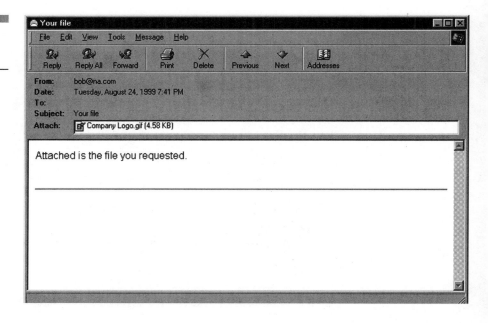

default it is set to 0, meaning UUEncode. But you can use base 64 by setting it to 1.

Let's say you have created the body of the email message that is HTML like this:

```
TheMessage = "<HTML>" _
  & "<HEAD>" _
  & "<TITLE>We've Got A Sale</TITLE>" _
  & "</HEAD>" _
  & "<BODY>" _
  & <img src=logo.gif>
  & "<H1><CENTER>Everything is <STRIKE>30%</STRIKE> 50%
    off!</CENTER></H1>" _
  & "<HR>" _
  & "<P>So stop by now! <A HREF=""http://www.na.com"">Click
    here!</A></P>" _
  & "</BODY>" _
  & "</HTML>"
```

Notice that the HTML includes an Image tag. You can use the AttachURL method to attach that graphic with the email message:

```
ObjMail.AttachURL "e:\inetpub\logo.gif", "logo.gif"
```

The graphic on the HTML email is now part of the message.

SetLocaleIDs Method

The *SetLocaleIDs method* is used to specify the locale of the message, which then appropriately formats numbers, currency, dates, and so forth. The method has the following syntax:

```
ObjMail.SetLocaleIDS LocaleID
```

The ObjMail object must be of type NewMail. The LocaleID needs to be a number in the range of the long data type and represents the locale of the message.

NewMail Object in Action

If you have read this chapter, you have probably already come up with many uses for the NewMail object. The ability to add email to your Web site can enhance it in numerous ways.

Many Web sites use the NewMail object to route requests from visitors for more information. A tool that I have used is to supply visitors with a form where they can include their email address, name, phone number, and so forth, and their message. It then prompts them for a topic from a list that their message goes with. This list would be of a select form element. The text list of the topics would be displayed to visitors, but an email address for the topic would be submitted with the form. So a different person could be in charge of each topic. You could also include a list of people, separated with a semicolon, to send the email message to.

So, if the form element had the name Topic, you would set the To property to that form element:

```
ObjMail.To = Request.Form("Topic")
```

Another frequent use of the NewMail object is to send out a notice that some event has occurred. For example, on e-commerce sites it may be necessary to store the order information in a database but you would also want to send a message out to the person in charge of the store that they have a new order that needs to be processed. You wouldn't want to send the entire order through email, since it may include secure information such as credit card numbers.

In Chapter 7, we looked at creating a Word document by creating an instance of that object using the CreateObject method of the Server object. The document was generated from a form like a form letter that was then displayed to the visitor. But you could modify the code so that visitors receive the document via email. Remember that your visitors may have a variety of systems with different tools installed, so offering a wide range of methods for the same task can be quite helpful.

Think about using HTML email instead of just plain text. This is better, especially for promotional material, and it really doesn't require much more work. Just use a simple HTML tool to design the page. Then view the source of the page and copy and paste it into your Active Server Page. Turn it into a string and set the Body property to that string. This simple change can make your email stand out among the numerous emails your visitors probably receive.

Another fun use of the NewMail object is with a postcard or birthday card page. These pages allow the visitor to send an email to friends or colleagues. The email tells recipients that they have a birthday card, postcard, or some other type of card to pick up at your site. They then click on a link that you send in the email message that transports them to your site. Once there, they see the message left by the original visitor. Not only does this technique get visitors coming back, it introduces new visitors to your site—and all it takes is a form for the original visitor to select the card type and the text for the card. You then would use the NewMail object to send out a message to the recipient of the card. When visitors return to the site, they see an Active Server Page that derives its content from the saved information of the original viewer.

The combinations of the different objects we have discussed thus far allow you to create an almost limitless variety of Active Server Page applications.

CHAPTER 10

ASP
Components

Objects that Extend Your ASP Capabilities

IIS comes with a variety of components that assist you in your Active Server Page development. We looked at one of those components in the last chapter, the Collaborative Data objects. But IIS also comes with a slew of other minor components that you can use in your code to perform a variety of tasks. In this chapter we focus on these minor components. Table 10-1 presents the names of the components and what they are used for.

Browser Capabilities Component

The *Browser Capabilities component* provides you with information about the visitor's browser and information about their system. The following is a simple call to the Browser Capabilities component:

```
set BC = server.createobject("MSWC.BrowserType")
Browser = BC.Browser & " " & BC.Version
FramesSupport = BC.frames
Platform = BC.platform
```

TABLE 10-1

ASP Components

Component	Purpose
Browser Capabilities	Supplies specific information about the browser used by the visitor and the capabilities of that browser.
Ad Rotator	Provides methods for easily managing the placement of banner ads on your site.
Page Counter	Gives you a way to display and keep track of the number of visitors to a page.
Counters	Provides a mechanism to maintain a number that is meant to be incremented through an Active Server Page application.
Content Linking	Allows you to create a series of pages that are ordered like a book and provides the navigational needs for such a style.
Content Rotator	Provides a way for you to supply random content to a page or to elements on a page.
MyInfo	Supplies an object with a variety of properties that you can use to store information about you and your company.

An instance of the Browser Capabilities component is created by using the CreateObject method:

```
set BC = server.createobject("MSWC.BrowserType")
```

The call creates an instance of the BrowserType class of the MSWC server and sets it to the object variable BC. After that call, the variable Browser is set to the name and version of the browser the visitor is using:

```
Browser = BC.Browser & " " & BC.Version
```

The FramesSupport variable is set to a value containing whether the visitor's browser supports frames:

```
FramesSupport = BC.frames
```

In addition, the Platform variable is set to the visitor's operating system based on the Platform property of the Browser Capabilities object:

```
Platform = BC.platform
```

The Browser Capabilities component works pretty simply. It retrieves an HTTP header variable, called User Agent, which contains a somewhat coded line with the visitor's information. That value retrieved is then used for a lookup in an INI file called browscap.ini, which is a text file that contains configuration information for a variety of browsers and operating systems. The browscap.ini file must be in the same directory as the library file for the component browscap.dll.

If you are using Internet Explorer on Windows NT, your User Agent may be set to this.

```
Mozilla/4.0 (compatible; MSIE 4.01; Windows NT)
```

The component would look through the browscap.ini file searching for this entry:

```
[Mozilla/4.0 (compatible; MSIE 4.01; Windows NT)*]
```

Under that list would be the following information about this system's configuration:

```
parent=IE 4.0
```

```
minorver=01
platform=WinNT
```

Notice the first line parent. That states that there is an entry in the `browscap.ini` file called IE 4.0. The library is to use the information here and, for any missing values, it is to use the values in the parent to this type.

Under the parent directory the following configuration would be noted for this particular system:

```
browser=IE
Version=4.0
majorver=#4
minorver=#0
frames=TRUE
tables=TRUE
cookies=TRUE
backgroundsounds=TRUE
vbscript=TRUE
javascript=TRUE
javaapplets=TRUE
ActiveXControls=TRUE
Win16=False
beta=False
AK=False
SK=False
AOL=False
crawler=False
CDF=True
```

If you were using Netscape's Navigator on a Windows 95 system, the Header would return this value:

```
Mozilla/4.0 * (Win95; U)
```

The Browser Capabilities component would look for that value in the `browscap.ini` file and find this entry:

```
parent=Netscape 4.0
platform=Win95
```

Notice that the parent entry is set to Netscape 4.0. The component would look for that value for the other properties and find these entries:

```
browser=Netscape
version=4.0
majorver=#4
minorver=#0
```

```
frames=TRUE
tables=TRUE
cookies=TRUE
backgroundsounds=FALSE
vbscript=FALSE
javascript=TRUE
javaapplets=TRUE
ActiveXControls=FALSE
beta=False
```

You can use the Browser Capabilities component to write code that determines the capabilities of the visitor's system. Take a look at this sample code:

```
<%
Option Explicit
Dim BC
set BC = server.createobject("MSWC.BrowserType")
Response.Write "Browser: " & BC.Browser & " " & BC.Version & "<BR>"
Response.Write "Platform: " & BC.Platform & "<BR>"
Response.Write "DHTML: " & BC.dhtml & "<BR>"
Response.Write "Frames: " & BC.frames & "<P>"
Response.Write "Tables: " & BC.tables & "<BR>"
Response.Write "Cookies: " & BC.cookies & "<BR>"
Response.Write "Background Sounds: " & BC.backgroundsounds & "<BR>"
Response.Write "VBScript: " & BC.vbscript & "<P>"
Response.Write "JavaScript: " & BC.javascript & "<BR>"
Response.Write "Java Applets: " & BC.javaapplets & "<BR>"
Response.Write "ActiveX Controls: " & BC.activexcontrols & "<BR>"
Response.Write "AOL: " & BC.AOL & "<P>"
Response.Write "Beta: " & BC.Beta & "<BR>"
Response.Write "CDF: " & BC.cdf
%>
```

First the code states that variables will be declared:

```
Option Explicit
```

Then a variable called BC is created:

```
Dim BC
```

The BC variable is set to become an instance of the Browser Capabilities component:

```
set BC = server.createobject("MSWC.BrowserType")
```

First, the name and version of the visitor's browser are written to the browser:

```
Response.Write "Browser: " & BC.Browser & " " & BC.Version & "<BR>"
```

Next, the platform, the operating system of the visitor is written to the browser:

```
Response.Write "Platform: " & BC.Platform & "<BR>"
```

Whether the browser supports Dynamic HTML is next written to the browser. Possible values for this property include True, False, and Unknown:

```
Response.Write "DHTML: " & BC.dhtml & "<BR>"
```

The next question asks if the visitor's browser supports the ability to display Frames. Possible values for this property include True, False, and Unknown:

```
Response.Write "Frames: " & BC.frames & "<P>"
```

Here the Browser Capabilities component reports whether the visitor's browser can display. Possible values for this property include True, False, and Unknown:

```
Response.Write "Tables: " & BC.tables & "<BR>"
```

Does the visitor's browser support cookies? Possible values for this property include True, False, and Unknown. Note that the browser could support cookies but the visitor may have some other tool in place that blocks cookies:

```
Response.Write "Cookies: " & BC.cookies & "<BR>"
```

Can the browser play background sound? Possible values for this property include True, False, and Unknown:

```
Response.Write "Background Sounds: " & BC.backgroundsounds & "<BR>"
```

Can the browser process client-side VBScript? Note this is client-side, so it has nothing to do with ASP, which is processed on your server. Possible values for this property include True, False, and Unknown:

```
Response.Write "VBScript: " & BC.vbscript & "<P>"
```

The same question is asked for JavaScript. Again we are referring to the client-side's capabilities. Possible values for this property include True, False, and Unknown:

```
Response.Write "JavaScript: " & BC.javascript & "<BR>"
```

Does the browser support Java Applets? That question is answered through the JavaApplets property of the Browser Capabilities component:

```
Response.Write "Java Applets: " & BC.javaapplets & "<BR>"
```

Can the browser work with ActiveX Components on the client-side? Possible values for this property include True, False, and Unknown:

```
Response.Write "ActiveX Controls: " & BC.activexcontrols & "<BR>"
```

Is the visitor using AOL? Possible values for this property include True, False, and Unknown:

```
Response.Write "AOL: " & BC.AOL & "<P>"
```

Is the browser a Beta version? Possible values for this property include True, False, and Unknown:

```
Response.Write "Beta: " & BC.Beta & "<BR>"
```

Finally, does the browser support the Channel Definition Format (CDF)? Possible values for this property include True, False, and Unknown:

```
Response.Write "CDF: " & BC.cdf
```

Figure 10-1 displays the output of this page on a Windows 98 system using Netscape Navigator 4.0.

Figure 10-2 shows the output of the code on a Windows NT system running Internet Explorer 5.0. The most important use of this code is for directing the visitor to the proper version of your Web site. You may include a Web site that is optimized for Internet Explorer, another that is optimized for Netscape Navigator, a third that is optimized for WebTV, and a fourth for other browsers. You could do that with code like this:

```
<%
Option Explicit
Dim BC
```

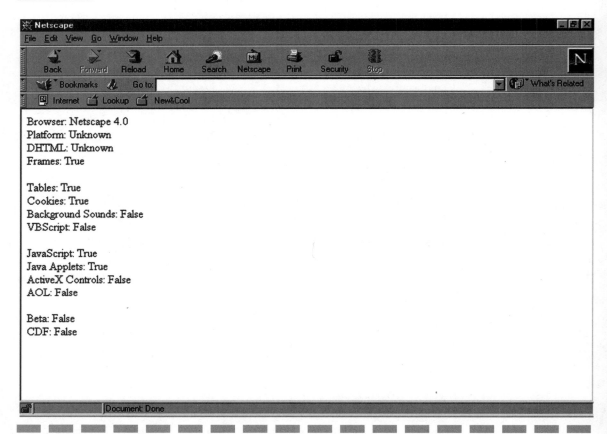

Figure 10-1 Output of Browser Capabilities code.

```
set BC = server.createobject("MSWC.BrowserType")
If BC.Browser = "IE" then
  Response.redirect "./IE/index.asp"
ElseIf BC.Browser = "Netscape" then
  Response.redirect "./Netscape/index.asp"
ElseIf BC.Browser = "WebTV" then
  Response.redirect "./WebTV/index.asp"
Else
  Response.redirect "./other/index.asp"
End If
%>
```

First variable declaration is required:

```
Option Explicit
```

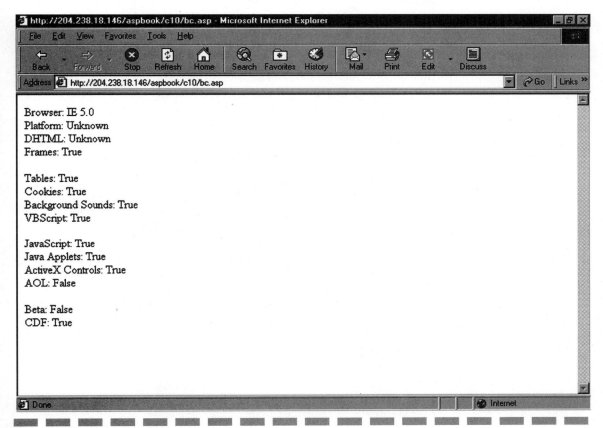

Figure 10-2 Output of Browser Capabilities code.

Then a variable named BC is created:

```
Dim BC
```

That variable is instantiated as a Browser Capabilities object:

```
set BC = server.createobject("MSWC.BrowserType")
```

We then query the Browser property of the Browser Capabilities object to see if it is an Internet Explorer browser:

```
If BC.Browser = "IE" then
```

If it is, the visitor is directed to a subdirectory that contains the pages for that browser:

```
Response.redirect "./IE/index.asp"
```

The code then checks to see if the visitor's browser is from Netscape:

```
ElseIf BC.Browser = "Netscape" then
```

If that is true, they are sent to the Netscape directory:

```
Response.redirect "./Netscape/index.asp"
```

A browser type becoming more popular every day is the WebTV browser. If your audience is large in that market, you will definitely want a version of your site specific to their viewing needs:

```
ElseIf BC.Browser = "WebTV" then
```

If that is their browser type, then they are redirected to the WebTV subdirectory:

```
Response.redirect "./WebTV/index.asp"
```

otherwise, visitors are sent to the default viewing of your site:

```
Response.redirect "./other/index.asp"
```

Another way that you may want to redirect your visitors into a special version of your site is by specific technologies. If you are concerned about older browsers visiting your site, then tables and frame support may be the method for what site your visitors see. Take a look at this code:

```
<%
Option Explicit
Dim BC
set BC = server.createobject("MSWC.BrowserType")
If BC.Tables = "True" and BC.Frames = "True" then
  Response.Redirect "./full/index.asp"
ElseIf BC.Tables = "True" then
  Response.Redirect "./noframes/index.asp"
Else
  Response.Redirect "./none/index.asp"
End If
%>
```

As usual we require variable declaration:

```
Option Explicit
```

The BC variable is created:

```
Dim BC
```

and set to be a Browser Capabilities object:

```
set BC = server.createobject("MSWC.BrowserType")
```

We start out with questions at the top level. Does the browser support tables and frames?

```
If BC.Tables = "True" and BC.Frames = "True" then
```

If the browser does support both, then visitors are redirected here:

```
Response.Redirect "./full/index.asp"
```

Next we step back a level in technology. Frames came after tables, so we then remove Frames from the equation and see if visitors' browsers at least support Tables:

```
ElseIf BC.Tables = "True" then
```

If it does, the Redirect method of the Response object is used to send visitors to this location:

```
Response.Redirect "./noframes/index.asp"
```

otherwise, visitors' browsers do not support either technology and we send them to a basic version of our site:

```
Else
 Response.Redirect "./none/index.asp"
```

Remember that the component just looks for the User Agent entry in the INI file that matches the User Agent value returned through the HTPP Header. The INI file it looks in is merely a text file with a bunch of different listings—that means if you do nothing—the INI file will quickly become out of date. In fact, when you install IIS new, it probably has an outdated version of the INI file. For that reason, if you use this tool you need to make an effort to keep it updated.

One of the places you can get an update form is cyScape, Inc. at http://www.cyscape.com/browscap. They frequently release a new version of the `browscap.ini` file with additions and corrections. You can sign up for their email update so they notify you with new versions of the file. They also have their own version of the Browser Capabilities component that supplies additional properties beyond the ones discussed in this section of the chapter.

Modifying the `Browser.INI` File

You can also update the file yourself. Remember it is just a text file that must be in a specific format, but that is all. If you want to modify the file yourself, first back it up. Then you can use the description for each section presented here to modify the file.

A comment in the file is any line that starts with a semicolon:

```
;;;;;;;;;;;;;;;;;;;;;;;;;;;
;;; My browser definition ;;
;;;;;;;;;;;;;;;;;;;;;;;;;;;
```

Each section of the file contains either the `User Agent` header, exactly, or it can define a parent section. Say, for example, that you wanted to define a browser that wasn't in the list that returned this string for the `User Agent`:

```
[My Browser/1.2.2beta (Windows 95)]
```

Notice that brackets surround the section definition. The properties for the section come next. Then continue until another section header is found. You could define the properties for your section like this:

```
parent=MyBrowser 1.0
platform=Win95
beta=True
```

Notice the special entry first called *parent*, which says that somewhere else in the INI file is an entry called MyBrowser 1.0. Go to that entry and use all its properties unless I specify something in this section. After that the platform is defined and the browser is a beta.

Somewhere else in the INI file we must add the parent section. That matches the name used here exactly, so it would look like this:

```
[MyBrowser 1.0]
browser=MyBrowser
version=1.0
majorver=#1
minorver=#0
frames=FALSE
tables=TRUE
cookies=TRUE
backgroundsounds=FALSE
vbscript=TRUE
javascript=FALSE
javaapplets=FALSE
platform=Windows95
beta=FALSE
```

Notice that some of the entries are repeated here in the parent. The one that is in the actual definition overrides what is in the parent entry, which simply stores the default values that are not redefined by the child entry.

Ad Rotator Component

The *Ad Rotator component* gives you a tool to manage the banner ads that appear on a Web page. The component will randomly display a banner ad on an Active Server Page each time the page is accessed. The component uses a separate schedule file that you create to determine how often to display one banner ad versus another banner ad. Making a call to the Banner Ad Rotator component looks like this:

```
set objAdRot = server.createobject("MSWC.AdRotator")
Response.write
objAdRot.GetAdvertisement("./html/AdFiles/AdFile.txt")
```

The first line creates an instance of the AdRotator class of the MSWC class placing it into an object variable called `objAdRot`.

```
set objAdRot = server.createobject("MSWC.AdRotator")
```

Then the GetAdvertisement method is called to retrieve the information about the banner ad to be displayed. The returned value is written to the browser with the Write method of the Response object:

```
Response.write objAdRot.GetAdvertisement("./html/AdFiles
   /AdFile.txt")
```

This is what is written to the browser:

```
<A HREF="http://www.netstats2000.com/nmaha/html/AdFiles/AdRedirect.
   asp?
url=http://www.netstats2000.com/nmaha/html/Adfiles/HA.html
&image=http://www.netstats2000.com/nmaha/html/Adfiles/ha.gif" >
<IMG SRC="http://www.netstats2000.com/nmaha/html/Adfiles/ha.gif"
ALT="Get your organization online" WIDTH=468 HEIGHT=60 BORDER=0>
```

The GetAdvertisement method is passed a single parameter, the path to the `Schedule` file, which contains the list of banner ads that are to be displayed and how often they are to be displayed. The `Schedule` file also contains the action to be taken if the person clicks on the banner ad, as well as the size of the image to be displayed, so the GetAdvertisement method looks up all the values in the `Schedule` file and produces the output as just shown.

The contents of the `Schedule` file for this real-world example are shown here:

```
Redirect http://www.netstats2000.com/nmaha/html/AdFiles/
   AdRedirect.asp
width 468
height 60
border 0
*
http://www.netstats2000.com/nmaha/html/Adfiles/ha.gif
http://www.netstats2000.com/nmaha/html/Adfiles/HA.html
Get your organization online
10
http://www.netstats2000.com/nmaha/html/Adfiles/sgianim.gif
http://www.silkgraph.com
Silkscreen Graphics Inc.
10
http://www.netstats2000.com/nmaha/html/Adfiles/forrent.gif
mailto:mcecchi@ibm.net
Space For Rent
10
```

The first section of the `Schedule` file contains configuration information. The first line contains the page to go to when visitors click on the banner ad:

```
Redirect http://www.netstats2000.com/nmaha/html/AdFiles/
   AdRedirect.asp
```

Passed to this page in the QueryString will be the name of the image that was clicked on and the address to go to for that banner ad.

The second and third lines of the first section contain the width and height of the banner ad:

```
width 468
height 60
```

which is followed by the border for the banner ad:

```
border 0
```

Look at the preceding HTML produced by the GetAdvertisement and you will see this configuration information. A single asterisk follows the configuration section on a line by itself:

```
*
```

After that, the schedule file contains a list of all the banner ads with their schedule. The first line for each of the banner ad's entries is the path to the banner ad:

```
http://www.netstats2000.com/nmaha/html/Adfiles/ha.gif
```

followed by the Web location that visitors should eventually be redirected to when they click on the banner ad:

```
http://www.netstats2000.com/nmaha/html/Adfiles/HA.html
```

The Alt text for the banner ad is on the third line:

```
Get your organization online
```

The fourth line contains the proportional amount that this banner ad should be displayed versus the other banner ads:

```
10
```

The output produced by this banner ad rotation file entry is displayed in Figure 10-3. Notice the banner at the top of this figure. It is produced from the first entry in the rotation file. So the Alt text matches that which is shown in Figure 10-3 and the link in the status bar shows the URL that the banner links to.

If you look back at the whole Schedule file, you will see that this structure repeats. The next item will display this graphic:

```
http://www.netstats2000.com/nmaha/html/Adfiles/sgianim.gif
```

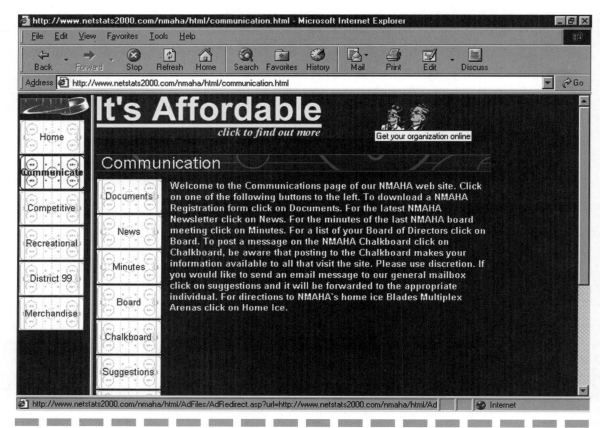

Figure 10-3   Banner ad produced by first rotation.

When this is clicked, the visitor will be sent to this URL:

```
http://www.silkgraph.com
```

The Alt text for the graphic is below:

```
Silkscreen Graphics Inc.
```

Its relative number of impressions compared to the other graphics in the file is this:

```
10
```

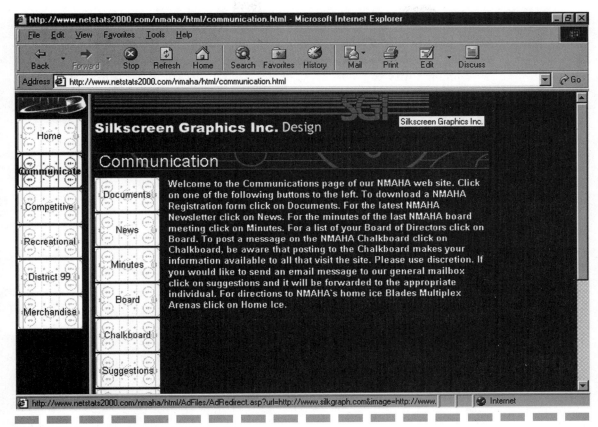

Figure 10-4 Second ad from rotation file.

This entry produces the page shown in Figure 10-4. Notice that this graphic matches what is in the rotation file. Also note that this is the same page as the other banner ad was on. That is because each time the page is viewed, a different graphic can appear, based on the graphic that is the most overdue.

You will also see that each page is scheduled the same proportion of impressions, 10, but they don't have to be. You could set the first one to 20 and the other two to 10. This would mean that the first would appear twice as often as the other two.

Remember that the first line of the Schedule file contains the location that visitors are sent to when they click on the banner ad:

```
Redirect http://www.netstats2000.com/nmaha/html/AdFiles/
  AdRedirect.asp
```

This Active Server Page would normally contain no output. It is your opportunity to record that visitors have clicked on a banner ad, called a *click-through,* in your database for later analysis. Here is a sample of what the code for such a page might look like.

```
<%
set conn = server.createobject ("adodb.connection")
conn.open "EmpDir", "sa", "yourpassword"
conn.execute "insert into Referrals (ReferredTo) values ('" _
  & Request.QueryString("url") & "')"
response.redirect(Request.QueryString("url"))
%>
```

The code first connects to the database:

```
set conn = server.createobject ("adodb.connection")
conn.open "EmpDir", "sa", "yourpassword"
```

The code then adds a record to a table called *Referrals,* adding to it the banner ad that visitors clicked on:

```
conn.execute "insert into Referrals (ReferredTo) values ('" _
& Request.QueryString("url") & "')"
```

Visitors are then redirected to the location of the Web site of the banner ad they clicked on:

```
response.redirect(Request.QueryString("url"))
```

Think about other fields that you would want included in this entry. For example, you would probably want to record the date and time that the visitor clicked on the banner ad. You may also want to use the Browser Capabilities component that we discussed in the last section to record extended information about the visitor who clicked on the banner ad.

On the other end, you would probably also want a page where your advertisers could come to see how many clicks there were on their banner ad. Such a page could look something like the page displayed in Figure 10-5.

By default the page loads displaying the year-to-date date range. When visitors press the Display Report page they see the results of their query as shown in Figure 10-6.

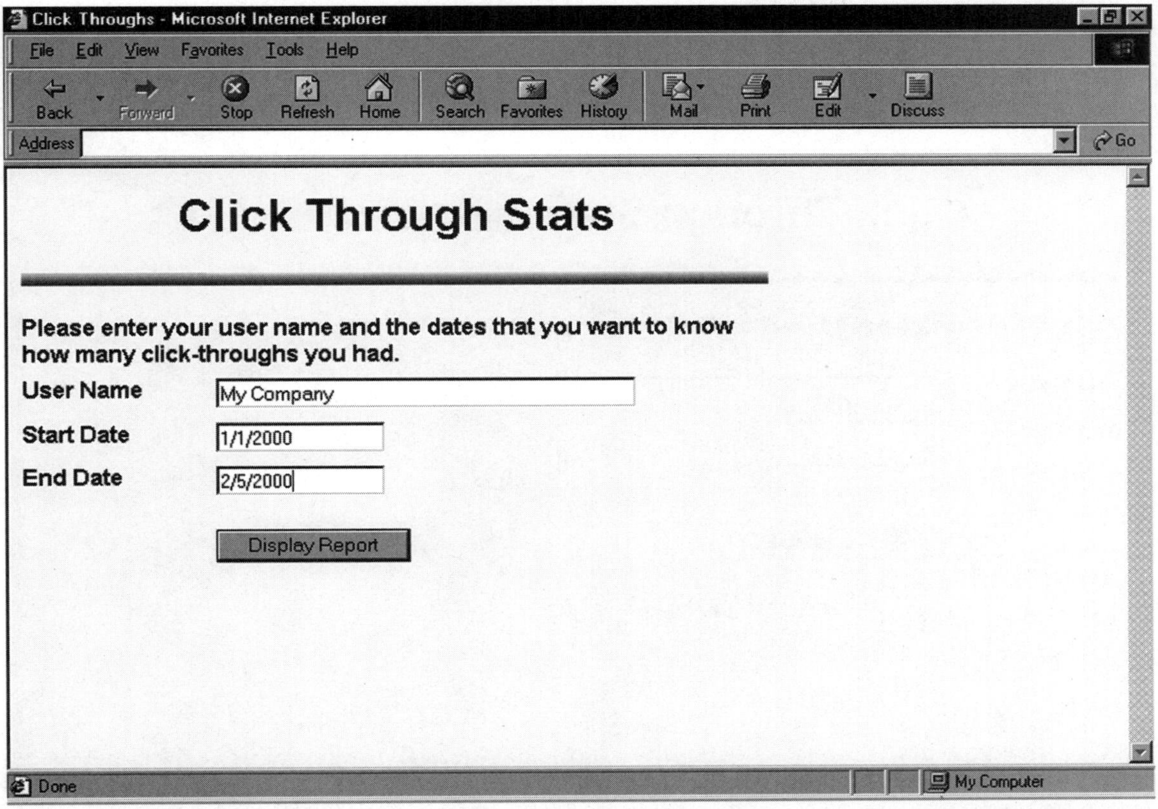

Figure 10-5   Sample Click-Through Report page.

The code on the page would query the database based on the requested information if the form was submitted. The code on the page also must display the year-to-date information. The main code block is:

```
<%
Option Explicit
Dim conn
Dim RSHits
Dim TheMessage
Dim StartDate
Dim EndDate
If Not IsEmpty(Request.Form("DisplayReport")) Then
    set conn = server.createobject ("adodb.connection")
    conn.open "EmpDir", "sa", "yourpassword"
    set RSHits = conn.Execute("select Count(ReferralID) as TheCount " _
      & "from Referrals " _
      & "where UserName = '" & Request.Form("UserName") & "' " _
        & "and HitDate >= '" & Request.Form("StartDate") & "' " _
```

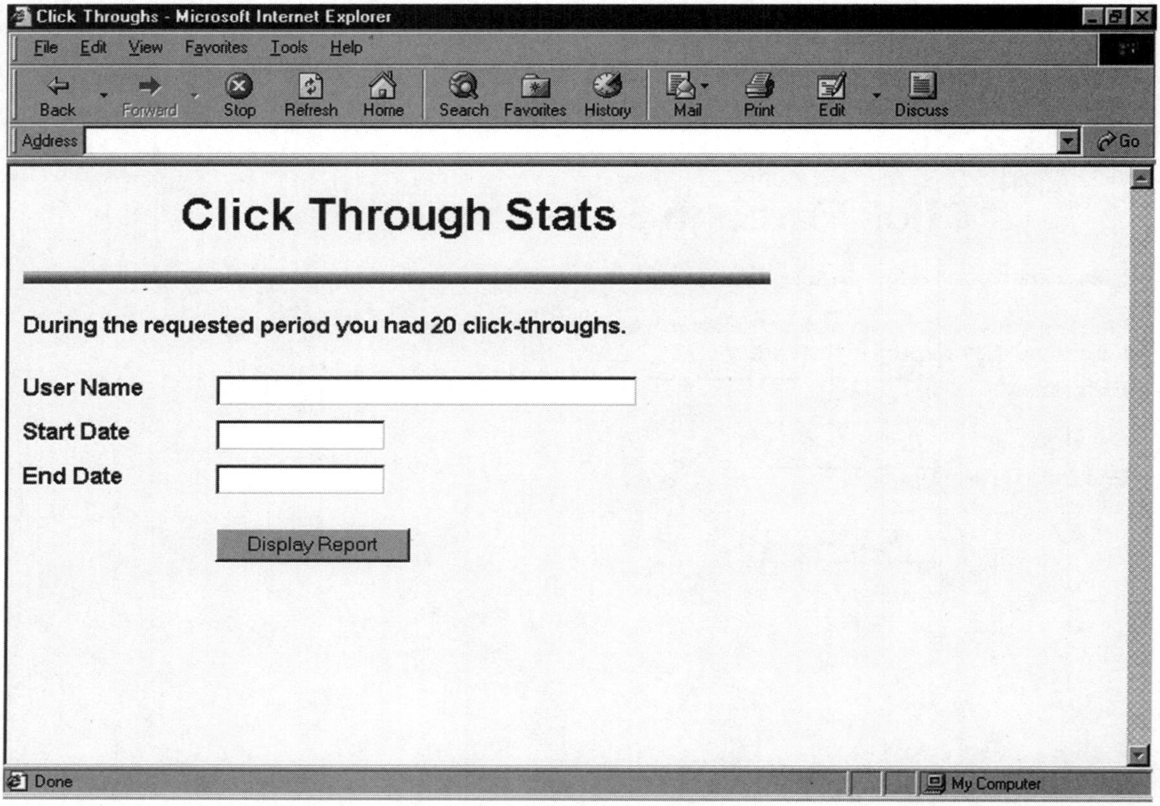

Figure 10-6 Click-throughs query result.

```
         & "and HitDate <= '" & Request.Form("EndDate") & "' ")
      TheMessage = "During the requested period you had " _
         & RSHits("TheCount") & " click-throughs."
   else
      TheMessage = "Please enter your user name and the dates that you
         want " _
         & "to know how many click-throughs you had."
   End If
   StartDate = "1/1/" & Year(Date)
   EndDate = Date
   %>
```

First we specify the Option Explicit directive:

```
Option Explicit
```

Then we declare a variable that will store the database connection:

```
Dim conn
```

Next a variable that will store the data from the database:

```
Dim RSHits
```

A message variable will display instructions or the result of the query to the browser:

```
Dim TheMessage
```

Another variable will store the default start date:

```
Dim StartDate
```

and one will store the default end date:

```
Dim EndDate
```

The page has two states. In the *initial state*, the page has just been entered and visitors need instruction displayed to them. In the *submitted state*, visitors have submitted the form and we need to process it. We determine the state by looking in the Form collection for the submit button called DISPLAYREPORT:

```
If Not IsEmpty(Request.Form("DisplayReport")) Then
```

If the form collection item is not empty, then the form has been submitted. In that case, we will need a connection to the database to establish the number of click-throughs. A Connection object is created:

```
set conn = server.createobject ("adodb.connection")
```

and is connected to the desired database:

```
conn.open "EmpDir", "sa", "yourpassword"
```

A query is run, which returns the count of number of records for this particular user between the selected dates:

```
set RSHits = conn.Execute("select Count(ReferralID) as TheCount " _
    & "from Referrals " _
    & "where UserName = '" & Request.Form("UserName") & "' " _
    & "and HitDate >= '" & Request.Form("StartDate") & "' " _
    & "and HitDate <= '" & Request.Form("EndDate") & "' ")
```

A variable is then set to the text to display to visitors that includes the click-through information that we just retrieved from the database:

```
TheMessage = "During the requested period you had " _
  & RSHits("TheCount") & " click-throughs."
```

If the form hasn't been submitted, then we just need to set the message variable to the instructions:

```
else
  TheMessage = "Please enter your user name and the dates that you
    want " _
      & "to know how many click-throughs you had."
```

In either case, we need to create the StartDate and EndDate variables. The start date is set to the first date of the current year:

```
StartDate = "1/1/" & Year(Date)
```

and the end date is set to the current system date:

```
EndDate = Date
```

Then inline with the HTML we use the Write method of the Response object to send the message variable back to the browser:

```
<P><B><% Response.Write TheMessage %></B>
```

The start date is written as the value for the STARTDATE text box:

```
<INPUT TYPE=TEXT NAME="StartDate" VALUE="<% Response.Write
StateDate %>"
SIZE=40 MAXLENGTH=50>
```

Then for the end date we supply the default in the value parameter:

```
<INPUT TYPE=TEXT NAME="StartDate" VALUE="<% Response.Write EndDate %>"
SIZE=40 MAXLENGTH=50>
```

Page Counter Component

The *Page Counter component* provides a simple way to track and display the number of hits on a Web page. The component is not installed by default with IIS. It is part of the IIS Resource Kit, which you can find at

Microsoft's Web site, or, if you subscribe to Microsoft Technet, it is included on a CD. You can manually install the component by placing the file from the Technet CD's location:

```
\IIS Resource Kit\Component\Page Counter\DLL\i386\PageCnt.dll
```

and place the file in your `WinNT\System32` directory. Then register the component by using the `Start\Run` command and entering:

```
Regsvr32 PageCnt.dll
```

You should see the message that the component was successfully registered, like the one displayed in Figure 10-7. Once the library is successfully registered, you can start using the component in code. You create the component like the other components by using the CreateObject method of the Server component.

Microsoft's documentation shows two different ways to create this object. I have found one doesn't work but let's look at both just in case a future version uses the other nonfunctional syntax. This declaration currently does not work:

```
Set MyPageCounter = Server.CreateObject("MSWC.PageCounter")
```

The `MyPageCounter` variable would contain an instance of the Page Counter component. The other syntax for creating an instance of this component uses a different application/class string:

```
Set MyPageCounter = Server.CreateObject("IISSample.PageCounter")
```

Again, here the `MyPageCounter` variable would be an object of the Page Counter class.

Internally the DLL creates a text file and stores the number of hits that a page is viewed. The component periodically dumps the hit information to

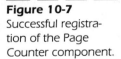

Figure 10-7
Successful registration of the Page Counter component.

the text file, so the data will persist if the server goes down. When the component is first initialized, it loads the values of the different page hits.

To record a hit on a page you need to call the *PageHit method* of the component:

```
<%
Option Explicit
Dim MyPageCounter
Set MyPageCounter = Server.CreateObject("IISSample.PageCounter")
MyPageCounter.PageHit
%>
```

First we code `Option Explicit`:

```
Option Explicit
```

Then a variable that will store the Page Counter object is created:

```
Dim MyPageCounter
```

That variable is set to be a Page Counter component:

```
Set MyPageCounter = Server.CreateObject("IISSample.PageCounter")
```

The PageHit method of the Page Counter object is used to increment the count for this particular page:

```
MyPageCounter.PageHit
```

so, internally, the counter for this page is incremented by one. The component stores the page name and its location with the value for that page to provide for uniqueness.

A Page Counter wouldn't be worth much if you couldn't display the page count. The component provides the Hit method for that purpose. That method has the following syntax:

```
TheCount = MyPageCounter.Hits(OptPageName)
```

The `MyPageCounter` variable must be a valid Page Counter component. Returned from the call would be the hit count into the variable `TheCount`. The method takes a single optional parameter, which is the name and the virtual path to the page for which you want to know the count. If you leave off that parameter, the method returns the hit count for the current page.

Let's take a look at a sample site that uses this component. First the Welcome page is shown in Figure 10-8.

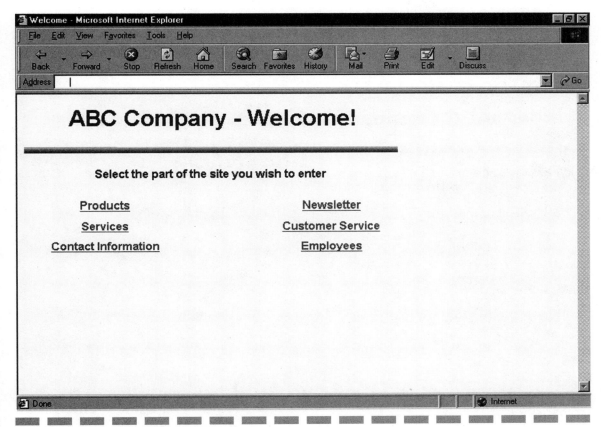

Figure 10-8   Welcome page from sample site.

The Welcome page records a hit to that page but does not display any hit information. The next page of this sample site records a hit on that page and displays the hit information for both pages on the site. It is displayed in Figure 10-9. Notice that the page displays the hit information for both pages.

The code on the Welcome page increments the hit counter for that page. The code block is:

```
<%
Option Explicit
Dim MyPageCounter
Set MyPageCounter = Server.CreateObject("IISSample.PageCounter")
MyPageCounter.PageHit
%>
```

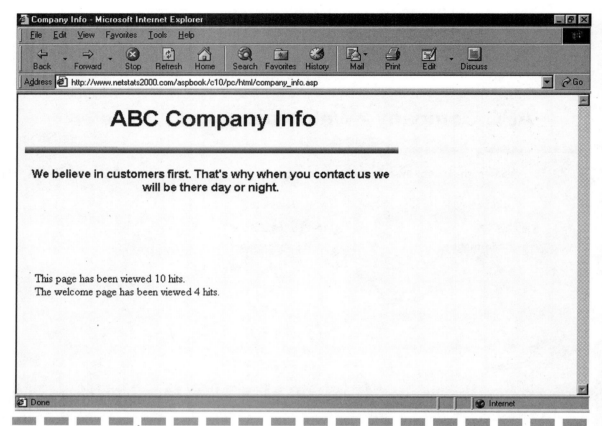

Figure 10-9   Page displaying hit information.

First we tell the compiler that variables will be declared:

```
Option Explicit
```

Next we declare the page counter variable:

```
Dim MyPageCounter
```

and instantiate it:

```
Set MyPageCounter = Server.CreateObject("IISSample.PageCounter")
```

The counter for this page is incremented:

```
MyPageCounter.PageHit
```

The code on the Company Info page increments the page counter for that page and then displays the hit information for both pages. The main code block is:

```
<%
Option Explicit
Dim MyPageCounter
Dim CompInfoCount
Dim WelcomeCount
Set MyPageCounter = Server.CreateObject("IISSample.PageCounter")
MyPageCounter.PageHit
If MyPageCounter.Hits = 1 Then
    CompInfoCount = "1 hit"
else
    CompInfoCount = MyPageCounter.Hits & " hits"
End If
If MyPageCounter.Hits("/aspbook/c10/pc/html/welcome.asp") = 1 Then
    WelcomeCount = "1 hit"
else
    WelcomeCount =
MyPageCounter.Hits("/aspbook/c10/pc/html/welcome.asp") _
    & " hits"
End If
%>
```

The first line of code sets `Option Explicit`:

```
Option Explicit
```

Next the page counter object variable is declared:

```
Dim MyPageCounter
```

A variable that will store the hit count for the Company Info page is created:

```
Dim CompInfoCount
```

This variable will store the hit count for the Welcome page:

```
Dim WelcomeCount
```

Next the page counter object is instantiated:

```
Set MyPageCounter = Server.CreateObject("IISSample.PageCounter")
```

The PageHit method is used to increment the hit count for this page:

```
MyPageCounter.PageHit
```

Next we need to create the text messages that display the hit information for both pages. The *Hits method* of the Page Counter object retrieves that value. First we look at the hits for this page:

```
If MyPageCounter.Hits = 1 Then
```

The code in this If block properly formats the singular or plural of the word hit:

```
CompInfoCount = "1 hit"
```

Notice that the Hits method is used without a parameter, since we are talking about the hits for this page:

```
else
    CompInfoCount = MyPageCounter.Hits & " hits"
End If
```

Next the same is done for the Welcome page. Notice the Hits method now contains a parameter, the virtual path to the page for which we want to know the number of hits:

```
If MyPageCounter.Hits("/aspbook/c10/pc/html/welcome.asp") = 1 Then
    WelcomeCount = "1 hit"
else
    WelcomeCount =
MyPageCounter.Hits("/aspbook/c10/pc/html/welcome.asp") _
    & " hits"
End If
```

Then within the HTML, the hit information is written using the two strings just created:

```
<P>This page has been viewed <% response.write CompInfoCount %>.
<BR>The welcome page has been viewed <% response.write WelcomeCount
    %>.
```

The Page Counter component has one more method, the *Reset method*, which sets the counter for a page back to zero. The method has the following syntax:

```
MyPageCounter.Refresh OptPage
```

The MyPageCounter variable must be a valid Page Counter object. The method takes an optional single parameter. The parameter contains the virtual path to the page for which you want the counter reset. If you leave off that parameter, then the current page is reset.

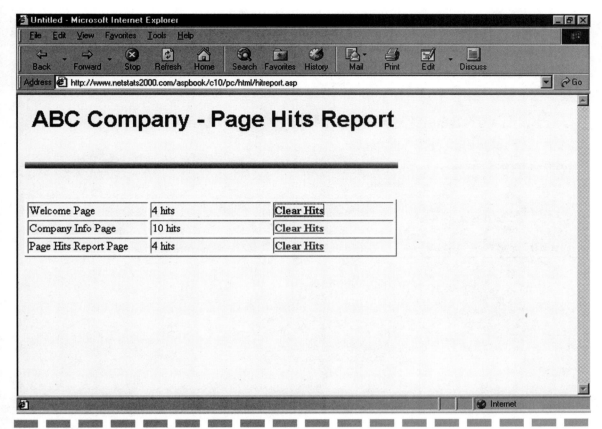

Figure 10-10 Hits Report page.

Let's add this method to our site example by presenting a Report page that lists the hits on all three pages and allows the visitor to reset the counter. Such a page is presented in Figure 10-10. The page lists the name of each page in the first column followed by the number of hits for that page and a link to reset the counter for that page. Clicking on the link will return that counter to 0 and the page is then redisplayed. For example, if you were to click on the CLEAR HITS link for the Company Info page, you would see the counter reset like it is in Figure 10-11. The code on this page must add a hit for this page, reset the counter for a page if requested, and display the hits for each page. The main code block is:

```
<%
Option Explicit
Dim MyPageCounter
Dim CompInfoCount
```

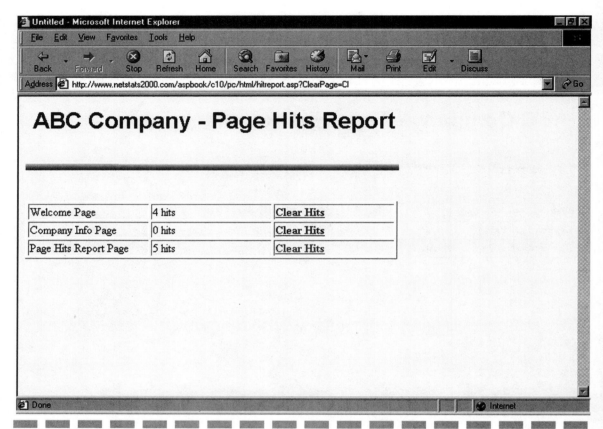

Figure 10-11 Hits Report page after a counter has been reset.

```
Dim WelcomeCount
Dim HitReportCount
Set MyPageCounter = Server.CreateObject("IISSample.PageCounter")
MyPageCounter.PageHit
If not isempty(Request.QueryString("ClearPage")) Then
  If Request.QueryString("ClearPage") = "Welcome" Then
    MyPageCounter.Reset("/aspbook/c10/pc/html/welcome.asp")
  ElseIf Request.QueryString("ClearPage") = "CI" Then
    MyPageCounter.Reset("/aspbook/c10/pc/html/company_info.asp")
  ElseIf Request.QueryString("ClearPage") = "Report" Then
    MyPageCounter.Reset
  End If
End If
If MyPageCounter.Hits("/aspbook/c10/pc/html/company_info.asp") = 1
  Then
    CompInfoCount = "1 hit"
else
    CompInfoCount =
MyPageCounter.Hits("/aspbook/c10/pc/html/company_info.asp") & "
  hits"
```

```
End If
If MyPageCounter.Hits("/aspbook/c10/pc/html/welcome.asp") = 1 Then
   WelcomeCount = "1 hit"
else
   WelcomeCount =
MyPageCounter.Hits("/aspbook/c10/pc/html/welcome.asp") & " hits"
End If
If MyPageCounter.Hits = 1 Then
   HitReportCount = "1 hit"
else
   HitReportCount = MyPageCounter.Hits & " hits"
End If
%>
```

First `Option Explicit` is noted:

```
Option Explicit
```

Then a variable for the Page Counter object is created:

```
Dim MyPageCounter
```

Next we will need variables to store the hit text for each of the three pages:

```
Dim CompInfoCount
Dim WelcomeCount
Dim HitReportCount
```

The Page Counter object is instantiated:

```
Set MyPageCounter = Server.CreateObject("IISSample.PageCounter")
```

A hit is recorded for this Report page:

```
MyPageCounter.PageHit
```

Next the code checks to see if any of the counters need to be reset. The links to reset a page counter, as you will see later, pass the name of the page to reset through the QueryString field ClearPage, so if that field is present we need to reset a page counter:

```
If not isempty(Request.QueryString("ClearPage")) Then
```

If Welcome is passed through that field, the Welcome counter needs to be reset:

```
If Request.QueryString("ClearPage") = "Welcome" Then
```

Notice that the Reset method passes the parameter referring to the virtual path of the page to reset since it is not the current page:

```
MyPageCounter.Reset("/aspbook/c10/pc/html/welcome.asp")
```

The same check and action is done for the Company Info page:

```
ElseIf Request.QueryString("ClearPage") = "CI" Then
   MyPageCounter.Reset("/aspbook/c10/pc/html/company_info.asp")
```

Notice for the Report page no parameter is sent to the Reset method. That is because we are clearing the hits for the current page so no parameter is necessary:

```
ElseIf Request.QueryString("ClearPage") = "Report" Then
   MyPageCounter.Reset
```

Next the code prepares the proper text for the Company Info hit information:

```
If MyPageCounter.Hits("/aspbook/c10/pc/html/company_info.asp") = 1
   Then
      CompInfoCount = "1 hit"
else
      CompInfoCount = MyPageCounter.Hits("/aspbook/c10/pc/html/
      company_info.asp") & " hits"
End If
```

The same is done for the Welcome page:

```
If MyPageCounter.Hits("/aspbook/c10/pc/html/welcome.asp") = 1 Then
      WelcomeCount = "1 hit"
else
      WelcomeCount = MyPageCounter.Hits("/aspbook/c10/pc/html/
      welcome.asp") & " hits"
End If
```

and also for the Report page:

```
If MyPageCounter.Hits = 1 Then
      HitReportCount = "1 hit"
else
      HitReportCount = MyPageCounter.Hits & " hits"
End If
```

Within the HTML, the HMTL table needs to be populated with the proper text for each of the pages.

```
<TD WIDTH=164><P>Welcome Page</TD>
<TD WIDTH=164><P><% response.write WelcomeCount %></TD>
<TD WIDTH=164><P><A HREF="./hitreport.asp?ClearPage=Welcome">
<B>Clear Hits</B></A></TD>
<TD WIDTH=164><P>Company Info Page</TD>
<TD WIDTH=164><P><% response.write CompInfoCount %></TD>
<TD WIDTH=164><P><A HREF="./hitreport.asp?ClearPage=CI">
<B>Clear Hits</B></A></TD>
<TD WIDTH=164><P>Page Hits Report Page</TD>
<TD WIDTH=164><P><% response.write HitReportCount %></TD>
<TD WIDTH=164><P><A HREF="./hitreport.asp?ClearPage=Report">
<B>Clear Hits</B></A></TD>
```

Notice that the first cell of the HTML table contains just the name of the page:

```
<TD WIDTH=164><P>Welcome Page</TD>
```

Then the text with the hit information is written to the browser:

```
<TD WIDTH=164><P><% response.write WelcomeCount %></TD>
```

Notice that the link to reset the counter goes back to this same page. Also note that passed in with the link through the QueryString is the name of the page to reset:

```
<TD WIDTH=164><P><A HREF="./hitreport.asp?ClearPage=Welcome">
<B>Clear Hits</B></A></TD>
```

Counters Component

The *Counters component* provides a simple interface for you to store integers that you can read, write, remove, and increment across all the pages in your site and even across the boundaries of Active Server Page applications. As with the last component this component, comes with the IIS Resource Kit. Within the resource kit it is located here:

```
\IIS Resource Kit\Component\Counters\DLL\i386\counters.dll
```

Place the file in your WinNT\System32 directory, then register the component by using the Start\Run command and entering:

```
Regsvr32 counters.dll
```

After successfully registering the component you can start using it.

The syntax for creating a Counters component is below:

```
set MyCounter = Server.CreateObject("MSWC.Counters")
```

A Counters component is instantiated using the CreateObject method of the Server object. You pass to the method the application/class string `MSWC.Counters`. An object of the Counters class is returned into the variable `MyCounter`.

The Counters component stores the values of the counters in a text file that is located in the same directory as the library file. The counters stored in the component are available to any page in your Web site, even if the site is in a different Active Server Page application.

These variables have a scope beyond any that we have discussed thus far. We looked at `Session` variables that are available to any page within a particular session of an Active Server Page application. We looked at `Application` variables that are available to any page and any session in an Active Server Page application. But the counter variables cross those boundaries to and are available to any page regardless of the Active Server Page application to which they belong.

A counter is created either by retrieving its value or by setting its value. You retrieve the value of a counter by using the *Get method* of the Counters component:

```
TheValue = MyCounter.Get (NameOfCounter)
```

The `MyCounter` variable must be a value instance of the Counters component. The Get method takes a single parameter, which is the name of the counter. The current value of the counter would be returned by the method and placed into the variable `TheValue`. If the counter does not exist, it is created and the value zero is returned.

In this example:

```
<%
Option Explicit
Dim MyCounter
set MyCounter = Server.CreateObject("MSWC.Counters")
Response.Write MyCounter.Get("Product10Views")
%>
```

The value of the counter Product10Views would be displayed in the browser. If the counter doesn't exist, it is created and displayed in the browser as the number 0.

To set a counter to a particular value you can use the *Set method*, which resets the counter to whatever value you indicate and if the counter doesn't exist the component creates the new counter. The method has the following syntax:

```
MyCounter.Set NameOfCounter, ValueOfCounter
```

The `MyCounter` variable must be a valid Counters object. Two parameters are passed to the Set method: the first parameter is the name of the counter whose value you want to set; the second parameter is the value to which you want to set the counter.

For example:

```
<%
Option Explicit
Dim MyCounter
set MyCounter = Server.CreateObject("MSWC.Counters")
MyCounter.Set "AllPageViews", 123
%>
```

This code would set the counter AllPageViews to the value 123. If the counter doesn't exist, it is created and set to that value.

Another method provided by this component is the *Increment method*, which increases the value of a counter by one. The method has the following syntax:

```
MyCounter.Increment NameOfCounter
```

The `MyCounter` variable must be a valid instance of the Counters component. NameOfCounter is the name of the counter that you want to increment.

Take a look at this example:

```
<%
Option Explicit
Dim MyCounter
set MyCounter = Server.CreateObject("MSWC.Counters")
MyCounter.Increment "AllPageViews"
%>
```

Here the counter AllPageViews is set to the value one greater than its previous value, so if it was 123 before, it is now 124.

The Counters component provides one more method, the *Remove method*, which removes the counter from the counter file. If the counter is referenced again, it is re-created and the value would be set to zero if the counter was created with the Set method.

The method has the following syntax:

```
MyCounter.Remove NameOfCounter
```

The `MyCounter` variable must be a valid instance of the Counters component. The method takes a single parameter, which is the name of the counter that you want to delete.

For example:

```
<%
Option Explicit
Dim MyCounter
set MyCounter = Server.CreateObject("MSWC.Counters")
MyCounter.Remove "AllPageViews"
%>
```

Here the counter named AllPageViews is removed from memory. If it is referenced again using the Get or Set method, it is re-created.

In this next code block all the methods are used to demonstrate the use of the component.

```
<%
Option Explicit
Dim MyCounter
set MyCounter = Server.CreateObject("MSWC.Counters")
Response.Write "<B>A new counter is now created.<P>"
Response.Write "Just by retrieving its value which is: "
Response.Write MyCounter.Get("Counter1") & "<P>"
MyCounter.Set "Counter1", 33
Response.Write "The counter has been set to: "
Response.Write MyCounter.Get("Counter1") & "<P>"
MyCounter.Increment "Counter1"
Response.Write "The counter has been incremented: "
Response.Write MyCounter.Get("Counter1") & "<P>"
MyCounter.Remove "Counter1"
Response.Write "The counter has been removed." & "<P>"
MyCounter.Set "Counter2", 250
Response.Write "A new counter has been set to the value: "
Response.Write MyCounter.Get("Counter2") & "<P>"
%>
```

First `Option Explicit` is specified:

```
Option Explicit
```

A variable is created to store the Counter object:

```
Dim MyCounter
```

That variable is then instantiated:

```
set MyCounter = Server.CreateObject("MSWC.Counters")
```

A counter is created through the Get method and the initial value is displayed:

```
Response.Write "<B>A new counter is now created.<P>"
Response.Write "Just by retrieving its value which is: "
Response.Write MyCounter.Get("Counter1") & "<P>"
```

That same counter is set to the number 33:

```
MyCounter.Set "Counter1", 33
```

which is then displayed in the browser using the Get method:

```
Response.Write "The counter has been set to: "
Response.Write MyCounter.Get("Counter1") & "<P>"
```

The Counter1 counter is next incremented:

```
MyCounter.Increment "Counter1"
```

The value of the counter is displayed again in the browser:

```
Response.Write "The counter has been incremented: "
Response.Write MyCounter.Get("Counter1") & "<P>"
```

The Remove method is used to delete the Counter1 counter:

```
MyCounter.Remove "Counter1"
Response.Write "The counter has been removed." & "<P>"
```

A second counter is created that will be displayed in another page that is in a different Active Server Page application:

```
MyCounter.Set "Counter2", 250
```

and the value for the counter is displayed here:

```
Response.Write "A new counter has been set to the value: "
Response.Write MyCounter.Get("Counter2") & "<P>"
```

The output of this page is shown in Figure 10-12.

Remember that the counters have a scope that goes beyond the scope of an Active Server Page application, so on another page in a

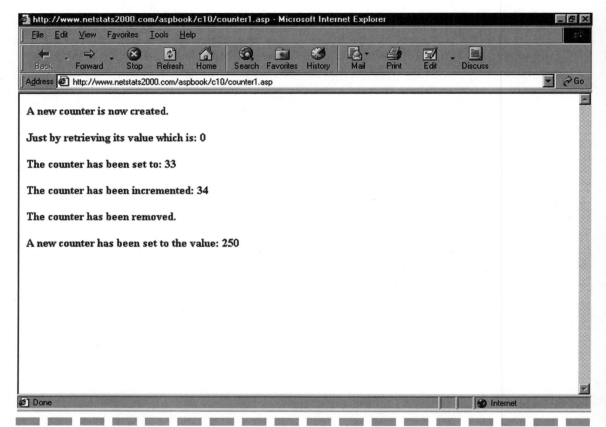

Figure 10-12 Output of counter code.

different Active Server Page application we can reference the counter created in this code:

```
<%
Option Explicit
Dim MyCounter
set MyCounter = Server.CreateObject("MSWC.Counters")
Response.Write "<B>This page retrieves the second counter "
Response.Write "created in a different Active Server Page "
Response.Write "Application.<P>The value is: "
Response.Write MyCounter.Get("Counter2") & ".<P>"
%>
```

First `Option Explicit` is set:

```
Option Explicit
```

Then the counter variable is created:

```
Dim MyCounter
```

and initialized:

```
set MyCounter = Server.CreateObject("MSWC.Counters")
```

The value of the counter we created in the other page is written to the browser by retrieving it through the Get method:

```
Response.Write "<B>This page retrieves the second counter "
Response.Write "created in a different Active Server Page "
Response.Write "Application.<P>The value is: "
Response.Write MyCounter.Get("Counter2") & ".<P>"
```

The output of this page that is part of a different Active Server Page application is displayed in Figure 10-13.

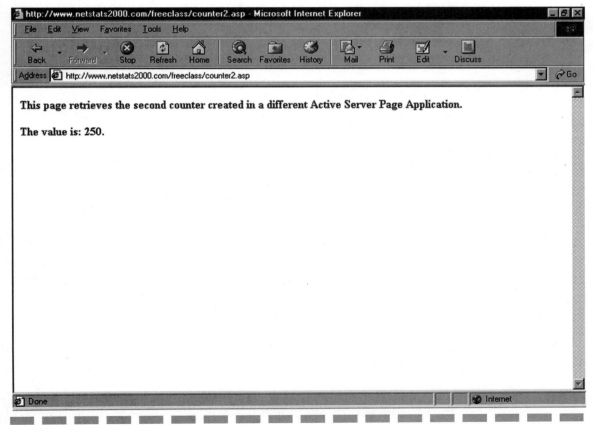

Figure 10-13 Output of the second page in the counters demonstration.

Content Linking Component

The *Content Linking component* provides a way for you to link pages that are to be viewed in a series, pages that have sequential meaning. For example, a book has sequential pages or a help file has a series of pages. When you have such a scenario, you frequently want links that dynamically take visitors to the next page or back to the last page. You also may want a Table of Contents for the series of pages. The Content Linking component provides methods to produce this type of functionality.

The component is part of the standard IIS Installation. The library file for the component is called `nextlink.dll`. The way the component works is that you supply a text file that contains all the pages that are linked together in the order in which you want them linked. In this special text file you supply not just the name of the page but the URL of the page. You don't have to name the text file anything special—it just needs to be accessible within the directory structure of the Web site where it will be used.

Each line of the text file has the following structure:

```
PageURL Description Comment
```

Each field is separated by a tab and each page entry must be placed on a separate line in the text index file. The first field on each line stores the URL to that page. The second field is the name or description of the page. The third field is optional and can contain any comments you like, which are just ignored by the component.

Take a look at this sample index file:

```
TOC.asp Table of Contents Page
Page1.asp   Page  1 of Chapter 1
Page2.asp       Page 2  of Chapter 1
```

Note that the URL and the description are separated with a tab. Also notice the order in which the entries are placed. The order is important because the navigational methods use this order to determine what the next page is and what the previous page is. I find that the best location to save this text file is in the same directory as the pages that will use it. This makes using the methods a little easier since the path to this page is the same as the pages themselves.

In your code you can then create an instance of the Content Linking component that uses this text file to determine what actions to take. To create an instance of the Content Linking component you code this:

```
Set MyCL = Server.CreateObject("MSWC.NextLink")
```

TABLE 10-2

ASP Components

Component	Purpose
GetListCount	Returns the number of entries in the index file.
GetListIndex	Returns the numeric position of the current page in the index file.
GetNextURL	Returns the URL of the next page is the list based on the position of the current page.
GetNextDescription	Returns the description of the next page is the list based on the position of the current page.
GetPreviousURL	Returns the URL of the previous page is the list based on the position of the current page.
GetPreviousDescription	Returns the description of the previous page is the list based on the position of the current page.
GetNthURL	Returns the URL for the item in the index based on the number passed to the method.
GetNthDescription	Returns the description for the item in the index based on the number passed to the method.

As with the other components, you use the CreateObject method of the Server object to create an instance of the component. In this case, the instance would be placed in the MyCL object variable. You can now use the text file in conjunction with the object you created to provide for the navigational needs of this type of application.

The component contains eight methods that are discussed below and summarized in Table 10-2.

The *GetListCount method* returns the number of items in the index file. The syntax for the method is as follows:

```
TheCount = MyCL.GetListCount(Path2IndexFile)
```

The virtual path to the location of the index file is passed to the method, so if the index file is in the same location as the page making the call, then just the name of the file needs to be entered. The number of entries in the index text file is returned from the method so if you coded this based on the index text file discussed earlier:

```
Response.Write MyCL.GetListCount("CLList.txt")
```

the number 3 would be written to the browser.

The next method to discuss is the *GetListIndex method*, which returns the numeric position of the current page within the index text file. The method has the following syntax:

```
TheIndex = MyCL.GetListIndex(Path2IndexFile)
```

The `MyCL` variable must be a valid Content Linking component. Passed to the method is the `Path2IndexFile` parameter, which contains the virtual path to the location of the index text file, so if we were viewing `Page1.asp` within the index file described earlier, and we coded this:

```
Response.Write MyCL.GetListIndex("CLList.txt")
```

the number2 would be written to the browser.

The *GetNextURL method* returns the URL for the next item in the index file. If the current page is the past page in the list, then the GetNextURL method returns the first page in the list, looping visitors back to the top. The method has the following syntax:

```
TheURL = MyCL.GetNextURL(Path2IndexFile)
```

The `MyCL` variable must be a valid Content Linking component. The `Path2IndexFile` parameter contains the virtual path to the text index file. The URL entry in the index page for the next entry is returned from the method, so if we were on `Page1.asp` and we coded this:

```
Response.Write MyCL.GetNextURL("CLList.txt")
```

the URL Page2.asp would be written to the browser.

The *GetNextDescription method* retrieves the description field for the entry in the index file that is one past the current page. If the current page is the last page, then the component returns the description for the first page. The method has the following syntax:

```
TheDescription = MyCL.GetNextDescription(Path2IndexFile)
```

The `MyCL` variable must be an instance of the Content Linking component. The path to the index file is passed to the method, and the description of the next page in the index file is returned from the method, so if you were on `Page1.asp` from the preceding index file description and you coded this:

```
Response.Write MyCL.GetNextDescription("CLList.txt")
```

this text would be written to the browser:

```
Page 2 of Chapter 1
```

The *GetPreviousURL method* returns the URL for the previous item in the text index file. If the current page is the first page in the list, then the GetNextURL method returns the last page in the list, looping visitors back to the bottom. The method has the following syntax:

```
TheURL = MyCL.GetPreviousURL(Path2IndexFile)
```

The `MyCL` variable must be a valid Content Linking component. The `Path2IndexFile` parameter contains the virtual path to the text index file. The URL entry in the index page for the previous entry is returned from the method, so if we were on `Page1.asp` and we coded this:

```
Response.Write MyCL.GetNextURL("CLList.txt")
```

the URL TOC.asp would be written to the browser.

The *GetPreviousDescription method* retrieves the description field for the entry in the index file that is one before the current page. If the current page is the first page then the component returns the description for the last page. The method has the following syntax:

```
TheDescription = MyCL.GetPreviosDescription(Path2IndexFile)
```

The `MyCL` variable must be an instance of the Content Linking component. Passed to the method is the path to the index file. The description of the previous page in the index file is returned from the method, so if you were on `Page1.asp` from the preceding index file description and you coded this:

```
Response.Write MyCL.GetPreviousDescription("CLList.txt")
```

this text would be written to the browser:

```
Table of Contents Page
```

We have one more pair of methods to discuss, the *GetNthURL method* and the *GetNthDescription method,* which also return a URL and a description from the index file, respectively. But with these methods you specify the numeric entry that you want returned from the function.

The GetNthURL method has the following syntax:

```
TheURL = MyCL.GetNthURL(Path2IndexFile, NumericPosition)
```

The `MyCL` variable must be a valid instance of the Content Linking component. Two parameters are passed to the method: the first parameter is the virtual location of the text index file; the second parameter stores the position of the URL that you want returned, and the URL of the requested item is returned from the method.

For example, if you coded this based in the index text file discussed earlier:

```
Response.Write MyCL.GetNthURL("CLList.txt", 2)
```

the link `Page1.asp` would be written to the browser.

The GetNthDescription method has the following syntax:

```
TheDescription = MyCL.GetNthDescription(Path2IndexFile,
    NumericPosition)
```

The `MyCL` variable must be a valid instance of the Content Linking component. Two parameters are passed to the method: the first parameter is the virtual location of the text index file; the second parameter stores the position of the description that you want returned, and the description of the requested item is returned from the method.

For example, if you coded this based in the index text file discussed earlier:

```
Response.Write MyCL.GetNthDescription("CLList.txt", 2)
```

the text `Page 1 of Chapter 1` would be written to the browser.

If you combine these methods together you can create a nice Active Server Page application that allows visitors to progress forward and backward through your site and supply them with a Table of Contents. Let's take a look at such a Web site that describes the methods of the component we discussed in the last section, the Counters component.

Listed next is the text of the index file that is located in the same directory as the Active Server Pages:

```
get_method.asp Get Method
set_method.asp Set Method
increment_method.asp Increment Method
remove_method.asp Remove Method
toc.asp Go to Table of Contents
```

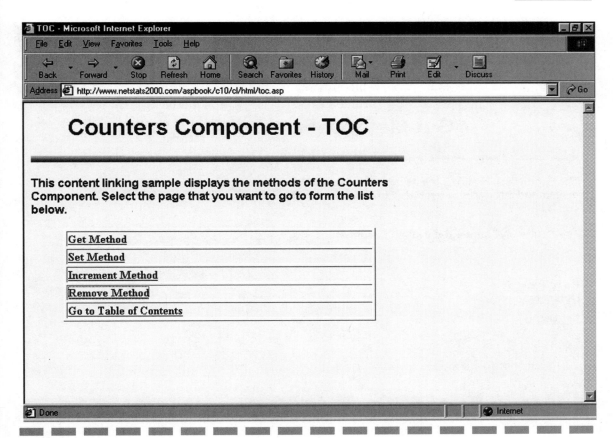

Figure 10-14 *Table of Contents page from the sample Content Linking site.*

Four pages are listed with their respective URLs and descriptions. The Table of Contents page produced from this index is displayed in Figure 10-14.

Notice that the order of the items listed in Figure 10-14 is the same as they are in the text index file. When visitors click on the Get Method link they see the page displayed in Figure 10-15.

Notice the links on the Get Method page. The previous link returns the visitor to the Table of Contents page, since this page is the first in the list. The next link displays the Set Method text, which if clicked displays the Set Method as shown in Figure 10-16.

After the Increment page is the Remove page, displayed in Figure 10-17. Notice that the next link on this page returns visitors to the Table of Contents page, since that item is listed last in the list. The previous link would take visitors to the Increment method.

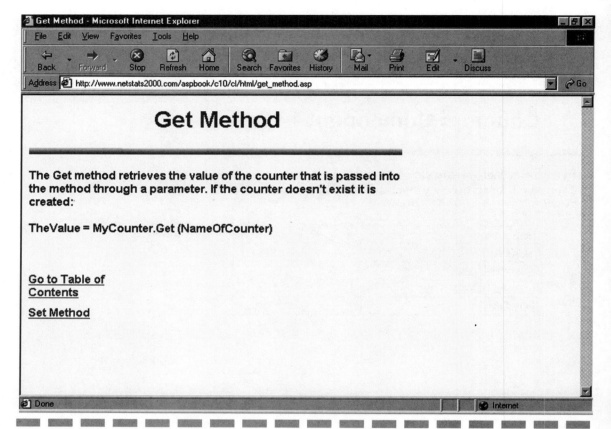

Figure 10-15 Get Method page from the sample Content Linking site.

The code used to create this site is of two types: one set of code is used to create the Table of Contents page; then each of the methods pages uses the same code structure to display the next and previous link information.

The first code block for the Table of Contents page is:

```
<%
Option Explicit
Dim MyCL
Dim TheCount
Dim I
Set MyCL = Server.CreateObject("MSWC.NextLink")
TheCount = MyCL.GetListCount("CLList.txt")
%>
```

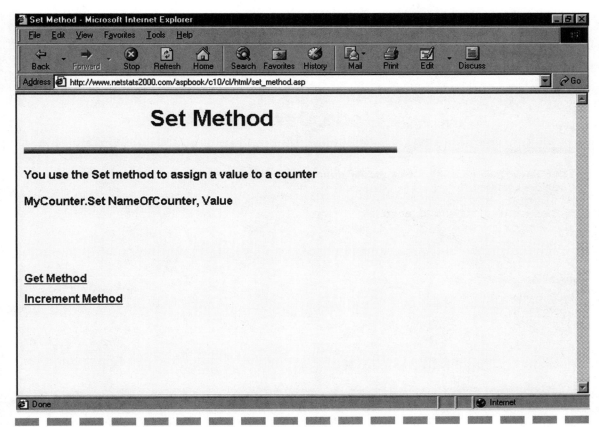

Figure 10-16 Set Method page from the sample Content Linking site.

First `Option Explicit` is noted:

```
Option Explicit
```

Then a variable that will store the Content Linking object is created:

```
Dim MyCL
```

Another variable is created that will store the total number of entries in the index text file:

```
Dim TheCount
```

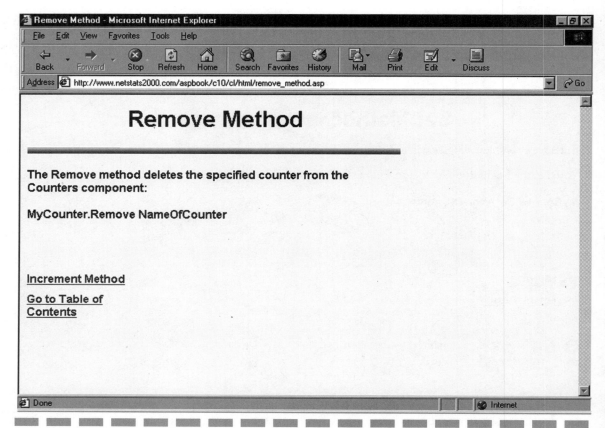

Figure 10-17 Remove Method page from the sample Content Linking site.

Another variable is created to store a number as we iterate through a loop in the second code block:

```
Dim I
```

An instance of the Content Linking component is initialized:

```
Set MyCL = Server.CreateObject("MSWC.NextLink")
```

The `TheCount` variable is then set to the number of items in the text index file:

```
TheCount = MyCL.GetListCount("CLList.txt")
```

The next code block produces the HTML table with all the items in the index file.

```
<%
For I = 1 to TheCount
%>
  <TR>
    <TD WIDTH=423><P><A HREF="
      <% Response.Write MyCL.GetNthURL("CLList.txt", i) %>">
      <B><% Response.Write MyCL.GetNthDescription("CLList.txt", i)
        %>
      </B></A>
    </TD>
  </TR>
<%
Next
%>
```

The code uses a `For` loop to iterate through each item in the text index file:

```
For I = 1 to TheCount
```

Then, each of the items is written to an HTML table. The URL is written using the GetNthURL and the description is written using the GetNthDescription method. The code then loops back to process the next record:

```
Next
```

The code on all the other pages is the same. The first code block creates the Content Linking component.

```
<%
Option Explicit
Dim MyCL
Set MyCL = Server.CreateObject("MSWC.NextLink")
%>
```

First `Option Explicit` is coded:

```
Option Explicit
```

Then a variable is created that will store the Content Linking component:

```
Dim MyCL
```

That object is then instantiated:

```
Set MyCL = Server.CreateObject("MSWC.NextLink")
```

The next code block writes the previous and next links to the browser.

```
<P><A HREF="<% Response.Write MyCL.GetPreviousURL("CLList.txt")
  %>"><B>
<% Response.Write MyCL.GetPreviousDescription("CLList.txt")
  %></A></B>
<P><A HREF="<% Response.Write MyCL.GetNextURL("CLList.txt") %>"><B>
<% Response.Write MyCL.GetNextDescription("CLList.txt") %></A></B>
```

First the previous link is written:

```
<P><A HREF="<% Response.Write MyCL.GetPreviousURL("CLList.txt")
  %>"><B>
```

Next the description for the previous link is written:

```
<% Response.Write MyCL.GetPreviousDescription("CLList.txt")
  %></A></B>
```

The link for the Next URL is written:

```
<P><A HREF="<% Response.Write MyCL.GetNextURL("CLList.txt") %>"><B>
```

Last is the description of the Next link:

```
<% Response.Write MyCL.GetNextDescription("CLList.txt") %></A></B>
```

Content Rotator Component

The *Content Rotator component* provides a way for you to have different content appear on your pages whenever the page is loaded. Things such as a quote of the day, different welcome messages, tips of the day, or fortunes are examples of use of this component. This same functionality could be done by loading data from a database but this component provides an alternative mechanism that does not require a database to be loaded just to change the tip of the day.

The component is not part of the standard IIS installation, but rather is part of the IIS Resource Kit. On the Resource Kit, the library is located in the following path:

```
\IIS Resource Kit\Component\Content Rotator\DLL\i386\controt.dll
```

Place the file in your WinNT\System32 directory, then register the component by using the Start\Run command and entering:

```
Regsvr32 controt.dll
```

Once you have installed it, you can instantiate the component with a line of code like this:

```
Set objCR = Server.CreateObject("IISSample.ContentRotator")
```

The CreateObject method of the Server object is used to create an instance of the component. In this example, the variable objCR would now be an instance of this component.

The component relies on a separate text file that contains the different content that should be displayed. Within the text file you give the content a relevancy rating that determines how often that content is viewed versus the rest of the content. You can supply a comment and then you enter in the content itself.

The content is placed directly into the HTML, so you can include HTML tags in the entries. The file should be saved as a plain text file and needs to be in a place that can be addressed from the page in which you want to use the content. I find it easiest to place the file in the same location as the page using the content, so the calls are a little clearer.

Each entry has the following structure:

```
%% #Ranking // A comment
The text of the content
```

Each entry starts with a double percent sign. That tag is optionally followed by a *ranking* for the entry, which refers to how often the entry should be viewed versus the other entries in the list file; if you leave off the ranking, it defaults to a ranking of one.

After the ranking or relevancy value is a comment, which is also optional. Then the next line contains the content for this entry. The content can cover multiple lines and is assumed to continue until another double percent sign is reached or the end of file is reached.

The component has two methods you use to retrieve the content from the content file, the first of which, *ChooseContent method*, returns an entry from the content list. The entry that is returned is more likely to appear if it has a higher ranking. The method has the following syntax:

```
TheText = objCR.ChooseContent(Path2ContentFile)
```

The objCR variable must be a valid instance of the Content Rotator file. The Path2ContentFile parameter is passed to the method. This is the virtual path to the file that contains the content entries, and the text of the entry retrieved from the content entries file is returned from the method.

The second method, *GetAllContent,* returns all the content entries from the file and writes them directly to the browser. The method has the following syntax:

```
objCR.GetAllContent(Path2ContentFile)
```

The `objCR` variable must be a valid instance of the Content Rotator component. The `Path2ContentFile` parameter needs to contain the path to the content text file. The method writes all the content directly to the browser. Each entry is written separated by HTML HR.

Let's take a look at a sample Quote of the Day page that uses this component. When visitors first enter the page, they see something like that in Figure 10-18.

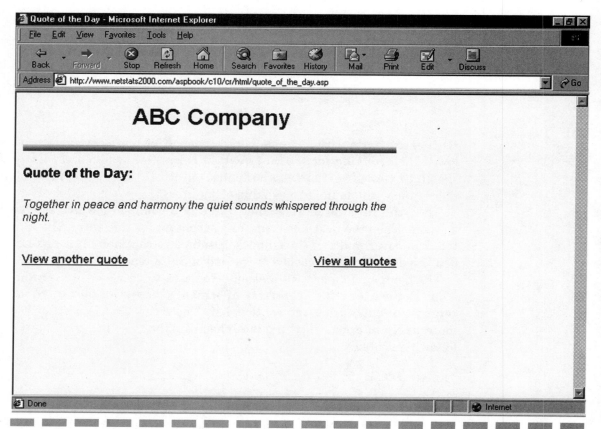

Figure 10-18   First page of the Quote of the Day.

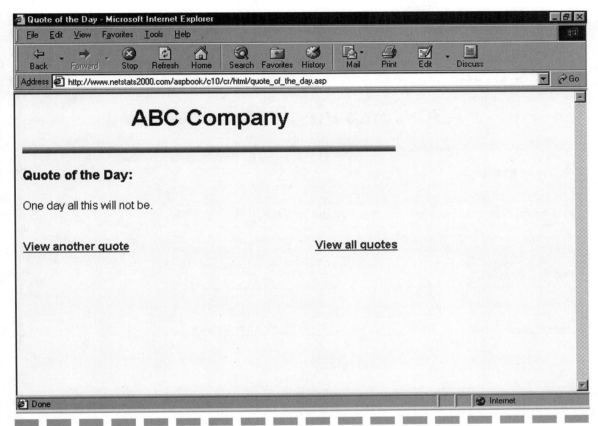

Figure 10-19 Page after the VIEW ANOTHER QUOTE link was clicked.

If visitors click on the VIEW ANOTHER QUOTE link, they could see another quote like the one shown in Figure 10-19.

If visitors click on the VIEW ALL QUOTES link, they see a page like the one displayed in Figure 10-20. The page uses a content scheduler text file that contains each quote as shown here:

```
%% #2 // This is a comment
<B><FONT FACE="Arial,Helvetica,Univers,Zurich BT">
Live all your days like they are your first day and your last.
</FONT></B>

%% #3
<I><FONT FACE="Arial,Helvetica,Univers,Zurich BT">
Together in peace and harmony the quiet sounds whispered through
the night.
</FONT></I>
```

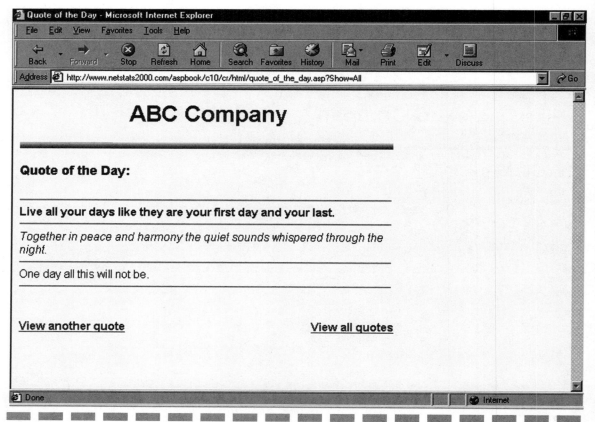

Figure 10-20 Quote of the Day with all the quotes present.

```
%% #1 // This quote has the lowest value
<FONT FACE="Arial,Helvetica,Univers,Zurich BT">
One day all this will not be.
</FONT>
```

The first entry has a ranking of 2. If we add up all the numbers we get 6. With a value of 2, this first entry has a 2/6 or 33 percent chance of being viewed:

```
%% #2 // This is a comment
<B><FONT FACE="Arial,Helvetica,Univers,Zurich BT">
Live all your days like they are your first day and your last.
</FONT></B>
```

Notice that the entry has a comment and that the content of the entry is across more than one line.

The second entry has a rating of 3 so it has 3/6 or a 50 percent chance of being viewed. Notice it doesn't have a comment:

```
%% #3
<I><FONT FACE="Arial,Helvetica,Univers,Zurich BT">
Together in peace and harmony the quiet sounds whispered through
the night.
</FONT></I>
```

The last entry has a rating of 1, so it should appear only once every six times the page is viewed:

```
%% #1 // This quote has the lowest value
<FONT FACE="Arial,Helvetica,Univers,Zurich BT">
One day all this will not be.
</FONT>
```

The code on the Quote of the Day page displays one of these entries or all of the entries based on the link clicked by the visitor. The first code block on the page creates the Content Rotator component.

```
<%
Option Explicit
Dim objCR
Set objCR = Server.CreateObject("IISSample.ContentRotator")
%>
```

We start the code in the typical fashion of including the Option Explicit variable. Remember that if you use Option Explicit, it must be the first line on the page:

```
Option Explicit
```

Next the Content Rotator variable is created:

```
Dim objCR
```

and initialized:

```
Set objCR = Server.CreateObject("IISSample.ContentRotator")
```

The next code block occurs in the spot on the page where we want the quote to appear, so it is embedded with the HTML:

```
<%
If IsEmpty(Request.QueryString("Show")) Then
  Response.Write objCR.ChooseContent("cr.txt")
```

```
Else
  objCR.GetAllContent("cr.txt")
End If
%>
```

The two links at the bottom of the page link back to this same page to display another quote. The difference is that when visitors click on the link to display all the quotes on the page, a parameter is passed through the QueryString, so in the code we first look for that field in the QueryString:

```
If IsEmpty(Request.QueryString("Show")) Then
```

If it is empty, that means that we just need to display a single quote:

```
Response.Write objCR.ChooseContent("cr.txt")
```

otherwise, we use the GetAllContent method to write all the quotes to the browser. Notice that this is not done with the Write method. That is because the GetAllContent method writes straight to the browser itself:

```
Else
  objCR.GetAllContent("cr.txt")
End If
```

MyInfo Component

Earlier in this chapter we looked at the Counters component. We talked about how it had an almost super-scope level because it was viewable by all the sessions and all the Active Server Page applications in your server. One drawback of this, however, was that the component stored only numbers. Although the MyInfo component doesn't have the Increment and Remove methods like the Counters component, it does allow you to have strings that persist across the server. The values persist if the server goes down because they are stored in a text file outside IIS.

The *MyInfo component* is made up of properties that you create just by setting their values and retrieve just by specifying their name. To create the component just use this line of code:

```
Set MyInfo = Server.CreateObject("MSWC.MyInfo")
```

The CreateObject method of the Server object is used to create the component. The variable `MyInfo` becomes an instance of the MyInfo component. Once the component is created, you can create and access properties as you like.

For example:

```
<%
Option Explicit
Dim MyInfo
Set MyInfo = Server.CreateObject("MSWC.MyInfo")
MyInfo.CompanyName = "ABC Company"
Response.Write "<B>" & MyInfo.CompanyName & "<P>"
%>
```

Here we first state that we will declare our variables:

```
Option Explicit
```

Then we declare the `MyInfo` variable:

```
Dim MyInfo
```

and instantiate it:

```
Set MyInfo = Server.CreateObject("MSWC.MyInfo")
```

Next we create a property for this component called CompanyName and set the value for that property in the same line of code. Note that if the property already exists, then we have replaced the value that it was before:

```
MyInfo.CompanyName = "ABC Company"
```

The value of this property is written to the browser:

```
Response.Write "<B>" & MyInfo.CompanyName & "<P>"
```

That output is displayed in Figure 10-21. Remember, though, that this property has super-scope, so we can also create a page with the following code that is in a totally different Active Server Page application on our server.

```
<%
Option Explicit
Dim MyInfo
Set MyInfo = Server.CreateObject("MSWC.MyInfo")
Response.Write "<B>This is from a different Active Server " _
  & "Page Application: " & MyInfo.CompanyName & "<P>"
%>
```

Figure 10-21
Output of first page
in MyInfo sample.

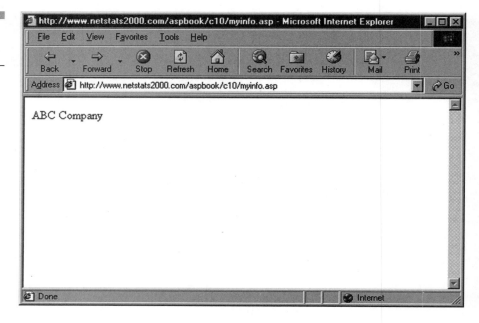

Here the property is written to the browser from a different Active Server Page application to demonstrate the scope of this component's properties. The output is shown in Figure 10-22.

Figure 10-22
Output of the
CompanyName
property from a dif-
ferent Active Server
Page application.

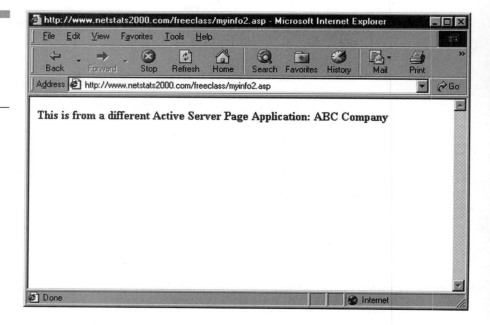

CHAPTER 11

Scripting Objects

Additional VBScript Components

Besides the components that come with ASP, VBScript itself has some additional components you can create. These components fall into three categories:

- The first category includes the objects that let you access files, folders, and drives on your system. With these objects you can read and write to files and browse the contents of folders.
- The second category is the Dictionary object, with which you can create a grouping or list of similar items. With this list you can add, remove, and delete items.
- The third category of objects included with VBScript is the Err object, which allows you to write protection code that takes some action when an error occurs. We discuss this object in the next chapter when we talk about issues of debugging.

The objects that we discuss in this chapter are summarized in Table 11-1.

TABLE 11-1

Scripting Objects

Object	Purpose
FileSystemObject Object	Provides a variety of methods to work with the file system.
Drives Collection	A collection of all the available drives.
Drive Object	Provides numerous properties for a single drive.
Folders Collection	A collection of subfolders that are in a folder or root.
Folder Object	Provides properties and methods for querying and manipulating a single folder.
Files Collection	A collection of all the file objects that are in a folder or root.
File Object	Provides methods and properties for manipulating and querying a file.
TextStream Object	Provides the capability for working with the information in a file.
Dictionary Object	Allows for the storage in related items that are key-value pairs.

Relationship of the File System Objects

You use eight different objects to access files, folders, and drives on your system. These items are the FileSystemObject object, Drives collection, Drive object, Folders collection, Folder object, Files collection, File object, and the TextStream object. The objects relate in a hierarchical format with the FileSystemObject object at the top level and the TextStream object at the bottom of the hierarchy as shown in Figure 11-1.

The objects and collections relate in a logical format starting at the system through the drives, folders, and files and down to a stream to a file. Notice that the relationship between the Folders collection and a Folder object is *bidirectional* because every Folder object has a Folders collection and every Folders collection has Folder objects. As you will see in the next sections of this chapter, there are also direct ways of accessing lower levels of the hierarchy from the top level without having to create each level down the line.

Figure 11-1

Relationship between the File System objects and collections.

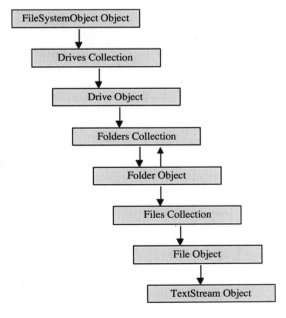

FileSystemObject Object

The redundantly named FileSystemObject object provides a single property and numerous methods to access the computer's file system. The object is at the top level of the File System Object hierarchy and is needed to create or reference any of the other objects and collections in the File System Object hierarchy.

You can create an instance of the FileSystemObject object by using the CreateObject method of the Server object:

```
Set objFileSys = Server.CreateObject("Scripting.FileSystemObject")
```

The name of the application/class you wish to create is passed to the CreateObject method. In this case, Scripting.FileSystemObject is created and returned into the variable objFileSys.

FileSystemObject Object Property

The FileSystemObject object contains a single property that is discussed below and summarized in Table 11-2.

Drives Property
The only property of the FileSystemObject object is the *Drives property*, which you use to return a reference to the drives on the system that the method is called on. The property has the following syntax:

```
Set objDrives = objFileSystem.Drives
```

The Drives collection would be returned into objDrives. Notice that the Set keyword is used at the beginning of this line. That is because the property returns an object, not a simple variable. So the Set keyword is required.

TABLE 11-2

Scripting Objects

Property	Purpose
Drives	Returns a Drives collection.

ObjFileSystem would need to be a valid FileSystemObject object. So you would need code like this to access the Drives property:

```
<%
Option Explicit
Dim objFileSys
Dim objDrives
Set objFileSys = Server.CreateObject("Scripting.FileSystemObject")
Set objDrives = objFileSys.Drives
%>
```

First, the `Option Explicit` variable is noted:

```
Option Explicit
```

Then a variable is created to store the FileSystemObject object and the Drives collection:

```
Dim objFileSys
Dim objDrives
```

Then the `objFileSys` variable is set to the File System:

```
Set objFileSys = Server.CreateObject("Scripting.FileSystemObject")
```

and the `objFileSys` variable is used to return the drives collection into `objDrives`:

```
Set objDrives = objFileSys.Drives
```

FileSystemObject Object Methods

The methods of the FileSystemObject object allow you to directly manipulate and query the Drives, Folders, and Files on the system. The numerous methods of this object are discussed below and summarized in Table 11-3.

BuildPath Method

The *BuildPath method* correctly builds a directory and/or file path from two parts: the first part is an existing path; the second part represents a deeper level to which you want to take your path. The method has the following syntax:

```
ThePath = objFileSys.BuildPath(OriginalPath, ExtendedPath)
```

TABLE 11-3

FileSystemObject
Object Methods

Method	Purpose
BuildPath	Adds a deeper path level to an existing path.
CopyFile	Copies a file or files from one location to another.
CopyFolder	Copies a folder and all its files and subfolders from one location to another.
CreateFolder	Creates a new folder or directory at the location indicated by the path.
CreateTextFile	Creates a new text file and returns a connection to that file.
DeleteFile	Permanently removes a file from the specified path.
DeleteFolder	Deletes a folder and all of its files and subfolders.
DriveExists	Checks for the existence of a drive and returns True or False based on that finding.
FileExists	Checks to see if a file exists at the path specified and returns True or False.
FolderExists	Checks to see if the specified folder exists at the path indicated.
GetAbsolutePathName	Returns the absolute path of a folder based on a logical or relative path.
GetBaseName	Returns the name of a file without its extension.
GetDrive	Returns a Drive object based on the path specified.
GetDriveName	Returns the name of a drive based on a specified path.
GetExtensionName	Returns the extension part of a file or folder name based on a path.
GetFile	Returns a File object based on a specified path.
GetFileName	Returns the full name of a file based on its path.
GetFolder	Returns a Folder object for the specified path.
GetParentFolderName	Returns the name of the parent directory based on a path.
GetSpecialFolder	Returns the path to certain system folders like Windows.
GetTempName	Returns a random file name that can be used to work with a temporary file.
MoveFile	Moves a file or files from one location to another.
MoveFolder	Moves a folder and all of its files and subfolders from one location to another.
OpenTextFile	Returns a TextStream object for the specified file.

The `objFileSys` variable must be a valid File System object. Two parameters are passed to the method: the first is the original path that you want to add to; the second is the deeper level that you want to take the path. The method returns the resulting full path with the correct placement of directory dividing characters.

The following code demonstrates the uses of the BuildPath method:

```
<%
Option Explicit
Dim objFileSys
Dim ThePath1
Dim ThePath2
set objFileSys = Server.CreateObject("Scripting.FileSystemObject")
ThePath1 = "c:\Program Files"
ThePath2 = "c:\Program Files\"
Response.Write objFileSys.BuildPath(ThePath1, "Office") & "<P>"
Response.Write objFileSys.BuildPath(ThePath1, "\Office") & "<P>"
Response.Write objFileSys.BuildPath(ThePath2, "Office") & "<P>"
Response.Write objFileSys.BuildPath(ThePath2, "\Office") & "<P>"
%>
```

First, we state that we will declare our variables:

```
Option Explicit
```

Then we create a variable that will store the File System object:

```
Dim objFileSys
```

Then two variables are created that will store paths:

```
Dim ThePath1
Dim ThePath2
```

The objFileSys object is instantiated:

```
set objFileSys = Server.CreateObject("Scripting.FileSystemObject")
```

Then we set the path variables to a beginning of a path. Notice that one ends with a directory-dividing character and one doesn't:

```
ThePath1 = "c:\Program Files"
ThePath2 = "c:\Program Files\"
```

We then append to these paths a subfolder, some of which start with a directory-dividing character and some that do not. The result of the method calls are written to the browser:

```
Response.Write objFileSys.BuildPath(ThePath1, "Office") & "<P>"
Response.Write objFileSys.BuildPath(ThePath1, "\Office") & "<P>"
Response.Write objFileSys.BuildPath(ThePath2, "Office") & "<P>"
Response.Write objFileSys.BuildPath(ThePath2, "\Office") & "<P>"
```

The output of this code is displayed in Figure 11-2. Notice that, regardless of the use of the directory-separating character, the method outputs a syntactically correct path.

CopyFile Method

The *CopyFile method* provides a way for you to copy a file or a group of files from one location to another location. The method has the following syntax:

```
ObjFileSys.CopyFile SourceLocation, DestinationLocation,
    OverWriteFlag
```

The `ObjFileSys` variable must be a valid instance of the FileSystemObject object. The `SourceLocation` parameter is the location of the file or files that you wish to copy and the `DestinationLocation` parameter is the place where you want the file copied.

The `OverWriteFlag` parameter is used to determine whether to overwrite files if they already exist. The parameter is optional and, if it

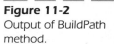

Figure 11-2
Output of BuildPath method.

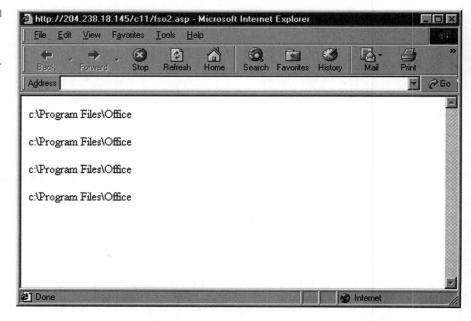

http://204.238.18.145/c11/fso2.asp - Microsoft Internet Explorer

File   Edit   View   Favorites   Tools   Help

Back   Forward   Stop   Refresh   Home   Search   Favorites   History   Mail   Print

Address

c:\Program Files\Office

c:\Program Files\Office

c:\Program Files\Office

c:\Program Files\Office

Done   Internet

is excluded, it is set to True. When the parameter is set to True, it means that you want to overwrite existing files; if you set the parameter to False, then you don't want to overwrite files.

As mentioned, the `SourceLocation` parameter can represent a file or a group of files. You can represent more than one file here by using wildcards. For example here:

```
ObjFileSys.CopyFile "c:\docs\*.txt", "d:\backup\"
```

All of the files with the extension .txt in the docs directory of the C drive would be copied into the backup directory on D drive.

If the destination is a folder, then the file is copied into that folder. So here:

```
ObjFileSys.CopyFile "c:\docs\file1.txt", "d:\backup"
```

if backup on D drive was a directory, then a file called file1.txt would be created in that directory. If backup did not exist, the method would assume you were trying to create a file called backup and the contents of file1.txt would be created in a new file called backup.

CopyFolder Method

The *CopyFolder method* is used to copy entire folders from one location to another location. The method has the following syntax:

```
ObjFileSys.CopyFolder SourceLocation, DestinationLocation,
    OverWriteFlag
```

The `ObjFileSys` variable must be a valid instance of the FileSystemObject object.

`SourceLocation` is the location of the folder or folders that you want to copy. As with the CopyFile method, the CopyFolder method permits the use of wildcards in the `SourceLocation` parameter, so you can specify a single folder:

```
ObjFileSys.CopyFolder "c:\docs\technical1", "d:\backup"
```

or you can use wildcards to match on more than one folder:

```
ObjFileSys.CopyFolder "c:\docs\technical*", "d:\backup"
```

The `DestinationLocation` parameter stores the location where you want the folder or folders copied. The third parameter, `OverWriteFlag`, is an optional parameter that specifies whether you want existing folders overwritten. The default for this property is True, which means that you want the folders overwritten. You can also set the parameter to False, which means that you don't want to overwrite files and folders.

CreateFolder Method

The *CreateFolder method* is used to create a new folder at the location specified. The method has the following syntax:

```
set TheNewFolder = objFileSys.CreateFolder(NewFolderLocation)
```

The ObjFileSys variable must be a valid instance of the FileSystemObject object. Passed to the method is a single parameter that stores the name and path to the new folder. Returned from the method is a Folder object that points to the folder just created.

If the folder specified already exists, an error will occur. If the path to the folder does not exist, an error will also occur. Take this example:

```
<%
Option Explicit
Dim objFileSys
Dim TheNewFolder
set objFileSys = Server.CreateObject("Scripting.FileSystemObject")
set TheNewFolder =
objFileSys.CreateFolder("c:\inetpub\wwwroot\myfolder")
%>
```

First, Option Explicit is set:

```
Option Explicit
```

Then the variables are defined:

```
Dim objFileSys
Dim TheNewFolder
```

The FileSystemObject is instantiated:

```
set objFileSys = Server.CreateObject("Scripting.FileSystemObject")
```

The CreateFolder method is used to create a new folder called Myfolder at the path indicated. A Folder object is returned into TheNewFolder variable. If the folder Myfolder already exists at this location, an error will occur. If the path to that folder c:\inetput\wwwroot\ does not exist, an error will also occur:

```
set TheNewFolder = objFileSys.CreateFolder("c:\inetpub\wwwroot\
  myfolder")
```

CreateTextFile Method

The *CreateTextFile method* can be used to create a new text file that is in ASCII or Unicode format. The method has the following syntax:

```
set TheNewFile = objFileSys.CreateFolder(Path2File, OverWriteFlag,
  UnicodeFormat)
```

The method returns a TextStream object, which in this case would be into the variable `TheNewFile`. As you will see later in this chapter, you can use the TextStream object to manipulate the contents of a file.

The CreateTextFile method is a method of the FileSystemObject object so ObjFileSys would have to be a valid instance of that object. The first parameter, `Path2File`, stores the location of the file you want to create.

The second parameter, `OverWriteFlag`, is optional. This flag is used to determine whether an existing file is to be overwritten. If the parameter is set to True, an existing file is overwritten; if the parameter is set to False, the default, files are not overwritten.

The third parameter, `UnicodeFormat`, is also an optional parameter, which is used to specify whether a Unicode or ASCII file is created. The default value for this parameter is False, which means that an ASCII file is created. If you set the parameter to True, a Unicode file is created.

DeleteFile Method

You use the *DeleteFile method* to delete files from the system. The method has the following syntax:

```
ObjFileSys.DeleteFile NameOfFile, DeleteReadOnly
```

The `ObjFileSys` variable must be a valid instance of the FileSystemObject object. The first parameter stores the name of the file or files you want to delete. This required parameter could contain wild cards. If no files are found that match the file name or wild card pattern, an error occurs.

The second parameter stores the action to take if the file or files encountered are read-only. This parameter is not required and is set to False by default, which means that read-only files cannot be deleted. If the parameter was set to True, read-only files would be deleted.

Take a look at this example.

```
<%
Option Explicit
Dim objFileSys
set objFileSys = Server.CreateObject("Scripting.FileSystemObject")
objFileSys.DeleteFile "c:\docs\mydoc.txt"
objFileSys.DeleteFile "c:\docs\*.txt"
%>
```

First, we tell the compiler that variables will be declared:

```
Option Explicit
```

Then a variable that will store an instance of the FileSystemObject object is created:

```
Dim objFileSys
```

That variable is instantiated:

```
set objFileSys = Server.CreateObject("Scripting.FileSystemObject")
```

Then a single file is deleted. If the file does not exist an error will occur. If the file is read-only, it will not be deleted:

```
objFileSys.DeleteFile "c:\docs\mydoc.txt"
```

And finally, a wild card is used to delete all the text files:

```
objFileSys.DeleteFile "c:\docs\*.txt"
```

DeleteFolder Method

The *DeleteFolder method* provides a way for you to delete folders or directories from your system. The method will delete the folder and any subfolders and files that it contains. The method has the following syntax:

```
ObjFileSys.DeleteFolder NameOfFolder, DeleteReadOnly
```

The `ObjFileSys` variable must be a valid instance of the FileSystemObject object. The `NameOfFolder` parameter stores the path to the folder that should be deleted. If the folder does not exist, an error occurs.

The second parameter, `DeleteReadOnly`, is optional and stores the action to take if the folder is read-only. The default for this parameter is False, which means that read-only folders are not removed. If you set the parameter to True, then read-only folders can be deleted.

DriveExists Method

The *DriveExists method* allows you to determine whether a drive letter is a valid drive. The method has the following syntax:

```
TheResult = ObjFileSys.DriveExists(DriveLetter)
```

The `ObjFileSys` variable must be a valid instance of the FileSystemObject object. Passed to the method is the drive letter that you want to test. A value of True or False is returned from the method: True is returned if the drive exists, False if the drive does not exist.

If the drive being tested has removable media like a floppy drive or a CD drive, the drive does not need to have the media in place for the method to work properly. Take a look at this code sample.

```
<%
Option Explicit
Dim objFileSys
set objFileSys = Server.CreateObject("Scripting.FileSystemObject")
Response.Write "Drive C is valid: " & objFileSys.DriveExists("C") &
    "<P>"
Response.Write "Drive A is valid: " & objFileSys.DriveExists("A") &
    "<P>"
Response.Write "Drive R is valid: " & objFileSys.DriveExists("R") &
    "<P>"
%>
```

First, `Option Explicit` is written, so variable declaration is required:

```
Option Explicit
```

Next, a variable is created to store the FileSystemObject object:

```
Dim objFileSys
```

That object is instantiated:

```
set objFileSys = Server.CreateObject("Scripting.FileSystemObject")
```

The code then checks for the existence of a fixed drive that is in place:

```
Response.Write "Drive C is valid: " & objFileSys.DriveExists("C") &
    "<P>"
```

Then the code checks for the existence of a drive with removable media:

```
Response.Write "Drive A is valid: " & objFileSys.DriveExists("A") &
    "<P>"
```

The code then checks for the existence of a drive that doesn't actually exist on this system:

```
Response.Write "Drive R is valid: " & objFileSys.DriveExists("R") &
    "<P>"
```

The result of this code is displayed in Figure 11-3.

FileExists Method

The *FileExists method* checks to see if a file exists in the path provided. The method has the following syntax:

```
TheResult = objFileSys.FileExists(Path2File)
```

The `ObjFileSys` variable must be a valid FileSystemObject object. Passed to the method is the single parameter, which is the path to the file to test for. The path can be either absolute or relative. Returned from the method is the value True or False: True is returned if the file was found and False is returned if the file was not found.

Figure 11-3
Result of drive exists.

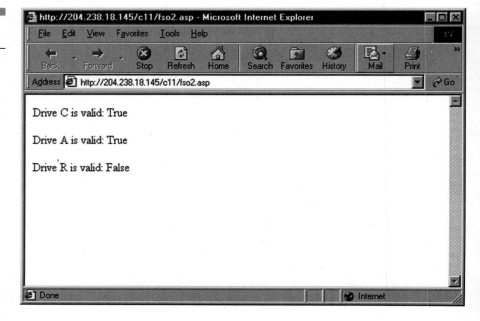

Since the path can be absolute or relative you can code this:

```
<%
Option Explicit
Dim objFileSys
set objFileSys = Server.CreateObject("Scripting.FileSystemObject")
Response.Write objFileSys.FileExists("myfile.txt") & "<P>"
Response.Write objFileSys.FileExists("..\myfile.txt") & "<P>"
Response.Write objFileSys.FileExists("c:\docs\myfile.txt") & "<P>"
%>
```

First Option Explicit is noted:

```
Option Explicit
```

Then the FileSystemObject object is declared and initialized:

```
Dim objFileSys
set objFileSys = Server.CreateObject("Scripting.FileSystemObject")
```

This line tests for a file in the current folder:

```
Response.Write objFileSys.FileExists("myfile.txt") & "<P>"
```

Here, the code tests for a file in the parent folder:

```
Response.Write objFileSys.FileExists("..\myfile.txt") & "<P>"
```

And in this line of code, the FileExists method is used to test for a file in an absolute path:

```
Response.Write objFileSys.FileExists("c:\docs\myfile.txt") & "<P>"
```

FolderExists Method

The *FolderExists method* of the FileSystemObject object tests for the existence of a folder. The method has the following syntax:

```
TheResult = objFileSys.FolderExists(Path2Folder)
```

The ObjFileSys variable must be a valid FileSystemObject object. Passed to the method is the relative or absolute location of the folder to test existence on. The value returned from the method is either True or False: True if the folder is found and False if the folder is not found.

Since the path to test can be absolute or relative, you can code like this:

```
<%
Option Explicit
Dim objFileSys
set objFileSys = Server.CreateObject("Scripting.FileSystemObject")
Response.Write objFileSys.FolderExists(".\Docs\MyFolder") & "<P>"
Response.Write objFileSys.FolderExists("MyFolder") & "<P>"
Response.Write objFileSys.FolderExists("..\..\MyFolder") & "<P>"
%>
```

First, `Option Explicit` is noted:

```
Option Explicit
```

Then a variable is created and instantiated to be a FileSystemObject object:

```
Dim objFileSys
set objFileSys = Server.CreateObject("Scripting.FileSystemObject")
```

The location of a folder called `MyFolder`, which is a subfolder of a folder called `Docs` that is in the current folder is tested:

```
Response.Write objFileSys.FolderExists(".\Docs\MyFolder") & "<P>"
```

Here, the code checks for the existence of a folder called `MyFolder` that is in the current folder:

```
Response.Write objFileSys.FolderExists("MyFolder") & "<P>"
```

Then the code looks for a folder called `MyFolder` that is located in the parent folder of the parent folder:

```
Response.Write objFileSys.FolderExists("..\..\MyFolder") & "<P>"
```

GetAbsolutePathName Method

The *GetAbsolutePathName method* returns an absolute path from a relative path. The method has the following syntax:

```
ThePath = objFileSys.GetAbsolutePathName(Path2Convert)
```

The GetAbsolutePathName method is a method of the FileSystemObject object, so the `ObjFileSys` variable must be a valid object of that type. The path that you want to determine the absolute path for is passed to the method. The absolute path is returned from the method.

Take a look at this code sample that is based on the current directory being the c:\winnt\system32 directory.

```
<%
Option Explicit
Dim objFileSys
set objFileSys = Server.CreateObject("Scripting.FileSystemObject")
Response.Write objFileSys.GetAbsolutePathName("") & "<P>"
Response.Write objFileSys.GetAbsolutePathName(".\") & "<P>"
Response.Write objFileSys.GetAbsolutePathName("..\") & "<P>"
Response.Write objFileSys.GetAbsolutePathName("..\..\") & "<P>"
%>
```

First, Option Explicit is noted:

```
Option Explicit
```

Then the FileSystemObject object is created and initialized:

```
Dim objFileSys
set objFileSys = Server.CreateObject("Scripting.FileSystemObject")
```

An empty string returns the path to the current directory:

```
Response.Write objFileSys.GetAbsolutePathName("") & "<P>"
```

This path also represents the current directory:

```
Response.Write objFileSys.GetAbsolutePathName(".\") & "<P>"
```

Here the parent path is requested:

```
Response.Write objFileSys.GetAbsolutePathName("..\") & "<P>"
```

The path to the parent directory of the parent directory is passed to the GetAbsolutePathName here:

```
Response.Write objFileSys.GetAbsolutePathName("..\..\") & "<P>"
```

The output of this code is displayed in Figure 11-4.

GetBaseName Method

The *GetBaseName method* returns the name of a file based on a path to the file without the file extension or any folder path. The file has the following syntax:

```
BaseName = objFileSys.GetBaseName(Path2File)
```

The ObjFileSys variable must be a valid instance of the FileSystem Object object. Passed to the function is the name of the file for which you

Figure 11-4
Output of the
GetAbsolutePathName
code.

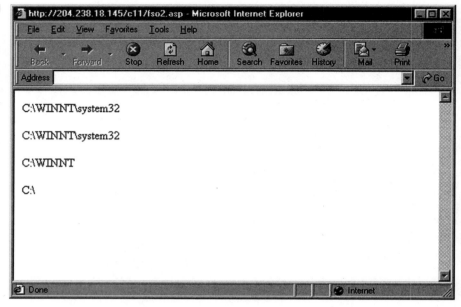

Figure 11-4
Output of the
GetAbsolutePathName
code.

want the base name. The base name of that file is returned from the method.

Take a look at this code:

```
<%
Option Explicit
Dim objFileSys
set objFileSys = Server.CreateObject("Scripting.FileSystemObject")
Response.Write objFileSys.GetBaseName("c:\docs\myfile.txt") & "<P>"
Response.Write objFileSys.GetBaseName("myfile.txt") & "<P>"
Response.Write objFileSys.GetBaseName("c:\docs\myfile") & "<P>"
%>
```

First, Option Explicit is noted:

```
Option Explicit
```

Then the FileSystemObject object is created and initialized:

```
Dim objFileSys
set objFileSys = Server.CreateObject("Scripting.FileSystemObject")
```

Then the base name of a file in an absolute path is written to the browser:

```
Response.Write objFileSys.GetBaseName("c:\docs\myfile.txt") & "<P>"
```

Here the base name of a file in the current directory is written to the browser:

```
Response.Write objFileSys.GetBaseName("myfile.txt") & "<P>"
```

Also written to the browser is the base name of a file that has no extension:

```
Response.Write objFileSys.GetBaseName("c:\docs\myfile") & "<P>"
```

The result of this code is displayed in Figure 11-5.

GetDrive Method

The *GetDrive method* returns a Drive object based on the parameter passed to the method. The GetDrive method has the following syntax:

```
Set TheDrive = objFileSys.GetDrive(DriveName)
```

The ObjFileSys variable must be a valid FileSystemObject object. Passed to the function is the drive letter of the drive to be returned or

Figure 11-5
Output of the GetBaseName method.

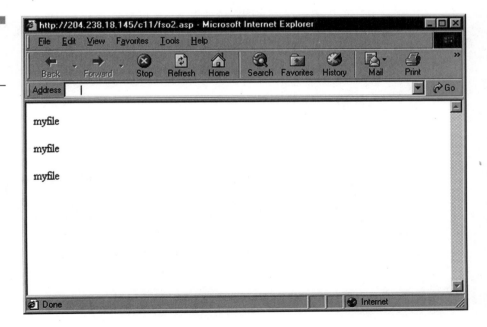

the drive letter with a colon or network share, so any of the following would be valid:

```
Set TheDrive = objFileSys.GetDrive("C")
Set TheDrive = objFileSys.GetDrive("C:")
Set TheDrive = objFileSys.GetDrive("\\share\path")
```

Returned from the method is a Drive object. The Drive object is discussed later in this chapter.

GetDriveName Method

The *GetDriveName method* returns the letter name of a drive from a path passed to the method, which has the following syntax:

```
TheDriveName = objFileSys.GetDriveName(Path)
```

the ObjFileSys variable must be a valid FileSystemObject object. Passed to the method is the path from which you want to parse the drive letter. Returned from the method is a string that contains the drive letter with a colon.

Take a look at this code sample:

```
<%
Option Explicit
Dim objFileSys
set objFileSys = Server.CreateObject("Scripting.FileSystemObject")
Response.Write "<B>" & objFileSys.GetDriveName("c:\docs\doc1.txt")
& "<P>"
Response.Write objFileSys.GetDriveName("c:\my documents") & "<P>"
Response.Write objFileSys.GetDriveName("a:") & "<P>"
%>
```

First, Option Explicit is noted:

```
Option Explicit
```

Then the FileSystemObject object is created and instantiated:

```
Dim objFileSys
set objFileSys = Server.CreateObject("Scripting.FileSystemObject")
```

First, the drive letter parsed from a path to a file will be written to the browser:

```
Response.Write "<B>" & objFileSys.GetDriveName("c:\docs\doc1.txt")
& "<P>"
```

Figure 11-6
Output of the
GetDriveName code.

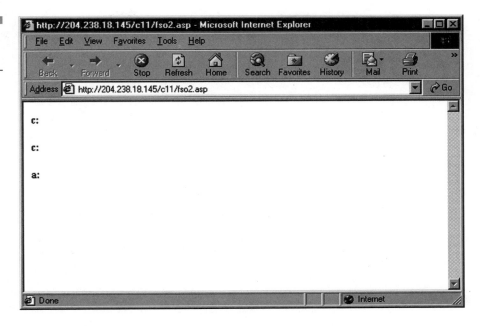

Then a drive letter based on a folder path is written to the browser:

```
Response.Write objFileSys.GetDriveName("c:\my documents") & "<P>"
```

Finally, just a drive letter is passed so that is what would be returned:

```
Response.Write objFileSys.GetDriveName("a:") & "<P>"
```

The output of this code is displayed in Figure 11-6.

GetExtensionName Method

The *GetExtensionName method* parses the extension of a file from a
path passed to the method. The method has the following syntax:

```
TheExtension = objFileSys.GetExtensionName(Path2File)
```

The `ObjFileSys` variable must be a valid instance of the
FileSystemObject object. Passed to the method is the path and name of
the file from which you want to parse the extension. The path can be
either absolute or relative; in fact, the file doesn't have to exist. The
method really just parses out the extension of the file based on the location of the dot separator.

This code sample uses the GetExtensionName method to parse out the extension of a few file names.

```
<%
Option Explicit
Dim objFileSys
set objFileSys = Server.CreateObject("Scripting.FileSystemObject")
Response.Write objFileSys.GetExtensionName("c:\docs\doc1.txt") &
"<P>"
Response.Write objFileSys.GetExtensionName("doc1.txt") & "<P>"
Response.Write objFileSys.GetExtensionName("doc1") & "<P>"
%>
```

First, `Option Explicit` is noted to the compiler:

```
Option Explicit
```

Then the FileSystemObject object is created and initialized:

```
Dim objFileSys
set objFileSys = Server.CreateObject("Scripting.FileSystemObject")
```

The extension for a file with a path specified is written to the browser:

```
Response.Write objFileSys.GetExtensionName("c:\docs\doc1.txt") &
   "<P>"
```

Next written to the browser is the extension of a file without a path specified:

```
Response.Write objFileSys.GetExtensionName("doc1.txt") & "<P>"
```

An empty string is then written to the browser here since the file has no extension:

```
Response.Write objFileSys.GetExtensionName("doc1") & "<P>"
```

The output of this code is displayed in Figure 11-7. Notice that there are only two lines of output in the browser window—that is because the third file had no extension name.

GetFile Method

The *GetFile method* returns a file object based on the parameter passed to the method. The method has the following syntax:

```
Set MyFile = objFileSys.GetFile(Path2File)
```

Figure 11-7
Output of the
GetExtensionName
code.

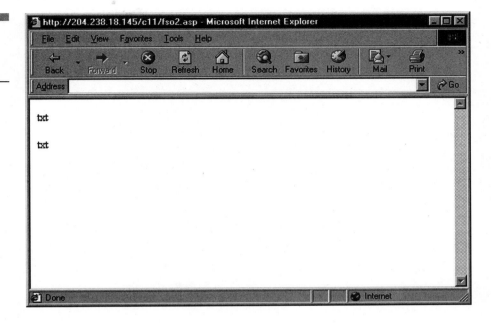

the `ObjFileSys` variable must be a valid FileSystemObject object. The name of the file to retrieve is passed to the method. The parameter can also include a path that can be absolute or relative.

A File object is returned from the method. We discuss the File object later in this chapter.

GetFileName Method

So far we have looked at a method called GetBaseName that returns the name portion without the extension of a file. We have also looked at the GetExtensionName method that returns the extension portion of the file name. The *GetFileName method* combines these two methods and returns the full file name based on a path that is either absolute or relative.

The method has the following syntax:

```
TheFileName = objFileSys.GetFileName(Path2File)
```

The `ObjFileSys` variable must be a valid instance of the FileSystemObject object. Passed to the method is the name of the file with a path that is either relative or absolute. Take a look at this sample use of the method.

```
<%
Option Explicit
Dim objFileSys
set objFileSys = Server.CreateObject("Scripting.FileSystemObject")
Response.Write "The file name is: " &
objFileSys.GetFileName("c:\docs\doc1.txt") & "<P>"
Response.Write "The file name is: " &
objFileSys.GetFileName(".\doc1.txt") & "<P>"
Response.Write "The file name is: " &
objFileSys.GetFileName("c:\docs\doc1") & "<P>"
%>
```

First, the `Option Explicit` directive is declared:

```
Option Explicit
```

Then the FileSystemObject object is created and instantiated:

```
Dim objFileSys
set objFileSys = ServerCreateObject("Scripting.FileSystemObject")
```

Written to the browser next is the file name from an absolute path:

```
Response.Write "The file name is: " & objFileSys.GetFileName
   ("c:\docs\doc1.txt") & "<P>"
```

Here the file name is parsed from a relative path:

```
Response.Write "The file name is: " & objFileSys.GetFileName
   (".\doc1.txt") & "<P>"
```

Finally, the file name is parsed without an extension. Note that the file does not have to exist. The method merely parses out the name of the file:

```
Response.Write "The file name is: " & objFileSys.GetFileName
   ("c:\docs\doc1") & "<P>"
```

The output of this code is displayed in Figure 11-8.

GetFolder Method

The *GetFolder method* returns a Folder object based on the path passed to the object. The syntax for the method is as follows:

```
Set MyFolder = objFileSys.GetFolder(Path2Folder)
```

The `ObjFileSys` variable must be a valid instance of the FileSystemObject object. Passed to the method is the path to the folder

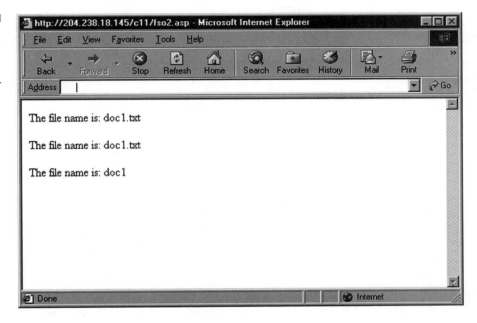

Figure 11-8
Output of code using the GetFileName method.

that you wish to retrieve. If the folder does not exist, an error occurs. A Folder object pertaining to the requested folder is returned from the method. The Folder object is discussed later in this chapter.

GetParentFolderName Method

The *GetParentFolderName method* returns the name of a parent folder based on a path passed to the method. The method has the following syntax:

```
TheName = objFileSys.GetParentFolderName(Path)
```

The `ObjFileSys` variable must be a valid instance of the FileSystemObject object. Passed to the method is the path from which you want to derive the parent folder. Returned from the method is the path to the parent folder.

This code sample uses the GetParentFolderName to return the parent folder for three entries:

```
<%
Option Explicit
Dim objFileSys
set objFileSys = Server.CreateObject("Scripting.FileSystemObject")
```

```
Response.Write objFileSys.GetParentFolderName("c:\support\docs\
   doc1.txt") & "<P>"
Response.Write objFileSys.GetParentFolderName("c:\support\docs") &
   "<P>"
Response.Write objFileSys.GetParentFolderName("c:\support") & "<P>"
%>
```

First, `Option Explicit` is noted:

```
Option Explicit
```

Then a FileSystemObject object is created and instantiated:

```
Dim objFileSys
set objFileSys = ServerCreateObject("Scripting.FileSystemObject")
```

Written to the browser here is the parent folder that the file is in:

```
Response.Write objFileSys.GetParentFolderName("c:\support\docs\
   doc1.txt") & "<P>"
```

Then the parent folder for that folder is written:

```
Response.Write objFileSys.GetParentFolderName("c:\support\docs") &
   "<P>"
```

The parent folder for the top-level is then written to the browser:

```
Response.Write objFileSys.GetParentFolderName("c:\support") & "<P>"
```

The output of this code is displayed in Figure 11-9.

GetSpecialFolder Method

The *GetSpecialFolder method* returns the path of certain system folders. The method has the following syntax:

```
ThePath = objFileSys.GetSpecialFolder(WhichFolder)
```

The `ObjFileSys` variable must be a valid instance of the FileSystemObject object. A number representing the path that you want returned is passed to the method. If you place a 0 in this parameter, then the path to the `Windows NT` folder is returned; if you pass a 1 to the method, the path to the `System` folder is returned; and if you pass a 2 to the method through the parameter, the path to the `Temporary` folder is returned. Returned from the method is the path as a string.

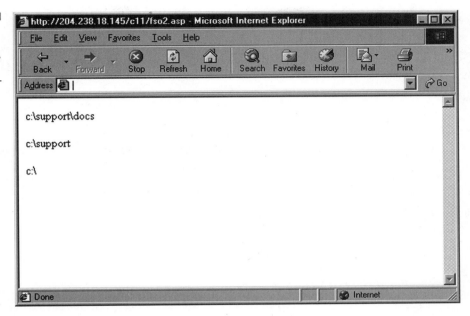

Figure 11-9
Output of the
GetParentFolderName
code.

The following code uses the GetSpecialFolder method to retrieve the paths to these three special folders.

```
<%
Option Explicit
Dim objFileSys
set objFileSys = Server.CreateObject("Scripting.FileSystemObject")
Response.Write "Path to Windows: " & objFileSys.GetSpecialFolder(0)
    & "<P>"
Response.Write "Path to Windows/System: " & objFileSys.GetSpecial
    Folder(1) & "<P>"
Response.Write "Path to Temp Folder: " & objFileSys.GetSpecial
    Folder(2) & "<P>"
%>
```

First, Option Explicit is coded:

```
Option Explicit
```

Then the FileSystemObject object is created and instantiated:

```
Dim objFileSys
set objFileSys = Server.CreateObject("Scripting.FileSystemObject")
```

The path to the Windows folder is written to the browser:

```
Response.Write "Path to Windows: " & objFileSys.GetSpecialFolder(0)
    & "<P>"
```

The GetSpecialFolder is used here to return the path to the System folder:

```
Response.Write "Path to Windows/System: " & objFileSys.GetSpecial
    Folder(1) & "<P>"
```

And the path to the Temporary folder is written to the browser:

```
Response.Write "Path to Temp Folder: " & objFileSys.GetSpecial
    Folder(2) & "<P>"
```

The result of this code is shown in Figure 11-10.

GetTempName Method

Sometimes in your code you will need to create a temporary file that you plan on taking some action with and will then later delete. You may have concerns about one temporary file overwriting another temporary file, so you will have a need to come up with unique temporary file names. The *GetTempName* method does just that.

Figure 11-10
Result of the
GetSpecialFolder
method.

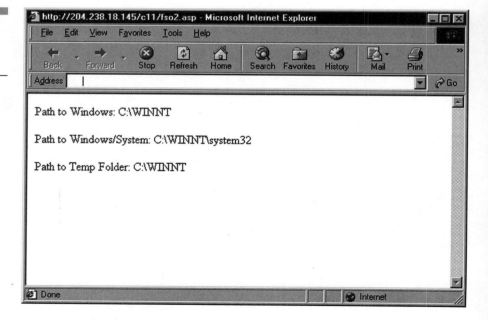

The method has the following syntax:

```
TheName = objFileSys.GetTempName
```

The method is a method of the FileSystemObject object so you will need a valid object of that type to make the call. The method has no parameters and returns a random file name in the form as shown here:

```
Name of first Temp file: rad19DA8.tmp
Name of second Temp file: radDBB77.tmp
Name of third Temp file: rad4C168.tmp
```

Notice that what is returned is just a file name, not a path. You may want to combine this function with the GetSpecialFolder to create a unique Temporary file name that is placed in the Temporary folder:

```
TempFileNameWithPath = objFileSys.GetTempName _
& objFileSys.GetSpecialFolder(2)
```

MoveFile Method
The *MoveFile method* can be used to move a file or a group of files from one location to another. Since the files are moved, they are deleted from the original location. The method has the following syntax:

```
ObjFileSys.MoveFile SourceLocation, DestinationLocation
```

MoveFile is a method of the FileSystemObject object, so in this code, the ObjFileSys variable would have to be an instance of that object. The method requires two parameters. The first parameter is the location of the file or files that you want to move. This parameter can be a single file:

```
ObjFileSys.MoveFile "c:\docs\mydoc.txt", "d:\backup\"
```

or, you can use wild cards to represent more than one file to move. Here, all files that have the extension .txt are moved:

```
ObjFileSys.MoveFile "c:\docs\*.txt", "d:\backup\"
```

The second parameter stores the location where you want the files moved to. This parameter cannot contain wildcards. If the parameter specifies a folder, then all the files are moved to that folder. If the parameter ends with a file name, then the file or files are moved into that new file.

MoveFolder Method

You use the *MoveFolder method* to move a folder and all of its files and subfolders to a new location. The method is a method of the FileSystemObject object and has the following syntax:

```
ObjFileSys.MoveFolder SourceLocation, DestinationLocation
```

The method takes two parameters. The first is the current location of the folder that you want to move. As with the MoveFile method, this parameter can contain wildcards, so you can match on a single folder or a group of folders. Remember that the method moves the folder and all the files and subfolders that it contains. The second parameter stores the location where you want to move the directory. For example, here:

```
ObjFileSys.MoveFolder "c:\docs", "d:\backup"
```

the folder `docs` and all of the files and subfolders in that directory are moved to the folder called `Backup`.

OpenTextFile Method

The *OpenTextFile method* is used to open a text file that can be manipulated from code. The method has the following syntax:

```
Set MyFile = objFileSys.OpenTextFile(NameOfFile, OpenMode,
    CreateNewFlag, TextFormat)
```

The method requires that the `ObjFileSys` variable be a valid instance of the FileSystemObject object. Passed to the method are four parameters, the first of which is the path to the file that you want to open.

You use the second parameter to indicate how you want the file opened. You can open the file for reading, writing, or appending. You use a 1 to open a file for read-only. The data in the file can only be read. You cannot write to this file. If you want to open the file for writing, you use a 2. That means that you will write to the file, but you cannot read the file. If you want to append to the file you use a value of 8. When you append to a file, all writes are added to the end of the file.

The third parameter is the `CreateNewFlag`, with which you specify what action to take if the file specified in the first parameter does not exist. The default for this parameter is False, which means that you do not want a new file created. If you specify True for this parameter, then a new file is created if the file requested is not found.

The last parameter is used to indicate the format of the text in the file, either ASCII or Unicode. If you specify 0 for this parameter, then the file is opened as ASCII; if you specify -1 for the format, then the file is opened as Unicode; you can also specify -2, which means that the file is opened as whatever is the system default.

Drives Collection

The *Drives collection* represents a collection of all the drives on the server. The drives can be fixed or removable like a floppy drive. You can use the Drives collection to iterate or work with all the Drives on the server or you can use the drives collection to refer to a specific drive. Additionally, you can use the Drives collection to return a single Drive object, which can be further manipulated.

The Drives collection has no methods but does contain two properties: the Count property and the Item property. The *Count property* returns a total count of the drives on the server. The *Item property* can be used to refer to a specific drive on the system.

Take a look at this sample that demonstrates the properties of the Drives collection. The code also iterates through the Drive objects in the collection.

```
<%
Option Explicit
Dim objFileSys
Dim MyDrives
Dim TheDrive
set objFileSys = Server.CreateObject("Scripting.FileSystemObject")
set MyDrives = objFileSys.Drives
Response.Write "Total Drives: " & MyDrives.Count & "<P>"
set TheDrive = MyDrives.Item("C")
Response.Write "Drive C is: " & TheDrive.DriveLetter & "<P>"
For Each TheDrive in MyDrives
  Response.Write "Drive: " & TheDrive.DriveLetter & "<P>"
Next
%>
```

First, `Option Explicit` is noted:

```
Option Explicit
```

Then we create a variable that will store FileSystemObject object:

```
Dim objFileSys
```

one that will store the Drives collection:

```
Dim MyDrives
```

and a Drive object:

```
Dim TheDrive
```

The FileSystemObject object is instantiated:

```
set objFileSys = Server.CreateObject("Scripting.FileSystemObject")
```

The Drives collection is accessed through objFileSys:

```
set MyDrives = objFileSys.Drives
```

The Count property is then used to write the total number of drives to the browser:

```
Response.Write "Total Drives: " & MyDrives.Count & "<P>"
```

The variable TheDrive is set to a specific drive in the Drives collection using the Item property:

```
set TheDrive = MyDrives.Item("C")
```

The letter for that Drive is written to the browser:

```
Response.Write "Drive C is: " & TheDrive.DriveLetter & "<P>"
```

Then a For...Each loop is used to iterate through each of the Drives in the collection:

```
For Each TheDrive in MyDrives
```

The letter for each of the drives is written to the browser:

```
Response.Write "Drive: " & TheDrive.DriveLetter & "<P>"
```

before looping to the next drive:

```
Next
```

The output of this code is displayed in Figure 11-11.

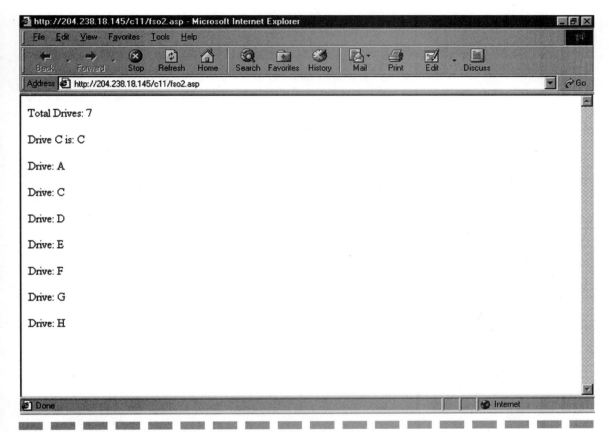

Figure 11-11 Output of the Drives collection code.

Drive Object

The *Drive object* is used to access a variety of informative properties about a specific drive. One of the properties also returns a Folder object so that you can start accessing Folder and File objects on a drive. The properties for the Drive object are discussed below and summarized in Table 11-4.

The code here demonstrates and annotates the use of the properties of the Drive object:

```
<%
Option Explicit
Dim objFileSys
Dim MyDrives
```

TABLE 11-4

Drive Object Properties

Properties	Purpose
AvailableSpace	Returns the total number of available bytes on the drive.
DriveLetter	Returns the letter designation for the drive.
DriveType	Numeric value that specifies the type of drive, for example, fixed or removable.
FileSystem	Structure of files on the drive, like FAT or NTFS.
FreeSpace	Returns the number of bytes that are not in use on the drive.
IsReady	Most helpful for drives like floppy drives, the property returns if the drive has its media inserted.
Path	Returns the path for the drive.
RootFolder	Returns a Folder object pointing to the root of the drive.
SerialNumber	Returns the serial number for the Drive object.
ShareName	Used to return the share name for a network drive.
TotalSize	Total number of bytes on the drive.
VolumeName	Returns the volume name for the drive.

```
Dim TheDrive
Dim TheRootFolder
set objFileSys = Server.CreateObject("Scripting.FileSystemObject")
set MyDrives = objFileSys.Drives
set TheDrive = MyDrives.Item("E")
Response.Write "Available Space: " &
FormatNumber(TheDrive.AvailableSpace, 0) & "<P>"
Response.Write "Drive Letter: " & TheDrive.DriveLetter & "<P>"
Response.Write "Drive Type: " & TheDrive.DriveType & "<P>"
Response.Write "File System: " & TheDrive.FileSystem & "<P>"
Response.Write "Free Space: " & FormatNumber(TheDrive.FreeSpace, 0)
& "<P>"
Response.Write "Is Ready: " & TheDrive.IsReady & "<P>"
Response.Write "Path: " & TheDrive.Path & "<P>"
set TheRootFolder = TheDrive.RootFolder
Response.Write "Serial Number: " & TheDrive.SerialNumber & "<P>"
Response.Write "Share Name: " & TheDrive.ShareName & "<P>"
Response.Write "Total Size: " & FormatNumber(TheDrive.TotalSize, 0)
& "<P>"
Response.Write "Volume Name: " & TheDrive.VolumeName & "<P>"
%>
```

First, `Option Explicit` is noted:

```
Option Explicit
```

Next, the variables are defined. First, a variable that will store the instance of the FileSystemObject object is created:

```
Dim objFileSys
```

Then one for the Drives collection is created:

```
Dim MyDrives
```

followed by a variable that will store a single Drive:

```
Dim TheDrive
```

A variable that will store a Folder object is also created:

```
Dim TheRootFolder
```

The FileSystemObject is then instantiated:

```
set objFileSys = Server.CreateObject("Scripting.FileSystemObject")
```

The Drives collection is returned into the MyDrives object:

```
set MyDrives = objFileSys.Drives
```

The variable `TheDrive` is set to a specific Drive:

```
set TheDrive = MyDrives.Item("E")
```

The AvailableSpace property is then used to write the number of bytes free on the drive to the browser. Note the use of the `FormatNumber` function so the number will be formatted with comma separators:

```
Response.Write "Available Space: " & FormatNumber(TheDrive.
   AvailableSpace, 0) & "<P>"
```

The DriveLetter property is used to write the drive letter to the browser:

```
Response.Write "Drive Letter: " & TheDrive.DriveLetter & "<P>"
```

Next, the drive type is written. A 0 indicates an unknown drive type; a 1 indicates a removable drive type, whereas a 2 indicates a fixed drive; a 3 is used for a Network drive; a 4 indicates a CD ROM; and a 5 indicates a RAM Disk:

```
Response.Write "Drive Type: " & TheDrive.DriveType & "<P>"
```

The FileSystem property returns FAT, NTFS, or CDFS:

```
Response.Write "File System: " & TheDrive.FileSystem & "<P>"
```

Next, the free space is written to the browser:

```
Response.Write "Free Space: " & FormatNumber(TheDrive.FreeSpace, 0)
  & "<P>"
```

If this drive had removable media, you could test for the media being ready with the IsReady property. True indicates that the drive is ready; False indicates that it is not:

```
Response.Write "Is Ready: " & TheDrive.IsReady & "<P>"
```

The Path, which is the drive letter with a colon, is written next:

```
Response.Write "Path: " & TheDrive.Path & "<P>"
```

Next, the RootFolder property is used to return a Folder object that is placed into the variable TheRootFolder:

```
set TheRootFolder = TheDrive.RootFolder
```

Next, the serial number for the drive is written to the browser:

```
Response.Write "Serial Number: " & TheDrive.SerialNumber & "<P>"
```

If the drive is a network drive, you can use the ShareName property to return the network share name for the drive:

```
Response.Write "Share Name: " & TheDrive.ShareName & "<P>"
```

Next the total size, in bytes, of the drive is written to the browser:

```
Response.Write "Total Size: " & FormatNumber(TheDrive.TotalSize, 0)
  & "<P>"
```

Finally, the volume name for the drive is written to the browser:

```
Response.Write "Volume Name: " & TheDrive.VolumeName & "<P>"
```

The output of this code is displayed in Figure 11-12.

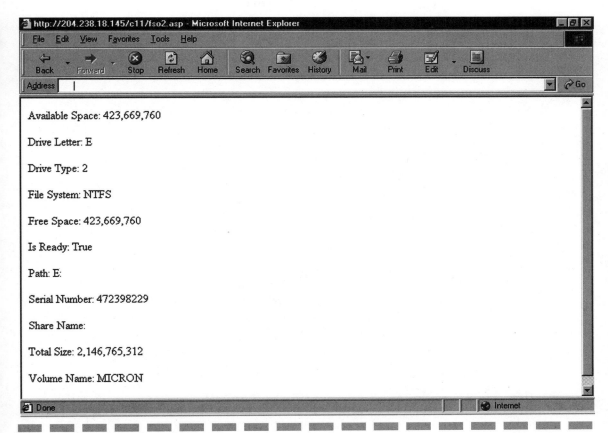

Figure 11-12 Output of the Drive object code.

Folders Collection

The *Folders collection* contains a collection of Folder objects. The properties of the collection allow you to refer to a specific Folder object in the collection as well as the count of the Folder objects in the collection. The collection also contains a single method that you can use to add a new folder to the collection.

The code here uses the method and properties of the Folders collection and iterates through all the folders in the collection.

```
<%
Option Explicit
Dim objFileSys
Dim MyDrives
```

```
Dim TheDrive
Dim TheRootFolder
Dim RootFolders
Dim SubFolder
set objFileSys = Server.CreateObject("Scripting.FileSystemObject")
set MyDrives = objFileSys.Drives
set TheDrive = MyDrives.Item("E")
set TheRootFolder = TheDrive.RootFolder
set RootFolders = TheRootFolder.SubFolders
Response.Write "Total Folders in root: " & RootFolders.Count &
"<P>"
set SubFolder = RootFolders.Item("Admin")
RootFolders.Add "NewFolder"
For Each SubFolder in RootFolders
  Response.Write SubFolder.Name & "<BR>"
Next
%>
```

First, `Option Explicit` is coded:

```
Option Explicit
```

Then variables are created to store the FileSystemObject object, the Drives collection, a Drive object, a root Folder object, a Folders collection, and an additional Folder object:

```
Dim objFileSys
Dim MyDrives
Dim TheDrive
Dim TheRootFolder
Dim RootFolders
Dim SubFolder
```

Next, the FileSystemObject is instantiated:

```
set objFileSys = Server.CreateObject("Scripting.FileSystemObject")
```

That object is used to return the Drives collection:

```
set MyDrives = objFileSys.Drives
```

The variable `TheDrive` is set to a specific Drive object from the Drives collection:

```
set TheDrive = MyDrives.Item("E")
```

A Folder object is set to the root folder of the Drive object:

```
set TheRootFolder = TheDrive.RootFolder
```

The Folder collection in the root of the Drive object is returned into the RootFolders object:

```
set RootFolders = TheRootFolder.SubFolders
```

The count of the Folder object in the Folders collection is written:

```
Response.Write "Total Folders in root: " & RootFolders.Count &
   "<P>"
```

A specific Folder object is returned from the Folders collection into the SubFolder variable:

```
set SubFolder = RootFolders.Item("Admin")
```

A new folder is created and added to the collection:

```
RootFolders.Add "NewFolder"
```

A For...Each loop will be used to iterate through all the folders in the collection:

```
For Each SubFolder in RootFolders
```

The name of each folder is written to the browser:

```
Response.Write SubFolder.Name & "<BR>"
```

The code then loops to the next Folder object in the collection:

```
Next
```

The output of this code is displayed in Figure 11-13. Notice that included in the text in the browser window is the folder that was added to the collection.

Folder Object

The *Folder object* contains numerous properties that allow you to manipulate the folder and the contents of the folder. The properties of the Folder object are discussed below and summarized in Table 11-5.

Figure 11-13
Output of the Folders
collection code.

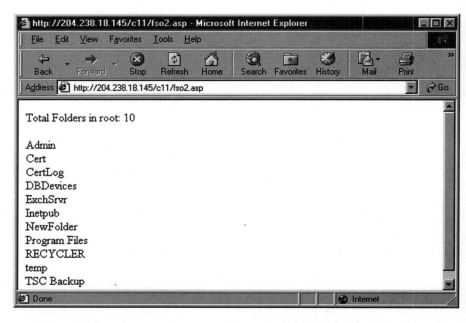

TABLE 11-5

Folder Object
Properties

Properties	Purpose
Attributes	Sets or returns the attributes of the folder.
DateCreated	Returns the date that the folder was created.
DateLastAccessed	Returns the date that the folder was last accessed.
DateLastModified	Returns the date that the folder was last modified.
Drive	Returns the letter for the drive that the folder is on.
Files	Returns a Files collection with all the files that are in this folder.
IsRootFolder	True or False property indicating whether this folder is the root of the drive.
Name	Returns the name of the folder.
ParentFolder	Returns the folder that is one level up from this folder.
Path	Returns the full absolute path to the folder.
ShortName	Returns the DOS name for the folder in the 8.3 format.
ShortPath	Returns the path in short name format to the folder.
Size	Returns the size in bytes of the contents of the folder including any subfolders.
SubFolders	Returns a Folders collection containing all the folders in this Folder object.

The code here uses each of these properties on a single Folder object.

```
<%
Option Explicit
Dim objFileSys
Dim TheFolder
Dim TheFiles
Dim TheSubFolders
set objFileSys = Server.CreateObject("Scripting.FileSystemObject")
set TheFolder = objFileSys.GetFolder("c:\my documents")
Response.Write "Attributes: " & TheFolder.Attributes & "<BR>"
Response.Write "Date Created: " & TheFolder.DateCreated & "<BR>"
Response.Write "Date Last Accessed: " & TheFolder.DateLastAccessed
    & "<BR>"
Response.Write "Date Last Modified: " & TheFolder.DateLastModified
    & "<BR>"
Response.Write "Drive: " & TheFolder.Drive & "<BR>"
Set TheFiles = TheFolder.Files
Response.Write "Is Root Folder: " & TheFolder.IsRootFolder & "<BR>"
Response.Write "Name: " & TheFolder.Name & "<BR>"
Response.Write "Parent Folder: " & TheFolder.ParentFolder & "<BR>"
Response.Write "Path: " & TheFolder.Path & "<BR>"
Response.Write "Short Name: " & TheFolder.ShortName & "<BR>"
Response.Write "Short Path: " & TheFolder.ShortPath & "<BR>"
Response.Write "Size: " & TheFolder.Size & "<BR>"
Set TheSubFolders = TheFolder.SubFolders
%>
```

First, `Option Explicit` is noted for the compiler:

```
Option Explicit
```

Next, the variables for a FileSystemObject object, the main Folder object, a Files collection, and a Folders collection are created:

```
Dim objFileSys
Dim TheFolder
Dim TheFiles
Dim TheSubFolders
```

Then the FileSystemObject object is instantiated:

```
set objFileSys = Server.CreateObject("Scripting.FileSystemObject")
```

The specific folder to work with is then retrieved through the GetFolder method of the FileSystemObject object:

```
set TheFolder = objFileSys.GetFolder("c:\my documents")
```

Next, the attributes for the folder are written. The Attributes value is a series of bits that are turned on or off, indicating things like read-only, system, hidden, and so forth. A value of 16, as we see here, means that this item is a folder:

```
Response.Write "Attributes: " & TheFolder.Attributes & "<BR>"
```

The date and time that the folder was created are written to the browser:

```
Response.Write "Date Created: " & TheFolder.DateCreated & "<BR>"
```

followed by the date and time that the folder was last accessed and modified:

```
Response.Write "Date Last Accessed: " & TheFolder.DateLastAccessed
    & "<BR>"
Response.Write "Date Last Modified: " & TheFolder.DateLastModified
    & "<BR>"
```

The drive that the folder is in is written to the browser:

```
Response.Write "Drive: " & TheFolder.Drive & "<BR>"
```

The File collection contained in this folder is placed into the variable TheFiles:

```
Set TheFiles = TheFolder.Files
```

If this folder was the root folder of the drive then the IsRootFolder would return true:

```
Response.Write "Is Root Folder: " & TheFolder.IsRootFolder & "<BR>"
```

The name of the folder is written to the browser:

```
Response.Write "Name: " & TheFolder.Name & "<BR>"
```

The path to the parent folder is retrieved through the ParentFolder property:

```
Response.Write "Parent Folder: " & TheFolder.ParentFolder & "<BR>"
```

The path to this folder is written to the browser:

```
Response.Write "Path: " & TheFolder.Path & "<BR>"
```

Here the DOS 8.3 name of the file and path are written to the browser:

```
Response.Write "Short Name: " & TheFolder.ShortName & "<BR>"
Response.Write "Short Path: " & TheFolder.ShortPath & "<BR>"
```

The size, in bytes, of the contents of the folder and any subfolders is written to the browser:

```
Response.Write "Size: " & TheFolder.Size & "<BR>"
```

The Folders collection of this folder is then retrieved and placed into the variable TheSubFolders:

```
Set TheSubFolders = TheFolder.SubFolders
```

The result of running this code is displayed in Figure 11-14.

The Folder object also contains a few methods that allow you to manipulate the contents of the folder directly. The Folder object contains a *Copy method*, which allows you to directly copy this folder to a new location. The method has the following syntax:

```
ObjFolder.Copy NewLocation, OverWriteFlag
```

Figure 11-14
Result of running the Folder object properties code.

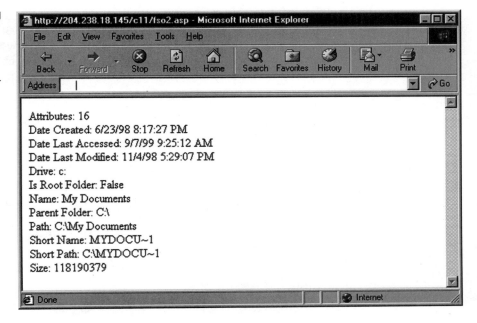

The `ObjFolder` variable must be a valid Folder object. Passed to the method are two parameters. The first is the location where you want the folder and all of its contents copied. The second parameter is optional and indicates what action to take if the folder already exists. The default, True, indicates that existing files and folders should be over-written. If you use False in this parameter, then the action will not over-write existing files.

The *Delete method* of the Folder object allows you to directly delete the Folder. It has the following syntax:

```
ObjFolder.Delete DeleteReadOnlyFlag
```

The `ObjFolder` variable must be a valid Folder object. Passed to the method is a single optional parameter, which stores what action to take if the folder is read-only. The default for the parameter is False, which does not delete read-only files. If you set this parameter to True, read-only folders are also deleted.

You can also move the folder to a new location with the *Move method*, which has the following syntax:

```
ObjFolder.Move NewLocation
```

The single parameter in this method is the location where you want to move the folder and all of its subfolders.

The Folder also has a *CreateTextFile method*, which creates a new text file and returns a TextStream object. This method is identical to the CreateTextFile method of the FileSystemObject object.

Files Collection

The *Files collection* is a collection of File objects that are contained within a Folder object. The collection can be used to iterate or take action on each of the files in a folder or to retrieve a single File object.

The following code uses the two properties of the collection, Count and Item. The code also iterates through all the File objects in the collection.

```
<%
Option Explicit
Dim objFileSys
Dim TheFolder
Dim TheFiles
```

```
Dim AFile
set objFileSys = Server.CreateObject("Scripting.FileSystemObject")
set TheFolder = objFileSys.GetFolder("c:\my documents")
Set TheFiles = TheFolder.Files
Response.Write "Total files in collection: " & TheFiles.Count &
  "<P>"
Set AFile = TheFiles.Item("nmaha.mdb")
For Each AFile in TheFiles
  Response.Write AFile.Name & "<P>"
Next
%>
```

First, we state that variables will be declared:

```
Option Explicit
```

Next, we will need a FileSystemObject object to access the file system:

```
Dim objFileSys
```

A Folder object will be needed so we can retrieve the Files collection:

```
Dim TheFolder
```

Here a Files collection variable is declared:

```
Dim TheFiles
```

A variable that will store a single File object is then created:

```
Dim AFile
```

The FileSystemObject object is instantiated:

```
set objFileSys = Server.CreateObject("Scripting.FileSystemObject")
```

A Folder object is retrieved:

```
set TheFolder = objFileSys.GetFolder("c:\my documents")
```

and from the object, the Files collection is retrieved:

```
Set TheFiles = TheFolder.Files
```

The count of the File object in that collection is written to the browser using the Count property:

```
Response.Write "Total files in collection: " & TheFiles.Count &
  "<P>"
```

Figure 11-15
Output of the Files
collection code.

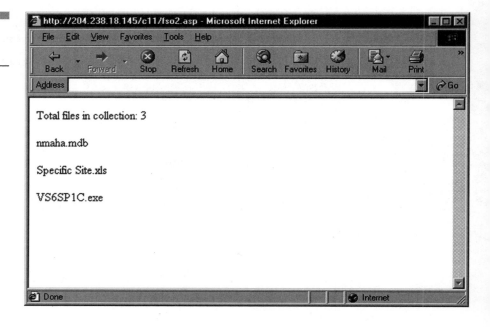

The Item property of the Files collection is used to retrieve a single File object, which is placed into the AFile variable:

```
Set AFile = TheFiles.Item("nmaha.mdb")
```

Then the code iterates through each file in the Files collection writing the Name of each object to the browser:

```
For Each AFile in TheFiles
  Response.Write AFile.Name & "<P>"
Next
```

The output of this code is displayed in Figure 11-15.

File Object

The *File object* contains numerous properties that you can use to retrieve information about a file. The properties are discussed below and summarized in Table 11-6.

TABLE 11-6

File Object
Properties

Properties	Purpose
Attributes	Sets or returns the attributes of the file.
DateCreated	Returns the date that the file was created.
DateLastAccessed	Returns the date that the file was last accessed.
DateLastModified	Returns the date that the file was last modified.
Drive	Returns the letter for the drive that the file is on.
Name	Returns the name of the file.
ParentFolder	Returns the folder that the file is in.
Path	Returns the full absolute path to the file.
ShortName	Returns the DOS name for the file in the 8.3 format.
ShortPath	Returns the path in short name format to the file.
Size	Returns the size of the file in bytes.
Type	Returns text information about the type of file the File object is.

The following code demonstrates the use of File object properties. Pay particular attention to the code that sets and resets the attributes of the file; the code uses bit manipulation to achieve this task.

```
<%
Option Explicit
Dim objFileSys
Dim TheFolder
Dim TheFiles
Dim TheFile
set objFileSys = Server.CreateObject("Scripting.FileSystemObject")
set TheFolder = objFileSys.GetFolder("c:\my documents")
Set TheFiles = TheFolder.Files
set TheFile = TheFiles.Item("nmaha.mdb")
If TheFile.Attributes and 1 Then
  Response.Write "The file is read only.<BR>"
else
  Response.Write "The file is not read only.<BR>"
End If
TheFile.Attributes = TheFile.Attributes or 1
If TheFile.Attributes and 1 Then
  Response.Write "The file is read only.<BR>"
else
  Response.Write "The file is not read only.<BR>"
End If
TheFile.Attributes = TheFile.Attributes and not 1
If TheFile.Attributes and 1 Then
  Response.Write "The file is read only.<BR>"
```

```
else
   Response.Write "The file is not read only.<BR>"
End If
Response.Write "Attributes: " & TheFile.Attributes & "<BR>"
Response.Write "Date Created: " & TheFile.DateCreated & "<BR>"
Response.Write "Date Last Accessed: " & TheFile.DateLastAccessed &
   "<BR>"
Response.Write "Date Last Modified: " & TheFile.DateLastModified &
   "<BR>"
Response.Write "Drive: " & TheFile.Drive & "<BR>"
Response.Write "Name: " & TheFile.Name & "<BR>"
Response.Write "Parent Folder: " & TheFile.ParentFolder & "<BR>"
Response.Write "Path: " & TheFile.Path & "<BR>"
Response.Write "Short Name: " & TheFile.ShortName & "<BR>"
Response.Write "Short Path: " & TheFile.ShortPath & "<BR>"
Response.Write "Size: " & TheFile.Size & "<BR>"
Response.Write "Type: " & TheFile.Type & "<BR>"
%>
```

First, Option Explicit is noted:

```
Option Explicit
```

The variables that will be needed in the code are created:

```
Dim objFileSys
Dim TheFolder
Dim TheFiles
Dim TheFile
```

The FileSystemObject object is instantiated:

```
set objFileSys = Server.CreateObject("Scripting.FileSystemObject")
```

A Folder object is set:

```
set TheFolder = objFileSys.GetFolder("c:\my documents")
```

as is the Files collection of that Folder object:

```
Set TheFiles = TheFolder.Files
```

A file from that collection is also retrieved into TheFile:

```
set TheFile = TheFiles.Item("nmaha.mdb")
```

Attributes in a file are things like whether it is hidden, or a system file. The attributes are stored as a bit so they are either on or off. Collectively the bits are stored together and referenced as a single num-

TABLE 11-7

Attribute Flag
Values

Flag	Purpose
0	Normal
1	Read-Only
2	Hidden
4	System
8	Volume
16	Directory
32	Archive
64	Alias
128	Compressed

ber with the Attribute property, so to check for a particular flag within the attributes, you need to check the value of the individual bit. You can do that by using bit arithmetic with the operators and, or, and not.

To use these operators you need to know the values of the different flags. These values are summarized in Table 11-7. Once you know these values you can use them to check to see if a bit is on and to turn a bit on or off. To test for a flag you use the and in an If statement like this:

```
If TheFile.Attributes and 1 Then
```

Here the attributes are checked with an And to see of the read-only flag is on. If so, then a message to that fact is written to the browser:

```
Response.Write "The file is read only.<BR>"
```

otherwise, a different message is written:

```
else
   Response.Write "The file is not read only.<BR>"
End If
```

Next, Or is used to turn on an attribute. Now the file is flagged as read-only:

```
TheFile.Attributes = TheFile.Attributes or 1
```

So written to the browser should be the message that the file is read-only:

```
If TheFile.Attributes and 1 Then
  Response.Write "The file is read only.<BR>"
else
  Response.Write "The file is not read only.<BR>"
End If
```

Here, an And Not combination is used to turn off a flag:

```
TheFile.Attributes = TheFile.Attributes and not 1
```

Now, the file should no longer be read-only:

```
If TheFile.Attributes and 1 Then
  Response.Write "The file is read only.<BR>"
else
  Response.Write "The file is not read only.<BR>"
End If
```

Here, the entire value of the attributes are written to the browser:

```
Response.Write "Attributes: " & TheFile.Attributes & "<BR>"
```

Next, the dates the file was created, last accessed, and last modified are written to the browser:

```
Response.Write "Date Created: " & TheFile.DateCreated & "<BR>"
Response.Write "Date Last Accessed: " & TheFile.DateLastAccessed &
  "<BR>"
Response.Write "Date Last Modified: " & TheFile.DateLastModified &
  "<BR>"
```

The drive that the file is on is written:

```
Response.Write "Drive: " & TheFile.Drive & "<BR>"
```

Then Name of the File is written:

```
Response.Write "Name: " & TheFile.Name & "<BR>"
```

The folder that the file is in is written to the browser using the ParentFolder property:

```
Response.Write "Parent Folder: " & TheFile.ParentFolder & "<BR>"
```

The path to the file is written here:

```
Response.Write "Path: " & TheFile.Path & "<BR>"
```

The 8.3 format of the file name and path are accessed through these properties:

```
Response.Write "Short Name: " & TheFile.ShortName & "<BR>"
Response.Write "Short Path: " & TheFile.ShortPath & "<BR>"
```

The size of the file in bytes is written next:

```
Response.Write "Size: " & TheFile.Size & "<BR>"
```

and the type of file, as defined by the file association for the file extension, is written here:

```
Response.Write "Type: " & TheFile.Type & "<BR>"
```

The output of this code is displayed in Figure 11-16.

The File object also has four methods: Copy, Delete, and Move methods that are identical to those that are part of the Folder object. The File

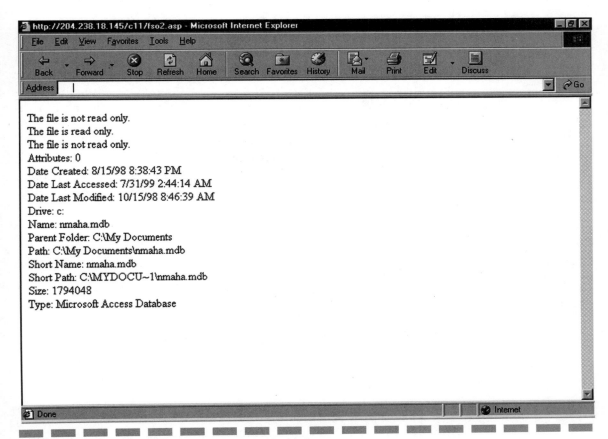

Figure 11-16 Output of the File object properties code.

object also contains one other method, the *OpenAsTextStream method*, which allows you to open a File object as a TextStream object. The method has the following syntax:

```
Set ObjTextStream = objFile.OpenASTextStream(OpenForMode, TextFormat)
```

The `ObjFile` variable must be a valid File object. Returned from the method is a TextStream object. Passed to the method are two optional parameters. The first is the `OpenForMode`, which is used to determine how the file is opened. Use 1 for reading, 2 for writing, and 8 for appending. The second parameter is for the format of the text in the file, either ACSII or Unicode. A value of 0 uses ASCII, -1 uses Unicode, and -2 is used for the system default.

TextStream Object

The *TextStream object* allows you to read and write to text files. This can be useful if you need to store persistent data outside of a database, or you want fast and easy access to text data without going through a database. The TextStream object provides a variety of properties and methods that enable you to manipulate a text file.

The properties of the TextStream object are summarized in Table 11-8.

The methods of the TextStream object provide a way for you to move around a text file and to read from and write to a TextStream object. The methods of the TextStream object are summarized in Table 11-9.

TABLE 11-8

TextStream Object
Properties

Property	Purpose
AtEndOfLine	A True/False flag that returns True if the pointer in the file is just before an end of line.
AtEndOfStream	Another True/False flag that returns True when the end of a text file is reached.
Column	Indicates the current character position of the pointer within a row within a text file.
Line	Indicates the current line number of the pointer in a TextStream object.

TABLE 11-9

TextStream Object
Methods

Method	Purpose
Close	Closes an open TextStream object.
Read	Reads a specified number of characters from a text file. The number of characters to read is passed as a parameter to this method.
ReadAll	Reads the entire contents of the TextStream object.
ReadLine	Reads characters from the current position in a TextStream object until a new line character is found.
Skip	Moves the pointer in the TextStream object ahead by the number of characters passed as a parameter to this method.
SkipLine	Moves the pointer within the TextStream object ahead of the next new line character.
Write	Writes characters to a TextStream object. Does not append a new line character to the end of the write.
WriteBlankLines	Writes a new line character or characters to the TextStream object. The number of new line characters written is passed as a parameter to this method.
WriteLine	Writes characters to a TextStream object and appends a new line character to the end of the write.

The following code uses almost all of these methods and properties to write to a TextStream object and then read from the file created.

```
<%
Option Explicit
Dim objFileSys
Dim TheTextStream
set objFileSys = Server.CreateObject("Scripting.FileSystemObject")
set TheTextStream = objFileSys.CreateTextFile("temp.txt", True)
TheTextStream.WriteLine "This is the first line."
TheTextStream.WriteLine "This is the second line."
TheTextStream.Write "No end of line."
TheTextStream.WriteBlankLines 2
TheTextStream.WriteLine "Another line."
TheTextStream.Close
set TheTextStream = objFileSys.OpenTextFile("temp.txt", 1)
Response.Write TheTextStream.ReadAll & "<P>"
TheTextStream.Close
set TheTextStream = objFileSys.OpenTextFile("temp.txt", 1)
Do Until TheTextStream.AtEndOfStream
   Response.Write TheTextStream.ReadLine & "<BR>"
Loop
TheTextStream.Close
set TheTextStream = objFileSys.OpenTextFile("temp.txt", 1)
Response.Write "<BR>" & TheTextStream.Read(6) & "<P>"
Response.Write "On Line: " & TheTextStream.Line & "<BR>Column: " &
   TheTextStream.Column
```

```
TheTextStream.Skip 4
Response.Write "<BR>" & TheTextStream.Read(3) & "<P>"
TheTextStream.SkipLine
Response.Write TheTextStream.ReadLine
%>
```

First, Option Explicit is specified:

```
Option Explicit
```

Two variables will be needed in this code sample—first, one that will store the FileSystemObject object:

```
Dim objFileSys
```

and then one that will store the TextStream object:

```
Dim TheTextStream
```

The FileSystemObject is instantiated:

```
set objFileSys = Server.CreateObject("Scripting.FileSystemObject")
```

The CreateTextFile method of the FileSystemObject object is used to create a new text file. Note that the second parameter, True, means that if the file exists it should be overwritten. Returned from the method is a TextStream object pointed to the file that was just created:

```
set TheTextStream = objFileSys.CreateTextFile("temp.txt", True)
```

A single line of text is written to the browser with the WriteLine method. Remember that this method appends a new line character to the end of the write:

```
TheTextStream.WriteLine "This is the first line."
```

A second line of text is written in the same way:

```
TheTextStream.WriteLine "This is the second line."
```

Now the Write method is used to write characters to the file without a new line character:

```
TheTextStream.Write "No end of line."
```

Here two new line characters are written to the file. The first ends the write that we did earlier and the second adds a blank line to the file:

```
TheTextStream.WriteBlankLines 2
```

Again, the WriteLine method is used to write an entire line to the file. You can think of the line as a record, since we have a method that allows us to read a full line back:

```
TheTextStream.WriteLine "Another line."
```

The file is then closed and released from memory:

```
TheTextStream.Close
```

Now the OpenTextFile method of the FileSystemObject object is used to open the file that we just created:

```
set TheTextStream = objFileSys.OpenTextFile("temp.txt", 1)
```

The ReadAll method of the TextStream object is used to retrieve the entire contents of the file we created earlier. This is then written to the browser:

```
Response.Write TheTextStream.ReadAll & "<P>"
```

The file is closed again:

```
TheTextStream.Close
```

and reopened, so we are pointing back to the beginning of the file:

```
set TheTextStream = objFileSys.OpenTextFile("temp.txt", 1)
```

Now we enter a loop where we will read one line of text at a time until the end of the file is reached:

```
Do Until TheTextStream.AtEndOfStream
```

Each line is retrieved using the ReadLine method and is written to the browser:

```
Response.Write TheTextStream.ReadLine & "<BR>"
```

The code then loops to the next line of text:

```
Loop
```

The file is once again closed:

```
TheTextStream.Close
```

and reopened:

```
set TheTextStream = objFileSys.OpenTextFile("temp.txt", 1)
```

The Read method is used to read the first six characters from the file:

```
Response.Write "<BR>" & TheTextStream.Read(6) & "<P>"
```

Next, the position of the pointer within the TextStream object is written through the Line and Column properties:

```
Response.Write "On Line: " & TheTextStream.Line & "<BR>Column: " &
    TheTextStream.Column
```

The pointer is then moved ahead four characters:

```
TheTextStream.Skip 4
```

and the next three characters are read and written to the browser:

```
Response.Write "<BR>" & TheTextStream.Read(3) & "<P>"
```

The pointer in the TextStream object is moved ahead past the next new line character:

```
TheTextStream.SkipLine
```

and the next line of text from the file is written to the browser:

```
Response.Write TheTextStream.ReadLine
```

Figure 11-17 shows the result of this code. Try to follow with the code to see why and where certain characters were written.

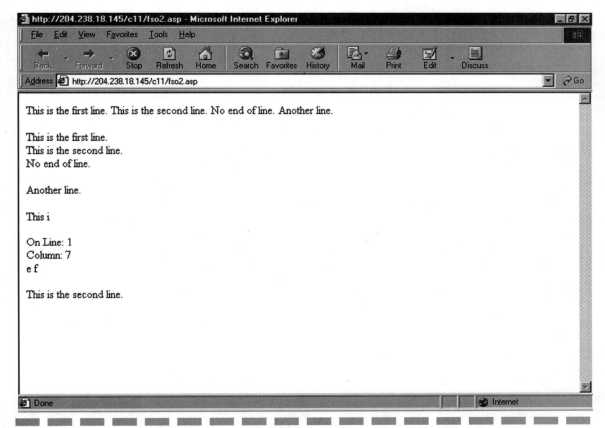

Figure 11-17   Result of the TextStream object code.

Dictionary Object

One more object to talk about in this chapter is the Dictionary object, which is separate from the other FileSystemObject objects and collections discussed thus far in this chapter. The *Dictionary object* allows you to create a group of related items each of which has a name and a value. For example, say that you needed to group together the names of Web pages with a description for each page. You could use a Dictionary object to satisfy such a need. The Dictionary object contains properties and methods that let you add, remove, access, and change items in the collection.

For example, if you did want to create a grouping of Web page names with their descriptions, you could use the Dictionary object like this:

```
<%
Option Explicit
Dim ThePages
set ThePages = Server.CreateObject("Scripting.Dictionary")
ThePages.Add "Home", "This is the home page of the site"
ThePages.Add "Support", "Here you will find our knowledge base"
ThePages.Add "Contact", "This page contains our contact information"
ThePages.Add "Sale", "List of our products currently on sale"
Response.Write ThePages.Item("Home") & "<P>"
Response.Write ThePages("Contact") & "<P>"
%>
```

First, `Option Explicit` is noted for the compiler:

```
Option Explicit
```

A single variable will be needed to store the Dictionary object:

```
Dim ThePages
```

A Dictionary object is created by using the CreateObject method of the Server object. Passed to the CreateObject method is the application/ class string `Scripting.Dictionary`:

```
set ThePages = Server.CreateObject("Scripting.Dictionary")
```

The Add method is used to add new items to the dictionary object. You specify the name for the item, which is called the *key* and the *value* for the item:

```
ThePages.Add "Home", "This is the home page of the site"
ThePages.Add "Support", "Here you will find our knowledge base"
ThePages.Add "Contact", "This page contains our contact
information"
ThePages.Add "Sale", "List of our products currently on sale"
```

You can then later reference the values stored within each key in one of two ways. You can reference an item through the Item property of the Dictionary object:

```
Response.Write ThePages.Item("Home") & "<P>"
```

or directly from the dictionary object since the Item property is the default property:

```
Response.Write ThePages("Contact") & "<P>"
```

Figure 11-18
Output of Dictionary
object code sample.

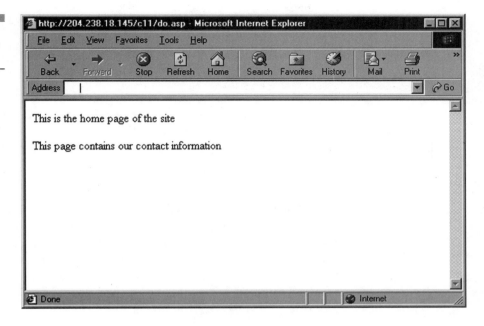

Figure 11-18
Output of Dictionary
object code sample.

The output of this code is displayed in Figure 11-18.

Once you've added an item to a Dictionary object you can remove the item by using the Remove method, so if we wanted to remove the entry for the Sale page we would code this:

```
ThePages.Remove "Sales"
```

You can clear out the entire contents of the Dictionary object with the RemoveAll method like this:

```
ThePages.RemoveAll
```

You can check to see if a key is already part of the Dictionary object using the Exists method. So if you coded this:

```
Response.Write ThePages.Exists("Sales")
```

True would be written to the browser. If you coded this:

```
Response.Write ThePages.Exists("Jobs")
```

False would be written to the browser since the key Jobs does not exist.

You can use the count property to determine the number of items in the Dictionary object. So if you coded this:

```
Response.Write ThePages.Count
```

the number 4 would be written to the browser.

You can also change the name of a key using the Key property, so if we wanted to change the name of the Sale page to Sales, we could code like this:

```
ThePages.Key("Sale") = "Sales"
```

By default, the Keys are stored as case sensitive. That means that you can have one key with the name *sale* and another with the name *Sale* as two separate keys. You can change this by using the CompareMode property. The default for this property is 0, which means a binary comparison should be used—that means that a lowercase "s" is different from a capital "S." But you can change the value of that property to one like this:

```
ThePages.CompareMode = 1
```

Now you could not create a key called *sale* if one called *Sale* already existed.

12

Error Handling
and the Script
Debugger

Error Handling

Unhandled Errors

The concept of *error handling* refers to what you do or don't do in your code when something goes wrong. An error can occur for a variety of reasons: an error can occur because some service you are using is not properly installed; an error can occur because your code has incorrect syntax; or, an error can occur because your code has created a situation that the system does not know how to deal with.

When an error occurs, you can take some action to correct the error or you can at least provide a more graceful response to the visitor—or, you can simply do nothing about the error. If you choose to do nothing, at least in the days of browsers, you don't see what they see when an application throws an error that is not handled. For example, Figure 12-1 shows what would happen to a user of an application written in Visual Basic if an unhandled error occurs.

When an unhandled error occurs for a program written in Visual Basic, the user is presented with a message box that for most users has absolutely no meaning. But even worse than the error message is when visitors press the OK button, they are totally thrown out of the application where the error occurred. Users would have to restart the application.

When a similar error occurs in an ASP application your visitor is treated a little better than the user of a desktop application. First, if an error occurs, it occurs on your server since that is where the code is being run. That means that you can take some action that can track

Figure 12-1
Unhandled error in a
desktop application.

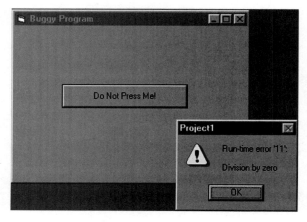

errors that are occurring instead of relying on your users to report errors. But it also means that visitors aren't thrown out of their browser. They may not be able to see your page but they can at least go to another page or try to refresh your page.

You also have some control of what visitors see when an unhandled error occurs. Say you had code like this in an Active Server Page application:

```
<%
x = 1 / 0
Response.Write "Won't see this."
%>
```

The Response.Write method should never get called because an error occurs before that line of code when we attempt to divide a number by zero. Since we don't have any error-handling code, IIS takes its own action when confronted with an error but, as mentioned, visitors will not get thrown out of their browser. They will see an error message like the one in Figure 12-2.

Although visitors don't get thrown out of their browser, they still see an error that really won't make much sense to them. But you can change what message is shown. Within the IIS view through the

Figure 12-2
Default error message displayed when an unhandled error occurs.

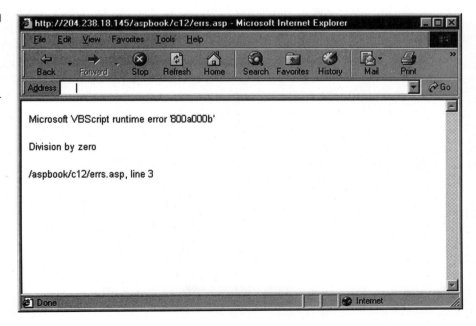

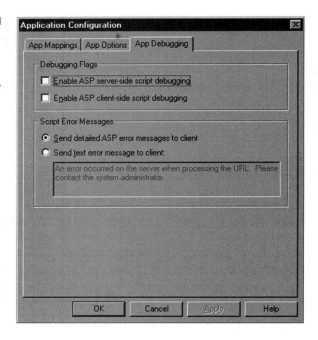

Microsoft Management Console, select the properties of the Active
Server Page application or directory in which you want to have a custom
error message displayed, then right-click on that item and select
Properties. Go to the DIRECTORY tab or HOME DIRECTORY tab and press
the CONFIGURATION button. Switch to the APP DEBUGGING tab and you
should see a dialog box like the one shown in Figure 12-3. Notice on this
dialog the Script Error Messages section, which is where you set what
you want displayed to visitors in the event of an unhandled error. Right
now, the Send Detailed ASP Error Message to Client message is displayed; that is why we saw the error message in Figure 12-2. We can
also enter a custom message into the text box below that option if we
select the Send Text Error Message to Client.

For example, you could place this text as the error message:

```
An error has occurred. Please try this page again in a few minutes.
   If the problem persists call tech support.
```

Now visitors would see this more informative message instead of the
raw error message as shown in Figure 12-4.

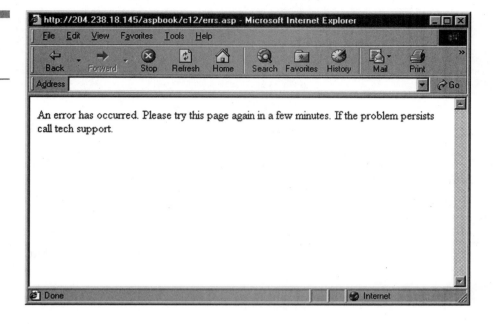

Figure 12-4
Unhandled error
with a graceful
message.

Handling Errors

Setting the preceding properties didn't do anything to handle the error condition, but it did provide a more graceful and understandable report to your visitor. But you can also write code that checks for an error and takes appropriate action based on that error.

If you do want to provide code that handles errors, then you will need to place an On Error statement, usually at the top of the code on your page but after the Option Explicit statement. (If you are a Visual Basic programmer, you will have some disappointment with the On Error statement in VB Script since you can't have the code flow to a label.) The On Error statement has the following form:

```
On Error Resume Next
```

What this On Error statement says is if a line of code produces an error, just skip that line of code and move on. The intention is that somewhere in your code you will then take care of the problem. For example, take a look at this code block:

```
<%
Option Explicit
```

```
On Error Resume Next
Dim x
x = Request.QueryString("Number1") / Request.QueryString("Number2")
If Err.Number <> 0 Then
  If Err.Number = 11 then
     Response.Write "You can not divide by zero. Please try again."
  ElseIf Err.Number = 6 Then
     Response.Write "You need to provide both numbers for this
        text. Please try again."
  ElseIf Err.Number = 13 Then
     Response.Write "Only numbers are allowed. Please try again."
  Else
     Response.write "An unexpected error has occurred. " _
        & "We are working on the problem, please try again later."
  End If
  Response.End
End If
Response.Write "The answer is: " & x
%>
```

First, we use `Option Explicit` to indicate that variable declaration will be required:

```
Option Explicit
```

Next, we use the `On Error` statement. Remember, the effect of this code is that, if an error occurs, you don't want the compiler to do anything about it; you want the code to flow on to the next line:

```
On Error Resume Next
```

A variable is defined that is used to store the result of our division:

```
Dim x
```

Here we place the result of dividing two numbers passed through the QueryString collection into the variable x. This is a dangerous line of code and a variety of errors could occur:

```
x = Request.QueryString("Number1") / Request.QueryString("Number2")
```

But if an error did occur at that line of code, the compiler will move on to the next line since we are using the `On Error Resume Next` statement. We can check for an error by looking at the Number property in the Err object. If no error occurred, then this property would be set to zero; otherwise, it would store the number of the error that occurred. Here we check the error number to see if it is 0:

```
If Err.Number <> 0 Then
```

If it is not zero, then we enter this code block and query the error number further. We then check to see if error 11 occurred:

```
If Err.Number = 11 then
```

If it did, that means that the second number provided in the QueryString collection is zero, so division by zero has occurred and we inform the visitor of that problem:

```
Response.Write "You can not divide by zero. Please try again."
```

Next we check for error 6:

```
ElseIf Err.Number = 6 Then
```

Error 6 is an overflow error. In that case it probably means that one or both of the numbers were not passed through the QueryString collection:

```
Response.Write "You need to provide both numbers for this text.
    Please try again."
```

We then check for error number 13:

```
ElseIf Err.Number = 13 Then
```

This is a type mismatch error, which in this case probably means that the visitor entered a nonnumeric value for one of the numbers. We write a message about that problem to the browser:

```
Response.Write "Only numbers are allowed. Please try again."
```

If the error that occurred was not one of the previous ones, then we display a general message to the visitor:

```
Else
  Response.write "An unexpected error has occurred. " _
    & "We are working on the problem, please try again later."
End If
```

We then stop all processing of the code. Since an error has occurred, we really probably don't want to continue on with this page until some proper values are entered.

```
Response.End
```

Figure 12-5
Output of Error
Handling code.

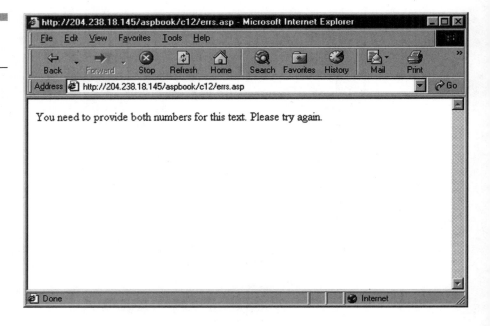

If the QueryString collection contained two valid numbers, then the code should flow here and we display the result of the division:

```
Response.Write "The answer is: " & x
```

Figure 12-5 shows what the output of the code would look like if no parameters were passed to the page.

Err Object

As you just saw in the last sample code segment, the *Err object* is used to determine what error has occurred. It also provides a variety of other properties and methods so you can query and manipulate the Err object, which is part of the ASP environment so you don't have to use the CreateObject method of the Server to instantiate it. You simply refer to the object directly.

Err Object Properties

The Err object contains five properties that contain details about an error. The properties are discussed below and summarized in Table 12-1.

TABLE 12-1

Err Object
Properties

Property	Purpose
Number	The numeric value for the error that has occurred. Set to zero if no error has occurred.
Description	Short, text description about the type of error that occurred.
Source	Name of the object or application that threw the error.
HelpFile	Returns the path to the Help file, if any, associated with the error number.
HelpContext	Returns the ID of the Topic within the Help file, if any, for the error that has occurred.

The *Number property* of the Err object returns the numeric value corresponding to the type of error that has occurred. In our previous code example we noted that an error number of 6 means that Divide by Zero has occurred. If no error has occurred, the value of this property is set to zero; so you typically provide code like this around your error handlers:

```
If Err.Number <> 0
   'error handling code
End If
```

The code in the If block will run only if an error has occurred; otherwise, the Number property would be zero.

The *Description property* provides for you a sometimes helpful, but often not very helpful, text message about what the error means. If a Divide by Zero error occurs, a descriptive message like this appears:

```
Division by zero
```

This message accurately describes the problem, but take a look at this code block:

```
<%
Option Explicit
On Error Resume Next
Dim TheDictionary
TheDictionary = Server.CreateObject("Scripting.Dictionary")
If Err.Number <> 0 Then
  Response.Write Err.Description
  Response.End
End If
Response.Write "No problems"
%>
```

If you run this code you get this error message:

```
Wrong number of arguments or invalid property assignment
```

because of this line of code:

```
TheDictionary = Server.CreateObject("Scripting.Dictionary")
```

This is an example of an uninformative error message. The first part says Wrong Number of Arguments. This is the correct number of arguments for the CreateObject method, so that's not the problem. The second half of the error message says Invalid Property Assignment. CreateObject is a method, not a property, so that message isn't helpful. Thus, the error message didn't provide us with any useful information. The problem is actually because we left the keyword Set off of the beginning of the line of code.

The *Source property* of the Err object returns the application or object that caused or returned the error. This can be an external application as shown in this code:

```
<%
Option Explicit
On Error Resume Next
Dim conn
set conn = server.createobject ("adodb.connection")
conn.open "WrongDSN", "sa", "yourpassword"
If Err.Number <> 0 Then
  Response.Write Err.Source
  Response.End
End If
Response.Write "No problems"
%>
```

Here the error occurs because the database connection is not correct, so displayed in the browser is the application that reported that error:

```
Microsoft OLE DB Provider for ODBC Drivers
```

which is an external application, so the error didn't occur in the ASP but in an external source. The external application found a problem with the parameters that were passed through the Open method and sent an error back to the caller. If the error was internal to your ASP code, such as the Divide by Zero error, you would see this text in the Source property:

```
Microsoft VBScript runtime error
```

As you will see in a later section, you can also create your own custom errors. If you do that and don't supply a source for the error, the Source property is set to an empty string.

The *HelpFile* and *HelpContext properties* report information about a help file associated with an error, if any. Since the help file and topic are located on the server, these properties don't have much application in server-side Active Server Pages.

Err Object Methods

The Err object contains two methods that you can use to manipulate the Err object. These methods are discussed below and summarized in Table 12-2.

The *Clear method* is used to remove an error from the Err object. For example, take a look at this code:

```
<%
Option Explicit
On Error Resume Next
Dim x
x = 1 / 0
Err.Clear
If Err.Number <> 0 Then
  Response.Write Err.Description
  Response.End
End If
Response.Write "No problems"
%>
```

First, we state that we will declare our variables:

```
Option Explicit
```

Then we use the On Error statement:

```
On Error Resume Next
```

and declare a temporary variable:

```
Dim x
```

TABLE 12-2

Err Object Methods

Method	Purpose
Clear	Resets the Err object as if an error never occurred.
Raise	Provides a mechanism for you to create your own custom errors.

A Divide by Zero error is created:

```
x = 1 / 0
```

But then the error is removed from the Err object:

```
Err.Clear
```

So the Number property of the error should be zero and we shouldn't enter this code block:

```
If Err.Number <> 0 Then
  Response.Write Err.Description
  Response.End
End If
```

Instead, we should see this in the browser window:

```
Response.Write "No problems"
```

If you look at Figure 12-6 that is what you will see.

The *Raise method* provides a way for you to generate your own error. This is often done for one of two reasons. First, you might generate your own error to see what would happen in your code if such an error

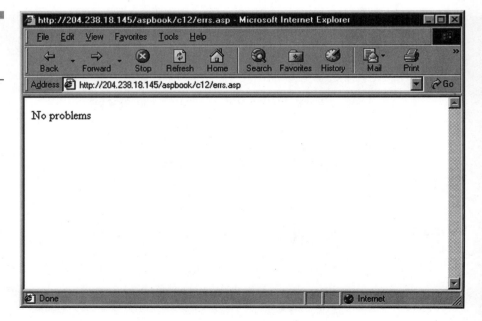

Figure 12-6
Result of using the Clear method of the Err object.

occurred. For example, you might generate an error that reports that a connection to a database could not be established. You could then test your code to see how it reacts to such a problem.

The other reason you might use this method is to return a custom error from your own procedure. For example, say that you had a procedure that was to parse a first name out of a full name. You would parse out the first name by looking for a space in the full name. Everything before the space would be assumed to be the first name. You may want to return an error if no space was found.

The Raise method has the following syntax:

```
Err.Raise Number, Source, Description, HelpFile, HelpContext
```

All the parameters of the Raise method are optional, except the first parameter, which is the number of the error that you want to throw. You can simulate an existing error number, such as the Divide by Zero error, just by supplying its number in this property. If you want to create your own custom error, you should use a number outside the normal range by adding some number to the vbObjectError constant like this:

```
MyNumber = 22 + vbObjectError
```

The second parameter, Source, refers to the source of the error. You can use the third parameter to create a description for your error, and you can also specify a help file and context for your error.

The following code creates a function that parses a first name out of a full name. If a space in the name is not found, a custom error occurs.

```
<%
Option Explicit
On Error Resume Next
Response.Write FirstName("Jan")
If Err.Number <> 0 Then
  Response.Write Err.Number & "<P>"
  Response.Write Err.Description & "<P>"
  Response.Write Err.Source & "<P>"
End If

Function FirstName (FullName)
  If InStr(FullName, " ") = 0 Then
    Err.Raise vbObjectError + 22, "MyFunction.FirstName", _
      "The FullName parameter of this function must contain a
        space!"
  Else
    FirstName = Left(FullName, InStr(FullName, " ") - 1)
  End If
End Function
%>
```

First, we specify `Option Explicit`:

```
Option Explicit
```

Then the `On Error` statement is written, telling the compiler to proceed past any errors by going to the next line of code:

```
On Error Resume Next
```

Next, a function called `FirstName` is called. The result of that function is written to the browser window:

```
Response.Write FirstName("Jan")
```

If an error occurred in our code we would enter the `If` block:

```
If Err.Number <> 0 Then
```

and write the information about the error to the browser:

```
Response.Write Err.Number & "<P>"
Response.Write Err.Description & "<P>"
Response.Write Err.Source & "<P>"
```

At the bottom of the code the `FirstName` function is defined:

```
Function FirstName (FullName)
```

First, the code in the function uses the `InStr` function to test the `FullName` parameter for a space:

```
If InStr(FullName, " ") = 0 Then
```

If a space is not found, the `InStr` function would return a 0 and we would enter the `If` portion of the `If` block. The Raise method of the Err object is then used to create a custom error:

```
Err.Raise vbObjectError + 22, "MyFunction.FirstName", _
    "The FullName parameter of this function must contain a space!"
```

If an error didn't occur, then the first name is parsed out of the full name by chopping off all the characters prior to the occurrence of a space:

```
FirstName = Left(FullName, InStr(FullName, " ") - 1)
```

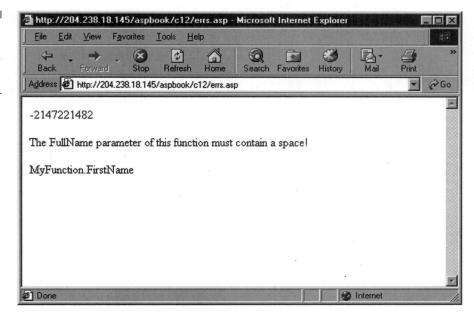

Figure 12-7
Result of the Raise
method code sample
when an error
occurs.

Since the name passed to the function does not have a space, an error would occur and we would see the error message shown in Figure 12-7.

Logging Errors to a File

One of the things that you can do with the Err object is to use it to help you identify problems with an Active Server Page. One of the more difficult problems you have to deal with is email from visitors that says something like:

```
I was trying to view your page and something went wrong. What
   should I do?
```

Based on your visitors' email, you believe that something did go wrong but you have no idea what page provided them difficulty; what the error was that occurred; or, even if the error occurred because of something on your server as opposed to something in their own browser going wrong.

What would be helpful would be a way to write information about an error and when and where it occurred to a text file for later retrieval. This would aid in fixing errors that were reported and also those that were never reported. The next code does just that:

```
<%
Option Explicit
On Error Resume Next
Response.Write FirstName("Jan")

Function FirstName (FullName)
    If InStr(FullName, " ") = 0 Then
      Err.Raise vbObjectError + 22, "MyFunction.FirstName", _
        "The FullName parameter of this function must contain a
          space!"
    Else
      FirstName = Left(FullName, InStr(FullName, " ") - 1)
    End If
End Function

If err.number <> 0 Then
    Dim objFileSys
    Dim ObjErrorFile
    set objFileSys =
Server.CreateObject("Scripting.FileSystemObject")
    set objErrorFile =
objFileSys.OpenTextFile("e:\inetpub\errorfile.txt", 8, True)
    objErrorFile.WriteLine Err.number & " - " & Err.Description & "
      - " _
      & Err.Source & " - " & Now & " - " & Request.ServerVariables
        ("Script_Name")
    Response.Write "An error has been logged to the log file. We
      will address " _
      & "the problem as soon as possible."
End If
%>
```

The code on the page starts in the normal way with `Option
Explicit`:

```
Option Explicit
```

and the `On Error` statement:

```
On Error Resume Next
```

The code is at the point where we think it will work fine; but we want to
monitor it for errors that we will log to a file, so we call the procedure
below:

```
Response.Write FirstName("Jan")
```

The procedure parses out the person's first name from a full name field:

```
Function FirstName (FullName)
```

If there is no space in the full name, an error is thrown:

```
If InStr(FullName, " ") = 0 Then
   Err.Raise vbObjectError + 22, "MyFunction.FirstName", _
        "The FullName parameter of this function must contain a space!"
```

otherwise, the code returns the first name parsed from the full name field:

```
FirstName = Left(FullName, InStr(FullName, " ") - 1)
```

Then, after all the code is run, we check to see if an error occurred:

```
If err.number <> 0 Then
```

If so, we want to write information about the error to a log file. So we will need a FileSystemObject object:

```
Dim objFileSys
```

and a connection to a text file:

```
Dim ObjErrorFile
```

The FileSystemObject object is instantiated:

```
set objFileSys = Server.CreateObject("Scripting.FileSystemObject")
```

and a text file is open. The file is open for append, so writes to the file will be written at the end of the file. The third parameter indicates that the file should be created if it doesn't already exist:

```
set objErrorFile = objFileSys.OpenTextFile("e:\inetpub\errorfile.
   txt", 8, True)
```

Then we use the WriteLine method of the TextStream object to write information about the error to the text error file. The error number and description are written:

```
objErrorFile.WriteLine Err.number & " - " & Err.Description & " - " _
```

followed by the source of the error, the date and time that it occurred, and the page on which the error occurred:

```
& Err.Source & " - " & Now & " - " & Request.ServerVariables
   ("Script_Name")
```

Figure 12-8
Result of error log file
code.

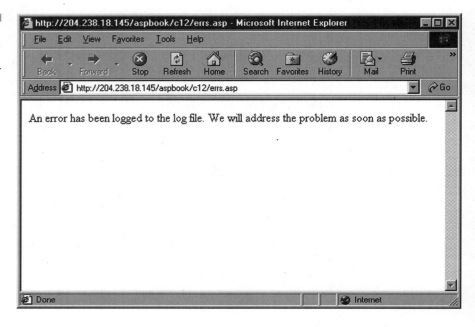

Then a message is displayed to the visitor through the browser:

```
Response.Write "An error has been logged to the log file. We will
   address " _
& "the problem as soon as possible."
```

Visitors to the page would see what is shown in Figure 12-8.
This entry would then be written to the log file:

```
11 - Division by zero - Microsoft VBScript runtime error -
9/9/99 7:39:40 PM - /aspbook/c12/errs.asp
```

So now when you get those anonymous emails about some problem at
your site, you could get at least a clue about what the problem was.

Script Debugger

Let's say you have this page with 500 lines of code on it and you are getting unexpected results. You need a way to look at the code when an
error occurs and to be able to step through that code one line at a time
to see what the effect is on the variables. You can do that with the *Script
Debugger*.

Figure 12-9
Setting server-side
debugging options.

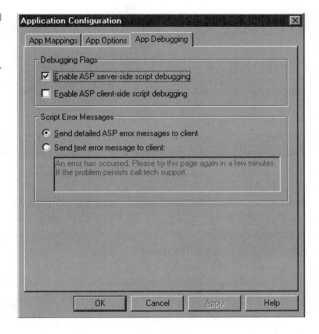

To make the Script Debugger available for an Active Server Page application, you need to browse to that application in IIS, then right-click on it and select Properties. From the DIRECTORY tab, press the CONFIGURATION button and then select the APP DEBUGGING tab. You should see the dialog displayed in Figure 12-9. From this dialog you can turn on server-side debugging by selecting the Enable ASP server-side script debugging. Use this option only while you are debugging a page. Once you are done debugging, turn off this option, because what this option does is automatically launch the Script Debugger when an error occurs on an Active Server Page.

Say that within this Active Server Page application you have a page with the following code:

```
<%
Option Explicit
Dim x
Dim y
Dim z
x = 1
y = 0
z = x / y
Response.Write z
z = z + 8
y = z - x
Response.Write y
%>
```

The code may be a few hundred lines long and you are getting a Divide by Zero error in the browser but you don't know how that could happen. You want to see the values of the variables on the page so you can work with them. Since you have turned on server-side debugging, when you next view that page, the Script Debugger opens on the server automatically and shows you the error message as well as the line of code that produced the error. This is shown in Figure 12-10.

Note that a message box in the Script Debugger shows the error that occurred. If you press the OK button, you are live in debug mode with the page that produced the error. An arrow will show you what line of code caused the error.

Notice the other window in the Script Debugger called the *Command Window*. If you don't see it, select it from the View menu. If you are familiar with Visual Basic, this window is like the Debug window. From

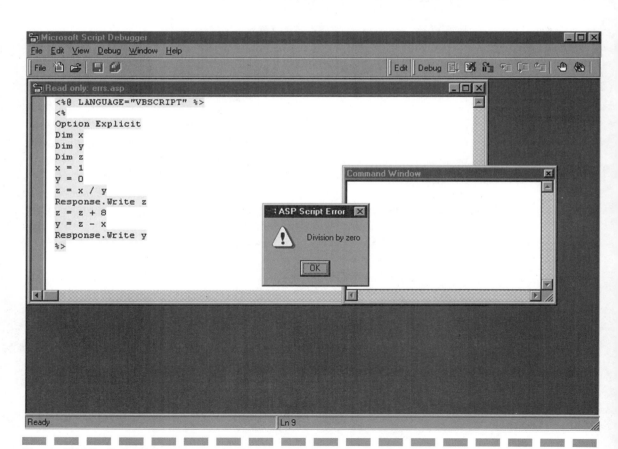

Figure 12-10 Script Debugger opening because an error occurred.

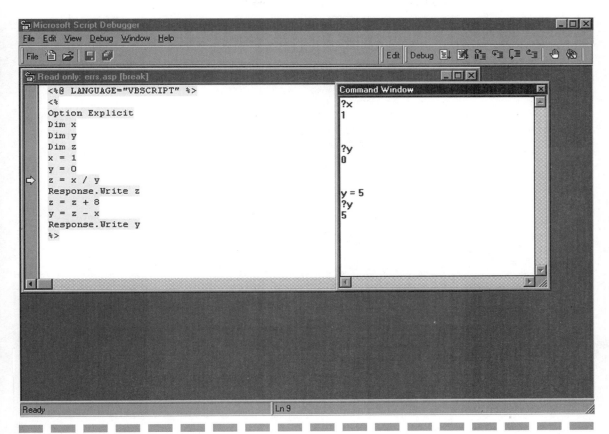

Figure 12-11 Using the Command Window.

here you can check the values of variables and expressions to see what values they have. Take a look at Figure 12-11. Notice the text in the Command Window. You can check the value of a variable here by prefacing the variable name with a question mark and then pressing ENTER. You can also assign a variable here as is done with the variable y, which is set to the value 5.

Using the Script Debugger in this way allows you to take a snapshot of what is happening on the page when an error occurs. You can then check the values of all your variables and read through your code to identify how the error occurred.

Sometimes, though, you don't get an error but you are getting unexpected results. In these cases, it is sometimes helpful to walk through the code on a page and study the values of the variables as you go, running one line of code at a time. You can also do this with the Script Debugger.

You can do this by placing a `Stop` statement in your code where you would like the Script Debugger to open as shown in this code:

```
<%
Option Explicit
Dim x
Dim y
Dim z
Stop
x = 1
y = 2
z = x / y
Response.Write z
z = z + 8
y = z - x
Response.Write y
%>
```

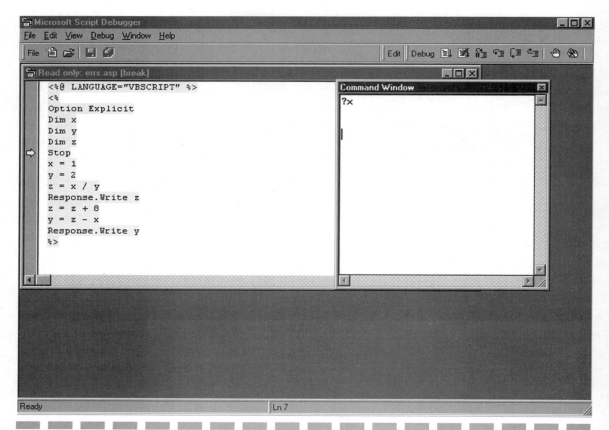

Figure 12-12   Script Debugger entered with the `Stop` statement.

An error will not occur in this code, but the result is not what we thought it should be. Notice the addition of the Stop statement. When this page is next run in the browser, the Script Debugger will launch and the code will cease running right at the Stop statement, as shown in Figure 12-12. Notice that the run arrow is pointing to the Stop statement.

We can now use the Command Window to check out the values of each of the variables in the Active Server Page. We can also run the code on the page one line at a time using the options under the Debug menu. These options are displayed in Figure 12-13.

The Debug menu item options give you the capability to run your code further and then stop again. Each time you can go to the Command Window to see what the values of the variables are as you are working

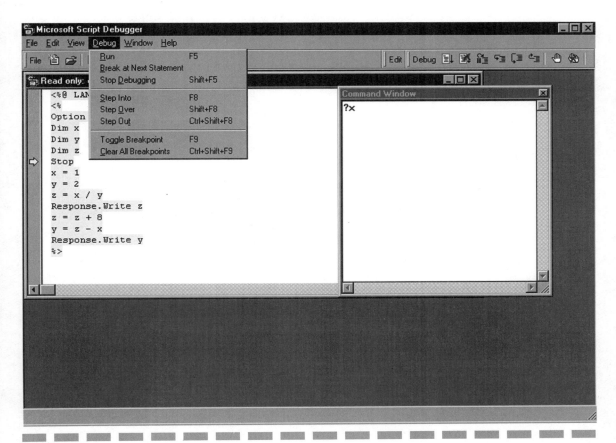

Figure 12-13 Debug menu item options.

with them. In fact, on the click-side you can see the result of each line of code, so when the code gets to a Response.Write method call, you can run that line of code and then look at the browser to see the effect of that line of code.

The first option under the Debug menu says Run. This option basically runs the code until another `Stop` statement is reached. The Stop Debugging ends the debugging session.

The most powerful options, however, are the Step Into, Step Over, and Step Out options. These options provide a way for you to run code one line at a time. You can then go to the Command Window and check the values of each variable as you go to better understand the logic of the page.

The Step Into option runs the next line of code, even if that next line of code branches you off to a Function somewhere else on the page. The Step Over option runs the next line of code as a single line of code even if it is a call to a function or sub. You use this option to prevent yourself from branching off to a procedure that you don't want to debug. The Step Out option provides a way for you to break out of a procedure that you have entered but no longer wish to run.

13

Structured Query Language, SQL Server, and Access

The Back End of an Active Server Page Application

Behind the scenes of most Active Server Page applications is a database—stored in that database is what makes the site dynamic. Your being able to communicate with that database effectively and efficiently will dictate the complexity and usability of your Active Server Page application.

In this chapter, we look first at the Structured Query Language or SQL, which is the language you use to request data from a database. We compare and contrast SQL Server's query language and Access's query language; then, later in the chapter, we look at Data Source Names, views, indexes, and security issues in the sections on SQL Server and Access.

Structured Query Language

In this part of the chapter, we look at the *Structured Query Language* (SQL), the language you use to communicate the records you want to retrieve or actions that you want to take on a database. We review two flavors often used in conjunction with Active Server Page applications: *T-SQL*, the language used with SQL Server; and *Access SQL*, the language used in Microsoft Access. We review these two flavors together so we can review their differences. If you are familiar with the SQL language used in Microsoft Access, you will find that the two are very similar, although they have some important differences.

Sample Database

Throughout this section of the chapter, we refer to a sample database to help demonstrate the use and structure of T-SQL and Access SQL. The sample database has two tables: one table contains information about an employee, the other contains departments to which the employees can belong.

The table specifications for the employee table in SQL Server, tblEmps, is shown in Table 13-1. The same table defined in Microsoft Access is displayed in Table 13-2. Notice the similarities and differences

TABLE 13-1

SQL Server tblEmps
Field Specifications

Field Name	Field Type	Notes
EmpID	int	Identity column, seeded at 1 and incremented by 1
FirstName	varchar	Length = 50
LastName	varchar	Length = 50
DepartmentID	int	Foreign Key
Salary	money	
BirthDate	datetime	

between the two table definitions. First, notice that the field names are the same; the name of a field in SQL Server can be called the same in Microsoft Access. Both tables also have a primary key, and both tables could have a primary key made up of more than one field.

The field types, however, are different in every case. Table 13-3 displays the field types for Microsoft Access and displays the matching field type in SQL Server.

In both of the tblEmps tables, the EmpID is the *primary key*, which is a field in which the values are unique across all records. For example, a person's Social Security number is usually considered a primary key because everyone has a different number. People can be uniquely identified by their Social Security number. In this case, an arbitrary number will be used in the EmpID field to uniquely identify the employee. In SQL Server, the field is set up as an Identity column, which means the SQL Server will fill in a unique number for you. In Microsoft Access, the field is set up as an AutoNumber field of subtype long.

TABLE 13-2

Microsoft Access
tblEmps Field
Specifications

Field Name	Field Type	Notes
EmpID	AutoNumber	Set as primary key
FirstName	text	Length = 50
LastName	text	Length = 50
DepartmentID	number, long	Foreign Key
Salary	currency	
BirthDate	Date/Time	

TABLE 13-3

Microsoft Access
and SQL Server
Field Types

Microsoft Access	SQL Server
AutoNumber, Long	int, Identity column
Text	varchar
Memo	text
Number, Byte	smallint
Number, Integer	smallint
Number, Long	int
Number, Single	real
Number, Double	float
Date/Time	datetime
Currency	money
Yes/No	bit
OLE Object	image

The FirstName and LastName fields are character fields that store the employee's name. In SQL Server, a character field is set up as a varchar field. In Microsoft Access we use text as the field type. Both of these fields can store a maximum of 255 characters. If you need the field to be longer than 255 characters in Access, you use a Memo type field and in SQL Server you would use the text field.

The DepartmentID is referred to as a *Foreign Key*. This field will be used to link the employee to the other table in this sample database. The Salary field stores the amount of money the employee makes. In Microsoft Access this is a currency field and in SQL Server it is a money field.

The BirthDate field stores the date on which the employee was born. In both SQL Server and Access, a field of this type can store a date or a time or both a date and a time in the same field.

For this section's demonstration, tblEmps is populated with the records shown in Table 13-4.

TABLE 13-4

Sample Records for
the tblEmps Table

EmpID	FirstName	LastName	DepartmentID	Salary	BirthDate
1	Michelle	Morgan	1	$35,000	5/1/62
2	Jack	Gordon	1	$35,000	6/15/48
3	Jamie	Lesser	2	$22,000	8/21/55
4	Amanda	Smith	5	$88,000	5/2/59

TABLE 13-5

SQL Server
tblDepartments
Field Specifications

Field Name	Field Type	Notes
DepartmentID	int	Identity column, seeded at 1 and incremented by 1
DepartmentName	varchar	Length = 100
Location	text	

The other table in the database is tblDepartments. The field specifications for that table in SQL Server are shown in Table 13-5.

The field specifications for the Department table in Microsoft Access are shown in Table 13-6. The DepartmentID is the primary key for this table. As with the other table, the field is set up in SQL Server as an Identity column and in Microsoft Access as an AutoNumber field so it will be automatically populated. The field is used by the tblEmps in providing the link between the tables. For example, if an employee's record indicates that he or she is in Department 1, that value in this table will tell you what the name and location of that department are. This is referred to as a *table relationship*, of which there are three types: a one-to-one relationship, a one-to-many relationship, and a many-to-many relationship.

Figure 13-1 shows examples of one-to-one relationships. In a one-to-one relationship a record in the first table has a match of one record in a second table. A record in the second table has only one match in the first table, so in the first relationship, an employee record has a single spouse record; each record in the Spouse table relates to just a single Employee record.

TABLE 13-6

Microsoft Access
tblDepartments
Field Specifications

Field Name	Field Type	Notes
DepartmentID	AutoNumber	Set as Primary Key
DepartmentName	text	Length = 100
Location	memo	

Figure 13-1
Examples of one-to-one relationships.

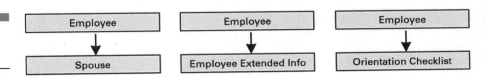

In the second example, we have an Employee table and an Employee extended information table. The Employee table would contain general, frequently accessed data about an employee. The Employee Extended Info table would contain additional information about an employee that was infrequently accessed. The two tables relate in a one-to-one relationship. Each Employee has a single record in the Employee Extended Info table and each record in the Employee Extended Info table goes with a single employee's record.

The third example shows the relationship between an Employee and an Orientation Checklist table. The Orientation Checklist table contains a list of Boolean fields that show which orientation items an employee has completed. Each record in the Employee table relates to a single record in the Orientation Checklist table and each record in the Orientation Checklist table relates to a single record in the Employee table.

Figure 13-2 shows examples of one-to-many relationships. In a one-to-many relationship, a single record in one of the tables relates to many records in a second table. The records in the second table, however, relate to only a single record in the other table, so in the first example of Figure 13-2, each employee can have many dependents, but each dependent relates to only a single employee.

In the second example, we have a Customer table and an Order table. Each customer can place many orders but a single order must be from a single customer.

The third example shows the relationship between records in a Building table and records in a Room table. A record in the Building table can have many Room records to which it relates, but a single Room record can belong to only a single Building.

The last type of relationship is a many-to-many relationship, examples of which are shown in Figure 13-3. In a many-to-many relationship, each

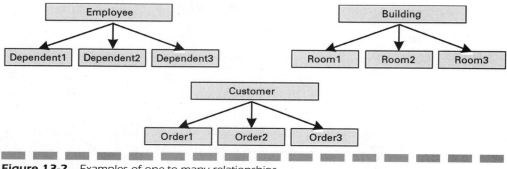

Figure 13-2   *Examples of one-to-many relationships.*

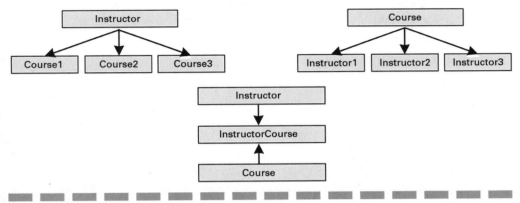

Figure 13-3   Examples of many-to-many relationships.

record in both tables relates to many records in the other table. In this example, we have an Instructor table and a Course table. The Instructor table contains information about instructors and the Course table contains a list of all the courses. An instructor can teach more than one course, so each record in the Instructor table can relate to many records in the Course table. A course can have more than one instructor, so each record in the Course table can relate to many records in the Instructor table.

When the relationship between two tables is bidirectionally one-to-many, you have a many-to-many relationship, although it cannot be expressed directly between two tables. The relationship requires that a third go-between table relate to the original tables in a one-to-many relationship. In Figure 13-3, note the third table called Instructor Course. Each Instructor record can have many records in the InstructorCourse table, and each record in the Course table can relate to many records in the Instructor table.

In our example, the tblEmps table and the tblDepartments table relate to each other in a one-to-many relationship. Each of the Employee records can relate to only a single record in the tblDepartments table, although each of the departments can have many employees.

The DepartmentName field stores the name of the department—in Access this is a text field and in SQL Server this is a varchar field. The Location field stores the descriptive location of the department. This field can contain extended, lengthy text. In SQL Server it is defined as a text field and in Access it is a memo field.

Don't get confused about the different meaning of the text field type in Access and SQL Server because they mean very different things. In

TABLE 13-7

Sample Records for
the tblDepartments
Table

DepartmentID	DepartmentName	Location
1	Administration	Top floor, west wing
2	IS	Bottom floor, by the vending machines
3	Human Resources	First floor, east wing

Access, a text field is a character field up to 255 characters; in SQL Server, a text field can go well beyond that length.

Table 13-7 shows sample records from the tblDepartments table that is used with our sample SQL statements.

Select Statements

The most basic SQL statement retrieves all the records and all the fields from a table. This `Select` statement would be identical in T-SQL and Access SQL:

```
Select * from tblEmps
```

When you use a `Select` statement, you are saying that you want to select fields and records to be returned from the database. In a basic SQL statement like this, the word `Select` is followed by the name of the fields that you want to return. Then the statement has the keyword `From`, which is followed by the name of the table that you want to retrieve records.

The result of that query is displayed in Table 13-8. The * in this query means that we want all the fields from the table indicated in the `From` clause.

TABLE 13-8

Result of Select
Query

EmpID	FirstName	LastName	DepartmentID	Salary	BirthDate
1	Michelle	Morgan	1	$35,000	5/1/62
2	Jack	Gordon	1	$35,000	6/15/48
3	Jamie	Lesser	2	$22,000	8/21/55
4	Amanda	Smith	5	$88,000	5/2/5

TABLE 13-9

Query Results

FirstName	LastName
Michelle	Morgan
Jack	Gordon
Jamie	Lesser
Amanda	Smith

But we often don't need all the fields. We should retrieve just the fields that we are going to use because it is much more efficient. Think about the number of bytes that would be required if you returned one of the fields versus all of the fields. So in Access SQL or T-SQL, if we just wanted the employees' names, the SQL statement would be this:

```
Select LastName, FirstName from tblEmps
```

The results of that query are shown in Table 13-9.

When we want to return specific fields we just list them separated by commas. We can also combine and extract from fields to produce fields that are outputted but are not part of the table. For example, we may want to display the full name of the employee as a single field. We would do that in T-SQL like this:

```
Select LastName + ', ' + FirstName as FullName from tblEmps
```

In Access SQL the query would be this:

```
Select LastName & ', ' & FirstName as FullName from tblEmps
```

Notice the difference between the two queries. In T-SQL we use the + to indicate concatenation; in Access SQL you use the &.

The results of that query are displayed in Table 13-10. The new field outputted is called FullName. Again, note that this does not become part

TABLE 13-10

Query Results

FullName
Morgan, Michelle
Gordon, Jack
Lesser, Jamie
Smith, Amanda

T-SQL	Access SQL	Purpose
DatePart(yy, date)	Year(Date)	Returns the year for the date passed to the function.
DatePart(mm, date)	Month(Date)	Returns the month for the date passed to the function.
DatePart(dd, date)	Day(Date)	Returns the day of the month for the date passed to the function.
DatePart(hh, time)	Hour(Time)	Returns the hour for the time passed to the function.
DatePart(mi, time)	Minute(Time)	Returns the minute for the time passed to the function.
DatePart(ss, time)	Second(Time)	Returns the second for the time passed to the function.
GetDate	Now	Returns the current system date and time.

of the table, but rather is merely a temporary field in this output. Whenever we create a field like this, we use the As keyword to indicate what the temporary field should be called. Also notice that the concatenation is in three parts. The first part is the last name of the employee, followed by a comma and a space; concatenated to that is the first name of the employee.

We can also extract parts of a field. This is where you will see a big difference between Access SQL and T-SQL. When you use a built-in function in Access SQL, you use the same VB Script functions that you use in your ASP. When you use T-SQL, the built-in functions are part of SQL Server.

Table 13-11 reviews some of the functions common between both languages and their purpose.

Say you want to retrieve just the month that the person was born and their first name. From T-SQL you would write this query:

```
Select FirstName, DatePart(mm, Birthdate) as MonthBorn from tblEmps
```

From Access SQL you would code this:

```
Select FirstName, Month(Birthdate) as MonthBorn from tblEmps
```

TABLE 13-12

Query Results

FirstName	MonthBorn
Michelle	5
Jack	6
Jamie	8
Amanda	5

The results of that query are shown in Table 13-12. This time, a temporary field called MonthBorn was outputted from the database with the employee's first name. The T-SQL function, DatePart, was used to extract the month from the BirthDate field. The first parameter of the function is the part of the date you want. The second part is the date to extract from. In Access SQL the function Month is used to return the month from the BirthDate field.

Sometimes you want to retrieve just the unique values for a field. For example, if you wanted to display a list of all the salaries, but didn't want to see duplicates, you would use this T-SQL or Access SQL statement:

```
Select Distinct Salary from tblEmps
```

The results of this query are shown in Table 13-13. Notice in this result that the salary amount $35,000 is shown only once even though it occurs in two records.

It is also simple to retrieve summary information about our data. For example, if we wanted to know the salary of the highest paid person we would code:

```
Select Max(Salary) as TopSalary from tblEmps
```

TABLE 13-13

Query Results

Salary
$35,000
$22,000
$88,000

The output of this query in Access SQL or T-SQL would be $88,000; the Max function retrieves the highest values for the field. We can also retrieve the lowest salary:

```
Select Min(Salary) as LowSalary from tblEmps
```

We can even add up all the salaries and get a total amount:

```
Select Sum(Salary) as TotalSalary from tblEmps
```

One more summary function is the Count function that counts the number of records as in the following:

```
Select Count(EmpID) as TotalRecords from tblEmps
```

That statement would return the value 4 since there are four records in the table.

Where Clause

So far we have limited our output to all the records, but we often want just some of the records. We limit the records outputted with the *Where clause*. For example, if we wanted to view only those people who made more than $30,000, we would use this statement:

```
Select * from tblEmps where Salary > 30000
```

That query would result in the output shown in Table 13-14. In both Access SQL and T-SQL, we can use =, <, >, >=, < >, or <= in the Where clause to limit output from the table.

If we are looking for a numeric field in the Where clause, as we did earlier with the search on the Salary field, we just put the number in

TABLE 13-14

Query Results

EmpID	FirstName	LastName	DepartmentID	Salary	BirthDate
1	Michelle	Morgan	1	$35,000	5/1/62
2	Jack	Gordon	1	$35,000	6/15/48
4	Amanda	Smith	5	$88,000	5/2/59

TABLE 13-15

Sample Records for
the tblEmps Table

EmpID	FirstName	LastName	DepartmentID	Salary	BirthDate
2	Jack	Gordon	1	$35,000	6/15/48

the query. If we have a text field we are searching in either T-SQL or Access SQL, we surround the text we are searching for with single quotes:

```
Select * from tblEmps where FirstName = 'Jack'
```

The results of that query are displayed in Table 13-15.

If we wanted to use a date in the Where clause, we would surround the date in single quotes for T-SQL:

```
Select * from tblEmps where BirthDate > '1/1/56'
```

The same query in Access SQL would look like this:

```
Select * from tblEmps where BirthDate > #1/1/56#
```

The results of either of these queries are displayed in Table 13-16.

Another way we can limit the output is with a *wild card*, which you use to represent any character combinations. For example, in T-SQL, if we wanted to display all the employees whose first name started with a J, we would have a query like this:

```
Select * from tblEMps where FirstName Like 'J%'
```

The same query in Access SQL would be this:

```
Select * from tblEMps where FirstName Like 'J*'
```

TABLE 13-16

Results of Select
Query

EmpID	FirstName	LastName	DepartmentID	Salary	BirthDate
1	Michelle	Morgan	1	$35,000	5/1/62
4	Amanda	Smith	5	$88,000	5/2/59

TABLE 13-17

Sample Records for
the tblEmps Table

EmpID	FirstName	LastName	DepartmentID	Salary	BirthDate
2	Jack	Gordon	1	$35,000	6/15/48
3	Jamie	Lesser	2	$22,000	8/21/55

The results of that query are displayed in Table 13-17. The Where clause selects all employees whose first name starts with the letter J. The % or * character is the wild card character.

We can also combine more than one criteria with an and or an or. If we wanted to see all those employees in department 5 that have a salary of more than $34,000, we would write:

```
Select * from tblEmps where DepartmentID = 5 and Salary > 34000
```

The result of that query is displayed in Table 13-18. This means that both criteria must match. If an or was used instead, the result of the query would be everyone in department 5 and also include anyone who makes more than $34,000. This result is shown in Table 13-19.

Order By Clause

The *Order By clause* allows us to sort the outputted records. The Order By clause comes after the Where clause and looks like this:

```
Select * from tblEMps order by Salary
```

TABLE 13-18

Result of Select
Query

EmpID	FirstName	LastName	DepartmentID	Salary	BirthDate
4	Amanda	Smith	5	$88,000	5/2/59

TABLE 13-19

Result of Select
Query

EmpID	FirstName	LastName	DepartmentID	Salary	BirthDate
1	Michelle	Morgan	1	$35,000	5/1/62
2	Jack	Gordon	1	$35,000	6/15/48
4	Amanda	Smith	5	$88,000	5/2/59

TABLE 13-20

Result of Select
Query

EmpID	FirstName	LastName	DepartmentID	Salary	BirthDate
4	Amanda	Smith	5	$88,000	5/2/59
1	Michelle	Morgan	1	$35,000	5/1/62
2	Jack	Gordon	1	$35,000	6/15/48
3	Jamie	Lesser	2	$22,000	8/21/55

The outputted records would now be sorted by employee salary as shown in Table 13-20.

We could also sort the records in the reverse order by using the *DESC* qualifier, which means descending:

```
Select * from tblEMps order by Salary
```

The outputted records would now be sorted from lowest to highest salary, as shown in Table 13-21.

You can also sort by more than one field in the Order By clause. If we wanted to sort the records by the LastName field and the FirstName field we would code this:

```
Select * from tblEMps order by LastName, FirstName
```

Joins

Sometimes we need to retrieve data that is across more than one table. For example, we may want to output the employee's name with the name of the department in which he or she works. To do this, we need to use the Join keyword.

```
Select tblEmps.FirstName, tblEmps.LastName, tblDepartments.
  DepartmentName from tblEmps
Inner Join tblDepartments on tblEmps.DepartmentID =
  tblDepartments.DepartmentID
```

TABLE 13-21

Result of Select
Query

EmpID	FirstName	LastName	DepartmentID	Salary	BirthDate
3	Jamie	Lesser	2	$22,000	8/21/55
2	Jack	Gordon	1	$35,000	6/15/48
1	Michelle	Morgan	1	$35,000	5/1/62
4	Amanda	Smith	5	$88,000	5/2/59

TABLE 13-22

Sample Records for
the tblEmps Table

FirstName	LastName	DepartmentName
Michelle	Morgan	Administrative
Jack	Gordon	Administrative
Jamie	Lesser	IS

This query combines both tables and displays just the name and department for each employee, as shown in Table 13-22. The words Inner Join are followed with the name of the table to join with, which is followed with the names of the fields that link the two tables together.

Notice that the employee Amanda Smith is not in this output. That is because the department for that employee is number 5 and there is no department 5 in tblDepartments. This is what an Inner Join does—it will output only matches in both tables. If we want to see all the employees, even if they don't have a matching department, we need to change Inner Join to Left Join. If we wanted to see all the departments, even if they didn't have an employee, then we would change Inner Join to Right Join.

Add, Edit, and Delete

Beyond viewing records in your database in Access SQL or T-SQL, you will need to Add, Edit, and Delete records.

To add records, we use an Insert statement as in this example:

```
Insert into tblEMps (FirstName, LastName, DepartmentID, Salary,
  BirthDate) values
('John', 'Doe', 2, 45000, '3/22/66')
```

Now the tblEmps table would have the records shown in Table 13-23. The Insert statement starts with the term Insert, followed with the

TABLE 13-23

Sample Records for
the tblEmps Table

EmpID	FirstName	LastName	DepartmentID	Salary	BirthDate
1	Michelle	Morgan	1	$35,000	5/1/62
2	Jack	Gordon	1	$35,000	6/15/48
3	Jamie	Lesser	2	$22,000	8/21/55
4	Amanda	Smith	5	$88,000	5/2/59
5	John	Doe	2	$45,000	3/22/66

TABLE 13-24

Sample Records for
the tblEmps Table

EmpID	FirstName	LastName	DepartmentID	Salary	BirthDate
1	Michelle	Morgan	3	$35,000	5/1/62
2	Jack	Gordon	1	$35,000	6/15/48
3	Jamie	Lesser	2	$22,000	8/21/55
4	Amanda	Smith	5	$88,000	5/2/59
5	John	Doe	2	$45,000	3/22/66

`into` keyword and the name of the table into which we are adding a
record. Then, surrounded by parentheses, are the names of all the fields
to which we are adding data for this new record. That is followed by the
keyword `values`. Then another set of parentheses surrounds the data
being inserted into the table.

We use an `Update` statement to edit an existing record. The `Update`
statement takes the following form:

```
Update tblEmps set Salary = 35000, DepartmentID = 3 where
    EmployeeID = 1
```

That action would result in the data looking like that displayed in Table
13-24. The `Update` statement begins with the `Update` keyword followed
by the name of the table to update. Then the `set` keyword is used, followed by field/value pairs that are each separated by commas. At the
end of the statement is usually a Where clause indicating which record
or records to update.

To delete a record or records, we use an SQL `Delete` statement,
which takes the following form:

```
Delete from tblEmps where EmployeeID = 2
```

This action would result in our table looking like that displayed in
Table 13-25. The statement starts with `Delete from`, followed by the

TABLE 13-25

Sample Records for
the tblEmps Table

EmpID	FirstName	LastName	DepartmentID	Salary	BirthDate
1	Michelle	Morgan	3	$35,000	5/1/62
3	Jamie	Lesser	2	$22,000	8/21/55
4	Amanda	Smith	5	$88,000	5/2/59
5	John	Doe	2	$45,000	3/22/66

name of the table where the record needed to be deleted is located. That is usually followed by a Where clause, limiting the records to be deleted.

Working with SQL Server in an Active Server Page Application

In this section, we look at things you can do within SQL Server to provide access to your database and to make your database more efficient.

Indexes

In the previous section, we had an Employee table with a variety of fields. With a table like that, you frequently search for an employee's record by his or her name. A field like this is an ideal candidate for being an *index*, which is a separate table of data maintained by SQL Server that stores the field index sorted. So if you were to search for an employee's name in a query and the name field was indexed, then the query would run quickly because SQL Server would have a list of employees sorted by name. If the field was not indexed, the SQL Server would have to look through the first names one at a time until a match was found.

Probably one of the easiest ways to work with databases in SQL Server is to use the Data View that comes with the Visual Studio products. There is a similar tool that comes with SQL Server 7.0. The Data View is displayed in Figure 13-4. Browse to the table to which you want to add indexes and right-click on it. Then select the Design option and you should see the Design view for the table, as displayed in Figure 13-5. Now right-click anywhere in the design view of the table and select Properties. Switch to the INDEXES/KEYS tab and you should see the dialog displayed in Figure 13-6. When you first enter this dialog you may see that your table already has an Index. That is because SQL Server automatically creates an Index for the field that is the primary key on the table.

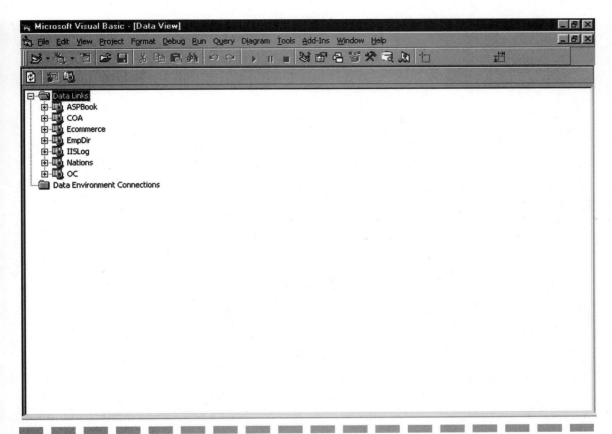

Figure 13-4 Data View window.

Let's say that we wanted to create an Index for the LastName field of the tblEmps table. To do this, first press the NEW button in the Indexes/Keys dialog. Then, under the section labeled Column Name, select the LastName field. Provide a name in the Index Name field. You should then see your new Index like that shown in Figure 13-7. If you select the CREATE UNIQUE check box, the Index requires that each entry in this field is unique. The Fill Factor option is used to determine how much space is on each page of the Index internally. By default, SQL Server uses its internal configuration for this field.

The Clustered option gives you the opportunity to determine the physical order of the records in the table. If you choose this option, the

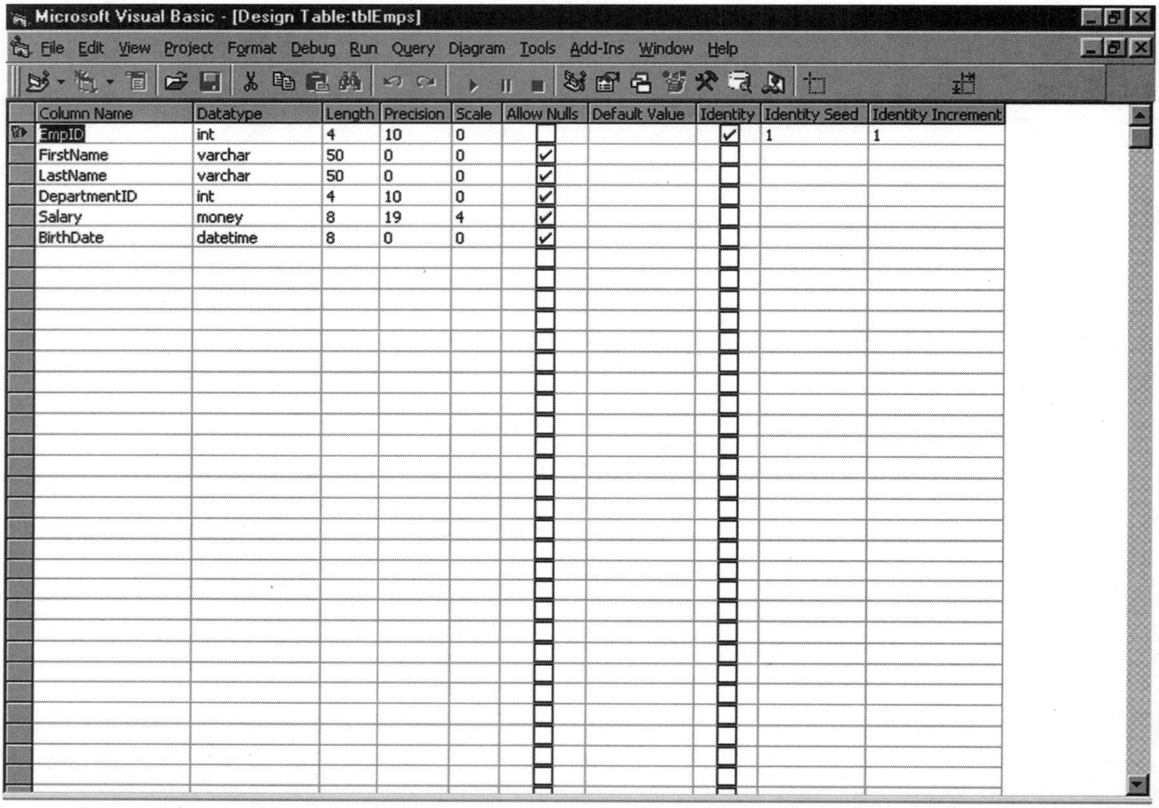

Figure 13-5 Table Design view.

records in the table will be stored based on this index. You are allowed only one Clustered Index per table.

You can also include more than one field in an Index. Say, for example, that you wanted to create an Index on the LastName field followed by the FirstName field. You would do this if you frequently had queries that searched both of these fields. For example, you may have a Web page that displayed information on an employee based on the Field collection passed into the page:

```
"Select * from tblEmps where from tblEmps LastName = '" &
    Request.Form("FirstName") & "'"
    & " and FirstName = '" & Request.Form("LastName") & "'"
```

Figure 13-6
Indexes/Keys view.

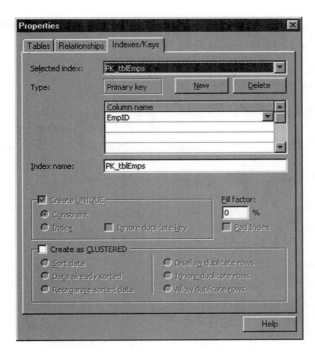

Figure 13-7
New Index
IndexLastName
created.

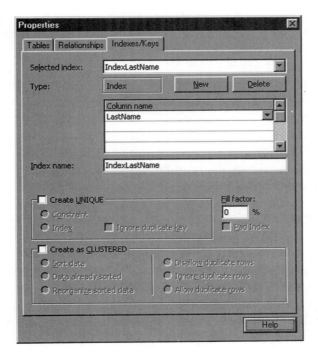

Figure 13-8
Creating a Composite
Index.

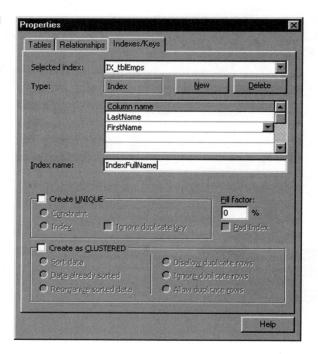

You would start to create an index in the same way as the first one, and you would give it a name like before. But under Column name you would select two fields as shown in Figure 13-8.

Once you create indexes, SQL Server will try to use the index that most optimizes the query. But sometimes SQL Server does not choose the correct index. You can force it to use a specific index by including the index name like this:

```
"Select * from tblEmps from tblEmps (Index = IndexFullName) " _
  & "where LastName = '" & Request.Form("FirstName") & "'" _
  & " and FirstName = '" & Request.Form("LastName") & "'"
```

As you decide what indexes to add and not to add, remember that each index adds additional overhead to the database. Every time a record is added, modified, or deleted it must also be added, modified, or deleted in the table where it resides, as well as the Index tables.

Views

Views are queries that stay the same and which you need to run over and over again. You don't have to use them but, as with indexes, they optimize your database. If you have a query that you are running, many times you can create it as a View. Then the query is internally compiled and optimized so the next time it is called, it will run more efficiently.

You can create a View by just entering the SQL or by using the New View option in the View window. In the View window, browse to the database to which you want to add a view, then right-click on the Views folder for that database and select New View as shown in Figure 13-9. You will then see the New View window as shown in Figure 13-10.

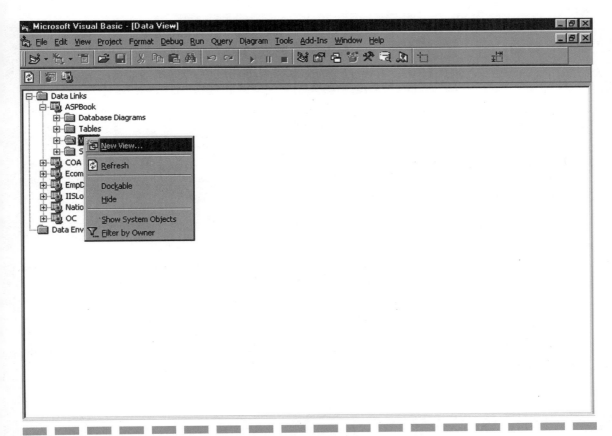

Figure 13-9   Creating a New View.

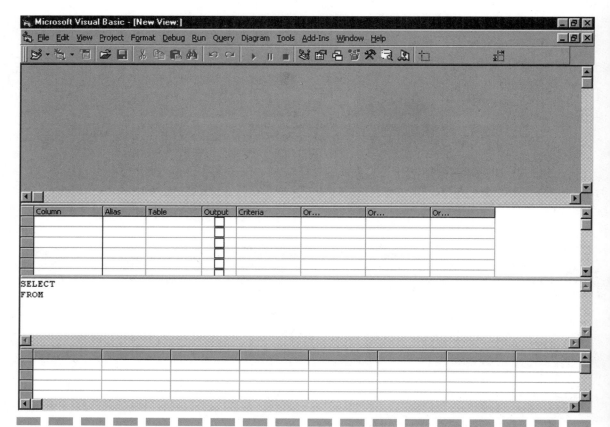

Figure 13-10   New View window.

If you are familiar with creating queries in SQL Server, you will find this tool easy to use. The top part of the page contains the table or tables that you want to include in the query. You can drag and drop the tables to be included onto the New View window or you can type the table name into the where clause. Figure 13-11 shows the New View window with the tblEmps table included. You can then add fields, criteria, and an Order clause to your query. Figure 13-12 shows a completed View. You can then save the View and call it from your code.

Creating a DSN for an SQL Server Database

To access a database from your Active Server Pages, you need to create an ODBC Data Source on the server, which then allows ADO to use the

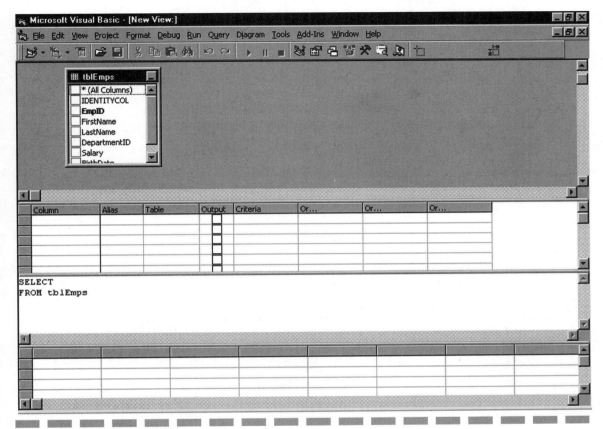

Figure 13-11   New View with table added.

Connection object to connect to your database. In this section, we create an ODBC Data Source for an SQL Server Database.

From the server, go to the Control Panel and double-click on ODBC as shown in Figure 13-13. When you enter the ODBC Data Source Administrator, you see the dialog box shown in Figure 13-14.

You need to change to the System DSN. The User DSN is available only to the person who is currently logged in to the Server. With the System DSN, the data source will be available to any user. When you select System DSN, you should see the dialog shown in Figure 13-15. On the System DSN, press the NEW button. You should see the dialog shown in Figure 13-16. Select SQL Server from this dialog and press FINISH.

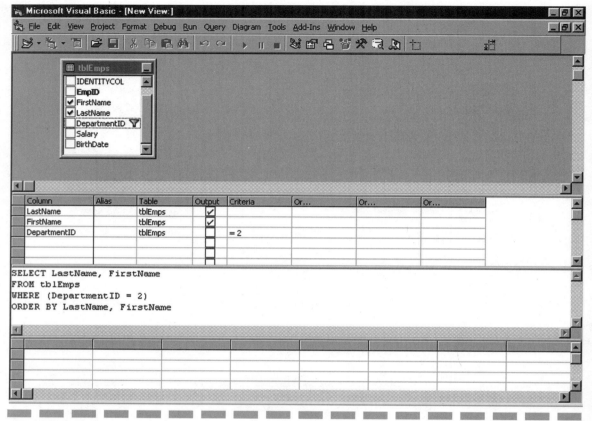

Figure 13-12 Completed View.

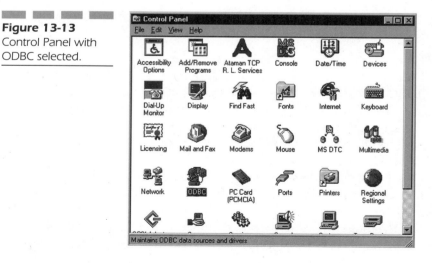

Figure 13-13
Control Panel with
ODBC selected.

Figure 13-14
ODBC Data Source
Administrator upon
initial entrance.

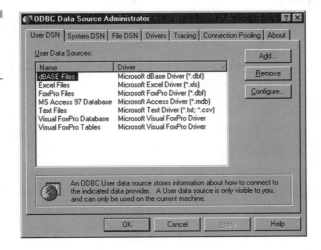

Figure 13-14
ODBC Data Source
Administrator upon
initial entrance.

You should then see the first page of the Create a New Data Source to SQL Server wizard as shown in Figure 13-17. This page is where you actually enter the name for the DSN. This name is very important and needs to be noted because you will use it in your connection statement in your Active Server Pages. You can also give your DSN a description and you need to select the SQL Server to which you are connecting. If the SQL Server is on this machine, then you could select Local.

Press NEXT to go to step two of the wizard as shown in Figure 13-18. Select the name of the database you created in SQL Server and press the NEXT button. You should see step three of the wizard as displayed in

Figure 13-15
System DSN tab.

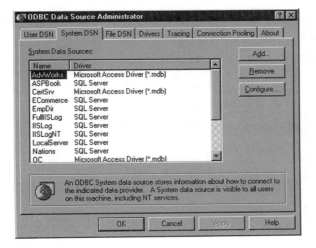

Figure 13-16
Create a New Data
Source dialog.

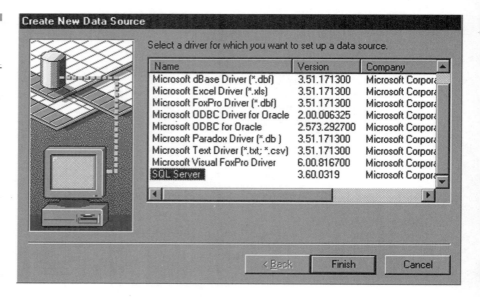

Figure 13-16
Create a New Data
Source dialog.

Figure 13-19. Select SQL Server Authentication and enter your SQL Server user name and password.

Press NEXT to see the dialog shown in Figure 13-20. Use the defaults on this page and press NEXT to see the fifth and final page in the wizard (Figure 13-21). Again, accept the defaults and then press the FINISH but-

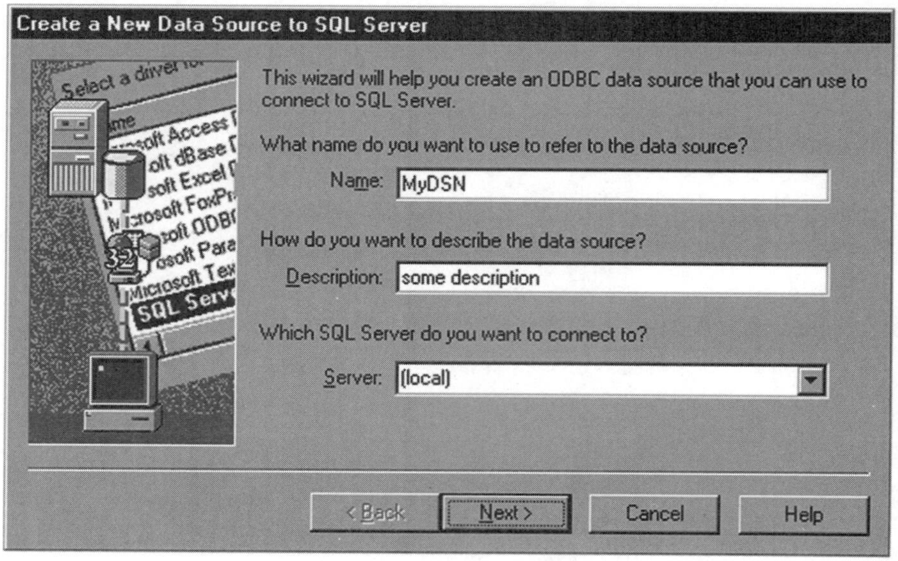

Figure 13-17
First page of the SQL
Server DSN wizard.

Figure 13-18
Page two of the SQL
Server DSN wizard.

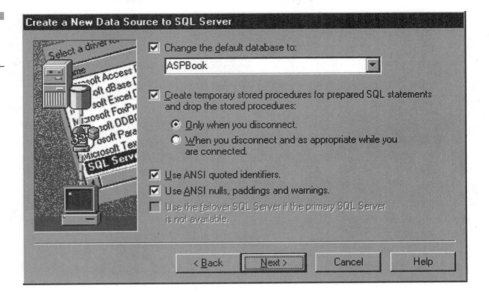

ton. You will then see the dialog shown in Figure 13-22. From here you will see a summary of your selections. You can press the TEST DATA SOURCE button to test your settings or you can just press OK to exit. Your DSN has now been completed and, if you entered it correctly, you should now be able to access the database from your Active Server Pages.

Figure 13-19
Page three of the
SQL Server DSN
wizard.

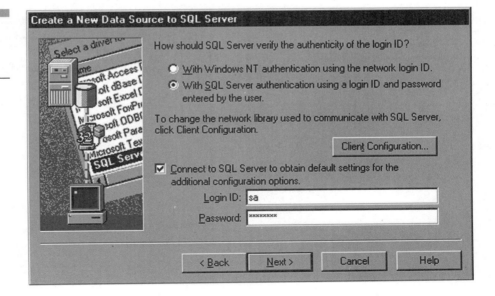

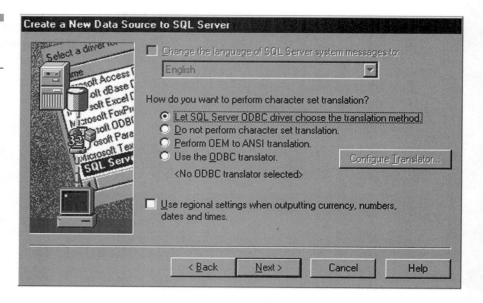

Figure 13-20
Page four of the SQL
Server DSN wizard.

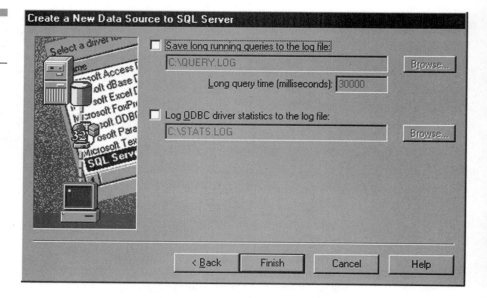

Figure 13-21
Final page of the
wizard.

Figure 13-22
SQL Server ODBC
confirmation screen.

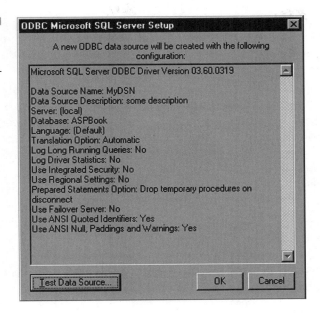

ODBC Microsoft SQL Server Setup

A new ODBC data source will be created with the following
configuration:

Microsoft SQL Server ODBC Driver Version 03.60.0319

Data Source Name: MyDSN
Data Source Description: some description
Server: (local)
Database: ASPBook
Language: (Default)
Translation Option: Automatic
Log Long Running Queries: No
Log Driver Statistics: No
Use Integrated Security: No
Use Regional Settings: No
Prepared Statements Option: Drop temporary procedures on
disconnect
Use Failover Server: No
Use ANSI Quoted Identifiers: Yes
Use ANSI Null, Paddings and Warnings: Yes

Test Data Source...   OK   Cancel

Working with Microsoft Access in an Active Server Page Application

In this part of the chapter we look at Microsoft Access and how we can connect to it and make our data safer.

Securing an Access Database

There are a variety of reasons that a company will elect to use Microsoft Access instead of something like SQL Server as the back-end database for its Active Server Page applications. First, for many people Access is easier to use. With the wizards and dialogs that come with Access, creating and setting up a database in Access is much easier than in SQL Server, and it is more widely available. Most companies can afford Microsoft Access but the requirements for SQL Server beyond just the software itself often squeeze out a smaller company.

Remember, though, that Access is not a database server. That means you don't have a server dedicated to shelling out query results, so it is not optimized for very heavy use. More important than that, though, is that you must address the issue of security if you are going to use an Access database in an Internet setting; that is, unless you don't mind your entire database being open to anyone in the world.

In this section we walk through the steps you need to take to secure an Access database. These steps are often misunderstood or sometimes a vital step is simply skipped—so follow them carefully and your data will be less accessible by the general population.

The unfortunate problem with securing a database in Access is that the database was generally first created in an unsecured environment. So, even if you secure that database, the default account will own it and always be able to access the database.

The way security works in Access is through your data database and a user database. The *data database* is the database with your tables, queries, forms, reports, macros, and modules. The *user database* stores user name passwords, identifiers, groups, and group membership information. All the user database does is validate a user and a password and provides group membership information; the data database then provides the specific permission within itself.

Security is always on in Access. You don't see any login because, by default, you are logging in as the default administrator without a password. The following steps focus on removing the privileges of the default account since this account is available to any Access installation.

Step 1: Create a New User Database

As mentioned earlier, the user database is where the logins for the database are stored. In this section, we create a new user database and then use that database to secure our data database. To create and join a new user database, you use a tool that comes with access called the *Microsoft Access Workgroup Administrator*.

This tool is not usually on your shortcut menu, so you will have to browse to find it. Normally there is a shortcut for the tool in the `Microsoft Office` directory. But you can also just search for the name of the file, which is `WRKGADM.EXE`. When you start that tool you should see the dialog shown in Figure 13-23.

We want to create and join a new user database, so press the CREATE button and you should see the dialog shown in Figure 13-24. From this dialog, supply a name for your user database. Then supply the organiza-

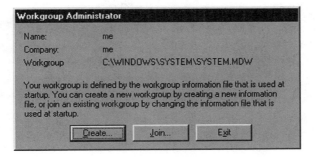

Figure 13-23
Microsoft Access
Workgroup
Administrator main
dialog.

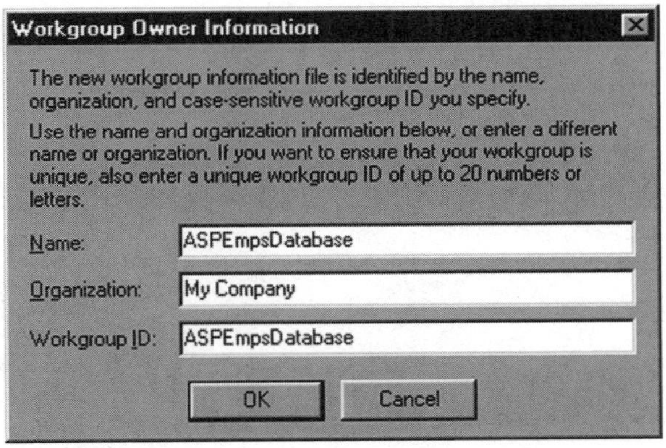

Figure 13-24
Creating a new user
database.

tion for the database as well as an ID for it. When you have done that, press the OK button.

Next, supply the location where you want to create this user database and the name of the file, as shown in Figure 13-25. Press OK when you have the file name and location complete.

You are then prompted to confirm all the information you have just supplied, as shown in Figure 13-26. If the information is correct, press the OK button; if not, press the CHANGE button. The tool then tells you that you have successfully created and joined the new user database.

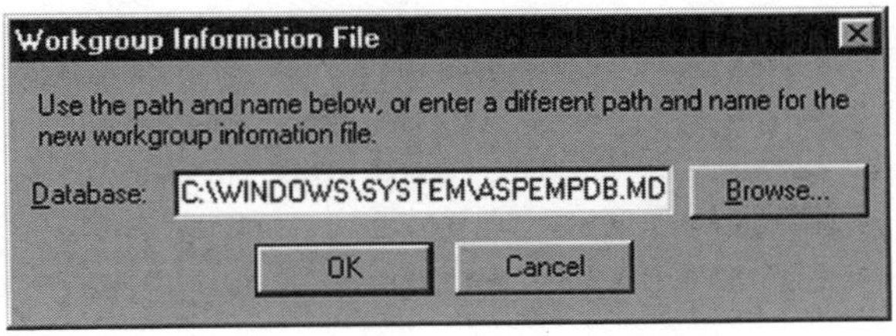

Figure 13-25
Supplying the file
name for your user
database.

Figure 13-26
Confirming the infor-
mation for your new
user database.

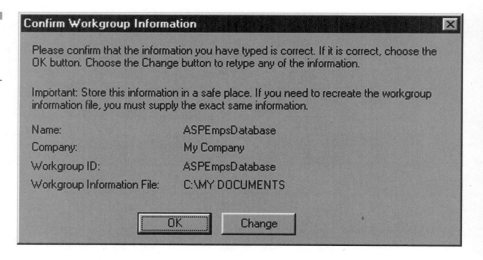

Confirm Workgroup Information

Please confirm that the information you have typed is correct. If it is correct, choose the OK button. Choose the Change button to retype any of the information.

Important: Store this information in a safe place. If you need to recreate the workgroup information file, you must supply the exact same information.

Name: ASPEmpsDatabase

Company: My Company

Workgroup ID: ASPEmpsDatabase

Workgroup Information File: C:\MY DOCUMENTS

OK   Change

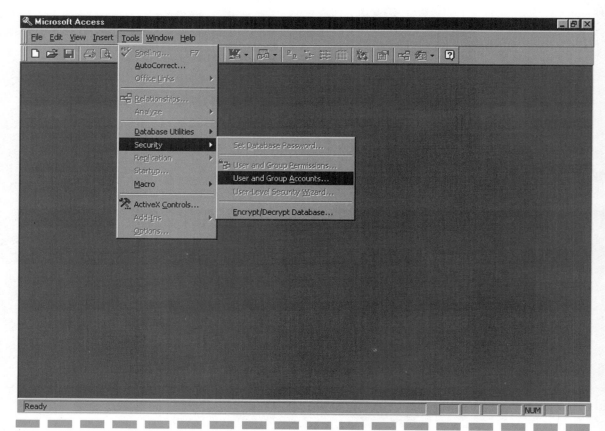

Figure 13-27   Accessing the User and Group Accounts menu option.

544

Step 2: Getting the Login Box to Appear

When you enter, Access security is on even though you don't log in. The reason a login box doesn't appear is that the default account that you are logging in through does not have a password, but in this step we will change that. Launch Access and don't open a database. Using the menu, select options Tools-Security-User and Group Accounts as shown in Figure 13-27.

Switch to the CHANGE LOGON PASSWORD tab as shown in Figure 13-28. The old password for the Admin account should be left blank. That is why you weren't required to log in to access before. Provide a new password for the Admin account and press the OK button. Now close Access and restart it. You should be prompted for a Name and Password. Supply the Admin for the name and the password you supplied for that account.

Step 3: Creating a New Admin

The default Admin through which you normally log in is an account available with every installation of Access. Even if you change the password in your own copy of the user database, like we did in the last step, someone can take your database and place it on a different computer and use the default Admin account without a password to access your database; so we need to create a new Admin.

Figure 13-28
Change Logon
Password dialog.

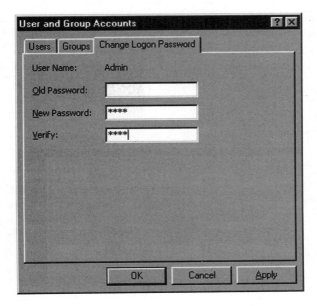

Figure 13-29
User dialog.

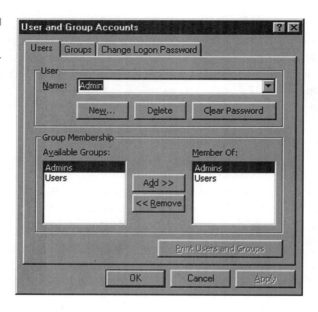

Launch Access and, again, don't open a database. From the menu, select options Tools-Security-User and Group Accounts. Select the USERS tab and you should see the dialog shown in Figure 13-29.

We need to add a new administrator, so press the NEW button. Supply the new administrator with a name and an identifier. The new administrator needs to belong to the Admins group. So, next highlight the Admins group in the Available Groups list and press the ADD button. Your new administrator account should look like the dialog shown in Figure 13-30. Press the OK button and the NewAdmin account is created.

The account, however, doesn't have a password since all new accounts are created without a password; so close Access and restart it. This time, log in as the new administrator that you just created and leave the password field blank—once again, don't open a database. Go straight to the Tools-Security-User and Group Accounts. Select the CHANGE LOGON PASSWORD tab and you should see that the current account is the NewAdmin account like that shown in Figure 13-31. For the old password, just leave it blank since this is a new user. Then supply a new password for the NewAdmin.

Figure 13-30
Creating the NewAdmin account.

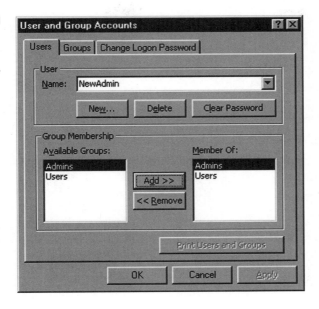

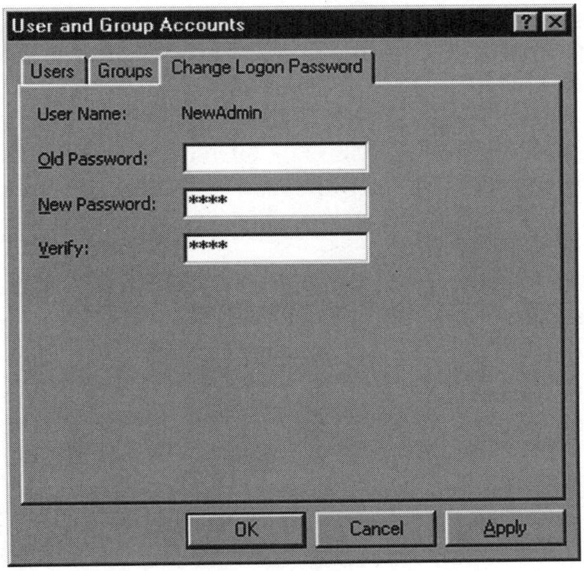

Figure 13-31
Supplying a password for the NewAdmin account.

Figure 13-32
Admin account not
belonging to the
Admins group.

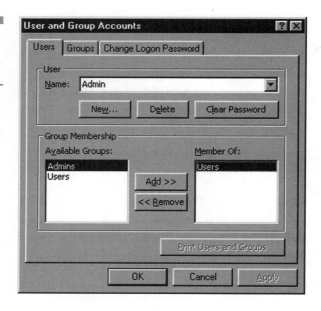

Figure 13-32
Admin account not
belonging to the
Admins group.

Step 4: Removing the Admin from the Admins Group

Unfortunately, you cannot just delete the original Admin account. However, you can remove the Admin from the Admins group so that the account won't be able to manage new databases.

Log in to the database as the NewAdmin account. Don't open a database; as before, just go to the Tools-Security-User and Group Accounts menu option. From the USERS tab, under name, select Admin. Then in the Member Of list, highlight the Admins group and click REMOVE. The Admin account should now look like that displayed in Figure 13-32.

Step 5: Taking Ownership of the Unsecured Database

Since the original database was created with the default Admin account in an unsecured environment, there is no way of removing ownership of that database from the Admin account; so, you need to create a new database and import all the objects from the unsecured database into the new database. Then, at some point, you may want to remove or delete the unsecured database.

Make sure you are logged in as the NewAdmin and create a new database. Then from the File menu, select options Get External Data-Import as shown in Figure 13-33. Then browse to the database

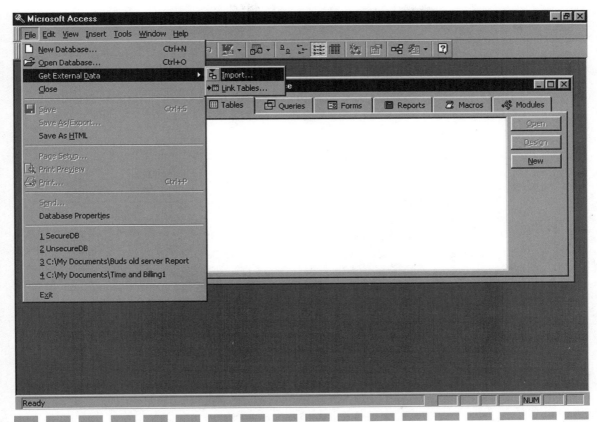

Figure 13-33 Importing data into the secured database.

that contains the unsecured data and objects. You will then be presented with the Import Objects dialog shown in Figure 13-34. From this dialog, select all the Tables, Queries, Forms, Reports, Macros, and Modules that you want to be part of your secured database. On the TABLES tab, make sure that you are importing the Definition and Data.

Step 6: Remove Privileges to the Secure Database

So far we have created a new administrator, assigned it to the Admins group and removed the Admin from the Admins group. We have created a secured database and imported objects into that database. But the Admin user is in the Users group, which still has privileges for this database—we need to remove those privileges.

Figure 13-34
Import Objects
dialog.

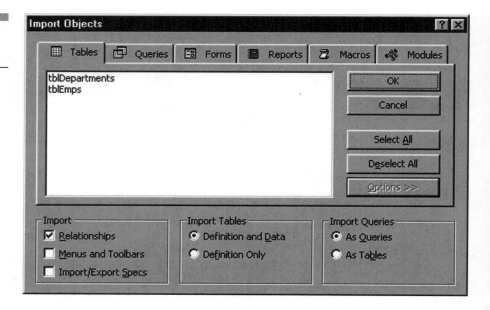

Figure 13-34
Import Objects
dialog.

Log in to Access as the NewAdmin and open the secured database. Now, from the menu select Tools-Security-User and Group Permissions as shown in Figure 13-35. Under List, select Groups. Then, in the User/Group Name list, select Users. Set the Object Type to Database and uncheck all the Permissions that are checked. Press the APPLY button and the dialog should now look like the one shown in Figure 13-36. The old Admin should now not be able to access this database.

To test your security, leave Access and reenter as the original Admin. Then try to open the newly secured database. You should get an error like the one displayed in Figure 13-37.

Step 7: Encrypting the Database

The database is now secure from entry, but one problem still remains. Access internally stores most of the data in the database as raw text, so someone could still easily see the contents of your database by looking at them through a text editor. The last step in securing the database is to *encrypt* it.

Log in to Access as the NewAdmin and open your secured database. From the menu, select Tools-Security-Encrypt/Decrypt Database as

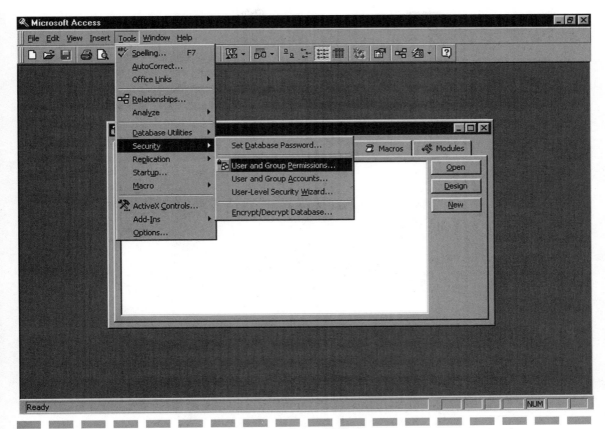

Figure 13-35 Selecting the User and Group Permissions menu option.

shown in Figure 13-38. Then browse to the database that you want to encrypt and then supply a name for the encrypted database.

Step 8: Additional Users

You now have a secure database that can be accessed by just a single user. You can stop there and then use the NewAdmin account to log in to the database through your Active Server Page applications. But you may want to create an additional Web user that has the specific privileges that will be needed by your code in the Active Server Page applications. For example, you may have some tables for which you only want to supply reading; or, you may have some tables to which you only want the Web site user to add records.

Figure 13-36
Users group with the
permission removed.

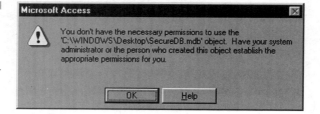

Figure 13-37
Error message
received by the
Admin user.

You would do this by creating a new user like you did with the NewAdmin; then give users permissions to the database and the specific permissions to the database, just like we did when we removed the permissions from the Admin user earlier in this section.

Creating a DSN for an Access Database

Just like with the SQL Server database, you will need to create an ODBC DSN for your Access database so it is accessible to your Active Server Page applications.

From the server, select the ODBC item listed in the Control Panel as shown in Figure 13-39. Switch to the SYSTEM DSN tab and you should see the dialog shown in Figure 13-40. Press the ADD button and you

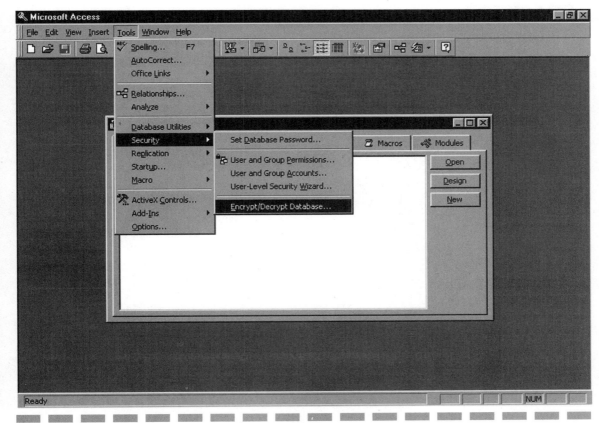

Figure 13-38 Selecting the Encrypt/Decrypt Database menu option.

Figure 13-39
Selecting the ODBC
Administrator.

Figure 13-40
System DSN tab of
the ODBC Data
Source Administrator.

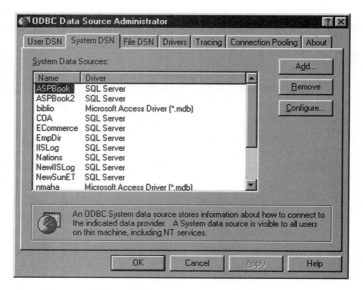

should see a list of drivers like those displayed in Figure 13-41. Select
the Microsoft Access Driver and press the FINISH button. Press the
OPTIONS button so you can see all the options as shown in Figure 13-42.

First, enter the Data Source Name. What you place here is important
because this is what you will use in code to specify the database to connect to. You can also supply a description, which is just for your own use.

Press the SELECT button next and browse to your secured database.
You also need to supply the database that contains the login information. You do this in the System Database part of the dialog. Change the
option to Database and then press the SYSTEM DATABASE button to

Figure 13-41
Creating a New Data
Source.

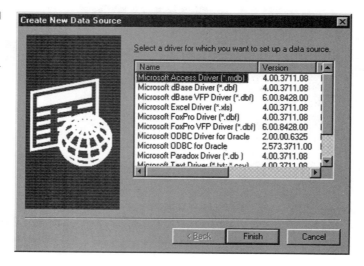

Figure 13-42
Setting the options
for the DSN.

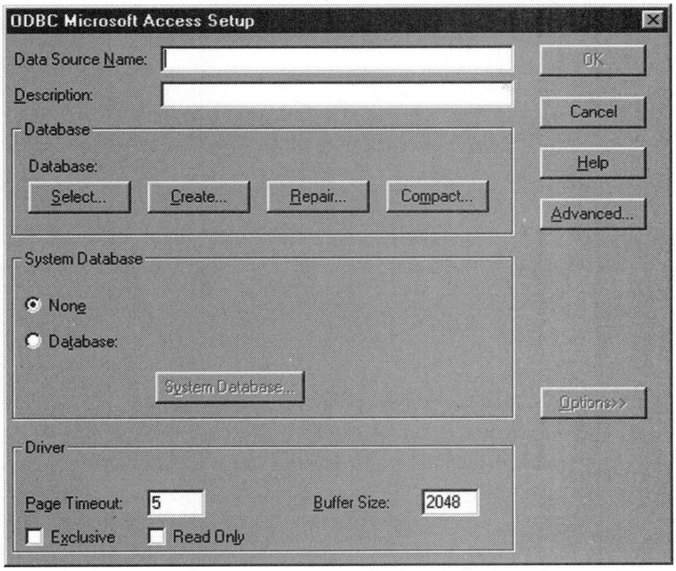

browse to the database you created that contains the login information
for your secured database.

The DSN options should now look like those displayed in Figure 13-43.
Press OK and your DSN for your Access should be complete. If you completed it correctly, you should now be able to connect to your Access database through your code.

Figure 13-43
Completed DSN
options.

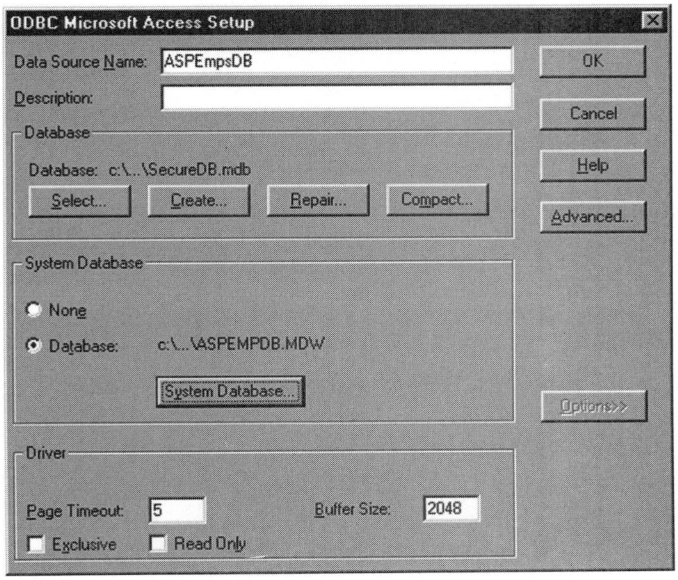

ADO

ActiveX Data Objects

The *ActiveX Data Objects library* provides the mechanism for you to connect to a database and to manipulate the data in the database. You can use the ActiveX Data Objects (ADO) library to view and browse through records in a database. You can also use the library to add, edit, and delete records from a database. In this chapter, we look at the different methods and properties of the objects in the ActiveX Data Objects library.

We have already used ADO in different examples throughout this book. In fact, you will find that without connecting to a database through ADO, or some other mechanism, the complexity of an Active Server Page application is limited. In Chapter 5, we looked at a page that would display the details of a product based on the data stored in a database. That code used ADO to connect to an SQL Server database and retrieve the information about the product. Let's take a closer look at that code:

```
<%
Option Explicit
Dim conn
Dim RSProduct
set conn = server.createobject ("adodb.connection")
conn.open "ASPBook", "sa", "yourpassword"
set RSProduct = conn.Execute("select * from Products where " _
  & "ProductID = " & Request.QueryString("ProductID"))
%>
```

First, we have the `Option Explicit` statement that tells the compiler that each of our variables and objects will be declared:

```
Option Explicit
```

The next object variable is used as a Connection object of the ADO library:

```
Dim conn
```

The RSProduct object is a Recordset object of the ADO library:

```
Dim RSProduct
```

Next, the CreateObject method is used to create the `Conn` variable as a Connection object:

```
set conn = server.createobject ("adodb.connection")
```

The Open method of the Connection object is used to connect to the database that is supplied through the ASPBook DSN. The second parameter indicates the user name to use in the connection and the third parameter indicates the password associated with that user name:

```
conn.open "ASPBook", "sa", "yourpassword"
```

The Execute method of the Connection object is used to return a Recordset object, which is placed in the variable RSProduct. An SQL statement that describes the record or records that are to be retrieved from the database is passed to the method.

```
set RSProduct = conn.Execute("select * from Products where " _
    & "ProductID = " & Request.QueryString("ProductID"))
```

So, with just a couple of objects and a couple of methods we are able to retrieve data from a database; however, the objects and collections of the ActiveX Data Objects library supply much more functionality.

Table 14-1 summarizes the collections and objects of the ADO library.

TABLE 14-1

ADO Objects and
Collections

Object/Collection	Purpose
Connection Object	Used to connect to a database.
Recordset Object	Returns records as the result of a query.
Fields Collection	All the field objects in a Recordset object.
Field Object	Used to access the data and properties of a specific field or column within a Recordset object.
Command Object	Used to execute a query or to manipulate a database. Can return a Recordset.
Parameters Collection	A collection of all the parameters contained in the Command object.
Parameter Object	Used to specify a value that is to be passed with the execution of a Command object like a Stored Procedure.
Errors Collection	A collection of all the Error objects generated when an action fails in the ADO library.
Error Object	Contains information about a single error that was generated when an action failed in the ADO library.

Connection Object

A *Connection object,* which contains a variety of properties and methods for connecting to a database and the behavior of that connection, is created using the CreateObject method of the Server object:

```
set Conn = Server.CreateObject("ADODB.Connection")
```

The Application/Class string, ADODB.Connection, is passed to the CreateObject method, and a valid instance of the Connection object is returned from the method.

Connection Object Properties

The properties of the Connection are summarized in Table 14-2. When we look at methods of the Connection object you will see that a transaction allows you to make modifications to a database in bulk. In other

TABLE 14-2

Connection Object Properties

Property	Purpose
Attributes	Stores information about what happens when a transaction ends or begins.
CommandTimeOut	Stores the number of seconds that a command can run without completing.
ConnectionString	Connect string that describes how to connect to a database.
ConnectionTimeOut	Specifies the amount of time in seconds that a connection can take to complete without timing out.
CursorLocation	Allows you to specify where the data in a recordset are stored, either on the client end or the server.
DefaultDatabase	Used to set or return the name of the default database used in the connection object.
IsolationLevel	Used to indicate how data in different transactions are viewed.
Mode	Indicates the modifications allowed to data through this connection.
Provider	Indicates the database provider for the connection.
State	Returns whether a connection is open or closed.
Version	Returns the Version number of the ActiveX Data Objects library.

words, you can decide to add a record to one table and delete one from another and have only the changes to both tables occur together. If something were to go wrong, and the record from the one table could not be deleted, then the record in the other table would not be added to the database. The Attributes property is used for some database servers to indicate whether a new transaction should be started after one is complete or aborted.

The property is read/write and has the following syntax:

```
Conn.Attributes = NewValue
```

Conn must be a valid instance of a Connection object. The new attributes are returned or set to the value. If you wanted a transaction to start automatically after one completed, you would set the property to this value:

```
Conn.Attributes = 131072
```

If you wanted a new transaction to start after one was canceled, you would code this:

```
Conn.Attributes = 262144
```

and if you wanted both attributes for the transaction set, you would add the numbers together and code this:

```
Conn.Attributes = 393216
```

When you create a Recordset, you do it by executing some command, either through the Connection object or through the Command object. Sometimes a query can take a long time to complete. You can modify how long you will allow a command to execute before it times out using the CommandTimeOut property.

This read/write property stores the amount of time in seconds and has the following syntax:

```
Conn.CommandTimeout = NumSeconds
```

Conn must be a valid instance of a connection object. The number of seconds a connection can run without timing out is returned or set to the property. In the next code block the default of the property is written to the browser and is then changed.

```
<%
Option Explicit
Dim conn
set conn = server.createobject ("adodb.connection")
conn.open "ASPBook", "sa", "yourpassword"
Response.Write "<B>The default time out value is: " & Conn.Command
  Timeout _
  & " seconds.<P>"
conn.CommandTimeout = 60
Response.Write "It has been changed to: " & Conn.CommandTimeout _
  & " seconds.<P>"
%>
```

First, Option Explicit is noted:

```
Option Explicit
```

Then a variable that will store a connection object is created:

```
Dim conn
```

and instantiated to a Connection object:

```
set conn = server.createobject ("adodb.connection")
```

A connection to a database is opened:

```
conn.open "ASPBook", "sa", "yourpassword"
```

The default value for the property is written to the browser:

```
Response.Write "<B>The default time out value is: " &
  Conn.CommandTimeout _
  & " seconds.<P>"
```

The value of the property is modified to 1 minute:

```
conn.CommandTimeout = 60
```

and that value is written to the browser:

```
Response.Write "It has been changed to: " & Conn.CommandTimeout _
  & " seconds.<P>"
```

The output of this code is displayed in Figure 14-1.

Thus far we have specified which database and server we want to connect to, as well as who we are, through the open method of the

Figure 14-1
Output of
CommandTimeOut
property code.

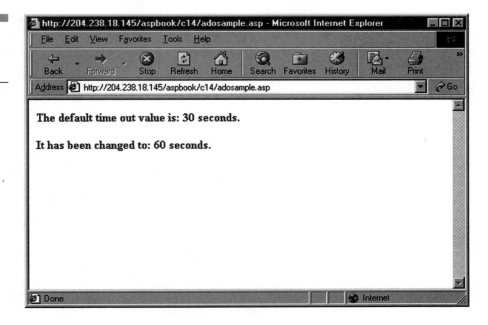

Connection object:

```
conn.open "ASPBook", "sa", "yourpassword"
```

But we don't have to use a DSN. We can supply a connect string that specifies all the information ADO needs to connect to a database. This is done through the ConnectionString property, which has the following syntax:

```
Conn.ConnectionString = ConnectStringText
```

Conn must be a valid instance of a Connection object. The string passed to the property contains a list of parameters needed to make the connection complete, as shown here:

```
conn.ConnectionString = "driver={SQL Server};" & _
  "server=NameOfServer;uid=sa;pwd=yourpassword;database=Database
    InServer"
```

Notice the different parameters supplied in the connection string. The first is the type of server to which you want to connect. The second parameter is the name or IP Address of the server. Then you supply the user name for the connection as well as the password. The last parameter in this connection string is the name of the database in the server.

Once the ConnectionString property is set, you still need to call the Open method:

```
conn.ConnectionString = "driver={SQL Server};" & _
"server=NameOfServer;uid=sa;pwd=yourpassword;database=Database
  InServer"
conn.open
```

If you specify connection information through the Open method, the ConnectionString property is not used.

You can set how long a Connection object should attempt to connect to a database with the ConnectionTimeOut property, which has the following syntax:

```
Conn.ConnectionTimeOut = NumSeconds
```

Conn must be a valid instance of the Connection object. The property is read/write and contains the number of seconds that the Connection object should attempt to connect to a database before timing out and throwing an error. The property must be set before the Open method of the Connection object is called. The default value for this property is 15 seconds.

When ADO is described, the term *cursor* is often used, where a cursor represents data from a database. Attributes of a cursor determine what actions can be taken on the data and where the data are stored as the cursor remains open. The CursorLocation property stores where the data in a recordset will be located.

This read/write property of the Connection object has the following syntax:

```
Conn.CursorLocation = LocationValue
```

Conn must be a valid instance of a Connection object. If you set the property to the value 2, then the cursor is located on the server; if you set the value of the CursorLocation property to 3, the cursor is located on the client.

The DefaultDatabase property indicates the name of the database opened through the Open method. The method has the following syntax:

```
DBName = Conn.DefaultDatabase
```

Conn must be a valid instance of the Connection object. Stored in the property is a string corresponding to the default database. Take a look at this sample code:

```
<%
Option Explicit
Dim conn
set conn = server.createobject ("adodb.connection")
conn.open "ASPBook", "sa", "yourpassword"
Response.Write "<B>The name of the default database in this SQL
 Server " _
  connection is: " & Conn.DefaultDatabase
conn.close
conn.open "EmpsDatabase", "Admin", ""
Response.Write "<P>The name of the default database in this
 Microsoft Access " _
  & connection is: " & Conn.DefaultDatabase
%>
```

First, `Option Explicit` is noted for the compiler:

```
Option Explicit
```

Then a variable called `Conn` is declared:

```
Dim conn
```

The variable is set to a Connection object:

```
set conn = server.createobject ("adodb.connection")
```

A connection to an SQL Server database is opened:

```
conn.open "ASPBook", "sa", "yourpassword"
```

The name of the database opened through the DSN ASPBook is written to the browser:

```
Response.Write "<B>The name of the default database in this SQL
 Server " _
  connection is: " & Conn.DefaultDatabase
```

The Close method is used to disconnect from the database:

```
conn.close
```

Now a connection is made to an unsecured Access database:

```
conn.open "EmpsDatabase", "Admin", ""
```

The name of the Access database opened through this connection is written to the browser:

```
Response.Write "<P>The name of the default database in this
   Microsoft Access " _
& connection is: " & Conn.DefaultDatabase
```

The output of this code is displayed in Figure 14-2. Notice that the path is included for the Access database.

The *IsolationLevel* property is used to indicate what the view of the data is across more than one transaction. The Read/Write property has the following syntax:

```
Conn.IsolationLevel = NewValue
```

Conn must be a valid instance of a Connection object. The property returns or sets the numeric value for the isolation. The possible values are indicated in Table 14-3.

The *Mode* property of the Connection object is used to indicate how the database should be opened, that is, read, write, or both. It is also

Figure 14-2
Output of
DefaultDatabase
sample code.

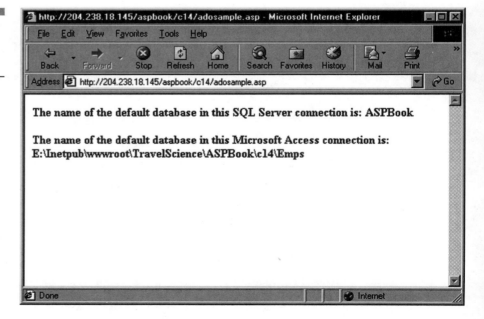

TABLE 14-3

IsolationLevel
Values

IsolationLevel	Purpose
-1	The isolation level cannot be determined.
16	Isolated transactions cannot be overwritten.
256	Changes in one transaction are visible in another transaction.
4096	Changes in other transactions are viewable only after a transaction is committed.
65536	Must rerun a query to see changes made in other transactions.
1048576	Transactions are completed isolated from other transactions.

used to indicate what restrictions should be placed on additional connections to the database.

The Read/Write property has the following syntax:

```
Conn.Mode = Value
```

Conn must be a valid instance of a Connection object. Possible values for this property are specified in Table 14-4.

The *Provider* property indicates the database service used to connect to the database. The property is read/write and has the following syntax:

```
TheProvider = Conn.Provider
```

Conn must be a valid Connection object. A string that stores the name of the provider used in the connection is returned from the property.

TABLE 14-4

Mode Property
Values

IsolationLevel	Purpose
0	Unknown value for the property.
1	The connection is opened for Read only.
2	The connection is opened for Write only.
3	The connection is opened for Read/Write.
4	Deny others from opening a Read only conneciton.
8	Deny others from opening a Write only conneciton.
12	Deny any other connections to the database.
16	Deny other connections to the database with any permissions set.

The *State* property returns a value indicating whether the connection is opened or closed. A value of 1 is returned if the connection is open and a value of 0 is returned if the connection is closed. The property has the following syntax:

```
TheValue = Conn.State
```

Conn must be an instance of the Connection object, and the value 0 or 1 is returned. The following code block displays the value of the State property while the connection is open and closed.

```
<%
Option Explicit
Dim conn
set conn = server.createobject ("adodb.connection")
Response.Write "<B>The current state of the connection is: " &
  Conn.State
conn.open "ASPBook", "sa", "yourpassword"
Response.Write "<P>The current state of the connection is: " &
  Conn.State
conn.close
Response.Write "<P>The current state of the connection is: " &
  Conn.State
%>
```

First, the `Option Explicit` line is written:

```
Option Explicit
```

Then a connection object is created:

```
Dim conn
```

and instantiated:

```
set conn = server.createobject ("adodb.connection")
```

The initial state of the connection is written to the browser:

```
Response.Write "<B>The current state of the connection is: " &
  Conn.State
```

The connection is opened:

```
conn.open "ASPBook", "sa", "yourpassword"
```

and the state of the connection is written:

```
Response.Write "<P>The current state of the connection is: " &
    Conn.State
```

The connection to the database is closed:

```
conn.close
```

Again, the connection state is written to the browser:

```
Response.Write "<P>The current state of the connection is: " &
    Conn.State
```

The output of the code is displayed in Figure 14-3.

The *Version* property of the connection object returns the version of the ActiveX Data Objects library. The property has the following syntax:

```
TheValue = Conn.Version
```

Conn must be a valid Connection object. The full version of the ActiveX Data Objects library is returned from the property.

Connection Object Methods

The methods of the Connection object, which allow you to open and manage connections, are summarized in Table 14-5. A *transaction* refers

Figure 14-3
Output of State property sample code.

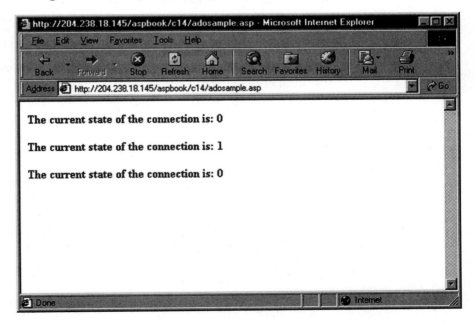

TABLE 14-5

Connection Object
Methods

Method	Purpose
BeginTrans	Initiates a transaction.
CommitTrans	Saves the changes made in a transaction to the database.
RollbackTrans	Undoes the changes made in a transaction.
Close	Closes a connection to a database.
Open	Opens a connection to a database.
Execute	Runs an SQL statement against a database.

to a group of actions that are taken. In database work, we group together actions on a database in a transaction. When we do that, we can then commit all the changes to a database at the same time and have assurance that all the changes will succeed or fail as a group.

Think about a situation in a database where your code is being used to transfer money from one bank account to another. One account will have a debit record added to the database, the other a credit record. But both actions on the database must occur together. You can't have the debit occurring without the credit and vice versa. Another example would involve products in an inventory. You want to remove a product from inventory and place it with a customer's order. You don't want either of these to occur without the other.

The Connection object provides three methods you can use to control this kind of behavior: BeginTrans, CommitTrans, and RollBackTrans.

You use the *BeginTrans* method of the Connection to indicate that you want to start a transaction. The method has the following syntax:

```
Conn.BeginTrans
```

Conn must be a valid Connection object. The Connection object must be open before the BeginTrans method is called.

Once the transaction has started, all changes to the database are buffered until you either call the *CommitTrans* method or the RollBackTrans method is used. If you use the CommitTrans method, then all the pending changes are made as a single change to the database. The method has the following syntax:

```
Conn.CommitTrans
```

Conn must be an instance of the Connection object. If your code dictates that the changes made to the database should be undone, then you can use the *RollBackTrans* method, which discards any changes in the buffer that were made within the scope of the current transaction through the current Connection object.

The method has the following syntax:

```
Conn.RollBackTrans
```

Conn must be a valid instance of a Connection object.

The next code block uses the three transaction methods.

```
<%
Option Explicit
Dim conn
Dim RS
set conn = server.createobject ("adodb.connection")
conn.open "AspBook", "sa", "yourpassword"
set RS = conn.execute("select * from tblEmps where LastName =
  'Doe'" _
  & " and FirstName = 'Jane'")
If RS.EOF Then
   Response.Write "<P>No Jane Doe in the database."
Else
  Response.Write "<P>Jane Doe was found!"
End If
conn.close
conn.open "AspBook", "sa", "yourpassword"
conn.BeginTrans
conn.execute "insert into tblEmps (FirstName, LastName) values (" _
  & "'Jane', 'Doe')"
conn.RollBackTrans
set RS = conn.execute("select * from tblEmps where LastName =
  'Doe'" _
  & " and FirstName = 'Jane'")
If RS.EOF Then
   Response.Write "<P>No Jane Doe in the database."
Else
  Response.Write "<P>Jane Doe was found!"
End If
conn.close
conn.open "AspBook", "sa", "yourpassword"
conn.BeginTrans
conn.execute "insert into tblEmps (FirstName, LastName) values (" _
  & "'Jane', 'Doe')"
conn.CommitTrans
set RS = conn.execute("select * from tblEmps where LastName =
  'Doe'" _
  & " and FirstName = 'Jane'")
If RS.EOF Then
   Response.Write "<P>No Jane Doe in the database."
Else
  Response.Write "<P>Jane Doe was found!"
End If
%>
```

First, the code specifies the `Option  Explicit` compiler option variable:

```
Option Explicit
```

Then one variable is declared that will store the Connection object:

```
Dim conn
```

Another variable will be used as a Recordset object:

```
Dim RS
```

Next, the Connection object is instantiated:

```
set conn = server.createobject ("adodb.connection")
```

and a Connection to a database is established:

```
conn.open "AspBook", "sa", "yourpassword"
```

Next, a Recordset object that contains a specific record from the employee table is returned:

```
set RS = conn.execute("select * from tblEmps where LastName =
    'Doe'" _
  & " and FirstName = 'Jane'")
```

That Employee record should not exist yet, since it will be added within a transaction. The code here verifies that it doesn't exist by checking the EOF property. If the Employee record does not exist, then the Recordset contains no records and EOF is True:

```
If RS.EOF Then
    Response.Write "<P>No Jane Doe in the database."
Else
    Response.Write "<P>Jane Doe was found!"
End If
```

We then close the Connection object:

```
conn.close
```

and reopen it:

```
conn.open "AspBook", "sa", "yourpassword"
```

The BeginTrans method is used to start a transaction:

```
conn.BeginTrans
```

An Employee record for Jane Doe is added to the database:

```
conn.execute "insert into tblEmps (FirstName, LastName) values (" _
& "'Jane', 'Doe')"
```

But since we are in a transaction, the record is not committed to the database. It is at this point that we use the RollBackTrans method to discard the Insert of the record into the tblEmps database:

```
conn.RollBackTrans
```

Here, we attempt to retrieve the Employee record for this employee:

```
set RS = conn.execute("select * from tblEmps where LastName =
  'Doe'" _
& " and FirstName = 'Jane'")
```

But since we discarded the database changes, the record should not be found and EOF should be True:

```
If RS.EOF Then
   Response.Write "<P>No Jane Doe in the database."
Else
  Response.Write "<P>Jane Doe was found!"
End If
```

The Connection to the database is closed:

```
conn.close
```

and then reopened:

```
conn.open "AspBook", "sa", "yourpassword"
```

Another transaction is started using the BeginTrans method:

```
conn.BeginTrans
```

and the Employee record is inserted into the database:

```
conn.execute "insert into tblEmps (FirstName, LastName) values (" _
& "'Jane', 'Doe')"
```

The CommitTrans method is used to apply the changes made within this transaction through this Connection object to the database:

```
conn.CommitTrans
```

Again, we attempt to retrieve the Employee record from the database:

```
set RS = conn.execute("select * from tblEmps where LastName =
   'Doe'"
 & " and FirstName = 'Jane'")
```

This time EOF should be False since the record was added to the database, so the code in the `Else` portion of the `If` statement should run:

```
If RS.EOF Then
   Response.Write "<P>No Jane Doe in the database."
Else
  Response.Write "<P>Jane Doe was found!"
End If
```

The output of this code is displayed in Figure 14-4.

Figure 14-4
Output of sample code using the transaction methods.

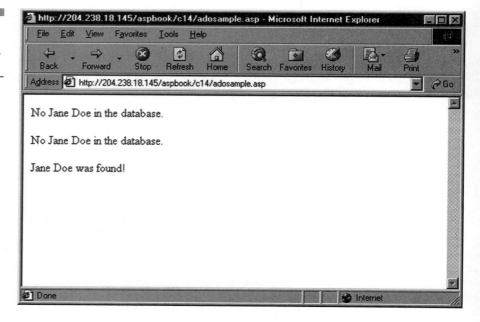

The *Close* method of the Connection object provides the mechanism for disconnecting a Connection object from a database. The method has the following syntax:

```
Conn.Close
```

Conn must be a valid instance of a Connection object.

As you have seen, the *Open* method is used to open a connection to the database. The Open method of the Connection object can be called without parameters if the ConnectionString property is set first:

```
Conn.ConnectionString = "driver={SQL Server};" & _
"server=NameOfServer;uid=sa;pwd=yourpassword;database=Database
  InServer"
Conn.Open
```

or the method can be called with the connection information as part of the call:

```
Conn.Open DSN, UserName, Password, Options
```

Conn must be a valid instance of a Connection object. All the parameters are optional; the first parameter of the Open method is the DSN to which you want to connect; the second parameter is the user name to log in to the database as; the third parameter is the password for that user; and the fourth parameter is used for additional options.

We have also used the Execute method of the Connection object in the code samples in this chapter and other chapters of this book. The Execute method runs a query, stored procedure, or some other database provider function. The method has the following syntax:

```
Conn.Execute SQLText, NumRecordsAffected, Options
```

The Conn object must be a valid instance of a Connection object. Only the first parameter is required and that parameter is the SQL passed that is to be run. The second parameter stores the number of records that were affected by the query. The last parameter stores options that can be passed to the database provider. Some of the values for this parameter are summarized in Table 14-6.

The Execute method can return nothing with an action query:

```
conn.execute "insert into tblEmps (FirstName, LastName) values (" _
& "'Jane', 'Doe')"
```

TABLE 14-6

Options for the
Execute Method

Option	Purpose
1	The SQLText parameter passed in should be evaluated as text.
2	The SQLText parameter is the name of a table and the table should be returned.
4	The SQLText being passed in is a stored procedure.
8	The command in the SQLText parameter is unknown.

or it can return a Recordset object:

```
set RS = conn.execute("select * from tblEmps where LastName =
   'Doe'" _
& " and FirstName = 'Jane'")
```

The following block uses the Execute method to update some records in a database. The number of records affected by the update are written to the browser. The code also uses the Execute method to return a Recordset object.

```
<%
Option Explicit
Dim conn
Dim RSEmps
Dim NumRecordsModified
set conn = server.createobject ("adodb.connection")
conn.open "AspBook", "sa", "yourpassword"
conn.Execute "Update tblEmps set LastName = 'Smith'", NumRecords
   Modified
Response.Write "The update query affected " & NumRecordsModified
   & " records."
set RSEmps = conn.execute("Select EmpID, LastName from tblEmps")
Do Until RSEmps.EOF
   Response.Write "<P>Employee ID: " & RSEmps("EmpID") _
      & "<BR>Last Name: " & RSEmps("LastName")
   RSEmps.MoveNext
Loop
%>
```

First, Option Explicit is noted:

```
Option Explicit
```

Then a variable to store a Connection object is created:

```
Dim conn
```

and one to store a Recordset object:

```
Dim RSEmps
```

This third variable will store the number of records modified by a query:

```
Dim NumRecordsModified
```

The Connection object is instantiated:

```
set conn = server.createobject ("adodb.connection")
```

The Open method is used to open a connection to a database:

```
conn.open "AspBook", "sa", "yourpassword"
```

Here the Execute method of the Connection object is used to run an Update query. The number of records changed by the query is placed in the second parameter of the Execute method:

```
conn.Execute "Update tblEmps set LastName = 'Smith'", NumRecords
   Modified
```

That value is written to the browser:

```
Response.Write "The update query affected " & NumRecordsModified _
   & " records."
```

Now the Execute method is used to return a Recordset object:

```
set RSEmps = conn.execute("Select EmpID, LastName from tblEmps")
```

The code then loops through all the records, displaying that the records were correctly updated in the preceding Update query.

```
Do Until RSEmps.EOF
   Response.Write "<P>Employee ID: " & RSEmps("EmpID") _
      & "<BR>Last Name: " & RSEmps("LastName")
   RSEmps.MoveNext
Loop
```

The output of this code is displayed in Figure 14-5.

Figure 14-5
Output of Execute
method code.

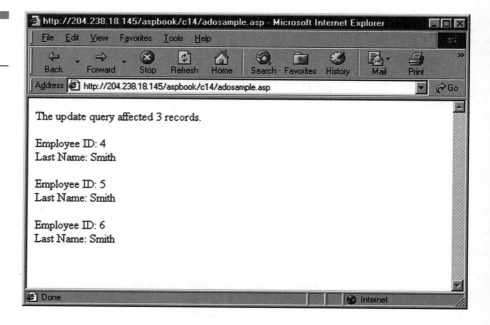

Recordset Object

Most of what you will want to do on your Web pages with ActiveX Data Objects can be done through the Connection object and the Recordset object. As you saw in the last section, the Connection object is used to connect to a database and to execute stored procedures and queries against the database. The Recordset object is used to browse through data returned from the Execute method of the Connection object, like this:

```
set RSEmps = conn.execute("Select EmpID, LastName from tblEmps")
```

Here, RSEmps is a Recordset object that contains all the records from the tblEmps table and only the EmpID and LastName fields from that table.

The records in a Recordset object are contained in three regions as shown in Figure 14-6. The Recordset is made up of the Beginning of File (BOF) region, the records themselves, and the End of File (EOF) region. The current record is the record we are currently working with, which is sometimes referred to as the *record pointer*. The current record can be any of the records, or it can be the BOF and EOF regions. In fact, if you open a recordset with no records, the record pointer will be pointing to both the BOF and the EOF.

Figure 14-6
Three regions of the
records.

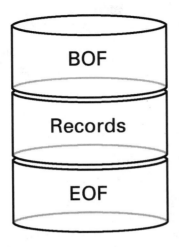

Recordset Object Properties

The Recordset object contains a variety of properties that are summarized in Table 14-7.

In ADO terms, a page of data is a logical division of records: a *page* is one or more records and that division is carried out through all the records in the recordset. So if you decide that the page size for the Recordset object should be 4 and you have 25 records then you have 7 pages of data. The first six pages have the full four records and the last page has just a single record. Pages allow you to jump ahead or back in the recordset at predictable points.

The Recordset object has three properties you can use to manipulate how the page size is configured and used. These properties are the AbsolutePage, PageCount, and PageSize.

The *AbsolutePage* property can be used to jump to a specific page or to report what the current page number is. The property has the following syntax:

```
RS.AbsolutePage = PageNumber
```

or

```
PageNumber = RS.AbsolutePage
```

RS must be a valid instance of a Recordset object. The current page number is set to or returned from the property. If you set the

TABLE 14-7

Recordset Object
Properties

Property	Purpose
AbsolutePage	Specifies the current page number for the current record.
PageCount	Number of pages within the recordset.
PageSize	Number of records on a single page.
AbsolutePosition	Specifies the sequential number for the current record.
ActiveConnection	Specifies the Connection object through which the Recordset was created.
BOF/EOF	Boolean properties indicating whether the record pointer is before or after the record region.
Bookmark	Used to return to a specific record after further navigation and modification has been performed within a Recordset object.
CacheSize	Number of records cached at one time in memory.
CursorLocation	Client/Server location of the records in the recordset.
CursorType	The type of cursor used in the Recordset object.
EditMode	Indicates whether an edit is currently being made.
Filter	Allows you to filter records out of the Recordset object.
Sort	Specifies the sorting to be done on a recordset.
LockType	The data locking currently in place with the recordset.
MaxRecords	Maximum number of records to return into a recordset.
RecordCount	Number of records in a Recordset object.
Source	Specifies the SQL text used to create the Recordset object.

AbsolutePage property, then the record pointer within the Recordset object moves to the first record on that page.

You can set or retrieve the number of records on a page with the *PageSize* property. This read/write property has the following syntax:

```
RS.PageSize = PageSize
```

or

```
PageSize = RS.PageSize
```

RS must be a Recordset object. If you modify this property, then the total number of pages will be recalculated based on the value.

You can find out how many pages there are in the Recordset with the *PageCount* property, which is read-only and returns the total number of pages in a Recordset object. The property has the following syntax:

```
PageCount = RS.PageCount
```

RS must be a valid instance of a Recordset object.

One of the places these properties are useful is with a page where you have too many results from a query to place on a single Web page. You see this often on search engines where each result page has a specific number of matches. In the following example, the page properties of the Recordset object are used to display employee names from an employee table.

```
<%
Option Explicit
Dim ConnectString
Dim CurrentPage
Dim RSEmps
Dim I
If IsEmpty(Request.QueryString("PageNumber")) Then
  CurrentPage = 1
Else
  CurrentPage = cint(Request.QueryString("PageNumber"))
End If
ConnectString = "DSN=EmpsDatabase;User Id=Admin;Password=;"
set RSEmps = Server.CreateObject("ADODB.Recordset")
RSEmps.CursorLocation = 3
RSEmps.Open "tblEmps", ConnectString, , , 2
RSEmps.PageSize = 3
RSEmps.AbsolutePage = CurrentPage
Do Until RSEmps.AbsolutePage <> CurrentPage or RSEmps.EOF
  Response.Write RSEmps("LastName") & ", " & RSEmps("FirstName") _
    & "<P>"
  RSEmps.MoveNext
Loop
Response.Write "Select page to view more employee records: "
For I = 1 to RSEmps.PageCount
  Response.Write "<A HREF=""./adosample.asp?PageNumber=" & I _
    & """>" & I & "</A> "
Next
%>
```

First, we specify that we will declare our variables:

```
Option Explicit
```

One variable will hold the text of the connect string:

```
Dim ConnectString
```

The next variable will store the value of the current page that needs to be viewed:

```
Dim CurrentPage
```

A variable that will store the Recordset object is created:

```
Dim RSEmps
```

Next, a variable that will be used to iterate through a `For...Next` structure is declared:

```
Dim I
```

The first time the visitor enters the Active Server Page we will set the current page number in the Recordset object to 1. We can tell if this is the first entrance to the page by looking for the PageNumber field in the QueryString collection, which is passed with any other page besides the initial viewing of the page. If the QueryString variable was not passed, then we set the current page to 1:

```
If IsEmpty(Request.QueryString("PageNumber")) Then
  CurrentPage = 1
```

otherwise, the current page is set to the one requested by the visitor:

```
Else
  CurrentPage = cint(Request.QueryString("PageNumber"))
End If
```

Next, we set the string variable `ConnectString` to the connection information needed to connect to the database. The connection is to an Access database with a Data Source Name of EmpsDatabase:

```
ConnectString = "DSN=EmpsDatabase;User Id=Admin;Password=;"
```

Then the `RSEmps` variable is instantiated as a Recordset object using the CreateObject method of the Server object:

```
set RSEmps = Server.CreateObject("ADODB.Recordset")
```

The location of the records is set to the client-side:

```
RSEmps.CursorLocation = 3
```

The Open method of the Recordset object, which is discussed in the next section of this chapter, is used to open a table directly:

```
RSEmps.Open "tblEmps", ConnectString, , , 2
```

The PageSize method is used to set the number of records on a page to 3:

```
RSEmps.PageSize = 3
```

The record pointer is then moved to the first record of the current page:

```
RSEmps.AbsolutePage = CurrentPage
```

Next, we enter a loop where we will display all the records on the current page or until we run out of records as defined by hitting the EOF (end of file) region:

```
Do Until RSEmps.AbsolutePage <> CurrentPage or RSEmps.EOF
```

Within the loop, the name of the employee is written to the browser:

```
Response.Write RSEmps("LastName") & ", " & RSEmps("FirstName") _
    & "<P>"
```

before we move on to the next record:

```
    RSEmps.MoveNext
Loop
```

After the page of data is written to the browser, we want to set up links for visitors to click on for all the pages within this recordset:

```
Response.Write "Select page to view more employee records: "
```

A For...Next block is used to iterate through numbers from 1 to the count of pages in the Recordset object:

```
For I = 1 to RSEmps.PageCount
```

A link is then written to the browser that links back to this page, passing back in the page number of the data that should be viewed:

```
Response.Write "<A HREF=""./adosample.asp?PageNumber=" & I _
    & """>" & I & "</A> "
```

before moving on to the next number:

```
Next
```

Figure 14-7
Initial Web page from
page properties sam-
ple code.

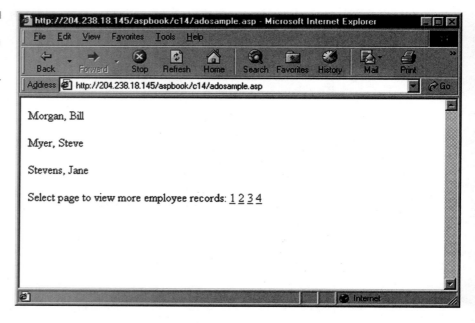

When visitors first enter the page they see what is displayed in Figure 14-7. Notice that three names are listed on the page. That is because we set the PageSize property to 3. Also notice that there are links to four pages in all. The table has ten records so the first three pages have three records and the last page has a single record.

If visitors were to click on the link to the second page they would see the page displayed in Figure 14-8. Notice again that three names are displayed. Also notice that the link in the Address box displayed the QueryString field for the PageNumber. This is how the single page displays the different pages of data.

Figure 14-9 shows what is displayed with the last page of data. The last page contains just a single record, since that page of data starts at the tenth record and there are a total of ten records.

The *AbsolutePosition* property of the Recordset object returns the exact position of the current record within the recordset. The property has the following syntax:

```
ThePosition = RS.AbsolutePosition
```

RS must be a valid Recordset object. The exact numeric position of the current record within the Recordset object is returned from the property.

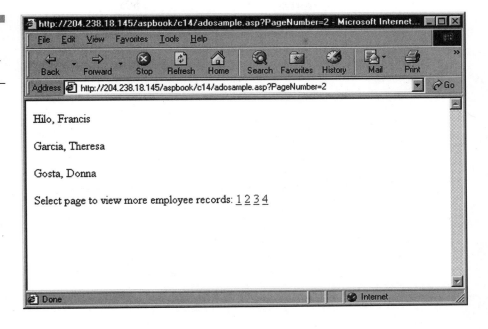

Figure 14-8
Second page from sample page properties site.

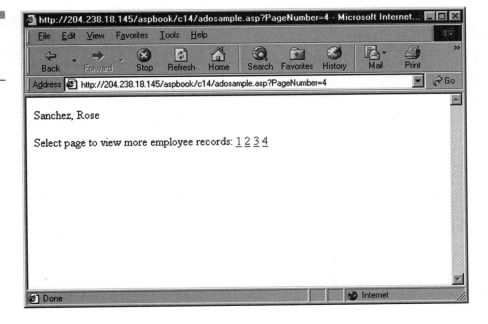

Figure 14-9
Last page of data from the sample page properties site.

This value is based, not on the position of the record within the table, but on the position of the record within the recordset. So we could modify the loop in our previous code example so that the record number is printed with the listing in the browser:

```
Do Until RSEmps.AbsolutePage <> CurrentPage or RSEmps.EOF
   Response.Write RSEmps.AbsolutePosition & ": " _
      & RSEmps("LastName") & ", " & RSEmps("FirstName") _
      & "<P>"
   RSEmps.MoveNext
Loop
```

The output in the browser with the record number included is displayed in Figure 14-10.

If you use the Execute method of a Connection object to return a Recordset object, you can use the ActiveConnection property of the Recordset object to retrieve extended information about how the connection was made. The ActiveConnection property has the following syntax:

```
ConnInfo = RS.ActiveConnection
```

RS must be a valid instance of a Recordset object. The text of this property, based on a connection to an Access database, is displayed in Figure 14-11.

Figure 14-10
Output of code using the AbsolutePosition property.

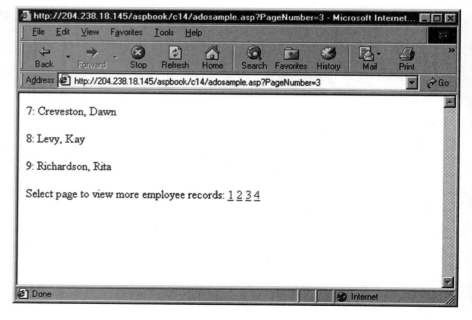

Figure 14-11
Output of the
ActiveConnection
property with an
Access database.

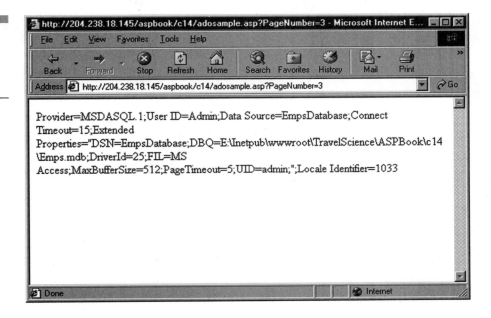

The *BOF* property and the *EOF* property report to you whether you are on the beginning of the file region or the end of the file region, respectively. The BOF region is where the record pointer points if you move the record pointer before the first record; the EOF region is the area after the last record. These Boolean read-only properties have the following syntax:

```
BOFValue = RS.BOF
EOFValue = RS.EOF
```

RS must be an instance of the Recordset object. The value True or False is returned from the properties, indicating whether you are on one of these regions.

One important use of these properties is testing for an empty Recordset. If your query did not return records, both EOF and BOF will be set to True, so you will frequently see code like this:

```
<%
Option Explicit
Dim Conn
Dim RSVisitor
set conn = server.createobject ("adodb.connection")
conn.open "EmpsDatabase", "Admin", ""
set RSVisitor = conn.execute("select VisitorID from Visitors
  where " _
```

```
     & "UserName = '" & Request.Form("UserName") & "' and " _
     & "Password = '" & Request.Form("Password") & "'")
If RSVisitor.EOF Then
  'Invalid log in
Else
  'Valid log in
End If
%>
```

First, we specify `Option Explicit` for the compiler:

```
Option Explicit
```

Then a variable to store a connection to the database is created:

```
Dim Conn
```

as is one for the Recordset object:

```
Dim RSVisitor
```

Next, the Connection object is instantiated:

```
set conn = server.createobject ("adodb.connection")
```

The Open method is used to connect to a database:

```
conn.open "EmpsDatabase", "Admin", ""
```

Here a query attempts to find a record based on the login information supplied by the visitor through the Form fields collection of the Request object:

```
set RSVisitor = conn.execute("select VisitorID from Visitors
  where " _
  & "UserName = '" & Request.Form("UserName") & "' and " _
  & "Password = '" & Request.Form("Password") & "'")
```

If a record was not found, then the visitor entered an invalid entry and the EOF property will be True. Note that we also could have used the BOF property:

```
If RSVisitor.EOF Then
  'Invalid log in
```

The `Else` portion of the `If` statement means that the login was valid. Since EOF was False, there must be a record. The only way the

Recordset can contain a record is if the visitor supplied a user name and password that match a record:

```
Else
  'Valid log in
End If
```

Another place that you will frequently see the EOF property used is to loop through all the records in a recordset and take some action with each record. The code would loop until EOF was reached. Take a look at the next sample code block:

```
<SELECT NAME="Question" >
<%
set RSAllQuestions = conn.Execute("select FAQID, FAQQuestion from
  WIFAQ")
Do Until RSAllQuestions.EOF
%>
    <OPTION VALUE="<% Response.Write RSAllQuestions("FAQID") %>">
    <% Response.Write RSAllQuestions("FAQQuestion") %></OPTION>
<%
     RSAllquestions.MoveNext
    Loop
%>
</SELECT>
```

This sample code loops through all the records in the Recordset object to populate a Select form element with the entire Question in a FAQ. First, the Recordset object is populated with all the questions from the database:

```
set RSAllQuestions = conn.Execute("select FAQID, FAQQuestion from
  WIFAQ")
```

Then the code enters a loop that will continue on until all the records have been processed, as indicated by the record pointer pointing to the EOF region:

```
Do Until RSAllQuestions.EOF
```

With each of the records an Option is added to the Select form element. The FAQID would be passed when the form is processed:

```
<OPTION VALUE="<% Response.Write RSAllQuestions("FAQID") %>">
```

The text of the question would be displayed to the visitor in the Select control:

```
<% Response.Write RSAllQuestions("FAQQuestion") %></OPTION>
```

The code then moves the record pointer on to the next record:

```
RSAllquestions.MoveNext
```

before looping:

```
Loop
```

As you are working with a Recordset, you may add and delete records from that Recordset. You may also have a need to return to a specific record after such actions have occurred. We have looked at the AbsolutePosition property, which returns to use the row number for a particular record in a Recordset. But if you add and delete records, a single record may be in a different location. For example, if you need to return to the fifth record, but you have deleted the second and third record, the fifth record is now the third record.

The *Bookmark* property provides the functionality of pointing to a specific record in a recordset. Regardless of the changes to a Recordset, a Bookmark always points to the same record. The read/write Bookmark property has the following syntax:

```
RS.Bookmark = MyBookmark
```

or

```
MyBookMark = RS.Bookmark
```

`RS` must be a valid instance of a Recordset object. You could use the property in an Active Server Page Application where you had a Recordset stored in a `Session` variable. You would allow the visitor to add and remove records and move around a Recordset. You could use the Bookmark property to provide a way for the visitor to return to a favorite or key record by clicking on a link.

When you retrieve records into a Recordset, the number of records retrieved at one time is specified by the *CacheSize* property. This read/write property has the following syntax:

```
RS.CacheSize = TheValue
```

or

```
TheValue = RS.CacheSize
```

The default value for this property is 1, so each time a record is requested it is retrieved from the database. But you can change the value of this property so more records are retrieved at one time. The following code reports the value of the CacheSize property and then changes that value.

```
<%
Option Explicit
Dim ConnectString
Dim RSEmps
ConnectString = "DSN=EmpsDatabase;User Id=Admin;Password=;"
set RSEmps = Server.CreateObject("ADODB.Recordset")
Response.Write RSEmps.CacheSize & "<P>"
RSEmps.CacheSize = 5
Response.Write RSEmps.CacheSize
%>
```

First, `Option Explicit` is noted for the compiler:

```
Option Explicit
```

Next, a variable that will store the connection string is created:

```
Dim ConnectString
```

as is one that will store the Recordset object:

```
Dim RSEmps
```

The connection string is set to an Access database:

```
ConnectString = "DSN=EmpsDatabase;User Id=Admin;Password=;"
```

The Recordset object is instantiated:

```
set RSEmps = Server.CreateObject("ADODB.Recordset")
```

The default size of the cache, which is 1, is written to the browser:

```
Response.Write RSEmps.CacheSize & "<P>"
```

The cache is now set so that five records will be retrieved at one time:

```
RSEmps.CacheSize = 5
```

and the value of the cache is written to the browser. This time the number 5 is written to the browser:

```
Response.Write RSEmps.CacheSize
```

The *CursorLocation* property sets the location of the data in the Recordset: either client-side or server-side. This read/write property of the Recordset object has the following syntax:

```
RS.CursorLocation = LocationValue
```

RS must be a valid instance of a Recordset object. If you set the property to the value 2, then the cursor is located on the server; if you set the value of the CursorLocation property to 3, the cursor is located on the client.

The *CursorType* property is used to specify the type of cursor that will be used in the recordset. Based on the type of cursor, different actions on the recordset are allowed and differing amounts of resources are used. The CursorType property has the following syntax:

```
RS.CursorType = CursorValue
```

RS must be a valid instance of a Recordset object. The allowable values are summarized in Table 14-8.

The *EditMode* property returns the modification mode that the Recordset is in. This property is useful for code where you have a

TABLE 14-8

CursorType Values

Value	Purpose
0	*Default value*. Represents a forward-only recordset. You can go forward only in this recordset type. Uses the fewest resources. Best for situations where you want to make a single pass through the records.
1	*Keyset cursor*. Allows free movement through the recordset. Can see changes and deletes made by other users, but does not show additions made by other users without refreshing the recordset.
2	*Dynamic cursor*. Most powerful cursor but uses the most resources. Allows full movement through the Recordset. Can see additons, edits, and deletions made by other users.
3	*Static cursor*. Fully scrollable Recordset but disconnects from server after the Recordset is populated. Additions, edits, and deletes made by other users are not viewable.

Value	Purpose
0	No edit or add is in progress.
1	The current record is in edit mode and the changes have not been saved.
2	The current record is in add mode and the changes have not been saved.
4	The current record has been deleted.

TABLE 14-9

EditMode Values

`Session level` Recordset and are loosely controlling the actions taken by visitors. This read-only property has the following syntax:

```
TheMode = RS.EditMode
```

RS must be a valid instance of a Recordset object. Possible values for this property are displayed in Table 14-9.

You can supply a `Where` clause and an `Order by` clause to an open, existing Recordset with the Filter and Sort properties, respectively. The *Filter* property allows you to supply a field name and a condition for that field. The Recordset is then automatically filtered based on that value. The Filter property has the following syntax:

```
RS.Filter = FilterText
```

RS must be a valid instance of a Recordset object. The property is set to text similar to a `Where` clause in an SQL statement without the word `Where`.

The *Sort* property allows you to supply a field or fields by which you want the records in an open Recordset sorted. The Sort property has the following syntax:

```
RS.Sort = SortText
```

RS must be a valid instance of the Recordset object. SortText would be the field name by which you wanted the records sorted. If you want to sort the records by more than one field, separate each with a comma.

The following code uses these two properties to add sorting and filtering functionality to an HTML table that displays Employee records.

```
<%
Option Explicit
Dim ConnectString
If IsEmpty(Session("RSEmps")) Then
```

```
    ConnectString = "DSN=EmpsDatabase;User Id=Admin;Password=;"
    set Session("RSEmps") = Server.CreateObject("ADODB.Recordset")
    Session("RSEmps").CursorLocation = 3
    Session("RSEmps").Open "tblEmps", ConnectString, , , 2
Else
    Session("RSEmps").MoveFirst
    If Not Isempty(Request.Form("Requery")) Then
        Session("RSEmps").Sort = Request.Form("SortField")
        If Request.Form("Filter") = "All" Then
            Session("RSEmps").Filter = "EmpID > 0"
        Else
            Session("RSEmps").Filter = "EmpID = " & Request.Form
                ("Filter")
        End If
    End If
End If
Response.Write "<TABLE>"
Response.Write "<TR><B>"
Response.Write "<TD>Employee ID</TD><TD>First Name</TD>" _
    & "<TD>Last Name</TD></B></TR>"
Do Until Session("RSEmps").EOF
    Response.Write "<TR>"
    Response.Write "<TD>" & Session("RSEmps")("EmpID") & "</TD>"
    Response.Write "<TD>" & Session("RSEmps")("FirstName") & "</TD>"
    Response.Write "<TD>" & Session("RSEmps")("LastName") & "</TD>"
    Response.Write "</TR>"
    Session("RSEmps").MoveNext
Loop
Response.Write "</TABLE>"
%>
```

First, the `Option Explicit` compiler statement is written:

```
Option Explicit
```

One variable will be needed to store the Connection string:

```
Dim ConnectString
```

The code on this page relies on a sessionwide Recordset object that stores the Employee records. The visitor will be able to sort and filter those records. If the visitor is first entering the page, then the Recordset object needs to be instantiated. We check for this by seeing if the Recordset object is empty:

```
If IsEmpty(Session("RSEmps")) Then
```

If it is, then this is the first viewing of this page. The connect string's value is set:

```
ConnectString = "DSN=EmpsDatabase;User Id=Admin;Password=;"
```

The Recordset object is instantiated:

```
set Session("RSEmps") = Server.CreateObject("ADODB.Recordset")
```

The location of the cursor is set to the client:

```
Session("RSEmps").CursorLocation = 3
```

and the table tblEmps is opened directly into the Recordset object:

```
Session("RSEmps").Open "tblEmps", ConnectString, , , 2
```

If the sessionwide Recordset object was already present, then the visitor must have submitted the form or is refreshing the page. Either way the Recordset object already exists:

```
Else
```

In that case, we need to move back to the first record. After the last viewing of the page, the record pointer is still pointing to the EOF region:

```
Session("RSEmps").MoveFirst
```

Then we check to see if the form was submitted by looking for the SUBMIT button (which is called REQUERY):

```
If Not Isempty(Request.Form("Requery")) Then
```

If it is present, then the Sort method is used to sort the records by the field selected on the form by the visitor:

```
Session("RSEmps").Sort = Request.Form("SortField")
```

We also may need to filter the recordset for a specific employee. This value is submitted with the form through the Filter form field. This select control contains a list of Employee IDs to select from, as well as the term All. If the visitor selects the term All:

```
If Request.Form("Filter") = "All" Then
```

Then we need to remove the filter and display all the records:

```
Session("RSEmps").Filter = "EmpID > 0"
```

otherwise, the Recordset is filtered based on the Employee ID selected by the visitor:

```
Else
Session("RSEmps").Filter = "EmpID = " & Request.Form("Filter")
```

Next, an HTML table is written to the browser. This table will display all the records based on the visitor's sort and filter:

```
Response.Write "<TABLE>"
```

The header for the table is written next:

```
Response.Write "<TR><B>"
Response.Write "<TD>Employee ID</TD><TD>First Name</TD>" _
 & "<TD>Last Name</TD></B></TR>"
```

The code will loop through each record in the Recordset until EOF is reached:

```
Do Until Session("RSEmps").EOF
```

Within that loop, a row is written to the HTML table:

```
Response.Write "<TR>"
```

Cells in the row contain the EmpID field:

```
Response.Write "<TD>" & Session("RSEmps")("EmpID") & "</TD>"
```

the FirstName field:

```
Response.Write "<TD>" & Session("RSEmps")("FirstName") & "</TD>"
```

and the LastName field:

```
Response.Write "<TD>" & Session("RSEmps")("LastName") & "</TD>"
Response.Write "</TR>"
```

The code then moves onto the next record before looping:

```
  Session("RSEmps").MoveNext
Loop
```

The End of Table tag is also written to the browser:

```
Response.Write "</TABLE>"
```

The HTML after the code creates a form that is posted back to this page when the SUBMIT button is pressed:

```
<FORM ACTION="./adosample.asp" Method="POST">
```

The form contains two select controls, one for the Sort field and the other for the filter. The form also contains a SUBMIT button.

When visitors first enter the page they see what is displayed in Figure 14-12.

Notice that the records are initially sorted by the Employee ID. Also note that all the records are displayed. If visitors were to select a specific Employee record in the Filter box, they would see just one record as displayed in Figure 14-13. Now just a single record is displayed. Visitors

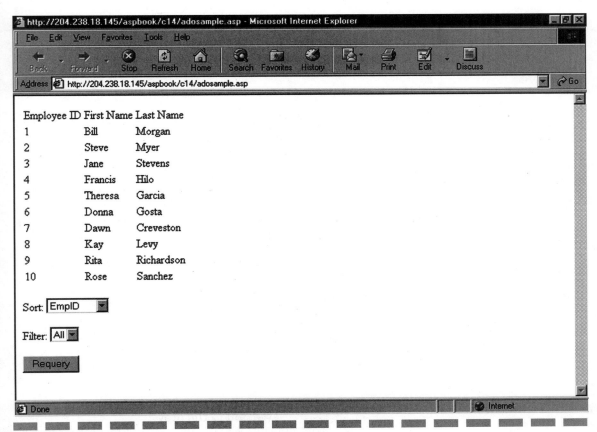

Figure 14-12   Initial page view of Sort and Filter code sample.

Figure 14-13
Recordset filtered.

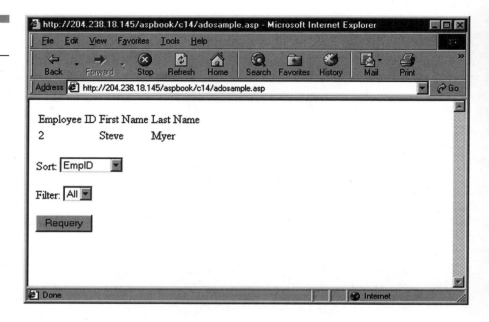

can then select All for the Filter to see all the records again; they can also choose to Sort the records, too. Figure 14-14 shows the sample page with the visitor having selected to sort by last name.

When you are dealing with a live Recordset, you need to concern yourself with *record locking*, which refers to what the database provider does to protect more than one person from editing the same record. You can tell the compiler how you want the locking to occur through the *LockType* property, which has the following syntax:

```
RS.LockType = LockValue
```

RS must be a Recordset object. The possible values for the property are summarized in Table 14-10.

The *MaxRecords* property provides a way for you to return a maximum number of records as the result of a query. The property has the following syntax:

```
RS.MaxRecords = NewValue
```

RS must be a valid Recordset object. The default for the property is 0, which returns all the records in the Recordset.

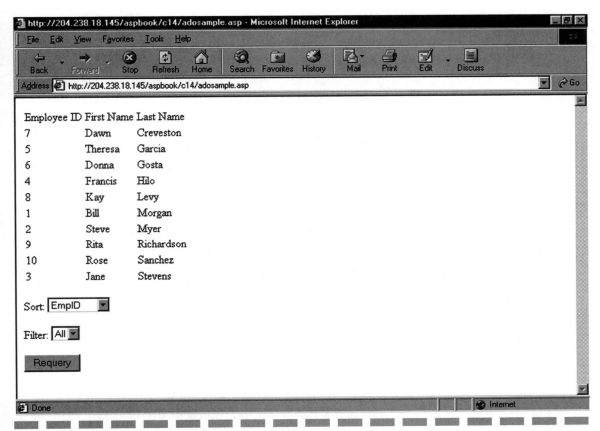

Figure 14-14 *Sample site with data sorted by last name.*

Whereas the MaxRecords property is used to supply the maximum number of records returned from a query, the *RecordCount* property returns the number of records in the Recordset. This read-only property has the following syntax:

```
TheCount = RS.RecordCount
```

TABLE 14-10

LockType Values

Value	Purpose
1	The records in the Recordset are read-only, so no modifcations are allowed.
2	The record is locked when it is first edited.
3	The record is locked while it is being updated.

RS must be a valid instance of a Recordset object. The total number of records in the Recordset object is returned from the property.

The Recordset object has one additional property, the *Source* property, which provides the underlying SQL statement used to generate the records in the Recordset object. The read-only property has the following syntax:

```
SQLText = RS.Source
```

RS must be a valid instance of a Recordset object. The query that produces the records in the Recordset object is returned from the property.

Recordset Object Methods

The Recordset object contains methods that let you navigate through the records in a Recordset object and to manipulate those records. Some of the methods of the Recordset object are summarized in Table 14-11.

For a cursor that can be updated, the *AddNew* method allows you to insert a new record into the database. The syntax for the method is as follows:

```
RS.AddNew
RS("Field1") = Value
RS.Update
```

After the method is called, each field name is populated with a value before the Update method adds the record to the database. The next code block opens a recordset and adds a record to that recordset.

TABLE 14-11

Recordset Object Methods

Method	Purpose
AddNew	Allows you to insert a new record into a Recordset.
CancelUpdate	Cancels any changes made to an existing or new record.
Clone	Creates a copy of an existing Recordset object.
Delete	Deletes the current record from the database.
Move methods	Allows forward and backward navigation through a Recordset.
Open	Directly opens a Recordset.
Requery	Reruns the query on which the recordset is based.
Update	Commits changes to a record or a new record to the database.

```
<%
Option Explicit
Dim ConnectString
ConnectString = "DSN=EmpsDatabase;User Id=Admin;Password=;"
set Session("RSEmps") = Server.CreateObject("ADODB.Recordset")
Session("RSEmps").CursorType = 1
Session("RSEmps").LockType = 2
Session("RSEmps").Open "tblEmps", ConnectString, , , 2
Session("RSEmps").AddNew
Session("RSEmps")("FirstName") = "Lila"
Session("RSEmps")("LastName") = "Lopez"
Session("RSEmps")("DepartmentID") = 1
Session("RSEmps").Update
%>
```

First, Option Explicit is noted:

```
Option Explicit
```

Then a variable that will store the connect string is created:

```
Dim ConnectString
```

The connect string is set to an Access database:

```
ConnectString = "DSN=EmpsDatabase;User Id=Admin;Password=;"
```

The Recordset object is instantiated:

```
set Session("RSEmps") = Server.CreateObject("ADODB.Recordset")
```

A keyset type of cursor is used:

```
Session("RSEmps").CursorType = 1
```

Locking will be done when the record is updated:

```
Session("RSEmps").LockType = 2
```

The recordset is then opened based on a table name:

```
Session("RSEmps").Open "tblEmps", ConnectString, , , 2
```

The AddNew method is used to add a record to the database:

```
Session("RSEmps").AddNew
```

The FirstName field from the table is set to a value for this new record:

```
Session("RSEmps")("FirstName") = "Lila"
```

The LastName field is similarly set:

```
Session("RSEmps")("LastName") = "Lopez"
```

as is the DepartmentID field:

```
Session("RSEmps")("DepartmentID") = 1
```

The Update method is then used to commit the new record to the database:

```
Session("RSEmps").Update
```

You can use the *CancelUpdate* method to discard changes made to an existing record or to discard a new record before it is added to the database. The method has the following syntax:

```
RS.CacelUpdate
```

The method takes no parameters. RS must be a valid instance of a Recordset object. The method must be called before the Update method is called.

If you want to create a copy of an existing Recordset into another Recordset object, you can use the *Clone* method. The method has the following syntax:

```
Set NewRS = OldRS.Clone
```

Both OldRSs must be a valid Recordset object. Passed in to NewRS is a copy of the OldRS Recordset object.

The *Delete* method of the Recordset object provides a way for you to delete a record or records from the Recordset. The method has two forms. In the first form, the record being pointed to by the record pointer is deleted:

```
RS.Delete
```

RS must be a Recordset object. The record pointer must be pointing to a record. After the method is called, the record is deleted.

In the second form of the method, a group of records can be deleted. This form has the following syntax:

```
RS.Filter = FilterText
RS.Delete 2
```

In this example, first the Filter property is set. Then the Delete method is called with the first parameter set to 2. This indicates that you want to delete all the records that apply to the first. For example, here:

```
RSEmps.Filter = "DepartmentID = 2"
RS.Delete 2
```

all the records with a DepartmentID of 2 would be deleted.

You have already seen some of the Move methods used in code. The *Move methods* allow you to navigate through the records in a Recordset object. The methods are MoveFirst, MovePrevious, MoveNext, MoveLast, and Move.

The MoveFirst method has the following syntax:

```
RS.MoveFirst
```

The method moves the record pointer to the first record. The MovePrevious method has similar syntax:

```
RS.MovePrevious
```

This method moves the record pointer to the previous record. If you are on the first record, calling the method puts you on the BOF region. If you are on the BOF region and you call the method, an error occurs.

The MoveLast method has the following syntax:

```
RS.MoveLast
```

When the method is called, the record pointer is moved to the last record. The MoveNext method has the following syntax:

```
RS.MoveNext
```

The method moves the record pointer onto the next record. If you are on the last record, then the method moves the record pointer onto the EOF region. If you are on the EOF region and you call the MoveNext, an error will occur.

The Move method allows you to move forward or backward a specific number of records. The method has the following syntax:

```
RS.Move NumToMove, StartPosition
```

RS must be a valid instance of a Recordset object. In the first parameter, the number of records you want to move is passed to the method. If you want to move forward, use a positive number. For example here:

```
RS.Move 3
```

The record pointer is moved ahead three records. If you want to move backward, use a negative number as is shown here:

```
RS.Move -4
```

The record pointer is moved backward four records.

The second parameter represents the start position for the move. The parameter is optional and, by default, the current record is the start position. But you can start at the first record by specifying 1 for the second parameter and you can start the move from the last record by specifying 2 for the second parameter.

As you have seen throughout this section, you can open a Recordset object directly using the Open method of the Recordset object. The method has the following syntax:

```
RS.Open SQLText, ConnectString, CursorType, LockType, Options
```

RS must be a valid instance of a Recordset object. All the parameters are optional and the first parameter is an SQL statement for the records you want to retrieve from the database. This can also be a table name or stored procedure.

The ConnectString parameter represents the connection information for the database that you want to connect to. The third parameter, CursorType, can have the same values as those that can be specified through the CursorType property. Similarly, the LockType parameter can be any value that is used in the LockType property. The Options parameter acts on the SQLText parameter and has the possible values displayed in Table 14-12.

The *Requery* method provides a way for you to refresh the records in the underlying Recordset object. The method has the following syntax:

```
RS.Requery
```

Option	Purpose
	TABLE 14-12
1	The SQLText parameter passed in should be evaluated as text.
2	The SQLText parameter is the name of a table and the table should be returned.
4	The SQLText being passed in is a stored procedure.
9	The command in the SQLText parameter is unknown.

Options for the Open Method

RS must be a Recordset object. The action of the method is like rerunning the query on which the Recordset is based.

One more method to discuss is the *Update* method, which commits the changes that you have made to a new or an existing record to the database. The method has the following syntax:

```
RS.Update
```

RS must be a valid instance of a Recordset object. If the record pointer is pointing to an existing record, then that record is saved; if the record pointer is pointing to a new record, then that record is added to the database.

Fields Collection and Field Object

Throughout the code in this chapter and throughout the code in this book, we have been using the Fields collection and Field object. These items provide a way for you to access the data in the columns or fields of a Recordset. We have been using these items indirectly, since they are the default collection of the Recordset object.

For example, earlier we had code that wrote records to an HTML table:

```
Response.Write "<TR>"
Response.Write "<TD>" & Session("RSEmps")("EmpID") & "</TD>"
Response.Write "<TD>" & Session("RSEmps")("FirstName") & "</TD>"
Response.Write "<TD>" & Session("RSEmps")("LastName") & "</TD>"
Response.Write "</TR>"
```

In this code, three fields were written to the browser. The fields were accessed through the Fields collection. Since it is the default collection we didn't have to explicitly state the collection name, but we could:

```
Response.Write "<TR>"
Response.Write "<TD>" & Session("RSEmps").Fields("EmpID") & "</TD>"
Response.Write "<TD>" & Session("RSEmps").Fields("FirstName") &
    "</TD>"
Response.Write "<TD>" & Session("RSEmps").Fields("LastName") &
    "</TD>"
Response.Write "</TR>"
```

Now each Fields collection is used to retrieve the data. Both sets of code produce the same results.

Since the fields in a Recordset are part of the Fields collection, we can use the Fields collection to iterate through all the fields instead of specifying each one. We could, therefore, display all the fields in all the records with code such as the following:

```
<%
Option Explicit
Dim ConnectString
Dim RSEmps
Dim MyField
ConnectString = "DSN=EmpsDatabase;User Id=Admin;Password=;"
set RSEmps = Server.CreateObject("ADODB.Recordset")
RSEmps.CursorLocation = 3
RSEmps.Open "select * from tblEmps where EmpID < 11", ConnectString
Response.Write "<TABLE>"
Response.Write "<TR>"
For Each MyField in RSEmps.Fields
    Response.Write "<TD>" & MyField.Name & "</TD>"
Next
Response.Write "</TR>"
Do Until RSEmps.EOF
  Response.Write "<TR>"
  For Each MyField in RSEmps.Fields
    Response.Write "<TD>" & RSEmps(MyField.Name) & "</TD>"
  Next
  Response.Write "</TR>"
    RSEmps.MoveNext
Loop
Response.Write "</TABLE>"
%>
```

First, `Option Explicit` is noted for the compiler:

```
Option Explicit
```

Next, the variables are declared, one for the connection string:

```
Dim ConnectString
```

one for the Recordset object:

```
Dim RSEmps
```

and one to store the Field object:

```
Dim MyField
```

The connection string is set:

```
ConnectString = "DSN=EmpsDatabase;User Id=Admin;Password=;"
```

Then the Recordset object is instantiated:

```
set RSEmps = Server.CreateObject("ADODB.Recordset")
```

The cursor location is set:

```
RSEmps.CursorLocation = 3
```

and a recordset is opened retrieving the first 10 employee records:

```
RSEmps.Open "select * from tblEmps where EmpID < 11", ConnectString
```

An HTML table tag is written to the browser:

```
Response.Write "<TABLE>"
```

as is the beginning of a table row:

```
Response.Write "<TR>"
```

Next we iterate through each field in the recordset object, setting each field in turn to the MyField object variable:

```
For Each MyField in RSEmps.Fields
```

The name of the field is written to the browser before moving on to the next field:

```
    Response.Write "<TD>" & MyField.Name & "</TD>"
Next
```

and the HTML table row ends:

```
Response.Write "</TR>"
```

Next, we iterate through each record in the Recordset object:

```
Do Until RSEmps.EOF
```

Each record is written as a row to the HTML table:

```
Response.Write "<TR>"
```

For each of the records we iterate through each of the fields in that record:

```
For Each MyField in RSEmps.Fields
```

and write the data in that field to the browser:

```
Response.Write "<TD>" & RSEmps(MyField.Name) & "</TD>"
Next
```

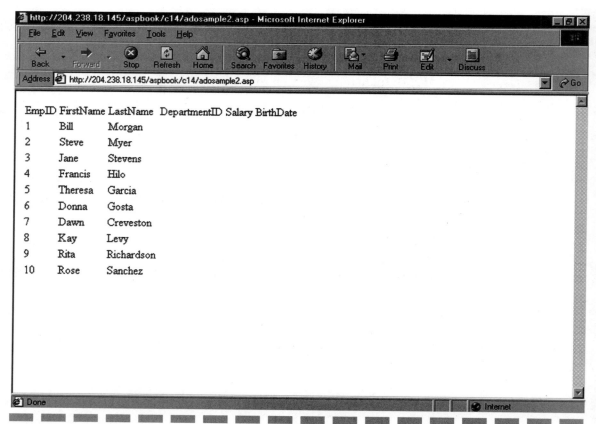

Figure 14-15 Output of Field collection code.

We then end that row in the table:

```
Response.Write "</TR>"
```

and loop to the next record:

```
RSEmps.MoveNext
Loop
```

The HTML table then ends:

```
Response.Write "</TABLE>"
```

The output of the code is displayed in Figure 14-15.

Command and Parameter Objects

So far you have seen that you can create a Recordset object through the Connection object. You have also seen that you can directly populate the records in a Recordset object through the Open method of the Recordset object. A third way to return a Recordset object is through the *Command* object.

Take a look at this sample code that uses a Connection, Command, and Recordset object to report the number of employees in Department 1.

```
<%
Option Explicit
Dim Conn
Dim CmdEmps
Dim RSEmps
set conn = server.createobject ("adodb.connection")
conn.open "EmpsDatabase", "Admin", ""
Set CmdEmps = Server.CreateObject("ADODB.Command")
Set CmdEmps.ActiveConnection = conn
CmdEmps.CommandText = "select Count(EmpID) as TheCount from
  tblEmps " _
    & "where DepartmentID = 1"
set RSEmps = CmdEMps.Execute
Response.Write "Total number of employees in Department 1 is: " _
    & RSEmps("TheCount")
%>
```

First, `Option Explicit` is noted:

```
Option Explicit
```

Then the variables are declared, one variable for the Connection object:

```
Dim Conn
```

one variable for the Command object:

```
Dim CmdEmps
```

and another for the Recordset object:

```
Dim RSEmps
```

Next, the Connection object is instantiated:

```
set conn = server.createobject ("adodb.connection")
```

and a database is opened through the Connection object:

```
conn.open "EmpsDatabase", "Admin", ""
```

Now, we instantiate a Command object using the CreateObject method of the Server object:

```
Set CmdEmps = Server.CreateObject("ADODB.Command")
```

The ActiveConnection property of the Command object needs to be set to the open Connection object, so the Command object inherits a database connection through the open Connection object:

```
Set CmdEmps.ActiveConnection = conn
```

The CommandText property of the Command object is used to set the query that the Command object will Execute. This can be a query, table name, or a stored procedure:

```
CmdEmps.CommandText = "select Count(EmpID) as TheCount from tblEmps " _
    & "where DepartmentID = 1"
```

The Execute method of the Command object executes the query in the CommandText property against the connection in the ActiveConnection property. The results of the query in a Recordset object are returned from the call:

```
set RSEmps = CmdEMps.Execute
```

The number of employees that are in Department 1 is written then to the browser, which is what the query executed:

```
Response.Write "Total number of employees in Department 1 is: " _
    & RSEmps("TheCount")
```

The result of this code is displayed in Figure 14-16.

The *Parameter* object is used in conjunction with the Command object to specify the values the parameters of a stored procedure. You don't have to do this through Parameter objects. For example, the following

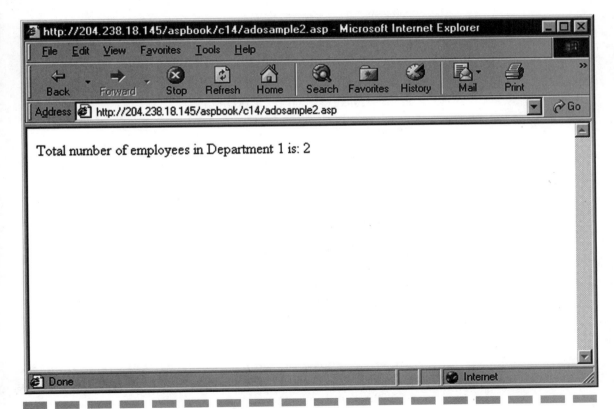

Figure 14-16 Output of Command object code.

code block calls a stored procedure through a Connection object, placing the output of the stored procedure into a Recordset object.

```
<%
Option Explicit
Dim conn
Dim RSResults
set conn = server.createobject ("adodb.connection")
conn.open "IISLog", "sa", "yourpassword"
conn.commandTimeout = 60
set RSResults = conn.execute ("getStats '" & Request.Form
  ("QueryName") _
   & "', '" & Request.Form("UserName") & "', '" & Request.Form
     ("Grouping") & "'")
Response.Write RSResults("TotalHits")
%>
```

First, `Option Explicit` is noted:

```
Option Explicit
```

A variable for a connection object is created:

```
Dim conn
```

A variable for a Recordset object is created:

```
Dim RSResults
```

The Connection object is instantiated:

```
set conn = server.createobject ("adodb.connection")
```

and a connection to a database is established:

```
conn.open "IISLog", "sa", "yourpassword"
```

The execution of the stored procedure through the Connection object is given 60 seconds to complete:

```
conn.commandTimeout = 60
```

The results of the stored procedure are placed into the `RSResults` recordset. Passed to the stored procedure are three parameters, which are passed in through the Form collection:

```
set RSResults = conn.execute ("getStats '" & Request.Form
  ("QueryName") _
```

```
& "', '" & Request.Form("UserName") & "', '" & Request.Form
("Grouping") & "'")
```

and the result of the stored procedure is written to the browser:

```
Response.Write RSResults("TotalHits")
```

You can achieve the same result by using a Command object with Parameter objects as shown in the next code block:

```
<%
Option Explicit
Dim Conn
Dim Cmd1
Dim RSResults
Dim Param1
Dim Param2
Dim Param3
set conn = server.createobject ("adodb.connection")
conn.open "IISLog", "sa", "yourpassword"
conn.commandTimeout = 60
Set Cmd1= Server.CreateObject("ADODB.Command")
Cmd1.CommandText = "getStats"
Cmd1.CommandType = 4
Set Param1 = Cmd1.CreateParameter("QueryName", 129, 1)
Cmd1.Parameters.Append Param1
Param1.Value = Request.Form("QueryName")
Set Param2 = Cmd1.CreateParameter("UserName", 129, 1)
Cmd1.Parameters.Append Param2
Param2.Value = Request.Form("UserName")
Set Param3 = Cmd1.CreateParameter("Grouping", 3, 1)
Cmd1.Parameters.Append Param3
Param3.Value = Request.Form("Grouping")
Set Cmd1.ActiveConnection = conn
set RSResults = Cmd1.Execute
Response.Write RSResults("TotalHits")
%>
```

First, `Option Explicit` is noted:

```
Option Explicit
```

Then the variables are declared. First, one for the Connection object:

```
Dim Conn
```

then one for the Command object:

```
Dim Cmd1
```

and the Recordset object:

```
Dim RSResults
```

Three Parameter objects will be needed:

```
Dim Param1
Dim Param2
Dim Param3
```

The Connection object is instantiated:

```
set conn = server.createobject ("adodb.connection")
```

and a connection to the database is opened:

```
conn.open "IISLog", "sa", "yourpassword"
```

A command in the Connection object can take 60 s to complete:

```
conn.commandTimeout = 60
```

The Command object is then instantiated:

```
Set Cmd1= Server.CreateObject("ADODB.Command")
```

The text of the Command object is set to a stored procedure:

```
Cmd1.CommandText = "getStats"
```

and the type of command is set to a stored procedure:

```
Cmd1.CommandType = 4
```

Next, the first parameter is created using the *CreateParameter* method of the Command object. The name of the parameter, the data type of the parameter, and the fact that this is an input parameter are passed to the method:

```
Set Param1 = Cmd1.CreateParameter("QueryName", 129, 1)
```

The parameter is appended to the Parameters collection of the Command object:

```
Cmd1.Parameters.Append Param1
```

and the value for the parameter is set:

```
Param1.Value = Request.Form("QueryName")
```

The same code is used to set up the second parameter of the stored procedure:

```
Set Param2 = Cmd1.CreateParameter("UserName", 129, 1)
Cmd1.Parameters.Append Param2
Param2.Value = Request.Form("UserName")
```

as well as the third parameter:

```
Set Param3 = Cmd1.CreateParameter("Grouping", 3, 1)
Cmd1.Parameters.Append Param3
Param3.Value = Request.Form("Grouping")
```

The connection for the Command object is set to conn:

```
Set Cmd1.ActiveConnection = conn
```

Finally, the Recordset object can be created:

```
set RSResults = Cmd1.Execute
```

and the result displayed:

```
Response.Write RSResults("TotalHits")
```

Error Object and Error Collection

Like the Error object we discussed in Chapter 12, ADO has its own Error object and collection you can use to query the library about the errors it encountered.

The next code block uses the On Error statement discussed in Chapter 12 to display the errors related to the problems encountered by the ADO library.

```
<%
Option Explicit
On Error Resume Next
Dim Conn
Dim MyError
set conn = server.createobject ("adodb.connection")
```

```
conn.Open "Garbage"
For Each MyError In conn.Errors
   Response.write "Error Number: " & MyError.Number & "<BR>"
   Response.write "Description: " & MyError.Description & "<BR>"
   Response.write "Source: " & MyError.Source & "<BR>"
   Response.write "State: " & MyError.SQLState & "<BR>"
   Response.write "Native Error: " & MyError.NativeError & "<P>"
Next
%>
```

First, variable declaration will be required:

```
Option Explicit
```

Then the On Error statement is written. Remember that this statement tells the compiler to blow past errors—you will handle them yourself:

```
On Error Resume Next
```

Then the variables are declared, one for the Connection object:

```
Dim Conn
```

and one for the Error object:

```
Dim MyError
```

The Connection object is instantiated:

```
set conn = server.createobject ("adodb.connection")
```

To produce an error, a nonexistent DSN is used in the connect string:

```
conn.Open "Garbage"
```

Since the Error objects are part of the Errors collection, we can iterate through that collection:

```
For Each MyError In conn.Errors
```

First, the number for the error is written to the browser:

```
Response.write "Error Number: " & MyError.Number & "<BR>"
```

Next, the description of the error is written:

```
Response.write "Description: " & MyError.Description & "<BR>"
```

as is the Source of the Error:

```
Response.write "Source: " & MyError.Source & "<BR>"
```

The SQL State property returns the error code from the database provider:

```
Response.write "State: " & MyError.SQLState & "<BR>"
```

and the native error is written to the browser:

```
Response.write "Native Error: " & MyError.NativeError & "<P>"
```

before looping to the next error:

```
Next
```

The output of this code is displayed in Figure 14-17.

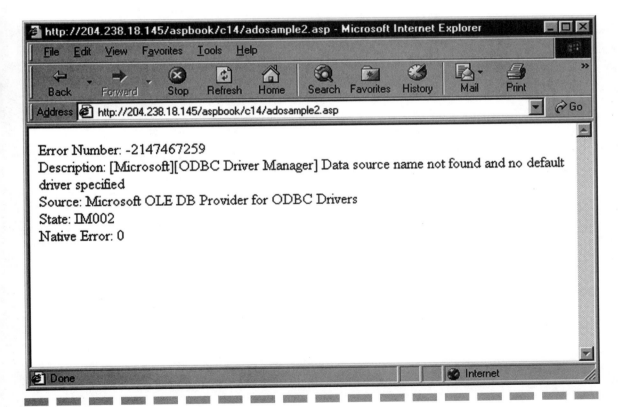

Figure 14-17   Output of Error object code.

15

Creating
Components

Using VB to Create Your Own Custom Libraries

In most of the code samples in this book, we have used components to extend the capabilities of Active Server Page applications. In the last chapter, we looked at the ADO components that provide a library of methods and properties for connecting to databases, greatly extending the capabilities of Active Server Page applications. In Chapter 9, we looked at the Collaborative Data Objects, a component that allows you to send email out through your Active Server Page applications. Again, this component extends the capabilities of what you can do with Active Server Page applications.

In fact, one of the excellent features of the ASP object model is the ability to include these extra components to extend what you can do in your code, so your code isn't limited by what ASP supports, but only by what the server can do—that includes creating your own components. In this chapter, you will learn how to create your own custom components using Visual Basic 6.0.

Why Should You Create Components?

Extending Capabilities of Active Server Page Applications

Probably the number one reason developers create their first component for an Active Server Page application is to perform some functionality that they cannot do from within ASP or to work around a bug in ASP.

Say, for example, that you have a Web site that needs to send a fax to someone when a certain page is submitted. Maybe it is a fax back service you offer to your customers. You will need some way of manipulating the modem on the server to send a fax. This is not something you can do directly with ASP, but you could create a component in Visual Basic that would take that action.

Maybe you want to have a page that displays extended information about the health of the server. You could do this by creating a component in Visual Basic. The VB component could make the low-level system calls to gather the desired information and then return the information through a method call to the Active Server Page application.

Encapsulation

Another reason to create your own components is for encapsulation. Say that you are using the same chunk of code across 30 different pages.

Maybe the code retrieves some sales information from the company's database. You use the exact same code across the 30 locations and then you find out that you need to revise the query you use to retrieve the value. If that is the case, you have 30 different places to fix the code. If, instead, you had placed the code in a component, you could just fix the component in one place and then recompile it. The pages that use the component would be updated.

Third-Party Tools

Another reason to create a component is to sell it or make it freely available to other developers. Maybe you have a series of Web pages that produce a chat board. You could place the function code (the code that displays threads, messages, handles responses, etc.) in a component that you create with Visual Basic. You could then compile your component and sell it to other developers as a way for them to easily implement a chat board.

Wrappers

One final reason that you may decide it is time to create your own components is to wrap functionality. When you wrap functionality you take a task that is complex or lengthy and place it in a component that requires a single call to that component to run the lengthy or complex code, which in turn makes your code more readable and easier to modify. You can also use this technique to protect novice or specialized developers from overly complex tasks.

Say for example, you specialize in Collaborative Data Objects with Exchange Server. You have mastered the art of manipulating the folders within Exchange. You could create a wrapper component that made performing standard Exchange tasks less complex for other developers from their Active Server Page applications.

Creating a Wrapper Component

In this section we create a wrapper component that provides easy access to records in a table for the purpose of manipulating them. The library provides methods for viewing, adding, editing, and deleting employees. It also provides methods that display the records in the table in HTML format.

Database Component

The database for this example is an Access database that uses a single table called *tblEmps*. The field specifications for that table are displayed

TABLE 15-1

tblEmps Field
Specifications

Field Name	Field Type	Notes
EmpID	AutoNumber	Primary Key
FirstName	Text	50
LastName	Text	50
DepartmentID	Number	Subtype Long
Salary	Currency	
BirthDate	Date/Time	

in Table 15-1. The EmpID field is an AutoNumber field, so it is automatically populated when a new record is added to the table.

Creating the Component

To create you own component, you need to create an ActiveX DLL project within Visual Basic. To do this, select New Project from the File menu or reopen Visual Basic and you should see the dialog shown in Figure 15-1.

Select ActiveX DLL from the menu and click OK. Visual Basic then sets up the environment of the project so that it will be treated as an ActiveX DLL. *DLL* stands for Dynamic Link Library. What this means is that you are creating a library that should be dynamically linked to whatever client is using your component. That means that the component will load in memory when it is needed and release its resources when it is no longer in use. Since the component is created as a DLL, as opposed to an EXE, it will run in-process. That means that your compo-

Figure 15-1
Creating an ActiveX
DLL.

nent will load in the same processing space as the client, so it will run more efficiently than an ActiveX DLL.

When you create an instance of a component in your Active Server Page applications you use the CreateObject method of the Server object like this:

```
Set MyObject = Server.CreateObject("App.Class")
```

The `App.Class` string is passed to the CreateObject method. When you create your own components, you and other developers will need to know your `App.Class` string so they can successfully instantiate your component.

The `App` portion of that string comes from the name you give your application in Visual Basic. To modify this entry, select Project-Project Properties from the menu. Then on the GENERAL tab enter the name of your application under Project Name as shown in Figure 15-2. Then change to the MAKE tab and supply the application title as displayed in Figure 15-3.

Adding the Employee Class

The SampleServer component implements two classes. One class provides the methods for working with a single employee, whereas the other class has methods for working with more than one employee. In this section, we add the Employee class and the code for that class. To

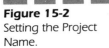

Figure 15-2
Setting the Project Name.

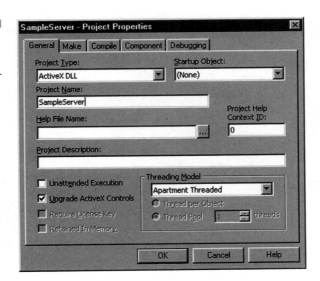

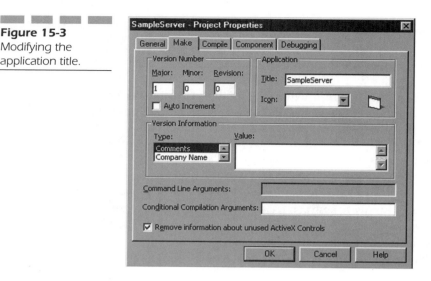

Figure 15-3
Modifying the
application title.

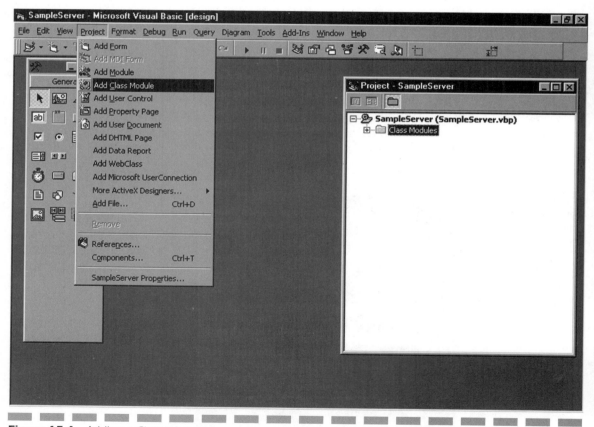

Figure 15-4   Adding a Class module.

add a class to your project, select from the menu Project-Add Class Module as shown in Figure 15-4.

The *Class module* is where you will define the methods of the component. The name that you give your component is very important because it will be used by you and other developers when instantiating your component with the CreateObject method. To assign a name to a Class, use the Properties window when the Class module has the focus. Use the Name property to name your class, as shown in Figure 15-5. Now with the Application name and Class name in place, the CreateObject method would be called like this when your component was to be instantiated:

```
MyObject = Server.CreateObject("SampleServer.Employee")
```

Adding the Methods to the Employee Class

The Employee Class module has a variety of methods that provide for the functionality of manipulating the records in the tblEmps table.

Figure 15-5
Naming the
Employee Class
module.

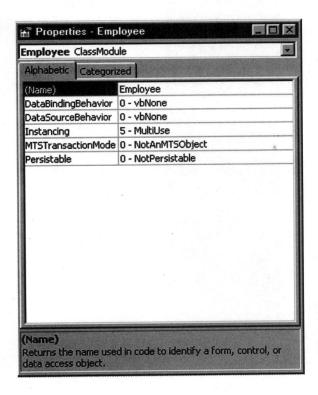

Method	Purpose
AddEmployee	Adds a new employee to the database.
DeleteEmployee	Deletes an existing employee from the database.
EditEmployee	Edits an existing employee.
DeleteEmployee	Views the contents of an existing employee.
EmpInfo	Displays the contents of the requested record in HTML format.
FormWithFields	Displays a form populated with the values for the requested record.

Table 15-2 summarizes the methods that are added to the Employee class.

First, let's add the AddEmployee method to the class. To do this, from the Tools menu select Add Procedure. You should see the dialog shown in Figure 15-6. The type selected for the AddEmployee method, Function, is chosen because the method will return a value. If the method does not return a value, use Sub. The scope of the method is Public, which means that it is visible to clients instantiating your component. If you make the scope of method Private, it is available only inside your component.

The code for the AddEmployee method is:

```
Public Function AddEmployee(LastName, FirstName, DepartmentID,
    Salary, BirthDate)
If IsNumeric(DepartmentID) = False Then
    Err.Raise vbObjectError + 3, "SampleServer", _
```

Figure 15-6
Adding the
AddEmployee
method.

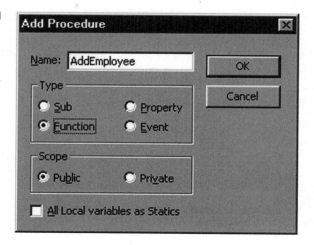

```
            "Department ID must be passed as a number!"
ElseIf IsNumeric(Salary) = False Then
    Err.Raise vbObjectError + 4, "SampleServer", _
        "Salary must be passed as a number!"
ElseIf IsDate(BirthDate) = False Then
    Err.Raise vbObjectError + 5, "SampleServer", _
        "BirthDate must be passed as a date!"
Else
    Dim Conn As New ADODB.Connection
    Dim RSEmpID As ADODB.Recordset
    Conn.Open "EmpsDatabase", "Admin", ""
    Conn.Execute "insert into tblEmps (LastName, FirstName,
        DepartmentID, " _
        & "Salary, BirthDate) values (" _
        & "'" & LastName & "', " _
        & "'" & FirstName & "', " _
        & DepartmentID & ", " _
        & Salary & ", " _
        & "'" & BirthDate & "')"
    Set RSEmpID = Conn.Execute("select Max(EmpID) as MaxID from
        tblEmps")
    AddEmployee = RSEmpID("MaxID")
End If
End Function
```

The first line in the method is the declaration:

```
Public Function AddEmployee(LastName, FirstName, DepartmentID,
    Salary, BirthDate)
```

In that line, the name of the method is defined, as well as the parameters. The method has five parameters, which are the data for the employee to be added to the database.

Next, we do some error checking. First, we test to see if the DepartmentID is a number:

```
If IsNumeric(DepartmentID) = False Then
```

Since the DepartmentID field is defined as a numeric field, we don't want to insert nonnumeric data into that field. If the field is not numeric, the Raise method of the Err object is used to throw a custom error back to the client application. The first parameter of the method is the number for the error. The constant vbObjectError takes the error number out of the normal error number range into the number that can be customized. The second parameter is the source of the error and the third parameter passed to the Raise method is the description for the error:

```
Err.Raise vbObjectError + 3, "SampleServer", _
    "Department ID must be passed as a number!"
```

If an error did occur there, no further code would run.

Next, we use the `IsNumeric` function to check the Salary field, which must also be numeric:

```
ElseIf IsNumeric(Salary) = False Then
```

If it is not, an error is thrown back to the client with a different number and description than the last error:

```
Err.Raise vbObjectError + 4, "SampleServer", _
    "Salary must be passed as a number!"
```

Next, we test the BirthDate field, which should be a date since it is defined as Date/Time in the database. The `IsDate` function is used to test the value passed through the parameter into this method:

```
ElseIf IsDate(BirthDate) = False Then
```

If the BirthDate field is not a date, then an error is thrown back to the client:

```
Err.Raise vbObjectError + 5, "SampleServer", _
    "BirthDate must be passed as a date!"
```

The `Else` portion of the main `If` statement means that the data passed in through the parameters pass the validation tests:

```
Else
```

In that case, we will need to add the new record to the database. A Connection object will be needed:

```
Dim Conn As New ADODB.Connection
```

Notice the use of the `New` keyword, which allows us to declare and instantiate the Connection object in a single line of code so we don't have to use the CreateObject method. Next, a Connection object is declared; the `New` keyword isn't used in this declaration since we don't want to instantiate the object here. It will be instantiated further down:

```
Dim RSEmpID As ADODB.Recordset
```

The Open method of the Connection object is used to open a connection to the Access database:

```
Conn.Open "EmpsDatabase", "Admin", ""
```

Next, the Execute method of the Connection object is used to add the new record to the tblEmps table. An SQL insert method is used, and the data are passed to that method:

```
Conn.Execute "insert into tblEmps (LastName, FirstName,
    DepartmentID, " _
        & "Salary, BirthDate) values (" _
        & "'" & LastName & "', " _
        & "'" & FirstName & "', " _
        & DepartmentID & ", " _
        & Salary & ", " _
        & "'" & BirthDate & "')"
```

From this method, we need to return the Employee ID for the employee that was just added to the database. Here, the Execute method of the Connection object is used to run a query that retrieves the ID of the employee record just added to the database:

```
Set RSEmpID = Conn.Execute("select Max(EmpID) as MaxID from
    tblEmps")
```

The function name is set to the value retrieved in the previous record-set. This is how we return a value from the method:

```
AddEmployee = RSEmpID("MaxID")
```

The DeleteEmployee method removes an employee record from the database. The method is added to the Employee class as a Public Sub, and does not return a value. The code for this method is:

```
Public Sub DeleteEmployee(EmpID)
    Dim Conn As New ADODB.Connection
    If IsNumeric(EmpID) = False Then
        Err.Raise vbObjectError + 1, "SampleServer", _
            "Employee ID must be passed as a number!"
    End If
    Conn.Open "EmpsDatabase", "Admin", ""
    Conn.Execute "Delete from tblEmps where EmpID = " & EmpID
End Sub
```

First, the method is declared:

```
Public Sub DeleteEmployee(EmpID)
```

Then a connection object is declared and instantiated:

```
Dim Conn As New ADODB.Connection
```

The ID of the Employee record that is to be deleted is then passed into the method. That ID should be a number, so the `IsNumeric` function is used to test the EmpID field:

```
If IsNumeric(EmpID) = False Then
```

If the `EmpID` parameter is not a number, then an error is thrown back to the client:

```
Err.Raise vbObjectError + 1, "SampleServer", _
  "Employee ID must be passed as a number!"
```

otherwise, the Open method of the Connection object is used to connect to the database:

```
Conn.Open "EmpsDatabase", "Admin", ""
```

The Execute method of the Connection object is then used to run an SQL Delete query, which deletes the desired employee record:

```
Conn.Execute "Delete from tblEmps where EmpID = " & EmpID
```

The Edit employee method is used to modify an existing employee record. The code block for that procedure is:

```
Public Sub EditEmployee(EmpID, LastName, FirstName, DepartmentID,
  Salary, BirthDate)
If IsNumeric(EmpID) = False Then
    Err.Raise vbObjectError + 1, "SampleServer", _
        "Employee ID must be passed as a number!"
ElseIf IsNumeric(DepartmentID) = False Then
    Err.Raise vbObjectError + 3, "SampleServer", _
        "Department ID must be passed as a number!"
ElseIf IsNumeric(Salary) = False Then
    Err.Raise vbObjectError + 4, "SampleServer", _
        "Salary must be passed as a number!"
ElseIf IsDate(BirthDate) = False Then
    Err.Raise vbObjectError + 5, "SampleServer", _
        "BirthDate must be passed as a date!"
Else
    Dim Conn As New ADODB.Connection
    Dim RSEmpID As ADODB.Recordset
    Conn.Open "EmpsDatabase", "Admin", ""
    Set RSEmpID = Conn.Execute("select EmpID from tblEmps where " _
        & "EmpID = " & EmpID)
    If RSEmpID.EOF Then
        Err.Raise vbObjectError + 2, "SampleServer", _
            "No such employee record was found to edit!"
    End If
    Conn.Execute "Update tblEmps set " _
```

```
            & "LastName = '" & LastName & "', " _
            & "FirstName = '" & FirstName & "', " _
            & "DepartmentID = " & DepartmentID & ", " _
            & "Salary = " & Salary & ", " _
            & "BirthDate = '" & BirthDate & "' " _
            & "where EmpID = " & EmpID
    End If
End Sub
```

First, the method is declared:

```
Public Sub EditEmployee(EmpID, LastName, FirstName, DepartmentID,
    Salary, BirthDate)
```

Notice that the method is declared as a Sub, since it does not return a value. Passed into the method are the EmpID, LastName, FirstName, DepartmentID, Salary, and BirthDate parameters.

The EmpID field should be numeric since it is stored as a Number of type Long in the database. Here, the IsNumeric function tests that field:

```
If IsNumeric(EmpID) = False Then
```

If the field is not a number, an error is thrown back to the client:

```
Err.Raise vbObjectError + 1, "SampleServer", _
    "Employee ID must be passed as a number!"
```

Next, the DepartmentID field is tested. It should also be a number:

```
ElseIf IsNumeric(DepartmentID) = False Then
```

If not, a different error is thrown back to the client that made the call:

```
Err.Raise vbObjectError + 3, "SampleServer", _
    "Department ID must be passed as a number!"
```

The Salary field should also be numeric:

```
ElseIf IsNumeric(Salary) = False Then
```

If not, the Raise method of the Err object is used to send an error back to the client:

```
Err.Raise vbObjectError + 4, "SampleServer", _
    "Salary must be passed as a number!"
```

The `IsDate` function is used to test the `BirthDate` parameter. This field must be a date:

```
ElseIf IsDate(BirthDate) = False Then
```

If `IsDate` returns False, we enter the `If` statement and throw an error:

```
Err.Raise vbObjectError + 5, "SampleServer", _
"BirthDate must be passed as a date!"
```

otherwise, the data passed in can be stored in the database:

```
Else
```

A connection to the database will be needed:

```
Dim Conn As New ADODB.Connection
```

as will a Recordset object:

```
Dim RSEmpID As ADODB.Recordset
```

The Open method of the Connection object is used to open a connection to the database:

```
Conn.Open "EmpsDatabase", "Admin", ""
```

Before we edit the record, we need to make one more check. The EmpID needs to exist in the database or nothing will be edited, so the Execute method of the Connection object is used to retrieve the record from the database matching the EmpID passed into this method:

```
Set RSEmpID = Conn.Execute("select EmpID from tblEmps where " _
& "EmpID = " & EmpID)
```

If a record was not found, EOF will be True:

```
If RSEmpID.EOF Then
```

If that is the case, an error is thrown back to the client:

```
Err.Raise vbObjectError + 2, "SampleServer", _
"No such employee record was found to edit!"
```

If the EmpID was found, then the modifications can be made to that record. The Execute method of the Connection object is used to execute an SQL Update statement. Notice the Where clause that limits the update to this single record:

```
Conn.Execute "Update tblEmps set " _
    & "LastName = '" & LastName & "', " _
    & "FirstName = '" & FirstName & "', " _
    & "DepartmentID = " & DepartmentID & ", " _
    & "Salary = " & Salary & ", " _
    & "BirthDate = '" & BirthDate & "' " _
    & "where EmpID = " & EmpID
```

Another method used in this class is the GetEmployee method, which returns a Recordset object containing a single record for the requested employee. The code for the procedure is:

```
Public Function GetEmployee(EmpID)
    Dim Conn As New ADODB.Connection
    If IsNumeric(EmpID) = False Then
        Err.Raise vbObjectError + 1, "SampleServer", _
            "Employee ID must be passed as a number!"
    End If
    Conn.Open "EmpsDatabase", "Admin", ""
    Set GetEmployee = Conn.Execute("select * from tblEmps where " _
        & "EmpID = " & EmpID)
    If GetEmployee.EOF Then
        Err.Raise vbObjectError + 2, "SampleServer", _
            "No employee record was found!"
    End If
End Function
```

The method is declared as a Public Function since it returns a value. A single parameter, the EmpID to retrieve from the database, is passed into the method.

```
Public Function GetEmployee(EmpID)
```

A Connection object will be needed:

```
Dim Conn As New ADODB.Connection
```

Since the EmpID field in the database is numeric, we need to check the EmpID field passed into the method:

```
If IsNumeric(EmpID) = False Then
```

If the value passed into the method is not a number, an error is thrown back to the client:

```
Err.Raise vbObjectError + 1, "SampleServer", _
  "Employee ID must be passed as a number!"
```

otherwise, we can connect to the database:

```
Conn.Open "EmpsDatabase", "Admin", ""
```

Next, the requested record is retrieved from the database. Notice that the recordset is returned into the name of this function. This is how we will return a Recordset object from a procedure:

```
Set GetEmployee = Conn.Execute("select * from tblEmps where " _
  & "EmpID = " & EmpID)
```

One more test is performed. If the Recordset object is empty, the EmpID requested was not found. The EOF property is checked to test this condition:

```
If GetEmployee.EOF Then
```

If a record was not found, an error is thrown back to the client:

```
Err.Raise vbObjectError + 2, "SampleServer", _
  "No employee record was found!"
```

The EmpInfo method returns HTML text that displays the requested employee record formatted. The code for the method is:

```
Public Function EmpInfo(EmpID)
    If IsNumeric(EmpID) = False Then
        Err.Raise vbObjectError + 1, "SampleServer", _
            "Employee ID must be passed as a number!"
    End If
    Dim Conn As New ADODB.Connection
    Dim RSEmp As ADODB.Recordset
    Conn.Open "EmpsDatabase", "Admin", ""
    Set RSEmp = Conn.Execute("select * from tblEmps where " _
        & "EmpID = " & EmpID)
    If RSEmp.EOF Then
        Err.Raise vbObjectError + 2, "SampleServer", _
            "No such employee record was found to edit!"
    End If
    EmpInfo = "Employee ID: " & RSEmp("EmpID") & "<BR>"
    EmpInfo = EmpInfo & "First Name: " & RSEmp("FirstName") &
"<BR>"
    EmpInfo = EmpInfo & "Last Name: " & RSEmp("LastName") & "<BR>"
```

```
        EmpInfo = EmpInfo & "Department: " & RSEmp("DepartmentID") &
          "<BR>"
        EmpInfo = EmpInfo & "Salary: " & FormatCurrency(RSEmp
          ("Salary")) & "<BR>"
        EmpInfo = EmpInfo & "Birth Date: " & RSEmp("BirthDate") &
          "<BR>"
    End Function
```

The method is declared as a `Public  Function` since it returns a value. The ID of the employee that is to be retrieved from the database is passed to the method.

```
    Public Function EmpInfo(EmpID)
```

Since the `EmpID` parameter is a number, and will be used to look for the record in the database, we need to make sure that what was passed is a number:

```
    If IsNumeric(EmpID) = False Then
```

If it is not, we throw an error back to the client that called the method:

```
    Err.Raise vbObjectError + 1, "SampleServer", _
      "Employee ID must be passed as a number!"
```

otherwise, we can attempt to retrieve the requested Employee record. To do that, we will need a connection to the database:

```
    Dim Conn As New ADODB.Connection
```

We will also need a Recordset object:

```
    Dim RSEmp As ADODB.Recordset
```

The Open method of the Connection object is used to make the connection to the Access database:

```
    Conn.Open "EmpsDatabase", "Admin", ""
```

Then a Select query is used to retrieve the contents of the requested employee record. The `Where` clause specifies the EmpID passed into this method:

```
    Set RSEmp = Conn.Execute("select * from tblEmps where " _
      & "EmpID = " & EmpID)
```

We then check to see if we found an employee record with that value. If no records were found, we would be on the EOF region:

```
If RSEmp.EOF Then
```

If that is the case, an error is thrown back to the client:

```
Err.Raise vbObjectError + 2, "SampleServer", _
  "No such employee record was found to edit!"
```

otherwise, we have a valid record and can prepare the text that is returned to the client. First, the EmpID is concatenated to the return value:

```
EmpInfo = "Employee ID: " & RSEmp("EmpID") & "<BR>"
```

Then the FirstName and LastName fields are concatenated to the output of the method:

```
EmpInfo = EmpInfo & "First Name: " & RSEmp("FirstName") & "<BR>"
EmpInfo = EmpInfo & "Last Name: " & RSEmp("LastName") & "<BR>"
```

as is the DepartmentID field:

```
EmpInfo = EmpInfo & "Department: " & RSEmp("DepartmentID") & "<BR>"
```

the Salary field:

```
EmpInfo = EmpInfo & "Salary: " & FormatCurrency(RSEmp("Salary")) &
  "<BR>"
```

and the BirthDate field:

```
EmpInfo = EmpInfo & "Birth Date: " & RSEmp("BirthDate") & "<BR>"
```

The FormWithFields method generates an HTML form that contains form elements for each of the fields in the tblEmps table that are populated with a specific Employee record. This method would allow the client a simple way to generate a form for an Employee record. The code for this method is:

```
Public Function FormWithFields(EmpID, FormAction, PostGet)
    If IsNumeric(EmpID) = False Then
        Err.Raise vbObjectError + 1, "SampleServer", _
            "Employee ID must be passed as a number!"
```

```
    End If
    Dim Conn As New ADODB.Connection
    Dim RSEmp As ADODB.Recordset
    Conn.Open "EmpsDatabase", "Admin", ""
    Set RSEmp = Conn.Execute("select * from tblEmps where " _
        & "EmpID = " & EmpID)
    If RSEmp.EOF Then
        Err.Raise vbObjectError + 2, "SampleServer", _
            "No such employee record was found to edit!"
    End If
    FormWithFields = "<FORM ACTION=""" & FormAction _
        & """ METHOD=""" & PostGet & """>"
    FormWithFields = FormWithFields & _
        "<INPUT TYPE=""hidden"" NAME=""EmpID"" VALUE=""" &
RSEmp("EmpID") & """>"
    FormWithFields = FormWithFields _
        & "First Name: <BR><INPUT TYPE=""text"" NAME="."FirstName""
            VALUE=""" _
        & RSEmp("FirstName") & """><P>"
    FormWithFields = FormWithFields _
        & "Last Name: <BR><INPUT TYPE=""text"" NAME=""LastName""
            VALUE=""" _
        & RSEmp("LastName") & """><P>"
    FormWithFields = FormWithFields _
        & "Department ID: <BR><INPUT TYPE=""text"" NAME="
            "DepartmentID"" VALUE=""" _
        & RSEmp("DepartmentID") & """><P>"
    FormWithFields = FormWithFields _
        & "Salary: <BR><INPUT TYPE=""text"" NAME=""Salary""
            VALUE=""" _
        & RSEmp("Salary") & """><P>"
    FormWithFields = FormWithFields _
        & "Birth Date: <BR><INPUT TYPE=""text"" NAME=""BirthDate""
            VALUE=""" _
        & RSEmp("BirthDate") & """><P>"
    FormWithFields = FormWithFields _
        & "<INPUT TYPE=""submit"" NAME=""Submit"" VALUE=""Submit"
            "></FORM>"
End Function
```

The method returns a value, so it is created as a `Public Function`. Passed into the method is the EmpID that the client wants to display, the Action to take when the Form is submitted, and the method for the submittal of the form, Post or Get:

```
Public Function FormWithFields(EmpID, FormAction, PostGet)
```

The method must find an employee record based on the EmpID field, so we need to make sure that that field is numeric:

```
If IsNumeric(EmpID) = False Then
```

If it is not, an error is thrown back to the client:

```
Err.Raise vbObjectError + 1, "SampleServer", _
    "Employee ID must be passed as a number!"
```

otherwise, we can connect to the database. A Connection object variable is declared:

```
Dim Conn As New ADODB.Connection
```

as is one for the Recordset object:

```
Dim RSEmp As ADODB.Recordset
```

A connection to the database is established:

```
Conn.Open "EmpsDatabase", "Admin", ""
```

and an SQL Select statement is used to retrieve the desired employee record:

```
Set RSEmp = Conn.Execute("select * from tblEmps where " _
    & "EmpID = " & EmpID)
```

We then check the EOF property of the Recordset object to make sure a record was found, based on the EmpID passed into this method:

```
If RSEmp.EOF Then
```

If one wasn't found, the Raise method of the Err object is used to throw an error back to the client:

```
Err.Raise vbObjectError + 2, "SampleServer", _
    "No such employee record was found to edit!"
```

otherwise, we are ready to generate the HTML form based on the employee record. First, the Form tag is defined with the Action and Method supplied to the parameters passed into this method:

```
FormWithFields = "<FORM ACTION=""" & FormAction _
    & """ METHOD=""" & PostGet & """>"
```

Then, concatenated with the return value is a Form Hidden field with the EmpID for the value. This would allow the client to know what record was being modified when the form was submitted:

```
FormWithFields = FormWithFields & _
```

```
"<INPUT TYPE=""hidden"" NAME=""EmpID"" VALUE=""" & RSEmp("EmpID")
    & """>"
```

Next, a Form text field is used to concatenate the FirstNameField to the output:

```
FormWithFields = FormWithFields _
    & "First Name: <BR><INPUT TYPE=""text"" NAME=""FirstName""
    VALUE=""" _
    & RSEmp("FirstName") & """><P>"
```

The same is done with the LastName field:

```
FormWithFields = FormWithFields _
    & "Last Name: <BR><INPUT TYPE=""text"" NAME=""LastName"" VALUE=""" _
    & RSEmp("LastName") & """><P>"
```

Notice that the value for each of the fields comes from the value for the field in the database:

```
FormWithFields = FormWithFields _
    & "Department ID: <BR><INPUT TYPE=""text"" NAME=""DepartmentID""
    VALUE=""" _
    & RSEmp("DepartmentID") & """><P>"
```

Also notice the use of the double quotes to embed a quote, within a quote since that is required for the HMTL tags:

```
FormWithFields = FormWithFields _
    & "Salary: <BR><INPUT TYPE=""text"" NAME=""Salary"" VALUE=""" _
    & RSEmp("Salary") & """><P>"
```

and the BirthDate field is concatenated to the return value:

```
FormWithFields = FormWithFields _
    & "Birth Date: <BR><INPUT TYPE=""text"" NAME=""BirthDate""
    VALUE=""" _
    & RSEmp("BirthDate") & """><P>"
```

Finally, we need to include a SUBMIT button on the Form and use the End Form tag:

```
FormWithFields = FormWithFields _
    & "<INPUT TYPE=""submit"" NAME=""Submit""
    VALUE=""Submit""></FORM>"
```

Adding the Employees Class
The other class in our SampleServer is the *Employees class*, which has methods that deal with a group of employees. To add the Employees

Figure 15-7
Adding a Class mod-
ule through the
Project Explorer.

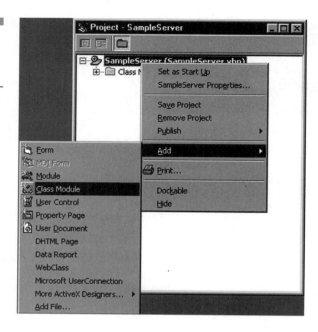

class, right-click on the SampleServer project in the Project Explorer and
select Add-Class Module, as shown in Figure 15-7. Once added, press the
F4 key to give your class a name, as shown in Figure 15-8. With your
class module given the name Employees, we can now know how the class
will be instantiated using the CreateObject method in code:

```
MyObject = Server.CreateObject("SampleServer.Employees")
```

Adding the Methods to the Employees Class
The Employees Class module has a variety of methods for working with
a group of records. Table 15-3 summarizes the methods that will be
added to the Employees class.

The *GetAllEmployees* method returns a Recordset object containing
all the fields and all the records in the tblEmps table.

```
Public Function GetAllEmployees()
    Dim Conn As New ADODB.Connection
    Conn.Open "EmpsDatabase", "Admin", ""
    Set GetAllEmployees = Conn.Execute("select * from tblEmps")
End Function
```

Figure 15-8
Naming the
Employees Class
module.

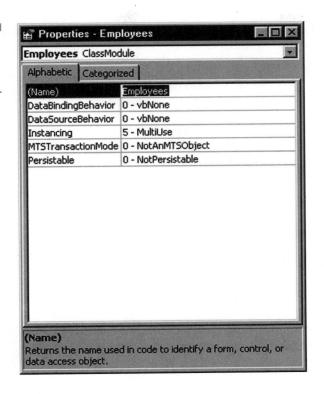

TABLE 15-3

Employees Class
Methods

Method	Purpose
GetAllEmployees	Returns a Recordset of all employee records.
LastNameRecords	Returns a Recordset for employees matching the passed filter.
GetAllEmployeesHTMLTable	Returns an HTML table of all the employee records.
FormWithSelectControl	Returns an HTML form with a Select control populated with the employee records.
SelectControl	Returns an HTML Select control populated with the employee records.

The method is declared as a `Public  Function` since it will return a value:

```
Public Function GetAllEmployees()
```

A Connection object will be needed:

```
Dim Conn As New ADODB.Connection
```

A connection to the database is established using the Open method of the Connection object:

```
Conn.Open "EmpsDatabase", "Admin", ""
```

A Recordset object is returned into the name of the function set. It will be returned to the client using the Execute method of the Connection object:

```
Set GetAllEmployees = Conn.Execute("select * from tblEmps")
```

The *LastName* records method provides a mechanism for clients to retrieve a subset of the records in the table based on criteria passed into the method.

```
Public Function LastNameRecords(LastNameLike)
    Dim Conn As New ADODB.Connection
    Conn.Open "EmpsDatabase", "Admin", ""
    Set LastNameRecords = Conn.Execute("select * from tblEmps " _
        & "where LastName Like '*" & LastNameLike & "*'")
End Function
```

This method is also declared as a `Public  Function` since it returns a Recordset object:

```
Public Function LastNameRecords(LastNameLike)
```

A connection to the database will be needed:

```
Dim Conn As New ADODB.Connection
```

and one is opened:

```
Conn.Open "EmpsDatabase", "Admin", ""
```

The SQL statement retrieves all the records with a LastName that matches the one passed into this method with wildcard characters. Note that these are the wildcard characters for an Access database. If you are using SQL Server, substitute a % character for the * characters:

```
Set LastNameRecords = Conn.Execute("select * from tblEmps " _
& "where LastName Like '*" & LastNameLike & "*'")
```

The next method in this class is the *GetAllEmployeesHTMLTable* method, which creates and returns an HMTL table based on all the records in the database.

```
Public Function GetAllEmployeesHTMLTable()
    Dim Conn As New ADODB.Connection
    Dim RSEmps As ADODB.Recordset
    Dim MyField
    Conn.Open "EmpsDatabase", "Admin", ""
    Set RSEmps = Conn.Execute("select * from tblEmps")
    GetAllEmployeesHTMLTable = "<TABLE><TR>"
    For Each MyField In RSEmps.Fields
        GetAllEmployeesHTMLTable = GetAllEmployeesHTMLTable &
            "<TD>" _
                & MyField.Name & "</TD>"
    Next
    GetAllEmployeesHTMLTable = GetAllEmployeesHTMLTable & "</TR>"
    Do Until RSEmps.EOF
        GetAllEmployeesHTMLTable = GetAllEmployeesHTMLTable &
            "<TR>"
        For Each MyField In RSEmps.Fields
            GetAllEmployeesHTMLTable = GetAllEmployeesHTMLTable &
                "<TD>" _
                    & RSEmps(MyField.Name) & "</TD>"
        Next
        GetAllEmployeesHTMLTable = GetAllEmployeesHTMLTable &
            "</TR>"
        RSEmps.MoveNext
    Loop
    GetAllEmployeesHTMLTable = GetAllEmployeesHTMLTable & "</Table>"
End Function
```

The method will return the text of an HTML table, so it is declared as a Public Function and receives no parameters:

```
Public Function GetAllEmployeesHTMLTable()
```

A Connection object will be needed:

```
Dim Conn As New ADODB.Connection
```

as will a Recordset object that contains the records from the tblEmps table:

```
Dim RSEmps As ADODB.Recordset
```

One more variable needs to be declared as Field object will be used in the `For...Each` loops:

```
Dim MyField
```

A connection to the database is established:

```
Conn.Open "EmpsDatabase", "Admin", ""
```

The Execute method is used to return all the rows and fields from the tblEmps table:

```
Set RSEmps = Conn.Execute("select * from tblEmps")
```

The HTML begin tags are placed into the name of the function so they will be returned:

```
GetAllEmployeesHTMLTable = "<TABLE><TR>"
```

Next, a `For...Each` structure is used to iterate through each of the fields in the Recordset object's Fields collection:

```
For Each MyField In RSEmps.Fields
```

The name of each of the fields with table cell tags is concatenated into the return value of the function:

```
GetAllEmployeesHTMLTable = GetAllEmployeesHTMLTable & "<TD>" _
    & MyField.Name & "</TD>"
```

Before looping to the next Field object in the collection:

```
Next
```

an end row tag for the field headers is concatenated into the return value of the method:

```
GetAllEmployeesHTMLTable = GetAllEmployeesHTMLTable & "</TR>"
```

Next, a `Do...Loop` is used to iterate through all the records in the Recordset object:

```
Do Until RSEmps.EOF
```

Each of the records from the Recordset object will be placed in its own row:

```
GetAllEmployeesHTMLTable = GetAllEmployeesHTMLTable & "<TR>"
```

Then another `For...Each` structure is used to iterate through the Field objects in the Fields collection of the Recordset object:

```
For Each MyField In RSEmps.Fields
```

Within the loop, each of the fields within each of the records is concatenated to the return value of the method:

```
GetAllEmployeesHTMLTable = GetAllEmployeesHTMLTable & "<TD>" _
    & RSEmps(MyField.Name) & "</TD>"
```

After each of the fields is concatenated to the return value, an end row tag is added to the return value:

```
GetAllEmployeesHTMLTable = GetAllEmployeesHTMLTable & "</TR>"
```

The code then moves onto the next record before looping:

```
    RSEmps.MoveNext
Loop
```

Finally, an HTML end table tag is concatenated to the return value:

```
GetAllEmployeesHTMLTable = GetAllEmployeesHTMLTable & "</Table>"
```

The *FormWithSelectControl* method outputs an HTML select control contained within a form that lists all the Employee names but internally submits the EmpID for the employee. The code for that method is:

```
Public Function FormWithSelectControl(FormAction, PostGet)
    Dim Conn As New ADODB.Connection
    Dim RSEmps As ADODB.Recordset
    Conn.Open "EmpsDatabase", "Admin", ""
    Set RSEmps = Conn.Execute("select EmpID, FirstName & ' ' &
      LastName " _
        & "as EmpName from tblEmps")
    FormWithSelectControl = "<FORM ACTION=""" & FormAction _
        & """ METHOD=""" & PostGet & """>EmpID:"
    FormWithSelectControl = FormWithSelectControl & "<SELECT
      NAME=""EmpID"" SIZE=1>"
    Do Until RSEmps.EOF
```

```
        FormWithSelectControl = FormWithSelectControl & "<OPTION
          VALUE=""" _
          & RSEmps("EmpID") & """>" & RSEmps("EmpName")
        RSEmps.MoveNext
    Loop
    FormWithSelectControl = FormWithSelectControl & "</SELECT><P>" _
        & "<INPUT TYPE=""submit"" NAME=""Submit""
VALUE=""Submit""></FORM>"
End Function
```

The method is declared as a `Public Function` since it returns a value. Passed into the method is the Action to take when the form is submitted and the method used in the submittal, Post or Get:

```
Public Function FormWithSelectControl(FormAction, PostGet)
```

A Connection object is required:

```
Dim Conn As New ADODB.Connection
```

as will a Recordset object:

```
Dim RSEmps As ADODB.Recordset
```

The Open method of the Connection object is used to establish a connection to the Access database:

```
Conn.Open "EmpsDatabase", "Admin", ""
```

A Select query is executed using the Execute method of the Connection object, which returns a Recordset object into the `RSEmps` variable. Retrieved from the database is the EmpID field and a concatenation of the FirstName field, a space, and the LastName field outputted as EmpName:

```
Set RSEmps = Conn.Execute("select EmpID, FirstName & ' ' &
  LastName " _
& "as EmpName from tblEmps")
```

The `Form` tag starts the text of the return value. Note that the `FormAction` parameter and the `PostGet` parameter are used to generate this tag:

```
FormWithSelectControl = "<FORM ACTION=""" & FormAction _
  & """ METHOD=""" & PostGet & """>EmpID:"
```

The beginning portion of the Select control tag is concatenated to the return value:

```
FormWithSelectControl = FormWithSelectControl & "<SELECT
    NAME=""EmpID"" SIZE=1>"
```

Then we set a Do...Loop to iterate through all the employee records:

```
Do Until RSEmps.EOF
```

Each record is added as an Option to the Select control. The name of the employee would be displayed to the visitor. The EmpID for that employee record would be returned when the form is submitted:

```
FormWithSelectControl = FormWithSelectControl & "<OPTION
    VALUE=""" _
    & RSEmps("EmpID") & """>" & RSEmps("EmpName")
```

The code then moves on to the next record before looping:

```
    RSEmps.MoveNext
Loop
```

The last line concatenates the ending tag for the Select control, a SUBMIT button, and the ending tag for the HTML Form:

```
FormWithSelectControl = FormWithSelectControl & "</SELECT><P>" _
    & "<INPUT TYPE=""submit"" NAME=""Submit"" VALUE=""Submit"">
        </FORM>"
```

One more method to discuss, the *SelectControl* method, returns an HTML Select control populated with the employee records. The code for this procedure is:

```
Public Function SelectControl()
    Dim Conn As New ADODB.Connection
    Dim RSEmps As ADODB.Recordset
    Conn.Open "EmpsDatabase", "Admin", ""
    Set RSEmps = Conn.Execute("select EmpID, FirstName & ' ' &
        LastName " _
        & "as EmpName from tblEmps")
    SelectControl = "<SELECT NAME=""EmpID"" SIZE=1>"
    Do Until RSEmps.EOF
        SelectControl = SelectControl & "<OPTION VALUE=""" _
            & RSEmps("EmpID") & """>" & RSEmps("EmpName")
        RSEmps.MoveNext
    Loop
```

```
        SelectControl = SelectControl & "</SELECT>"
End Function
```

The method accepts no parameters and is declared as a `Public Function` since it returns a value:

```
Public Function SelectControl()
```

A Connection object is needed, so one is declared:

```
Dim Conn As New ADODB.Connection
```

as is one for the Recordset object:

```
Dim RSEmps As ADODB.Recordset
```

A connection to the database is established:

```
Conn.Open "EmpsDatabase", "Admin", ""
```

and a Recordset is returned from the Connection object's Execute method that contains the names and IDs of all the employee records:

```
Set RSEmps = Conn.Execute("select EmpID, FirstName & ' ' &
  LastName " _
& "as EmpName from tblEmps")
```

The return value from the function is set to the opening tag for the Select control:

```
SelectControl = "<SELECT NAME=""EmpID"" SIZE=1>"
```

Then we start a loop that will take us through all the employee records:

```
Do Until RSEmps.EOF
```

Each record is concatenated to the return value as an Option of the Select control:

```
SelectControl = SelectControl & "<OPTION VALUE="""  _
  & RSEmps("EmpID") & """>" & RSEmps("EmpName")
```

The code then moves to the next record before looping:

```
RSEmps.MoveNext
Loop
```

Finally, the end tage for the Select control is concatenated to the return value:

```
SelectControl = SelectControl & "</SELECT>"
```

Compiling the Component into a DLL

Now that the component is properly named, has classes and method, we can compile the component into a DLL so that it can be used in our ASP code. To compile the component, select File-Make from the menu as shown in Figure 15-9. A File dialog opens and asks for the location to save the DLL to; save it to `Windows/System` directory.

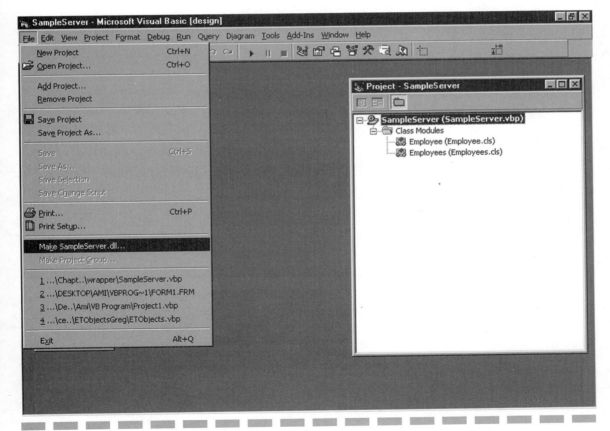

Figure 15-9 Compiling the SampleServer component.

Using Your Component in Your Active Server Page Applications

To use the AddEmployee method of the Employee class we would have code like the following:

```
<%
Option Explicit
Dim MyObject
Dim TheID
Set MyObject = Server.CreateObject("SampleServer.Employee")
TheID = MyObject.AddEmployee("Jackson", "Timmy", "two", 65000,
  "4/4/45")
Response.Write TheID
%>
```

First, we state that variables will be declared:

```
Option Explicit
```

Next, a variable called MyObject is declared:

```
Dim MyObject
```

and set to the Employee class of the SampleServer application. Notice that the App.Class string is just as we set it in the VB project:

```
Set MyObject = Server.CreateObject("SampleServer.Employee")
```

The AddEmployee method returns the value of the EmpID for the new employee. Notice that this call should produce an error, since the DepartmentID is not a number:

```
TheID = MyObject.AddEmployee("Jackson", "Timmy", "two", 65000,
  "4/4/45")
```

Then the EmpID is written to the browser:

```
Response.Write TheID
```

The error message displayed in the browser is shown in Figure 15-10.

Notice that the source of the error is the SampleServer. Also note that the error message that we supplied in the method is what is displayed in the Browser window. This line calls the method correctly:

```
TheID = MyObject.AddEmployee("Jackson", "Timmy", 2, 65000,
  "4/4/45")
```

The ID of the new employee would be displayed in the browser, as shown in Figure 15-11.

Figure 15-10
The AddEmployee
method producing
an error.

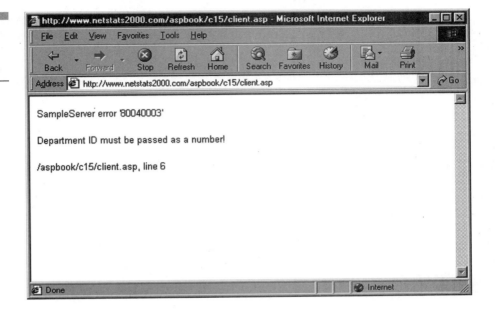

Figure 15-11
Output of code
when the
AddEmployee
method was used
correctly.

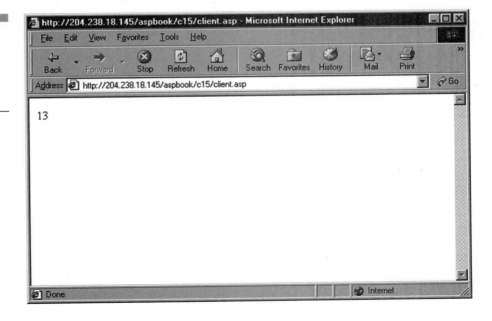

The next code block edits the data in the employee record that was just added and then displays the contents of that record.

```
<%
Option Explicit
Dim MyObject
Dim TheEmpObject
Set MyObject = Server.CreateObject("SampleServer.Employee")
MyObject.EditEmployee 13, "Jackson", "Tim", 3, 50000, "4/4/45"
Set TheEmpObject = MyObject.GetEmployee (13)
Response.Write "Employee ID: " & TheEmpObject("EmpID") & "<BR>"
Response.Write "First Name: " & TheEmpObject("FirstName") & "<BR>"
Response.Write "Last Name: " & TheEmpObject("LastName") & "<BR>"
Response.Write "Department: " & TheEmpObject("DepartmentID") &
    "<BR>"
Response.Write "Salary: " & FormatCurrency(TheEmpObject("Salary"))
    & "<BR>"
Response.Write "Birth Date: " & TheEmpObject("BirthDate") & "<BR>"
%>
```

First, `Option Explicit` is used to require variable declaration:

```
Option Explicit
```

Then the `MyObject` variable is declared, which will be used to instantiate the server object:

```
Dim MyObject
```

Also, a variable to store the returned Recordset with the contents of an employee record is declared:

```
Dim TheEmpObject
```

The `MyObject` variable is instantiated as an instance of our server:

```
Set MyObject = Server.CreateObject("SampleServer.Employee")
```

The EditEmployee method of the Employee object is used to modify this employee's record:

```
MyObject.EditEmployee 13, "Jackson", "Tim", 3, 50000, "4/4/45"
```

Then the GetEmployee method is used to return the contents of the record with the ID of 13:

```
Set TheEmpObject = MyObject.GetEmployee (13)
```

Figure 15-12
Output of
EditEmployee and
GetEmployee code.

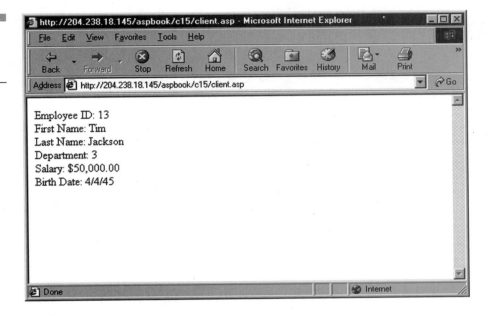

Each of the fields in that record is written to the browser:

```
Response.Write "Employee ID: " & TheEmpObject("EmpID") & "<BR>"
Response.Write "First Name: " & TheEmpObject("FirstName") & "<BR>"
Response.Write "Last Name: " & TheEmpObject("LastName") & "<BR>"
Response.Write "Department: " & TheEmpObject("DepartmentID") &
    "<BR>"
Response.Write "Salary: " & FormatCurrency(TheEmpObject("Salary"))
    & "<BR>"
Response.Write "Birth Date: " & TheEmpObject("BirthDate") & "<BR>"
```

Figure 15-12 displays the output of this code. Notice that the data are displayed as they were modified with the EditEmployee method.

The next code block deletes an employee record from the tblEmps table and then tries to retrieve the record. An error results from this code:

```
<%
Option Explicit
Dim MyObject
Dim TheEmpObject
Set MyObject = Server.CreateObject("SampleServer.Employee")
MyObject.DeleteEmployee 3
Set TheEmpObject = MyObject.GetEmployee (3)
Response.Write "Employee ID: " & TheEmpObject("EmpID") & "<BR>"
Response.Write "First Name: " & TheEmpObject("FirstName") & "<BR>"
Response.Write "Last Name: " & TheEmpObject("LastName") & "<BR>"
```

```
Response.Write "Department: " & TheEmpObject("DepartmentID") &
  "<BR>"
Response.Write "Salary: " & FormatCurrency(TheEmpObject("Salary"))
  & "<BR>"
Response.Write "Birth Date: " & TheEmpObject("BirthDate") & "<BR>"
%>
```

First, `Option Explicit` is written:

```
Option Explicit
```

Next, the `MyObject` variable is declared:

```
Dim MyObject
```

as is the object variable that will store an employee record:

```
Dim TheEmpObject
```

The `MyObject` variable is instantiated as an instance of our Employee class:

```
Set MyObject = Server.CreateObject("SampleServer.Employee")
```

The DeleteEmployee method is used to delete the employee record with an ID of 3:

```
MyObject.DeleteEmployee 3
```

The code then attempts to retrieve the record we just deleted. This line will produce an error:

```
Set TheEmpObject = MyObject.GetEmployee (3)
```

If the code didn't error out, the contents of the employee record would be displayed:

```
Response.Write "Employee ID: " & TheEmpObject("EmpID") & "<BR>"
Response.Write "First Name: " & TheEmpObject("FirstName") & "<BR>"
Response.Write "Last Name: " & TheEmpObject("LastName") & "<BR>"
Response.Write "Department: " & TheEmpObject("DepartmentID") &
  "<BR>"
Response.Write "Salary: " & FormatCurrency(TheEmpObject("Salary"))
  & "<BR>"
Response.Write "Birth Date: " & TheEmpObject("BirthDate") & "<BR>"
```

The output of this code is displayed in Figure 15-13.

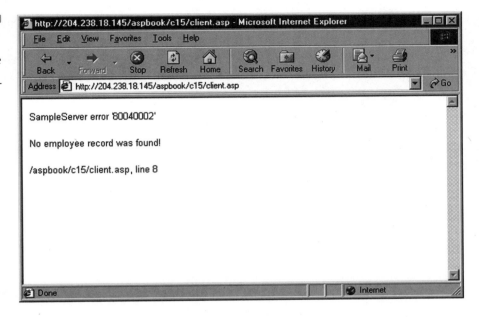

Figure 15-13
Output of error code
attempting to retrieve
a deleted record.

The next code block uses the EmpInfo method to display an employee record:

```
<%
Option Explicit
Dim MyObject
Set MyObject = Server.CreateObject("SampleServer.Employee")
Response.Write MyObject.EmpInfo(13)
%>
```

First, `Option Explicit` is used to state that variables will be declared:

```
Option Explicit
```

Next, we declare a variable for the SampleServer Employee class:

```
Dim MyObject
```

Here, the object is instantiated:

```
Set MyObject = Server.CreateObject("SampleServer.Employee")
```

The Write method of the Response object is simply used to write the employee record to the browser as returned from the EmpInfo method:

```
Response.Write MyObject.EmpInfo(13)
```

Figure 15-14
Output of EmpInfo code.

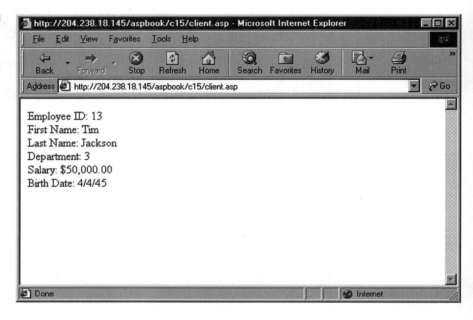

The output for this code is displayed in Figure 15-14.

The next code block demonstrates the use and output of the FormWithFields method:

```
<%
Option Explicit
Dim MyObject
Set MyObject = Server.CreateObject("SampleServer.Employee")
Response.Write MyObject.FormWithFields(13, "./index.asp", "POST")
%>
```

As usual, we start with `Option Explicit`:

```
Option Explicit
```

Next, we declare a variable for our SampleServer:

```
Dim MyObject
```

and instantiate it:

```
Set MyObject = Server.CreateObject("SampleServer.Employee")
```

Then we call the FormWithFields method, passing to it the employee record we want, the action for the Form, and the method for the submittal of the form:

```
Response.Write MyObject.FormWithFields(13, "./index.asp", "POST")
```

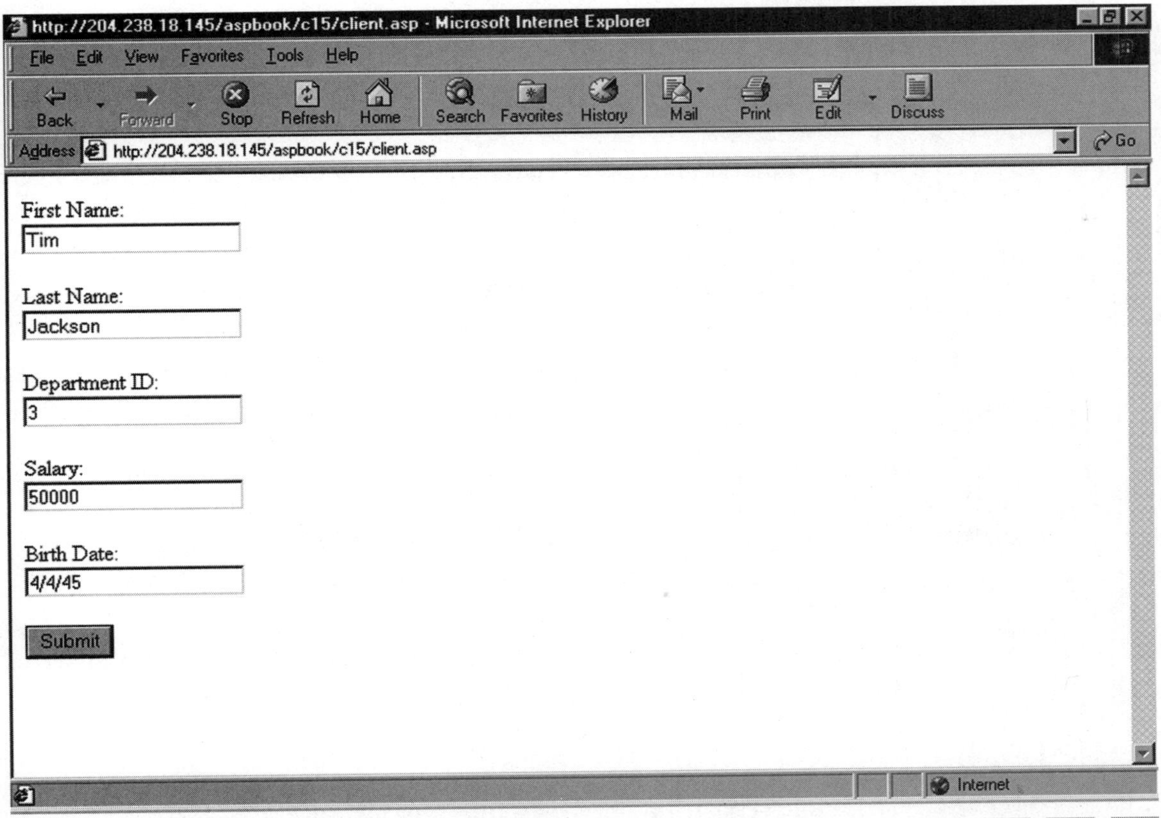

Figure 15-15 Output of EmpInfo code.

The output of the code is displayed in Figure 15-15.

The next code block uses the Employees class to retrieve all the records from the tblEmps table:

```
<%
Option Explicit
Dim MyObject
Dim EmpRecords
Set MyObject = Server.CreateObject("SampleServer.Employees")
Set EmpRecords = MyObject.GetAllEmployees
Do Until EmpRecords.EOF
    Response.Write "<B>Name: </B>" & EmpRecords("FirstName") & " " _
        & EmpRecords("LastName") & "<P>"
    EmpRecords.MoveNext
Loop
%>
```

First, the Option Explicit directive is written:

```
Option Explicit
```

Then a variable that will store the instance of the Employees class is declared:

```
Dim MyObject
```

as is a variable that will store the Recordset object:

```
Dim EmpRecords
```

Next, the Employees class is instantiated:

```
Set MyObject = Server.CreateObject("SampleServer.Employees")
```

The GetAllEmployees method of the Employees class is used to retrieve a Recordset object that will contain all the employee records from the tblEmps table. Notice that Set is used at the beginning of the statement. This is used because our Server is returning a complex object, a Recordset object, not a simple variable:

```
Set EmpRecords = MyObject.GetAllEmployees
```

The code then starts a loop through all the records in the EmpRecords Recordset:

```
Do Until EmpRecords.EOF
```

The name of each employee is written to the browser:

```
Response.Write "<B>Name: </B>" & EmpRecords("FirstName") & " " _
    & EmpRecords("LastName") & "<P>"
```

before moving on to the next record and looping:

```
    EmpRecords.MoveNext
Loop
```

Figure 15-16 shows the output of this code.

The next code block implements the LastNameRecords method:

```
<%
Option Explicit
Dim MyObject
Dim EmpRecords
Set MyObject = Server.CreateObject("SampleServer.Employees")
Set EmpRecords = MyObject.LastNameRecords("M")
Do Until EmpRecords.EOF
    Response.Write "<B>Name: </B>" & EmpRecords("FirstName") & " " _
```

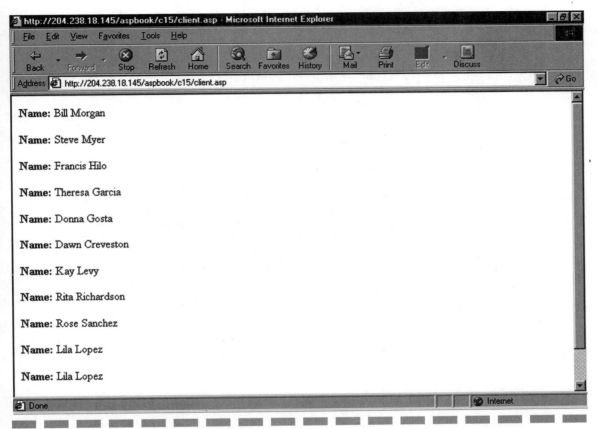

Figure 15-16 Output of GetAllEmployees method code.

```
            & EmpRecords("LastName") & "<P>"
        EmpRecords.MoveNext
    Loop
%>
```

First, Option Explicit is coded:

```
Option Explicit
```

An object variable that will store the Employees class is declared:

```
Dim MyObject
```

as is one for the Recordset object:

```
Dim EmpRecords
```

The Employees object is instantiated:

```
Set MyObject = Server.CreateObject("SampleServer.Employees")
```

The LastNameRecords method is called:

```
Set EmpRecords = MyObject.LastNameRecords("M")
```

The code then loops through all the records in the Recordset object:

```
Do Until EmpRecords.EOF
```

For each record, the name for that employee is written to the browser:

```
Response.Write "<B>Name: </B>" & EmpRecords("FirstName") & " " _
    & EmpRecords("LastName") & "<P>"
```

before moving to the next record and looping:

```
EmpRecords.MoveNext
Loop
```

The next code block shows the use of the GetAllEmployees HTMLTable method.

```
<%
Option Explicit
Dim MyObject
Set MyObject = Server.CreateObject("SampleServer.Employees")
Response.Write MyObject.GetAllEmployeesHTMLTable
%>
```

In this code block `Option Explicit` is the first line:

```
Option Explicit
```

The Employees class variable is declared:

```
Dim MyObject
```

and instantiated:

```
Set MyObject = Server.CreateObject("SampleServer.Employees")
```

The return of the GetAllEmployeesHTMLTable method is then written to the browser:

```
Response.Write MyObject.GetAllEmployeesHTMLTable
```

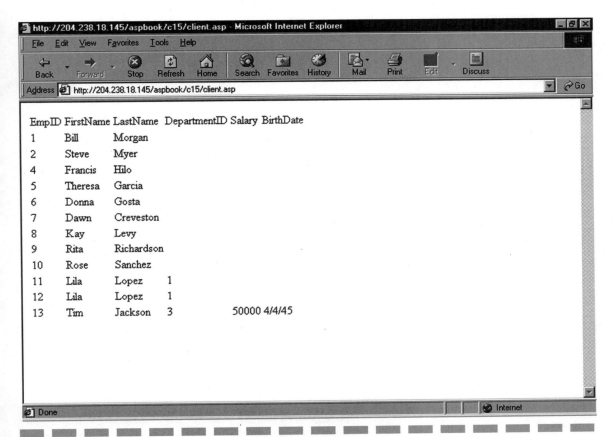

Figure 15-17 Output of GetAllEmployeesHTMLTable method code.

The output of this code is displayed in Figure 15-17.

The FormWithSelectControl method of the Employees class generates an HTML Form that contains a Select control populated with the employee records. The following code block demonstrates the use of the method:

```
<%
Option Explicit
Dim MyObject
Set MyObject = Server.CreateObject("SampleServer.Employees")
Response.Write MyObject.FormWithSelectControl("./index.asp",
"POST")
%>
```

The method is very simple to use. First, we write `Option Explicit`:

```
Option Explicit
```

Then we declare a variable that will store the SampleServer object:

```
Dim MyObject
```

and instantiate it:

```
Set MyObject = Server.CreateObject("SampleServer.Employees")
```

We then call the FormWithSelectControl method, passing to it the action to take on the form and the method for the submittal:

```
Response.Write MyObject.FormWithSelectControl("./index.asp",
   "POST")
```

Figure 15-18 shows the output of this code. Note that the Select control displays the employee names but the EmpID is submitted with the form.

One more method to demonstrate, the SelectControl method, is another simple call as demonstrated next. Remember, the purpose of creating this component was as a wrapper, so it should be simple to use.

```
<%
Option Explicit
```

Figure 15-18
Output of the
FormWithSelect
Control method.

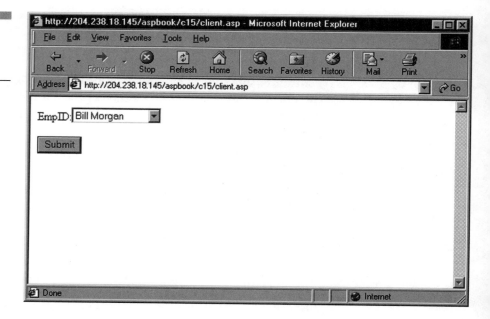

```
Dim MyObject
Set MyObject = Server.CreateObject("SampleServer.Employees")
Response.Write MyObject.SelectControl
%>
```

Once again, we start with `Option Explicit`:

```
Option Explicit
```

Then we declare our object variable:

```
Dim MyObject
```

and instantiate it:

```
Set MyObject = Server.CreateObject("SampleServer.Employees")
```

We then write the output of the SelectControl method to the browser using the Write method of the Response object:

```
Response.Write MyObject.SelectControl
```

The output of this code is displayed in Figure 15-19.

Figure 15-19
Output of the
SelectControl
method.

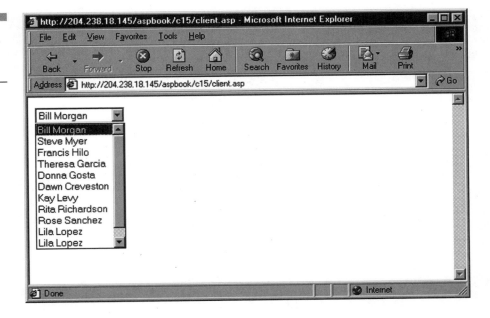

16

ASP in Action: Product Catalog

ASP in Action

In the next three chapters we explore an entire Active Server Page application, which provides an e-commerce solution. As you will see in the next three chapters, the site allows for the displaying, browsing, and searching of products. The site also has a shopping cart component that allows visitors to add, view, and delete items ordered and allows visitors to check out. When visitors check out they are presented with a secure page to supply their personal information. The site also shows you how you can work with your customers, providing them feedback and communication. The site also has numerous general site pages.

This chapter focuses on the Product Catalog portion of the site, as well as general pages for the site. In Chapter 17, we look at the Shopping Cart component and in Chapter 18 we look at the Customers component. As you look at the site, you will notice that every page is an Active Server Page. Most of the text on each of the pages is generated from the database, so the Web site is easily modified to sell many different products. Also, code on every page tracks visitors through your Web site so that you can later review your customers' viewing habits, as well as which pages are more popular than others.

Product Catalog Web Site

As mentioned previously, in this chapter we focus on the Product Catalog component of the Web site. This component contains pages that allow visitors to browse through a hierarchy of products, search through those products, and display detailed information about those products. Visitors can view comments about the products, add their own comments, and browse through the items on clearance. Other pages in this component allow visitors to read information about the company and about placing orders through the site.

Sample Usage

When visitors first enter the site they see the Home page displayed in Figure 16-1. Each page has a consistent look and feel. Below the title

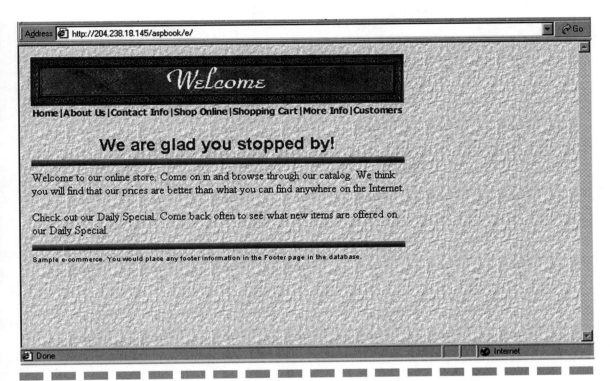

Figure 16-1 Home page.

of each page is a Navigation bar that allows visitors to go to any of the Top Level sections of the site. In this chapter, we focus on the first four Top Level sections, the Home, About Us, Contact Info, and Shop Online pages. As you will see when we look at the code, all the text below the Navigation bar comes from the database, so this page is entirely configurable.

Figure 16-2 displays the About Us page, which would be used to convey to the visitor information about the company hosting the Web site and things like where they are located and the company's philosophy. Again, all the text below the Navigation bar comes from the database, so the page is entirely configurable. Notice the footer text, which also comes from the database and is used across most of the pages at the site.

If visitors clicked on the Contact Info page they would see what is displayed in Figure 16-3. The Contact Info page also contains elements

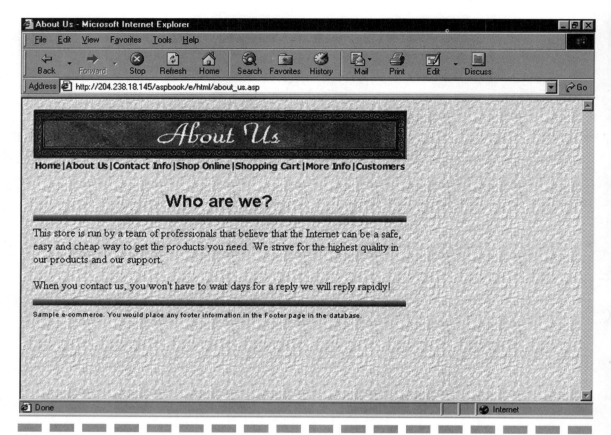

Figure 16-2 About Us page.

from the database that give the page a title and basic text as well as the footer. But this page adds an HTML table of contacts populated from a table in the database.

When visitors are ready to shop, they click on the SHOP ONLINE link and see the menu displayed in Figure 16-4. The Product Catalog menu page provides the mechanism for your visitors to view the products in your database. The menu also provides links to other pages within the Product Catalog.

If visitors wanted to read about the ordering process, they could click on the HOW TO ORDER link and would see the page displayed in Figure 16-5. On the How to Order page you would include the text that describes the ordering process to visitors. Again, all the text below the

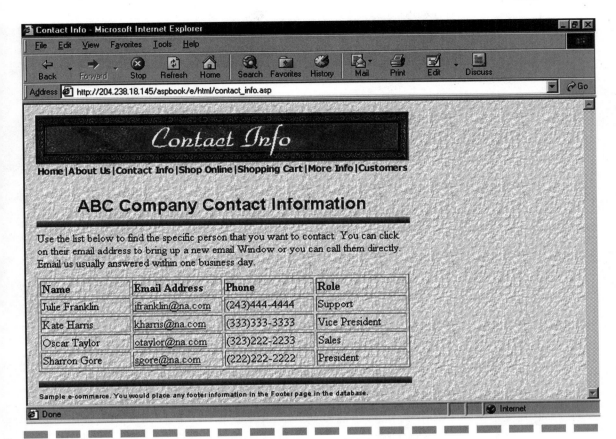

Figure 16-3 Contact Info page.

Navigation bar comes from the database. Also note that, as we are browsing through the site, every page we go to is recorded in the database, so we keep a trail of all the pages viewed by every visitor.

If visitors click on the RETURN POLICY link from the Product Catalog menu page they will see the page, shown in Figure 16-6. On this page you would state your company's return policy. You may want to include email links for further information, in addition to a phone number. The text on this page comes from the database, so it is easily modified.

If visitors select the SHIPPING INFO link on the Product Catalog menu page, they would see the page displayed in Figure 16-7. The Shipping Info page contains the title, description, and footer populated from the

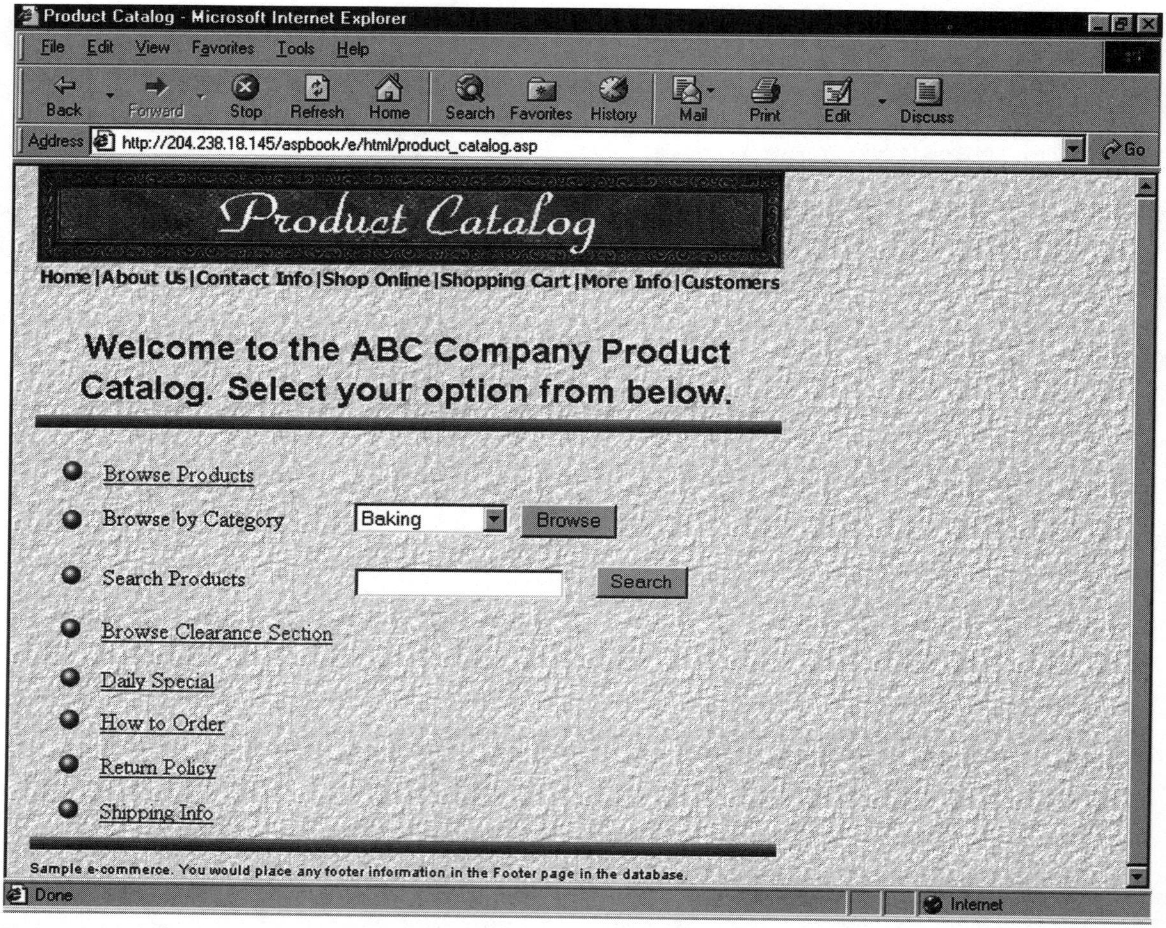

Figure 16-4   Product Catalog menu page.

database. This page could be used to describe the different shipping methods you use, where they go, how long they take, and approximate charges.

Back on the Product Catalog menu page, visitors have a variety of ways to see the products in the catalog. The catalog is organized by categories, where each category can have subcategories. Each category is a subcategory of another category, except for the Top Level category. Each category can also have products, and each product can belong to more than one category.

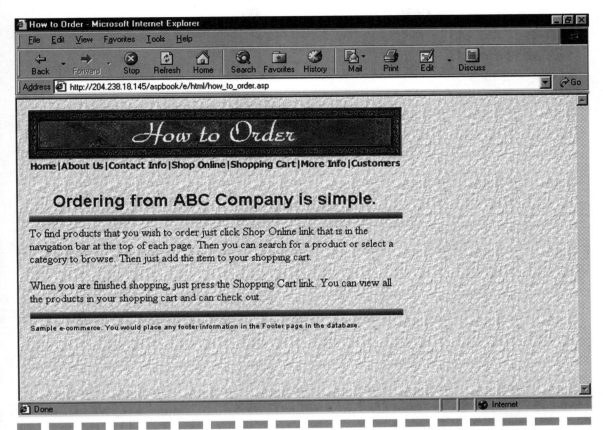

Figure 16-5 How to Order page.

What you end up with, then, is a completely customizable hierarchy-based product catalog, where products can be included in multiple locations. If visitors click on the BROWSE PRODUCTS link, they start viewing the product catalog from the top and can work their way down through the hierarchy of categories. The page seen when visitors select that link is shown in Figure 16-8. First notice that the subject of this sample site is Food. But remember that all the data comes from the database, so you can easily substitute other products to sell.

At the top of the Products page is the text Top Level /, which shows visitors where they are within the hierarchy of the Product Catalog. Since we are at the Top Level of the catalog, that is the full path to where we are. The next section lists the subcategories under the Top

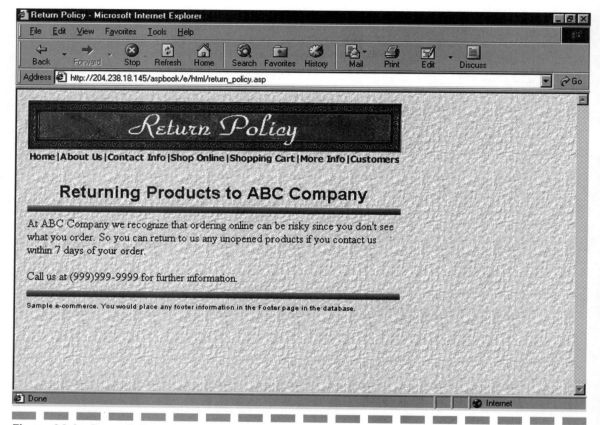

Figure 16-6   Return Policy page.

Level category. Remember that each of these categories can have its own subcategories, and each of the subcategories links back to this page, displaying the information for that category.

In the section after the subcategories is the list of any products in this category, although this category has none. Figure 16-9 shows the page displayed when the Breakfast subcategory is selected. Notice now that the top of the page contains the text Top Level/Breakfast, which is the path to where we are now in the hierarchy. We can go back to the Top Level by clicking on the Top Level text. Beneath that is the section of subcategories. The Breakfast category has three subcategories; beneath that is the single product that is in the Breakfast category.

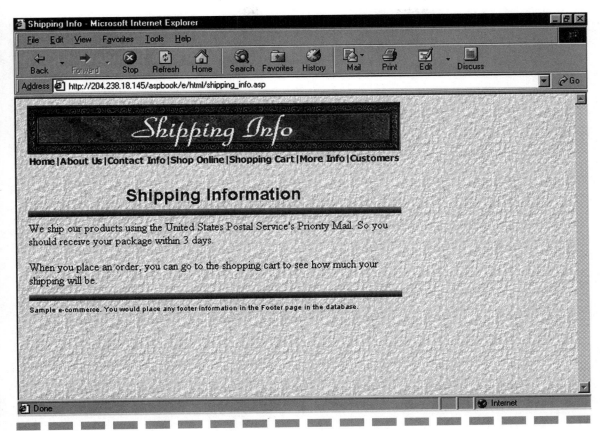

Figure 16-7   Shipping Info page.

If visitors were to click on the Cereal category, they would see the page displayed in Figure 16-10. Notice at the top of the page that we now see the full path to this category. Again, visitors can click on any part of the path to get back to that category. This category has no subcategories, so none is listed. Under that section are the products in the Breakfast category.

Each product entry lists the name of the item and a brief description; under that is the price. The code supports a standard price and a clearance price, so based on the database, the price for the product will be listed or it will be listed along with the clearance price. For example, take a look at Figure 16-11. The regular price for the pasta is crossed out because it is marked as a clearance item.

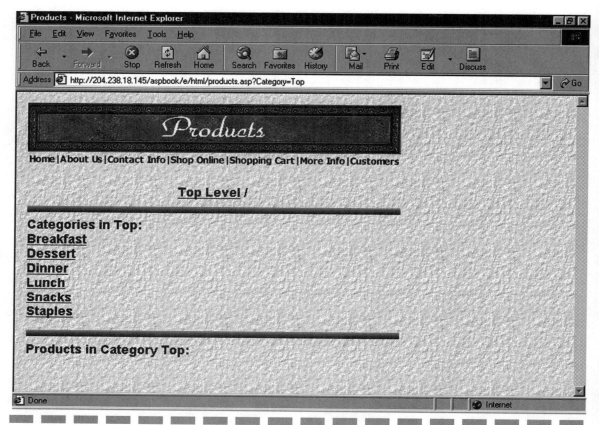

Figure 16-8 Products page displaying the Top Level category.

If visitors click on the icon of the product or the link beneath it, they see a large picture of the product as shown in Figure 16-12. The product icons are all the same size, but the full-size image can be any size the page displays the image itself. An ASP router page records a hit to the picture before redirecting visitors to the large image.

On the products page there is a link beneath each product that says, CLICK HERE FOR MORE INFORMATION OR TO ORDER THIS ITEM. If visitors click on that link, they see the extended information about the product as shown in Figure 16-13. At the top of the page, visitors see the name of the product and the brief description. They also see the icon picture of the product and can click on the icon to display the full-size picture. Beneath that is space for extended information about the product; under

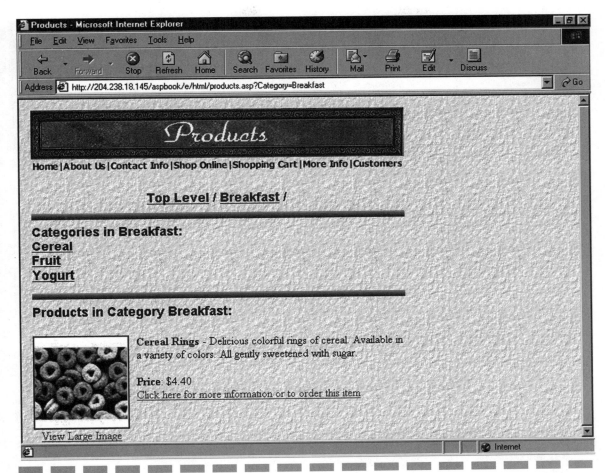

Figure 16-9 Product page displaying the Breakfast category.

that is a section where visitors can specify a quantity and add the item to their Shopping Cart.

At the bottom of the page is the section that displays the comments made by visitors. The visitors' name, location, and comments are displayed. Visitors can also click on the ADD YOUR OWN COMMENT link to add their own comment. That page is shown in Figure 16-14.

Customers can supply their name and their location as well as a comment, which is specifically for the product that they were looking at. When visitors press the ADD COMMENT button, their comment is added

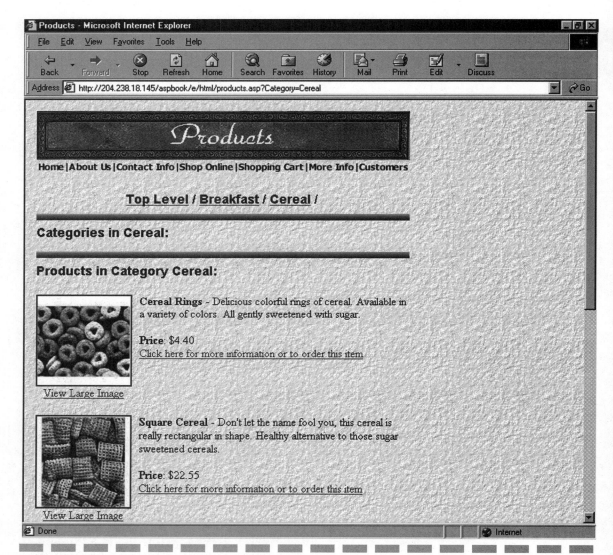

Figure 16-10 Products page displaying the Breakfast category.

to the database and they are redirected back to the product page they were looking at with their comment appended to the list, as shown in Figure 16-15.

Take a look at the product displayed in Figure 16-16. Notice that, besides the quantity field, visitors need to select the Candy Type and the

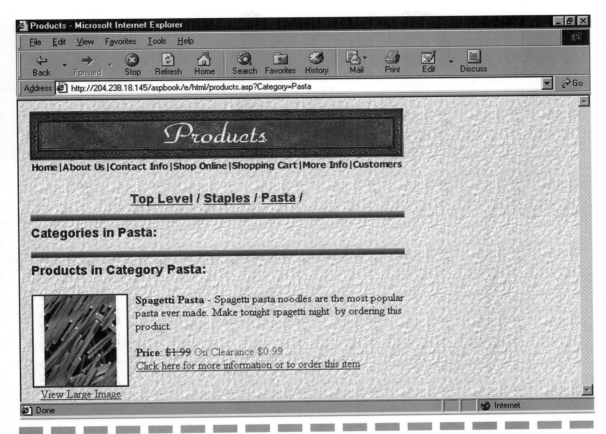

Figure 16-11 Pasta category displaying a product on clearance.

Candy Color for this item. As you will see when we look at the code, the Product Catalog component allows each product to have as many select controls as necessary to prompt visitors for additional selections. Each of the sections comes from the database and each product can contain zero or more selections. So if you are selling shirts, you can prompt visitors for color, size, and style.

Back on the Product Catalog menu page, visitors can also go directly to the category that they want to view. The Browse by Category Select control contains a list of all the categories in the database, so visitors can go directly to the Chips category, as shown in Figure 16-17.

Visitors can also select to search for products by using the Search option on the Product Catalog menu page. For example, if visitors want

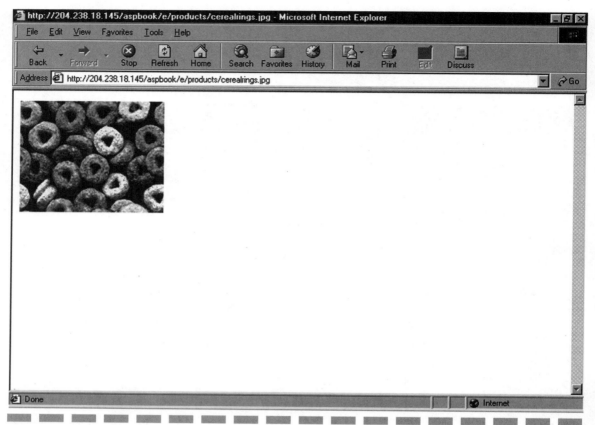

Figure 16-12 Product image.

to find something sweet, they can enter that into the search box and see the page shown in Figure 16-18. The Search page displays any category that has the search text in it. Also displayed on the Search page is any product for which the name contains the search phrase or has the search phrase in the description of the product.

Visitors can also select to view the clearance section from the Product Catalog menu page as shown in Figure 16-19. The Clearance page lists the products that are marked with a clearance price.

One more page to look at in the Product Catalog component is the Daily Special page, which is displayed in Figure 16-20. On this page you would place some product that has a special value, or you could offer promotions through this page such as free shipping or "buy one get one free."

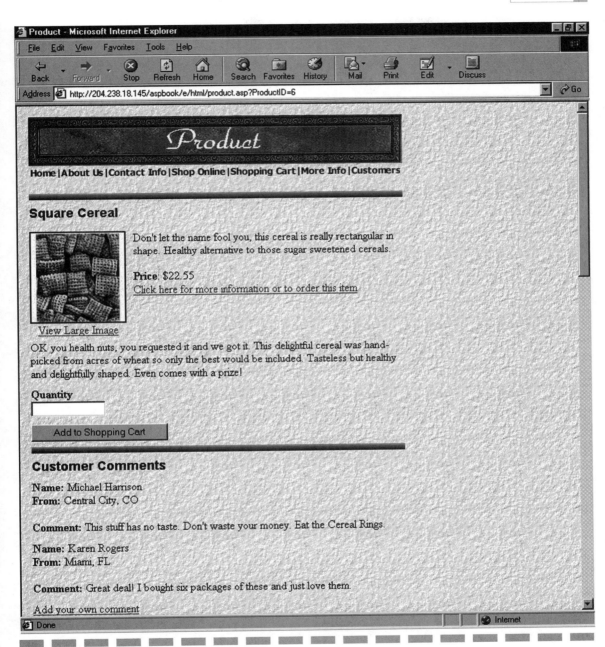

Figure 16-13 Product page.

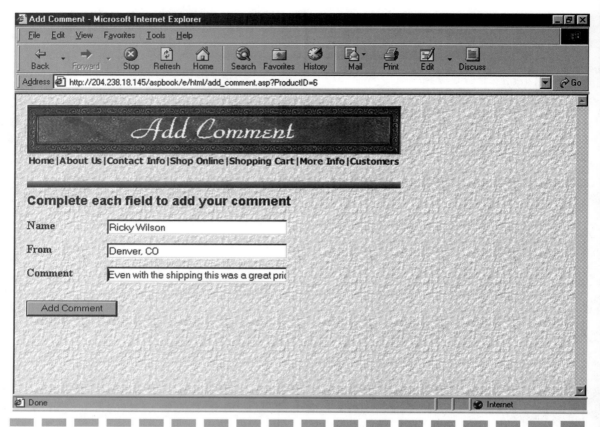

Figure 16-14 Customer comment.

Product Catalog Database Component

The database used in the Product Catalog component uses 11 tables. In this section, we define those tables, and then look at the relationships between the tables. We also define the fields in the tables.

NOTE: *The tables defined here are from an SQL Server database. To convert the tables into Access tables, refer to the information in Chapter 13.*

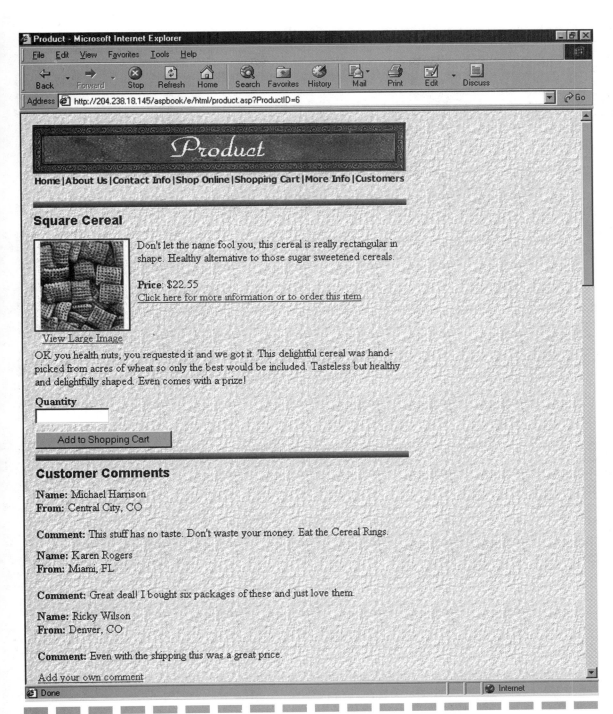

Figure 16-15 Product page displaying new comment.

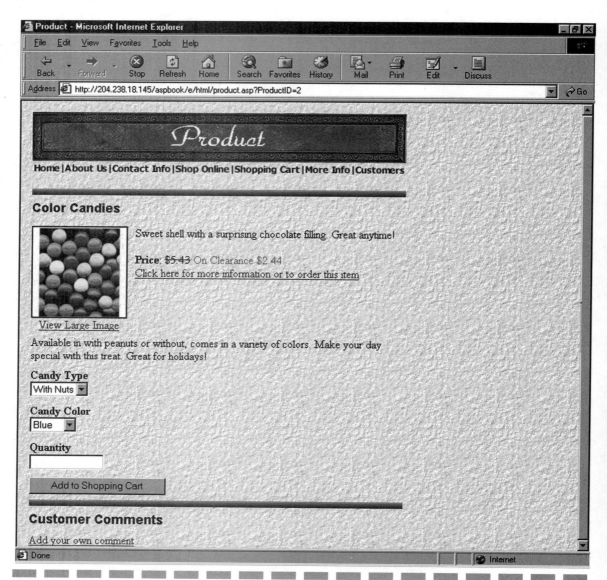

Figure 16-16 Product displaying select options.

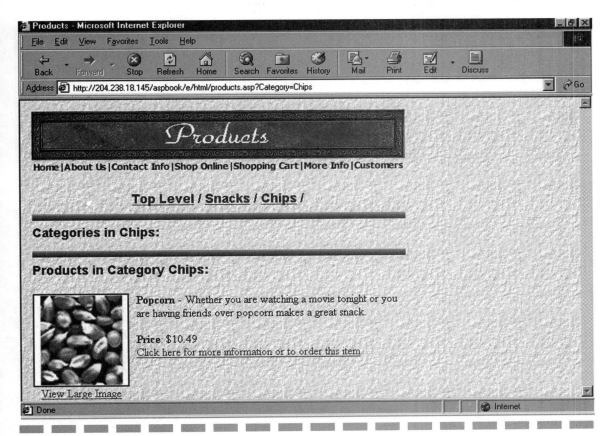

Figure 16-17 Chips category.

Table Definitions

ASPCategories
The *ASPCategories* table contains the information about the categories used in the Product Catalog. The table contains information about the categories and the parent of each category.

ASPContacts
The *ASPContacts* table is used for the Contact Info page. The fields in this table contain the contact information listed on that page.

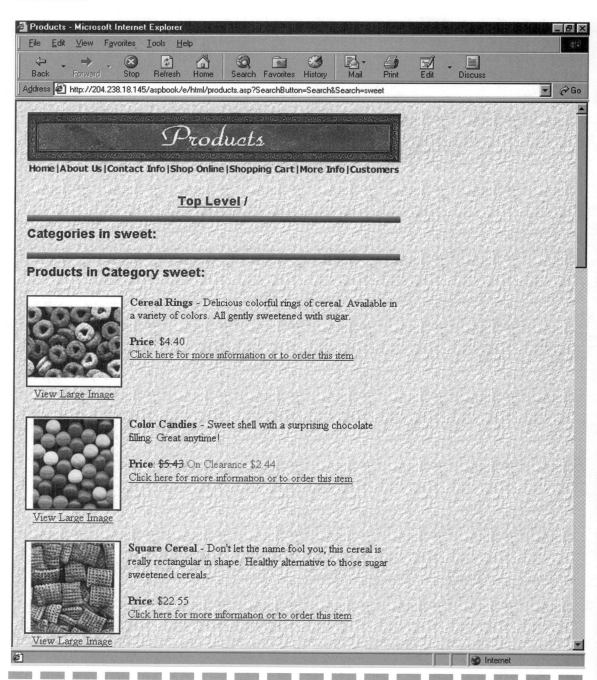

Figure 16-18 Results of a search.

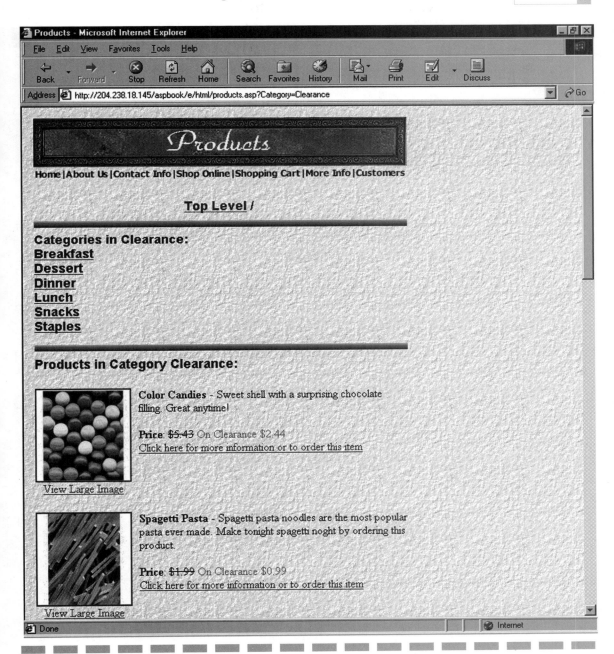

Figure 16-19 Clearance page.

Figure 16-20 Daily Special page.

ASPPageText

The *ASPPageText* table contains the general text used on most of the pages at the site. For example, the text from the Home page and the Footer text are contained in this table.

ASPProductCategories

Each product can belong to one or more categories; and each category can have more than one product. That means we have a many-to-many relationship between products and categories; and that means we need a go-between table—the *ASPProductCategories* table takes that action.

ASPProductComments

The *ASPProductComments* table contains all the comments entered by visitors regarding the products. Each comment is for a single product.

ASPProducts

The *ASPProducts* table stores information about the products themselves. Stored here are the descriptions of the products, price information, and paths to the images for the products.

ASPProductSelectLists

Each of the products can have lists from which visitors select some
option about the product like size, color, or type. Each of these options
can be used on more than one product. For example, you may use a shirt
size Select control for numerous products. So the relationship between
the products and the Select controls is many-to-many. That means
another go-between table is needed—the *ASPProductSelectLists* acts as
that table.

ASPSelectListItems

Each Select control has many options. For example, if you defined a
color Select control, then you could have red, yellow, and green for the
color choices. The *ASPSelectListItems* contains the records for each of
the options with the Select controls.

ASPSelectLists

The *ASPSelectLists* table contains the information about each of the
Select controls. This table is used to supply the text that appears before
each Select control and the name of each Select control on the Product
page.

ASPSessionPages

As visitors traverse the site, a record is added to the database to indicate each page hit. The *ASPSessionPages* records the hit for each page.

ASPSessions

The *ASPSessions* table contains the top-level information about visitors
to your site. This table records when visitors enter your site and other
information about the visitors.

Data Diagram and Relationships

Figure 16-21 displays the Data Diagram for the tables used in the
Product Catalog component. Each of the categories can have many products that are in that category, and each of the products can be listed in

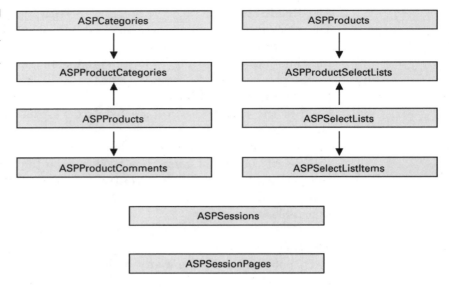

more than one category. So the ASPCategories table and the ASPProducts table are in a many-to-many relationship. The ASPProductCategories table satisfies the many-to-many relationship by acting as the go-between table. The ASPCategories and the ASPProductCategories table exist in a one-to-many relationship and the ASPProducts and ASPProductCategories tables exist in a one-to-many relationship.

Each of the products can have multiple comments made by customers, although each comment is for a single product. Thus, the ASPProducts table and the ASPProductComments table exist in a one-to-many relationship.

Each of the products in the database can have more than one select option for customers to supply additional information about the product they want, and each of the select options can be used with more than one product. Thus, the ASPProducts table and the ASPSelectLists table are in a many-to-many relationship. The go-between table for this relationship is the ASPProductSelectLists table, which is in a many-to-many relationship with the other two tables.

Each of the Select controls can have more than one option, although each option belongs to a single select control. The ASPSelectLists table is thus in a one-to-many relationship with the ASPSelectListItems table.

Each visitor can visit more than one page. That means that the

TABLE 16-1

ASPCategories Field Specifications

Field Name	Field Type	Notes
CategoryID	int	Identity column, seeded at 1 and incremented by 1
CategoryName	varchar	Length = 100
ParentCategory	varchar	Length = 100

ASPSessions table is in a one-to-many relationship with the ASPSessionPages table.

Field Specifications

ASPCategories Field Specifications
Table 16-1 shows the field specifications for the ASPCategories table. The CategoryID field is the primary key for the table. It is an identity column, so the field is automatically populated when a record is inserted into this table. The CategoryName field contains the name of the category. The ParentCategory field is used to store the name of the category that is one up above this category. A special value of Top for this field means that this is a Top Level category.

ASPContacts Field Specifications
Table 16-2 shows the field specifications for the ASPContacts table. The records in this table are used to build the HTML table in the Contact Info page.

TABLE 16-2

ASPContacts Field Specifications

Field Name	Field Type	Notes
ContactID	int	Identity column, seeded at 1 and incremented by 1
ContactName	varchar	Length = 100
ContactEmailAddress	varchar	Length = 100
ContactPhone	varchar	Length = 50
ContactRole	varchar	Length = 100

TABLE 16-3

*ASPProduct
Categories Field
Specifications*

Field Name	Field Type	Notes
ProductCategoryID	int	Identity column, seeded at 1 and incremented by 1
CategoryID	int	Foreign Key
ProductID	int	Foreign Key

ASPProductCategories Field Specifications

Table 16-3 shows the field specifications for the ASPProductCategories table, which is the go-between table that satisfies the many-to-many relationship for the ASPProducts table and ASPCategories table. The CategoryID field connects this table to the ASPCategories table. The ProductID field connects this table to the ASPProducts table.

ASPProductComments Field Specifications

Table 16-4 shows the field specifications for the ASPProductComments table. The ProductCommentID field is the primary key for the table. The ProductID field is a foreign key and connects this table with the ASPProducts table. The other fields contain the comment information about a product supplied by visitors.

ASPPageText Field Specifications

Table 16-5 shows the field specifications for the ASPPageText table, which contains the data used to populate the text for most of the pages. The PageTextID field is the primary key for the table. The PageName is important, as it is used in the code to retrieve the specific record for the page being viewed. For example, the PageName AboutUs is used for the

TABLE 16-4

*ASPProduct
Comments Field
Specifications*

Field Name	Field Type	Notes
ProductCommentID	int	Identity column, seeded at 1 and incremented by 1
ProductID	int	Foreign Key
CommentName	varchar	Length = 100
CommentFrom	varchar	Length = 100
Comment	varchar	Length = 255

TABLE 16-5

ASPPageText Field Specifications

Field Name	Field Type	Notes
PageTextID	int	Identity column, seeded at 1 and incremented by 1
PageName	varchar	Length = 50
BriefText	varchar	Length = 100
ExtendedText	text	

About Us page. The BriefText is used on most pages as the title text of the page. The Extended text field contains the bulk of the text for the page.

ASPProducts Field Specifications

Table 16-6 shows the field specifications for the ASPProducts table. The ProductID field is the primary key for the table. The Path2Icon field contains the name of the `Icon` file for this product. The code expects the icons to be in a `Products` directory. The Path2Image field contains the name of the full-size image for the product. The Price field contains the normal price for the product. If the product is currently on clearance, then the OnClearance field is set to the value 1; if the item is not on clearance, then the field is set to 0. The ClearancePrice field contains the price for the product if it is on clearance.

TABLE 16-6

ASPProducts Field Specifications

Field Name	Field Type	Notes
ProductID	int	Identity column, seeded at 1 and incremented by 1
ProductName	varchar	Length = 50
ShortDescription	varchar	Length = 250
LongDescription	varchar	Length = 255
Path2Icon	varchar	Length = 150
Path2Image	varchar	Length = 150
Price	money	
OnClearance	int	
ClearancePrice	money	

Field Name	Field Type	Notes
ProductSelectListID	int	Identity column, seeded at 1 and incremented by 1
ProductID	int	Foreign Key
SelectListID	int	Foreign Key

ASPProductSelectLists Field Specifications

Table 16-7 shows the field specifications for the ASPProductSelectLists table. The ProductSelectListID field is the primary key for the table. The ProductID field is a foreign key connecting this table to the ASPProducts table. The SelectListID field is also a foreign key connecting this table to the ASPSelectLists table.

ASPSelectListItems Field Specifications

Table 16-8 shows the field specifications for the ASPSelectListItems table. The SelectListItemID is the primary key for the table. The SelectListID fields is a foreign key connecting this table to the ASPSelectLists table. The ItemText field contains the text used to populate the options of the Select control.

ASPSelectLists Field Specifications

Table 16-9 shows the field specifications for the ASPSelectLists table. Each of the Select controls on the product page has text that names the select control and is used to display a label to visitors. That text comes from the SelectListName field.

Field Name	Field Type	Notes
SelectListItemID	int	Identity column, seeded at 1 and incremented by 1
SelectListID	int	Foreign Key
ItemText	varchar	Length = 50

Field Name	Field Type	Notes
SelectListID	int	Identity column, seeded at 1 and incremented by 1
SelectListName	varchar	Length = 50

ASPSessionPages Field Specifications
Table 16-10 shows the field specifications for the ASPSessionPages table. Each time visitors view a page at the site, a record is added to this table. The SessionPageID field is the primary key for the table. The SessionID field links this table to the ASPSessions table. The PageName field records the name of the page that was viewed by the visitor.

ASPSessions Field Specifications
Table 16-11 shows the field specifications for the ASPSessions table. The SessionID is the primary key for the table. The SessionStarted field stores the date and the time that visitors entered the site. The SessionEnded field stores the time that the session time-outs. The

Field Name	Field Type	Notes
SessionPageID	int	Identity column, seeded at 1 and incremented by 1
SessionID	int	Foreign Key
PageName	varchar	Length = 75

Field Name	Field Type	Notes
SessionID	int	Identity column, seeded at 1 and incremented by 1
SessionStarted	datetime	
SessionEnded	datetime	
RefSource	varchar	Length = 200
Browser	varchar	Length = 75
OS	varchar	Length = 75

RefSource field stores the location, if any, that visitors were at when they linked to your site, such as through a search engine. The Browser field stores the name of the browser that the visitor is using to view your site, and the OS field stores the visitor's operating system.

Active Server Page Application

Setup

Since we need to track visitors as they travel through the site to monitor the pages that they are going to and to maintain their Shopping Cart, we need the Web site to be installed as an Active Server Page application. To do this, enter the Microsoft Management Console and browse to the location where the site files are, right-click on the folder for the site, and select Properties. Select the DIRECTORY tab and you should see the dialog displayed in Figure 16-22. Press the CREATE button to set this directory structure as an Active Server Page application.

Figure 16-22
Adding the Active Server Page application.

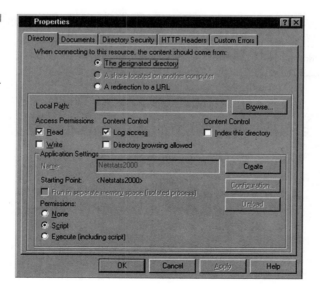

The `global.asa` File

The `global.asa` file is used in this Active Server Page application to have code run when visitors start a session and when the session ends. The Session_Start event initiates the visitor's session. The code for the Session_Start event is:

```
Sub Session_OnStart
   Dim conn
   Dim BC
   Dim Browser
   Dim Platform
   Dim Referer
   Dim RSSessionID
   set conn = server.createobject ("adodb.connection")
   conn.open "ASPBook", "sa", "yourpassword"
   set BC = server.createobject("MSWC.BrowserType")
   Browser = BC.Browser & " " & BC.Version
   Platform = cstr(BC.Platform)
   Referer = Request.ServerVariables("HTTP_REFERER")
   conn.execute "insert into ASPSessions (SessionStarted,
     RefSource, " _
      & "Browser, OS) values (" _
      & "'" & Now & "', " _
      & "'" & Referer & "', " _
      & "'" & Browser & "', " _
      & "'" & Platform & "')"
   set RSSessionID = conn.execute("select Max(SessionID) as MaxID
     from " _
      & "ASPSessions")
   Session("SessionID") = RSSessionID("MaxID")
End Sub
```

First, a few variables are declared. One is used for the Connection object:

```
Dim conn
```

The next is used to instantiate a Browser Capabilities component:

```
Dim BC
```

Another stores the browser that the visitor is using:

```
Dim Browser
```

the Platform of the visitor:

```
Dim Platform
```

and the referrer information:

```
Dim Referer
```

The next variable is used to retrieve the SessionID for the new visitor:

```
Dim RSSessionID
```

The connection object is instantiated:

```
set conn = server.createobject ("adodb.connection")
```

and a connection is opened:

```
conn.open "ASPBook", "sa", "yourpassword"
```

The Browser Capabilities component is instantiated:

```
set BC = server.createobject("MSWC.BrowserType")
```

Here the Browser Capabilities component is used to retrieve the name and version of the browser being used by the visitor:

```
Browser = BC.Browser & " " & BC.Version
```

The platform is retrieved from the Browser Capabilities component:

```
Platform = cstr(BC.Platform)
```

The referrer information is retrieved through the ServerVariables collection of the Request object:

```
Referer = Request.ServerVariables("HTTP_REFERER")
```

Then the Execute method of the Connection object is used to add the data about the visitor to the database:

```
conn.execute "insert into ASPSessions (SessionStarted, RefSource, " _
   & "Browser, OS) values (" _
   & "'" & Now & "', " _
   & "'" & Referer & "', " _
   & "'" & Browser & "', " _
& "'" & Platform & "')"
```

The SessionID of the record just added is retrieved from the database:

```
set RSSessionID = conn.execute("select Max(SessionID) as MaxID
  from " _
& "ASPSessions")
```

and is used to populate the Session variable SessionID:

```
Session("SessionID") = RSSessionID("MaxID")
```

The Session_OnEnd event writes the time that the session ended for the visitor to the database. This is the time that the session timed-out, not when the visitor left your site. The code for this event is:

```
Sub Session_OnEnd
  Dim conn
  set conn = server.createobject ("adodb.connection")
  conn.open "ASPBook", "sa", "yourpassword"
  conn.execute "Update ASPSessions set SessionEnded = '" & Now _
    & "' where SessionID = " & Session("SessionID")
End Sub
```

First, a Connection object variable is declared:

```
Dim conn
```

The connection object is instantiated:

```
set conn = server.createobject ("adodb.connection")
```

and opened:

```
conn.open "ASPBook", "sa", "yourpassword"
```

An Update query updates the visitor's session record by placing the current date and time in the SessionEnded field:

```
conn.execute "Update ASPSessions set SessionEnded = '" & Now _
  & "' where SessionID = " & Session("SessionID")
```

Home Page

The code on the Home page records a hit to the page and displays the dynamic text. The main code block is:

```
<%
Option Explicit
```

```
Dim conn
Dim RSPageText
Dim RSFooter
Dim PageText
set conn = server.createobject ("adodb.connection")
conn.open "ASPBook", "sa", "yourpassword"
conn.execute "insert into ASPSessionPages (SessionID, PageName)
 values (" _
   & Session("SessionID") & ", " _
   & "'Home')"
set RSPageText = conn.execute("select ExtendedText, BriefText from
 ASPPageText " _
   & "where PageName = 'Home'")
PageText= RSPageText("ExtendedText")
set RSFooter = conn.execute("select BriefText from ASPPageText " _
   & "where PageName = 'Footer'")
%>
```

First, Option Explicit is coded:

```
Option Explicit
```

A Connection object variable is declared:

```
Dim conn
```

as is a Recordset object for the text on the page:

```
Dim RSPageText
```

and the text for the footer:

```
Dim RSFooter
```

This variable will store the extended text information about the page:

```
Dim PageText
```

The Connection object is instantiated:

```
set conn = server.createobject ("adodb.connection")
```

and opened:

```
conn.open "ASPBook", "sa", "yourpassword"
```

The execute method is used to record a hit for this page with this particular visitor:

```
conn.execute "insert into ASPSessionPages (SessionID, PageName)
values (" _
 & Session("SessionID") & ", " _
 & "'Home')"
```

Then the text information for the page is retrieved. The values from the record will be written inline with the HTML:

```
set RSPageText = conn.execute("select ExtendedText, BriefText from
ASPPageText " _
& "where PageName = 'Home'")
```

PageText is set to the extended text for the page:

```
PageText= RSPageText("ExtendedText")
```

and a second Recordset object is used to retrieve the footer text for the page:

```
set RSFooter = conn.execute("select BriefText from ASPPageText " _
& "where PageName = 'Footer'")
```

Then, inline with the HTML, the title text for the page is written:

```
<% Response.Write RSPageText("BriefText") %>
```

as is the extended text:

```
<% Response.Write PageText %>
```

and the footer text:

```
<% Response.Write RSFooter("BriefText") %>
```

About Us Page

The code on the About Us page displays the dynamic text for that page and records the hit for that page. The main code block is:

```
<%
Option Explicit
Dim conn
Dim RSPageText
Dim RSFooter
Dim PageText
set conn = server.createobject ("adodb.connection")
```

```
conn.open "ASPBook", "sa", "yourpassword"
conn.execute "insert into ASPSessionPages (SessionID, PageName)
 values (" _
  & Session("SessionID") & ", " _
  & "'AboutUs')"
set RSPageText = conn.execute("select ExtendedText, BriefText from
 ASPPageText " _
  & "where PageName = 'AboutUs'")
PageText= RSPageText("ExtendedText")
set RSFooter = conn.execute("select BriefText from ASPPageText " _
  & "where PageName = 'Footer'")
%>
```

The code starts with the `Option Explicit` statement:

```
Option Explicit
```

Then the variables for the Connection object, two Recordset objects, are declared:

```
Dim conn
Dim RSPageText
Dim RSFooter
```

The `PageText` variable will store the extended text for the page:

```
Dim PageText
```

The Connection object is instantiated:

```
set conn = server.createobject ("adodb.connection")
```

and opened to the SQL Server database:

```
conn.open "ASPBook", "sa", "yourpassword"
```

A hit to the About Us page is recorded:

```
conn.execute "insert into ASPSessionPages (SessionID,
  PageName)    values (" _
    & Session("SessionID") & ", " _
& "'AboutUs')"
```

The main text for the page is retrieved from the **ASPPageText** table:

```
set RSPageText = conn.execute("select ExtendedText, BriefText from
  ASPPageText " _
& "where PageName = 'AboutUs'")
```

The extended information is stored in the `PageText` variable:

```
PageText= RSPageText("ExtendedText")
```

And the footer text is retrieved from the ASPPageText table:

```
set RSFooter = conn.execute("select BriefText from ASPPageText " _
& "where PageName = 'Footer'")
```

Then, inline with the HTML, the title, extended text, and footer fields are written.

Contact Info Page

The code on the Contact Info page records a hit for that page and displays the standard text for that page. An HTML table is also populated with contact information. The main code block is:

```
<%
Option Explicit
Dim conn
Dim RSPageText
Dim RSFooter
Dim PageText
Dim RSContacts
set conn = server.createobject ("adodb.connection")
conn.open "ASPBook", "sa", "yourpassword"
conn.execute "insert into ASPSessionPages (SessionID, PageName)
 values (" _
   & Session("SessionID") & ", " _
   & "'ContactUs')"
set RSPageText = conn.execute("select ExtendedText, BriefText from
 ASPPageText " _
   & "where PageName = 'ContactUs'")
PageText= RSPageText("ExtendedText")
set RSFooter = conn.execute("select BriefText from ASPPageText " _
   & "where PageName = 'Footer'")
set RSContacts = conn.execute("select * from ASPContacts order by
   ContactName")
%>
```

First, `Option Explicit` is used to require variable declaration:

```
Option Explicit
```

Then variables are declared for the Connection object and the Recordsets for the page text:

```
Dim conn
Dim RSPageText
Dim RSFooter
```

The `PageText` variable will store the extended information about the page:

```
Dim PageText
```

Another Recordset object is needed to display the Contact HTML table:

```
Dim RSContacts
```

The Connection object is instantiated:

```
set conn = server.createobject ("adodb.connection")
```

and opened:

```
conn.open "ASPBook", "sa", "yourpassword"
```

A hit for this page is recorded:

```
conn.execute "insert into ASPSessionPages (SessionID, PageName)
  values (" _
    & Session("SessionID") & ", " _
  & "'ContactUs')"
```

The title and extended text for the page are retrieved from the database:

```
set RSPageText = conn.execute("select ExtendedText, BriefText from
  ASPPageText " _
& "where PageName = 'ContactUs'")
```

The `PageText` variable is set to the ExtendedText field:

```
PageText= RSPageText("ExtendedText")
```

and the footer text is retrieved from the database:

```
set RSFooter = conn.execute("select BriefText from ASPPageText " _
  & "where PageName = 'Footer'")
```

All the contact records are retrieved into the `RSContacts` Recordset object:

```
set RSContacts = conn.execute("select * from ASPContacts order by
   ContactName")
```

An HTML table is built from this Recordset object.

```
<%
Do Until RSContacts.EOF
%>
   <TR>
   <TD WIDTH=121><P><% Response.Write RSContacts("ContactName")
    %></TD>
   <TD WIDTH=121><P><A HREF="mailto:<% Response.Write
     RSContacts("ContactEmailAddress") %>">
    <% Response.Write RSContacts("ContactEmailAddress")
      %></A></TD>
   <TD WIDTH=121><P><% Response.Write RSContacts("ContactPhone")
    %></TD>
   <TD WIDTH=122><P><% Response.Write RSContacts("ContactRole")
    %></TD>
   </TR>
<%
   RSContacts.MoveNext
Loop
%>
```

The code will loop through all the RSContacts Recordsets:

```
Do Until RSContacts.EOF
```

A row is added to the HTML table for each of the records:

```
<TR>
```

The field for the contact's name, email address, phone number, and role are added to that row:

```
<TD WIDTH=121><P><% Response.Write RSContacts("ContactName")
   %></TD>
<TD WIDTH=121><P><A HREF="mailto:<% Response.Write
   RSContacts("ContactEmailAddress") %>">
   <% Response.Write RSContacts("ContactEmailAddress") %></A></TD>
<TD WIDTH=121><P><% Response.Write RSContacts("ContactPhone")
   %></TD>
<TD WIDTH=122><P><% Response.Write RSContacts("ContactRole")
   %></TD>
```

The code then moves to the next record before looping:

```
   RSContacts.MoveNext
Loop
```

Product Catalog Page

The code on the Product Catalog page records a hit to the page and displays the basic textual information retrieved from the database. A second code block populates the select control used by visitors to browse to a specific category. The first code block is:

```
<%
Option Explicit
Dim conn
Dim RSPageText
Dim RSFooter
set conn = server.createobject ("adodb.connection")
conn.open "ASPBook", "sa", " yourpassword "
conn.execute "insert into ASPSessionPages (SessionID, PageName)
Values (" _
    & Session("SessionID") & ", " _
    & "'ProductCatalog')"
set RSPageText = conn.execute("select BriefText from ASPPageText " _
    & "where PageName = 'ProductCatalog'")
set RSFooter = conn.execute("select BriefText from ASPPageText " _
    & "where PageName = 'Footer'")
%>
```

First, Option Explicit is coded:

```
Option Explicit
```

Then the variables are declared for the Connection object, the Recordset object:

```
Dim conn
Dim RSPageText
Dim RSFooter
```

The Connection object is instantiated:

```
set conn = server.createobject ("adodb.connection")
```

and opened:

```
conn.open "ASPBook", "sa", "yourpassword"
```

A hit for the Product Catalog page is recorded:

```
conn.execute "insert into ASPSessionPages (SessionID, PageName)
  values (" _
    & Session("SessionID") & ", " _
  & "'ProductCatalog')"
```

and the BriefText for this page is retrieved from the database:

```
set RSPageText = conn.execute("select BriefText from ASPPageText " _
 & "where PageName = 'ProductCatalog'")
```

The footer text is also retrieved from the database:

```
set RSFooter = conn.execute("select BriefText from ASPPageText " _
 & "where PageName = 'Footer'")
```

Then, inline with the HTML, the title and footer text are written to the browser.

The next code block populates the options for the category Select control.

```
<%
Dim RSCategories
set RSCategories = conn.execute("select CategoryName from
 ASPCategories " _
 & "order by CategoryName")
Do Until RSCategories.EOF
%>
  <OPTION VALUE="<% Response.Write RSCategories("CategoryName")
   %>">
  <% Response.Write RSCategories("CategoryName") %></OPTION>
<%
  RSCategories.MoveNext
Loop
%>
```

The RSCategories variable is declared:

```
Dim RSCategories
```

and is set to contain all the categories in the ASPCategories table sorted by the category name:

```
set RSCategories = conn.execute("select CategoryName from
 ASPCategories " _
 & "order by CategoryName")
```

The code will loop through all the records in the Recordset:

```
Do Until RSCategories.EOF
```

Each record is written as an Option to the Select control:

```
<OPTION VALUE="<% Response.Write RSCategories("CategoryName") %>">
 <% Response.Write RSCategories("CategoryName") %></OPTION>
```

The code then moves to the next record before looping:

```
RSCategories.MoveNext
Loop
```

How to Order Page

The code on the How to Order page records a hit for that page for the visitor and writes the text to the page. The main code block is:

```
<%
Option Explicit
Dim conn
Dim RSPageText
Dim RSFooter
Dim PageText
set conn = server.createobject ("adodb.connection")
conn.open "ASPBook", "sa", " yourpassword "
conn.execute "insert into ASPSessionPages (SessionID, PageName)
 values (" _
   & Session("SessionID") & ", " _
   & "'HowToOrder')"
set RSPageText = conn.execute("select ExtendedText, BriefText from
ASPPageText " _
   & "where PageName = 'HowToOrder'")
PageText= RSPageText("ExtendedText")
set RSFooter = conn.execute("select BriefText from ASPPageText " _
   & "where PageName = 'Footer'")
%>
```

First, `Option Explicit` is coded:

```
Option Explicit
```

Then variables are declared for the Connection object, the page text Recordset, the footer text Recordset, and a variable to store the extended text:

```
Dim conn
Dim RSPageText
Dim RSFooter
Dim PageText
```

The CreateObject of the Server object is to return an instance of a Connection object into the `Conn` variable:

```
set conn = server.createobject ("adodb.connection")
```

The Open method is used to establish a connection to the SQL Server database:

```
conn.open "ASPBook", "sa", "yourpassword"
```

A hit is recorded for the How to Order page:

```
conn.execute "insert into ASPSessionPages (SessionID, PageName)
  values (" _
    & Session("SessionID") & ", " _
  & "'HowToOrder')"
```

The brief and extended text are retrieved for this page:

```
set RSPageText = conn.execute("select ExtendedText, BriefText from
  ASPPageText " _
  & "where PageName = 'HowToOrder'")
```

The `PageText` variable is set to extended text:

```
PageText= RSPageText("ExtendedText")
```

and the footer text is retrieved:

```
set RSFooter = conn.execute("select BriefText from ASPPageText " _
  & "where PageName = 'Footer'")
```

Inline with the HTML, the text of the page is written to the browser.

Return Policy Page

The Return Policy page is another standard page that records a hit and displays the text for the page. The main code block is:

```
<%
Option Explicit
Dim conn
Dim RSPageText
Dim RSFooter
Dim PageText
set conn = server.createobject ("adodb.connection")
conn.open "ASPBook", "sa", "yourpassword"
conn.execute "insert into ASPSessionPages (SessionID, PageName)
values (" _
    & Session("SessionID") & ", " _
    & "'ReturnPolicy')"
```

```
set RSPageText = conn.execute("select ExtendedText, BriefText from
   ASPPageText " _
   & "where PageName = 'ReturnPolicy'")
PageText= RSPageText("ExtendedText")
set RSFooter = conn.execute("select BriefText from ASPPageText " _
   & "where PageName = 'Footer'")
%>
```

First, `Option Explicit` is written to require variable declaration:

```
Option Explicit
```

The Connection object, Recordset objects, and text variable are declared:

```
Dim conn
Dim RSPageText
Dim RSFooter
Dim PageText
```

The Connection object is instantiated:

```
set conn = server.createobject ("adodb.connection")
```

and opened:

```
conn.open "ASPBook", "sa", "yourpassword"
```

A hit is recorded for the Return Policy page:

```
conn.execute "insert into ASPSessionPages (SessionID, PageName)
   values (" _
   & Session("SessionID") & ", " _
& "'ReturnPolicy')"
```

The text for the page is retrieved from the database:

```
set RSPageText = conn.execute("select ExtendedText, BriefText from
   ASPPageText " _
   & "where PageName = 'ReturnPolicy'")
PageText= RSPageText("ExtendedText")
```

as is the text for the footer:

```
set RSFooter = conn.execute("select BriefText from ASPPageText " _
   & "where PageName = 'Footer'")
```

Then, inline with the HTML, the data are written to create the custom page. First, the BriefText field is written:

```
<% Response.Write RSPageText("BriefText") %>
```

The extended text is then written to the browser:

```
<% Response.Write PageText %>
```

At the bottom of the page, the footer text is also written to the browser:

```
<% Response.Write RSFooter("BriefText") %>
```

Shipping Info Page

The code on the Shipping Info page, like the other standard pages, records a hit for that page and displays text for that page retrieved from the database. The main code block is:

```
<%
Option Explicit
Dim conn
Dim RSPageText
Dim RSFooter
Dim PageText
set conn = server.createobject ("adodb.connection")
conn.open "ASPBook", "sa", "yourpassword"
conn.execute "insert into ASPSessionPages (SessionID, PageName)
  values (" _
    & Session("SessionID") & ", " _
    & "'ShippingInfo')"
set RSPageText = conn.execute("select ExtendedText, BriefText from
  ASPPageText " _
    & "where PageName = 'ShippingInfo'")
PageText= RSPageText("ExtendedText")
set RSFooter = conn.execute("select BriefText from ASPPageText " _
    & "where PageName = 'Footer'")
%>
```

`Option Explicit` is used to require variable declaration:

```
Option Explicit
```

The variables needed to connect to the database and retrieve and display the data are declared:

```
Dim conn
Dim RSPageText
Dim RSFooter
Dim PageText
```

The Connection object is instantiated:

```
set conn = server.createobject ("adodb.connection")
```

and opened:

```
conn.open "ASPBook", "sa", "yourpassword"
```

A hit is then recorded into the ASPSessionPages table for this visitor's session to the Shipping Info page:

```
conn.execute "insert into ASPSessionPages (SessionID, PageName)
  values (" _
   & Session("SessionID") & ", " _
 & "'ShippingInfo')"
```

The text for the Shipping Info page is retrieved from the ASPPageText table:

```
set RSPageText = conn.execute("select ExtendedText, BriefText from
  ASPPageText " _
 & "where PageName = 'ShippingInfo'")
```

The PageText variable is set to the ExtendedText field:

```
PageText= RSPageText("ExtendedText")
```

The footer data is also retrieved from the database:

```
set RSFooter = conn.execute("select BriefText from ASPPageText " _
 & "where PageName = 'Footer'")
```

These data are then written inline to the browser.

Products Page

The code on the Products page also records a hit to that page. Additionally, it displays products, categories, and links based on the data passed into the page. The first code block is:

```
<%
Option Explicit
Dim conn
Dim ParentPath
Dim RSParents
Dim LastPath
```

```
Dim RSChildren
Dim CurrentCategory
Dim RSProducts
set conn = server.createobject ("adodb.connection")
conn.open "ASPBook", "sa", "yourpassword"
conn.execute "insert into ASPSessionPages (SessionID, PageName)
 values (" _
  & Session("SessionID") & ", " _
  & "'Products')"
If Isempty(Request.QueryString("Category")) and
Isempty(Request.QueryString("Search")) Then
  ParentPath = "<A HREF=""../html/products.asp?Category=Top"">Top
    Level</A> / "
  set RSChildren = conn.execute("select CategoryName from
   ASPCategories " _
    & "where ParentCategory = 'Top' order by CategoryName")
  CurrentCategory = "Top"
  set RSProducts = conn.execute("SELECT ASPProducts.ProductID,
   ASPProducts.ProductName, " _
  & "ASPProducts.ShortDescription, ASPProducts.Path2Icon,
    ASPProducts.Price, " _
  & "ASPProducts.OnClearance, ASPProducts.ClearancePrice " _
  & "FROM (ASPProducts INNER JOIN ASPProductCategories ON " _
  & "ASPProducts.ProductID = ASPProductCategories.ProductID) INNER
    JOIN " _
  & "ASPCategories ON ASPProductCategories.CategoryID =
    ASPCategories.CategoryID " _
  & "WHERE ASPCategories.CategoryName = 'Top'")
ElseIf Request.QueryString("Category") = "Top" Then
  ParentPath = "<A HREF=""../html/products.asp?Category=Top"">Top
    Level</A> / "
  set RSChildren = conn.execute("select CategoryName from
   ASPCategories " _
    & "where ParentCategory = 'Top' order by CategoryName")
  CurrentCategory = "Top"
  set RSProducts = conn.execute("SELECT ASPProducts.ProductID,
   ASPProducts.ProductName, " _
    & "ASPProducts.ShortDescription, ASPProducts.Path2Icon,
      ASPProducts.Price, " _
    & "ASPProducts.OnClearance, ASPProducts.ClearancePrice " _
    & "FROM (ASPProducts INNER JOIN ASPProductCategories ON " _
    & "ASPProducts.ProductID = ASPProductCategories.ProductID)
      INNER JOIN " _
    & "ASPCategories ON ASPProductCategories.CategoryID =
      ASPCategories.CategoryID " _
    & "WHERE ASPCategories.CategoryName = 'Top'")
ElseIf Request.QueryString("Category") = "Clearance" Then
  ParentPath = "<A HREF=""../html/products.asp?Category=Top"">Top
    Level</A> / "
  set RSChildren = conn.execute("select CategoryName from
   ASPCategories " _
    & "where ParentCategory = 'Top' order by CategoryName")
  CurrentCategory = "Clearance"
  set RSProducts = conn.execute("SELECT ASPProducts.ProductID,
   ASPProducts.ProductName, " _
    & "ASPProducts.ShortDescription, ASPProducts.Path2Icon,
      ASPProducts.Price, " _
    & "ASPProducts.OnClearance, ASPProducts.ClearancePrice " _
    & "FROM ASPProducts " _
```

```
                    & "WHERE OnClearance = 1")
        ElseIf Not Isempty(Request.QueryString("Category")) Then
            LastPath = Request.QueryString("Category")
            Do Until LastPath = "Top"
                ParentPath = "<A HREF=""../html/products.asp?Category=" _
                    & LastPath & """>" & LastPath & "</A> / " & ParentPath
                set RSParents = conn.execute("select ParentCategory from
                ASPCategories " _
                    & "where CategoryName = '" & LastPath & "'")
                LastPath = RSParents("ParentCategory")
            Loop
            ParentPath = "<A HREF=""../html/products.asp?Category=Top"">Top
            Level</A> / " _
                & ParentPath
            set RSChildren = conn.execute("select CategoryName from
            ASPCategories " _
                & "where ParentCategory = '" & Request.QueryString
                ("Category") _
                & "' order by CategoryName")
            CurrentCategory = Request.QueryString("Category")
            set RSProducts = conn.execute("SELECT ASPProducts.ProductID,
            ASPProducts.ProductName, " _
                & "ASPProducts.ShortDescription, ASPProducts.Path2Icon,
                ASPProducts.Price, " _
                & "ASPProducts.OnClearance, ASPProducts.ClearancePrice " _
                & "FROM (ASPProducts INNER JOIN ASPProductCategories ON " _
                & "ASPProducts.ProductID = ASPProductCategories.ProductID)
                INNER JOIN " _
                & "ASPCategories ON ASPProductCategories.CategoryID =
                ASPCategories.CategoryID " _
                & "WHERE ASPCategories.CategoryName = '" & Request.Query
                String("Category") & "'")
        Else
            ParentPath = "<A HREF=""../html/products.asp?Category=Top"">Top
            Level</A> / "
            set RSChildren = conn.execute("select CategoryName from
            ASPCategories " _
                & "where ParentCategory like '%" & Request.QueryString
                ("Search") _
                & "%' or CategoryName like '%" & Request.QueryString("Search") _
                & "%' order by CategoryName")
            CurrentCategory = Request.QueryString("Search")
            set RSProducts = conn.execute("SELECT ASPProducts.ProductID,
            ASPProducts.ProductName, " _
                & "ASPProducts.ShortDescription, ASPProducts.Path2Icon,
                ASPProducts.Price, " _
                & "ASPProducts.OnClearance, ASPProducts.ClearancePrice " _
                & "FROM ASPProducts " _
                & "WHERE ProductName Like '%" & Request.QueryString("Search") &
                "%' "
                & "or ShortDescription Like '%" & Request.QueryString("Search") &
                "%'")
        End If
%>
```

First, `Option Explicit` is noted:

```
Option Explicit
```

A variety of variables will be needed, a Connection object being one of them:

```
Dim conn
```

This variable will be used in building the path to the current category:

```
Dim ParentPath
```

These variables will also help in building that path:

```
Dim RSParents
Dim LastPath
```

This variable will be a Recordset containing all the subcategories in the current category:

```
Dim RSChildren
```

Another variable will store the current category:

```
Dim CurrentCategory
```

and one more will store the products in the current category:

```
Dim RSProducts
```

A Connection object is instantiated:

```
set conn = server.createobject ("adodb.connection")
```

and opened:

```
conn.open "ASPBook", "sa", "yourpassword"
```

Here the Execute method of the Connection object is used to record a hit for this page:

```
conn.execute "insert into ASPSessionPages (SessionID, PageName)
   values (" _
     & Session("SessionID") & ", " _
   & "'Products')"
```

The category and products displayed on this page are dependent on which item visitors clicked on from the Product Catalog menu page.

First, we deal with a scenario where they came to this page without passing any parameters. In that case, the Top Level category will be used. We test for that by checking for a Search field or a category:

```
If Isempty(Request.QueryString("Category")) and
Isempty(Request.QueryString("Search")) Then
```

If both are empty, we build a parent path that contains only the Top Level category:

```
ParentPath = "<A HREF=""../html/products.asp?Category=Top"">Top
    Level</A> / "
```

The subcategories are based on the Top Level category:

```
set RSChildren = conn.execute("select CategoryName from
    ASPCategories " _
        & "where ParentCategory = 'Top' order by CategoryName")
```

The current category is set to Top:

```
CurrentCategory = "Top"
```

and the products retrieved are based on any that are in the Top category:

```
set RSProducts = conn.execute("SELECT ASPProducts.ProductID,
    ASPProducts.ProductName, " _
        & "ASPProducts.ShortDescription, ASPProducts.Path2Icon,
    ASPProducts.Price, " _
        & "ASPProducts.OnClearance, ASPProducts.ClearancePrice " _
        & "FROM (ASPProducts INNER JOIN ASPProductCategories ON " _
        & "ASPProducts.ProductID = ASPProductCategories.ProductID)
    INNER JOIN " _
        & "ASPCategories ON ASPProductCategories.CategoryID =
        ASPCategories.CategoryID " _
            & "WHERE ASPCategories.CategoryName = 'Top'")
```

The next condition deals with indicating that they want to browse through the categories. Again, in this scenario we start them at the Top Level:

```
ElseIf Request.QueryString("Category") = "Top" Then
```

We build the path to the current folder as just the Top Level, since it contains no parent folders:

```
ParentPath = "<A HREF=""../html/products.asp?Category=Top"">Top
    Level</A> / "
```

We set the subcategories Recordset to any categories having Top as their parent:

```
set RSChildren = conn.execute("select CategoryName from
  ASPCategories " _
      & "where ParentCategory = 'Top' order by CategoryName")
```

We set the current category to Top:

```
CurrentCategory = "Top"
```

and retrieve a Recordset of products that are in the category Top:

```
set RSProducts = conn.execute("SELECT ASPProducts.ProductID,
  ASPProducts.ProductName, " _
      & "ASPProducts.ShortDescription, ASPProducts.Path2Icon,
        ASPProducts.Price, " _
      & "ASPProducts.OnClearance, ASPProducts.ClearancePrice " _
      & "FROM (ASPProducts INNER JOIN ASPProductCategories ON " _
      & "ASPProducts.ProductID = ASPProductCategories.ProductID)
        INNER JOIN " _
      & "ASPCategories ON ASPProductCategories.CategoryID =
        ASPCategories.CategoryID " _
        & "WHERE ASPCategories.CategoryName = 'Top'")
```

In the next scenario, visitors have indicated that they want to see clearance products:

```
ElseIf Request.QueryString("Category") = "Clearance" Then
```

Since the Clearance option isn't a category, we again set the category to Top:

```
ParentPath = "<A HREF=""../html/products.asp?Category=Top"">Top
  Level</A> / "
```

and will display all the subcategories of Top:

```
set RSChildren = conn.execute("select CategoryName from
  ASPCategories " _
      & "where ParentCategory = 'Top' order by CategoryName")
```

But set the current category to Clearance:

```
CurrentCategory = "Clearance"
```

and retrieve any products from the database that are marked as on clearance. Remember that a value of 1 for the OnClearance field means that the item is on clearance:

```
set RSProducts = conn.execute("SELECT ASPProducts.ProductID,
  ASPProducts.ProductName, " _
    & "ASPProducts.ShortDescription, ASPProducts.Path2Icon,
  ASPProducts.Price, " _
    & "ASPProducts.OnClearance, ASPProducts.ClearancePrice " _
    & "FROM ASPProducts " _
      & "WHERE OnClearance = 1")
```

In the next condition, visitors have selected a specific category that they want to view:

```
ElseIf Not Isempty(Request.QueryString("Category")) Then
```

Now we need to build a path to that category that is many deep. We need to start at the selected category:

```
LastPath = Request.QueryString("Category")
```

and work our way up until we get to the Top Level category:

```
Do Until LastPath = "Top"
```

Notice that the path displayed contains a link back to this page for that part of the path. This is how visitors can click on any part of the path and view that category:

```
ParentPath = "<A HREF=""../html/products.asp?Category=" _
         LastPath & """>" & LastPath & "</A> / " & ParentPath
```

We then grab from the database the parent of the current level in the path that we are at:

```
set RSParents = conn.execute("select ParentCategory from
  ASPCategories " _
      & "where CategoryName = '" & LastPath & "'")
```

and set that to the last path:

```
LastPath = RSParents("ParentCategory")
```

before looping and once again testing to see if we are at the top yet:

```
Loop
```

The Top Level path is then added as the top of the path to the current category:

```
ParentPath = "<A HREF=""../html/products.asp?Category=Top"">Top
  Level</A> / " _
      & ParentPath
```

The children of this category are retrieved from the database:

```
set RSChildren = conn.execute("select CategoryName from
ASPCategories " _
    & "where ParentCategory = '" & Request.QueryString("Category") _
    & "' order by CategoryName")
```

The current category is set to the one requested by the visitor:

```
CurrentCategory = Request.QueryString("Category")
```

and products in the requested category are retrieved:

```
set RSProducts = conn.execute("SELECT ASPProducts.ProductID,
ASPProducts.ProductName, " _
    & "ASPProducts.ShortDescription, ASPProducts.Path2Icon,
    ASPProducts.Price, " _
    & "ASPProducts.OnClearance, ASPProducts.ClearancePrice " _
    & "FROM (ASPProducts INNER JOIN ASPProductCategories ON " _
    & "ASPProducts.ProductID = ASPProductCategories.ProductID)
    INNER JOIN " _
    & "ASPCategories ON ASPProductCategories.CategoryID =
    ASPCategories.CategoryID " _
      & "WHERE ASPCategories.CategoryName = '" & Request.Query
        String("Category") & "'")
```

We get to the Else condition if visitors are performing a search on the catalog:

```
Else
```

In that case, we set the path to the Top Level path:

```
ParentPath = "<A HREF=""../html/products.asp?Category=Top"">Top
  Level</A> / "
```

and set the children to any category containing the search criteria or having a parent with the search criteria:

```
set RSChildren = conn.execute("select CategoryName from
ASPCategories " _
    & "where ParentCategory like '%" & Request.QueryString("Search") _
    & "%' or CategoryName like '%" & Request.QueryString("Search") _
      & "%' order by CategoryName")
```

We set the current category to their search string:

```
CurrentCategory = Request.QueryString("Search")
```

and retrieve from the database any products that have a name or description with the search term included:

```
set RSProducts = conn.execute("SELECT ASPProducts.ProductID,
   ASPProducts.ProductName, " _
      & "ASPProducts.ShortDescription, ASPProducts.Path2Icon,
         ASPProducts.Price, " _
      & "ASPProducts.OnClearance, ASPProducts.ClearancePrice " _
      & "FROM ASPProducts " _
      & "WHERE ProductName Like '%" & Request.QueryString("Search")
         & "%' " _
         & "or ShortDescription Like '%" & Request.QueryString
            ("Search") & "%'")
```

Then inline with the HTML, the path to the category:

```
<% Response.Write ParentPath %>
```

and the name of the current category are written:

```
Categories in <% Response.Write CurrentCategory %>:
```

The next code block writes all the subcategories to the browser:

```
<%
Do Until RSChildren.EOF
%>
<A HREF="../html/products.asp?Category=<
% Response.Write RSChildren("CategoryName") %>">
<B><FONT COLOR="#660000" SIZE="+1"
FACE="Arial,Helvetica,Univers,Zurich BT">
<% Response.Write RSChildren("CategoryName") %></FONT></B></A><BR>
<%
   RSChildren.MoveNext
Loop
%>
```

The code will loop through all the records in the RSChildren **Recordset**:

```
Do Until RSChildren.EOF
```

Displayed for each subcategory is its name with a link back to this page to display that category:

```
<A HREF="../html/products.asp?Category=<
```

```
% Response.Write RSChildren("CategoryName") %>">
<B><FONT COLOR="#660000" SIZE="+1"
FACE="Arial,Helvetica,Univers,Zurich BT">
<% Response.Write RSChildren("CategoryName") %></FONT></B></A><BR>
```

The code then moves to the next record before looping:

```
RSChildren.MoveNext
Loop
```

The next code block displays all the products for the category or search selected.

```
<%
Do Until RSProducts.EOF
%>
<A HREF="./image_router.asp?ProductID=<% Response.Write
  RSProducts("ProductID") %>">
<IMG HEIGHT=130 WIDTH=130
SRC="../products/<% Response.Write RSProducts("path2icon") %>"
BORDER=2 ALT="<% Response.Write RSProducts("ProductName") %>"></A>
<P ALIGN=CENTER><A HREF="./image_router.asp?ProductID=
<% Response.Write RSProducts("ProductID") %>">View Large Image</A>
<P><B><% Response.Write RSProducts("ProductName") %></B> -
<% Response.Write RSProducts("ShortDescription") %>
<%
If RSProducts("OnClearance") = 1 Then
%>
  <P><B>Price</B>: <STRIKE><% Response.Write FormatCurrency
    (RSProducts("Price"))
  %></STRIKE> <FONT COLOR="#FF0000">On Clearance
  <% Response.Write FormatCurrency(RSProducts("ClearancePrice")) %>
  <BR></FONT><A HREF="../html/product.asp?ProductID=
  <% Response.Write RSProducts("ProductID") %>">
  Click here for more information or to order this item</A></TD>
<%
Else
%>
  <P><B>Price</B>: <% Response.Write
FormatCurrency(RSProducts("Price")) %>
  <BR><A HREF="../html/product.asp?ProductID=
  <% Response.Write RSProducts("ProductID") %>">
  Click here for more information or to order this item</A></TD>
<%
End If
%>
<%
  RSProducts.MoveNext
Loop
%>
```

The code will loop through all the product records:

```
Do Until RSProducts.EOF
```

Displayed for each record first is the icon of the product with a link to the large image of the product:

```
<A HREF="./image_router.asp?ProductID=<% Response.Write
  RSProducts("ProductID") %>">
<IMG HEIGHT=130 WIDTH=130
SRC="../products/<% Response.Write RSProducts("path2icon") %>"
BORDER=2 ALT="<% Response.Write RSProducts("ProductName") %>"></A>
```

as well as a text link to that large image:

```
<P ALIGN=CENTER><A HREF="./image_router.asp?ProductID=
<% Response.Write RSProducts("ProductID") %>">View Large Image</A>
```

The name of the product and description are displayed:

```
<P><B><% Response.Write RSProducts("ProductName") %></B> -
<% Response.Write RSProducts("ShortDescription") %>
```

Then we check to see if the product is on clearance:

```
<%
If RSProducts("OnClearance") = 1 Then
%>
```

If it is, the price is crossed out and the clearance price is displayed:

```
<P><B>Price</B>: <STRIKE><% Response.Write FormatCurrency
  (RSProducts("Price")) %>
</STRIKE> <FONT COLOR="#FF0000">On Clearance
<% Response.Write FormatCurrency(RSProducts("ClearancePrice")) %>
<BR></FONT><A HREF="../html/product.asp?ProductID=
<% Response.Write RSProducts("ProductID") %>">
Click here for more information or to order this item</A></TD>
```

If not, just the current price is displayed:

```
<P><B>Price</B>: <% Response.Write
FormatCurrency(RSProducts("Price")) %>
  <BR><A HREF="../html/product.asp?ProductID=
  <% Response.Write RSProducts("ProductID") %>">
Click here for more information or to order this item</A></TD>
```

The code then moves to the next record prior to looping:

```
RSProducts.MoveNext
Loop
```

Image Router Page

The Image Router page redirects visitors to the large picture of the product. It first records a hit to that large image, so you could later analyze the database to see what products were more popular than others. The code for this page is:

```
<%
Option Explicit
Dim conn
Dim RSProduct
If IsEmpty(Request.QueryString("ProductID")) Then
    Response.Redirect "./product_catalog.asp"
End If
set conn = server.createobject ("adodb.connection")
conn.open "ASPBook", "sa", "yourpassword"
conn.execute "insert into ASPSessionPages (SessionID,
  PageName)      values (" _
    & Session("SessionID") & ", " _
    & "'ProductPicture" & Request.QueryString("ProductID") & "')"
set RSProduct = conn.execute("select Path2Image from ASPProducts
  where " _
    & "ProductID = " & Request.QueryString("ProductID"))
Response.Redirect "../products/" & RSProduct("Path2Image")
%>
```

Variable declaration is required:

```
Option Explicit
```

A Connection object will be needed:

```
Dim conn
```

and we will need to retrieve the path to the large product image:

```
Dim RSProduct
```

But we shouldn't get to this page without the ProductID being passed in through the QueryString:

```
If IsEmpty(Request.QueryString("ProductID")) Then
```

If the field is not present, visitors are redirected to the Product Catalog menu page:

```
Response.Redirect "./product_catalog.asp"
```

otherwise, the Connection object is instantiated:

```
set conn = server.createobject ("adodb.connection")
```

and opened:

```
conn.open "ASPBook", "sa", " yourpassword "
```

A hit to this image is recorded:

```
conn.execute "insert into ASPSessionPages (SessionID, PageName)
   values (" _
     & Session("SessionID") & ", " _
   & "'ProductPicture" & Request.QueryString("ProductID") & "')"
```

We then retrieve the path to the large image:

```
set RSProduct = conn.execute("select Path2Image from ASPProducts
   where " _
   & "ProductID = " & Request.QueryString("ProductID"))
```

and redirect the visitor to that location:

```
Response.Redirect "../products/" & RSProduct("Path2Image")
```

Product Page

The code on the Product page must display all the information about the product as well as any comments about the product. The main code block is:

```
<%
Option Explicit
If IsEmpty(Request.QueryString("ProductID")) Then
   Response.Redirect "./product_catalog.asp"
End If
Dim conn
Dim RSProduct
Dim LongDescription
Dim ShortDescription
Dim RSSelects
Dim RSSelectItems
Dim RSComments
set conn = server.createobject ("adodb.connection")
conn.open "ASPBook", "sa", "aspbook"
conn.execute "insert into ASPSessionPages (SessionID, PageName)
   values (" _
     & Session("SessionID") & ", " _
   & "'Product" & Request.QueryString("ProductID") & "')"
set RSProduct = conn.execute("SELECT ASPProducts.LongDescription, " _
   & "ASPProducts.ProductID, ASPProducts.ProductName, " _
   & "ASPProducts.ShortDescription, ASPProducts.Path2Icon,
     ASPProducts.Price, " _
```

```
                & "ASPProducts.OnClearance, ASPProducts.ClearancePrice " _
                & "FROM ASPProducts " _
                & "WHERE ProductID = " & Request.QueryString("ProductID"))
        LongDescription = RSProduct("LongDescription")
        ShortDescription = RSProduct("ShortDescription")
        set RSSelects = conn.execute("SELECT ASPSelectLists.SelectListID, _
                & "ASPSelectLists.SelectListName FROM ASPProductSelectLists " _
                & "INNER JOIN ASPSelectLists ON ASPProductSelectLists.SelectListID
                    = " _
                & "ASPSelectLists.SelectListID WHERE " _
                & "ASPProductSelectLists.ProductID = " & Request.QueryString
                    ("ProductID"))
        set RSComments = conn.execute("select CommentName, CommentFrom, _
            Comment from " _
                & "ASPProductComments where ProductID = " & Request.QueryString
                    ("ProductID"))
    %>
```

This page requires variable declaration:

```
Option Explicit
```

If no ProductID was passed into this page:

```
If IsEmpty(Request.QueryString("ProductID")) Then
```

Visitors are sent back to the Product Catalog menu page:

```
Response.Redirect "./product_catalog.asp"
```

A connection to the database will be needed:

```
Dim conn
```

and the information about the product is needed:

```
Dim RSProduct
```

These variables will store fields from the table:

```
Dim LongDescription
Dim ShortDescription
```

We will also need to build any Select controls for this product:

```
Dim RSSelects
```

and we will need any items in each Select control:

```
Dim RSSelectItems
```

Another Recordset will be needed for the comments on this product:

```
Dim RSComments
```

The Recordset object is instantiated:

```
set conn = server.createobject ("adodb.connection")
```

and opened:

```
conn.open "ASPBook", "sa", "aspbook"
```

A hit to the Product page for this specific ProductID is recorded:

```
conn.execute "insert into ASPSessionPages (SessionID, PageName)
   values (" _
     & Session("SessionID") & ", " _
   & "'Product" & Request.QueryString("ProductID") & "')"
```

The `RSProduct` Recordset is set to contain the data about this product:

```
set RSProduct = conn.execute("SELECT ASPProducts.LongDescription, " _
   & "ASPProducts.ProductID, ASPProducts.ProductName, " _
   & "ASPProducts.ShortDescription, ASPProducts.Path2Icon,
ASPProducts.Price, " _
   & "ASPProducts.OnClearance, ASPProducts.ClearancePrice " _
   & "FROM ASPProducts " _
   & "WHERE ProductID = " & Request.QueryString("ProductID"))
LongDescription = RSProduct("LongDescription")
ShortDescription = RSProduct("ShortDescription")
```

and we retrieve any Select controls that are needed for this product:

```
set RSSelects = conn.execute("SELECT ASPSelectLists.SelectListID, " _
   & "ASPSelectLists.SelectListName FROM ASPProductSelectLists " _
   & "INNER JOIN ASPSelectLists ON ASPProductSelectLists.SelectList
     ID = " _
   & "ASPSelectLists.SelectListID WHERE " _
   & "ASPProductSelectLists.ProductID = " & Request.QueryString
     ("ProductID"))
```

In addition, all the comments are retrieved from the database for this product:

```
set RSComments = conn.execute("select CommentName, CommentFrom,
   Comment from " _
   & "ASPProductComments where ProductID = " & Request.QueryString
     ("ProductID"))
```

Then, inline with the HTML, the information about the product is written. The next code block displays the Select controls, if any, for this product:

```
<%
Do Until RSSelects.EOF
  Set RSSelectItems = conn.execute("select ItemText from
    ASPSelectListItems " _
    & "where SelectListID = " & RSSelects("SelectListID"))
%>
<P><B><% Response.Write RSSelects("SelectListName") %></B>
<BR><SELECT NAME="<% Response.Write RSSelects("SelectListName")
  %>">
<%
  Do Until RSSelectItems.EOF
%>
    <OPTION VALUE="<% Response.Write RSSelectItems("ItemText") %>">
    <% Response.Write RSSelectItems("ItemText") %></OPTION>
<%
    RSSelectItems.MoveNext
  Loop
%>
</SELECT>
<%
  RSSelects.MoveNext
Loop
%>
```

The outer loop will go through each of the records in the RSSelects Recordset:

```
Do Until RSSelects.EOF
```

All the items for the current Select control are retrieved from the database:

```
Set RSSelectItems = conn.execute("select ItemText from
  ASPSelectListItems " _
  & "where SelectListID = " & RSSelects("SelectListID"))
```

The beginning tag for the Select control is written to the browser:

```
<P><B><% Response.Write RSSelects("SelectListName") %></B>
<BR><SELECT NAME="<% Response.Write RSSelects("SelectListName")
  %>">
```

We then enter the inner loop, which displays the items in the Select control:

```
Do Until RSSelectItems.EOF
```

Each item is written to the browser as an option for the current Select control:

```
<OPTION VALUE="<% Response.Write RSSelectItems("ItemText") %>">
<% Response.Write RSSelectItems("ItemText") %></OPTION>
```

The code then moves on to the next item:

```
RSSelectItems.MoveNext
Loop
```

Then the Select control ends:

```
</SELECT>
```

and we loop to the next Select control:

```
RSSelects.MoveNext
Loop
```

One more code block is needed to display all the comments for this particular product.

```
<%
Do Until RSComments.EOF
%>
<P><B>Name: </B><% Response.Write RSComments("CommentName") %>
<BR><B>From: </B><% Response.Write RSComments("CommentFrom") %><
P><B>Comment:</B><% Response.Write RSComments("Comment") %></TD>
<%
   RSComments.MoveNext
Loop
%>
```

The code will loop through all the records in the RSComments Recordset:

```
Do Until RSComments.EOF
```

For each of these records, the name of the person who made the comment is displayed:

```
<P><B>Name: </B><% Response.Write RSComments("CommentName") %>
```

followed by the customer's location:

```
<BR><B>From: </B><% Response.Write RSComments("CommentFrom") %><
```

and the customer's comment:

```
P><B>Comment:</B><% Response.Write RSComments("Comment") %></TD>
```

The code then uses the MoveNext method of the Recordset object to move on to the next record before looping:

```
RSComments.MoveNext
Loop
```

Add Comment Page

The Add Comment page gives visitors the opportunity to add their own comment about a particular product. The code on the page records their feedback in the database. The main code block is:

```
<%
Option Explicit
If IsEmpty(Request.QueryString("ProductID")) and _
  IsEmpty(Request.Form("ProductID"))Then
  Response.Redirect "./product_catalog.asp"
End If
Dim conn
set conn = server.createobject ("adodb.connection")
conn.open "ASPBook", "sa", " yourpassword "
conn.execute "insert into ASPSessionPages (SessionID, PageName)
  values (" _
  & Session("SessionID") & ", " _
  & "'Product" & Request.QueryString("ProductID") & "')"
If not IsEmpty(Request.Form("ProductID")) Then
  conn.execute "insert into ASPProductComments (ProductID,
  CommentName, " _
  & "CommentFrom, Comment) values (" _
  & Request.Form("ProductID") & ", " _
  & "'" & Request.Form("CommentName") & "', " _
  & "'" & Request.Form("CommentFrom") & "', " _
  & "'" & Request.Form("Comment") & "')"
  Response.Redirect "./product.asp?ProductID=" & Request.Form
  ("ProductID")
End If
%>
```

Option Explicit is first declared:

```
Option Explicit
```

This page should not be viewed if a ProductID was not passed in:

```
If IsEmpty(Request.QueryString("ProductID")) and _
    IsEmpty(Request.Form("ProductID"))Then
```

If none is present, visitors are sent back to the menu page:

```
Response.Redirect "./product_catalog.asp"
```

otherwise, we will need to connect to the database:

```
Dim conn
```

The Connection object is instantiated:

```
set conn = server.createobject ("adodb.connection")
```

and opened:

```
conn.open "ASPBook", "sa", "yourpassword"
```

A hit to this page is recorded:

```
conn.execute "insert into ASPSessionPages (SessionID, PageName)
    values (" _
    & Session("SessionID") & ", " _
    & "'Product" & Request.QueryString("ProductID") & "')"
```

If the form variable `ProductID` is found, then the form has been submitted:

```
If not IsEmpty(Request.Form("ProductID")) Then
```

In that case, we need to add the visitor's comment to the database:

```
conn.execute "insert into ASPProductComments (ProductID,
    CommentName, " _
    & "CommentFrom, Comment) values (" _
    & Request.Form("ProductID") & ", " _
    & "'" & Request.Form("CommentName") & "', " _
    & "'" & Request.Form("CommentFrom") & "', " _
    & "'" & Request.Form("Comment") & "')"
```

and then Redirect visitors back to the Product page for the product concerning which they just made a comment:

```
Response.Redirect "./product.asp?ProductID=" & Request.Form
    ("ProductID")
```

Daily Special Page

The code on the Daily Special page records a hit to that page and displays the dynamic content for that page. The main code block is:

```
<%
Option Explicit
Dim conn
Dim RSPageText
Dim RSFooter
Dim PageText
set conn = server.createobject ("adodb.connection")
conn.open "ASPBook", "sa", "yourpassword"
conn.execute "insert into ASPSessionPages (SessionID, PageName)
  values (" _
    & Session("SessionID") & ", " _
    & "'DailySpecial')"
set RSPageText = conn.execute("select ExtendedText, BriefText from
  ASPPageText " _
    & "where PageName = 'DailySpecial'")
PageText= RSPageText("ExtendedText")
set RSFooter = conn.execute("select BriefText from ASPPageText " _
    & "where PageName = 'Footer'")
%>
```

First, Option Explicit is coded:

```
Option Explicit
```

A connection object will be needed:

```
Dim conn
```

as will variables to retrieve and display the dynamic text for this page:

```
Dim RSPageText
Dim RSFooter
Dim PageText
```

The Connection object is instantiated:

```
set conn = server.createobject ("adodb.connection")
```

and opened:

```
conn.open "ASPBook", "sa", "yourpassword"
```

A hit to the Daily Special page is recorded:

```
conn.execute "insert into ASPSessionPages (SessionID, PageName)
values (" _
  & Session("SessionID") & ", " _
& "'DailySpecial')"
```

and the title and extended text for the page are retrieved:

```
set RSPageText = conn.execute("select ExtendedText, BriefText from
  ASPPageText " _
& "where PageName = 'DailySpecial'")
```

The PageText variable is set to the ExtendedText field:

```
PageText= RSPageText("ExtendedText")
```

Also, the footer text is retrieved from the database:

```
set RSFooter = conn.execute("select BriefText from ASPPageText " _
& "where PageName = 'Footer'")
```

The dynamic text is then written inline with the HTML.

ASP in Action: Shopping Cart

Shopping Cart Component

In the last chapter we completed the first part of our e-commerce site. We created the basic structure of the pages and the Online Catalog. The visitor was given a variety of ways to browse through the products in the catalog.

In this chapter, we expand on that site and add the pages that allow visitors to add products to a shopping cart, remove items from that shopping cart, and check out. Figure 17-1 displays the Web site hierarchy with the two components in place. In Chapter 16 we completed the Home, About Us, Product Catalog, and Contact Info portions of the site. In this chapter, we flow though the Product Catalog into the Shopping Cart as visitors add and remove products and check out of the online store.

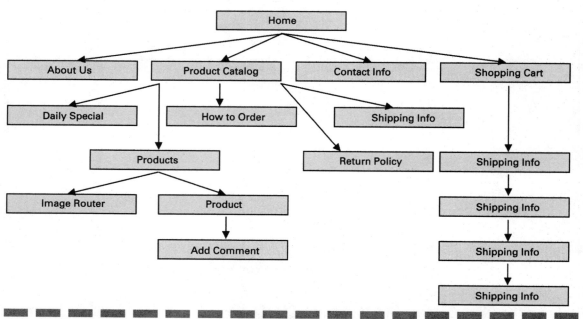

Figure 17-1   Site hierarchy.

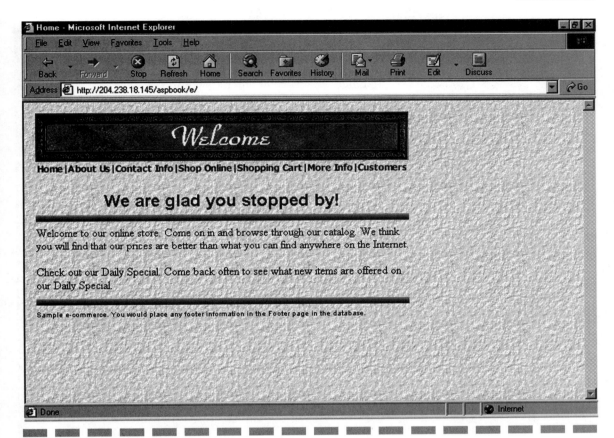

Figure 17-2 Home page from e-commerce site.

Sample Usage

Visitors enter the site through the Home page as shown in Figure 17-2. Visitors press the link labeled SHOP ONLINE to begin their shopping and eventually get to a product that they want to purchase. Figure 17-3 shows the Product page for the Color Candies. Visitors supply the type, color, and quantity for this product and press the ADD TO SHOPPING CART link. That product is added to their shopping cart as seen in Figure 17-4.

Visitors can then shop around and add another item to their Shopping Cart, as displayed in Figure 17-5.

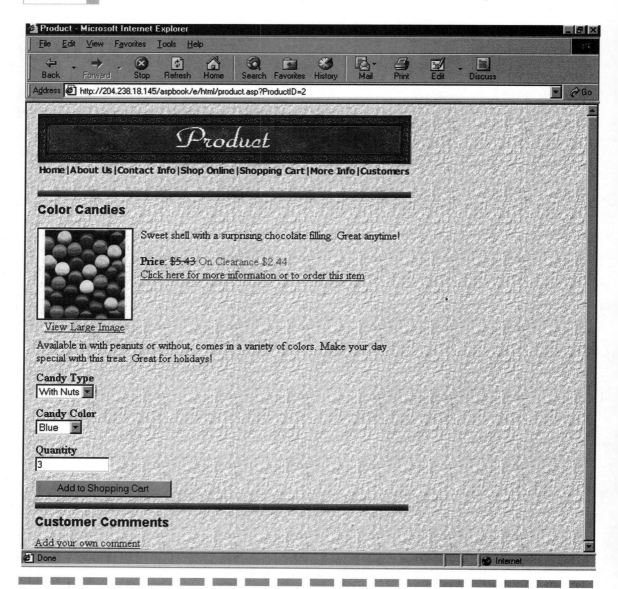

Figure 17-3   Color Candies Product page.

Visitors can then add this item to their Shopping Cart, which now has two products in it, as shown in Figure 17-6.

Take a close look at the format of the Shopping Cart. The page displays information about each item in the shopping cart, the name, quantity, price, and options selected. Below each product is a link to remove

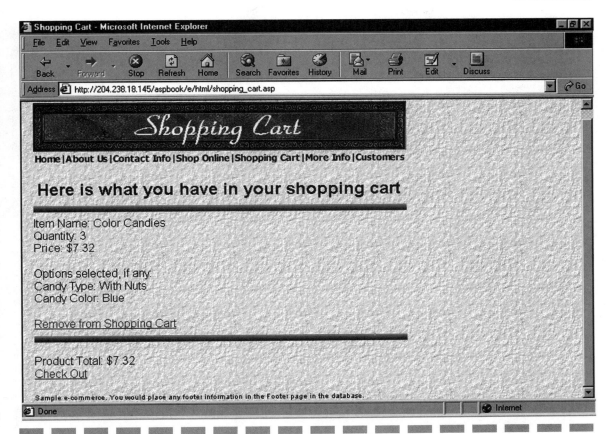

Figure 17-4 Shopping Cart with one product.

the product from the Shopping Cart. The link redisplays this page with the product removed. So if visitors were to click on the link to remove the Color Candies, they would see the Shopping Cart as displayed in Figure 17-7.

The bottom of the Shopping Cart displays the visitors' overall product total. When visitors are ready to check out, they click on the CHECK OUT link and see the first page of the wizard, as displayed in Figure 17-8. On this page visitors select their location so the shipping charge can be calculated. The Location field comes from the database, so you can have as much refinement as you want in your calculation of shipping total. As you will see in the code, the shipping is calculated based on the weight of each product, as well as a base shipping charge and a minimum shipping charge.

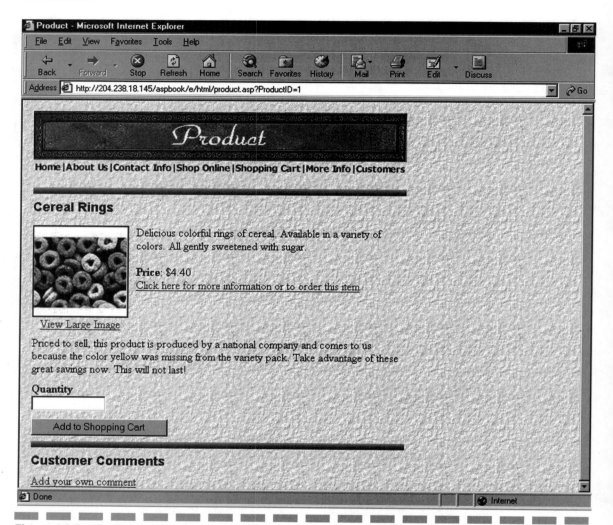

Figure 17-5 Product page displaying cereal rings.

Once visitors select their location, they would click on the CALCULATE SHIPPING button. That page is displayed in Figure 17-9. At the top of the Tax page, visitors see their product total as well as the shipping charge based on their location. They then select their location so the order can be taxed appropriately. This location field also comes from a database table but different from the one used in the Shipping page.

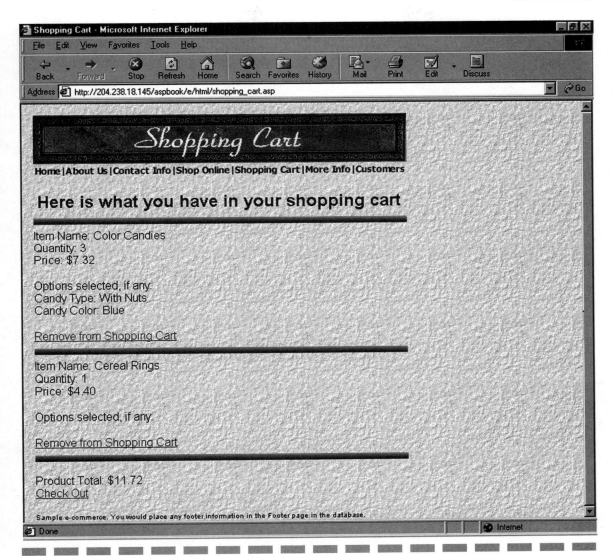

Figure 17-6 Shopping Cart with two products.

This allows you to have a different level of refinement for these charges, so you could have shipping based on the part of the country in which the person is located and have the tax based on the state in which the visitor is located.

When visitors click on the CALCULATE TAX button, they see the page

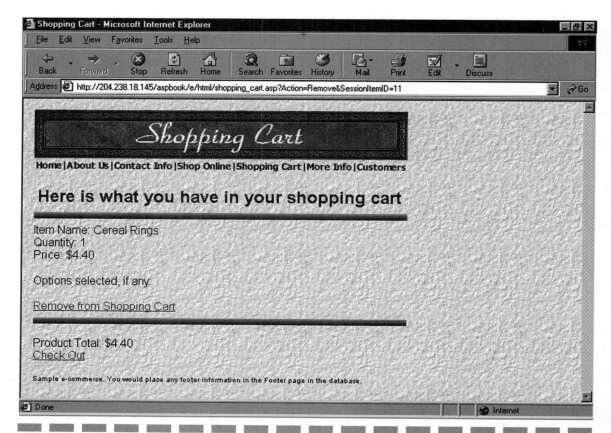

Figure 17-7　Shopping Cart with product removed.

displayed in Figure 17-10. At the top of the Check Out page visitors can see their full charge. If they decide to process their order, they use this secure page to supply their shipping and billing information. As you will see in the code, the Credit Card type comes from the database, so the options in that control are easily modified.

When visitors press the CHECK OUT button, their order is processed, their session ends, and they see the page displayed in Figure 17-11. This page processes the visitors' order and displays this response text that comes out of the database. This ends the visitors' session, so their shopping cart is emptied.

Since personal information is being transmitted with this page, the Check Out and Check Out Complete pages need to be marked as requiring secure communications. To do this, browse to the page in the

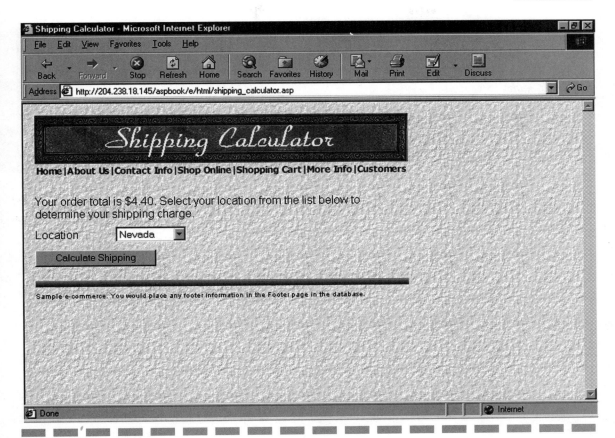

Figure 17-8 Shipping Calculator page.

Microsoft Management Console and select the properties for that page. Select the FILE SECURITY tab as shown in Figure 17-12. Then press the EDIT button in the Secure Communications section. You should see the dialog displayed in Figure 17-13. Check the box that says "Require Secure Channel when accessing this resource" to require that the page be accessed securely. In the HTML, one links to these pages with the https protocol instead of the http protocol.

Shopping Cart Database Component

In this section of the chapter we look at the tables that were added or modified for the Shopping Cart component of the e-commerce site. First,

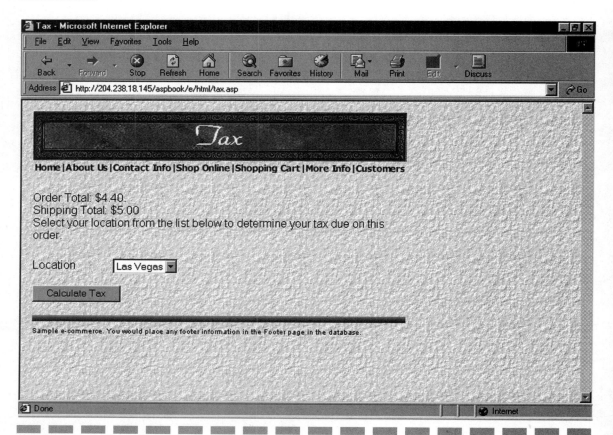

Figure 17-9 Tax page.

we will define the tables, then we will look at their relationships, and finally, we will look at the field specifications for those tables.

Table Definitions

ASPCCTypes
The *ASPCCTypes* table is used to populate the CCType field on the Check Out form. You could modify the form slightly and add other payment methods to this list such as Check, Money Order, and so forth.

ASPProducts
The *ASPProducts* table also has a role in the Shopping Cart component as it did in the Product Catalog component. In fact, it really ties the two components together. A new field is added to this table for shipping purposes.

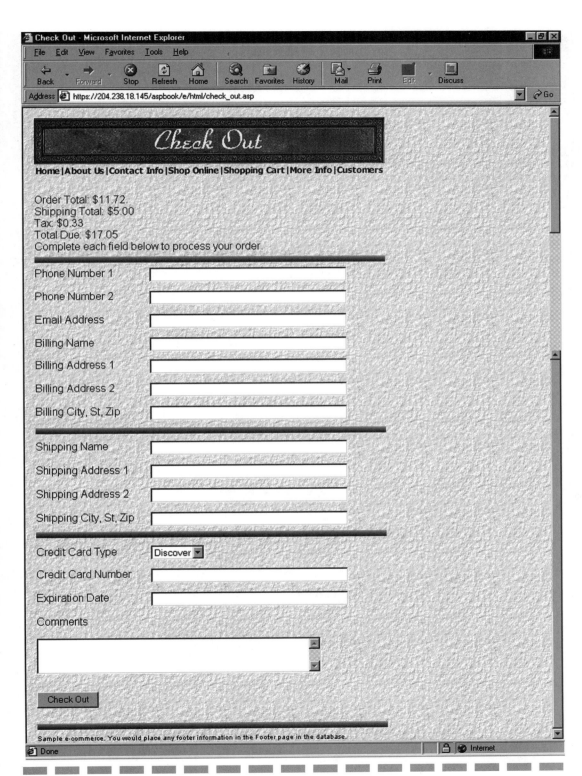

Figure 17-10 Check Out page.

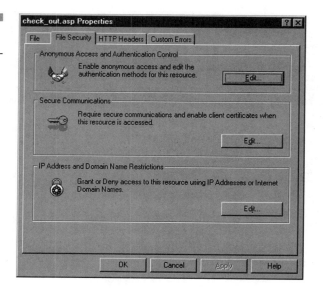

Figure 17-11 Check Out Complete page.

Figure 17-12
File Security tab.

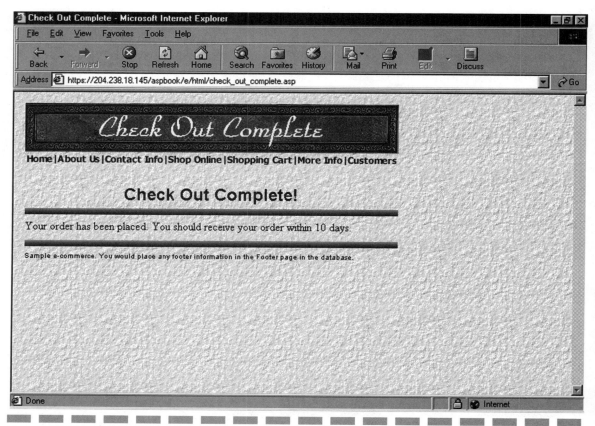

Figure 17-13
Secure
Communications
dialog.

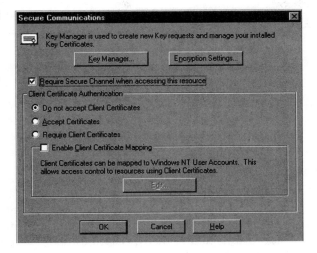

ASPSessionItems
The *ASPSessionItems* table is used to store the products that visitors have in their shopping cart and that they end up ordering. This table satisfies the many-to-many relationship between the products and the sessions.

ASPSessions
The *ASPSessions* table has numerous new fields. These fields store information about the visitor's order as well as the shipping and billing information about the visitor.

ASPShippingCharge
The *ASPShippingCharge* table is used to populate the locations for the shipping destination. Fields in the table are then used to calculate the shipping charge for the order for a particular area.

ASPTaxTable
The *ASPTaxTable* table is used to store the tax rate for different locations. Visitors pick a location and the applicable tax, if any, is added to their order.

Data Diagram and Relationships

Figure 17-14 shows the relationships for the tables in the Shopping Cart component. Each customer can order many products. Each product can

Figure 17-14
Shopping Cart data
diagram.

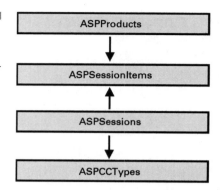

Figure 17-14
Shopping Cart data
diagram.

be ordered by many different customers. So the ASPSessions table and the ASPProducts table exist in a many-to-many relationship. A many-to-many relationship cannot be expressed directly; it requires a go-between table. The ASPSessionItems table is that go-between table and is in a one-to-many relationship with the ASPProducts table and the ASPSessions table.

The ASPSessions table and the ASPCCTypes table are in a one-to-many relationship. Each customer selects a single credit card type and each credit card type can be used by multiple customers. The other table, ASPShippingCharge and ASPTaxTable, do relate to the ASPSessions indirectly. They are used to calculate fields in the ASPSessions table.

Field Specifications

ASPCCTypes Field Specification
Table 17-1 shows the field specification for the ASPCCTypes table. The CCType field is used to populate the Options in the Credit Card Type select control on the Check Out page. The CCType field is also the primary key for the table.

ASPProducts Field Specifications
Table 17-2 shows the field specifications for the ASPProducts table. The ProductID field is the primary key for the table and is automatically

TABLE 17-1

ASPCCTypes Field
Specifications

Field Name	Field Type	Notes
CCType	varchar	Length = 50

TABLE 17-2

ASPProducts Field
Specifications

Field Name	Field Type	Notes
ProductID	int	Identity column, seeded at 1 and incremented by 1
ProductName	varchar	Length = 50
ShortDescription	varchar	Length = 250
LongDescription	varchar	Length = 255
Path2Icon	varchar	Length = 150
Path2Image	varchar	Length = 150
Price	money	
OnClearance	int	
ClearancePrice	money	
Weight	float	

populated since it is an identity column. The Weight field stores the number of pounds each product weighs. This field is used in calculating the shipping charge.

ASPSessionItems Field Specifications

Table 17-3 shows the field specifications for the ASPSessionItems table. This table is the connecting table between the ASPProducts table and the ASPSessions table. The SessionID field connects the table to the ASPSessions table and the ProductID field connects this table to the ASPProducts table. The Quantity field stores the number of products ordered and the SelectText field contains the concatenation of the options that the visitor chose for this item, such as color and size. The ItemPrice field stores the amount that the visitor is charged for that product.

TABLE 17-3

ASPSessionItems
Field Specifications

Field Name	Field Type	Notes
SessionItemID	int	Identity column, seeded at 1 and incremented by 1
SessionID	int	Foreign Key
ProductID	int	Foreign Key
Quantity	int	
SelectText	varchar	255
ItemPrice	money	

ASPSessions Field Specifications

Table 17-4 shows the field specifications for the ASPSessions table. The first few fields are the same as before and store information about visitors, where they came from, when they got here, and when their session ended. The Bill fields store information on the person being billed for the order; the Ship fields store the Shipping address to be used; the CC fields store the Credit Card information for visitors.

TABLE 17-4

ASPSessions Field Specifications

Field Name	Field Type	Notes
SessionID	int	Identity column, seeded at 1 and incremented by 1
SessionStarted	datetime	
SessionEnded	datetime	
RefSource	varchar	Length = 200
Browser	varchar	Length = 75
OS	varchar	Length = 75
BillName	varchar	Length = 50
Phone	varchar	Length = 50
Phone2	varchar	Length = 50
BillAddress1	varchar	Length = 100
BillAddress2	varchar	Length = 100
BillCSZ	varchar	Length = 100
ShipName	varchar	Length = 50
ShipAddress1	varchar	Length = 100
ShipAddress2	varchar	Length = 100
ShipCSZ	varchar	Length = 100
CCType	varchar	Length = 50
CCNumber	varchar	Length = 50
CCExpiration	varchar	Length = 50
Comments	text	
ProductTotal	money	
ShippingTotal	money	
TaxTotal	money	
OrderTotal	money	

Visitors use the Comments field to convey any additional information about their order.

The ProductTotal field stores the total cost of the products ordered; the ShippingTotal field stores the amount charged for shipping for this order; the TaxTotal field stores the amount charged for tax on this order; and the OrderTotal field stores the total amount due for this order.

ASPShippingCharge Field Specifications

Table 17-5 shows the field specifications for the ASPShippingCharge table. The ASPShippingCharge table is used to calculate the shipping charge for the order. The ShippingChargeID field is the primary key for the table and is an identity column. Based on the Locations elected by the visitor, the shipping rate is calculated by multiplying the number of pounds in the order by the PerPoundShipping field and adding to that the BaseRate. If that result is less than the MinimumShipping field, then that value is used.

ASPTaxTable Field Specifications

Table 17-6 shows the field specifications for the ASPTaxTable table. This table is used to calculate the amount of tax on the order. The TaxTableID field is the primary key for the table and is an identity column. Visitors select their Location and the TaxRate field is multiplied by the order total, which results in the tax on the order.

TABLE 17-5

ASPShipping
Charge Field
Specifications

Field Name	Field Type	Notes
ShippingChargeID	int	Identity column, seeded at 1 and incremented by 1
Location	varchar	Length = 50
MinimumShipping	money	
PerPoundShipping	money	
BaseRate	money	

TABLE 17-6

ASPTaxTable Field
Specifications

Field Name	Field Type	Notes
TaxTableID	int	Identity column, seeded at 1 and incremented by 1
Location	varchar	Length = 50
TaxRate	float	

Active Server Page Code

Code for the Shopping Cart Page

The code on the Shopping Cart page adds items to the Shopping Cart, removes items from the Shopping Cart, and displays the contents of the Shopping Cart. The page also records a hit to this page and displays the footer text. The main code block is:

```
<%
Option Explicit
Dim conn
Dim RSProduct
Dim RSProducts
Dim NewProductCost
Dim NewSelectText
Dim FormField
Dim RSFooter
Dim RSTotal
set conn = server.createobject ("adodb.connection")
conn.open "ASPBook", "sa", "yourpassword"
conn.execute "insert into ASPSessionPages (SessionID, PageName)
 values (" _
   & Session("SessionID") & ", " _
   & "'ShoppingCart')"
set RSFooter = conn.execute("select BriefText from ASPPageText " _
   & "where PageName = 'Footer'")
If not IsEmpty(Request.Form("AddToShoppingCart")) Then
   set RSProduct = conn.execute("select Price, OnClearance,
     ClearancePrice from " _
       & "ASPProducts where ProductID = " & Request.Form("ProductID"))
   If RSProduct("OnClearance") = 1 Then
   NewProductCost = RSProduct("ClearancePrice") * Request.Form
     ("Quantity")
Else
   NewProductCost = RSProduct("Price") * Request.Form("Quantity")
End If
For Each FormField in Request.Form
   If FormField <> "AddToShoppingCart" _
     and FormField <> "Quantity" _
     and FormField <> "ProductID" Then
     NewSelectText = NewSelectText & FormField & ": " _
         & Request.Form(FormField) & "<BR> "
   End If
Next
conn.execute "Insert into ASPSessionItems (SessionID, ProductID, " _
   & "Quantity, SelectText, ItemPrice) values (" _
   & Session("SessionID") & ", " _
   & Request.Form("ProductID") & ", " _
   & Request.Form("Quantity") & ", " _
   & "'" & NewSelectText & "', " _
   & NewProductCost & ")"
set RSTotal = conn.execute("select Sum(ItemPrice) as TheTotal from " _
   & "ASPSessionItems where SessionID = " & Session("SessionID"))
```

```
conn.execute "update ASPSessions set ProductTotal = " & RSTotal _
 ("TheTotal") _
 & "Where SessionID = " & Session("SessionID")
End If
If Not IsEmpty(Request.QueryString("Action")) Then
 conn.execute "Delete from ASPSessionItems where " _
 & "SessionItemID = " & Request.QueryString("SessionItemID")
set RSTotal = conn.execute("select Sum(ItemPrice) as TheTotal from " _
 & "ASPSessionItems where SessionID = " & Session("SessionID"))
conn.execute "update ASPSessions set ProductTotal = " & RSTotal _
 ("TheTotal") _
 & "Where SessionID = " & Session("SessionID")
End If
set RSProducts = conn.execute("SELECT ASPSessionItems.Session
 ItemID, " _
 & "ASPSessionItems.Quantity, ASPSessionItems.SelectText, " _
 & "ASPSessionItems.ItemPrice, ASPProducts.ProductName " _
 & "FROM ASPSessionItems INNER JOIN ASPProducts ON " _
 & "ASPSessionItems.ProductID = ASPProducts.ProductID " _
 & "WHERE ASPSessionItems.SessionID = " & Session("SessionID"))
set RSTotal = conn.execute("select Sum(ItemPrice) as TheTotal from " _
 & "ASPSessionItems where SessionID = " & Session("SessionID"))
%>
```

The code starts with `Option Explicit`:

```
Option Explicit
```

Then variables are declared. We will need to connect to the database:

```
Dim conn
```

and may need information on a product to add:

```
Dim RSProduct
```

and will need to display all the products in this session:

```
Dim RSProducts
```

We will need variables to calculate the order table:

```
Dim NewProductCost
```

and the options selected for a new item in the Shopping Cart:

```
Dim NewSelectText
```

This variable will be used as we iterate through the Form fields collection:

```
Dim FormField
```

The next Recordset will retrieve the text for the footer:

```
Dim RSFooter
```

and one more Recordset will be used to display the total for this order:

```
Dim RSTotal
```

A Connection object is returned into the `Conn` variable through the CreateObject method:

```
set conn = server.createobject ("adodb.connection")
```

and the Connection to the database is established:

```
conn.open "ASPBook", "sa", "yourpassword"
```

A hit is recorded to the ASPSessionPages table for this page:

```
conn.execute "insert into ASPSessionPages (SessionID, PageName)
  values (" _
  & Session("SessionID") & ", " _
& "'ShoppingCart')"
```

The footer text is then retrieved from the database:

```
set RSFooter = conn.execute("select BriefText from ASPPageText " _
  & "where PageName = 'Footer'")
```

If the ADDTOSHOPPINGCART button is present in the Form collection, the visitor entered this page by selecting a product and that product needs to be added to the Shopping Cart. The code checks for that field:

```
If not IsEmpty(Request.Form("AddToShoppingCart")) Then
```

The `RSProduct` Recordset object is set to contain the information for the product that is to be added to the Shopping Cart:

```
set RSProduct = conn.execute("select Price, OnClearance,
  ClearancePrice from " _
  & "ASPProducts where ProductID = " & Request.Form("ProductID"))
```

Next, we need to determine the price to charge for this item. If it is on clearance:

```
If RSProduct("OnClearance") = 1 Then
```

then the clearance price is used:

```
NewProductCost = RSProduct("ClearancePrice") * Request.Form
    ("Quantity")
```

otherwise, the standard price is used:

```
NewProductCost = RSProduct("Price") * Request.Form("Quantity")
```

Each of the products can have options that go with it that the visitor must select when ordering the item, such as size and color. We need to record those choices and since we don't know how many choices there were, we iterate through the Form collection:

```
For Each FormField in Request.Form
```

If the Form field is not the ADD button:

```
If FormField <> "AddToShoppingCart" _
```

and not the Quantity field:

```
and FormField <> "Quantity" _
```

and not the ProductID field:

```
and FormField <> "ProductID" Then
```

Then it must be one of the select items. If it is, it is appended to a variable called NewSelectText. Notice that an HTML <BR> tag is concatenated between each selection:

```
NewSelectText = NewSelectText & FormField & ": " _
    & Request.Form(FormField) & "<BR> "
```

The code then loops to the next field in the Form collection:

```
Next
```

The item selected by the visitor is then inserted into the Shopping Cart:

```
conn.execute "Insert into ASPSessionItems (SessionID, ProductID, " _
    & "Quantity, SelectText, ItemPrice) values (" _
    & Session("SessionID") & ", " _
    & Request.Form("ProductID") & ", " _
    & Request.Form("Quantity") & ", " _
```

```
      & "'" & NewSelectText & "', " _
   & NewProductCost & ")"
```

Next, the current order total is retrieved from the database:

```
   set RSTotal = conn.execute("select Sum(ItemPrice) as TheTotal
      from " _
   & "ASPSessionItems where SessionID = " & Session("SessionID"))
```

The ProductTotal field in the ASPSessions table is updated to the value
of the order total, so as new items are added to the order, the
ProductTotal field is kept updated:

```
   conn.execute "update ASPSessions set ProductTotal = " & RSTotal
      "TheTotal") _
   & "Where SessionID = " & Session("SessionID")
```

The next case to deal with is the visitor wanting to remove something
from the Shopping Cart. To determine this condition we look for the
Action property:

```
   If Not IsEmpty(Request.QueryString("Action")) Then
```

If it is present, then a product needs to be removed from the Shopping
Cart. An SQL Delete statement takes that action:

```
   conn.execute "Delete from ASPSessionItems where " _
   & "SessionItemID = " & Request.QueryString("SessionItemID")
```

The order total needs to be recalculated:

```
set RSTotal = conn.execute("select Sum(ItemPrice) as TheTotal from " _
   & "ASPSessionItems where SessionID = " & Session("SessionID"))
conn.execute "update ASPSessions set ProductTotal = " & RSTotal
 ("TheTotal") _
   & "Where SessionID = " & Session("SessionID")
```

Now that all the actions for the Shopping Cart have been taken care
of, we can display the contents of the Shopping Cart. First, we retrieve
all the products from the Shopping Cart:

```
   set RSProducts = conn.execute("SELECT
ASPSessionItems.SessionItemID, " _
      & "ASPSessionItems.Quantity, ASPSessionItems.SelectText, " _
      & "ASPSessionItems.ItemPrice, ASPProducts.ProductName " _
      & "FROM ASPSessionItems INNER JOIN ASPProducts ON " _
       & "ASPSessionItems.ProductID = ASPProducts.ProductID " _
     & "WHERE ASPSessionItems.SessionID = " & Session("SessionID"))
```

Then we retrieve the current order total:

```
set RSTotal = conn.execute("select Sum(ItemPrice) as TheTotal from " _
& "ASPSessionItems where SessionID = " & Session("SessionID"))
```

The next code block loops through each of the products in the Shopping Cart.

```
<%
Do Until RSProducts.EOF
%>
<P ALIGN=LEFT>Item Name: <% Response.Write RSProducts("ProductName")
  %>
<BR>Quantity: <% Response.Write RSProducts("Quantity") %>
<BR>Price: <% Response.Write FormatCurrency(RSProducts("ItemPrice"))
  %>
<P>Options selected, if any: <BR><% Response.Write RSProducts
  ("SelectText") %>
<P><A HREF="./shopping_cart.asp?Action=Remove&SessionItemID=
<% Response.Write RSProducts("SessionItemID") %>" >
Remove from Shopping Cart</A>
<%
  RSProducts.MoveNext
Loop
%>
```

The code will loop through the records in the RSProducts Recordset:

```
Do Until RSProducts.EOF
```

The values in each of the records is written to the browser:

```
<P ALIGN=LEFT>Item Name: <% Response.Write RSProducts("ProductName")
  %>
<BR>Quantity: <% Response.Write RSProducts("Quantity") %>
<BR>Price: <% Response.Write FormatCurrency(RSProducts("ItemPrice"))
  %>
<P>Options selected, if any: <BR><% Response.Write
RSProducts("SelectText") %>
<P><A HREF="./shopping_cart.asp?Action=Remove&SessionItemID=
<% Response.Write RSProducts("SessionItemID") %>" >
Remove from Shopping Cart</A>
```

and the record pointer is moved to the next record before looping:

```
RSProducts.MoveNext
```

Inline with the HTML, the order total is written:

```
<BR>Product Total: <% Response.Write FormatCurrency(RSTotal
  ("TheTotal")) %>
```

As is the text of the footer:

```
<% Response.Write RSFooter("BriefText") %>
```

Shipping Calculator Page

The Shipping Calculator page records a hit to that page and displays a list of locations for the visitor to select so shipping can be calculated.

```
<%
Option Explicit
Dim conn
Dim RSFooter
Dim RSTotal
Dim RSShipping
set conn = server.createobject ("adodb.connection")
conn.open "ASPBook", "sa", "yourpassword"
conn.execute "insert into ASPSessionPages (SessionID, PageName)
 values (" _
   & Session("SessionID") & ", " _
   & "'Shipping')"
set RSFooter = conn.execute("select BriefText from ASPPageText " _
   & "where PageName = 'Footer'")
set RSTotal = conn.execute("select Sum(ItemPrice) as TheTotal from
 " _
   & "ASPSessionItems where SessionID = " & Session("SessionID"))
set RSShipping = conn.execute("select ShippingChargeID, Location " _
   & "From ASPShippingCharge")
%>
```

First, Option Explicit is written:

```
Option Explicit
```

Then a Connection object is declared:

```
Dim conn
```

A Recordset will be needed to retrieve the footer for the page:

```
Dim RSFooter
```

and one will be needed to retrieve the order total:

```
Dim RSTotal
```

as well as the shipping locations:

```
Dim RSShipping
```

The Connection object is instantiated:

```
set conn = server.createobject ("adodb.connection")
```

and opened:

```
conn.open "ASPBook", "sa", "yourpassword"
```

A hit is then recorded for this page:

```
conn.execute "insert into ASPSessionPages (SessionID, PageName)
values (" _
  & Session("SessionID") & ", " _
& "'Shipping')"
```

and the text of the footer is retrieved from the database:

```
set RSFooter = conn.execute("select BriefText from ASPPageText " _
  & "where PageName = 'Footer'")
```

The order total will need to be displayed, so it is retrieved:

```
set RSTotal = conn.execute("select Sum(ItemPrice) as TheTotal from " _
& "ASPSessionItems where SessionID = " & Session:("SessionID"))
```

The shipping locations are retrieved into the RSShipping Recordset:

```
set RSShipping = conn.execute("select ShippingChargeID, Location " _
& "From ASPShippingCharge")
```

Inline with the HTML, the order total is written:

```
Your order total is <% Response.Write FormatCurrency(RSTotal
  ("TheTotal")) %>
```

Then the next code block populates the options for the Select control.

```
<%
Do Until RSShipping.EOF
%>
<OPTION VALUE="<% Response.Write RSShipping("ShippingChargeID") %>">
<% Response.Write RSShipping("Location") %></OPTION>
<%
  RSShipping.MoveNext
Loop
%>
```

The code will iterate through the records in the RSShipping Recordset:

```
Do Until RSShipping.EOF
```

The visitor will see the text of the location, but the `ShippingChargeID` will be passed with the form when it is submitted:

```
<OPTION VALUE="<% Response.Write RSShipping("ShippingChargeID") %>">
<% Response.Write RSShipping("Location") %></OPTION>
```

The record pointer is moved forward before looping to the next record:

```
RSShipping.MoveNext
Loop
```

The text of the footer is then written inline at the bottom of the page:

```
<% Response.Write RSFooter("BriefText") %>
```

Tax Page

The code on the Tax page calculates the shipping charge for the order, as well as displaying the choices for a location for tax purposes. The page also records a hit and displays the footer. The main code block is:

```
<%
Option Explicit
If IsEmpty(Request.Form("CalculateShipping")) Then
  Response.Redirect "./shopping_cart.asp"
End If
Dim conn
Dim RSFooter
Dim RSTotal
Dim RSTotalWeight
Dim RSShipping
Dim ShippingPrice
Dim RSTaxes
set conn = server.createobject ("adodb.connection")
conn.open "ASPBook", "sa", "yourpassword"
conn.execute "insert into ASPSessionPages (SessionID, PageName)
 values (" _
  & Session("SessionID") & ", " _
  & "'Tax')"
set RSFooter = conn.execute("select BriefText from ASPPageText " _
  & "where PageName = 'Footer'")
set RSTotalWeight = conn.execute("SELECT Sum(ASPSessionItems.
 Quantity * " _
  & "ASPProducts.Weight) as TotalWeight " _
  & "FROM ASPSessionItems INNER JOIN ASPProducts ON " _
   & "ASPSessionItems.ProductID = ASPProducts.ProductID " _
  & "WHERE ASPSessionItems.SessionID = " & Session("SessionID"))
set RSShipping = conn.execute("Select MinimumShipping,
 PerPoundShipping, " _
  & "BaseRate From ASPShippingCharge where " _
  & "ShippingChargeID = " & Request.Form("Location"))
```

```
ShippingPrice = (RSTotalWeight("TotalWeight") * RSShipping
 ("PerPoundShipping")) _
  + RSShipping("BaseRate")
If ShippingPrice < RSShipping("MinimumShipping") Then
  ShippingPrice = RSShipping("MinimumShipping")
End If
conn.execute "update ASPSessions set ShippingTotal = " &
 ShippingPrice _
  & "Where SessionID = " & Session("SessionID")
set RSTotal = conn.execute("select Sum(ItemPrice) as TheTotal from " _
  & "ASPSessionItems where SessionID = " & Session("SessionID"))
set RSTaxes = conn.execute("select Location, TaxRate from ASP
 TaxTable " _
  & "order by Location")
%>
```

First, `Option Explicit` is written:

```
Option Explicit
```

The page should be viewed only if it was entered by selecting a location on the Shipping Calculator page:

```
If IsEmpty(Request.Form("CalculateShipping")) Then
```

If it wasn't, the visitor is sent back to the Shopping Cart page:

```
Response.Redirect "./shopping_cart.asp"
```

otherwise, we will need to take action for this page. We will need a Connection object:

```
Dim conn
```

a Recordset object for the footer:

```
Dim RSFooter
```

one for the order total:

```
Dim RSTotal
```

as well as the total weight of the order:

```
Dim RSTotalWeight
```

and shipping information:

```
Dim RSShipping
Dim ShippingPrice
```

Plus, we will need to display the locations for tax rates:

```
Dim RSTaxes
```

The Connection object is then instantiated:

```
set conn = server.createobject ("adodb.connection")
```

and opened:

```
conn.open "ASPBook", "sa", "yourpassword"
```

A hit is recorded for this page in the ASPSessionPages table:

```
conn.execute "insert into ASPSessionPages (SessionID, PageName)
values (" _
  & Session("SessionID") & ", " _
  & "'Tax')"
```

The footer text is retrieved from the database:

```
set RSFooter = conn.execute("select BriefText from ASPPageText " _
  & "where PageName = 'Footer'")
```

The total weight of the order is returned by summing the quantities multiplied by the weight per item:

```
set RSTotalWeight = conn.execute("SELECT
Sum(ASPSessionItems.Quantity * " _
  & "ASPProducts.Weight) as TotalWeight " _
  & "FROM ASPSessionItems INNER JOIN ASPProducts ON " _
    & "ASPSessionItems.ProductID = ASPProducts.ProductID " _
  & "WHERE ASPSessionItems.SessionID = " & Session("SessionID"))
```

The shipping charge information for the location, selected by the visitor, is retrieved from the database:

```
set RSShipping = conn.execute("Select MinimumShipping, PerPound
Shipping, " _
  & "BaseRate From ASPShippingCharge where " _
  & "ShippingChargeID = " & Request.Form("Location"))
```

The shipping price is determined by multiplying the total weight by the price per pound and then adding the base rate to that value:

```
ShippingPrice = (RSTotalWeight("TotalWeight") * RSShipping
  ("PerPoundShipping")) _
  + RSShipping("BaseRate")
```

If that result is less than the minimum shipping charge for the location selected:

```
If ShippingPrice < RSShipping("MinimumShipping") Then
```

the minimum amount is used:

```
ShippingPrice = RSShipping("MinimumShipping")
```

The code then updates the session record to indicate this shipping charge:

```
conn.execute "update ASPSessions set ShippingTotal = " & 
  ShippingPrice _
  & "Where SessionID = " & Session("SessionID")
```

The current totals are retrieved from the database for this order:

```
set RSTotal = conn.execute("select Sum(ItemPrice) as TheTotal from " _
 & "ASPSessionItems where SessionID = " & Session("SessionID"))
```

and one more Recordset is opened and set to the Tax locations:

```
set RSTaxes = conn.execute("select Location, TaxRate from
  ASPTaxTable " _
  & "order by Location")
```

Inline with the HTML, the order totals are written:

```
Order Total: <% Response.Write FormatCurrency(RSTotal("TheTotal")) %>.
<BR>Shipping Total: <% Response.Write FormatCurrency(ShippingPrice) %>
```

The next code block populates the Location Select control:

```
<%
Do Until RSTaxes.EOF
%>
<OPTION VALUE="<% Response.Write RSTaxes("TaxRate") %>">
<% Response.Write RSTaxes("Location") %></OPTION>
<%
  RSTaxes.MoveNext
Loop
%>
```

The code will loop through the records in the RSTaxes Recordset:

```
Do Until RSTaxes.EOF
```

The `TaxRate` will be passed through the Select control, but the location is displayed to the visitor:

```
<OPTION VALUE="<% Response.Write RSTaxes("TaxRate") %>">
<% Response.Write RSTaxes("Location") %></OPTION>
```

The code then moves on to the next record before looping:

```
RSTaxes.MoveNext
Loop
```

One more line of code writes the footer text inline with the HTML:

```
<% Response.Write RSFooter("BriefText") %>
```

Check Out Page

The Check Out page calculates the tax charged to the visitor, displays the Credit Card Types, and records a hit to this page. The main code block is:

```
<%
Option Explicit
If IsEmpty(Request.Form("CalculateTax")) Then
  Response.Redirect "./shopping_cart.asp"
End If
Dim conn
Dim RSFooter
Dim RSTotal
Dim RSCCTypes
set conn = server.createobject ("adodb.connection")
conn.open "ASPBook", "sa", "yourpassword"
conn.execute "insert into ASPSessionPages (SessionID, PageName)
 values (" _
  & Session("SessionID") & ", " _
  & "'CheckOut')"
set RSFooter = conn.execute("select BriefText from ASPPageText " _
  & "where PageName = 'Footer'")
set RSTotal = conn.execute("select Sum(ItemPrice) as TheTotal from " _
  & "ASPSessionItems where SessionID = " & Session("SessionID"))
conn.execute "update ASPSessions set TaxTotal = " & (RSTotal
 ("TheTotal") _
  * Request.Form("Location")) _
  & " Where SessionID = " & Session("SessionID")
set RSTotal = conn.execute("Select ProductTotal, ShippingTotal, " _
  & "TaxTotal from ASPSessions " _
  & " Where SessionID = " & Session("SessionID"))
conn.execute "update ASPSessions set OrderTotal = " & (RSTotal
 ("ProductTotal") _
  + Request.Form("ShippingTotal") + Request.Form("TaxTotal")) _
  & " Where SessionID = " & Session("SessionID")
```

```
set RSCCTypes = conn.execute("select CCType from ASPCCTypes order by
  CCType")
%>
```

First, `Option Explicit` conveys to the compiler that we plan on declaring variables:

```
Option Explicit
```

This page should be viewed only after the Tax page:

```
If IsEmpty(Request.Form("CalculateTax")) Then
```

If it wasn't, the visitor is sent back to the Shopping Cart:

```
Response.Redirect "./shopping_cart.asp"
```

A Connection to the database will be needed:

```
Dim conn
```

as will the footer text:

```
Dim RSFooter
```

the order totals:

```
Dim RSTotal
```

and the Credit Card Types allowed:

```
Dim RSCCTypes
```

The Connection object is instantiated:

```
set conn = server.createobject ("adodb.connection")
```

and a Connection to the database is opened:

```
conn.open "ASPBook", "sa", "yourpassword"
```

A hit is recorded for this page:

```
conn.execute "insert into ASPSessionPages (SessionID, PageName)
  values (" _
```

```
     & Session("SessionID") & ", " _
     & "'CheckOut')"
```

Next, the text of the footer is retrieved:

```
     set RSFooter = conn.execute("select BriefText from ASPPageText " _
     & "where PageName = 'Footer'")
```

The product total is then retrieved from the database for this order:

```
set RSTotal = conn.execute("select Sum(ItemPrice) as TheTotal from " _
& "ASPSessionItems where SessionID = " & Session("SessionID"))
```

That value is used to calculate the tax due on the order:

```
conn.execute "update ASPSessions set TaxTotal = " & (RSTotal
("TheTotal") _
 * Request.Form("Location")) _
& " Where SessionID = " & Session("SessionID")
```

Next, all the totals are retrieved from the database:

```
set RSTotal = conn.execute("Select ProductTotal, ShippingTotal, " _
& "TaxTotal from ASPSessions " _
& " Where SessionID = " & Session("SessionID"))
```

The grand total due is set by adding the product total with the shipping and tax amounts:

```
conn.execute "update ASPSessions set OrderTotal = " & (RSTotal
("ProductTotal") _
 + Request.Form("ShippingTotal") + Request.Form("TaxTotal")) _
& " Where SessionID = " & Session("SessionID")
```

The next line of code retrieves the Credit Card Types allowed with the order:

```
     set RSCCTypes = conn.execute("select CCType from ASPCCTypes order
        by CCType")
```

Inline with the HTML, the order totals are displayed:

```
Order Total: <% Response.Write FormatCurrency(RSTotal("ProductTotal"))
   %>.
<BR>Shipping Total: <% Response.Write FormatCurrency(RSTotal
   ("ShippingTotal")) %>
<BR>Tax: <% Response.Write FormatCurrency(RSTotal("TaxTotal")) %>
<BR>Total Due: <% Response.Write FormatCurrency(RSTotal
   ("ProductTotal")
+ RSTotal("ShippingTotal") + RSTotal("TaxTotal")) %>
```

as is the text of the Footer:

```
<% Response.Write RSFooter("BriefText") %>
```

One more code block is needed to display the options for the Credit Card Types field.

```
<%
Do Until RSCCTypes.EOF
%>
<OPTION VALUE="<% Response.Write RSCCTypes("CCType") %>">
<% Response.Write RSCCTypes("CCType") %></OPTION>
<%
   RSCCTypes.MoveNext
Loop
%>
```

The code will loop through the records in the RSCCTypes Recordset:

```
Do Until RSCCTypes.EOF
```

Next, each record is written as an Option to the Select control:

```
<OPTION VALUE="<% Response.Write RSCCTypes("CCType") %>">
<% Response.Write RSCCTypes("CCType") %></OPTION>
```

The record pointer moves on to the next record before looping:

```
RSCCTypes.MoveNext
Loop
```

Check Out Complete Page

The Check Out Complete page writes the visitor's shipping and billing information to the database. It displays closing text and ends the visitor's session. The main code block is:

```
<%
Option Explicit
If IsEmpty(Request.Form("CheckOut")) Then
  Response.Redirect "./shopping_cart.asp"
End If
Dim conn
Dim RSPageText
Dim RSFooter
Dim PageText
set conn = server.createobject ("adodb.connection")
conn.open "ASPBook", "sa", "yourpassword"
conn.execute "insert into ASPSessionPages (SessionID, PageName)
  values (" _
```

```
   & Session("SessionID") & ", " _
   & "'CheckOutComplete')"
set RSPageText = conn.execute("select ExtendedText, BriefText from
 ASPPageText " _
   & "where PageName = 'CheckOutComplete'")
PageText= RSPageText("ExtendedText")
set RSFooter = conn.execute("select BriefText from ASPPageText " _
   & "where PageName = 'Footer'")
conn.Execute "update ASPSessions set " _
   & "BillName = '" & ConvertIt(Request.Form("BillName"),"'","'")
     & "', " _
   & "EmailAddress = '" &
ConvertIt(Request.Form("EmailAddress"),"'","'") & "', " _
   & "Phone = '" & ConvertIt(Request.Form("Phone"),"'","'") & "', " _
   & "BillAddress1 = '" & ConvertIt(Request.Form
     ("BillAddress1"),"'","'") & "', " _
   & "BillAddress2 = '" &
ConvertIt(Request.Form("BillAddress2"),"'","'") & "', " _
   & "BillCSZ = '" & ConvertIt(Request.Form("BillCSZ"),"'","'")
     & "', " _
   & "ShipName = '" & ConvertIt(Request.Form("ShipName"),"'","'")
     & "', " _
   & "ShipAddress1 = '" & ConvertIt(Request.Form("ShipAddress1"),
     "'","'") & "', " _
   & "ShipAddress2 = '" & ConvertIt(Request.Form("ShipAddress2"),
     "'","'") & "', " _
   & "ShipCSZ = '" & ConvertIt(Request.Form("ShipCSZ"),"'","'")
     & "', " _
   & "CCType = '" & ConvertIt(Request.Form("CCType"),"'","'") & "', " _
   & "CCNumber = '" & ConvertIt(Request.Form("CCNumber"),"'","'")
     & "', " _
   & "CCExpiration = '" & ConvertIt(Request.Form("CCExpiration"),
     "'","'") & "', " _
   & "Comments = '" & ConvertIt(Request.Form("Comments"),"'","'")
     & "', " _
   & "Phone2 = '" & ConvertIt(Request.Form("Phone2"),"'","'") & "' " _
   & "where SessionID = " & Session("SessionID")
%>
```

First, `Option Explicit` is noted:

```
Option Explicit
```

This page should be viewed only after the Check Out page:

```
If IsEmpty(Request.Form("CheckOut")) Then
```

If it wasn't, the visitor is sent back to the Shopping Cart page:

```
Response.Redirect "./shopping_cart.asp"
```

A Connection object will be needed:

```
Dim conn
```

as will the text for the page:

```
Dim RSPageText
```

and the footer text will be needed:

```
Dim RSFooter
Dim PageText
```

The Connection object is instantiated

```
set conn = server.createobject ("adodb.connection")
```

and opened:

```
conn.open "ASPBook", "sa", "aspbook"
```

A hit is recorded for this page:

```
conn.execute "insert into ASPSessionPages (SessionID, PageName)
values (" _
  & Session("SessionID") & ", " _
  & "'CheckOutComplete')"
```

Then the text for this page is retrieved:

```
set RSPageText = conn.execute("select ExtendedText, BriefText from
ASPPageText " _
  & "where PageName = 'CheckOutComplete'")
PageText= RSPageText("ExtendedText")
```

as is the text for the footer:

```
set RSFooter = conn.execute("select BriefText from ASPPageText " _
  & "where PageName = 'Footer'")
```

All the fields entered by visitors are updated in their session record:

```
conn.Execute "update ASPSessions set " _
  & "BillName = '" & ConvertIt(Request.Form("BillName"),"'","'")
    & "', " _
  & "EmailAddress = '" & ConvertIt(Request.Form("EmailAddress"),
    "'","'") & "', " _
  & "Phone = '" & ConvertIt(Request.Form("Phone"),"'","'") & "', " _
  & "BillAddress1 = '" & ConvertIt(Request.Form("BillAddress1"),
    "'","'") & "', " _
  & "BillAddress2 = '" & ConvertIt(Request.Form("BillAddress2"),
    "'","'") & "', " _
```

```
      & "BillCSZ = '" & ConvertIt(Request.Form("BillCSZ"),"'","'")
         & "', " _
      & "ShipName = '" & ConvertIt(Request.Form("ShipName"),"'","'")
         & "', " _
      & "ShipAddress1 = '" & ConvertIt(Request.Form("ShipAddress1"),
         "'","'") & "', " _
      & "ShipAddress2 = '" & ConvertIt(Request.Form("ShipAddress2"),
         "'","'") & "' , " _
      & "ShipCSZ = '" & ConvertIt(Request.Form("ShipCSZ"),"'","'")
         & "', " _
      & "CCType = '" & ConvertIt(Request.Form("CCType"),"'","'") & "', " _
      & "CCNumber = '" & ConvertIt(Request.Form("CCNumber"),"'","'")
         & "', " _
      & "CCExpiration = '" & ConvertIt(Request.Form("CCExpiration"),
         "'","'") & "', " _
      & "Comments = '" & ConvertIt(Request.Form("Comments"),"'","'")
         & "', " _
      & "Phone2 = '" & ConvertIt(Request.Form("Phone2"),"'","'") & "' " _
   & "where SessionID = " & Session("SessionID")
```

Note the use of the ConvertIt function. We need to get rid of the apostrophe characters because they will throw an error in SQL Server. The code for the ConvertIt function is:

```
Function ConvertIt(StringToConvert, ReplaceChar, ConversionChar)
   Dim TempString
   Dim LastFound
   TempString = StringToConvert
   LastFound = instr(TempString, ReplaceChar)
   do until LastFound = 0
     TempString = left(TempString, LastFound - 1) & ConversionChar _
        & right(TempString, Len(TempString) - LastFound)
     LastFound = instr(TempString, ReplaceChar)
   loop
   ConvertIt = TempString
End Function
```

Passed into the ConvertIt function is the string to convert, the character to convert, and what to convert it to:

```
Function ConvertIt(StringToConvert, ReplaceChar, ConversionChar)
```

A couple of temporary variables will be needed:

```
Dim TempString
Dim LastFound
```

Then the TempString variable is set to the string to convert:

```
TempString = StringToConvert
```

We then look for the character to replace in the string:

```
LastFound = instr(TempString, ReplaceChar)
```

and will loop until no more characters to replace are found:

```
do until LastFound = 0
```

Each one found is replaced with the replacement character:

```
TempString = left(TempString, LastFound - 1) & ConversionChar _
    & right(TempString, Len(TempString) - LastFound)
```

Before looking for the replace character again:

```
    LastFound = instr(TempString, ReplaceChar)
Loop
```

the converted value is returned from the function:

```
ConvertIt = TempString
```

Inline with the HTML, the footer and text of the page are written. That is followed by the end of visitors' session, since at this point their Shopping Cart has been processed:

```
Session.Abandon
```

CHAPTER 18

ASP in Action: Customers

Working with Customers

So far our Web site contains the Product Catalog component that we built in Chapter 16 and the Shopping Cart component that we discussed in Chapter 17. In this chapter, we look at pages that provide ways for you to get information from visitors and to provide them with information. Figure 18-1 shows the hierarchical view of the pages that we discuss in this chapter. The Customers component adds sections to the top of the site: the More Info section and the Customers section. These sections are accessible from any of the pages within the site because they are linked through the navigation bar.

Notice the two pages that are not part of the site hierarchy, the Send Email 1 and the Send Email 2 pages, which, although not part of the site, are related to it. As you will see in this chapter, they allow you to send email out to customers of your site. For that reason you should place these pages in a different location that is not accessible by visitors through the Internet.

Sample Usage

When visitors click on the MORE INFO link on the navigation bar, they see the page displayed in Figure 18-2. The text on the More Info page

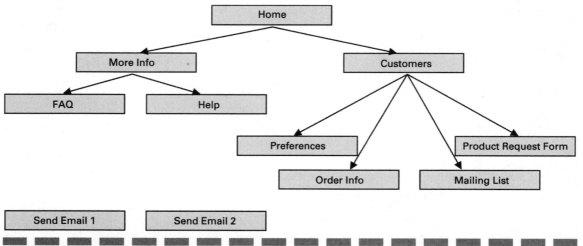

Figure 18-1   Site hierarchy for the Customers component.

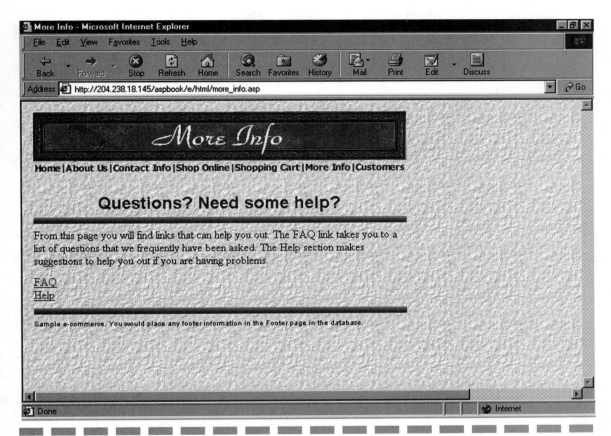

Figure 18-2 More Info page.

comes from the database, so it is entirely configurable without modifying the code or HTML on the page. The page has links to the FAQ page and the Help page. The FAQ page is displayed in Figure 18-3. The FAQ page displays at the top a list of questions that have been or may be asked by visitors to the site. The item selected in the QUESTION SELECT box is the current question and displayed in the bottom is the answer to that question. When visitors first enter this page, they see the answer to the first question on the list. But they can select a different question and press the ANSWER button to see the answer to that question as shown in Figure 18-4. Notice that the Select control now displays the question selected by the visitor and in the body of the page we see the answer to that question. The questions and answers come from a table in the data-

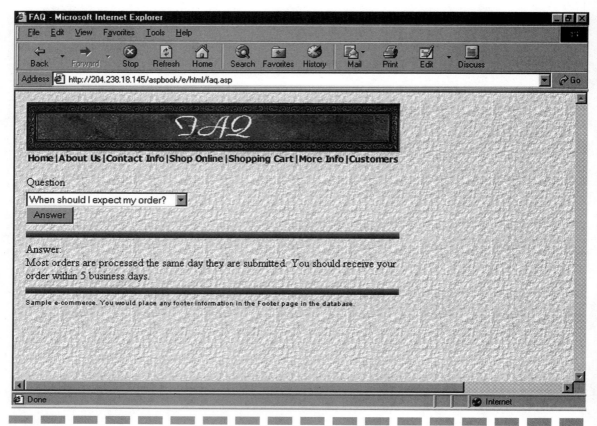

Figure 18-3 FAQ page.

base, so adding, editing, and deleting questions and answers is done through the database.

Figure 18-5 displays the Help page. The Help page displays a list of support problems that the customer may experience and beneath that problem displays a possible solution for that problem. The list of problems comes from a database table. When visitors first view the page, they see the first problem in the list with the accompanying solution.

If visitors select the CUSTOMERS link from the Navigation bar, they see the page displayed in Figure 18-6. The Customers page provides the links to the PREFERENCES, ORDERING INFO, MAILING LIST, and

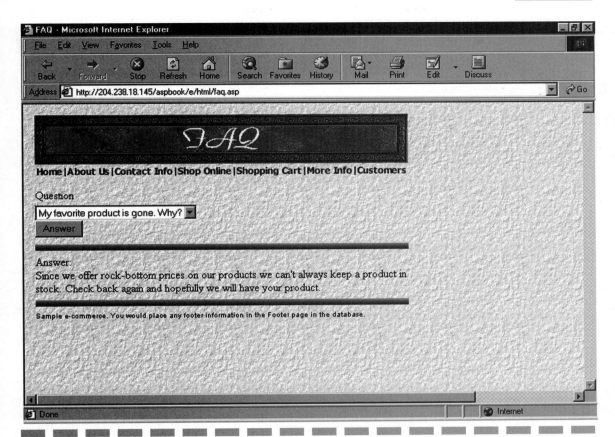

Figure 18-4 *FAQ page with new question selected.*

PRODUCT REQUEST FORM. Notice the text of the footer. It is the same text used throughout the site, which comes from a single record in the database.

If visitors click on the PREFERENCES link, they see the page displayed in Figure 18-7. This page allows visitors to pick their favorite category and to enter their email address so they can be informed when there are changes to this category. The Favorite Category Select control contains a list of all the categories in the Product Catalog. When visitors press the SUBMIT button, their email address and category are added to a table in the database. They are then redirected back to the Customers page.

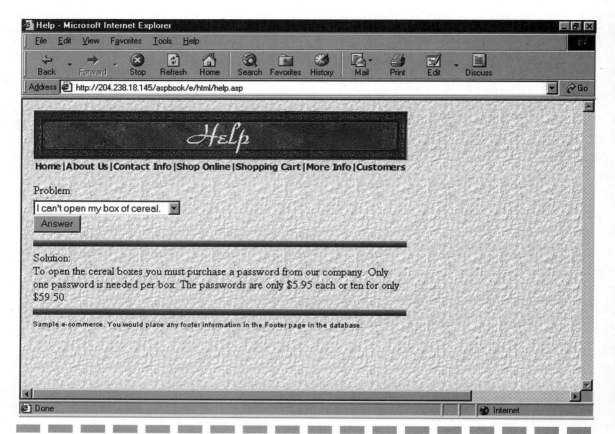

Figure 18-5 Help page.

Figure 18-8 shows the Order Info page in its initial view. The page allows visitors to enter their Order ID. When they do, they see the status of that order, as shown in Figure 18-9. If visitors enter an invalid Order ID, they see a message telling them that the Order ID does not exist.

Figure 18-10 shows the Mailing List page. The Mailing List page allows visitors to enter their email address, which is added to a table in the database when they press the SUBMIT button. This would provide you with a way for you to communicate with your customers when you have some sale or special planned.

Figure 18-11 shows the Product Request Form. This page provides a

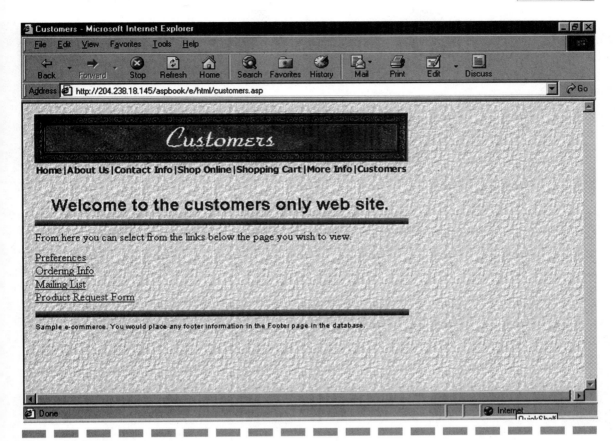

Figure 18-6 Customers page.

way for visitors to let you know if there is a product that they would like to see in your store. Visitors enter the name of the product and the description of that product. When they press the SUBMIT button, their request is added as a record to a table in the database.

The other two pages in this site are the Send Email pages. These pages provide a way for you to easily send a batch email out to those visitors who wish to be on one of your mailing lists. The Send Email 1 page is displayed in Figure 18-12. The Send Email 1 page is used to send an email out to all those who have signed up on the Preferences page for a particular category. You just select the category, enter a From Email Address, the subject of the message, and the text of the message. When

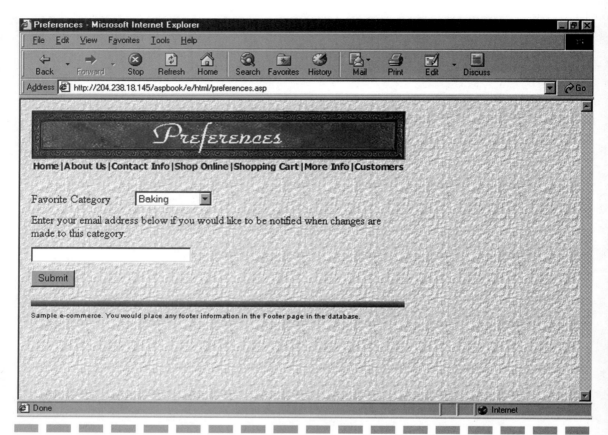

Figure 18-7   Preferences page.

you press the SEND button, an email is sent out to each person in that category, as displayed in Figure 18-13.

The Send Email 2 page provides another way for you to communicate with your visitors. This page is displayed in Figure 18-14.

The Send Email 2 page provides a way for you to send a general email out to all those people who signed up through the Mailing List page. Those who send the email supply their email address, the subject of the message, and the text of the message. When the sender presses the SEND button, the code sends emails out to each of the recipients.

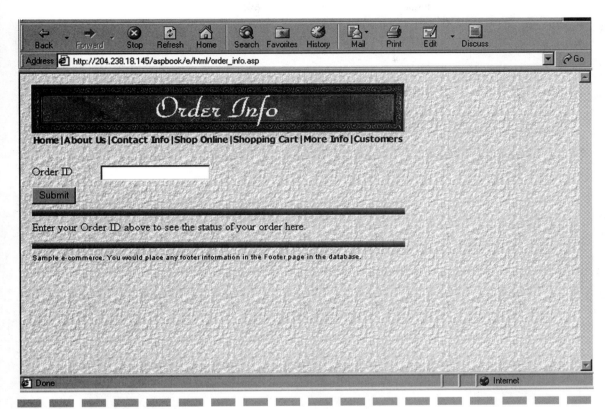

Figure 18-8 Order Info page.

Customers Database Component

In this section of the chapter, we define the tables that are involved in the Customers component, and then look at the fields in each of these tables.

Table Definitions

ASPCustomer

The *ASPCustomer* table is used to store the email addresses of customers who want to be on the mailing list. The table is then used to send a bulk email out to the subscribers.

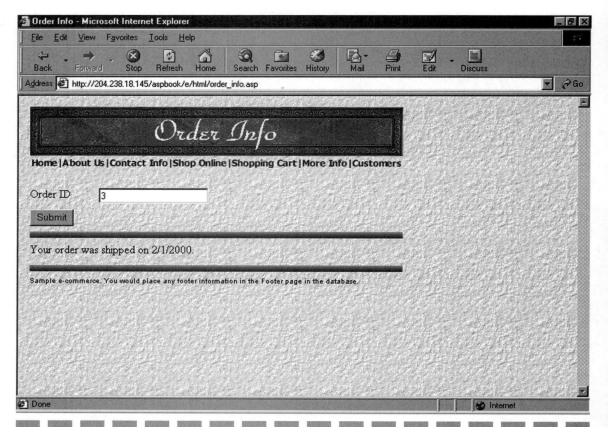

Figure 18-9 Order Info page displaying status of an order.

ASPCustomerWithCategory

The other table that stores customer email addresses is the *ASPCustomerWithCategory* table. This table stores customers' email address with the specific category that they want to subscribe to. The table is then used to send emails out to subscribers of a specific category.

ASPFAQ

The *ASPFAQ* table stores the questions and answers displayed in the FAQ page. Each question is listed in the Select control on that page.

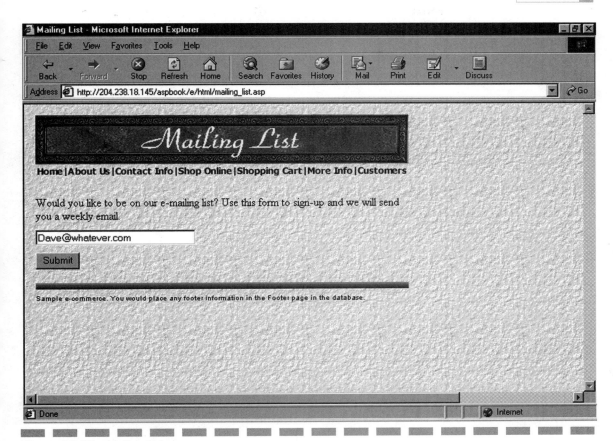

Figure 18-10 Mailing List page.

ASPHelp
The *ASPHelp* table stores the problems and solutions that are displayed on the Help page. The first record in this table is displayed by default when the page is first viewed, so that record could contain a more general statement rather than a specific problem.

ASPProductRequests
When a visitor requests that a product be included at the site, a record is added to the *ASPProductRequests* table. The table stores the name and description of the product requested.

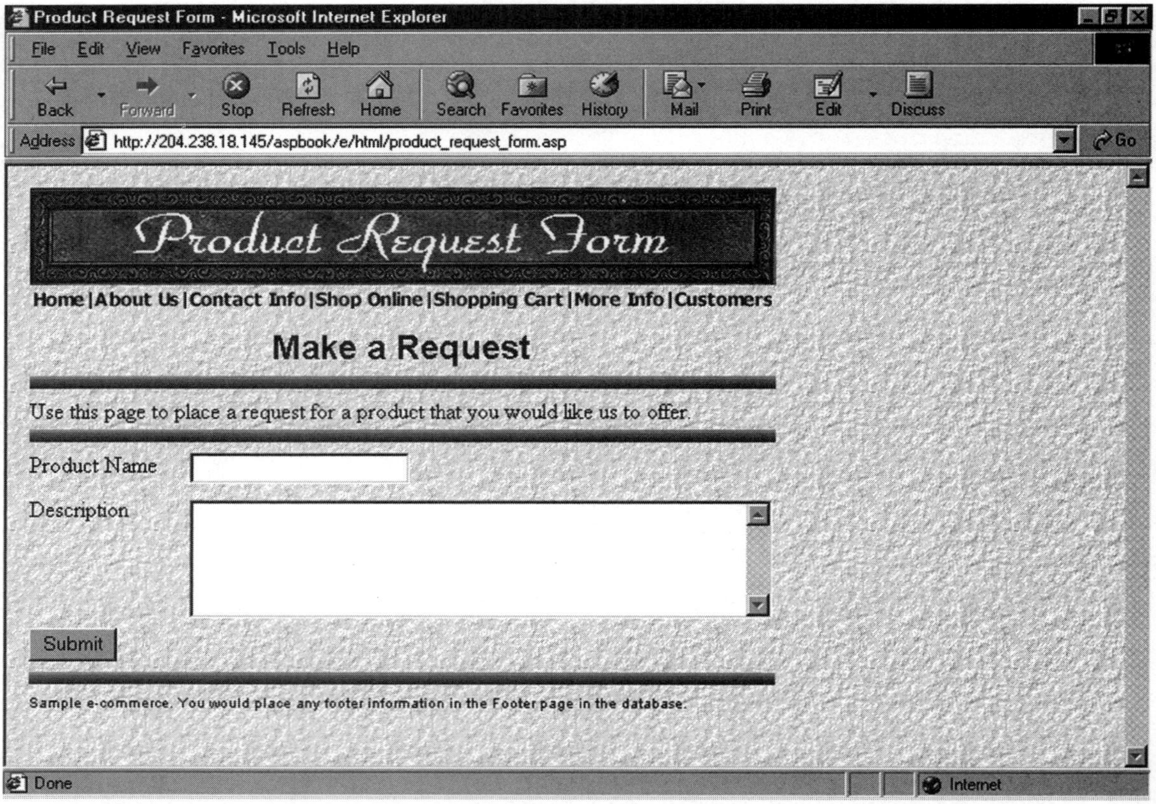

Figure 18-11   Product Request Form.

ASPSessions

The *ASPSessions* table, as we saw in the last chapter, is used to store information about the visitor placing an order. The table includes a new field here that stores the status of the visitor's order. This information is then used on the Order Info page.

Field Specifications

ASPCustomer Field Specifications

Table 18-1 shows the field specifications for the ASPCustomer table. The CustomerID field is the primary key for the table. Since it is an

Figure 18-12   Send Email 1 page.

identity column, the field is automatically populated when a new record is added to the table. The EmailAddress field stores the email address of the customer who has signed up on the Mailing List page.

ASPCustomerWithCategory Field Specifications

Table 18-2 shows the field specifications for the ASPCustomerWith Category table. The ASPCustomerWithCategory records an entry for each customer that signs up on the Preferences page. The EmailAddress field stores the email address of visitors and the Category field stores the name of the category that they wish to receive news about.

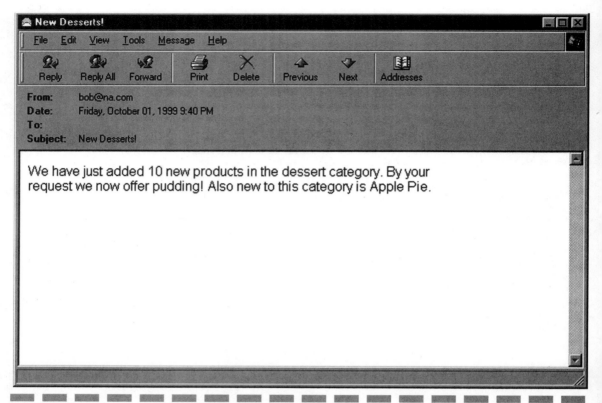

Figure 18-13   *Resulting email sent through the Send Email 1 page.*

ASPFAQ Field Specifications

Table 18-3 shows the field specifications for the ASPFAQ table. The FAQID is the primary key for the table and is automatically populated since it is an identity column. The Question field stores the different FAQ questions and is used to populate the options for the Question Select control on the FAQ page. The Answer field stores the answers to the questions.

ASPHelp Field Specifications

Table 18-4 shows the field specifications for the ASPHelp table. The fields in the ASPHelp table are used on the Help page. The Problem field populates the Select control on that page and the Solution field provides a possible solution to the visitor's problem.

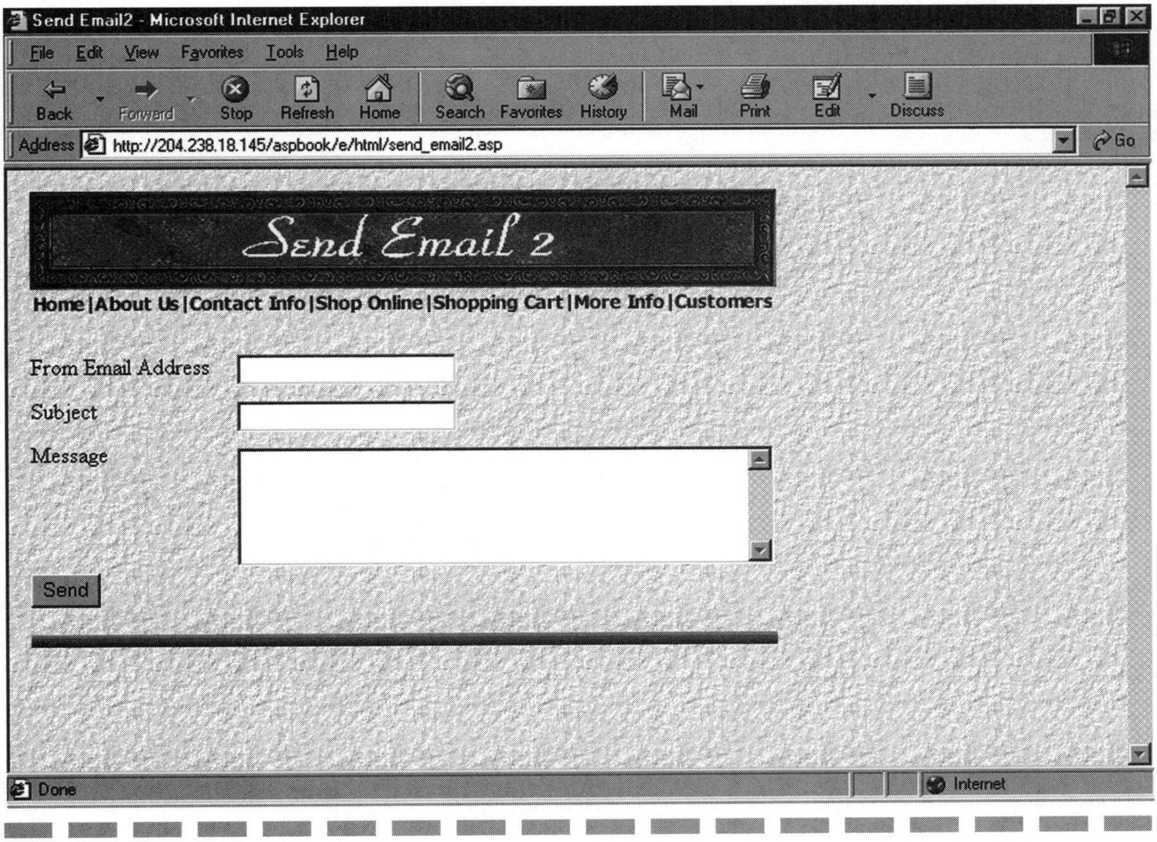

Figure 18-14 Send Email 2 page.

ASPProductRequests Field Specifications

Table 18-5 shows the field specifications for the ASPProductRequests table. The ProductRequestID field is the primary key for the table, uniquely identifying each record. The ProductName field stores the name of the product that the visitor is requesting and the Description field stores the description of the product that the visitor is requesting.

TABLE 18-1

ASPCustomer Field
Specifications

Field Name	Field Type	Notes
CustomerID	int	Identity column, seeded at 1 and incremented by 1
EmailAddress	varchar	Length = 100

TABLE 18-2

ASPCustomerWith
Category Field
Specifications

Field Name	Field Type	Notes
CustomerID	int	Identity column, seeded at 1 and incremented by 1
EmailAddress	varchar	Length = 100
Category	varchar	Length = 100

TABLE 18-3

ASPFAQ Field
Specifications

Field Name	Field Type	Notes
FAQID	int	Identity column, seeded at 1 and incremented by 1
Question	varchar	Length = 50
Answer	varchar	Length = 255

TABLE 18-4

ASPHelp Field
Specifications

Field Name	Field Type	Notes
HelpID	int	Identity column, seeded at 1 and incremented by 1
Problem	varchar	Length = 50
Solution	varchar	Length = 255

TABLE 18-5

ASPProductRequests
Field Specifications

Field Name	Field Type	Notes
ProductRequestID	int	Identity column, seeded at 1 and incremented by 1
ProductName	varchar	Length = 100
Description	text	

ASPSessions Field Specifications

Table 18-6 shows the field specifications for the ASPSessions table. New to the ASPSessions table is the Status field. This field stores the status of the visitor's order. As you process customers' orders, you would update this field so customers could come to the site and see where their order is in the process.

	Field Name	Field Type	Notes
TABLE 18-6	SessionID	int	Identity column, seeded at 1 and incremented by 1
ASPSessions Field Specifications	SessionStarted	datetime	
	SessionEnded	datetime	
	RefSource	varchar	Length = 200
	Browser	varchar	Length = 75
	OS	varchar	Length = 75
	BillName	varchar	Length = 50
	Phone	varchar	Length = 50
	Phone2	varchar	Length = 50
	BillAddress1	varchar	Length = 100
	BillAddress2	varchar	Length = 100
	BillCSZ	varchar	Length = 100
	ShipName	varchar	Length = 50
	ShipAddress1	varchar	Length = 100
	ShipAddress2	varchar	Length = 100
	ShipCSZ	varchar	Length = 100
	CCType	varchar	Length = 50
	CCNumber	varchar	Length = 50
	CCExpiration	varchar	Length = 50
	Comments	text	
	ProductTotal	money	
	ShippingTotal	money	
	TaxTotal	money	
	OrderTotal	money	
	Status	varchar	Length = 255

Active Server Page Code

Code for the More Info Page

The code on the More Info page is responsible for recording a hit to that page and placing the dynamic text on that page. The main code block is:

```
<%
Option Explicit
Dim conn
Dim RSPageText
Dim RSFooter
Dim PageText
set conn = server.createobject ("adodb.connection")
conn.open "ASPBook", "sa", "yourpassword"
conn.execute "insert into ASPSessionPages (SessionID, PageName)
 values (" _
   & Session("SessionID") & ", " _
   & "'MoreInfo')"
set RSPageText = conn.execute("select ExtendedText, BriefText from
ASPPageText " _
   & "where PageName = 'MoreInfo'")
PageText= RSPageText("ExtendedText")
set RSFooter = conn.execute("select BriefText from ASPPageText " _
   & "where PageName = 'Footer'")
%>
```

First, we tell the compiler that we will declare our variables:

```
Option Explicit
```

Next, a Connection object will be needed:

```
Dim conn
```

as will a Recordset object that retrieves the text for the page:

```
Dim RSPageText
```

and one for the footer of the page:

```
Dim RSFooter
```

This variable will store the main text blurb for the page:

```
Dim PageText
```

Then, a Connection object is returned into the variable Conn through the CreateObject method:

```
set conn = server.createobject ("adodb.connection")
```

The connection is opened to the SQL Server database:

```
conn.open "ASPBook", "sa", "yourpassword"
```

Next, a record is inserted into the ASPSessionPages table, recording a hit for this page:

```
conn.execute "insert into ASPSessionPages (SessionID, PageName)
 values (" _
  & Session("SessionID") & ", " _
 & "'MoreInfo')"
```

Next, the text for the page is retrieved from the database:

```
set RSPageText = conn.execute("select ExtendedText, BriefText from
  ASPPageText " _
 & "where PageName = 'MoreInfo'")
```

Then the PageText variable is set to the body text for the page:

```
PageText= RSPageText("ExtendedText")
```

and the footer text is retrieved from the database:

```
set RSFooter = conn.execute("select BriefText from ASPPageText " _
 & "where PageName = 'Footer'")
```

Then, inline with the HTML, the title text is written to the browser:

```
<% Response.Write RSPageText("BriefText") %>
```

Also within the HTML, the page text is written:

```
<% Response.Write PageText %>
```

as is the text for the footer:

```
<% Response.Write RSFooter("BriefText") %>
```

Code for the FAQ Page

The code on the FAQ page displays a list of questions to the visitor and the answer for the selected question. The page also records a hit and displays the text of the footer. The main code block is:

```
<%
Option Explicit
Dim conn
```

```
Dim RSFooter
Dim RSCurrentQuestion
Dim RSQuestions
Dim CurrentFAQID
Dim TheAnswer
Dim TheQuestion
set conn = server.createobject ("adodb.connection")
conn.open "ASPBook", "sa", "yourpassword"
conn.execute "insert into ASPSessionPages (SessionID, PageName)
 values (" _
  & Session("SessionID") & ", " _
  & "'FAQ')"
set RSFooter = conn.execute("select BriefText from ASPPageText " _
  & "where PageName = 'Footer'")
If IsEmpty(Request.Form("Answer")) Then
  set RSCurrentQuestion = conn.execute("select Min(FAQID) as MinID " _
    & "from ASPFAQ")
  CurrentFAQID = RSCurrentQuestion("MinID")
else
  CurrentFAQID = Request.Form("FAQID")
End If
set RSCurrentQuestion = conn.execute("select Answer, Question from
 ASPFAQ " _
  & "where FAQID = " & CurrentFAQID)
TheAnswer = RSCurrentQuestion("Answer")
TheQuestion = RSCurrentQuestion("Question")
set RSQuestions = conn.execute("select FAQID, Question from ASPFAQ")
%>
```

First, we code for requiring variable declaration:

```
Option Explicit
```

Then we have our variable declaration section. The first variable declared is for the Connection object:

```
Dim conn
```

A Recordset object will be needed to retrieve the footer text:

```
Dim RSFooter
```

one will be needed to retrieve the current question:

```
Dim RSCurrentQuestion
```

and another for all the questions in the ASPFAQ table:

```
Dim RSQuestions
```

This variable will store the ID of the current question:

```
Dim CurrentFAQID
```

This variable will store the text of the current answer:

```
Dim TheAnswer
```

Another variable will store the text of the question:

```
Dim TheQuestion
```

Here, the Connection object is instantiated:

```
set conn = server.createobject ("adodb.connection")
```

and opened:

```
conn.open "ASPBook", "sa", "yourpassword"
```

Next, a hit is recorded for this page:

```
conn.execute "insert into ASPSessionPages (SessionID, PageName)
 values (" _
  & Session("SessionID") & ", " _
  & "'FAQ')"
```

and the text of the footer is retrieved:

```
set RSFooter = conn.execute("select BriefText from ASPPageText " _
 & "where PageName = 'Footer'")
```

If the visitor is first viewing the page then the first question in the list is used as the current question; otherwise, the question selected is the current question. If the visitor is first viewing the page, the ANSWER button should not be present in the Form fields collection:

```
If IsEmpty(Request.Form("Answer")) Then
```

In that case, the first question in the table will be used. The ID for that question is retrieved here:

```
set RSCurrentQuestion = conn.execute("select Min(FAQID) as MinID " _
 & "from ASPFAQ")
```

The CurrentFAQID variable is set to that value:

```
CurrentFAQID = RSCurrentQuestion("MinID")
```

otherwise, the ID of the question selected by the visitor is used:

```
CurrentFAQID = Request.Form("FAQID")
```

Regardless of whether this is the first viewing of the page or we need to display the question requested by the visitor, the CurrentFAQID variable contains the correct ID. That value is used to retrieve the question and answer for that ID:

```
set RSCurrentQuestion = conn.execute("select Answer, Question from
  ASPFAQ " _
& "where FAQID = " & CurrentFAQID)
```

The answer is stored in the TheAnswer variable:

```
TheAnswer = RSCurrentQuestion("Answer")
```

The question is stored in the TheQuestion variable:

```
TheQuestion = RSCurrentQuestion("Question")
```

and one more Recordset is needed to retrieve all the questions that will be displayed in the Select control:

```
set RSQuestions = conn.execute("select FAQID, Question from ASPFAQ")
```

The next code block populates the options for the select control.

```
<OPTION VALUE="<% Response.Write CurrentFAQID %>" SELECTED>
<% Response.Write TheQuestion %></OPTION>
<%
Do Until RSQuestions.EOF
%>
  <OPTION VALUE="<% Response.Write RSQuestions("FAQID") %>">
  <% Response.Write RSQuestions("Question") %></OPTION>
<%
  RSQuestions.MoveNext
Loop
%>
```

First, the selected option in the Select control is set to the current option:

```
<OPTION VALUE="<% Response.Write CurrentFAQID %>" SELECTED>
<% Response.Write TheQuestion %></OPTION>
```

The code then sets a `Do...Loop` that will iterate through all the records in the `RSQuestions` Recordset:

```
Do Until RSQuestions.EOF
```

Within the loop, each of the records is written as an option to the Select control. The text of the question is displayed to the visitor, but the FAQID, when it is submitted, is passed with the form:

```
<OPTION VALUE="<% Response.Write RSQuestions("FAQID") %>">
<% Response.Write RSQuestions("Question") %></OPTION>
```

The record pointer is then moved to the next record before looping:

```
 RSQuestions.MoveNext
Loop
```

Within the HTML, the text of the answer is written:

```
<P>Answer:<BR><% Response.Write TheAnswer %>
```

as is the text of the footer:

```
<% Response.Write RSFooter("BriefText") %>
```

Code for the Help Page

The code for the Help page displays all the Problems and Solutions from the ASPHelp table. The code also records a hit to that page and displays the text of the footer.

```
<%
Option Explicit
Dim conn
Dim RSFooter
Dim RSCurrentProblem
Dim RSProblems
Dim CurrentHelpID
Dim TheProblem
Dim TheSolution
set conn = server.createobject ("adodb.connection")
conn.open "ASPBook", "sa", "yourpassword"
conn.execute "insert into ASPSessionPages (SessionID, PageName)
 values (" _
  & Session("SessionID") & ", " _
  & "'Help')"
```

```
set RSFooter = conn.execute("select BriefText from ASPPageText " _
  & "where PageName = 'Footer'")
If IsEmpty(Request.Form("Answer")) Then
  set RSCurrentProblem = conn.execute("select Min(HelpID) as MinID " _
    & "from ASPHelp")
  CurrentHelpID = RSCurrentProblem("MinID")
else
  CurrentHelpID = Request.Form("HelpID")
End If
set RSCurrentProblem = conn.execute("select Solution, Problem from
 ASPHelp " _
  & "where HelpID = " & CurrentHelpID)
TheSolution = RSCurrentProblem("Solution")
TheProblem = RSCurrentProblem("Problem")
set RSProblems = conn.execute("select HelpID, Problem from ASPHelp")
%>
```

First, `Option Explicit` is coded:

```
Option Explicit
```

Then we declare the Connection object variable:

```
Dim conn
```

Recordsets will be needed for the text of the footer, the fields for the current problem, and a list of all the problems:

```
Dim RSFooter
Dim RSCurrentProblem
Dim RSProblems
```

The ID for the current problem will be stored in this variable:

```
Dim CurrentHelpID
```

and the text of the problem and solution will be stored in these variables:

```
Dim TheProblem
Dim TheSolution
```

The Connection object is then instantiated:

```
set conn = server.createobject ("adodb.connection")
```

and opened:

```
conn.open "ASPBook", "sa", "yourpassword"
```

A hit is recorded for this page for this particular visitor:

```
conn.execute "insert into ASPSessionPages (SessionID, PageName)
  values (" _
  & Session("SessionID") & ", " _
  & "'Help')"
```

and the text of the footer is retrieved:

```
set RSFooter = conn.execute("select BriefText from ASPPageText " _
  & "where PageName = 'Footer'")
```

If this is the initial viewing of the page, then the first problem in the table will be used; otherwise, the problem selected by the visitor will be used. This state is determined by looking for the ANSWER button in the Form fields collection:

```
If IsEmpty(Request.Form("Answer")) Then
```

If the button is not present, we enter this portion of the If statement and use the first problem in the ASPHelp table. That value is retrieved:

```
set RSCurrentProblem = conn.execute("select Min(HelpID) as MinID " _
  & "from ASPHelp")
```

and set as the current ID:

```
CurrentHelpID = RSCurrentProblem("MinID")
```

otherwise, the ID selected by the visitor is used:

```
CurrentHelpID = Request.Form("HelpID")
```

In either case, the text of the problem and solution are retrieved from the database:

```
set RSCurrentProblem = conn.execute("select Solution, Problem from
  ASPHelp " _
  & "where HelpID = " & CurrentHelpID)
```

The variable TheSolution is set to the text of the solution for this problem:

```
TheSolution = RSCurrentProblem("Solution")
```

The variable `TheProblem` is set to the text of the current problem:

```
TheProblem = RSCurrentProblem("Problem")
```

One more Recordset object retrieves all the problems with their IDs that will be used to populate the options of the Select control:

```
set RSProblems = conn.execute("select HelpID, Problem from
   ASPHelp")
```

The next code block populates that Select control.

```
<OPTION VALUE="<% Response.Write CurrentHelpID %>" SELECTED>
<% Response.Write TheProblem %></OPTION>
<%
Do Until RSProblems.EOF
%>
   <OPTION VALUE="<% Response.Write RSProblems("HelpID") %>">
   <% Response.Write RSProblems("Problem") %></OPTION>
<%
   RSProblems.MoveNext
Loop
%>
```

The selected option is set to the current problem:

```
<OPTION VALUE="<% Response.Write CurrentHelpID %>" SELECTED>
<% Response.Write TheProblem %></OPTION>
```

The code then initiates a loop that will iterate through all the problems in the `RSProblems` Recordset object:

```
Do Until RSProblems.EOF
```

Each record is then written as an option to the Select control. The text of the problem is displayed to the visitor but the ID for the problem is passed through the form:

```
<OPTION VALUE="<% Response.Write RSProblems("HelpID") %>">
<% Response.Write RSProblems("Problem") %></OPTION>
```

The code then moves on to the next record before looping:

```
   RSProblems.MoveNext
Loop
```

The solution to the current problem is written inline with the HTML:

```
<P>Solution:<BR><% Response.Write TheSolution %>
```

as is the text of the footer:

```
<% Response.Write RSFooter("BriefText") %>
```

Code for the Customers Page

The code on the Customers page records a hit to that page and displays
the dynamic text for that page. The main code block is:

```
<%
Option Explicit
Dim conn
Dim RSPageText
Dim RSFooter
Dim PageText
set conn = server.createobject ("adodb.connection")
conn.open "ASPBook", "sa", "yourpassword"
conn.execute "insert into ASPSessionPages (SessionID, PageName)
 values (" _
   & Session("SessionID") & ", " _
   & "'Customers')"
set RSPageText = conn.execute("select ExtendedText, BriefText from
 ASPPageText " _
   & "where PageName = 'Customers'")
PageText= RSPageText("ExtendedText")
set RSFooter = conn.execute("select BriefText from ASPPageText " _
   & "where PageName = 'Footer'")
%>
```

First, Option Explicit is written:

```
Option Explicit
```

A Connection object will be needed:

```
Dim conn
```

as will Recordset objects for the footer and page text:

```
Dim RSPageText
Dim RSFooter
Dim PageText
```

The Connection object is instantiated:

```
set conn = server.createobject ("adodb.connection")
```

and opened:

```
conn.open "ASPBook", "sa", "yourpassword"
```

A hit is recorded for this page:

```
conn.execute "insert into ASPSessionPages (SessionID, PageName)
 values (" _
   & Session("SessionID") & ", " _
 & "'Customers')"
```

and the dynamic text for the page is retrieved:

```
set RSPageText = conn.execute("select ExtendedText, BriefText from
  ASPPageText " _

& "where PageName = 'Customers'")
PageText= RSPageText("ExtendedText")
```

as is the text for the footer:

```
set RSFooter = conn.execute("select BriefText from ASPPageText " _
 & "where PageName = 'Footer'")
```

Within the HTML, the title text is written to the browser:

```
<% Response.Write RSPageText("BriefText") %>
```

as is the page text:

```
<% Response.Write PageText %>
```

and the footer text:

```
<% Response.Write RSFooter("BriefText") %>
```

Code for the Preferences Page

The code on the Preferences page adds a record to the database, indicating the email address and the selected category for the visitor. The code also records a hit for this page and displays the text of the footer. The main code block is:

```
<%
Option Explicit
Dim conn
Dim RSFooter
Dim RSCategories
set conn = server.createobject ("adodb.connection")
conn.open "ASPBook", "sa", "yourpassword"
If not IsEmpty(Request.Form("Submit")) Then
```

```
conn.execute "insert into ASPCustomerWithCategory (EmailAddress,
  Category) " _
  & "values (" _
  & "'" & Request.Form("EmailAddress") & "', " _
  & "'" & Request.Form("Category") & "')"
Response.Redirect "./customers.asp"
End If
conn.execute "insert into ASPSessionPages (SessionID, PageName)
  values (" _
  & Session("SessionID") & ", " _
  & "'FAQ')"
set RSFooter = conn.execute("select BriefText from ASPPageText " _
  & "where PageName = 'Footer'")
set RSCategories = conn.execute("select CategoryName from
 ASPCategories " _
  & "order by CategoryName")
%>
```

First, Option Explicit is coded:

```
Option Explicit
```

Then the variables are declared. One variable is for the Connection object:

```
Dim conn
```

and the other two are Recordset objects that will be used to retrieve the footer text and the list of categories:

```
Dim RSFooter
Dim RSCategories
```

The CreateObject method is used to return a Connection object:

```
set conn = server.createobject ("adodb.connection")
```

and the connection to the database is opened:

```
conn.open "ASPBook", "sa", "yourpassword"
```

If the SUBMIT button is present, the form has been submitted and we need to process the request:

```
If not IsEmpty(Request.Form("Submit")) Then
```

If that is the case, we add a record to the ASPCustomerWithCategory table inserting the email address and the category selected by the visitor:

```
conn.execute "insert into ASPCustomerWithCategory (EmailAddress,
  Category) " _
  & "values (" _
  & "'" & Request.Form("EmailAddress") & "', " _
& "'" & Request.Form("Category") & "')"
```

The visitor is then redirected to the Customers page:

```
Response.Redirect "./customers.asp"
```

otherwise, the page is in the initial view and a hit needs to be recorded
for this page:

```
conn.execute "insert into ASPSessionPages (SessionID, PageName)
  values (" _
  & Session("SessionID") & ", " _
& "'FAQ')"
```

The text of the footer needs to be retrieved:

```
set RSFooter = conn.execute("select BriefText from ASPPageText " _
  & "where PageName = 'Footer'")
```

Also, the Select control will need to be populated with all the categories:

```
set RSCategories = conn.execute("select CategoryName from
  ASPCategories " _
  & "order by CategoryName")
```

The next code block uses that Recordset to populate the Select control.

```
<%
Do Until RSCategories.EOF
%>
  <OPTION VALUE="<% Response.Write RSCategories("CategoryName") %>">
  <% Response.Write RSCategories("CategoryName") %></OPTION>
<%
  RSCategories.MoveNext
Loop
%>
```

The code will loop through all the records in the RSCategories
Recordset:

```
Do Until RSCategories.EOF
```

Each record is written as an option to the Select control:

```
<OPTION VALUE="<% Response.Write RSCategories("CategoryName") %>">
<% Response.Write RSCategories("CategoryName") %></OPTION>
```

The record pointer moves to the next record before looping:

```
RSCategories.MoveNext
Loop
```

One more line of code at the bottom of the page writes the text of the footer:

```
<% Response.Write RSFooter("BriefText") %>
```

Code for the Order Info Page

The code for the Order Info page displays the status of the visitor's order. The page also records a hit and writes the text of the footer to the browser. The main code block is:

```
<%
Option Explicit
Dim conn
Dim RSFooter
Dim RSStatus
Dim TheMessage
set conn = server.createobject ("adodb.connection")
conn.open "ASPBook", "sa", "yourpassword"
conn.execute "insert into ASPSessionPages (SessionID, PageName)
 values (" _
  & Session("SessionID") & ", " _
  & "'OrderInfo')"
set RSFooter = conn.execute("select BriefText from ASPPageText " _
  & "where PageName = 'Footer'")
If IsEmpty(Request.Form("Submit")) Then
  TheMessage = "Enter your Order ID above to see the status of your
    order here."
Else
  Set RSStatus = Conn.execute("select Status from ASPSessions " _
    & "where SessionID = " & Request.Form("SessionID"))
  If RSStatus.EOF Then
    TheMessage = "The Order ID you entered was not found"
  Else
    TheMessage = RSStatus("Status")
  End If
End If
%>
```

First, `Option Explicit` is coded requiring variable declaration:

```
Option Explicit
```

Then variables are declared that will store the Connection object:

```
Dim conn
```

the text of the footer:

```
Dim RSFooter
```

the status of the order:

```
Dim RSStatus
```

and the text of that status:

```
Dim TheMessage
```

The Connection object is then instantiated:

```
set conn = server.createobject ("adodb.connection")
```

and opened:

```
conn.open "ASPBook", "sa", "yourpassword"
```

A hit is then recorded for this page:

```
conn.execute "insert into ASPSessionPages (SessionID, PageName)
values (" _
 & Session("SessionID") & ", " _
 & "'OrderInfo')"
```

and the text of the footer is retrieved from the database:

```
set RSFooter = conn.execute("select BriefText from ASPPageText " _
 & "where PageName = 'Footer'")
```

Then we check to see if the SUBMIT button is present in the Form fields collection:

```
If IsEmpty(Request.Form("Submit")) Then
```

If it is not present, we will write a generic message to the browser:

```
TheMessage = "Enter your Order ID above to see the status of your
 order here."
```

otherwise, we need to retrieve the status for the requested order:

```
Set RSStatus = Conn.execute("select Status from ASPSessions " _
 & "where SessionID = " & Request.Form("SessionID"))
```

If the order is not found, EOF will be True, since no records would be returned:

```
If RSStatus.EOF Then
```

In that case, we store a warning message in the TheMessage variable:

```
TheMessage = "The Order ID you entered was not found"
```

If a record is found, the status for that record will become the message displayed to the visitor:

```
TheMessage = RSStatus("Status")
```

Then, in the HTML, the text of the status is written:

```
<P><% Response.Write TheMessage %>
```

As is the text of the footer:

```
<% Response.Write RSFooter("BriefText") %>
```

Code for the Mailing List Page

The code on the Mailing List page adds a record to the database, indicating the email address of visitors that want to be on your mailing list. The code also records a hit and displays the text of the footer.

```
<%
Option Explicit
Dim conn
Dim RSFooter
Dim RSPageText
set conn = server.createobject ("adodb.connection")
conn.open "ASPBook", "sa", "yourpassword"
If not IsEmpty(Request.Form("Submit")) Then
  conn.execute "insert into ASPCustomer (EmailAddress) " _
    & "values (" _
    & "'" & Request.Form("EmailAddress") & "')"
  Response.Redirect "./customers.asp"
End If
conn.execute "insert into ASPSessionPages (SessionID, PageName)
 values (" _
  & Session("SessionID") & ", " _
  & "'MailingList')"
set RSFooter = conn.execute("select BriefText from ASPPageText " _
  & "where PageName = 'Footer'")
```

```
set RSPageText = conn.execute("select ExtendedText from ASPPage
  Text " _
  & "where PageName = 'MailingList'")
%>
```

First, `Option Explicit` is written:

```
Option Explicit
```

Then the variables are declared, one for the Connection object:

```
Dim conn
```

one for the footer text:

```
Dim RSFooter
```

and one for the text that appears on the page:

```
Dim RSPageText
```

The Connection object is instantiated:

```
set conn = server.createobject ("adodb.connection")
```

and opened:

```
conn.open "ASPBook", "sa", "yourpassword"
```

Then we check for the presence of the SUBMIT button:

```
If not IsEmpty(Request.Form("Submit")) Then
```

If it is present, that means the form has been submitted and we need to add a record to the ASPCustomer table, indicating the email address supplied by the visitor:

```
conn.execute "insert into ASPCustomer (EmailAddress) " _
  & "values (" _
  & "'" & Request.Form("EmailAddress") & "')"
```

Then the visitor is redirected to the Customers page:

```
Response.Redirect "./customers.asp"
```

otherwise, the page is to be displayed. A hit is recorded for the page:

```
conn.execute "insert into ASPSessionPages (SessionID, PageName)
values (" _
  & Session("SessionID") & ", " _
  & "'MailingList')"
```

The footer text is retrieved:

```
set RSFooter = conn.execute("select BriefText from ASPPageText " _
  & "where PageName = 'Footer'")
```

as is the text for the blurb that goes in the body of the page:

```
set RSPageText = conn.execute("select ExtendedText from ASPPage
  Text " _
  & "where PageName = 'MailingList'")
```

Then, inline with the HTML, that text blurb is written to the browser using the Write method of the Response object:

```
<P><% Response.Write RSPageText("ExtendedText") %>
```

Similarly, the text of the footer is written:

```
<% Response.Write RSFooter("BriefText") %>
```

Code for the Product Request Form

The code on the Product Request Form records the visitor's request to the database. The page also records a hit and displays dynamic text content for the page. The main code block is:

```
<%
Option Explicit
Dim conn
Dim RSPageText
Dim RSFooter
Dim PageText
set conn = server.createobject ("adodb.connection")
conn.open "ASPBook", "sa", "yourpassword"
If not IsEmpty(Request.Form("Submit")) Then
  conn.execute "insert into ASPProductRequests (ProductName,
    Description) " _
    & "values (" _
    & "'" & Request.Form("ProductName") & "', " _
    & "'" & Request.Form("Description") & "')"
```

```
    Response.Redirect "./customers.asp"
End If
conn.execute "insert into ASPSessionPages (SessionID, PageName)
 values (" _
   & Session("SessionID") & ", " _
   & "'ProductRequestForm')"
set RSPageText = conn.execute("select ExtendedText, BriefText from
 ASPPageText " _
   & "where PageName = 'ProductRequestForm'")
PageText= RSPageText("ExtendedText")
set RSFooter = conn.execute("select BriefText from ASPPageText " _
   & "where PageName = 'Footer'")
%>
```

First, Option Explicit is coded:

```
Option Explicit
```

Then the variables are declared. One is needed for the Connection object:

```
Dim conn
```

The others are used for the dynamic text content of the page:

```
Dim RSPageText
Dim RSFooter
Dim PageText
```

The CreateObject method returns an instance of a Connection object into the variable Conn:

```
set conn = server.createobject ("adodb.connection")
```

The Open method of the Connection object is used to connect to the SQL Server database:

```
conn.open "ASPBook", "sa", "yourpassword"
```

Then we check to see if the form has been submitted:

```
If not IsEmpty(Request.Form("Submit")) Then
```

If it has, we need to add the visitor's product request to the ASPProductRequests table:

```
conn.execute "insert into ASPProductRequests (ProductName,
 Description) " _
```

```
    & "values (" _
    & "'" & Request.Form("ProductName") & "', " _
    & "'" & Request.Form("Description") & "')"
```

Then we redirect the visitor to the Customers page:

```
Response.Redirect "./customers.asp"
```

otherwise, the page needs to be displayed, so we record a hit to this page:

```
conn.execute "insert into ASPSessionPages (SessionID, PageName)
    values (" _
    & Session("SessionID") & ", " _
    & "'ProductRequestForm')"
```

and retrieve the body text for this page:

```
set RSPageText = conn.execute("select ExtendedText, BriefText from
    ASPPageText " _
    & "where PageName = 'ProductRequestForm'")
PageText= RSPageText("ExtendedText")
```

and the footer text:

```
set RSFooter = conn.execute("select BriefText from ASPPageText " _
    & "where PageName = 'Footer'")
```

The title text is then written inline with the HTML:

```
<% Response.Write RSPageText("BriefText") %>
```

as is the page text:

```
<P><% Response.Write PageText %>
```

and the footer text:

```
<% Response.Write RSFooter("BriefText") %>
```

Code for the Send Email 1 Page

The code on the Send Email 1 page sends an email out to all the visitors who have signed up to receive email for a particular category. The main code block is:

```
<%
Option Explicit
Dim conn
Dim RSCategories
Dim RSCustomers
Dim ObjMail
set conn = server.createobject ("adodb.connection")
conn.open "ASPBook", "sa", "yourpassword"
If not IsEmpty(Request.Form("Send")) Then
   set RSCustomers = conn.execute("select EmailAddress from " _
      & "ASPCustomerWithCategory where Category = '" _
      & Request.Form("Category") & "'")
  Do Until RSCustomers.EOF
     Set objMail = CreateObject("CDONTS.NewMail")
     objMail.Send Request.Form("FromEmailAddress"), _
        RSCustomers("EmailAddress"), Request.Form("Subject"), _
        Request.Form("Message")
     Set objMail = Nothing
     RSCustomers.MoveNext
  Loop
End If
set RSCategories = conn.execute("select CategoryName from
 ASPCategories " _
   & "order by CategoryName")
%>
```

First, `Option Explicit` is coded:

```
Option Explicit
```

Next, we will need a Connection object:

```
Dim conn
```

a Recordset object for the categories:

```
Dim RSCategories
```

and a Recordset object for the customers to send an email to:

```
Dim RSCustomers
```

Next, a variable that will store the Collaborative Data Objects is declared:

```
Dim ObjMail
```

Next, the Connection object is instantiated:

```
set conn = server.createobject ("adodb.connection")
```

and opened:

```
conn.open "ASPBook", "sa", "yourpassword"
```

Then we check to see if the form has been submitted:

```
If not IsEmpty(Request.Form("Send")) Then
```

If it has been, we need to send out the email. Based on the category selected on the form, the email addresses for those customers in that category are retrieved:

```
set RSCustomers = conn.execute("select EmailAddress from " _
    & "ASPCustomerWithCategory where Category = '" _
    & Request.Form("Category") & "'")
```

Then we start a loop that will take us through each of the customers:

```
Do Until RSCustomers.EOF
```

We will need to send an email out to each customer, so the Collaborative Data Objects is instantiated:

```
Set objMail = CreateObject("CDONTS.NewMail")
```

and the Send method is used to send an email to the customer:

```
objMail.Send Request.Form("FromEmailAddress"), _
    RSCustomers("EmailAddress"), Request.Form("Subject"), _
    Request.Form("Message")
```

The object is then released:

```
Set objMail = Nothing
```

and we move to the next record before looping:

```
    RSCustomers.MoveNext
Loop
```

Next, we retrieve the categories that will be used to populate the options of the Select control:

```
set RSCategories = conn.execute("select CategoryName from
    ASPCategories " _
    & "order by CategoryName")
```

That Recordset is used in the next code block:

```
<%
Do Until RSCategories.EOF
%>
  <OPTION VALUE="<% Response.Write RSCategories("CategoryName")
    %>">
  <% Response.Write RSCategories("CategoryName") %></OPTION>
<%
  RSCategories.MoveNext
Loop
%>
```

The code will loop through all the records in the RSCategories Recordset:

```
Do Until RSCategories.EOF
```

Each of the records is added as an option to the Select control:

```
<OPTION VALUE="<% Response.Write RSCategories("CategoryName") %>">
<% Response.Write RSCategories("CategoryName") %></OPTION>
```

The record pointer is moved to the next record using the MoveNext method of the Recordset object before looping:

```
  RSCategories.MoveNext
Loop
```

Code for the Send Email 2 Page

The code on the Send Email 2 page sends an email blast out to all the customers who have entered their email address through the Mailing List page. The main code block is:

```
<%
Option Explicit
Dim conn
Dim RSCustomers
Dim ObjMail
set conn = server.createobject ("adodb.connection")
conn.open "ASPBook", "sa", "yourpassword"
If not IsEmpty(Request.Form("Send")) Then
  set RSCustomers = conn.execute("select EmailAddress from " _
    & "ASPCustomer")
  Do Until RSCustomers.EOF
    Set objMail = CreateObject("CDONTS.NewMail")
    objMail.Send Request.Form("FromEmailAddress"), _
      RSCustomers("EmailAddress"), Request.Form("Subject"), _
```

```
                Request.Form("Message")
        Set objMail = Nothing
        RSCustomers.MoveNext
    Loop
End If
%>
```

First, `Option Explicit` is coded:

```
Option Explicit
```

Then the variables are declared, one for the Connection object:

```
Dim conn
```

a Recordset object for the email addresses of the visitors:

```
Dim RSCustomers
```

and an instance of the Collaborative Data Objects:

```
Dim ObjMail
```

The Connection object is instantiated:

```
set conn = server.createobject ("adodb.connection")
```

and opened:

```
conn.open "ASPBook", "sa", "yourpassword"
```

Then we check to see if the form has been submitted:

```
If not IsEmpty(Request.Form("Send")) Then
```

If it has, we need to retrieve all the customers on the mailing list:

```
set RSCustomers = conn.execute("select EmailAddress from " _
    & "ASPCustomer")
```

The code will loop through each of the records in the `RSCustomers` Recordset:

```
Do Until RSCustomers.EOF
```

All customers need an email sent out to them:

```
Set objMail = CreateObject("CDONTS.NewMail")
```

The Send method is used to send the email out to visitors. The first parameter of the Send method is whom the email is from:

```
objMail.Send Request.Form("FromEmailAddress"), _
```

The second parameter is whom the email is to. The third parameter is the subject of the email:

```
RSCustomers("EmailAddress"), Request.Form("Subject"), _
```

and the last parameter of the send method is the text of the email message:

```
Request.Form("Message")
```

The resources used by the Collaborative Data Objects are released:

```
Set objMail = Nothing
```

The code then moves the record pointer to the next record:

```
RSCustomers.MoveNext
```

before looping back to the top of the Do . . . Loop and processing the next record:

```
Loop
```

APPENDIX A

VBScript QUICK REFERENCE

In this appendix many of the procedures available in VBScript are defined. Each procedure is listed with the description of the procedures, any parameters, any return value, and a sample use of the procedures.

Abs
DEFINITION:

Returns the absolute value of a number.

SYNTAX:

```
X = Abs(Num)
```

Num is a numeric value that the absolute value needs to be determined. Returned from the function is the absolute value of Num.

EXAMPLE:

```
Response.Write Abs(5) & "<P>"
Response.Write Abs(-5) & "<P>"
```

Written to the browser would be:

```
5
5
```

Asc
DEFINITION:

Returns the numeric ASCII value of a character.

SYNTAX:

```
X = Asc(TheLetter)
```

TheLetter is the character whose ASCII value you want to determine. Returned from the method would be the numeric ASCII value.

EXAMPLE:

```
Response.Write Asc("B") & "<P>"
Response.Write Asc("?") & "<P>"
```

Written to the browser would be:

```
66
63
```

Conversion Functions (CBool, Cbyte, Ccur, CDate, CDbl, CInt, CLng, CSng, CStr)
DEFINITION:

Converts a variable of one type to a variable of another type.

SYNTAX:

```
X = CStr(ValueToConvert)
```

The syntax is the same for all the conversion functions. Passed to the function is the value you wish to convert. Returned from the function is the converted number.

EXAMPLE:

```
X = CInt("44")
```

X would contain an integer with the value 44.

Chr
DEFINITION:

Converts an ASCII value to its character representation.

SYNTAX:

```
X = Chr(TheValue)
```

TheValue is the ASCII number you wish to return a character from. Returned from the function is the value converted.

EXAMPLE:

```
Response.Write Chr(72) & "<P>"
Response.Write Chr(74) & "<P>"
```

Written to the browser would be:

```
H
J
```

Date
DEFINITION:

Returns the current system date.

SYNTAX:

```
X = Date
```

X would contain the current system date.

EXAMPLE:

```
Response.Write Date
```

Written to the browser is the current system date.

DateAdd
DEFINITION:

Adds a value to a date or time.

SYNTAX:

```
X = DateAdd(Part2Add, Number2Add, Date)
```

The first parameter, `Part2Add`, is a string representing what you want to add to a date, like days or hours. For this parameter: yyyy represents years, q represents quarters, m represents months, y represents day of year, d represents days, w represents weekdays, ww represents week of year, h represents hours, n represents minutes, and s represents seconds.

Num2Add is the quantity that you want to add. Use a negative number to perform date subtraction. `Date` is the date that you want to add to.

EXAMPLE:

```
Response.Write DateAdd("h", 4, "5:15") & "<P>"
Response.Write DateAdd("yyyy", -3, "5/5/1940") & "<P>"
```

Written to the browser would be:

```
9:15:00 AM
5/5/37
```

DateDiff
DEFINITION:

Subtracts two dates and returns the difference.

SYNTAX:

```
X= DateDiff(Part2Diff, Date1, Date2)
```

The first parameter is a string representing what you want to use to subtract, like days or hours. For this parameter: yyyy represents years, q represents quarters, m represents months, y represents day of year, d represents days, w represents weekdays, ww represents week of year, h represents hours, n represents minutes, and s represents seconds.

The second parameter is the date that you want to subtract from the third parameter.

EXAMPLE:

```
Response.Write DateDiff("yyyy", "4/1/1952", "3/1/2005") & "<P>"
Response.Write DateDiff("n", "1:15", "1:25") & "<P>"
```

Written to the browser would be:

```
53
10
```

DatePart
DEFINITION:

Returns a portion of a date or time.

SYNTAX:

```
X = DatePart(Part2Return, Date)
```

The first parameter is a string representing what part you want to return, like day or hour. For this parameter: yyyy represents years, q represents quarters, m represents months, y represents day of year, d represents days, w represents weekdays, ww represents week of year, h represents hours, n represents minutes, and s represents seconds.

The second parameter is the date that you want to parse from. Returned is the portion of the date requested.

EXAMPLE:

```
Response.Write DatePart("yyyy", "4/1/1952") & "<P>"
Response.Write DatePart("n", "1:15") & "<P>"
```

Written to the browser would be:

```
1952
15
```

DateSerial
DEFINITION:

Returns a date from the parts year, month, day.

SYNTAX:

```
X = DateSerial(year, month, day)
```

Returned from the function is the concatenation of the date parts.

EXAMPLE:

```
Response.Write DateSerial("1955", "4", "22") & "<P>"
Response.Write DateSerial("2022", "8", "11") & "<P>"
```

Written to the browser would be:

```
4/22/55
8/11/22
```

Day
DEFINITION:

Returns the day portion of a date.

SYNTAX:

```
X = Day(Date)
```

Returned from the function would be the day of the Date.

EXAMPLE:

```
Response.Write Day("5/1/1971 5:15:32") & "<P>"
Response.Write Day("9/21/2002 12:32:54") & "<P>"
```

Written to the browser would be:

```
1
21
```

Do...Loop
DEFINITION:

Repeats a chunk of code until a condition is met.

SYNTAX:

```
Do Condition
   'Code Block
Loop
```

The code would run until the condition was met.

EXAMPLE:

```
Do Until Second(Time) = 0
  Response.Write "Not Yet"
Loop
```

The text "Not Yet" would be written over and over again to the browser until the seconds on the system time were zero.

Fix
DEFINITION:

Returns the integer portion of a number.

SYNTAX:

```
X = Fix(TheNumber)
```

X would be set to the integer portion of `TheNumber`.

EXAMPLE:

```
Response.Write Fix(2.999) & "<P>"
Response.Write Fix(0.1) & "<P>"
```

Written to the browser would be:

```
2
0
```

For...Each
DEFINITION:

Allows you to iterate through a collection of objects.

SYNTAX:

```
For Each MyItem in TheCollection
  'take action on the collection
Next
```

The code would perform the code block through each of the items in `TheCollection`.

EXAMPLE:

```
For Each TheField in RS.Fields
  Response.Write TheField.Name
Next
```

Written to the browser would be the name of each field in a Recordset object.

For...Next
DEFINITION:

Iterates from one number to another performing a block of code with each cycle.

SYNTAX:

```
For TheNumber = Start to End
  'code block
Next
```

The block would iterate until `TheNumber` was equal to `End`.

EXAMPLE:

```
For I = 1 to 5
  Response.Write I
Next
```

Written to the browser would be the numbers 1 through 5.

FormatCurrency
DEFINITION:

Formats a number as currency.

SYNTAX:

```
X = FormatCurrency(Number2Format)
```

X is set to Number2Format converted to currency.

EXAMPLE:

```
Response.Write FormatCurrency(2.999) & "<P>"
Response.Write FormatCurrency(0.1) & "<P>"
```

Written to the browser would be:

```
$3.00
$0.10
```

FormatDateTime
DEFINITION:

Formats a string in a date format.

SYNTAX:

```
X = FormatDateTime(TheDate)
```

X would be set to the formatted date version of TheDate.

EXAMPLE:

```
Response.Write FormatDateTime("12/6/1989", 0) & "<P>"
Response.Write FormatDateTime("12/6/1989", 1) & "<P>"
Response.Write FormatDateTime("12/6/1989", 2) & "<P>"
```

Written to the browser would be:

```
12/6/89
Wednesday, December 06, 1989
12/6/89
```

FormatNumber
DEFINITION:

Formats a number.

SYNTAX:

```
X = FormatNumber(TheNumber)
```

X will be set to the formatted version of TheNumber.

EXAMPLE:

```
Response.Write FormatNumber(1234567) & "<P>"
Response.Write FormatNumber(.1) & "<P>"
```

Written to the browser would be:

```
1,234,567.00
0.10
```

FormatPercent

DEFINITION:

Formats a number as a percent.

SYNTAX:

```
X = FormatPercent(TheNumber)
```

X would be set to the value of TheNumber written as a percentage.

EXAMPLE:

```
Response.Write FormatPercent(12.1) & "<P>"
Response.Write FormatPercent(.1877) & "<P>"
```

Written to the browser would be:

```
1,210.00%
18.77%
```

Hex

DEFINITION:

Returns a string representing the hexadecimal value of a number.

SYNTAX:

```
X = Hex(TheNumber)
```

X is set to a string containing the hexadecimal value of TheNumber.

EXAMPLE:

```
Response.Write Hex(255) & "<P>"
Response.Write Hex(16) & "<P>"
```

Written to the browser would be:

```
FF
10
```

Hour

DEFINITION:

Returns the hour portion of a time.

SYNTAX:

```
X = Hour(TheTime)
```

X would be set to the hour of TheTime.

EXAMPLE:

```
Response.Write Hour("5/1/1971 5:15:32") & "<P>"
Response.Write Hour("9/21/2002 12:32:54") & "<P>"
```

Written to the browser would be:

```
5
12
```

If
DEFINITION:

Provides for code to run based on a condition.

SYNTAX:

```
If Condition1 Then
  'Code block
ElseIf Condition2 Then
  'Code block
Else
  'Code block
End If
```

If Condition1 evaluates to True, then the first code block would run; if not, the code would test Condition2. If it evaluated to True, then the second code block would run; otherwise, the code in the third code block would run. The ElseIf and Else portions of an If statement are not required.

EXAMPLE:

```
If Month(Date) = 9 then
  Response.Write "September"
Else
  Response.Write "Not September"
End If
```

Written to the browser would be September if the current month is September; otherwise, Not September would be written.

InStr
DEFINITION:

Searches for a string within a string.

SYNTAX:

```
X = Instr(String2Search, SearchString)
```

X is set to the first occurrence of the `SearchString` within the `String2Search`. If the `SearchString` is not found, the function returns 0.

EXAMPLE:

```
Response.Write Instr("Hello", "e") & "<P>"
Response.Write Instr("Hello", "R") & "<P>"
```

Written to the browser would be:

```
2
0
```

InStrRev
DEFINITION:

Same as Instr, except the search begins at the end of the string.

SYNTAX:

```
X = Instr(String2Search, SearchString)
```

X would be set to the last occurrence of the `SearchString` within the `String2Search`.

EXAMPLE:

```
Response.Write InstrRev("Hello World", "l") & "<P>"
Response.Write InstrRev("Hello", "R") & "<P>"
```

Written to the browser would be:

```
10
5
```

Int
DEFINITION:

Returns the integer portion of a number.

SYNTAX:

```
X = Int(TheNumber)
```

X would be set to the integer portion of `TheNumber`.

EXAMPLE:

```
Response.Write Int(2.999) & "<P>"
Response.Write Int(0.1) & "<P>"
```

Written to the browser would be:

```
2
0
```

IsDate
DEFINITION:

Tests a value to see if it is a date.

SYNTAX:

```
X = IsDate(TheDate)
```

X will be set to True or False, depending on whether TheDate is actually a date.

EXAMPLE:

```
Response.Write IsDate("12/44/55") & "<P>"
Response.Write IsDate("12/14/55") & "<P>"
```

Written to the browser would be:

```
False
True
```

IsEmpty
DEFINITION:

Tests to see if a variable is empty.

SYNTAX:

```
X = IsEmpty(TheVariable)
```

X will be set to True or False, depending on whether TheVariable is empty or not.

EXAMPLE:

```
If Not IsEmpty(Request.Form("Submit")) Then
  'form submitted
Else
  'Form not submitted
End If
```

In this code example, if a form field called Submit was present, then the first code block would run; otherwise, the second code block would run.

IsNumeric
DEFINITION:

Tests to see if a value is a number.

SYNTAX:

```
X = IsNumeric(TheValue)
```

X would be set to True or False, depending on whether TheValue was a number.

EXAMPLE:

```
Response.Write IsNumeric("Hello") & "<P>"
Response.Write IsNumeric("33") & "<P>"
```

Written to the browser would be:

```
False
True
```

LCase
DEFINITION:

Converts text to lowercase.

SYNTAX:

```
X = LCase(TheValue)
```

X would be set to the lowercase text of the variable TheValue.

EXAMPLE:

```
Response.Write LCase("HELLO") & "<P>"
Response.Write LCase("123") & "<P>"
```

Written to the browser would be:

```
hello
123
```

Left
DEFINITION:

Chops characters off the left side of a string.

SYNTAX:

```
X = Left(String2Chop, NumCharacters)
```

String2Chop is the string from which you want to chop characters. NumCharacters is the number of characters you want to chop. Returned to X would be the chopped string.

EXAMPLE:

```
Response.Write Left("Hello", 2) & "<P>"
```

Written to the browser would be:

```
He
```

Len
DEFINITION:

Returns the length, in characters of a string.

SYNTAX:

```
X = Len(TheString)
```

X would be set to the number of characters in TheString.

EXAMPLE:

```
Response.Write Len("Hello") & "<P>"
Response.Write Len("Hello World") & "<P>"
```

Written to the browser would be:

```
5
11
```

LTrim
DEFINITION:

Returns a string without any leading spaces.

SYNTAX:

```
X = Ltrim(TheString)
```

X would be set to TheString without any leading spaces.

EXAMPLE:

```
X = Ltrim(" Hello ")
```

X would be set to the string, "Hello ".

Mid
DEFINITION:

Returns characters from the middle of the string.

SYNTAX:

```
X = Mid(TheString, StartPosition, NumCharacters)
```

TheString is the string from which to pull characters. StartPosition is the spot from which to start retrieving characters. NumCharacters is the number of characters to chop out of the middle. If the third parameter is left off, the function returns all characters after the start position.

EXAMPLE:

```
Response.Write Mid("Hello", 2, 3) & "<P>"
Response.Write Mid("Hello", 2) & "<P>"
```

Written to the browser would be:

```
ell
ello
```

Minute
DEFINITION:

Returns the minute from a time.

SYNTAX:

```
X = Minute(TheTime)
```

X would be set to the minutes within the `TheTime` variable.

EXAMPLE:

```
Response.Write Hour("5/1/1971 5:15:32") & "<P>"
Response.Write Hour("9/21/2002 12:32:54") & "<P>"
```

Written to the browser would be:

```
15
32
```

Month
DEFINITION:

Returns the month portion of a date as a number.

SYNTAX:

```
X = Month(TheDate)
```

X would be set to the month of `TheDate`.

EXAMPLE:

```
Response.Write Month("5/1/1971 5:15:32") & "<P>"
Response.Write Month("9/21/2002 12:32:54") & "<P>"
```

Written to the browser would be:

```
5
9
```

MonthName
DEFINITION:

Returns the month name for a number from 1 to 12.

SYNTAX:

```
X = MonthName(TheNumber)
```

X will be set to the text name of the month based on the number in `TheNumber`.

EXAMPLE:

```
Response.Write Month(3) & "<P>"
```

Written to the browser would be:

```
March
```

Now
DEFINITION:

Returns the current system date and time.

SYNTAX:

```
X = Now
```

X would be set to the current system date and time.

EXAMPLE:

```
Response.Write Now
```

Written to the browser would be the current system date and time.

Oct
DEFINITION:

Returns the octal value of a number.

SYNTAX:

```
X = Oct(TheNumber)
```

X would contain a string representing the octal value of TheNumber.

EXAMPLE:

```
Response.Write Oct(9) & "<P>"
Response.Write Oct(12) & "<P>"
```

Written to the browser would be:

```
11
14
```

Randomize
DEFINITION:

Initializes the random-number generator.

SYNTAX:

```
Randomize
```

The random number generator would be initialized.

EXAMPLE:

```
Randomize
```

Replace
DEFINITION:

Replaces one character in a string with another.

SYNTAX:

```
X = Replace(String2Fix, Character2Replace, What2ReplaceWith)
```

X would contain a converted String2Fix that would have Character2Replace substituted with What2ReplaceWith.

EXAMPLE:

```
Response.Write Replace("Mississippi", "i", "o") & "<P>"
```

Written to the browser would be:

```
Mossossoppo
```

Right
DEFINITION:

Chops characters off the right side of a string.

SYNTAX:

```
X = Right(String2Chop, NumCharacters)
```

X would contain the rightmost characters of String2Chop, based on the number in NumCharacters.

EXAMPLE:

```
Response.Write Right("Hello", 2)
```

Written to the browser would be:

```
lo
```

Rnd
DEFINITION:

Returns a random number.

SYNTAX:

```
X = Rnd
```

X would contain a random number.

EXAMPLE:

```
Response.Write Int(Rnd * 6) + 1
```

Written to the browser would be a number between 1 and 6.

Round
DEFINITION:

Rounds a number based on the number of decimal places specified.

SYNTAX:

```
X = Round(TheNumber, NumPlaces)
```

X would contain the rounded TheNumber rounded to NumPlaces.

EXAMPLE:

```
Response.Write Round(4.555, 2)
```

Written to the browser would be:

```
4.56
```

RTrim
DEFINITION:

Returns a string with any trailing spaces removed.

SYNTAX:

```
X = Rtrim(TheString)
```

X is set to TheString without any trailing spaces.

EXAMPLE:

```
X = Rtrim(" Hello ")
```

X would be set to the string, " Hello".

Second
DEFINITION:

Returns the seconds from a time.

SYNTAX:

```
X = Second(TheTime)
```

Returns a number representing the number of seconds chopped from a time.

EXAMPLE:

```
Response.Write Second("5/1/1971 5:15:32") & "<P>"
Response.Write Second("9/21/2002 12:32:54") & "<P>"
```

Written to the browser would be:

```
32
54
```

Select...Case
DEFINITION:

The Select...Case structure allows you to have code run, based on a condition.

SYNTAX:

```
Select Case X
   Case 1
      'first code block
   Case 2
      'second code block
   Case Else
End Select
```

The code will run a code block based on the value of X. If X is 1, the first code block will run; if X is 2, the second code block will run. Otherwise, the Else code block will run.

EXAMPLE:

```
X = 1
Select Case X
   Case 1
      Response.Write "This one."
   Case 2
      Response.Write "Not this one."
   Case Else
      Response.Write "Not this one."
End Select
```

Written to the browser would be the text This one.

Space
DEFINITION:

Returns a number of spaces as a string.

SYNTAX:

```
X = Space(TheNumber)
```

X would contain a string of TheNumber spaces.

EXAMPLE:

```
X = Space(5)
```

X would be set to the value "   ".

Sqr
DEFINITION:

Returns the square root of a number.

SYNTAX:

```
X = Sqr(TheNumber)
```

X would be set to the square root of the number.

EXAMPLE:

```
Response.Write Sqr(9) & "<P>"
```

Written to the browser would be:

```
3
```

StrComp
DEFINITION:

Compares two strings and returns a value based on that comparison.

SYNTAX:

```
X = StrComp(String1,String2)
```

If the two strings are equal, X will contain 0. If string 1 is greater, X will contain 1; otherwise, X will contain -1.

EXAMPLE:

```
Response.Write StrComp("Hello", "Hello") & "<P>"
Response.Write StrComp("Hello", "World") & "<P>"
Response.Write StrComp("World", "Hello") & "<P>"
```

Written to the browser would be:

```
0
-1
1
```

String
DEFINITION:

Returns a character repeated based on the parameters passed.

SYNTAX:

```
X = String(TheNumber, TheCharacter)
```

X will contain the character TheCharacter repeated TheNumber times.

EXAMPLE:

```
Response.Write String(4,"R")
```

Written to the browser would be:

```
RRRR
```

StrReverse
DEFINITION:

Reverses the characters in a string.

SYNTAX:

```
X = StrReverse(TheString)
```

X will contain TheString backwards.

EXAMPLE:

```
Response.Write StrReverse("Hello") & "<P>"
```

Written to the browser would be:

```
olleH
```

Time
DEFINITION:

Returns the current system time.

SYNTAX:

```
X = Time
```

X would contain the current system time.

EXAMPLE:

```
Response.Write Time
```

Written to the browser would be the current system time.

TimeSerial
DEFINITION:

Returns a time concatenated from an hour, minute, and second.

SYNTAX:

```
X = TimeSerial(Hour, Minute, Second)
```

X would contain the time based on the values of Hour, Minute, and Second.

EXAMPLE:

```
X = TimeSerial("5", "17", "32")
```

X would contain the time 5:17:32.

Trim

DEFINITION:

Removes the spaces from both ends of a string.

SYNTAX:

```
X = Trim(TheString)
```

X would contain the string `TheString` with all the spaces removed.

EXAMPLE:

```
X = Trim("  Hello  ")
```

X would be set to the string, `"Hello"`.

Ucase

DEFINITION:

Converts a string to its uppercase value.

SYNTAX:

```
X = UCase(TheString)
```

X would contain the string `TheString` with all the characters in uppercase.

EXAMPLE:

```
Response.Write UCase("hello")
```

Written to the browser would be:

```
HELLO
```

Weekday

DEFINITION:

Returns the numeric weekday of a date from 1 to 7.

SYNTAX:

```
X = WeekDay(TheDate)
```

X will contain a number 1 to 7 based on the weekday of `TheDate`.

EXAMPLE:

```
Response.Write Weekday("5/1/1971 5:15:32") & "<P>"
Response.Write Weekday("9/21/2002 12:32:54") & "<P>"
```

Written to the browser would be:

```
7
7
```

WeekdayName
DEFINITION:

Returns the name of a weekday based on its number.

SYNTAX:

```
X = WeekdayName(TheNumber)
```

X will contain the name of the day based on the number, where Sunday is 1 and Saturday is 7.

EXAMPLE:

```
Response.Write WeekdayName(1) & "<P>"
Response.Write WeekdayName(7) & "<P>"
```

Written to the browser would be:

```
Sunday
Saturday
```

Year
DEFINITION:

Returns the year portion of a date.

SYNTAX:

```
X = Year(TheDate)
```

X will be set to the year portion of TheDate.

EXAMPLE:

```
Response.Write Year("5/1/1971 5:15:32") & "<P>"
Response.Write Year("9/21/2002 12:32:54") & "<P>"
```

Written to the browser would be:

```
1971
2001
```

APPENDIX B

CD CONTENTS

The CD contains much of the code used throughout this book. For the first 15 chapters, a text file with the chapter number contains the major code blocks, if any.

For Chapters 15-18 where the e-commerce site was presented, the CD contains the entire solution. The `Web Site` folder contains all of the ASP and graphics that make up the site. In the `SQL Server Script` folder, you will find an SQL Server script that generates the tables for this solution. In the `Access DB` folder, you will find an Access database with the same tables. If you decide to use the Access database, please refer to Chapter 13 for other changes you may need to make to the code.

ABOUT THE AUTHOR

Greg Buczek is an author, a Microsoft Certified Solutions Developer, and a Microsoft Certified Trainer working as an Independent Consultant in Albuquerque, New Mexico. He is the Webmaster of over 20 Web sites where he strives to bring dynamic, data-driven content to the Internet. In his role as Webmaster, Greg has extensive experience with Active Server Pages. Greg also has extensive Visual Basic and SQL Server experience. He has developed numerous Visual Basic applications, ActiveX Components, and ActiveX Controls. As an MCT, Greg has taught and developed curriculum for the MCSD courses. In addition, he runs a vanguard Web site statistical service. This service allows customers to view live information about their site hit numbers, referrers of the hits, and Browser/OS info of the visitors through a Web interface, as well as weekly Excel Spreadsheets. All of this is automated through ASP and VB components. Greg's previous titles include *Instant ASP Scripts*. You can email Greg at asp@netstats2000.com.